L. G. Alexander

LONGMAN ADVANCED GRAMMAR

Reference and Practice

INSTITUTE FOR APPLIED LANGUAGE STUDIES
UNIVERSITY OF EDINBURGH
21 Hill Place
Edinburgh EH8 9DP

Addison Wesley Longman Limited
Edinburgh Gate
Harlow
Essex
CM20 2JE
England

Distributed in the United States of America by
Longman Publishing, New York

First published 1993
Sixth impression 1996

British Library Cataloguing in Publication Data
Alexander, L. G. (Louis George), *1932–*
    Longman advanced grammar practice.
    I. Title
    428.2
    ISBN 0–582–07978–0

Library of Congress Cataloging-in-publication Data
Alexander, L. G.
    Longman advanced grammar practice/L. G. Alexander
        p. cm.
    Includes bibliographical references and index.
    ISBN 0–582–07978–0: £6.95
    1. English language—Textbooks for foreign speakers.
    2. English language—Grammar—1950- —Problems,
    exercises, etc. I. Title.
    PE1128.A4573 1992
    428.2′4-dc20
                                            91-46008
                                            CIP

Set in Garamond/Frutiger by Tradespools Ltd, Somerset

Produced by Longman Singapore Publishers Pte Ltd
Printed in Italy

ISBN 0 582 07978 0

Acknowledgements

We are grateful to the following for permission to reproduce copyright material:

the author's agent for an extract from *Akenfield* by Ronald Blythe (Penguin Books Ltd, 1972); the author's agents for an extract from the story 'The Crowd' by Ray Bradbury, copyright © 1943, renewed 1970 by R Bradbury; British Museum Press for an extract from *The Innocent Anthropologist* by Nigel Barley (1986); Constable & Co Ltd for an extract from *The Comforts of Madness* by Paul Sayer (1988); the author's agent for an extract from the story 'The Kindness of Mrs Radcliffe' by Noel Coward from *Noel Coward: The Complete Stories* (Methuen, 1985), copyright © 1939 the Estate of Noel Coward; Andre Deutsch Ltd for an extract from *The Land of the Rising Yen* by George Mikes (1970); The Economist Newspaper Ltd for an extract from the article 'Forbidding Fruit' from *The Economist* magazine 6.4.88; Express Newspapers Ltd for the article 'The cuppa that's fit for the Queen' by Ross Benson from *Daily Express* newspaper, 14.5.88; The Financial Times Ltd for the article 'Alaska's dirty dollars' by David Thomas from *Financial Times* newspaper, 4.3.90; the author, Leslie Goffe for his article 'Planeload of 400 lobsters' from *The Guardian* newspaper, 20.8.88, copyright © L J T G Goffe; Victor Gollancz Ltd & Random House, Inc for an extract from *Castaway* by Lucy Irvine, copyright © 1983 by Lucy Irvine; the author's agent for an extract from *England Made Me* by Graham Greene (Penguin Books Ltd/William Heinemann Ltd, 1935), © Verdant SA 1935; the author's agent for an extract from *Joyce by herself and her friends* by Joyce Grenfell (Futura, 1981), © The Joyce Grenfell Memorial Trust 1980; Hamish Hamilton Ltd & Alfred A Knopf, Inc for an extract from *The High Window* by Raymond Chandler, copyright © 1942 by R Chandler & renewed 1970 by Helga Greene, Executor of the Estate of Raymond Chandler (Hamish Hamilton, 1951) & an extract from *Oscar Wilde* by Richard Ellmann, copyright © 1987 by The Estate of Richard Ellmann; HarperCollins Publishers for an extract from *Elephant and Other Stories* by Raymond Carver (Collins Harvill, 1988), an extract from *The Fords, An American Epic* by Peter Collier & David Horowitz (Futura, 1988) & an extract from *Arabia Through the Looking Glass* by Jonathan Raban (Fontana, 1980); William Heinemann Ltd for an extract from *A Writer's Notebook* by W Somerset Maugham (1967); William Heinemann Ltd & the author's agent for an extract from *Love and*

Friendship by Alison Lurie (1986), copyright © 1986 by Alison Lurie; William Heinemann & the author, Peter Ustinov for an extract from *Dear Me*; the author's agent, on behalf of Heller Arts Ltd, for an extract from *The Naked Manager* by Robert Heller (Coronet, 1974); the author's agent for an extract from *Unreliable Memoirs* by Clive James (Jonathan Cape Ltd/Picador, 1981); Macmillan Magazines Ltd for the article 'Dinosaurs on a tidal wave?' by Alun Anderson from *Nature* magazine (date unknown), copyright © Macmillan Magazines Ltd; Ewan MacNaughton Associates for the articles 'Pigeons 'not so bird brained'' by Adrian Berry from *Daily Telegraph* newspaper, 6.5.89 & 'Long distance duel over la belle Monique' by Suzanne Lowry from *Daily Telegraph* newspaper, 23.7.88 & the abridged article 'Underground gets fire message in plain English' by A J McIlroy from *Daily Telegraph* newspaper, 20.2.89, © The Daily Telegraph plc, 6.5.89, 23.7.88 & 20.2.89; The New Yorker Magazine, Inc for an extract from the article 'Notes and Comment' by Suzannah Lessard from *The New Yorker* magazine 9.10.89, © 1989 The New Yorker Magazine, Inc; Newspaper Publishing plc for the article 'Patients get the message on operating tables' by Oliver Gillie from *The Independent* newspaper, 26.8.88 & the abridged articles 'Roman soldiers had regimental brewery' by David Keys from *The Independent* newspaper, 26.9.88 & 'Armageddon larder yields its sickly secrets' by Andrew Marr from *The Independent* newspaper, 29.4.88; The Observer Ltd for the article 'Little queens sweep the board' by Lawrence Marks from *The Observer* newspaper, 30.10.88 & the abridged articles 'Tribal past flows through our veins' by Robin McKie from *The Observer* newspaper, 21.5.89 & 'Spot of mutiny on the High Cs' by Robin Smyth from *The Observer* newspaper, 31.7.88; Martin Secker & Warburg Ltd for an extract from *Wilt* by Tom Sharpe (1978); Penguin Books Ltd & the author's agent for an extract from *What's Bred in the Bone* by Robertson Davies (Viking, 1985), copyright © R Davies, 1985; the author's agent for the extract 'The least successful attempt to clear molehills' from *The Return of Heroic Failures* by Stephen Pile (Penguin Books Ltd); Random Century Group, on behalf of the author's Estate, for an extract from *In Patagonia* by Bruce Chatwin (Jonathan Cape Ltd 1979); Random House, Inc for extracts from *Random House Dictionary of the English Language* (Second Edition, Unabridged), copyright © 1987 Random House, Inc; The Reader's Digest Association Ltd for an extract from *Reader's Digest Book of Strange Stories and Amazing Facts* (1975), copyright © Reader's Digest Association Ltd; the author's agent for an extract from *Live Flesh* by Ruth Rendell (Hutchinson Books Ltd, 1986); the author, Judy Sadgrove for her abridged article 'Homeopathy? A drop in the bucket' from *The Guardian* newspaper, 20.7.88; Scientific American, Inc, for an extract from 'What is Happening at the Center Our Galaxy?' by Charles H Townes & Reinhard Genzel from *Scientific American* magazine, April 1990, copyright © 1990 Scientific American, Inc. All rights reserved; Sidgwick & Jackson Ltd for an extract from *An Actor and His Time* by John Gielgud (1981) & an extract from *The Professional Decision Thinker* by Ben Heirs with Peter Farrell (1986); Time, Inc Magazines for an extract from the article 'Japan's Underground Frontier' by Seiichi Kanise from *Time* magazine, 6.2.89, an extract from the article 'Invasion of the Data Snatchers!' from *Time* magazine, 26.9.88 & an extract from the article 'The Ultimate Quest' from *Time* magazine, 16.4.90; Times Newspapers Ltd for the abridged article 'Fax-mad New Yorkers try facsimilie therapy' by Charles Bremner from *The Times* newspaper, 2.1.89, the articles 'Expert explains 'the criminal look'' by Frances Gibb from *The Times* newspaper (date unknown) & 'Junket for robbers was police trap' by Michael Leapman from *The Times* newspaper, 18.3.81 & the abridged article 'A-levels or £1m?' by Amrit Roy from *The Sunday Times* newspaper, 25.3.90; © Times Newspapers Ltd 1989, 1981 & 1990; US News & World Report for the article 'Alzheimer's telltale protein' from *US News & World Report* magazine 2.10.89, copyright © 1989 US News & World Report; the author, Carolyn Webber for an extract from her essay 'The Politics of Taxation' from *The Wilson Quarterly* magazine, Vol XIII, No 2, Spring 1989; the author, Bibi Wein for an extract from her article 'Trust Your Impressions?' from *New Woman* magazine, April 1990, copyright © Bibi Wein, 1990.

We have been unable to trace the copyright holders in the following & would appreciate any information that would enable us to do so;

the article 'The Changing Role of Fathers' by Roger M Barkin from *USA Today* magazine, July 1989; the article 'Ready to break the Portland Vase' by Andrew Billen from *The Times* newspaper 2.6.88; the article 'Rubbish!' by William J Rathje from *The Atlantic* magazine, Dec 1989; the article 'Pop Art Absurdists' from *Sunday Telegraph* newspaper 8.5.88; the article 'Drug-war overkill' from *New York* magazine, 2.10.89.

We are grateful to the following for their permission to reproduce copyright material and photographs:

The Economist//Robert Hunt for page 248. Mary Evans Picture Library for page 104. Sally & Richard Greenhill for page 12. Greenpeace Communications/Merjenburgh for page 84. Gary Hallgren for illustration on page 176. The Hulton Picture Company for pages 144, 208, 216/Bettmann for page 64. Impact Photos/Michael Dent for page 198. Longman Photographic Unit for pages 108, 188. Mansell Collection for page 228. The Observer/Neil Libbert for page 28. Panos Pictures/J Hartly for page 196. Science Photo Library for pages 140, 156/David Parrer for page 212/David A Hardy for page 232. Frank Spooner Pictures for page 160. Taisei Corporation for page 132. Times Newspapers Ltd for page 124/Bob Collier for page 48. Zefa Picture Library UK Ltd for pages 164, 168, 220.

Illustrated by Edward McLachlan, Joseph McEwan and David Parkins.

Acknowledgements

Early versions of these materials were tried out with students in four countries. The book is in its present form partly as a result of the useful reports and in many cases the very detailed comments received while the work was being developed. I would like to thank the following:

Brazil	Vera Regina A Couto Rose Haberfeld Rosa Lenzuen	Cultura Inglesa, Rio
Germany	Hans Mettke	Humboldt University, Berlin
Greece	Nicholas Begley	The Moraïtis School, Athens
United Kingdom	Steve Moore	Eurocentre, Lee Green

I would also like to thank:

- Roy Kingsbury for his comprehensive report on the original proposal.

- my personal assistant, Penelope Parfitt, for her research and editorial work.

- my wife, Julia, for reading the entire manuscript, doing all the exercises and making detailed comments.

I am especially grateful to my publishers and their representatives for administering and monitoring the development of this project in various locations and for exercising such care and skill to see the work through to publication.

Longman English Grammar Series
by L.G. Alexander

Longman English Grammar: A Reference Grammar for English as a Foreign Language
Step by Step 1-3: Graded Grammar Exercises: Beginners' to Pre-Intermediate Level
Longman English Grammar Practice (Intermediate Level)
Longman Advanced Grammar

Contents

Study Section

Reference Section

Conventions used in this book

LEG	Longman English Grammar
LAG	Longman Advanced Grammar
BrE	British English
AmE	American English
Not *...*	likely student error
[>]	cross reference
[> App]	appendix reference (LEG)
/ /	phonetic transcription
n.	note (in cross references)
l./ll.	line/lines

Introduction

Who is this book for?

This book is for advanced students of English as a foreign or second language, working on their own or with a teacher. It begins at about the level of the Cambridge First Certificate, builds up to the level of the Cambridge Advanced English Examination and culminates at the level of the Cambridge Certificate of Proficiency. The material can be used for short-term or long-term courses and is suitable for students of the appropriate standard, whether they are preparing for examinations or not. In any event, its use is not intended to span more than a two-year period.

What does it do?

Longman Advanced Grammar has three aims:

1 To serve as an advanced 'text decoder', using the analysis of syntax as the key to understanding difficult text.

2 To provide practice in advanced points of grammar.

3 To serve as an advanced *reference* grammar, where citations are to be found in context, and not just quoted at sentence-level in isolation from their source.

The work combines the functions of a Reader, a Practice Book and a Reference Book for students whose previous learning history has not prepared them to cope with texts at an advanced level.

Rationale: what is an 'advanced level'?

There are two common misconceptions about the meaning of 'advanced', which have to be cleared up right away. The first is that students encounter ever more difficult structures which they have never met before, and the second is that there is a lot of 'difficult vocabulary'. The first assumption is simply not true. Structures do not exist in an ever-mounting spiral of increasing difficulty: the old, by now familiar, structures continue to be present at advanced levels. And while it is true that there is or may be a lot of 'difficult vocabulary' at advanced levels, that in itself does not constitute a difficulty which a competent dictionary cannot resolve. It is true that the way words are drawn to each other (*collocation*) is generally recognized to be a major feature of language acquisition and therefore a source of difficulty. Students may not always be able to produce correct and sometimes idiomatic collocations, but they have less difficulty understanding them. The capacity for reception always exceeds the capacity for production.

There are four principal factors (other than mere lexis) which account for 'difficulty' at the advanced level: *content, allusion, syntax, grammar points.*

1 *Content*

Advanced texts assume an extensive 'knowledge of the world': the kind of knowledge individuals need to bring with them before they can decode the information in a piece of writing. For the purposes of this book, we have to assume reasonable 'knowledge of the world', otherwise learners would not be aspiring advanced students. The more specialized a text, the more difficult it is, and this applies to native speakers as much as it does to language students. It follows that highly specialized texts must be excluded from a book of this kind. Texts drawn from a broad range of fields must reflect the same assumptions that are made by the editors of quality newspapers: namely, that their readers, regardless of their age, are *adult*. Texts must present the kind of English, both journalistic and general, which educated people, with a lively and intelligent awareness of the world around them, encounter on a more-or-less daily basis.

2 *Allusion*

What writers allude to is connected with the assumptions they make about their readers. So, for example, if a writer alludes to 'the double helix', he or she is assuming that the reader has encountered this concept before and therefore doesn't need to have it explained. Allusions may also be culture-bound, referring to aspects of life in the English-speaking world which might be obscure to the learner. A reference to, say, 'the old-boy network' has implications for a native speaker which may not be available to a learner.

3 *Syntax*

What makes language difficult is not just *words*, but the way words are combined to make sentences: i.e. *syntax*. A sentence is a sum-total of words and this sum-total is greater than its parts. Among the features of syntax that cause difficulty are: participle constructions, relative clauses, apposition, adverbial clauses, complementation after verbs, adjectives and nouns.

It is common knowledge that after years of study, non-native learners may still have difficulty in coping with publications like *Time Magazine*, *The Times* and *The Economist* and the 'quality' press, because they have never been trained to decode the (often relatively simple) structures that are combined syntactically into complex sentences. The key to comprehension at the advanced level is therefore the competent analysis of syntax. Analyzing and synthesizing train students to understand what difficult language is all about.

4 *Grammar points*

Familiar grammar points pose unusual problems because, all their learning lives, students have been given an over-simplified view of them. Common rules, such as the use of the present progressive to describe actions and events in progress at the moment of speaking, must be extended to account for sentences like *People are becoming less tolerant of smoking these days*. Advanced level material therefore requires a deeper understanding of grammatical structures and what they convey, as well as the elimination of persistent errors.

A description of the material

General organization

The book is divided into two parts: a study section and a reference section.

The study section contains sixty, four-page, units. Each unit begins with a text, followed by exercises laid out on facing pages. The exercises beneath the text, on the left-hand page, concentrate on sentence structure and are concerned with *coherence* (syntax); the exercises on the right-hand page are devoted to a selection of advanced, but *discrete*, grammar points. Inevitably, there is a degree of overlap, depending on whether a structure has been dealt with from the point of view of syntax, or as a discrete item. The two pages of exercises are immediately followed by two pages of Notes, also laid out on facing pages. The Notes provide a key to the preceding exercises and a commentary. They contain cross-references to other parts of the book and also to the *Longman English Grammar* for students requiring additional information. The study section occupies 240 pages.

The reference section (pages 252–304) contains the following: an explanation of text references to interpret difficult allusions (e.g. *the ark of the tabernacle*, Unit 15); a glossary of grammar terms and concepts; a detailed structural index.

The Texts

It is beyond the scope of this work to provide realia-type texts (advertisements and the like). The authentic texts chosen represent the kind of thing we would read for pleasure or information. They are drawn from a wide range of British and American sources. The source of each text is quoted in every unit, in the contents pages and in the *Text references* section, each indicating whether a text is British English (BrE) or American English (AmE). The range of topics covered is extremely wide and likely to appeal to the non-specialist general reader who is interested in anything and everything, from human interest stories to the latest big developments in space research. The texts are arranged roughly in order of increasing difficulty. Spelling is exactly as it appears in the original source (apart from a few glaring errors, which have been corrected). The original punctuation is left unaltered, even when it is arguably incorrect. Taken together, the texts are a representative sample of current English and reflect a great deal of stylistic variety: e.g. factual, humorous, descriptive, reflective, narrative and argumentative.

The Exercises

The structures to be covered are not pre-defined, as they generally are in practice books at lower levels (in *Step by Step 1–3*, and *Longman English Grammar Practice*, for example). Instead, they are derived from the texts themselves, which set the basic syllabus. We work from text to structure, not from structure to text. This means the exercises (unlike the texts) are not *graded*. Students have been conditioned to dealing only with graded materials all their learning lives. If they continue to do this at an advanced level, they may never gain the linguistic independence that is necessary for them to cope with really advanced English. At this level, students acquire command of new structures and vocabulary in the way they do in their own language: that is, by *random accretion*, as they encounter new items in their everyday reading.

The syntactical exercises on the left-hand pages cover the most commonly used devices for connecting ideas: participle constructions, relative clauses, apposition, etc. Inevitably, these devices occur in every text, so students have abundant practice in decoding sentences through analysis and synthesis. The range of exercise-types is extremely varied. They are also self-correcting because students compare their own answers with the syntax in the original text. This gives students the opportunity to emulate the style of the original.

The grammatical points on the right-hand pages are also suggested by the texts. They are designed to reinforce, systematize and actively extend what the students may already know. They will be found to vary in level and style: what is easy for one student may be difficult for another. Some exercises that have been included for remedial purposes may seem, at first glance, to be relatively elementary, but may not be so easy after all.

Grammar is concerned with *form* and *use* and is the key to meaning. Some exercises concentrate on form where this is likely to be a barrier to understanding; others concentrate on use. The points that are studied are derived from *texts*, so that we never lose sight of the fact that our underlying concern is with *meaning*, not with the sterile analysis of language for its own sake.

The Notes

In the Notes that follow each set of exercises, there is as much commentary on sentence structure and grammatical points as space will allow. Abundant cross-referencing to other parts of the book and to the *Longman English Grammar* enables students to find out more about the points covered if they wish to. Answers to all exercises are provided to help students working on their own and/or to help to settle arguments in class!

Course materials compared with LAG

When working with LAG , it is easy to forget that it is mainly a *practice book*, not a *course*. A multi-skills course can be expected to contain elements like the following: 'lead-in' activities in the form of pre-questions through which to present the texts; skimming and scanning exercises to develop reading skills; comprehension questions to test understanding, interpretation and implication; 'lead-out' activities to develop listening, speaking and writing skills, with suggested topics for discussion and exercises in summary-writing and composition. By comparison, LAG aims to get to grips with what advanced grammar really is, in a way that is quite beyond the scope of ordinary course materials. It goes without saying that teachers are free to add their own 'lead-in' and 'lead-out' activities if they wish to use LAG as a course.

Study skills

LAG   does not have study skills built into it, so answers to exercises are readily available. LAG   treats students as adults responsible for their own learning. If students 'cheat' by looking up the answer before doing an exercise, they should be aware it is their own time they are wasting.

Variable answers

There are many possible ways of organizing a sentence, so there may be numerous correct answers to the syntax exercises. The notes in LAG   concentrate on the syntax contained in the text. Where space permits, an alternative answer may be discussed in the notes, but it is clearly impossible to gloss every permutation.

How to use the book

Each unit contains two phases: PRESENTATION and ACTIVATION. How these are covered depends on whether students are working on their own or with a teacher.

TO THE STUDENT *(students working on their own)*

Begin at the beginning of the book, and work through it systematically doing the following:

PRESENTATION

1 Read the text silently, using a good dictionary, like the *Longman Dictionary of Contemporary English*, to find out the meanings of words you don't understand. Don't worry if you know the meanings of all the words in a sentence, but still can't understand the meaning of the sentence itself. The exercises that follow will help you to do this.

ACTIVATION

2 Cover the text and do the exercises that follow. Resist the temptation to look up the answers in the text until you have finished the exercise. Then study the notes that follow.

3 Go on to the exercises on the page opposite the text, following the style given in the model answers. Then study the notes and answers that follow on the next two pages. For more information about particular grammatical points, follow up the references to the *Longman English Grammar*.

4 If you want to revise or practise particular points of grammar, refer to the Index at the end of the book, or follow up cross-references to other parts of LAG.

TO THE TEACHER *(for teachers working with students)*

Work through the book either in sequence or selectively, doing the following:

PRESENTATION

1 You may use a wide variety of scanning and silent reading techniques to present the texts. Students may be trained to read for gist and/or detail by, for example, seeking the answers to pre-set questions. Alternatively, you may present the texts through listening comprehension techniques, or a combination of listening and reading. The presentation style recommended for students working on their own (see above) is also available. Whatever you do as a teacher, do *not* explain difficulties in advance. Train the students to become self-reliant by asking them to cope with the texts as best they can before you help them.

ACTIVATION

2 Ask the students to cover the text and then get them to tackle the exercises that follow. Explain the importance of not referring to the text until an exercise has been completed. Then take the students through the answers and commentary, discussing each point and answering individual queries.

3 Invite the students to tackle the exercises on the page opposite the text, then take them through the notes, answering individual queries. Exercises may be set as homework, so that the lessons are devoted to the discussion of the points covered. Follow up the references to the *Longman English Grammar* for more detailed information.

4 Use the cross references to other parts of LAG   and the Index at the end of the book to locate particular points of grammar you want your students to revise or practise.

Watching children

WATCHING children, particularly when they don't know you are doing so, is a particular pleasure. Those quick changes of mood, for instance. Small boys who dribble
5 an imaginary football down the street and then get more interested in trying to balance on the edge of the kerb. And then stand quite still to think for a few seconds before jumping up and down with their feet together for no
10 special reason, except that they feel like jumping up and down. Maybe the fact that I no longer feel in the least like jumping up and down adds to the interest.

I once watched a child of about two-and-a-half trying to
15 stamp on little waves breaking across a wide Cornish beach. She stretched her hands out in pleasure with every little stamp and her bathing pants fell lower and lower, till she jumped them off altogether but didn't notice it, so intent was she on the important job of stamping on those
20 waves. She sang to herself a sort of monotone running commentary on what she was doing and the sound of it, mingled with soft sea noises, made a most pleasing music.

Some time ago my housekeeper had to go away for a while, and her place was taken by an Austrian friend with
25 a five-year-old daughter. Liesl couldn't be left at home, so she came to work too. She was very fair, nicely rounded, with fierce blue eyes and more curiosity than any human being I have ever met. In her it was an energy that if harnessed could have run an entire electrical plant. There
30 was nothing idle about it, she wanted to know, and nothing short of picking her up bodily and removing her from the room could stop her knowing.

Small Fry by Joyce Grenfell *(BrE)*

Sentence structure

A Say why these three statements are not true sentences in the traditional sense. What's missing?

1 Those quick changes of mood, for instance. (lines 3–4)
2 Small boys who dribble an imaginary football down the street and then get more interested in trying to balance on the edge of the kerb. (ll. 4–7)
3 And then stand quite still to think for a few seconds before jumping up and down with their feet together for no special reason, except that they feel like jumping up and down. (ll. 7–11)

....

B Join these sentences using the suggestions in brackets and making any necessary changes. Then check against the text.

1 I once watched a child of about two-and-a-half. She was trying to stamp on little waves. The waves were breaking across a wide Cornish beach. (ll. 14–16) [-*ing* form]

....
....

2 She stretched her hands out in pleasure with every little stamp. Her bathing pants fell lower and lower. She jumped them off altogether. She didn't notice it. She was so intent on the important job of stamping on those waves. (ll. 16–20) [*and, till, but, so intent*]

....
....
....

3 She sang to herself. It was a sort of monotone running commentary on what she was doing. The sound of it was mingled with soft sea noises. It made a most pleasing music. (ll. 20–22) [*and*, commas]

....
....
....

C Why do these sentences begin with *It*?

   a *It is a particular pleasure **watching** children.* → **Watching** *children is a particular pleasure.* (ll.1–3)

   b *It is a particular pleasure **to watch** children.* → **To watch** *children is a particular pleasure.*

Combine these sentences beginning each one with an *-ing* form. Make any necessary changes.

1 I hate waiting at bus stops. It's always boring.
   Waiting at bus stops is always boring.
2 Nobody likes to fill in forms. It's an unpleasant task.

3 If you jog round the block every morning, you get tired. It's exhausting.

D Which of these two sentences is right and why? (ll. 4–7)

   a *Small boys get interested to try to balance on the edge of the kerb.*
   b *Small boys get interested in trying to balance on the edge of the kerb.*

Join or rewrite these sentences using the *-ing* form.

1 I don't want to try to balance on the edge of the kerb at my age. I'm not interested.
   I'm not interested in trying to balance on the edge of the kerb at my age.
2 They stand still for a few seconds before they jump up and down with their feet together.

3 She was stamping on the waves. She was really intent on this important job.

4 I went to the office without my briefcase this morning. I didn't take it with me.

E Why do we use *-ing* in sentence **a** (*jumping*), but a *to*-infinitive in sentence **b** (*to know*)?

   a *I no longer **feel** in the least **like jumping** up and down.* (l. 12)
   b *She **wanted to know** and nothing could stop her knowing.* (ll. 30–32)

Use the *to*-infinitive or the *-ing* form of the verbs in brackets.

1 You'll have to wait for ages for another driving test if you fail *to pass* this time. (pass)
2 The people in the flat below have refused................the Residents' Association. (join)
3 Katy doesn't really enjoy................in public. (sing)
4 Jill thinks we should phone now, but John suggests................later. (phone)
5 I think you should stop................and leave at five o'clock like everyone else. (work)
6 I don't want to join them on holiday. I can't afford................money the way they do. (spend)

F How do the words in bold italics in sentence **a** differ from the words in bold italics in **b**?

   a *We must **stop him telling**.* (compare l. 32)
   b ***Imagine his/him telling** the chef how to cook an omelette!*

Put in the missing words.

1 I don't want to catch *him climbing* over my fence again! (him/his, climb)
2 He is often late. I don't mind................late. (him/his, be)
3 I like to watch................. It's such a rare sight! (you/your, work)
4 Listen to those kids! Fancy................able to speak Spanish as well as that! (them/their, be)
5 I can't imagine................of what you're doing! (your mother/your mother's, approve)
6 Don't say that! You'll start................again. (him/his, complain)

SENTENCE STRUCTURE

A Answers and commentary

The three statements are not true sentences, in the traditional sense, because they do not have a finite main verb. (A verb is *finite* when it has a subject and tense.) This doesn't mean the statements are wrong. The writer has written statements without verbs to keep the rhythms of speech. If you read the text aloud, you will be able to 'hear' the poetic effect of these statements as they build up a series of images to supply different elements in a picture. [> LEG 1.2, LAG 14A, 42B, 48Bn.2b]

1 *Those quick changes of mood, for instance.*
This is a phrase (that is, a group of words that can be part of a sentence [> LEG 1.2]) and it contains no verb at all.

2 *Small boys who dribble an imaginary football...*
This contains a relative clause (*small boys who dribble*... [> LEG 1.25, LAG 5A, etc.]) but it doesn't contain a main verb. If we delete *who*, we get two simple sentences joined by *and* to make a complete compound sentence [> LEG 1.17]:
*Small boys dribble an imaginary football down the street **and** then get more interested...*
Alternatively, we could turn this into a true sentence, in the traditional sense, by adding a main finite verb:
*Small boys who dribble an imaginary football down the street and then get more interested in trying to balance on the edge of the kerb **may not know** that anyone is watching them.*

3 *And then stand quite still to think for a few seconds...*
Stand is not a finite verb because it doesn't have a subject. In ordinary English, the subject must be expressed, or it must be strongly implied. [> LEG 1.2, 4.5, 4.12] We can make this a true sentence by adding a subject (it's all right to begin a sentence with *And* for stylistic effect [> LAG 48Bns.2a–b]):
*And then **they stand** quite still to think for a few seconds before jumping up and down with their feet together...*

B Answers and commentary

1 *I once watched a child of two-and-a-half **trying** to stamp on little waves **breaking**...*
We can use the -*ing* form present participle to join sentences in place of relative clauses [> LEG 1.58.6, LAG 9An.1, etc.]:
*I once watched a child of two-and-a-half (**who was**) **trying** to stamp on little waves (**which were**) **breaking** across a wide Cornish beach.*

2 *She stretched her hands out in pleasure with every little stamp **and** her bathing pants fell lower and lower, **till** she jumped them off altogether **but** didn't notice it, **so intent was she** on the important job of stamping on those waves.*
We use *and* and *but* to make compound sentences. [> LEG 1.17]
We use *till* to introduce an adverbial clause of time. [> LEG 1.45.1, LAG 6Bn.1, 53Bn.1]
When we introduce a clause of reason with *so* + adjective or adverb, we change the order of subject and verb:
*...**so intent was she**...* [> LEG 7.59.3, LAG 33C]
It would also have been possible to write:
*...but she didn't notice **because she was so intent** on the important job of stamping...*
So is used as an intensifying adverb here. [> LEG 7.51.1, compare > LAG 3C, 33D]

3 *She sang to herself **a sort of monotone running commentary on what she was doing**...*
Normally, we avoid putting anything between the verb and its object: *...she sang a commentary to herself*... unless (as in this case) the object is very long. [> LEG 7.16.1]
*...**and** the sound of it, **mingled** with soft sea noises, **made** a most pleasing music.*
Which was has been deleted from the relative clause: *...**which was** mingled with soft sea noises...* [> LEG 1.62.3, compare > LAG 6Bn.1]
We use commas round this abbreviated clause because it is non-defining, that is, it adds extra information. [> LEG 1.26, LAG 31An.2, etc.]
The main clause is: *...the sound of it* (subject) *made* (main finite verb) *a most pleasing music* (object). [> LEG 1.21]

GRAMMAR POINTS

C Gerund and infinitive constructions
[> LEG 4.13, 16.26–33, 16.47–48]

a *It is a particular pleasure watching* ...
It is a preparatory subject, preparing us for the true subject *watching* [gerund > LAG 20D].

b *It is a particular pleasure to watch* ...
It is a preparatory subject, preparing us for the true subject *to watch* (infinitive).
We generally prefer to begin sentences of this kind with *It* (*It's a pleasure* + *to* or *-ing*). We rarely begin statements with the *to*-infinitive, but we often begin with *-ing* especially when we are making general statements [> LAG 37E]:
Watching children is a particular pleasure.
Rather than:
To watch children is a particular pleasure.

1 Waiting at bus stops is always boring.
2 Filling in forms is an unpleasant task.
3 Jogging round the block every morning is exhausting.

D Preposition + -ing [> LEG 16.50–56]

b is right because *get interested* is followed by the preposition *in*. Verbs after prepositions like *in* must be *-ing* forms:
Work quietly without talking. (Not *without to talk*)
Many adjectives are followed by prepositions [> LEG 16.53, LAG 9D, 52D]: *afraid of, bored with, interested in, keen on, sorry for.*
That's why we have to say:
They get interested in trying. (Not *They get interested to try/They are interested in to try*)

1 I'm not interested in trying to balance on the edge of the kerb at my age.
2 They stand still for a few seconds before jumping up and down with their feet together.
3 She was really intent on this important job of stamping on the waves.
4 I went to the office this morning without taking my briefcase with me.

E Verb + -ing and verb + to-infinitive
[> LEG 16.42, 16.19–20, Apps 45.3, 46.1]

a *feel like* is followed by *-ing*:
I no longer feel like jumping.
When we want to use another verb after *feel like*, the second verb can only be an *-ing* form, never

a *to*-infinitive. A few other verbs like this are: *admit, avoid, consider, deny, dislike, enjoy, excuse, finish, imagine, report, suggest.*

b *want* is followed by a *to*-infinitive:
She wanted to know.
When we want to use another verb after *want*, the second verb can only be a *to*-infinitive, never an *-ing* form. A few other verbs like this are: *aim, apply, can('t) afford, fail, hasten, hesitate, hurry, long, manage, offer, prepare, refuse, seek.*

1 to pass 2 to join 3 singing 4 phoning
5 working 6 to spend

F Verb (+ accusative or possessive) + -ing form: 'excuse me/my asking' [> LEG 16.45]

a We use the object ('accusative') form (*him*) after *stop*, not the possessive form (*his*).

b We use the possessive form (*his*) after *imagine*, but we can also use the object form (*him*).

With some of the verbs which can be followed by an *-ing* form, we can put another word between the verb and *-ing*. Sometimes this word must be an 'accusative' (e.g. an object pronoun like *me*, a name like *John*); sometimes it must be a possessive (e.g. *my*, or *John's*); sometimes it can be either.

After *hear, keep, smell, start, stop, watch* and verbs like them, we use the *-ing* form as a participle:
Is he working? Why doesn't he start?
→ *Why doesn't he start working?*
What can we do to start him working? (Not *his*)

After verbs like *avoid, enjoy* and *suggest* we use a possessive + *-ing*:
I don't enjoy your/his/John's teasing. (Not *I don't enjoy you/him/John teasing*)

After verbs like *dislike, excuse, fancy, forgive, imagine, like, love, mind, miss* and *prevent*, we can use an object or a possessive. Not all native speakers approve of the use of the object (accusative):
Please excuse his not writing to you. Or:
Please excuse him not writing to you.

1 him climbing 2 him/his being 3 you working 4 them/their being 5 your mother/your mother's approving 6 him complaining

Pop Art absurdists

ON Tuesday, a large painting by Jasper Johns, the 57-year-old Pop Art absurdist, sold at Christie's, New York, for £2.2 million. This was an auction record for the work of a living artist, according to my friend Geraldine Norman.

I suppose it is the pressure of the great American foundations which keeps this particular pantomime on the road. They have spent so much money on the same sort of rubbish already that they have to go on buying it or their previous investment in 'modern art' will be seen to be worthless.

But then I read of an enterprising Austrian who has offered Mick Jagger a vast sum of money for his ashes, hoping to sell them eventually in hour-glasses for many hundreds of thousands of pounds each. A spokesman for Jagger was quoted as saying 'It's going to be a heavy thing for Mick to figure out and give an answer.' Even if it is in death, what's he going to value more - his body or his money?

Few of us, I imagine, would be prepared to pay 50p for the whole collection of Rolling Bones. But the fact that money is available for this sort of nonsense might make us revise Marx's theory of Surplus Value. Technological capitalism produces so much more wealth than there are useful things to spend it on that we have to spend it on rubbish.

The Sunday Telegraph (BrE)

Sentence structure

A Three of these sentences contain an extra word, or extra words, not in the text. Cross out the extra words where necessary, and say why you have done so. Then check against the text.

1 On Tuesday, a large painting by Jasper Johns, he is the 57-year-old Pop Art absurdist, sold at Christie's. (ll. 1–5)

2 I suppose it is the pressure of the great American foundations which it keeps this particular pantomime on the road. (ll. 10–13)

3 Even if it is in death, what's he going to value more – his body or his money? (ll. 31–33)

4 But the fact that money is available for this sort of nonsense might make us to revise Marx's theory of Surplus Value. (ll. 37–40)

B Join these sentences using the suggestions in brackets and making any necessary changes. Then check against the text.

1 They have spent money on the same sort of rubbish already. They have to go on buying it. Their previous investment in 'modern art' will be seen to be worthless. (ll.13–19) [*so much, that , or*]

2 But then I read of an enterprising Austrian. He has offered Mick Jagger a vast sum of money for his ashes. He is hoping to sell them eventually in hour-glasses for many hundreds of thousands of pounds each. (ll. 20–26) [*who, -ing*]

Grammar points

C Comment on the form of the verbs.

   a *Jasper Johns **sold** a large painting for £2.2 million.*
   b *A large painting by Jasper Johns **was sold** for £2.2 million.*
   c *A large painting by Jasper Johns **sold** for £2.2 million.* (ll. 1–6)

....

Rewrite these sentences a) in the passive b) with an active verb that has a passive meaning.

1 They *have sold* some of Van Gogh's paintings for millions of dollars.
   Some of Van Gogh's paintings have been sold/have sold for millions of dollars.

2 They're already *reprinting* his book.

....

3 You *can wash* this new material at high temperatures.

....

4 How much *do you let* this flat *for* during the summer months?

....

D Why can't you use *alive* in sentence **a**?

   a *This was an auction record for the work of a **living** artist.* (ll. 6–8)
   b *This was an auction record for the work of an artist who's still **alive**.*

Complete these sentences using adjectives beginning with *a-*.

1 The *frightened* people ran out of the building. They all looked terribly *afraid* ....
2 We looked at the *floating* vessel. We were glad to know it was still ....
3 I could never touch a *live* lobster. I could never touch a lobster that is still ....
4 The *burning* forest glowed in the darkness. The forest was .... for days.
5 I never feel *lonely* when I am ....

E Read **a–d**, then make up rules for the use of *according to, in (my) opinion* and *by*.

   a ***According to Geraldine/In Geraldine's opinion**, this is a record.* (Not **by Geraldine**) (ll. 6–9)
   b ***According to** the weather forecast it'll be wet tomorrow.* (Not **by the weather forecast**)
   c ***In my opinion**, Geraldine may very well be right.* (Not **by me/according to me**)
   d ***By/According to** my watch, the time is exactly 8.27.*

....
....

Supply *according to, in ... opinion* or *by*. Sometimes more than one answer is possible.

1 I know what my verdict would be. *In my opinion* the man's innocent.
2 He's such a fusspot. He does everything exactly .... the book.
3 .... her, it's all right to eat fruit that hasn't been washed first.
4 .... an announcement I've just heard, the next train's been cancelled.
5 .... my solicitor, they haven't got a case.

F Why do we use *much* in **a** and *many* in **b**?

   a *Technological capitalism produces **much more** wealth than ...* (ll. 41–43)
   b *Technological capitalism produces **many more** goods than we need.*

....

Supply *much* or *many*. Suggest other words in place of *much/many* that will fit in these spaces.

1 Have you had enough to eat? – Yes, thank you. I can't eat *much/any* more.
2 That's just about all I know. I wasn't able to get .... more information than that.
3 .... more people are in favour of heavy penalties for drunken drivers than you think.
4 I wish you'd stop that noise! I really can't take .... more.

SENTENCE STRUCTURE

A Answers and commentary

Numbers **1**, **2** and **4** contain an extra word or extra words which are not in the text.

1 *On Tuesday, a large painting by Jasper Johns,* ~~*he is*~~ *the 57-year old Pop Art absurdist, ...*
He is the 57-year-old Pop Art absurdist is a complete sentence and therefore cannot stand in the middle of another sentence in formal writing without some kind of connecting word:
      ... Jasper Johns, **who is** *...*
We can avoid a relative clause by placing phrases side-by-side, separating them by commas, so that the second adds information to the first. Phrases like this are in apposition and are common in journalism [> LEG 1.39, 3.30, LAG 5A*ns*.2,4, etc.]:
      ... Jasper Johns, **the 57-year-old Pop Art absurdist**, *...*

2 *I suppose it is the pressure of the great American foundations which* ~~*it*~~ *keeps this ...*
Which refers to *pressure* and is a relative pronoun subject:
      There is **pressure**. *It keeps this pantomime on the road.*
      → *It is this* **pressure which** *keeps ...*
We never use a subject pronoun and a relative pronoun together to refer to the subject [> LEG 1.29, 1.31, LAG 37A*n*.3, etc.]:
      This is the **cat which/that** *caught the mouse.* (Not *This is the cat which it caught the mouse.*)

It is the pressure of the great American foundations which keeps this pantomime on the road is a cleft sentence, that is a simple sentence split into two clauses. [> LEG 4.14, LAG 28B*n*.2, 34D]

3 The sentence is all right as it is. The phrase *in death* is the opposite of the phrase *in life*:
      I didn't like him much **in life** *and I won't pretend to like him any better* **in death**.
      (= ... while he was alive ... now that he is dead)

4 *... this sort of nonsense might make us* ~~*to*~~ *revise Marx's theory of Surplus Value.*
We use the bare infinitive after *make* (= compel, cause to). We use *to* after *make* only in passive constructions [> LEG 16.4.3, LAG 25E]:
      They **made** *him* **work** *twenty hours a day.* (Not *made him to work*)
      → *He* **was made to work** *twenty hours a day.*

B Answers and commentary

1 *They have spent* **so much** *money on the same sort of rubbish already* **that** *they have to go on ...*
We can introduce clauses of result with *so + much/many/few/little*, etc. + *(that)*. [> LAG 10A*n*.2, 16A*n*.3]
Though *that* may normally be omitted, it would probably be included here because of the long phrase *on the same sort of rubbish already* that separates *so much money* from the clause of result. Compare:
      There was **so much** *to lose* **(that)** *we couldn't take any risks.* [> LEG 1.52.1]

... or their previous investment in 'modern art' will be seen to be worthless.
Or is a conjunction which can join nouns, adjectives or verbs. We would normally put a comma in front of it when it introduces a clause to suggest a pause in speech or writing [> LEG 1.16–18]:
      He speaks French, **or** *perhaps he understands it.*

2 *But then I read of an enterprising Austrian* **who** *has offered Mick Jagger a vast sum of money for his ashes, ...*
Who refers to *an Austrian* and is a relative pronoun subject:
      He is **an Austrian**. *He has offered ...*
      → *He is* **an Austrian who** *has offered ...*
(Not * *... who he has offered ...* *) [> LEG 1.29]

... **hoping** *to sell them eventually in hour-glasses for many hundreds of thousands of pounds each.*
The present participle is used in place of a clause of reason:
      He has offered a vast sum of money, **because** *he is* **hoping** *to ...*
      → *He has offered a vast sum of money,* **hoping** *to ...* [> LEG 1.58.3 and compare > LEG 1.48, LAG 24A*n*.8, 41A*n*.1]

GRAMMAR POINTS

C Active verbs with a passive meaning: 'it sold for £2.2m' [> LEG 12.3 n.9]

a *Jasper Johns* **sold** *a large painting*: the verb *sold* is active; its subject is *Jasper Johns*.

b *A large painting by Jasper Johns* **was sold**: *was sold* is the normal passive form of *sold*.

c *A large painting by Jasper Johns* **sold** *for £2.2 million*: *sold* is active in form, but passive in meaning.

A few active verbs like *clean*, *sell*, *show* and *wash* can be used with a passive meaning:
His picture **was sold** *for £2.2 million.*
→ *His picture* **sold** *for £2.2 million.*
There is often a link with 'ability':
This surface **cleans** *easily* really means 'It can be cleaned easily/It is cleaned easily.'

1 Some of Van Gogh's paintings have been sold/have sold for millions of dollars.

2 His book is already being reprinted/is already reprinting.

3 This new material can be washed/washes at high temperatures.

4 How much is this flat let for/does this flat let for during the summer months?

D Predicative adjectives beginning with 'a-': 'he is alive' [> LEG 6.8.2]

a We can't use *alive* before a noun:
He is a **living** *artist.* (But not *He is an alive artist**)

b But we can say:
This was an auction record for the work of an artist who's still **alive**/*who's still* **living**.

We say that an adjective is *predicative* or that it is used *predicatively* when it comes directly after *be*, *seem*, etc. A predicative adjective can be used on its own as a complement [> LEG 1.9, 6.7]:
This ticket **is old**. *Your mother* **seems angry**.
There are a few adjectives beginning with *a-* which are used only predicatively:
afloat, *afraid*, *alight*, *alike*, *alive*, *ashamed*, *asleep* and *awake*.

1 afraid
2 afloat
3 alive
4 alight/ablaze
5 alone

E 'According to', 'in my opinion' and 'by' [> LEG App 25.2, LAG 8An.1]

a We can say *according to* a person or *in the opinion of* a person. (Not *by a person*):
According to Geraldine . . . In Geraldine's opinion . . . (= as stated by).

b We can say *according to* a source of information (other than oneself):
According to the weather forecast . . . (Not **by the weather forecast**)

c When we want to refer to ourselves, we have to say *in my opinion*. (Not **by me/according to me**)

d We can use *by* in place of *according to* only when we are referring to something highly specific, like a watch, which no one can argue with:
By my watch/According to my watch, the time is exactly 8.27.

1 In my opinion
2 according to the book/by the book
3 According to her/In her opinion
4 According to an announcement
5 According to my solicitor/In my solicitor's opinion/In the opinion of my solicitor

F The use of 'much' or 'many' before 'more' [> LEG 5.6.1]

a *Much* goes with uncountable nouns; *wealth* is uncountable, so we have to say *much more wealth*.

b *Many* goes with plural countable nouns; *goods* is a plural countable noun, so we have to say *many more goods*. [> LAG 7E]
Note that *more* goes with both uncountable and countable nouns.

uncountable nouns:
We can say:
some more/any more, hardly any more, a little more, a lot more, much more, no more + **wealth**, **sugar**, etc.

plural countable nouns:
We can say:
some more/any more, a few more, hardly any more, a lot more, many more, no more + **goods**, **apples**, etc.

1 much, any
2 much, any
3 Many, A lot
4 much, any, a lot

The man who discovered Britain

He described frozen seas - but no one believed him

ON HIS RETURN from a sea journey north to the Atlantic, the Greek explorer said of Britain: 'The island is thickly populated ... has an extremely chilly
5 climate ...' Of its people, he wrote: 'They are unusually hospitable and gentle in manner ... Their diet is inexpensive and quite different from the luxury that is born of wealth ... It (Britain) has many kings and
10 potentates who live for the most part in a state of mutual peace ...'

Yet no one believed him. It was the year 304 BC, and the explorer was Pytheas of Marseilles.

For 2000 years historians labelled him a charlatan,
15 although they enjoyed his accounts of his travels as masterpieces of fabrication. Yet Pytheas was the first Greek to visit and describe Britain and its people and, possibly, to sail within sight of the Norwegian coast. He wrote: 'The people of Britannia are simple in their habits
20 and far removed from the cunning and knavishness of modern man ... they do not drink wine, but a fermented liquor made from barley, which they call *curmi*.'

At the time of his epic journey, the northern waters of the Atlantic were unknown to Pytheas's contemporaries.
25 How could they - familiar only with the warm waters of the Mediterranean - believe that he had seen chunks of floating ice larger than his ship? Or that further north the sea was entirely frozen and the sun never set?

Pytheas was discredited, and although later Greek
30 historians included references to his travels in their books, their attitude was typified by Strabo (born about 63 BC). He wrote: 'Pytheas tells us that Thule [believed then to be an undiscovered northernmost land] is one day's sail from the congealed sea ... and this Pytheas saw
35 with his own eyes - or so he would have us believe.'

The Reader's Digest *Book of Strange Stories Amazing Facts (AmE)*

Sentence structure

A Refer to the text, then write another word or words in place of the words in italics.

1 *Yet* no one believed him. (l. 12) ....

2 For 2000 years historians labelled him a charlatan, *although* they
enjoyed his accounts of his travels as masterpieces of fabrication. (ll. 14–16) ....

3 Pytheas was discredited, and *although* later Greek historians included
references to his travels in their books, their attitude was typified
by Strabo (born about 63 BC). (ll. 29–32) ....

B Rewrite these sentences as one sentence beginning with the words provided. Then check against the text.

1 He returned from a sea journey north to the Atlantic. The Greek explorer said of Britain: 'The island is thickly populated ...' (ll. 1–4)
On ....

2 There are (in Britain) many kings and potentates. They live for the most part in a state of mutual peace. (ll. 9–11)
It (Britain) ....

3 How was it possible for them to believe that he had seen chunks of floating ice larger than his ship? They were familiar only with the warm waters of the Mediterranean. (ll. 25–27)
How could ....
....

Grammar points

C What do the words in bold italics mean?

*The island is **thickly** populated ... has an **extremely** chilly climate* (ll. 3–5)
*Or that further north the sea was **entirely** frozen ...* (ll. 27–28)

Match a word in column **A** with a word in column **B**, then write sentences with them.

A	B	
thickly	respected	*thickly covered*
highly	disappointed	
utterly	ill	
painfully	covered	
gravely	stupid	
bitterly	embarrassed	

1 *The floor of the forest was thickly covered with moss.*
2
3
4
5
6

D Suggest other verbs which you could use in place of *labelled* here:

*For 2000 years historians **labelled** him a charlatan.* (l. 14)

Rewrite these sentences in the active.

1 Pytheas was labelled a charlatan by historians.
  Historians labelled Pytheas a charlatan.
2 Washington was elected president by the people of America.

3 Jane Austen is considered a great novelist by most readers.

4 James Henderson has been appointed chairman by the board of directors.

5 She was named Sarah Jane by her godparents.

E Use another phrase in place of the words in bold italics.

*This Pytheas saw with his own eyes – or so **he would have us believe**.* (ll. 34–35)

Rewrite these sentences using the correct forms of *have*.

1 John wants us to believe that he is a qualified engineer, but I know he isn't.
  John will/would have us believe that he is a qualified engineer.
2 Ask the next patient to come in now please, nurse.

3 We got Mr Saunders to paint our kitchen plain white.

4 Ask your secretary to make a list of companies that will be interested in our service.

5 I want you to know that I've already been on two trips up the Amazon.

SENTENCE STRUCTURE

A Answers and commentary

Possible answers

1 *But*: We can introduce contrast with *but* and *yet*. [> LEG 1.20.2, LAG 1B*n*.2] Some people avoid using *but* to begin a sentence [> LEG 1.17–20], but this is a matter of individual style. There is generally no objection to beginning a sentence with *But* or with *Yet*, as in the text. [> LAG 56A*n*.7]

2 *but*: *But* can sometimes replace *though* and *although* in contrast clauses [> LEG 1.50, LAG 11B*n*.2, 30A*n*.4], as long as it's not used to begin a sentence:
   Although they enjoyed his accounts of his travels, historians labelled him …
   (Not *But they enjoyed … , historians … *)

3 *even though* or *even if* [> LEG 1.50, LAG 15A*n*.2]: The use of *and* in front of *although* prevents us from using *but* in place of *although* here:
   *Pytheas was discredited, and although later Greek historians … *(Not *and but**)

B Answers and commentary

1 We could rewrite this sentence in two ways:

a *On returning from a sea journey north to the Atlantic, the Greek explorer said of Britain: …*
In this sentence we are using *On* + present participle in place of *When* in an adverbial clause of time [> LEG 1.58.2, compare > LAG 4B*n*.3, 28A*n*.3a, 53A*n*.2, 57A*n*.4]:
   When he returned from a sea journey …
   → *On returning from a sea journey …*

b *On his return from a sea journey north to the Atlantic, the Greek explorer said of Britain: …*
In this sentence we are using a noun in place of a verb [> LEG 16.33]:
   When he returned from a sea journey north to the Atlantic, the Greek explorer said of Britain: …
   → *On his return from a sea journey north to the Atlantic, the Greek explorer said of Britain: …*

2 *It (Britain) has many kings and potentates who live for the most part in a state of mutual peace.*
(The author has found it necessary to put *Britain* in brackets after *It*, to remind us that *Britain* is the true subject of the sentence.)

The relative pronoun *who* refers to people (*kings and potentates*) and remains unchanged whether it refers to masculine, feminine, singular or plural. *Who* is the relative pronoun subject of the relative clause [> LEG 1.27–29, compare > LAG 5A, etc.]:
   *It has many kings and potentates. **They** live for the most part in a state of mutual peace.*
   → *It has many kings and potentates **who** live for the most part in a state of mutual peace.*

3 *How could they – familiar only with the warm waters of the Mediterranean – believe (it)?*
Could refers to possibility in the past. [> LEG 11.27–30] In this context, *How could they believe … ?* is not a question that requires an answer. It means 'Of course they couldn't possibly believe it'.

– familiar only with the warm waters of the Mediterranean – is used in place of a relative clause: *who were familiar only with the warm waters of the Mediterranean*. The clause is non-defining because it adds extra information, which could be omitted. [> LAG 5A, 22A*n*.5, etc.] To emphasize this idea of extra information, dashes (– … –) are used to separate the clause from the body of the sentence. [> LEG 1.26, LAG 16A*n*.1]

GRAMMAR POINTS

C -ly intensifiers used in place of 'very': 'extremely tall' [> LEG 7.52–53, App 16]

Thickly and *extremely* mean 'very'; *entirely* means 'completely'.

We can use *-ly* intensifiers in front of adjectives (*extremely* **tall**) or adjectival past participles (*extremely* **bored**).
These *-ly* intensifiers fall broadly into three classes:

1 Adverbs like *extremely* and *terribly* which we often use for extra emphasis instead of *very*:
   John was **very hungry/tired** *last night.* = *John was* **extremely hungry/tired** *last night.*

2 Adverbs like *absolutely*, *completely* and *entirely* which retain their basic meaning:
   We are **entirely happy** *with the way the conference has been arranged.* (= completely happy)

3 Adverbs like *bitterly*, *gravely* and *thickly* which combine with small sets of words. We often use the term 'collocation' to describe the way words attract each other in this way: e.g.
   thickly +
   covered, populated, spread, wooded
   highly +
   critical, educated, intelligent, respected
   utterly +
   different, convinced, mistaken, stupid
   painfully +
   aware, embarrassed, obvious, true
   gravely +
   concerned, damaged, ill, mistaken
   bitterly +
   cold, disappointed, humiliated, envious

Sample answers

1 The floor of the forest was thickly covered with moss.
2 Our mayor is highly respected by everyone in the community.
3 I can't imagine how anyone so utterly stupid can be appointed to such an important job.
4 John laughed when he finished telling his joke, but we were all painfully embarrassed.
5 Martha has been gravely ill for six weeks now and may not recover.
6 Mayhew was bitterly disappointed when he failed to get a first class degree.

D Word order: subject + verb + object + complement: 'called him a fool'
[> LEG 1.14 and compare > LEG 12.8, 16.22, LAG 18D, 30F]

Other verbs in place of *labelled* could be e.g. *called, considered, declared*.

Verbs like *appoint, baptize, call, consider, crown, declare, elect, label, make, name* and *vote* can be followed by an object and a complement: *They labelled* **him** (object) *a charlatan* (noun complement).
The complement can sometimes be an adjective:
   They considered **him** (object) **stupid** (adjectival complement).
Verbs in this pattern are often used in the passive:
   They **appointed** *him chairman.* (active)
   → *He* **was appointed** *chairman.* (passive)

1 Historians labelled Pytheas a charlatan.
2 The people of America elected Washington president.
3 Most readers consider Jane Austen a great novelist.
4 The board of directors has appointed James Henderson chairman.
5 Her godparents named her Sarah Jane.

E 'Have' + personal object + bare infinitive: 'he would have us believe' [> LEG 16.10 and compare > LEG 12.10–12]

This Pytheas saw with his own eyes – or **so he wanted us to believe** (= so he would have us believe).

We can use *have* + personal object + bare infinitive to show that one person is causing another to do something:
   We **had Mr Saunders** (personal object) **paint** (bare infinitive) *our kitchen.*
We should not confuse this construction with the true causative form with an impersonal object:
   We **had our kitchen** (impersonal object) **painted** (past participle) *white.* [> LAG 26F]

1 John will/would have us believe that he is a qualified engineer.
2 Have the next patient come in now please, nurse.
3 We had Mr Saunders paint our kitchen plain white.
4 Have your secretary make a list of companies that will be interested in our service.
5 I'll/I'd have you know that I've already been on two trips up the Amazon.

Heroic failures

The least successful attempt to clear molehills

TIRED of the 10 large molehills that flourished on his lawn, Mr Oscar Ejiamike decided to remove them. After a vigorous campaign of bombing, gassing and waiting round in the dark with a raised shovel, he found that the 10 molehills survived intact. There were also 22 new ones.

At this point our man decided to 'surprise the moles' with a midnight poisoning raid. In May 1984 he drove his Jaguar 2.4 automatic to the edge of the lawn and trained the headlamps upon the enemy zone. While reaching across for the poison, Mr Ejiamike knocked the car into reverse and accelerated through the wall of his cottage, knocking over the electric heater, bursting his petrol tanks, setting fire to his newly decorated sitting room, and wrecking his car.

While this certainly surprised the moles, it had no effect on the 32 molehills. Next morning Mr Ejiamike bought 22 bags of ready-mixed cement and announced that he was going to concrete the lawn over.

The Sunday Times (BrE)

Sentence structure

A Put the words in the right order in each sentence to prepare yourself for exercise **B** below.

1 a tired Mr Oscar Ejiamike was of the 10 large molehills that on his lawn flourished.

....

b to remove them he decided. (ll. 1–4)

....

2 a his Jaguar 2.4 automatic in May 1984 to the edge of the lawn he drove.

....

b the headlamps the enemy zone he trained upon. (ll. 12–15)

....

3 a Mr Ejiamike for the poison was reaching across.

....

b into reverse the car he knocked.

....

c through of his cottage the wall he accelerated.

....

d the electric heater he knocked over. his petrol tanks burst he.

....

e his newly decorated sitting room he set fire to.

....

f his car he wrecked. (ll. 15–22)

....

B Join the above into three separate sentences, then check against the text.

1 ....

....

2 ....

....

3 ....

....

....

Grammar points

C Which prepositions would you use in these spaces and why?

a ... *May 1984 he drove his Jaguar 2.4 automatic to the edge of the lawn.* (ll. 12–14)
b ... *May 21, 1984, he drove his Jaguar 2.4 automatic to the edge of the lawn.*
c ... *Monday, May 21, 1984, ... 12.15 a.m. he drove his Jaguar 2.4 to the edge of the lawn.*

Supply the missing prepositions (*on*, *at* or *in*) in the following sentences.

1 I was born _*on*_ a Friday _*at*_ 7 _*in*_ the morning.
2 He claims he could read .... the age of 3 from a book he received .... his third birthday.
3 I'll see you .... the morning .... around 10 o'clock.
4 He was arrested .... the morning of Monday, April 24 .... precisely 10 a.m.
5 The roads are so crowded .... August, we've delayed our holiday till September.
6 Did you say you saw him .... May 25th, or .... 31st May?
7 He's so predictable. He does his washing .... Mondays and his shopping .... the weekend.

D Which of these sentences doesn't sound 'right' and why?

a *Mr Ejiamike knocked over the electric heater.* (ll. 19–20)
b *Mr Ejiamike knocked the electric heater over.*
c *He knocked the child over while driving to work.*
d *He knocked over the child while driving to work.*

Rewrite these sentences changing the position of the object where possible.

1 I knocked the heater over.   *I knocked over the heater.*
2 I paid the money back.
3 We rang Carlos back.
4 The teacher hurried the children along.
5 Bring your own food along.
6 I invited my friends down for the weekend.
7 Let the people off the bus.
8 The boy pulled off his jumper.
9 Ask your friends round.
10 Pass these chocolates round.

E What do the verbs *said* and *announced* do in sentences **a** and **b**?

a *He **said** that he was going to concrete the lawn over.*
b *He **announced** that he was going to concrete the lawn over.* (ll. 27–29)

Report the following statements using one of the following verbs in place of ***said***. Use each verb only once: *announced, complained, concluded, replied, promised, suggested.*

1 'I'm going to get engaged,' he said.
   He announced (that) he was going to get engaged.
2 'We should go by taxi,' she said.

3 'I'm not at all satisfied with this car,' he said.

4 'They must be out,' she said.

5 'I really don't agree with you,' he said.

6 'I'll phone you back tomorrow,' she said.

SENTENCE STRUCTURE

A Answers and commentary

In English, the order of words is essential to the meaning of a sentence. [> LEG 1.1] Although variations are possible [> LAG 1B*n*.2, 16C, etc.], the basic word order in a sentence that is not a question or a command is usually:

Subject   Verb   Object
I   *phoned* *my mother*
Manner   **Place**   **Time** [> LEG 1.3]
                    this morning.

We can also put Time at the beginning of a sentence [> LEG 7.19.1, 7.22]:

> ***This morning*** *I phoned my mother.*

When the verb is *be*, or a verb related to *be* like *seem*, the word order is:

Subject   Verb   Complement.

We cannot use an object after *be, seem,* etc. A complement is usually a noun, adjective or pronoun, or a combination as in **1a** below:

> *Frank is **an architect**. Frank is **clever**.*

[> LEG 1.9, 1.11, LAG 2D, 14E, 46D]

1a *Mr Oscar Ejiamike* (S) *was* (V) *tired of the 10 large molehills* (C) *that* (S) *flourished* (V) *on his lawn* (P).
b *He* (S) *decided* (V) *to remove them* (O).

2a (*In May 1984*) (T) *he* (S) *drove* (V) *his Jaguar 2.4 automatic* (O) *to the edge of the lawn* (P) (*in May 1984*) (T).
b *He* (S) *trained* (V) *the headlamps* (O) *upon the enemy zone* (P).

3a *Mr Ejiamike* (S) *was reaching across for* (V) *the poison* (O).
b *He* (S) *knocked* (V) *the car* (O) *into reverse* (P).
c *He* (S) *accelerated* (V) *through the wall of his cottage* (P).
d *He* (S) *knocked over* (V) *the electric heater* (O). *He* (S) *burst* (V) *his petrol tanks* (O).
e *He* (S) *set fire to* (V) *his newly decorated sitting room* (O).
f *He* (S) *wrecked* (V) *his car* (O).

B Answers and commentary

We combine simple sentences to make compound and/or complex sentences. [> LEG 1.19, 1.21] Suggestions for joining these sentences were not provided in the exercise, so there are many possible answers. The commentary is based on the way the sentences have been joined in the text.

1 ***Tired*** *of the 10 large molehills that flourished on his lawn,* ***Mr Oscar Ejiamike*** *...*
We can use an adjectival past participle (*tired*) in place of a clause (*Because he was tired*). [> LEG 1.62.1, 1.63, LAG 51A*ns*.2–3]

2 *In May 1984 he drove his Jaguar 2.4 automatic to the edge of the lawn* ***and trained*** *the headlamps ...*
Two simple sentences are joined by *and* to make a compound sentence. When the subject is the same in all parts of the sentence, it is usual not to repeat it, so we say *... and trained*, rather than *and he trained* (though *and he trained* would not necessarily be wrong). [> LEG 1.20, LAG 9B*n*.3, etc.]

3 ***While reaching*** *... , Mr Ejiamike knocked ...* ***and*** *accelerated ... , knocking ... , bursting ... , setting fire to ... , and wrecking ...*
We can join sentences with present participle constructions [> LEG 1.58, LAG 3B*n*.1]:
> *During the time he was reaching ...*
> *While he was reaching ...*
> → ***While reaching*** *...*
We could also omit *while* here and say:
> ***Reaching*** *across for the poison ...*
The main clause is *Mr Ejiamike knocked the car into reverse.* [> LEG 1.21]
(*He*) *accelerated through the wall of his cottage* is a co-ordinate main clause joined by *and*. [> LEG 1.17–18, LAG 1B*n*.2]
The remaining clauses (*he knocked over, he burst, he set fire to, he wrecked*) are joined to the main clause as present participle constructions (*-ing* forms). [> LEG 1.57–58, LAG 7B*n*.2, etc.] These present participles make up a list, separated by commas and a final *and*. The comma before *and* and the final item in a list like this is optional. [> LEG 6.21.2]

GRAMMAR POINTS

C Prepositions of time: 'at', 'on' and 'in'
[> LEG 8.10–14]

a: *In*; **b**: *On*; **c**: *On . . . at.*
The general rule is that we use:
– *at* with clock time (*at 4 o'clock*);
– *on* with days of the week (*on Monday*) and dates (*on May 21*);
– *in* with months of the year (*in July*) and years (*in 2002*). We can expand this rule as follows:

at for meal times (*at lunch time*); points of time (*at night*); festivals (*at Christmas*).

on for parts of specific days (*on Monday morning*); particular occasions (*on that day*); anniversaries (*on your birthday*); festivals (*on Christmas day*).

in (= during) for parts of the day (*in the evening*); seasons (*in (the) spring*); centuries (*in the 19th century*); periods of time (*in the holidays, in Ramadan*).

1 on . . . at . . . in
2 at . . . on
3 in . . . (at)
4 on . . . at
5 in
6 on . . . on
7 on . . . at

D Type 2 phrasal verbs: 'knocked the heater over'
[> LEG 8.28, App 32, LAG 13C, 27C, 44D]

d doesn't sound right: **He knocked over the child.** We can't put the object (a person, in this case) after the particle.

With Type 2 phrasal verbs like *knock over*, we can usually put the object, if it is a noun, either after or before the particle:
 Mr Ejiamike knocked over the electric heater. (object, *the electric heater*, after the particle, *over*)
 Mr Ejiamike knocked the electric heater over. (object, *the electric heater*, before the particle, *over*)

However, there are many occasions when we can't put a noun object after a particle, especially when the object refers to a person. There is no plausible rule for this and we can only learn from experience what is or is not possible.

If the object is a pronoun, it always comes before the particle: *He knocked it over*. (Not **He knocked over it.**)

Note how the personal noun objects in these answers go in front of the particles, whereas the inanimate ones can go in front or after. Also see the marked examples in LEG Appendix 32:

1 I knocked over the heater.
2 I paid back the money.
3 We rang Carlos back. (No change possible: Not **We rang back Carlos.**)
4 The teacher hurried the children along. (No change possible: Not **The teacher hurried along the children.**)
5 Bring along your own food.
6 I invited my friends down for the weekend. (No change possible: Not **I invited down my friends for the weekend.**)
7 Let the people off the bus. (No change possible: Not **Let off the people.**)
8 The boy pulled his jumper off.
9 Ask your friends round. (No change possible: Not **Ask round your friends.**)
10 Pass round these chocolates.

E Reporting verbs in indirect speech: 'he said . . . /explained . . .' [> LEG 15.6, 15.24, 16.22, App 45]

Said and *announced* are both reporting verbs which we can use to introduce indirect statements.

We don't always have to use *say*, *tell* [> LAG 20C] and *ask* to introduce indirect statements and questions. We should use the reporting verb which is appropriate for what we want to report:
 He warned me that the road ahead was closed. [> LAG 38E]
is more precise than:
 He said that the road ahead was closed.

1 He announced (that) he was going to get engaged.
2 She suggested (that) we (should) go by taxi.
3 He complained (that) he was not at all satisfied with this (or *that*) car.
4 She concluded (that) they must be out.
5 He replied that he really didn't agree with me.
6 She promised (that) she would phone me back tomorrow/the next day.

Little queens sweep the board

'HOT-HOUSING' is the technical word for it - but the precocious Polgar sisters from Hungary, who have been zapping the male chess community, certainly don't look like overbred hot-house blossoms.

Judit, 12, who won men's international master status at the unprecedented age of 11 (three years earlier than Bobby Fischer and Gary Kasparov), and Zsofi, who has just become a women's grandmaster at 13 (another record), started playing chess before they were five, never went to school, were educated by their parents, and now put in five or six hours a day at the board. They seem very natural children. Between moves in the Duncan Lawrie mixed tournament which ends today at London's Ecclestone Hotel, they jump up for a gossip or a joke together. Their elder sister Zsuzsa, back in Budapest, is halfway to men's international grandmaster status at the age of 19. The three girls, who will represent Hungary at the Chess Olympiad in Salonika in two weeks' time, have begun to demolish the assumption that, at the top level of world chess, men will always prevail.

Their father, Laszlo, once a lecturer in psychology, now their business manager, wanted to test the hot-housing theory: that if you subject a normally intelligent child to intensive, specialised training in a particular discipline at a very early age, you will produce excellence. His claim that his daughters were not endowed by nature with any special intellectual gifts is central to his argument. The girls' mother, Klara, a language teacher, says: 'It's improbable that three children in the same family would all be naturally gifted. They are normal - just like other children, except that they spend more time concentrating on chess. We hope one of them will be world champion one day.'

The Polgar blitz on male dominance has subverted some old physiological and psychoanalytical explanations of women's inferiority in top-level chess, and is likely to encourage other parents to push their daughters. Sooner or later, this should produce a woman world champion.

The Observer (BrE)

Sentence structure

A Supply commas in these sentences, where they are necessary.
Consider why you have or haven't used them, then check against the text.

1 ... the precocious Polgar sisters from Hungary who have been zapping the male chess community certainly don't look like overbred hot-house blossoms. (ll. 2–7)

2 Judit 12 who won men's international master status at the unprecedented age of 11 (three years earlier than Bobby Fischer and Gary Kasparov) and Zsofi who has just become a women's grandmaster at 13 (another record) started playing chess before they were five never went to school were educated by their parents and now put in five or six hours a day at the board. (ll. 8–20)

3 Between moves in the Duncan Lawrie mixed tournament which ends today at London's Ecclestone Hotel they jump up for a gossip or a joke together. (ll. 21–26)

4 Their father Laszlo once a lecturer in psychology now their business manager wanted to test the hot-housing theory: that if you subject a normally intelligent child to intensive specialized training in a particular discipline at a very early age you will produce excellence. (ll. 38–47)

5 His claim that his daughters were not endowed by nature with any special intellectual gifts is central to his argument. (ll. 47–51)

Grammar points

B *The three girls will represent Hungary in two weeks' time.* (ll. 30–34)
  a Why is the apostrophe after the *s* here? ....
  b Can we rewrite the phrase *the book of the film* with an apostrophe? ....
  c Rewrite the phrase *in two weeks' time* without the word *time*. ....

Rewrite with an apostrophe the phrases in italics that don't 'sound right'.
  1 I've just wasted *the work of two weeks*.   *two weeks' work*
  2 Tibet is often called *the roof of the world*.
  3 There's a lot of treasure at *the bottom of the sea*.
  4 The explorers returned after *the absence of a year*.
  5 This car cost me *the salary of six months*.
  6 It's almost impossible to keep up with *the cost of living*.
  7 *The edge of this ruler* is very sharp.
  8 We stood near *the edge of the cliff*.

C What's the difference in meaning between these two sentences?
  a *The three girls will represent Hungary in two weeks' time.* (ll. 30–34)
  b *The teams play a great many games in two weeks.*
  ....

Where possible, add *'s + time* in these sentences.
  1 The tournament will begin *in two weeks*.   *in two weeks' time*
  2 I finished the test *in two hours*.
  3 The race starts *in a minute*.
  4 I eat my breakfast *in a minute*.
  5 I'll return your book *in two days*.
  6 I read your book *in two days*.
  7 The explorers completed the journey *in a year*.

D What's the difference in meaning between the phrases in bold italics?
  a *At the top level of world chess, **men will always prevail**.* (ll. 36–37)
  b *It will be a tough match, but many people think **men will prevail**, as they have in the past.*
  ....

Rewrite the phrases in italics using *will*. Put an F beside the phrases that refer only to the future.
  1 *She often spends* hours reading stories to her children.   *She will often spend*
  2 *I intend to spend* an hour on this report tomorrow.   *I will spend (F)*
  3 *Grandpa generally has* a nap after lunch.
  4 *Grandpa arrives* here tomorrow afternoon.
  5 *You keep* criticizing me!
  6 *I intend to keep* this book for a week or so.
  7 The trouble with Harry is that *he never keeps* a secret.

E What do you notice about the form of the verb after *spend more time*?
*They are normal, except that they spend more time **concentrating** on chess.* (ll. 56–59)
  ....

Think of four phrases like *spend time + -ing* and write a sentence using each phrase:
  1 *They spend time wandering round London museums whenever they can.*
  2 ....
  3 ....
  4 ....
  5 ....

SENTENCE STRUCTURE

A Answers and commentary

1 *... the precocious Polgar sisters from Hungary,* ***who have been zapping the male chess community****, certainly don't look ...*
The relative clause in bold type is *non-defining*: that is, it supplies extra information, which we could omit if we wanted to, so we put commas before and after the clause. [> LEG 1.26 and e.g. 1.29.2] Here is part of the sentence with the relative clause omitted:
... the precocious Polgar sisters from Hungary certainly don't look like overbred hot-house blossoms.

2 *Judit, 12, who won ...*
The age (12) is in place of a relative clause: *Judit, who is 12, ...* . To express ourselves economically, we can avoid a relative clause by placing phrases side-by-side, separating them by commas, so that the second adds information to the first (in this case, Judit's age). Phrases like this are in apposition and are common in journalism. [> LEG 1.39, 3.30, LAG 2An.1]

Judit, 12, ***who won men's international master status at the unprecedented age of 11 (three years earlier than Bobby Fischer and Gary Kasparov)****, started ...*
The clause in bold type is *non-defining* (see **1** above). Note how the clause takes in all the information in brackets. We could omit this information and say:
Judit, 12, started playing chess before she was five.

... Kasparov), and Zsofi, ***who has just become a women's grandmaster at 13 (another record)****, started ...*
A second *non-defining* clause about Zsofi follows the first one about Judit and therefore needs commas before and after it. Again the second comma takes in the information in brackets. We could omit the information and say:
Zsofi started playing chess before she was five.

... record), started playing chess before they were five, never went to school, were educated by their parents, and now ...
Lists are normally separated by commas. [> LEG 6.21.1–2] Here we have a list of co-ordinate main clauses [> LEG 1.17]:

Judit and Zsofi started playing chess before they were five (main clause) ***and*** *never went to school* ***and*** *were educated by their parents* ***and*** *now put in five or six hours a day at the board* (co-ordinate main clauses).
Instead of using all these *ands*, the writer has separated the clauses by commas, so that they are in apposition to the main clause. We don't usually put a comma in front of the final *and* [> LEG 1.20, 6.21.2], but we may if we wish to emphasize separate activities, or if there is a particularly long list (as here).

3 *... the Duncan Lawrie mixed tournament which ends today at London's Ecclestone Hotel, ...*
A comma hasn't been used before *which* because the writer considers *which ends today at London's Ecclestone Hotel* essential information and part of the subject. It is a *defining* clause.
[> LEG 1.26 and e.g. 1.31.1, LAG 9Bn.2, 22Ans.4–5]

4 *Their father, Laszlo, once a lecturer in psychology, now their business manager, ...*
This combines a number of ideas:
He is their father. His name is Laszlo. Once he was a lecturer in psychology. Now he is their business manager.
The ideas are condensed, divided by commas, and are in apposition (see **2** above) to *their father*.

... if you subject a normally intelligent child to intensive, specialized training in a particular discipline at a very early age, you will produce excellence.
The comma after *intensive* separates two adjectives of equal importance (*intensive* and *specialized*). [> LEG 6.21.1] The second comma, after *age*, separates the conditional clause (beginning with *if*) from the main clause. [> LEG Chapter 14 *passim*, LAG 9E]

5 *His claim that his daughters were not endowed by nature with any special intellectual gifts is central to his argument.*
We don't use commas round *that ... gifts* because *that* introduces a noun clause reporting information after the noun *claim*:
his ***claim*** *that ...* → *he* ***claimed*** *that ...*
[> LEG 1.23.2, 15.5–16, App 45.1, LAG 4E, 14B, 38Bn.1]

GRAMMAR POINTS

B The genitive with non-living things: 'in two weeks' time' [> LEG 2.49–50, LAG 51D]

a The apostrophe is after the *s* here because it shows possession with a plural form. The singular would be *a week's time*.

b We can't rewrite the phrase *the book of the film* with an apostrophe as it refers to a non-living thing. As we can't make a compound noun (Not *the bookfilm* or *the filmbook*), we must use an *of*-construction. Compare *the leg of the table* where we can say *the table-leg* (but not *the table's leg*). [Compare > LAG 17C]

c We can rewrite the phrase as follows: *The three girls will represent Hungary in two weeks*. (no apostrophe) The addition of *'(s)* + *time* is optional. [> LEG 8.14]

We use *'s* and *s'* mainly to show possession for people and some living things: *Gus's car, the horses' stables*. [> LEG 2.42–48] We also use *'s* and *s'* for some non-living things, particularly time references (*a day's work*). We can only learn from experience when *'s* and *s'* 'sound right' with non-living things. If in doubt, use the *of*-construction, which is nearly always right. So, for example, if we don't know that *the cliff's edge* 'sounds right', then we can say *the edge of the cliff*, which is right here and 'safer' than *'s*.

1 two weeks' work **2** the roof of the world (no change) **3** the bottom of the sea (no change) **4** a year's absence **5** six months' salary **6** the cost of living (no change) **7** The edge of this ruler (no change) **8** the cliff's edge/the edge of the cliff

C 'In' to refer to stated periods of time: 'in two weeks' [> LEG 8.14]

a *The three girls will represent Hungary in two weeks ('time)*. (= That's when they will do it.)

b *The teams play a great many games in two weeks*. (= during that period; Not *in two weeks' time*)

We use *in* (and sometimes the more formal *within* [> LAG 27An.2]) to mean 'before the end of' a stated period of time:
I always eat my breakfast in ten minutes.
When we refer to the future in phrases like *in ten days* or *in ten days' time*, we mean 'at the

end of a period of time starting from now'. The use of *'s* or *s'* + *time* is optional:
The material will be ready in ten days/in ten days' time.

1 in two weeks' time **2** in two hours (no change) **3** in a minute's time **4** in a minute (no change) **5** in two days' time **6** in two days (no change) **7** in a year (no change)

D 'Will' to describe characteristic habit/behaviour: 'she will spend hours reading stories' [> LEG 11.63, compare > LAG 29C, 34Bn.1, 41C]

a The phrase *men will always prevail* refers to what usually happens. We can use the simple present instead:
At the top level of world chess, men always prevail.

b *... many people think men will prevail* refers to a future event (a match).

We sometimes use *will* in place of the simple present to refer to a person's characteristic habits or behaviour:
In fine weather, he will often sit in the sun for hours. (= he often sits)

1 She will often spend **2** I will spend (F) **3** Grandpa will generally have **4** Grandpa will arrive (F) **5** You will keep **6** I will keep (F) **7** he will never keep/he never will keep (more emphatic)

E Common expressions followed by '-ing': 'it's no use crying' [> LEG 16.49, compare > LAG 30E]

We use an *-ing* form after the phrase *spend time*:
spend more time concentrating ...

Some typical expressions after which we use the *-ing* form of a verb are listed in the exercise (e.g. *it's no use, it's no good, it's hardly worth*).

Sample answers
1 They spend time wandering round London museums whenever they can.
2 It's no good complaining that you never get any attention, because you know it isn't true.
3 'It's no use crying over spilt milk' is a common saying.
4 It's hardly worth wasting time on people who aren't willing to learn.
5 What's the use of worrying about the future? It may never happen!

The cup that cheers

AT the moment it reaches 212 degrees Fahrenheit, Sam Twining takes the kettle he had filled with fresh, cold water off the
5 boil and pours it carefully over the tea leaves. 'In the morning,' he was telling me, 'I will start with bright and brisk English breakfast tea. After lunch, I will have a cup of Darjeeling
10 - a mellow, rounded drink. If the afternoon is especially hot, I will have a cup of Lapsang Souchong which has a smoky taste from being smoked over oak chips. If the
15 afternoon is warm, I will have a cup of Earl Grey,' the bergamot-flavoured tea first blended for the Earl by Sam Twining's forebear - some 150 years ago. 'If it is cold and
20 miserable I'll probably have a cup of Assam which is rich and malty. And, if the weather is really awful, I'll have a cup of Vintage Darjeeling, which has a muscatel flavour.'
25 And so Twining's day progresses, a cup of tea never far from the hand of a man whose family have been teamen ever since they went into the business 'as a
30 gimmick' nine generations ago in 1706.

Another cup of low-caffeine Earl Grey at night. A cup of rose Pouchong, which is sprinkled with
35 real rose petals, if he happens to be at home in the evening. Fine black Russian Caravan, so named after the caravan route that first bore it out of China - after red wine. Oolong - to
40 tea what rosé is to wine - after white. 'As a complement, to enhance the flavours,' he explained.

The comparison with wine is a reasonable one. Having found a way
45 5,000 years ago of making water more palatable by infusing it with leaves of the *thea sinensis* plant, the Chinese went on to discover that tea, like the grape, draws its taste and
50 character from the soil in which it grows. And for all those intervening years, men have been transporting it, growing it and blending it in search of the perfect cup for the
55 occasion.

The Daily Express (BrE)

Sentence structure

A The first sentence in the text contains two careless errors. Can you spot them yourself?
A word is missing from three of these sentences. Put it in and consider why you have done so.

1 At the moment reaches 212 degrees Fahrenheit, Sam Twining takes the kettle he had filled with fresh, cold water off the boil and pours it carefully over the tea leaves. (ll. 1–6)

2 'In the morning,' he was telling me, 'will start with bright and brisk English breakfast tea.' (ll. 6–8)

3 'If the afternoon is especially hot, I will have a cup of Lapsang Souchong which has a smoky taste from being smoked over oak chips.' (ll. 10–14)

4 'If is cold and miserable I'll probably have a cup of Assam which is rich and malty.' (ll. 19–21)

B Replace or delete the word or words in italics. Then refer to the text.

1 *When* it reaches 212 degrees Fahrenheit, Sam Twining takes the kettle *which* he had filled with fresh, cold water off the boil. (ll. 1–5)

2 '*When* the afternoon is especially hot, I *will have* a cup of Lapsang Souchong which has a smoky taste *because it was* smoked over oak chips.' (ll. 10–14)

3 And so Twining's day progresses, a cup of tea never far from the hand of *the man. His* family have been teamen *from the time* they went into the business in 1706. (ll. 25–31)

4 Fine black Russian Caravan, *named like this* after the caravan route. (ll. 36–38)

5 'As a complement, *in order to enhance* the flavours,' he explained. (ll. 41–42)

Grammar points

C Break this sentence down into two sentences, then explain the use of *being*:
Lapsang Souchong has a smoky taste from being smoked over oak chips. (ll. 12–14)

Join these sentences using the words in brackets.

1 The laundry has a nice fresh smell. It was dried in the sun. (from)
The laundry has a nice fresh smell from being dried in the sun.

2 The children make their own beds. They aren't told to. (without)

3 The engine of this car will soon be worn out. It's driven too hard. (from)

4 John retired immediately. He was informed he would get a full pension. (on)

5 Jane decided to have an operation. She was examined by a specialist. (after)

6 It's the price he has to pay. He wasn't taught how to work when he was a boy. (for)

D What does *some* mean in these two sentences?

a *When I visited Sam Twining, he immediately offered me **some** tea.*
b *Earl Grey was first blended by Sam Twining's forebear – **some** 150 years ago.* (ll. 16–19)

Suggest meanings for *some* in these sentences.

1 Jim and his wife retired *some* years ago and moved to Brighton.   *several*
2 There were *some* 400 noisy people protesting against the new tax.
3 Surely there must be *some* person in this country who can read Sanskrit.
4 He's a professor at the age of 25 – that's *some* achievement!
5 You've broken four plates drying the dishes – that's *some* help, I must say.
6 I hear you've joined *some* club or other.
7 We've had a good crop of apples this year. Would you like *some*?
8 The programme you want to watch began *some* minutes ago.

E Compare the meanings of the verb phrases in bold italics in these three sentences.

a *He has a cup of rose Pouchong if **he is** at home in the evening.*
b *He has a cup of rose Pouchong if **he happens to be** at home in the evening.* (see ll. 33–36)
c *He has a cup of rose Pouchong if **it happens that he's** at home in the evening.*

Rewrite each sentence in two ways using the verb *happen*.

1 You're always rude about John's pictures, but *he's* a successful portrait painter.
  a *You're always rude about John's pictures, but he happens to be a successful portrait painter.*
  b *You're always rude about John's pictures, but it happens that he's a successful portrait painter.*
2 Joanna isn't late. She hasn't come in to work today because *she's* ill.
  a
  b
3 I'm not a football fan, but I go to matches because *I live* next door to the stadium.
  a
  b
4 *It's* my pen you've just put into your pocket.
  a
  b

33

SENTENCE STRUCTURE

A Answers and commentary

The two careless errors are:

1 The tense shifts from present to past perfect:
*... he **takes** the kettle he **had filled**...*
This should be:
*... he **takes** the kettle he **has filled** ...*

2 The writer hasn't thought what *it* refers to:
*... he takes **the kettle** he has filled and pours **it** ...*
This should be:
*... he takes **the kettle** he has filled and pours **boiling water** over the leaves.* (Not **pours the kettle**)

These are examples of native speaker error, or careless writing of a kind often found in popular journalism.

Numbers **1**, **2** and **4** have a word missing. In each case, the word that is missing is the subject of a sentence. In English, the subject must be expressed or strongly implied. [> LEG 1.2, 4.5, 4.12, LAG 21B*n*.1a, 60A*n*.5]

1 *At the moment **it** reaches 212 degrees Fahrenheit* ... (Not **At the moment reaches**)

2 *'In the morning,' he was telling me, '**I** will start with ...'* (Not **'... will start with ...'**)

3 This sentence is correct.

4 *If **it** is cold and miserable* ... (Not **If is cold**)

B Answers and commentary

1 ***At the moment** it reaches 212 degrees* ...
We can say *At the moment* or *The moment* here. (Note that *it* = 'the water in the kettle', not the temperature in general.) Time conjunctions like *after*, *as soon as*, *before*, *by the time*, *directly*, *the moment* and *when* introduce adverbial clauses of time. We normally use the simple present where other languages might use a simple future [> LEG 1.45.2]:
***It will reach** 212 degrees Fahrenheit. Sam Twining **will take** the kettle off the boil.*
→ ***At the moment/When** it reaches 212 degrees Fahrenheit, Sam Twining **takes** the kettle off the boil.* (Not **At the moment/When it will reach**)

*... Sam Twining takes **the kettle** he **had filled** with fresh, cold water off the boil.*
We can omit *which* (or *that*) because it is the object of a relative clause referring to a thing [> LEG 1.34, LAG 22A*n*.2, 36A*n*.1, 40A*n*.3]:
*Sam Twining takes **the kettle** off the boil. He had filled **it** with fresh, cold water.*
→ *Sam Twining takes the kettle (which/that) he had filled with fresh, cold water off the boil.*

2 ***If** the afternoon is especially hot, I will have a cup of Lapsang Souchong* ...
If doesn't introduce a conditional sentence here. It means 'on those occasions when' and it can be replaced by *when*. [> LEG 14.23.1, LAG 10B*n*.1, 16A*n*.5, etc.]
*... **I will have** a cup of Lapsang Souchong* is not a future after Type 1, *if* + present. [> LEG 14.2, 14.4–6, LAG 9E] *I will have* refers to 'characteristic behaviour' and can be replaced by the simple present [> LEG 11.63, LAG 5D]:
***If/When** the afternoon **is** especially hot, **I have** a cup of Lapsang Souchong.*

*... which has a smoky taste **from being** smoked over oak chips.*
We use the *-ing* form after a preposition. [> LEG 16.50–56 and see LEG 1.60 for *being*; LAG 1D, 6C]

3 *... a cup of tea never far from the hand of **a man whose** family have been teamen* ...
We can use *whose* in place of possessive adjectives (*my*, *your*, *his*, *her*, etc.) when joining sentences. [> LEG 1.32, LAG 11B*n*.1, 23B*n*.3, 51A*n*.1]

*... whose family have been teamen **ever since** they went into the business* ...
(Ever) since introduces an adverbial clause of time. [> LEG 1.45.1, LAG 8B*n*.1, 8E*n*.5]

4 *Fine black Russian Caravan, **so named** after the caravan route* ...
The past participle *named* replaces a relative clause (= which has been named in this way). [> LEG 1.62.3, LAG 8A*n*.2]
The adverb *so* means *like this* here [> LEG App 25.25 for *like* as a preposition], or *in this way*. [> LEG 1.47.1, LAG 13A*n*.1, 14E, 47A*n*.4, 60A*n*.13]

5 *'As a complement, **to enhance** the flavours,' he explained.*
The infinitive markers *to*, *in order to* and *so as to*, used to express purpose, are interchangeable. [> LEG 16.12.1]

GRAMMAR POINTS

C Preposition + 'being': 'from being smoked'

[> LEG 16.38–39, 16.51, 1.60, 1.62.2, 12.3*n*.8]

Two possible sentences are:

Lapsang Souchong has a smoky taste. It is smoked/It has been smoked over oak chips. *Being* is used after the preposition *from (from being smoked)* in place of *it is.*

Being can replace *(he) is, (he) was* and sometimes *(he) has been.* It is a feature of formal style:

He is *so ill he can't go back to work yet.*
→ **Being** *so ill, he can't go back to work yet.*
He was *so ill he couldn't go back to work for a month.*
→ **Being** *so ill, he couldn't go back to work for a month.* [> LAG 30A*ns*.2–3]

This also applies when the verb is in the passive:

We were *informed that the flight would be delayed, so we made other arrangements.*
→ **Being** *informed that the flight would be delayed, we made other arrangements.*

We may use the *-ing* form of a verb after a preposition [> LAG 1D]:

On/After being *informed that the flight would be delayed, we made other arrangements.*

1 The laundry has a nice fresh smell from being dried in the sun.
2 The children make their own beds without being told to.
3 The engine of this car will soon be worn out from being driven too hard.
4 John retired immediately on being informed he would get a full pension.
5 Jane decided to have an operation after being examined by a specialist.
6 It's the price he has to pay for not being (*having been* is also possible) taught how to work when he was a boy. [> LAG 26B*n*.1]

D Special uses of 'some': 'some 150 years ago'

[> LEG 5.12.1, and compare > LEG 5.3, 5.10, and LAG 39E]

a *a little, a quantity of*
b *about, approximately*

In its basic use, *some* refers to an indefinite number or amount:

*There are **some apples** in the bag.* (We are not told how many.)
*There is **some milk** in the fridge.* (We are not told how much.)

We commonly use *some* as a quantifier to refer to an indefinite number or amount and it is unstressed in speech. When we use *some* to refer to an unspecified person or thing, we generally stress it in speech: /sʌm/. See the answers to the exercise for possible meanings.

Some possible meanings of 'some':

1 several
2 about
3 one/a or *an unknown*
4 an extraordinary
5 no kind of
6 an unknown (dismissive here)
7 a quantity (unspecified)
8 several

E Verbs related in meaning to 'be': e.g. 'happen to/ happen that' [> LEG 10.24–25, App 45]

a . . . **he is** *at home* is certain. (neutral)
b . . . **he happens to be** *at home* means 'by chance'.
c . . . **it happens that he's** *at home* is a variation of **b** above.

We can use *happen to* + verb if we want to express the idea of 'by chance'.
In place of the form *he happens* + infinitive, we can use *It happens that . . .*
The basic meaning of *happen* is 'occur' and in this sense it is used like any other verb:

*Something awful **happened** when we were away on holiday.*

Happen (= by chance) combines with *be* (*happen to be*) or 'continuity verbs' like *live* (*happen to live*). [> LEG 9.33.1]

1 You're always rude about John's pictures, but he happens to be/it happens that he's a successful portrait painter.
2 Joanna isn't late. She hasn't come in to work today because she happens to be/it happens that she's ill.
3 I'm not a football fan, but I go to matches because I happen to live/it happens that I live next door to the stadium.
4 It happens to be/It happens that it's my pen you've just put into your pocket.

Junket for robbers was police trap

THE HAND-DRAWN sign in the front window of the charabanc read: 'Good Buy Charter'. It should have been spelt differently, for the coach party of 25, who had been expecting a jolly day's gambling and drinking at the casinos in Atlantic City, were instead driven to prison. It was the culmination of another of those police undercover operations which cause such merriment when they are disclosed. Good Buy was the name the police gave to a shop they established five months ago in Manhattan's Diamond District, on West 47th Street off Fifth Avenue, for the purpose of buying stolen property. During that time, police say they bought goods worth $2.5m although they paid only $8,000 for them. The discrepancy was caused by the fact that much of the property was stolen bonds which are hard to sell and therefore command a low price on the undercover market.

After they set up the shop, describing themselves as 'buyers of gold and silver', the police said it was not long before word of their willingness to buy stolen property circulated in the underworld. They received a steady flow of offers and propositions, including one from a man who wanted their help in killing and robbing a Brooklyn couple.

Soon the operators of Good Buy informed their clients that, to celebrate the imminence of spring, they would be organizing a gambling trip to Atlantic City to reward their loyal patrons. There would be free champagne and $1,000 of stake money each. The day trippers were to meet yesterday morning at Sullivan's Bar on Eighth Avenue at 46th Street, not far from the Diamond District. When the group of 25 had assembled they were all placed under arrest. Then they were loaded on to the coach and driven, not to the seaside, but to the police station. There, 11 of the 25 were charged with possessing stolen goods and the remainder held for questioning. Police are still looking for 18 of their customers who, with apparent foresight, did not go.

The Times (BrE)

Sentence structure

A Circle the item that fits the space, then refer to the text.

The hand-drawn sign in the front window of the charabanc read: 'Good Buy Charter'. [1]........ should have been spelt differently, [2]........ the coach party of 25, [3]........ had been expecting a jolly day's gambling and drinking at the casinos in Atlantic City, were instead driven to prison. [4]........ was the culmination of another of those police undercover operations [5]........ cause such merriment [6]........ they are disclosed. Good Buy was the name [7]........ the police gave to a shop [8]........ they established five months ago in Manhattan's Diamond District. (ll. 1–16)

1 a Which	b It	c –
2 a for	b why	c because of
3 a whom	b –	c who
4 a It	b Which	c –
5 a who	b –	c which
6 a when	b as	c while
7 a who	b whom	c –
8 a who	b whom	c –

B Supply the connecting words, then check against the text.

[1] *After* they set up the shop, [2](*describe*) .... themselves as 'buyers of gold and silver', the police said it was not long [3].............. word of their willingness [4](*buy*) .... stolen property circulated in the underworld. [5].............. received a steady flow of offers and propositions, [6](*include*) .... one from a man [7].............. wanted their help in [8](*kill*) .... and [9](*rob*) .... a Brooklyn couple. [10].............. the operators of Good Buy informed their clients that, [11](*celebrate*) .... the imminence of spring, they would be organizing a gambling trip to Atlantic City [12](*reward*) .... their loyal patrons. [13].............. would be free champagne and $1,000 of stake money each. The day trippers were to meet yesterday morning at Sullivan's Bar on Eighth Avenue at 46th Street. (ll. 27–47)

C *The **hand-drawn** sign in the front window of the charabanc read: ... (ll. 1–3)*
What part of speech is *hand-drawn*? Write the phrase from which it has been formed.

....

Complete each unfinished sentence.
1 They make all this pottery by hand.   It's all *hand-made*.............................
2 They pick these strawberries by hand.   They're all ....
3 They build these cars by hand.   They're all ....
4 They write these letters by hand.   They're all ....
5 They feed these calves by hand.   They're all ....
6 They paint this pottery by hand.   It's all ....

D What's the difference in meaning between these two sentences?
   a *It read: 'Good Buy Charter'. It **should have been spelt** differently. (ll. 3–5)*
   b *The letter was so urgent, it **had to be sent** by special delivery.*

....

Write the active and passive forms of *should have*.
1 They didn't spell it correctly. (differently)   a *They should have spelt it differently.*
                                                   b *It should have been spelt differently.*
2 They didn't teach us well. (better)   a ....
                                                   b ....
3 They didn't fry the chops long enough. (longer) a ....
                                                   b ....

E *Goods* has no singular form. Can you think of other nouns like this?
*During that time, police say they bought **goods** worth $2.5m. (ll.19–20)*

....

Supply suitable nouns in these sentences.
1 They bought a lot of things from us and we sent the ...*goods*... by air freight.
2 I don't want to spend too much on what I wear. I buy all my.........................at the sales.
3 I hear you won first prize! Well done! ....!
4 Diana is a very clever woman. She really has ....
5 It doesn't matter what you look like.........................aren't everything, you know.
6 I'd like to bet on Black Star winning the race. What are the ....?

F Why is *would* used here, rather than *will*?
*Good Buy informed their clients that they **would** be organizing a gambling trip. (ll. 37–41)*

....

Rewrite these lines in the past, then check against the text. (ll. 37–50)

The operators of Good Buy inform their clients that, to celebrate the imminence of spring, they will be organizing a gambling trip to Atlantic City to reward their loyal patrons. There will be free champagne and $1,000 of stake money each. The day trippers are to meet this morning at Sullivan's Bar on Eighth Avenue at 46th Street, not far from the Diamond District. When the group of 25 has assembled, they will all be placed under arrest.

....
....
....
....
....

SENTENCE STRUCTURE

A Answers and commentary

1 b *It*: the subject of *should have been spelt*, referring to the hand-drawn sign. [> LEG 4.5.5]

2 a *for*: could be replaced by *because*. We often use *for* to give the reason for something that has just been stated. This use is common in written English. [> LEG 1.18, 1.20.5, LAG 54A*n*.9]

3 c *who*: because the writer has thought of them as *25 people* (= they) and used the subject relative pronoun *who*. The writer could also have thought of *the party* (= it) and used the subject relative pronoun *which*. [> LEG 1.27, 1.29, 1.31]

4 a *It*: subject of *was*, referring back to the whole event. [> LEG 4.5.5, LAG 30A*n*.1]

5 c *which*: subject relative pronoun introducing a relative clause (*which cause such merriment*). *Which* remains unchanged whether it refers to singular or plural. [> LEG 1.31, LAG 24A*n*.5]

6 a *when*: conjunction introducing time clause (*when they are disclosed*). [> LEG 1.45.1]

7 c –: The object relative pronoun *which* or *that* is omitted here [> LEG 1.34, LAG 6B*n*.1]:
> *This was the name. The police gave **it** to a shop.*
> → *This was the name the police gave to a shop.*

8 c –: The object relative pronoun *which* or *that* is omitted here [> LEG 1.34]:
> *This was the shop. They established **it** five months ago.*
> → *This was the shop they established ....*

B Answers and commentary

1 *After*: time conjunction, introducing an adverbial clause of time (*After they set up the shop*). [> LEG 1.45.1] It is not necessary to use the past perfect here to describe the first of two actions (*After they had set up the shop*), because the sequence of events is clear. [> LEG 9.30]

2 *describing*: The present participle replaces a co-ordinate clause with *and* [> LEG 1.58.1]:
> *They set up the shop **and described** themselves ...*
> → *They set up the shop, **describing** themselves ...*

3 *before*: *It was not long before ...* is another way of saying *It didn't take a long time before ...* [> LEG 16.21]

4 *to buy*: noun + *to*-infinitive: *their **willingness to buy** circulated ....* Many adjectives which can be followed by *to*-infinitives have equivalent nouns (usually different in form, e.g. *willing – willingness*) [> LEG 16.34]:
> *They were **willing to buy** and this circulated*
> → *Their **willingness to buy** circulated ...*

5 *They*: We often use personal pronouns to refer back to something that has already been mentioned. Here *they* refers to *the police*. [> LEG 4.2.1, 4.5.7]

6 *including*: The present participle replaces a relative clause with *which/that* [> LEG 1.58.6]:
> *They received a steady flow of offers and propositions, **which/that included** one from a man ...*
> → *They received a steady flow of offers and propositions, **including** one from a man ...*

7 *who*: subject relative pronoun, introducing a relative clause to refer to a person. We can't omit the subject [> LEG 1.29, LAG 3B*n*.2, 9B*n*.2]:
> *He was a man. **He** wanted their help.*
> → *He was a **man who** wanted their help.*

8 (and **9**) *killing* and *robbing*: The writer could have used a *to*-infinitive after *help*:
> *He wanted their **help to kill** and (**to**) **rob** a Brooklyn couple.*
This would be a noun + *to*-infinitive construction, as in **4** above. But it is possible to use prepositions after some nouns and then we are obliged to use an *-ing* form after the preposition [> LEG 16.34, 16.53, LAG 1D]:
> *He wanted their **help in killing** and **robbing** a Brooklyn couple.*

10 *Soon* (= A short time after that): This adverb helps the progress of the narrative and connects with what has gone before. Similar adverbs are: *afterwards, at last, at once, eventually, now, recently*. [> LEG 7.23]

11 *to celebrate*: infinitive of purpose, interchangeable with *so as to* and *in order to* [> LEG 16.12.1]:
> *They would be organizing a gambling trip. **They wanted to** celebrate ...*
> → *They would be organizing a gambling trip **to/so as to/in order to celebrate**.*

12 *to reward*: infinitive of purpose, as in **11** above.

13 *There*: *There* combines not only with *is, was, has been*, etc., but also with modal forms (*may, will, would*, etc.). The sequence of tenses requires *would* here to follow on from the past form of the reporting verb *informed*. [> LEG 10.17–19, 11.76, LAG 7F]

GRAMMAR POINTS

C Compound adjectives formed with participles: 'hand-drawn' [> LEG 6.3.1]

For regular/irregular past participles [> LEG Apps 39–40, LAG 32F, 47D]
Hand-drawn is an adjective. It has been formed from *which had been hand-drawn/drawn by hand*.

We can form compound adjectives with participles. In the exercise, all the compound adjectives are formed with *hand* + past participle, but there are any number of possibilities: *a **self-employed** author*, *a **man-made** fibre*, etc.

1 hand-made   2 hand-picked   3 hand-built
4 hand-written   5 hand-fed   6 hand-painted

D Advisability/necessity: the perfect and past: 'should have' [> LEG 11.51, 11.57.2, passive > LEG 12.2]

should have been spelt differently means it was desirable to spell it differently, but it wasn't spelt differently.
had to be sent means it was necessary to send it and it was sent. [> LAG 17D]

Should have (also *ought to have*) refers to whatever is desirable or necessary, but did not happen. We can express:
– criticism:
   You **should have paid** the electricity bill on time. (but you didn't)
   You **shouldn't have paid** the plumber in advance. (but you did)
– failure to observe a prohibition:
   You **should have stopped** at the red light. (but you didn't)
   You **shouldn't have stopped** on the motorway. (but you did)
Had to suggests that the action was performed in the past because this was necessary (there was no choice):
   I **had to catch** an early train to be at the meeting on time. (and I did)

Active and passive forms of *should have* are contrasted in the exercise:
1 a They should have spelt it differently.
   b It should have been spelt differently.
2 a They should have taught us better.
   b We should have been taught better.
3 a They (= people) should have fried them longer.
   b They (= the chops) should have been fried longer.

E Nouns with a plural form + plural verb: 'goods' [> LEG 2.32, compare > LAG 19E]

Goods is one of a small group of nouns which is plural in form and is used with a plural verb. Other examples are in the exercise.

1 goods
2 clothes
3 Congratulations
4 brains
5 Looks
6 odds

F The sequence of tenses [> LEG 9.5, 15.12–16]

Would is used here rather than *will* because it matches the past form of the reporting verb *informed*. [compare > LAG 8E, 10C]

In extended speech or writing we usually select a governing tense which affects all other tense forms. If we start from the point of view of *now*, we usually maintain 'now' as our viewpoint:
   Our postman usually **delivers** our mail at 7 every morning. **It's** nearly lunch-time and the mail still **hasn't arrived**.

If we start from the point of view of *then*, we usually maintain 'then' as our viewpoint:
   When I **lived** in London the postman usually **delivered** our mail at 7 every morning.

Though present attracts present and past attracts past, speakers and writers can vary tenses according to their viewpoint [> LAG 29B]:
   He told me he **is** a good tennis-player. (he still is)
   He tells me he **used to be** a good tennis player.

The operators of Good Buy **informed** their clients that, to celebrate the imminence of spring, they **would be organizing** a gambling trip to Atlantic City to reward their loyal patrons. There **would be** free champagne and $1,000 of stake money each. The day trippers **were to meet yesterday morning** at Sullivan's Bar on Eighth Avenue at 46th Street, not far from the Diamond District. When the group of 25 **had assembled**, they **were** all **placed** under arrest.

Roman regimental brewery

MILITARY units in the Roman Empire appear to have run their own regimental breweries, according to new evidence from archaeological excavations near Hadrian's Wall. One of a large collection of wooden writing tablets found at Vindolanda Roman fort in Northumberland reveals that troops were sent by their officers to work in what seems to have been an army-run brewery, as well as the regimental bakery, clay pits, lime kilns, bath house and cobbler's workshop. At least eight soldiers ran the regimental brewery and supplied six gallons of beer a day to the commanding officer's household and presumably large quantities to the troops.

Another tablet reveals that at least 5 per cent of soldiers were suffering from conjunctivitis. This medical detail is contained in a copy of a military report sent from Vindolanda to the provincial governor in London. Known as a *pridianum* and written on a 1.5 millimetre thin sheet of oak, it is the only document of its sort found in Western Europe. So far this year, a team under Robin Birley, archaeologist with the Vindolanda Trust, has unearthed 165 writing tablets, and since the current excavations began four years ago 1,100 tablets have been found. The texts date from 85-120 AD, just before the construction of Hadrian's Wall.

Perhaps the most entertaining tablet unearthed is one presumably written by a child, probably one of the sons of Flavius Cerialis, prefect of the 9th cohort of Batavians - troops from what is now Holland. Written in capitals, rather than joined-up writing, it is an inaccurately reproduced excerpt from Book Nine of Virgil's *Aeneid*, under which is written, in joined-up writing, *segnis* (sloppy) - presumably the opinion of the child's tutor.

Texts in more than 600 different hands have been found, indicating the high degree of literacy in the Roman army. Slaves at the fort also appear to have been literate.

The Independent (BrE)

Sentence structure

A Complete the sentences, choosing from the words in brackets, then refer to the text.

1 Military units in the Roman Empire appear to have run their own regimental breweries, [*by/according to*] new evidence from archaeological excavations near Hadrian's Wall. (ll. 1–7)

2 One of a large collection of wooden writing tablets [*found/was found*] at Vindolanda Roman fort in Northumberland reveals that troops were sent by their officers to work in [*what/which*] seems to have been an army-run brewery, [*also/as well as*] the regimental bakery. (ll. 7–15)

3 Texts in more than 600 different hands have been found, [*indicated/indicating*] the high degree of literacy in the Roman army. (ll. 59–62)

B Join these sentences using the suggestions in brackets and making any necessary changes. Then check against the text.

1 So far this year, a team under Robin Birley has unearthed 165 writing tablets. He is an archaeologist with the Vindolanda Trust. The current excavations began four years ago. 1,100 tablets have been found. (ll. 33–40) [commas, *and since*]

....

....

2 Perhaps the most entertaining tablet unearthed is one presumably written by a child. He was probably one of the sons of Flavius Cerialis. He was prefect of the 9th cohort of Batavians. They were troops from what is now Holland. (ll. 44–50) [commas, dash]

....

....

Grammar points

C Supply *a/an*, *the* or zero (–) where necessary in this paragraph, then refer to the text. (ll. 1–22) Give a reason or reasons beside each choice.

[1]......... military units in
[2]......... Roman Empire appear to have run their
own regimental breweries, according to [3]......... new evidence
from archaeological excavations near [4]......... Hadrian's Wall. One of
[5]......... large collection of
[6]......... wooden writing tablets found at
[7]......... Vindolanda Roman fort in
[8]......... Northumberland reveals that
[9]......... troops were sent by their officers to work
in what seems to have been [10]......... army-run brewery, as well as
[11]......... regimental bakery, clay pits, lime kilns, bath house
and cobbler's workshop. At least eight soldiers ran [12].........
regimental brewery and supplied six gallons of [13]......... beer
[14]......... day to
[15]......... commanding officer's household and presumably large
quantities to [16]......... troops.

....
....
....
....
....
....
....
....
....
....
....
....
....
....

D We have to say: ... *5 per cent of soldiers **were suffering from** conjunctivitis.* (ll. 24–25)
Why can't we say: ... *5 per cent of soldiers ***were suffering** conjunctivitis **from***?*

....

Supply the missing prepositions.

1 I often suffer *from* a bad back.
2 What time did you arrive .... Bangkok?
3 I must apologize .... my mistake.
4 I've borrowed some money .... the bank.
5 You can rely .... me.
6 He confessed .... everything in the end.
7 I advise you .... going to law.
8 My hands smell .... soap.
9 What's become .... old Mrs Harris?
10 He quarrels .... everybody.

11 I insist .... knowing what happened.
12 I read .... it in the papers.
13 Success is something you dream ....
14 She identified .... her mother.
15 I can't deal .... this problem.
16 This article refers .... you.
17 Who's going to pay .... all this?
18 He's failed .... his efforts to find her.
19 They all laughed .... me.
20 How dare you interfere .... my work.

E Supply the right forms and tenses of the verbs in brackets, then refer to the text. (ll. 23–48) In each case, give your reason for the tense you have chosen.

Another tablet reveals that at least 5 per cent of soldiers
[1](*suffer*).................from conjunctivitis.
This medical detail [2](*contain*).................in a copy of a military
report sent from Vindolanda to the provincial governor in London.
Known as a *pridianum* and written on a 1.5 millimetre
thin sheet of oak, it [3](*be*).................the only document
of its sort found in Western Europe. So far this year,
a team under Robin Birley, archaeologist with the Vindolanda Trust,
[4](*unearth*) ....165 writing tablets, and
since the current excavations [5](*begin*).................four years ago
1,100 tablets [6](*find*) ....
The texts [7](*date*).................from 85–120 AD,
just before the construction of Hadrian's Wall. Perhaps the most
entertaining tablet unearthed [8](*be*) .... one presumably
written by a child, probably one of the sons of Flavius Cerialis.

....
....

....

....

....
....

....

41

SENTENCE STRUCTURE

A Answers and commentary

1 *Military units in the Roman Empire appear to have run their own regimental breweries,* **according to** *new evidence* ...
We can say *according to* + a source of information. (Not *by new evidence*) [> LEG App 25.2, LAG 2E]

2 *One of a large collection of wooden writing tablets* **found** *at Vindolanda* ...
(= *which were* or *which have been found*) The past participle *found* is used in place of a relative clause. [> LEG 1.62.3]

... *troops were sent by their officers to work in* **what** *seems to have been* ...
What is a conjunction here, the equivalent of *that which*, or *the thing that*. [> LEG 1.24.2, LAG 42D]

... *seems to have been an army-run brewery,* **as well as** *the regimental bakery.* (= in addition to)
[For some uses of *also* and *as well*, *as well as* > LEG 7.56, 8.4.4, LAG 36Bn.2, 56An.2]

3 *Texts in more than 600 different hands have been found,* **indicating** *the high degree of literacy* ...
A present participle construction is used in place of a co-ordinate clause with *and* [> LEG 1.58.1, LAG 4Bn.3, 43Ans.11–12, 47Bn.4]:
Texts in more than 600 different hands have been found **and these indicate** ... → **indicating** ...

B Answers and commentary

1 *So far this year, a team under Robin Birley, archaeologist with the Vindolanda Trust, has unearthed 165 writing tablets* ...
We can place two noun phrases side-by-side, separating the phrases by commas, so that the second adds information to the first. The phrases are in apposition, the second replacing a relative clause [> LEG 1.39, LAG 2An.1, 5Ans.2,4]:
So far this year, a team under Robin Birley, **who is** *an archaeologist with the Vindolanda Trust, has unearthed* ...

The use of phrases in apposition to identify a named person by his/her occupation, etc. is very common in journalism.

The omission of the article before *archaeologist* suggests that *Robin Birley* is well-known. [> LEG 3.30, LAG 18An.4] Compare:
Robin Birley, **an** *archaeologist with the Vindolanda Trust* which suggests the reader may not have heard of him, or that there may be other archaeologists there as well.
Robin Birley, **the** *archaeologist with the Vindolanda Trust* which suggests that many people have heard of him, or that he is the only one.
Robin Birley, archaeologist with the Vindolanda Trust which suggests he is well known.

... *has unearthed 165 writing tablets,* **and since** *the current excavations began four years ago 1,100 tablets have been found.*
and since (= and from the time when) introduces an adverbial clause of time. [> LEG 1.45.1]
The sentence divides into two compound/complex sentences. In the first half, the main clause is *So far this year, a team under Robin Birley has unearthed 165 writing tablets*. In the second half (after *and*) the main clause is *(So far this year) 1,100 tablets have been found*. [> LEG 1.21]

2 *Perhaps the most entertaining tablet unearthed* (= which was/has been unearthed) *is one presumably written* (= which was presumably written) *by a child, probably one of the sons of Flavius Cerialis, prefect of the 9th cohort of Batavians* ...

Two phrases in apposition are used in succession in place of relative clauses [> LEG 1.39, LAG 2An.1, 5Ans.2,4]:
Perhaps the most entertaining tablet unearthed is one presumably written by **a child, who was** *probably one of the sons of* **Flavius Cerialis, who was** *prefect of the 9th cohort of Batavians* ...

... *Flavius Cerialis, prefect of the 9th cohort of Batavians – troops from what is now Holland.*
The dash (–) is used here like a colon (:). [> LAG 16An.6, 22An.6]
Explanatory information is given after it, equivalent to *that is*:
... *the 9th cohort of Batavians,* **that is**, *troops from what is now Holland.*

GRAMMAR POINTS

C Articles [> LEG Chapter 3, LAG 11C, etc.]

1 (–) *Military units*: in general, therefore zero article with plural countable (*units*). [> LEG 3.25–26] However, we could use *the* if we wanted to specify these particular military units. [> LEG 3.20]

2 *the Roman Empire*: *Empire* is a noun like *Kingdom* or *Republic* which needs *the* in front of it. [> LEG 3.31]

3 (–) *new evidence*: in general, therefore zero article with uncountable noun (*evidence*). [> LEG 3.25–26]

4 (–) *Hadrian's Wall*: Proper noun, therefore zero article. [> LEG 2.13.1, 3.25–27, 3.31]

5 *a large collection*: not specifying any particular *collection*, therefore indefinite article. [> LEG 3.8, 3.10]

6 (–) *wooden writing tablets*: in general, therefore zero article with plural countable (*tablets*). [> LEG 3.25–26]. We don't use *the* in partitives: *a collection of writing tablets*. (Not *the writing tablets*) [> LEG 2.18, App 5]

7 (–) *Vindolanda*: Proper noun, therefore zero article. [> LEG 2.13.1, 3.25–27, 3.31]

8 (–) *Northumberland*: Proper noun, therefore zero article. [> LEG 2.13.1, 3.25–27, 3.31]

9 (–) *troops*: in general, therefore zero article with plural countable (*troops*). [> LEG 3.25–26]

10 *an army-run brewery*: not specifying any particular *brewery*, therefore indefinite article. [> LEG 3.8, 3.10]

11 *the regimental bakery*: specifying in this context, therefore *the*. However, *a* would have been possible if the author had decided not to specify. [> LEG 3.20.4]

12 *the regimental brewery*: not specified at first mention (*an army-run brewery* – see 10 above), now specified, therefore *the*. [> LEG 3.10.2, 3.20.1]

13 *six gallons of* (–) *beer*: in general, therefore zero article with uncountable noun (*beer*). [> LEG 3.25–26] Note that this is a partitive, relating to a measure (like *two kilos of sugar*). [> LEG 2.18.2, LAG 17C]

14 *a day*: *a* (= per) is used in the sense of 'each' (like *40 km an/per hour*). [> LEG 3.12]

15 *the commanding officer's household*: specific reference, therefore *the*. (There is only one *commanding officer's household*.) [> LEG 3.20.4]

16 *the troops*: general statement about a specified group (like *the unions*). [> LEG 3.19.4]

D Type 1 phrasal verbs, non-idiomatic meanings: 'suffer from' [> LEG 8.27, App 28, LAG 24C, 27C, 47E]

In *suffer from*, *from* is a preposition, and it must be followed by an object. We can't put the preposition after the object in the same way as we can put an adverb particle after the object (*Turn the light on*). [> LEG 8.28, LAG 4D, 13C]

Phrasal verbs in this group are used in their obvious sense. The problem is to remember which prepositions are associated with which verbs. This awareness can only come from experience.

1 suffer from   2 arrive in/at/from
3 apologize for   4 borrowed some money from
5 rely on   6 confessed to   7 advise you against   8 smell of   9 become of
10 quarrels with   11 insist on   12 read about
13 dream about/of   14 identified with
15 deal with   16 refers to   17 pay for
18 failed in   19 laughed at   20 interfere with

E Verbs and verb tenses [> LEG Chapter 9]

1 *5 per cent of soldiers were suffering from*: The action was in progress at some time in the past, therefore the past progressive is appropriate here. [> LEG 9.20.1, LAG 27Bn.1] However, the simple past (*suffered*) would not be wrong here to describe the situation at the time. [> LEG 9.17.1]

2 *This medical detail is contained*: The governing tense is the present (*Another tablet reveals* . . .), so the simple present passive [> LEG 12.2–3] follows on naturally. [> LEG 9.5, LAG 7F] The stative verb *contain* cannot be used in the progressive. [> LEG 9.3, App 38.5, LAG 51E]

3 *is*: The simple present of *be* is a full verb here, not an auxiliary. [> LEG 10.1, 10.5–7]

4 *has unearthed*: Only the present perfect is possible after *so far* suggesting 'up to the present'. [> LEG 9.18, 9.25.1]

5 *since the current excavations began four years ago*: *Since* is a conjunction here, referring to an exact point of time in the past. [> LEG 1.45.1, 9.25.2, compare LAG 10An.2]

6 *have been found*: that is, up to the present time, therefore present perfect. [> LEG 9.25, passive > LEG 12.2–3, LAG 25C, 33B, 60An.8]

7 *The texts date from 85–120 AD*: The simple present is the governing tense (see 2 above), so this tense follows on naturally here. [> LAG 7F]

8 *is*: as for 3 above.

Plane-load of 400 lobsters

Hope you're all enjoying the flight

FOUR HUNDRED Hebridean lobsters facing certain death were given a brief reprieve when the plane taking them to France to become lobster pot, bisque, and quadrille was forced to make an emergency landing behind Wormwood Scrubs prison in west London yesterday. The lobsters were *en route* from the Outer Hebrides in Scotland to Le Touquet in northern France when the Cessna 206 light aircraft transporting them developed engine trouble. The Danish pilot, 46-year-old Mr Carsten Petersen, managed to guide the plane down on to land 200 yards from the Scrubs. Mr Petersen, who lives in County Offaly in the Irish Republic, had made earlier abortive attempts to land on Clapham Common or Battersea Park in south London.

A spokesman for Heathrow Airport said Mr Petersen had radioed them, saying his plane was suffering from severe vibration and he needed to make a speedy landing. The airport was put on emergency alert but in the end, he was forced to put it down in London. It seems he found some open space and had a very lucky escape. The pilot and his cargo emerged unscathed.

'The lobsters are sick of flying,' said Mr Petersen before dashing off to sell his cargo at Billingsgate fish market before it died of natural causes. 'If you go into a good London restaurant, you might get one.'

Mr Petersen hoped his crippled aircraft would be hauled away this morning. Scotland Yard confirmed that the plane and its lobster cargo were being treated as an emergency landing and no charges will be brought. Residents who live around the prison are more used to break-out dramas than forced landings.

One commented: 'Why don't they give the lobsters to the prisoners?'

Leslie Goffe, *The Guardian (BrE)*

Sentence structure

A Three of these sentences contain a word that is wrong. Provide the right words where necessary and give reasons for your choice. Then check against the text.

1 Four hundred Hebridean lobsters facing certain death were given a brief reprieve when the plane took them to France to become lobster pot, bisque, and quadrille was forced to make an emergency landing behind Wormwood Scrubs prison in west London yesterday. (ll. 1–10)

2 The lobsters were *en route* from the Outer Hebrides in Scotland to Le Touquet in northern France when the Cessna 206 light aircraft transporting them developed engine trouble. (ll. 10–16)

3 The airport was put on emergency alert so in the end, he was forced to put it down in London. (ll. 31–34)

4 Mr Petersen hoped his crippled aircraft to be hauled away this morning. (ll. 46–48)

B Join these notes to make sentences. Then check against the text.

1 Danish pilot – 46 – Mr Carsten Petersen – managed – guide plane down – land 200 yards - Scrubs (ll. 16 20)

2 Mr Petersen – lives – County Offaly – Irish Republic – made earlier abortive attempts – land – Clapham Common – Battersea Park – south London (ll. 20–25)

3 It seems – found – open space – very lucky escape (ll. 34–36)

Grammar points

C What different kinds of ability are expressed by *could* and *managed to* here?

  a *When I was younger, I could walk for hours without getting tired.*
  b *Mr Carsten Petersen managed to guide the plane down on to land.* (ll. 17–19)

Could is more appropriate than *managed to* in some of these sentences. Which ones?

1 Elsie was so clever she ......*could*...... read before she was five.
2 .... get tickets for the show last night? – Yes, we did.
3 When the Titanic went down, very few of the passengers.........................get on to lifeboats.
4 I........................read without glasses till I was 55.
5 I am pleased to say I.........................finish writing the report last night.
6 My son........................drive long before he was allowed to take his driving test.
7 When she was at her peak, Maria Callas .... sing better than anyone I have ever heard.
8 Susan........................make a million before she was thirty.

D Which preposition fits in here? List a few adjectives and the prepositions that follow them.
'The lobsters are sick .... flying,' said Mr Petersen. (ll. 39–40)

Supply the missing prepositions.

  1 I'm sorry ...*for*.... the trouble I've caused.
  2 The south is different .... the north.
  3 Don't trust him. He's capable .... anything.
  4 I was surprised .... his attitude.
  5 You can have this free .... charge.
  6 I'm curious .... Tony's background.
  7 Old Alf is very careful .... his money.
  8 We're quite safe .... danger.
  9 Bill is now married .... the girl next door.
10 Businessmen can't be certain .... success.
11 Contrary .... expectations, she won!
12 I wasn't aware .... Pam's absence.
13 This magazine is full .... ads.
14 Frank's quite careless .... danger.
15 We're very sad .... Jane's departure.
16 It's no good being angry .... me.
17 John is jealous .... his wife's success.
18 We should be kind .... dumb animals.
19 I'm very fond .... anything sweet.
20 We're really excited .... the wedding.

E What's the difference in meaning between these two sentences?

  a *If you go into a good London restaurant, you will get one.*
  b *If you go into a good London restaurant, you might get one.* (ll. 43–45)

Rewrite these sentences using modals (*will, may, might, must,* etc.) to express precise meanings.

1 If you catch an early train, it's certain you'll get to the meeting on time.
  If you catch an early train, you will get to the meeting on time.
2 If you leave here too late, it's possible you'll be late for your meeting.

3 If you want good accommodation in Brighton, it's advisable to book in advance.

4 If it's fine tomorrow, we would be able to go on an excursion.

5 If you want him to succeed, it isn't advisable to criticize him all the time.

6 If you want to spend the week-end here, it's necessary for you to let me know in advance.

7 If you don't want the neighbours to complain, it's necessary not to play loud music.

8 If I don't go to the sales soon, it's possible I won't find anything I like.

SENTENCE STRUCTURE

A Answers and commentary

There are mistakes in numbers **1**, **3** and **4**.

1 *Four hundred Hebridean lobsters facing certain death were given a brief reprieve when the plane* **taking** *them to France ...* (Not *took*). The sentence is made up as follows: *Four hundred Hebridean lobsters were facing certain death. They were given a brief reprieve. [This happened when] a plane was taking them to France to become lobster pot, bisque, and quadrille. The plane was forced to make an emergency landing behind Wormwood Scrubs prison in west London yesterday.* These sentences have been joined with present participles (*facing ... taking*) in place of relative clauses ([*which*] *were facing ...* [*which*] *was taking*). [> LEG 1.58.6, LAG 12An.5]

2 This sentence is correct. It is made up as follows: *The lobsters were en route from the Outer Hebrides in Scotland to Le Touquet in Northern France. A Cessna 206 light aircraft was transporting them. It developed engine trouble.*

3 *The airport was put on emergency alert* **but in** *the end, he was forced to put it down in London.* (Not *so*)
So is incorrect here because it expresses consequence or result [> LAG 56An.6]; *but* expresses contrast. [> LEG 1.18, 1.20.2, 1.20.4, LAG 1Bn.2]

4 *Mr Petersen hoped his crippled aircraft* **would be hauled** *away ...* (Not **to be hauled away**)
We can use a *to*-infinitive or a *that*-clause after *hope* [> LEG 16.12.3, 16.23]:
   I **hope to see** *you soon.*
   I **hope to be cured**.
   I **hope that I will see** *you soon.*
   I **hope that I will/shall/'ll be cured**.
However, we can't use a noun or pronoun object + *to*-infinitive after *hope*. (Not **I hope John/you to be cured**) [> LEG 16.20, LAG 10D]
We have to use a *that*-clause + future [> LEG 9.37.3]:
   He **hopes (that) it will be hauled** *away.*
   → *He* **hoped (that) it would be hauled** *away.*

B Answers and commentary

1 *The Danish pilot,* **46-year-old Mr Carsten Petersen**, ...
The second noun phrase is used in place of a relative clause (*The Danish pilot, who is 46-year-old ...*). It is in apposition and adds information to the first noun phrase. [> LEG 1.39, LAG 2An.1, 5Ans.2,4] This style is common in journalism, particularly when providing someone's age with a hyphenated compound adjective (*46-year-old*). [> LEG 6.3.2]

... managed **to guide** *the plane down* **on to** *land 200 yards* **from the** *Scrubs.*
We use *managed to, was able to* or *succeeded in* + *-ing* (Not *could*) for the successful completion of a specific action. [> LEG 11.12.3, LAG 9C, 48C] Note that *land* is a noun here. The verb is *guide* + adverb particle (*down*) + preposition (*on to* or *onto*). [> LEG 8.9.4, 8.18, 8.30.2, LAG 13C, 16B]

2 *Mr Petersen,* **who lives in County Offaly in the Irish Republic**, *had made ...*
We use commas before and after *who lives in County Offaly in the Irish Republic* because this is a non-defining clause. This means it provides extra information which could easily be omitted (we don't need to know that Mr Petersen lives in County Offaly): *Mr Petersen had made earlier abortive attempts to land on Clapham Common.* [> LEG 1.26, compare > LAG 5A]
Compare a defining clause where we don't use commas because the information is essential and can't be omitted [> LAG 19Bn.1, 22Ans.4,5]:
   Residents **who live around the prison** *are more used to break-out dramas than forced landings.* (Not **Residents, who live around the prison, are more used to break-out dramas than forced landings.**)

3 *It seems he found some open space* **and had** *a very lucky escape.*
When the subject is the same in all parts of the sentence, it is usual not to repeat it. We do not usually put a comma in front of *and*. [> LEG 1.20]
It would not be wrong to write:
   It seems he found some open space **and he had** *a very lucky escape.*
But the extra *he* is unnecessary. [> LAG 4Bn.2, 13B, 16An.2]

GRAMMAR POINTS

C 'Could' and 'managed to' [> LEG 11.8.3, 11.12, LAG 48C, 22C]

a This use of *could* refers to general ability in the past.

b This use of *managed to* refers to the successful completion of a specific action. We cannot use *could* in place of *managed to* in this context.

When talking about ability, we can use *could*:
– to talk about general ability in the past. We can also use *was able to*:

Jim **could** *run/**was able to** run very fast when he was a boy.* (= he had that ability)
– to talk about specific events, only when we use verbs of perception [> LEG 11.13, LAG 48C]:

When I was out this morning, the atmosphere was so clear I **could see** *as far as the coast.*

We use *managed to*, *was/were able to* [> LAG 15Bn.2] and *succeeded in* (+ -ing) to describe the successful completion of a specific action:

For a change, I **managed to** *get to work on time this morning.* (Not *could*)

For a change, I **succeeded in getting** *to work on time this morning.* (Not *could get* or *succeed to get*)

1 *could* (general ability in the past); *managed to* if we think of it as a specific action 'after effort'.

2 *Did you manage to ... ?* (specific action, but *could* is also possible in questions like this. [> LEG 11.12.3])

3 *managed to* if we think of it as a specific action; *could* if we think of it as general ability.

4 *could* (general ability in the past); *managed to* to suggest 'but with increasing difficulty'.

5 *managed to* (specific action). (Not *could*)

6 *could* (general ability). (Not *managed to*)

7 *could* (general ability). (Not *managed to*)

8 *managed to* (specific action). (Not *could*)

D Adjective + preposition: 'sick of' [> LEG 16.53, App 27, LAG 1D, 52D]

sick of; examples of adjectives + preposition occur in the exercise.

Many adjectives are associated with particular prepositions. The problem is to remember which prepositions. This awareness can only come from experience.

1 sorry for	**11** contrary to
2 different from	**12** aware of
3 capable of	**13** full of
4 surprised at/by	**14** careless of/about
5 free of	**15** sad about/at
6 curious about	**16** angry with
7 careful with	**17** jealous of
8 safe from	**18** kind to
9 married to	**19** fond of
10 certain of	**20** excited about

E Type 1 conditionals with 'will' and other modals: 'if you go ... you will/might' [> LEG 14.4–7, compare > LAG 22C, 37D (Type 2), 16C, 50D (Type 3)]

a suggests certainty because of the use of *will*.

b suggests possibility because of the use of *might*.

You have probably been taught that Type 1 conditionals require the use of *will*:
If + present + will:

If the weather **is** *fine,* **we'll** *go for a walk.*
In fact, we can use any modals in Type 1 conditionals to express ability, possibility, advisability, etc.:

If the weather **is** *fine,* **we may** *go for a walk.*

1 If you catch an early train, you will get to the meeting on time. (it's certain)

2 If you leave here too late, you may/might be late for your meeting. (*might* is more 'tentative')

3 If you want good accommodation in Brighton, you should (or *ought to*) book in advance. (= it's advisable)

4 If it's fine tomorrow, we could go on an excursion. (= we would be able to)

5 If you want him to succeed, you shouldn't (or *oughtn't to/mustn't*) criticize him all the time. (= it isn't advisable to)

6 If you want to spend the week-end here, you must let me know in advance. (= it's necessary)

7 If you don't want the neighbours to complain, you mustn't play loud music. (= it's necessary not to)

8 If I don't go to the sales soon, I may not/mightn't find anything I like. (*mayn't* is rare [> LEG 11.5.1])

A-Levels or £1m?

WHEN, at the age of three, David Bolton began using a calculator, his proud parents foresaw that he would do well at school. They could not have anticipated the problem he would face 14 years later. While most pupils his age are struggling with A-levels, he is trying to perform an uneasy balancing act between schoolwork and making his first £1m from a computer consultancy. He is meeting his headmaster tomorrow for a showdown that could mean he will have to leave school. Since his early days, Bolton has progressed from computer to computer with such ease that he now sells his own programmes to property firms and to doctors wanting to put their patients' records on disk.

'It is a quandary,' said the schoolboy, who has turned up for morning assembly in his Porsche 924. 'The business opportunities may not come again if I don't seize them now, and I also understand why my parents and my headmaster would prefer me to stay at school. However, I cannot concentrate on my lessons if I need to meet clients, and sometimes the problem will not wait.'

Since Bolton is over 16, he can

legally decide whether or not to stay on at school. He is apprehensive that business opportunities, if not immediately exploited, may not be repeated, but he does not want to destroy his parents' dream of him achieving a Cambridge degree.

Bolton is a pupil at Wilson's, a highly academic grammar school (founded 1615) in Wallington, Surrey. Last week he was plunged into controversy when his father, Bill Bolton, a retired hospital worker, told John Simpson, the headmaster, that his son wished to leave so that he could devote himself to his computer consultancy (which the boy runs from his bedroom). Bolton Jnr has made it clear that he will quit unless the school rules are modified to allow him to attend urgent business meetings. At school, meanwhile, Bolton sat 10 GCSEs a year early and obtained four A grades, four Bs, and two Cs. He also wrote persuasive letters to companies offering himself as a computer consultant - usually omitting to mention his age.

The Sunday Times (BrE)

Sentence structure

A Replace the word or words in italics. Then refer to the text.

1 *During the time that* most pupils his age are struggling with A-levels, he is trying to perform an uneasy balancing act. (ll. 3–5) ....

2 *From* his early days, Bolton has progressed from computer to computer *so easily* that he now sells his own programmes to property firms. (ll. 9–13) ....

3 The business opportunities may not come again *unless I seize* them now. (ll. 19–21) ....

4 *As* Bolton is over 16, he can legally decide *to stay on at school or not.* (ll. 28–30) ....

5 Bolton Jnr has made it clear that he will quit *if the school rules are not* modified. (ll. 46–48) ....

B Join these sentences using the suggestions in brackets and making any necessary changes. Then check against the text.

1 I cannot concentrate on my lessons. I need to meet clients. Sometimes the problem will not wait. (ll. 24–27) [*However, if, and*]

....

2 Last week he was plunged into controversy. His father, Bill Bolton, is a retired hospital worker. He told John Simpson, the headmaster, that his son wished to leave. His son wanted to devote himself to his computer consultancy. The boy runs it from his bedroom. (ll. 39–46) [*when, commas, so that, which*]

....

....

....

Grammar points

C Combine modals (*can, may,* etc.) with the verbs in brackets. Then refer to the text. (ll. 1–9, 16–27) Alternatives are possible. In each case give a reason for your choice.

When, at the age of three, David Bolton began using a calculator, his proud parents foresaw that he ¹(*do*) .... well at school.
They ²(*not anticipate*) .... the problem
he ³(*face*) .... 14 years later. While most pupils his age are struggling with A-levels, he is trying to perform an uneasy balancing act between schoolwork and making his first £1m from a computer consultancy. He is meeting his headmaster tomorrow for a showdown that ⁴(*mean*) ....
he ⁵(*have to*) .... leave school.
'It is a quandary,' said the schoolboy, who has turned up for morning assembly in his Porsche 924. 'The business opportunities ⁶(*not come*) .... again if I don't seize them now, and I also understand why my parents and my headmaster ⁷(*prefer*) .... me to stay at school.
However, I ⁸(*not concentrate*) .... on my lessons
if I need to meet clients, and sometimes the problem ⁹(*not wait*).' ....

D What's the difference in meaning between these two sentences?

   a *My headmaster would prefer to stay at school.*
   b *My headmaster would prefer me to stay at school.* (ll. 22–23)

   ....

Write sentences with an object using the suggestions in brackets.

   1 I don't want to write to him. (I'd prefer you) *I'd prefer you to write to him.*
   2 I don't want to phone her. (want your mother) ....
   3 I don't want to make the supper. (I'd like you) ....
   4 I don't want to answer this letter. (expect the boss) ....
   5 I don't want to speak to him. (intend you) ....

E With an arrow, show a possible different position for *or not* in this sentence.
*Since Bolton is over 16, he can legally decide whether **or not** to stay on at school.* (ll. 28–30)

Rewrite each sentence in two ways, using *whether or not.*

   1 He'll decide if he wants to buy it.   *He'll decide whether or not he wants to buy it.*
                                                    He'll decide whether he wants to buy it or not.

   2 I don't know if the stock market has fallen. ....
                                                    ....

   3 She didn't say if she would be back for dinner. ....
                                                    ....

F You can use *unless* in place of *if ... not* in one of these sentences. Which one?

   a *He's made it clear that he will quit **if** the school rules **aren't** modifed.* (ll. 46–48)
   b *She'd be better company **if** she **didn't** complain so much.*

Show with a tick (✓) the sentences in which we can use *unless* in place of *if ... not.*

   1 If she doesn't apply for a university place soon, she'll be too late. (✓)
   2 The atmosphere is bound to get warmer if we don't stop producing so much carbon dioxide.
   3 It will be really amazing if the present government doesn't win the next election.
   4 I'm really surprised if you aren't upset by all this bad news.
   5 If we don't all follow the same fishing rules, there won't be many fish left in the sea.
   6 It would be better for everybody if we didn't take too many fish out of the sea.
   7 Some companies wouldn't make so much profit if they weren't monopolies.

SENTENCE STRUCTURE

A Answers and commentary

1 *While most pupils his age are struggling with A-levels, he is trying to . . .*
While means 'during the time that' (Not **During most pupils . . . **). We often use it to describe two parallel actions in progress at the same time [> LEG 9.20.3, LAG 20Bn.1, 40An.5, 41An.4]:

> *While most pupils are struggling with A-levels, he is trying to . . .* (present progressive)
> *While most pupils were struggling with A-levels, he was trying to . . .* (past progressive)
> *While most pupils have been struggling with A-levels, he has been trying to . . .* (present perfect progressive)

2 *Since his early days, Bolton has progressed from computer to computer . . .*
Since usually refers to a fixed point of time. It can't be replaced by *from* in all cases:

> *I have been waiting here since 4 o'clock.* (Not **from 4 o'clock**) [> LEG 7.31, 9.25.2, 10.13.5, compare > LAG 8Bn.1, 8En.5]

> *. . . Bolton has progressed from computer to computer with such ease that . . .*
So + adjective/adverb + *(that)* and *such (a/an)* + noun + *(that)* introduce adverbial clauses of result. [> LEG 1.52.1, LAG 2Bn.1]

3 *The business opportunities may not come again if I don't seize them now.*
When *unless* means 'except on the condition that', it can replace *if . . . not*. [> LEG 14.20, LAG 10F] For example, *unless* cannot replace *if . . . not* here:

> *I'll be surprised if he doesn't win.*

4 *Since Bolton is over 16, he can legally decide . . .*
We use *since* with time references (see **2** above) and also in the sense of 'because' (as here). [> LEG 1.48, LAG 24An.12, 30An.6, 34An.3]

> *. . . whether or not to stay on at school.*
Note that *. . . or not* can be used optionally with *whether*. [> LEG 1.24.1, 14.21, 15.18, LAG 10E, 24An.18] It is also correct to say:

> *Bolton can legally decide whether to stay on at school (or not).*

5 *Bolton Jnr has made it clear that he will quit unless the school rules are modified.*
Unless means 'except on the condition that' and can replace *if . . . not* (see **3** above).

B Answers and commentary

1 *However, I cannot concentrate on my lessons if I need to meet clients, and sometimes . . .*
We often use *however*, as a connecting adverb, to introduce a contrast. [> LEG 7.58, App 18, LAG 37Bn.1, 45An.2]
If does not mean 'on the condition that' here and does not introduce a conditional clause. It means 'on those occasions when' [> LAG 6Bn.2] and can be replaced by *when*. Note the use of a comma before *and* here to mark off the preceding clause. This use is at the writer's discretion.

2 *Last week he was plunged into controversy when his father . . . told John Simpson . . .*
When introduces an adverbial clause of time. [> LEG 1.45.1, LAG 3Bn.1, 6Bn.1]

> *. . . when his father, Bill Bolton, a retired hospital worker, told John Simpson, the headmaster, . . .*
The two noun phrases *Bill Bolton* and *a retired hospital worker* are in apposition with *his father*: each phrase adds information to the one that went before. The phrases replace relative clauses:

> *His father, whose name is Bill Bolton, who is a retired hospital worker, . . .*
The phrases *John Simpson, the headmaster,* are also in apposition. [> LEG 1.39, LAG 2An.1]

> *. . . that his son wished to leave so that he could devote himself to his computer consultancy . . .*
We can introduce adverbial clauses of purpose with *so that* and *in order that*. When the verb in the main clause is in the simple past, we use *should, could, might* or *would* after *so that*. [> LEG 1.51.1–2] Of course, it is much easier to use a *to*-infinitive to express purpose. Instead of using *so that* we could say [> LEG 16.12.1]:

> *. . . his son wished to leave to/so as to/in order to devote himself to his computer consultancy . . .*

> *. . . consultancy (which the boy runs from his bedroom).*
The brackets aren't strictly necessary and a comma after *consultancy* would have been enough. *Which* is a relative pronoun object, replacing *it* (= the boy runs it from his bedroom). [> LEG 1.34]

GRAMMAR POINTS

C Modals and related verbs [> LEG Chapter 11, LAG 37C]

1 *would/might do*: normal sequence of tenses after the reporting verb *foresaw*: past attracts past [> LEG 9.5, 15.12–13, LAG 7F]:

> *They **foresee** that he **will** do well.*
> →*They **foresaw** that he **would** do well.*

2 *could not have anticipated*: (= it would not have been possible to anticipate). [> LEG 11.28–29]

3 *would face*: normal sequence of tenses after the reporting verb *could have anticipated*: past attracts past [> LEG 9.5, 15.12–13, LAG 7F]:

> *They **can't anticipate** the problem he **will** face.*
> → *They **couldn't anticipate**/They **couldn't have anticipated** the problem he **would** face.*

4 *could/might mean*: (= it is possible that it will mean, it might mean). [> LEG 11.28–29]

5 *will have to*: simple future reference (prediction). [> LEG 9.35–38, LAG 29C] As we can't say **will must**, we may use *will have to*, or simply *has to* to refer to advisability in the future. [> LEG 11.50, LAG 17D, 23F]

6 *may/might not come*: (= it is possible that they won't). [> LEG 11.28–29, LAG 37Cn.5]

7 *would prefer me to*: This use of *would* makes the statement less definite than the simple present [> LEG 11.74.2, LAG 41C]:

> *My headmaster **prefers** me to stay at school.* (definite)
> → *My headmaster **would prefer** me to stay at school.* (less definite)

8 *cannot concentrate*: (= am not able to concentrate). [> LEG 11.11] Note that *cannot* is always written as one word, unlike other modal full-form negatives (*could not*, *may not*, etc. Not **couldnot**, etc.). [> LEG 11.5.1]

9 *will not/can't wait*: simple future reference (*will not*), but also with the idea of 'refusal' (*can't*). [> LEG 9.35–38, 11.74.1, LAG 29C]

D Verb + optional noun/pronoun + *to*-infinitive: 'want (me) to' [> LEG 16.20]

a *My headmaster **would prefer to stay** at school.* (so that *he* will stay at school.)

b *My headmaster **would prefer me to stay** at school.* (so that *I* will stay at school.)

Some verbs like *prefer*, *want*, *wish*, etc. may be followed by a *to*-infinitive:

> *I **want to stay** at school.*

or by a noun/pronoun object + *to*-infinitive:

> *I **want you/my son to stay** at school.* (Not **I want that you stay at school.**)

1 I'd prefer you to write to him.
2 I want your mother to phone her.
3 I'd like you to make the supper.
4 I expect the boss to answer this letter.
5 I intend you to speak to him.

E Reporting Yes/No questions with 'or not': 'he wants to know if/whether … or not' [> LEG 1.24.1, 14.21, 15.18n.7, LAG 14B, 24An.18, 29B]

*Since Bolton is over 16, he can legally decide **whether** to stay on at school **or not**.*
We can say:

> *He wants to know **if/whether** we want any dinner **or not**.*

Or:

> *He wants to know **whether or not** we want any dinner.* (Not **if or not**)

1 He'll decide whether or not he wants to buy it.
He'll decide whether he wants to buy it or not.

2 I don't know whether or not the stock market has fallen.
I don't know whether the stock market has fallen or not.

3 She didn't say whether or not she would be back for dinner.
She didn't say whether she would be back for dinner or not.

F Negatives with 'if … not' and 'unless' [> LEG 14.20, LAG 9E, 10An.3, 20A]

a We can only replace *if … not* by *unless* when the meaning is 'except on the condition that'. Note that *unless* often occurs with a verb in the affirmative:

> *He's made it clear he will quit **if** the school rules **aren't** modified.*
> *He's made it clear he will quit **unless** the school rules **are** modified.*

The following require ticks: **1**, **2**, **5**.
1 Unless she applies
2 unless we stop
5 Unless we all follow

Memories of a great actress

PERHAPS the most legendary theatrical figures of that time [1904-1921] were the international star actresses, those great creatures whose names alone could fill a
5 theatre. I saw Eleonora Duse in *Ghosts* at the New Oxford Theatre in Tottenham Court Road, long since demolished. I stood at the back of the packed theatre at a matinée. Every actor in London was there and the
10 feeling in the audience was unforgettable, a mixture of respect and awe, a sense that we would never see this great woman again. When Duse came on, the atmosphere was already electric, and she could hardly fail to
15 make the most wonderful impression. I did not know the play very well, but Duse looked infinitely sad and distinguished with her white hair, and wearing a plain black dress with a shawl draped over her shoulders. I remember that her acting seemed very, very simple. She
20 had marvellous hands and all her movements were weary and poetic. Here was a legendary figure whose career had spanned fifty or sixty years of the nineteenth-century theatre, and she succeeded, to my mind, in living up to her legend, although she was evidently old and tired.
25   Many years later, in 1952, at a cocktail party in Hollywood, I was introduced to Charlie Chaplin. He took me aside and began to talk to me about his boyhood in London when he used to see Tree's productions from the gallery at His Majesty's. For some reason we talked about
30 Duse. Chaplin described an occasion on which he saw her act. He began to imitate the actor who had appeared that night with Duse. He whipped out a chair and sat astride it and began to jabber bogus Italian. In a brilliant mime, he showed how the actor was enthralling the audience with
35 a long speech when suddenly the curtains behind began to move and a little old lady came out very quietly and glided across the stage and put her hands towards the fire. Duse. And at this point the poor actor who had seemed so remarkable a moment before was completely blotted out.

An Actor and His Time by John Gielgud *(BrE)*

Sentence structure

A Put the words in the right order in each sentence, inserting necessary commas. This exercise prepares you for **B** below.

1 a those great creatures | of that time | the international star actresses | perhaps the most legendary theatrical figures | were

....

b alone | their names | a theatre | could fill (ll. 1–5)

....

2 a a legendary figure | here | was

....

b of the nineteenth-century theatre | her career | fifty or sixty years | had spanned

....

c in living up to her legend | she succeeded | to my mind

....

d old and tired | evidently | she was (ll. 21–24)

....

B Join the above into two separate sentences, then check against the text.

1 ....

....

....

2 ....

....

....

....

Grammar points

C Why do we use *the most* in **a**, and *most* in **b**?

    a *Perhaps **the most legendary** theatrical figures ... were the international star actresses.*
    (ll. 1–3)
    b ***Most legendary** theatrical figures are remembered long after their time.*

Supply *most* or *the most* in these sentences.

1 *Most* of the output of this factory is exported.
2 .... of our competitors are trying to create new markets for their products.
3 The building of the Channel Tunnel has been one of.............ambitious European projects.
4 We are.............grateful to you for all the help you have given us.
5 We expect.............products on sale to the public to be clearly labelled these days.
6 .... good wine improves with keeping.
7 He'll be lucky to scrape through with a bare pass in his exams. It's.............you can expect.

D Why can we use only *every* in **a** but *every* or *each* in **b**?

    a ***Every actor** in London was there and the feeling in the audience was unforgettable.*
    (ll. 9–10)
    b *At the end of the play **every/each actor** bowed to the enthusiastic audience.*

Supply *every* or *each*, noting where both are possible.

1 It's often said that *every* cloud has a silver lining.
2 .... time I wash the car it rains!
3 .... house in the district is set in its own garden.
4 Nearly.............house in the village was damaged during the recent storms.
5 We are careful to respond to.............single inquiry we receive.
6 At the end of Timmy's birthday party, a present was given to.............child.
7 They both worked hard and they.............received a bonus.

E Which of these sentences is wrong and why? (ll. 13–15)

    a *When Duse came on, she could hardly fail to make the most wonderful impression.*
    b *When Duse came on, she couldn't hardly fail to make the most wonderful impression.*

Express agreement with each of these statements. Use *hardly* in each of your answers.

1 I was so moved, I couldn't speak.   *Yes, you could hardly speak!*
2 But that isn't what I wanted.
3 You don't really know the Wentworths.
4 She isn't the person for the job.
5 Trains in this country aren't ever on time.
6 Les isn't tall enough to be a policeman.
7 Speak up, I can't hear what you're saying.

F What's the passive of:
They introduced me to Charlie Chaplin. (l. 26)

Put these into the passive. In which sentence is it possible to have two versions of the passive?

1 They described him to me.   *He was described to me.*
2 They explained the situation to me.
3 They entrusted the money to her.
4 They have mentioned the case to me.
5 They're reporting the matter to the police.
6 They've already said something to him.
7 They suggested an alternative idea to him.

SENTENCE STRUCTURE

A Answers and commentary

1a *Perhaps* (adverb) *the most legendary theatrical figures of that time* (subject) *were* (verb) *the international star actresses* (complement), *those great creatures* (in apposition to the complement).

Perhaps is a viewpoint adverb which reveals the writer's attitude (in this case being tentative). We often express a viewpoint with adverbs like *frankly*, *normally*, at the beginning of a sentence to prepare the reader for our attitude. [> LEG 7.57, App 17] The rest of the sentence follows the normal subject, verb, complement order of an English sentence. [> LEG 1.3, 1.11, LAG 4A] *Those great creatures* adds information to the statement that went before. [> LEG 1.39, 3.30]

b *Their names* (subject) *alone* (focus adverb) *could fill* (verb) *a theatre* (object).

We can use *alone* in different positions, depending on the focus we want. [> LEG 7.54–55, compare > LAG 21Bn.1b] We can also say:

Alone, their names could fill a theatre.
Their names could alone fill a theatre.
Their names could fill a theatre alone.

2a *Here* (adverb complement) *was* (verb) *a legendary figure* (subject).

We often begin a statement with *here is/was* in order to identify something to draw attention to it. If we do this, the noun subject comes after the verb [> LEG 7.59.1]:

Here's your tea.

Rather than:

Your tea (subject) *is* (verb) *here* (adverb complement).

b *Her career* (subject) *had spanned* (verb) *fifty or sixty years of the nineteenth-century theatre* (object).

Though we tend to follow the subject/verb/object pattern strictly, we often lengthen the subject or the object with a phrase or clause. In this case *of the nineteenth-century theatre* expands the object (*fifty or sixty years*). [> LEG 1.5]

c *She* (subject) *succeeded* (verb), *to my mind* (adverb), *in* (preposition) *living up to her legend* (object).

To my mind expresses the writer's viewpoint (= in my opinion). The position of this phrase

can vary according to the emphasis we wish to make. [> LEG 7.57, App 17] We can also say:

To my mind, she succeeded in living up to her legend.

She succeeded in living up to her legend, to my mind.

d *She* (subject) *was* (verb) *evidently* (viewpoint adverb) *old and tired* (adjectival complement).

Again, *evidently* expresses the writer's viewpoint (= I am drawing that conclusion). The position of the adverb can vary according to the emphasis we wish to make. [> LEG 7.57, App 17] We can also say:

Evidently, she was old and tired.
She was old and tired, evidently.

B Answers and commentary

1 *Perhaps the most legendary theatrical figures of that time were the international star actresses, those great creatures **whose** names alone could fill a theatre.*

Whose names is the subject of the relative clause. *Whose* remains unchanged whether it refers to masculine, feminine, singular or plural. We use it in place of possessive adjectives (*my*, *your*, *his*, etc.). Here, it is used in place of *their*, referring to *international star actresses*. [> LEG 1.32]

2 *Here was a legendary figure **whose** career had spanned fifty or sixty years of the nineteenth-century theatre, **and** she succeeded, to my mind, in living up to her legend, **although** she was evidently old and tired.*

Whose replaces *her*. (See **1** above.) [> LEG 1.32]

and introduces a co-ordinate clause, adding information. [> LEG 1.18, LAG 1Bn.2] Because the sentence is so long, the clause with *and* is marked off by commas. [> LEG 1.20]

although introduces an adverbial clause of concession by adding an element of contrast. *But* and *even though* would do the same job as *although* here. We could begin the sentence with *Although* or *Even though*, but not with *But*:

Although she was evidently old and tired, she was a legendary figure whose career had spanned fifty or sixty years of the nineteenth-century theatre, and she succeeded, to my mind, in living up to her legend.

GRAMMAR POINTS

C 'Most' and 'the most' [> LEG 5.5, 6.27.4]

a *The most legendary figures* is a superlative and therefore requires *the*. (= compared with all the others) [> LEG 6.28, LAG 32D]

b *Most legendary theatrical figures* means 'the largest number of'. (= the largest number of theatrical figures)

When we make general statements to refer to the class as a whole, we use zero (–), not *a/an* or *the* [> LEG 3.24–26, LAG 8C, 15C, 22B, etc.]:

(–) *Legendary theatrical figures are remembered long after their time.* (general statement with adjective + plural countable)

To refer to 'the greatest number of', we simply put *most* in front of a plural noun phrase:

(–) *Most legendary theatrical figures are remembered long after their time.*

We can also use *most* (Not *the most*) as an adverb of degree: *I'm **most obliged** to you.* (= very) [> LEG 7.51.1, LAG 21C]

1 Most
2 Most
3 the most
4 most
5 most
6 Most
7 the most

D 'Every' and 'each' [> LEG 5.26, 5.30]

a *Every* suggests *all (of the actors)*; **b** *Every* and *each* can both suggest 'separately'.

Every and *each* refer to particular people or things. They can point to more than two. *Each* is more individual and suggests 'one by one' or 'separately'. We use *each* to refer to a definite and usually limited number.

1 Every (suggests *all*)
2 Every/Each (suggests separate occasions)
3 Every/Each (suggests separate houses)
4 Nearly every (we can modify *every*, but not *each*)
5 every single (we can use *single* after *every*, but not after *each*)
6 every/each (suggests separate children)
7 each (*each*, but not *every*, can also refer to *two*)

E Negative statements with 'hardly': 'she could hardly fail' [> LEG 7.39, 13.8–10, compare > LAG 14G, 34A, 46E]

b *She couldn't hardly fail* is wrong because *not* and *hardly* are both negative words and we normally have only one negative in any one clause, not a 'double negative'.

1 Yes, you could hardly speak!
(Not *you couldn't hardly speak*)
2 Yes, that's hardly what you wanted.
(Not *that isn't hardly what you wanted*)
3 Yes, I hardly know the Wentworths!
(Not *I hardly don't know*)
4 Yes, she's hardly the person for the job!
(Not *she isn't hardly the person*)
5 Yes, they're hardly ever on time!
(Not *they aren't hardly ever on time*)
6 Yes, he's hardly tall enough to be a policeman!
(Not *he isn't hardly tall enough*)
7 Yes, you can hardly hear what I'm saying!
(Not *you can't hardly hear*)

F Passive forms of verbs like 'explain': 'it was explained to me' [> LEG 1.12.1]

As the emphasis is on *me*, the passive is: *I was introduced to Charlie Chaplin*.
Verbs like *explain* and *repeat* do not have two possible passive forms [> LAG 53An.3]:

*The situation **was explained to me**.* (Not *I was explained the situation.* or *To me was explained the situation.*)
Compare:

They gave me a pen.
→ *I was given a pen.*
→ *A pen was given to me.* [> LEG 1.13.2–4, chapter 12, 12.3n.4]

In the case of *introduce*, we could also say *Charlie Chaplin was introduced to me*, but it's the meaning of *introduce* that makes this possible. Compare *entrust* in **3** below.

1 He was described to me.
2 The situation was explained to me.
3 The money was entrusted to her. (or *she was entrusted with*)
4 The case has been mentioned to me.
5 The matter is being reported to the police.
6 Something has already been said to him.
7 An alternative idea was suggested to him.

La belle Monique

You can see the movie titles now: 'Passion and Pursuit on the Motorway', 'Jealousy of the Long Distance Lorry Driver'; or, as one French paper had it, 'Rodeo on the Autoroute'. In a terrifying but farcical scenario, two lorry drivers fought a motorway duel in their 38-ton vehicles over a course of more than 60 miles in the Auvergne, south-west France: a furious chase at 80mph which ended with one man in hospital, the other in jail and blood all over the road. The cause? La belle Monique, wife of driver number 1, who was riding in the cab of driver number 2.

The story began with Jöel André, 31, and apparently well known as a tough guy, leaving home in Clermont-Ferrand early in the morning and driving peacefully towards Saint Étienne. Observing all the rules of the road, he was keeping well to the right when he saw the driver of a lorry behind pull out to overtake him. When it drew level, Jöel glanced into the cabin and saw, to his stupefaction, his wife Monique, whom he imagined safe at home in bed, sitting next to the driver, who turned out to be Patrick Monron, 47.

Monique paled, Jöel turned purple with rage and put his foot down, while his horrified rival tried desperately to escape. First on the motorway, then on the Route Nationale, they engaged in a mad and dangerous chase through the Puy-de-Dôme, across the Upper Loire and then the Loire itself, passing and repassing each other and forcing other motorists off the road until they finally crashed into each other. That was not the end.

The knights of the road climbed out and continued the battle with what weapons they could find - a crowbar and the handle of an axe. It was a bloody struggle: one duellist (Patrick) had his arm cut to shreds and the other had deep head wounds. Honour still unsatisfied, they got back into their lorries and were off again, this time trying to edge each other into a deep ravine that fell away at one side of the road. But Patrick, the adulterer, had lost so much blood that he passed out, and Monique, who had stayed in his cab all the time, had to take the wheel. She managed to stop the truck and call the police, fire brigade and an ambulance. Yesterday Patrick was in hospital and Jöel in prison. History does not record whether Monique is at bedside or bars.

The film rights are presumably still available.

The Daily Telegraph (BrE)

Sentence structure

A Supply the connecting words, then check against the text.

In a terrifying ¹........ farcical scenario, two lorry drivers fought a motorway duel in their 38-ton vehicles over a course of more than 60 miles in the Auvergne, south-west France: a furious chase at 80mph ²........ ended with one man in hospital, the ³........ in jail and blood all over the road. The cause? La belle Monique, wife of driver number 1, ⁴........ was riding in the cab of driver number 2. The story began with Jöel André, 31, and apparently well known as a tough guy, ⁵(*leave*) .... home in Clermont-Ferrand early in the morning ⁶........ driving peacefully towards Saint Étienne. ⁷(*Observe*) .... all the rules of the road, he was keeping well to the right ⁸........ he saw the driver of a lorry behind pull out ⁹(*overtake*) .... him. ¹⁰........ it drew level, Jöel glanced into the cabin ¹¹........ saw, to his stupefaction, his wife Monique, ¹²........ he imagined safe at home in bed, ¹³(*sit*) .... next to the driver, ¹⁴........ turned out to be Patrick Monron, 47. Monique paled, Jöel turned purple with rage ¹⁵........ put his foot down, ¹⁶........ his horrified rival tried desperately to escape. First on the motorway, then on the Route Nationale, they engaged in a mad and dangerous chase through the Puy-de-Dôme, across the Upper Loire and ¹⁷........ the Loire itself, ¹⁸(*pass*) .... and ¹⁹(*repass*) .... each other and ²⁰(*force*) .... other motorists off the road ²¹........ they finally crashed into each other. That was not the end. The knights of the road climbed out ²²........ continued the battle with what weapons they could find – a crowbar and the handle of an axe. It was a bloody struggle: ²³........ duellist (Patrick) had his arm cut to shreds and the other had deep head wounds. Honour still ²⁴(*unsatisfy*) ...., they got back into their lorries and were off again, this time ²⁵(*try*) .... to edge each other into a deep ravine ²⁶........ fell away at one side of the road. But Patrick, the adulterer, had lost ²⁷........ much blood ²⁸........ he passed out. (ll. 7–66)

Grammar points

B Supply the missing prepositions. Then refer to the text. (ll. 1–36) Give reasons for each choice, where you can. Alternatives are possible.

You can see the movie titles now: 'Passion and Pursuit ^{1}............... the
Motorway', 'Jealousy ^{2}............... the Long Distance Lorry Driver';
or, as one French paper had it, 'Rodeo ^{3}............... the Autoroute'.
^{4}............... a terrifying but farcical scenario, two lorry drivers
fought a motorway duel ^{5}............... their 38-ton vehicles
^{6}............... a course
^{7}............... more than 60 miles
^{8}............... the Auvergne, south-west France: a furious chase
^{9}............... 80mph which
ended ^{10}............... one man
^{11}............... hospital,
the other ^{12}............... jail and blood
all ^{13}............... the road. The cause? La belle Monique,
wife ^{14}............... driver number 1, who was riding
^{15}............... the cab
^{16}............... driver number 2.
The story began ^{17}............... Jöel André, 31, and apparently well known
^{18}............... a tough guy, leaving home
^{19}............... Clermont-Ferrand early
^{20}............... the morning and driving peacefully
^{21}............... Saint Étienne.
Observing all the rules ^{22}............... the road,
he was keeping well ^{23}............... the right
when he saw the driver ^{24}............... a lorry
behind pull out to overtake him. When it drew level, Jöel glanced
^{25}............... the cabin and saw,
^{26}............... his stupefaction, his wife Monique,
whom he imagined safe ^{27}............... home
^{28}............... bed, sitting
^{29}............... the driver, who turned out to be Patrick Monron, 47.

C What's the difference between:

a *It was a bloody struggle: one duellist **had his arm cut** to shreds ...* (ll. 55–57)
b *It was a bloody struggle: one duellist **had cut his arm** to shreds ...*

....
....

Supply the correct forms with *had* in these sentences.

1 I couldn't understand the problem until the teacher (explain it) *had explained it*
   again.
2 You should understand the problem now. You (explain it) *had it explained* to you
   yesterday.
3 John has to drive carefully now. He (endorse his licence) .... twice last week.
4 John couldn't drive because the police (endorse his licence) .... three times.
5 John couldn't afford any luxuries, because his landlord (increase his rent) ....
6 John couldn't afford any luxuries because he had (increase his rent) ....
7 I recently (steal my car) .... when I parked it in the street.
8 As I was walking to the station, two youths drove past me and I noticed with dismay that
   they (steal my car) ....
9 I wasn't comfortable until the dentist (extract the painful tooth) ....
10 I wasn't comfortable until I had (extract the painful tooth) ....

SENTENCE STRUCTURE

A Answers and commentary

1 *but*: The scenario **was terrifying but it was farcical**. → It was **a terrifying but farcical** scenario. [> LEG 1.20.6]

2 *which/that*: relative pronoun subject of a relative clause, replacing *it* (= the event) [> LEG 1.31]:
  It was a furious chase at 80mph. **It** ended ...
  → *It was a furious chase* **which/that** *ended ...*

3 *other*: We can refer to two people/things with the pronouns *(the) one ... the other.* [> LEG 4.11]

4 *who* (optional): relative pronoun subject, replacing *she* [> LEG 1.29, LAG 5Ans.1–2]:
  She was the wife of driver number 1. **She was riding in the cab ...** → *... the wife of driver number 1,* **who** *was riding ...*

5 *leaving*: present participle construction in place of a relative clause [> LEG 1.58.6, LAG 9An.1]:
  ... a tough guy, **who was leaving** *home in Clermont-Ferrand ...* → *... a tough guy,* **leaving** *home in Clermont-Ferrand ...*

6 *and*: + participle construction [> LEG 1.18]:
  ... **who was leaving** *home ...* **and who was driving** *peacefully ...* → *...* **leaving** *home ...* **and driving** *peacefully ...*

7 *Observing*: present participle construction in place of the past progressive [> LEG 1.57]:
  He was observing *all the rules of the road* **and was keeping** *...* → **Observing** *all the rules of the road, he* **was keeping** *...*

8 *when*: time conjunction, introducing a clause of time *(when he saw ...).* [> LEG 1.45.1]

9 *to overtake*: infinitive of purpose. We could also use *so as to* and *in order to.* [> LEG 16.12.1]

10 *When/As*: time conjunction, introducing an adverb clause *(When it drew level).* [> LEG 1.45.1]

11 *and*: conjunction introducing a co-ordinate clause. We don't usually repeat the subject after *and* [> LEG 1.20]:
  Jöel **glanced** *into the cabin.* **He saw** *...* → *Jöel* **glanced** *...* **and saw** *... (= and he saw).*

12 *whom*: relative pronoun object replacing *her.* [> LEG 1.33, LAG 27An.3, 40An.3]:
  ... his wife Monique. He imagined **her** *safe at home.* → *... his wife Monique,* **whom** *he imagined safe at home.*

13 *sitting*: present participle construction in place of a co-ordinate clause [> LEG 1.58.1]:
  ... wife Monique **and she was sitting** *...* → *... wife* **Monique** *sitting ...*

14 *who*: relative pronoun subject of a relative clause, replacing *he* [> LEG 1.29, LAG 5Ans.1–2]:
  He was the driver. **He** *turned out to be Patrick Monron.* → *... the driver,* **who** *...*

15 *and*: conjunction introducing a co-ordinate clause *(and put his foot down).* We don't usually repeat the subject (see **11** above). [> LAG 1Bn.2]

16 *while* (= during the time when): We often use the progressive with *while* to emphasize an action in progress [> LAG 10An.1]:
  Jöel put his foot down, **while** *his horrified rival* **was trying** *desperately to escape.* However, the simple past *(while he tried)* can also describe the action in progress. [> LEG 9.20.2]

17 *then*: We often use *and then* to connect a sequence of events in a narrative. [> LEG 1.18]

18, 19, 20: *passing* and *repassing ... forcing*: present participle constructions in place of the past progressive [> LEG 1.57, LAG 4Bn.3]:
  They engaged in a mad and dangerous chase. **They were passing** *and* **repassing** *each other.* **They were forcing** *...* → *a mad and dangerous chase,* **passing** *and* **repassing** *each other and* **forcing** *...*

21 *until/till*: time conjunction, introducing a clause of time *(until they finally crashed).* [> LEG 1.45.1]

22 *and*: conjunction introducing a co-ordinate clause *(and continued).* We don't usually repeat the subject (see **11** above).

23 *one*: We can refer to two people or things with the pronouns *(the) one ... the other.* [> LEG 4.11]

24 *unsatisfied*: past participle construction in place of the passive [> LEG 1.62.1, LAG 6Bn.4]:
  (Their) honour **was still unsatisfied, so** *they got back into their lorries ...* → *Honour still* **unsatisfied, they** *...*

25 *trying*: present participle construction in place of the past progressive [> LEG 1.57]:
  They were off again. **They were trying** *to edge each other ...* → *They were off again,* **trying** *to edge each other ...*

26 *that*: relative pronoun subject of a relative clause, replacing *it* [> LEG 1.31, LAG 5An.3]:
  It was a deep ravine. **It** *fell away.* → *It was a deep ravine* **that** *(or* **which***) fell away ...*

27 *so*: adverbial clause of result introduced by *so much.* [> LEG 1.52.1, LAG 2Bn.1, 10An.2]

28 *that*: continuation of the clause: *so much blood (that).* [> LEG 1.52.1] *That* is often omitted: *He had lost* **so much** *blood (that)* **he passed out** *...*

GRAMMAR POINTS

B Prepositions [> LEG Chapter 8, Apps 25–30, LAG 31C, 32C, 46B, 55C]

The choice of prepositions of place and direction often depends on the viewpoint of the speaker or writer. That's why more than one preposition is sometimes possible.

1 *on*: *on* a surface (*the motorway*). [> LEG 8.6]

2 *of*: noun (*jealousy*) + associated preposition. Compare adjective: *jealous of*; also possession (*driver's jealousy*). [> LEG App 27, LAG 1D, 9D, 52D]

3 *on*: *on* a surface (*the Autoroute*). [> LEG 8.6]

4 *in*: 'enclosed' *in a scenario*. [> LEG 8.6]

5 *in*: 'enclosed' *in their 38-ton vehicles* [> LEG 8.6]; or *with* (vehicles as 'instruments').

6 *over* (= from one end of the course to the other): *across* would also be possible. However, *over* is probably more appropriate because the course is 'here and there' (not in a straight line). [> LEG App 25.3]

7 *of*: genitive (= of more than 60 miles' distance). We can say [> LEG 2.49, LAG 5B]: *a course of 60 miles* or *a 60 mile course*.

8 *in*: 'enclosed' *in the Auvergne*. [> LEG 8.6]

9 *at*: + speed: *at 80mph* (= 80 miles per hour). [> LEG App 25.7]

10 *with*: verb + preposition (*end with*). [compare > LEG App 28, LAG 8D]

11 *in*: preposition + zero article noun (*in hospital*). [> LEG 3.28.3, 8.9.2, App 22.5, LAG 45E]

12 *in*: preposition + zero article noun (*in jail*). [> LEG 3.28.3, 8.9.2, App 22.5, LAG 45E]

13 *over* (= here and there): intensified by *all* (*all over*). [> LEG App 25.3]

14 *of*: genitive (*wife of driver number 1*). *Driver number 1's wife* would also be possible, but more awkward. [> LEG 2.42–44]

15 *in*: 'enclosed' *in the cab*. [> LEG 8.6]

16 *of*: genitive. ... *who was riding in driver number 2's cab* would also be possible, but more awkward. [> LEG 2.42–44, compare > LAG 57E]

17 *with*: verb + preposition (*begin with*). [> LEG App 28, LAG 8D]

18 *as* (= in the capacity of): *known **as a tough guy***. [> LEG App 25.25, LAG 25An.17]

19 *in*: 'enclosed' *in Clermont-Ferrand*. [> LEG 8.6]

20 *in*: time phrase with *in* (*in the morning*). [> LEG 7.21, 8.13, App 48, LAG 4C]

21 *towards* (= in the general direction of). [> LEG App 25.34]

22 *of*: genitive (*of the road*). The apostrophe *s* construction is not a possible alternative (**the road's rules**), nor is a compound noun (**the road rules**). [> LEG 2.47, LAG 5B, compare > LAG 17C]

23 *to* (= in the direction of): prepositional phrase (*to the right*). [> LEG 8.9, 8.17]

24 *of*: genitive (*of a lorry*). The apostrophe *s* construction is not a possible alternative (**a lorry's driver**), but a compound could fit here, though not with precisely the same meaning (*a lorry driver*). [> LEG 2.10.6, 2.47, LAG 5B]

25 *into*: The normal preposition after the verb *glance* (= look) is *at*. However, the writer wants to convey the idea of 'a searching look' and *into*, suggesting movement, is used; *in* would also have been possible. [> LEG 8.9.5, LAG 31Cn.6]

26 *to*: prepositional phrase (*to his stupefaction*). Compare *to his surprise*, etc. [compare > LEG App 26.8]

27 *at*: + *home*. [> LEG 10.9.7, LAG 45E]

28 *in*: preposition + zero article noun (*in bed*). [> LEG 3.28.3, 8.9.2, App 22.5]

29 *next to*: *beside* or *by* would also have been possible. [> LEG App 25.15, LAG 21E]

C The simple past perfect tense and the causative with 'had' ('had something done') [> LEG 9.28–31, 12.11n.1, 12.12.3]

a (= *he was injured*) This is a variation of the causative and means 'this is what someone did to him'. It is a simple past.

b (= *he had injured himself*) This is a past perfect and means 'this is what he (previously) did to himself'.

The past perfect points to an earlier action [> LAG 26Ans.3–4, 27Bn.3, 37Bn.3, 52B]:

> The patient **had died** before the doctor **arrived**.

The use of the causative in this context suggests you've experienced something; it was beyond your control [> LAG 26F, 35E]:

> In the duel, he **had his arm cut** to shreds.

1 had explained it
2 had it explained to you
3 had his licence endorsed
4 had endorsed his licence
5 had increased his rent
6 had his rent increased
7 had my car stolen
8 had stolen my car
9 had extracted the painful tooth
10 had the painful tooth extracted

Patagonia

15 I was half asleep when the country boy reeled in, flung himself on the other bed and groaned and sat up and was sick. He was sick on and off for an hour and then he snored. I did not sleep that night for the smell of the sick and the snoring.

20 So next day, as we drove through the desert, I sleepily watched the rags of silver cloud spinning across the sky, and the sea of grey-green thornscrub lying off in sweeps and rising in terraces and the white dust streaming off the saltpans, and, on the horizon, land and sky dissolving into 25 an absence of colour.

Patagonia begins on the Río Negro. At mid-day the bus crossed an iron bridge over the river and stopped outside a bar. An Indian woman got off with her son. She had filled up two seats with her bulk. She chewed garlic and wore 30 real gold jangly earrings and a hard white hat pinned over her braids. A look of abstract horror passed over the boy's face as she manoeuvred herself and her parcels on to the street.

The permanent houses of the village were of brick with 35 black stove pipes and a tangle of electric wires above. Where the brick houses gave out, the shacks of the Indians began. These were patched out of packing cases, sheet plastic and sacking.

A single man was walking up the street, his brown felt 40 hat pulled low over his face. He was carrying a sack and walking into the white dustclouds, out into the country. Some children sheltered in a door-way and tormented a lamb. From one hut came the noise of the radio and sizzling fat. A lumpy arm appeared and threw a dog a bone. The dog 45 took it and slunk off.

In Patagonia by Bruce Chatwin *(BrE)*

BAHÍA BLANCA is the last big place before the Patagonian desert. Bill dropped me at the hotel near the bus station. The barroom was green and brightly lit and full of 5 men playing cards. A country boy stood by the bar. He was shaky on his feet but he kept his head up like a gaucho. He was a nice-looking boy with curly black hair and was really very drunk. The owner's wife showed 10 me a hot airless room, painted purple, with two beds in it. The room had no window and the door gave out on to a glassed-in courtyard. It was very cheap and the woman said nothing about having to share.

Sentence structure

A There are two simple sentences in each exercise. Put the words in the right order, then join the simple sentences to make compound sentences. Check against the text.

1 shaky on his feet was he. like a gaucho up his head he kept. (ll. 6–7)

2 with curly black hair a nice-looking boy was he. really very drunk was he. (ll. 7–9)

3 no window the room had. out on to a glassed-in courtyard gave the door. (ll. 11–12)

4 on and off was he sick for an hour. he snored. (l. 17)

5 over the river at mid-day an iron bridge crossed the bus. a bar outside stopped it. (ll. 26–28)

6 a sack he was carrying. out into the country into the white dustclouds he was walking. (ll. 40–41)

7 in a door-way sheltered some children. a lamb they tormented. (ll. 42–43)

8 appeared a lumpy arm. a bone a dog threw it. (l. 44)

B Write a rule saying when we normally have to use a second subject in a compound sentence.

C What effect does *up* have on the basic meaning of the verb *keep*?
*He **kept** his head **up** like a gaucho.* (ll. 6–7)

Check back against the text, then suggest possible meanings for the adverb particles in italics.

1 He kept his head *up* like a gaucho. (ll. 6–7)   *in an upward direction*
2 The door gave *out* on to a glassed-in courtyard. (l. 12)
3 He was sick *on and off* for an hour. (l. 17)
4 ... the sea of grey-green thornscrub lying *off* in sweeps. (l. 22)
5 An Indian woman got *off* with her son. (l. 28)
6 She had filled *up* two seats with her bulk. (ll. 28–29)
7 Where the brick houses gave *out*, the shacks began. (ll. 36–37)
8 The dog took it and slunk *off*. (ll. 44–45)

D *He was a **nice-looking** boy with curly black hair.* (ll. 7–8)
What part of speech is *nice-looking*? Write the phrase from which it has been formed.

Complete each unfinished sentence.

1 He's a boy who looks nice.   He's a *nice-looking boy*
2 It's a record which plays for a long time.   It's a
3 It's a job which consumes a lot of time.   It's a
4 They're parents who suffer a lot.   They're
5 They're rules which have stood for a long time.   They're
6 It's a house which looks funny.   It's a
7 He's a salesman who talks fast.   He's a

E What's the difference between:

a *He was **sick** on and off for an hour.* (l. 17)
b *He's a **sick** boy.*

Supply suitable adjectives (most of which relate to health).

1 He's been in hospital for a month. He's a *sick* man.
2 Jane's in hospital and we're not allowed to visit her. She's still very
3 As soon as I stopped the car, my son jumped out and was very
4 John has been ill for a long time, but he's very .... now.
5 Quick! Bring me some smelling salts. I feel quite
6 There was a .... square mark on the wall where the picture had hung.
7 I'm fed up with these colds. I just want to be

F Write this sentence in a different way and then explain why this is possible (l. 44):
*A lumpy arm appeared and **threw a dog a bone**.*

Rewrite these sentences.

1 Jane has given a present to her mother.   *Jane has given her mother a present.*
2 Jane cooked a nice meal for the family.
3 They're paying a higher salary to the staff.
4 The Smiths found a good job for their daughter.
5 I've written a long letter to my aunt.
6 He left a fortune to his children.
7 Why don't you sing a song to the audience?

SENTENCE STRUCTURE

A Answers and commentary

1 *He* (subject) *was* (be) *shaky* (complement) *on his feet* (place). [> LEG 1.7, 1.11]
He (subject) *kept* (transitive verb) *his head* (object) *up like a gaucho* (manner). [> LEG 1.12]
Like is a preposition and is followed by a noun (*a gaucho*). We can't use *as* here. [> LEG App 25.25, LAG 45A]
→ *He was shaky on his feet **but he kept** his head up like a gaucho.*
But (or *yet*) introduces contrast. [> LEG 1.18–20, LAG 1B*n*.2] The author has chosen to repeat the subject here, but he could have omitted it:
  *He was shaky on his feet **but kept** his head up like a gaucho.*
Alternatively, we could combine the two simple sentences with *although* to express contrast [> LEG 1.50, LAG 3A*n*.2]:
  ***Although** he was shaky on his feet, he kept his head up like a gaucho.*

2 *He* (subject) *was* (be) *a nice-looking boy with curly black hair* (complement). [> LEG 1.11]
Note the use of *with* to describe physical characteristics. [> LEG App 25.37, LAG 14D]
He (subject) *was* (be) *really very drunk* (complement). [> LEG 1.11]
Really intensifies *was* (= he really was); *very* intensifies *drunk*. [> LEG 7.52]
→ *He was a nice-looking boy with curly black hair **and was** really very drunk.*
Though *and he was really ...* would be possible, the subject is not repeated here. [> LAG 4B*n*.2]

3 *The room* (subject) *had* (transitive verb) *no window* (object). [> LEG 1.12, LAG 14G]
We could also say *didn't have any window(s)*. [> LEG 5.11.1, compare >LAG 25D, 49G]
The door (subject) *gave out on to* (or *onto*) (transitive phrasal verb) *a glassed-in courtyard* (object). [> LEG 1.12, for three-part phrasal verbs of this type > LEG 8.30, LAG 16B]
→ *The room had no window **and the door** gave out on to a glassed-in courtyard.*
We have to use a second subject (*the door*) because we are talking about two different things. [> LEG 1.20.1, LAG 13B]

4 *He* (subject) *was sick* (verb phrase) *on and off for an hour* (time). [> LEG 1.11]
He (subject) *snored* (intransitive verb). [> LEG 1.10]
→ *He was sick on and off for an hour **and then he** snored.*
We often use *and then* to show continuation. The second subject could have been omitted. [> LEG 1.18, 1.20.1, LAG 4B*n*.2, 13B]

5 *At mid-day* (time) *the bus* (subject) *crossed* (transitive verb) *an iron bridge* (object) *over the river* (place). [> LEG 1.12]
It (subject) *stopped* (intransitive verb) *outside a bar* (place). [> LEG 1.10.2]
→ *At mid-day the bus crossed an iron bridge over the river **and stopped** outside a bar.*
The subject is not repeated. [> LEG 1.20]

6 *He* (subject) *was carrying* (transitive verb) *a sack* (object). [> LEG 1.12]
He (subject) *was walking* (intransitive verb) *into the white dustclouds, out into the country* (place). [> LEG 1.10.1]
→ *He was carrying a sack **and walking** into the white dustclouds, out into the country.*
The subject + *was* are not repeated. [> LEG 1.20]

7 *Some children* (subject) *sheltered* (intransitive verb) *in a door-way* (place). [> LEG 1.10.2]
They (subject) *tormented* (transitive verb) *a lamb* (object). [> LEG 1.12]
→ *Some children sheltered in a door-way **and tormented** a lamb.* The subject is not repeated. [> LEG 1.20]

8 *A lumpy arm* (subject) *appeared* (intransitive verb). [> LEG 1.10]
It (subject) *threw* (verb + two objects) *a dog a bone.* [> LEG 1.13.2, LAG 13F]
→ *A lumpy arm appeared **and threw** a dog a bone.* The subject is not repeated. [> LEG 1.20]

B Possible answer

There is no need to repeat the subject if it is the same in both parts of a compound sentence:
  ***The room** had no window **and was** bare.*
When the subjects in a compound sentence are different, they must both be used [> LEG 1.20.1]:
  ***The room** had no window **and the door** gave out on to a glassed-in courtyard.*

GRAMMAR POINTS

C Particles that strengthen or extend the effect of the verb: 'keep your head up' [> LEG 8.28.4, App 32, LAG 4D, 16B, 27C, 44D]

Up (= upright) extends the basic meaning of *keep* (= hold).

Some adverb particles (*up*, *down*, etc.) strengthen the effect of the verb:
> ***Write*** *their names.*
> → ***Write down*** *their names.*
> → ***Write*** *their names* ***down***. (the effect of *write* is 'strengthened')

Some adverb particles extend the meaning of a verb:
> ***Give out*** *these leaflets.*
> ***Give*** *these leaflets* ***out***. (= distribute; the meaning of *give* is 'extended')

Particles like *out* can have slightly different meanings and affect verbs in different ways.

1 kept up (= in an upward direction) [> LEG App 32.14.1]
2 gave out (= movement from inside to outside) [> LEG App 32.10.1]
3 on and off (= intermittently) [compare > LEG App 25.29]
4 lying off (= at a distance) [> LEG App 32.8.2]
5 got off (= separated from) [> LEG App 32.8.3] (*get off* = leave a vehicle.)
6 filled up (= completely) [> LEG App 32.14.3]
7 gave out (= exhaustion, i.e. the houses came to an end) [> LEG App 32.10.4]
8 slunk off (= away) [> LEG App 32.8.2]

D Compound adjectives formed with participles: 'nice-looking' [> LEG 6.3.1 and compare > LEG 6.14]

Nice-looking is an adjective. It has been formed from *who looks nice.*

We can form compound adjectives with present participles (ending in *-ing*). [compare > LAG 7C, 20D, 23E] The compound adjective is always hyphenated. [compare > LEG 2.7, 2.11n.3]

1 nice-looking boy 2 long-playing record
3 time-consuming job 4 long-suffering parents 5 long-standing rules 6 funny-looking house 7 fast-talking salesman

E Adjectives with different meanings when used before a noun or on their own: 'he was sick/he's a sick boy' [> LEG 6.8.1]

a ***He was sick*** *on an off for an hour.* (= he vomited); b *He's* ***a sick boy***. (= he's ill)

Some adjectives (often those concerning health) can have a different meaning when used before a noun or on their own. Or they may be used only in restricted ways. For example, we can say:
> *He is ill.* But: *He's a sick man.* (though *he's an ill man* is also sometimes heard)
> *The boy is well.* (But not *He's a well boy.*)
> *He's healthy. He's a healthy boy.*

1 sick
2 ill/poorly
3 sick
4 well
5 faint (= about to lose consciousness)
6 faint (= light)
7 healthy/well

F Subject + verb + indirect object + direct object: 'threw a dog a bone' [> LEG 1.13]

A lumpy arm ... ***threw a bone to a dog***.
After some verbs, like *throw* and *bring*, we can use an indirect object followed by a direct object:
> *He threw* ***a dog a bone***.
> *He bought* ***his son a bike***.

or a direct object + *to* or *for*:
> *He threw* ***a bone to a dog***.
> *He bought* ***a bike for his son***.

When there are two nouns present after verbs in this category, it is important not to put *to* or *for* after the verb:
> *Jane has given* ***her mother a present***.
> → *Jane has given* ***a present to her mother***.
> (But not *Jane has given to her mother a present.*)
> *Jane has cooked* ***the family a nice meal***.
> → *Jane has cooked* ***a nice meal for the family***.
> (But not *Jane has cooked for the family a nice meal.*)

1 Jane has given her mother a present.
2 Jane cooked the family a nice meal.
3 They're paying the staff a higher salary.
4 The Smiths found their daughter a good job.
5 I've written my aunt a long letter.
6 He left his children a fortune.
7 Why don't you sing the audience a song?

You're Marlowe?

IT was a cosy sort of office, not too large. There was a built-in upholstered corner seat by the french windows and a man in a white dinner-jacket was standing with his
5 back to the room, looking out. He had grey hair. There was a large black and chromium safe, some filing-cases, a large globe in a stand, a small built-in bar, and the usual broad heavy executive desk with the usual
10 high-backed padded leather chair behind it.

I looked at the ornaments on the desk. Everything standard and all copper. A copper lamp, a pen set and a pencil tray, a glass and copper ashtray with a copper elephant on the rim, a copper letter opener, a copper
15 thermos bottle on a copper tray, copper corners on the blotter holder. There was a spray of almost copper-coloured sweet peas in a copper vase.

It seemed like a lot of copper.

The man at the window turned around and showed me
20 that he was going on fifty and had soft ash-grey hair and plenty of it, and a heavy handsome face with nothing unusual about it except a short puckered scar in his left cheek that had almost the effect of a deep dimple. I remembered the dimple. I would have forgotten the man.
25 I remembered that I had seen him in pictures a long time ago, at least ten years ago. I didn't remember the pictures or what they were about or what he did in them, but I remembered the dark heavy handsome face and the puckered scar. His hair had been dark then.
30 He walked over to his desk and sat down and picked up his letter opener and poked at the ball of his thumb with the point. He looked at me with no expression and said: 'You're Marlowe?'

I nodded.

The High Window by Raymond Chandler *(AmE)*

Sentence structure

A Say why these statements are not true sentences in the traditional sense. What is missing from them?

1 Everything standard and all copper. (ll. 11–12)

....

2 A copper lamp, a pen set and a pencil tray, a glass and copper ashtray with a copper elephant on the rim, a copper letter opener, a copper thermos bottle on a copper tray, copper corners on the blotter holder. (ll. 12–16)

....

B Find a reporting verb in each of these sentences. Which word can we omit after each verb?

1 The man at the window turned around and showed me that he was going on fifty and had soft ash-grey hair and plenty of it, and a heavy handsome face with nothing unusual about it except a short puckered scar in his left cheek that had almost the effect of a deep dimple. (ll. 19–23)

....

2 I remembered that I had seen him in pictures a long time ago, at least ten years ago. (ll. 25–26)

....

C Join these sentences using the suggestions in brackets and making any necessary changes. Then check against the text.

I didn't remember the pictures. What were the pictures about? What did he do in them? I remembered the dark heavy handsome face and the puckered scar. (ll. 26–29) [*or, or, but*]

....

....

Grammar points

D Which preposition would you expect to use in these sentences and why?

a *A man* .... *a white dinner-jacket was standing with his back to the room.* (ll. 3–5)
b *[He had] a heavy handsome face* .... *a short puckered scar in his left cheek.* (ll. 21–23)

....

Supply the missing prepositions in these sentences.

1 He was described to me as a tall man *with* a red beard.
2 She was .... red shoes .... a large red handbag to match.
3 Which man do you mean? The one .... the grey coat, or the one .... the umbrella?
4 Will I look all right this evening .... a long dress, or should I wear something less dressy?
5 .... your blue eyes and a bit of make-up, you'll look smashing .... that outfit.
6 If you think I'm going through Customs .... so much stuff in my pockets, you're mistaken!
7 .... a suit like that and .... a moustache, you'll look at least ten years older.

E Is it possible to omit *like* in this sentence? Why?/Why not?
It seemed like a lot of copper. (l. 18)

....

In which of these sentences could you delete *like*?

1 It seemed like a lot of copper.
2 Your friend sounds like just the right person for the job to me.
3 I can't describe the flavour to you, but it tastes a bit like pineapple.
4 You say this object in the sky looked like a round dish. Did you see a little green man as well?
5 I know it looks like a real mess, but it's not really as bad as it looks.
6 If you touch this stuff, it feels like leather, but it's actually plastic.
7 Listen carefully. It sounds like a symphony orchestra, but there are only a dozen instruments.

F What would you have to add if you wanted to rewrite this sentence beginning with *Except*?
Which complex prepositions (two in all) could you use in place of *except*?
There was nothing unusual about his face except a short puckered scar in his left cheek.
(ll. 21–23)

....

Rewrite these sentences beginning with *Except*.

1 The deer have eaten everything in our garden except a few apples left on the trees.
Except for a few apples left on the trees, the deer have eaten everything in our garden.
2 Nobody knows what the decision will be except a few people who are close to the Minister.

....

3 There's nothing to distinguish her from anyone else, except her background.

....

G What change would you have to make to rewrite this sentence with *any* in place of *no*?
He looked at me with no expression and said: 'You're Marlowe?' (ll. 32–33)

....

Write the phrase with *any*, *a/an* or zero (–) that could be used in place of a phrase with *no*.

1 I don't think you'll be able to manage with no legal advice.   *without (any) legal advice*
2 I don't think one can enjoy life with no friends.   ....
3 How do you get through the day with no watch?   ....
4 You can't expect a torch to work with no battery.   ....
5 Children can't succeed with no encouragement.   ....
6 A country can't function with no government.   ....
7 The editor accepted my article with no comments.   ....
8 I resigned my job with no regrets.   ....

SENTENCE STRUCTURE

A Answers and commentary

The two statements are not true sentences, in the traditional sense, because they don't contain verbs. A sentence must contain a finite main verb. A verb is *finite* when it has a subject and tense. For example, *he writes*, *she wrote* and *he has written* are finite, but *written* by itself is not. This doesn't mean the statements are wrong. We can speak or write statements without verbs, especially when we want to keep the rhythms of speech, as is the case in this passage. The effect here is of 'listing', as the narrator mentally records what he sees. [> LAG 1A, 42B, 48B*n*.2b]

1 *Everything standard and all copper.*
We can turn this into a grammatical sentence by adding *was*:
*Everything **was** standard and all copper.*

2 We can turn the list into a grammatical sentence by adding *(There was) . . . and (there were)*:
***There was** a copper lamp, a pen set and a pencil tray, a glass and copper ashtray with a copper elephant on the rim, a copper letter opener, a copper thermos bottle on a copper tray **and** (**there were**) copper corners on the blotter holder.*
Informally, we often use *there is* or *there was* to refer to a plural [> LEG 10.18, compare > LAG 48B*n*.2b]:
***There's a man and a dog** in our garden.*
Rather than:
There are a man and a dog in our garden.

B Answers and commentary

We could omit *that* after *showed me* in the first sentence and after *remembered* in the second. We use reporting verbs to report statements or questions. Statements are reported with a noun clause introduced by *that* (often called a *that-*clause). [> LAG 4E] Yes/No questions are reported with *if* or *whether*. [> LAG 10E, 29B] It is possible to omit *that* after most reporting verbs, but it isn't possible to omit *if* or *whether* [> LEG 1.23.2, 15.6, App 45]:
*He said (**that**) he would see me later.*
*He asked me **if/whether** he would see me later.*

1 *The man at the window turned around and **showed me** (that) he was going on fifty . . .*
That is often included after *show*, but can be omitted. [> LAG 4E]

2 *I **remembered** (that) I had seen him in pictures . . .*
Remembered could also be followed by an -*ing* form here [> LEG 16.59, LAG 57D]:
*I remembered **having seen/seeing** him in pictures . . .*

C Answer and commentary

*I didn't remember the pictures **or what they were** about **or what he did** in them, . . .*
Remember is a reporting verb which introduces two indirect question-word questions with *what* here. The direct question word order changes back to statement word order (subject + verb) in indirect speech [> LEG 15.20, LAG 29B, 50E]:
*What **were they** about? What **did he do** in them?*
→ *I didn't remember **what they were** about or **what he did** in them, . . .*

*. . ., **but** I remembered the dark heavy handsome face and the puckered scar.*
Co-ordinate main clauses are joined by *or . . . or . . . but . . .* [> LEG 1.17–18]:
*I didn't remember the pictures **or** what they were about **or** what he did in them, **but** I remembered the dark heavy handsome face and the puckered scar.*
Though the repetition of the subject *I* is optional here, it is desirable because the first statement is a negative which contrasts with the affirmative that follows [compare > LAG 13A*n*.1]:
*I didn't remember . . . , **but** I remembered . . .*

GRAMMAR POINTS

D 'In' and 'with' to describe people and their possessions: 'in a jacket/with a scar' [> LEG 10.31*ns*. 4–5, App 25.37]

a *A man **in** a white dinner jacket* ... (because he's wearing it; = dressed in)

b ... *a heavy handsome face **with** a short puckered scar* ... (*with* for physical characteristics)

We use *in* to mean 'dressed in' or 'wearing' and *with* to mean 'having'. We also use *with* to mean 'carrying', or 'accompanied by':

*Do you see that man **with the umbrella**?*
*There was a copper ashtray **with a copper elephant** on the rim.*

1 with (= having)
2 in (= wearing) with (= carrying)
3 in (= wearing) with (= carrying)
4 in (= wearing)
5 with (= having) in (= wearing)
6 with (= carrying)
7 in (= wearing) with (= having)

E Verbs related in meaning to 'be': 'seem', etc. [> LEG 10.23–25, LAG 4A, 6E, 16D, 46D]

Yes, it's possible to omit *like* after *seem*. The use of *like* before a noun is optional after *seem*.

We use *like* after *feel, look, seem, smell, sound* and *taste* only when we are comparing one thing with another directly. In such cases we cannot omit *like*:

*This **looks/tastes/smells/feels like** an orange* (obligatory *like*).

After *seem*, and verbs that may be used like *seem* to mean 'give the impression', *like* is optional:

*Jennifer **seems/sounds/looks** (like) the right person for the job.*

You could delete *like* in numbers **1**, **2** and **5**:

1 It seemed a lot of copper.
2 Your friend sounds just the right person ...
5 I know it looks a real mess ...

F 'Except' and 'except for' [> LEG App 25.14 and compare > LEG App 20.3]

If you wanted to begin the sentence with *except*, you would have to add *for*:

***Except for** a short puckered scar in his left cheek, there was nothing unusual about his face.*

Two other complex prepositions you could use in place of *except* here are *but for* and *apart from*. *With the exception of* would also be possible.

Except (for) is a preposition which means 'with the exception of'. We can use *except* or *except for* in the middle of a sentence:

*No one has offered to help us **except John**. = No one has offered to help us **except for John**.*

But if we begin a sentence with *except*, we normally use *for* after it:

***Except for** John, no one has offered to help us.* (Not **Except John**)

1 Except for a few apples left on the trees, the deer have eaten everything in our garden.
2 Except for a few people who are close to the Minister, nobody knows what the decision will be.
3 Except for her background, there's nothing to distinguish her from anyone else.

G 'Not ... any' and 'no' [> LEG 5.11.1, 13.10 and compare > LEG Apps 25.36–37, LAG 25D, 49G, 53D]

We would have to say:

*He looked at me **without any** expression and said: 'You're Marlowe?'*

We could also omit *any* here if we wanted to.

The preposition *without* contains the negative, so we use *any* in place of *no*.

We can use *without any* in place of *with no* with uncountables and plural countables:

*She arrived **with no money** and **with no qualifications**.*
→ *She arrived **without any money** and **without any qualifications**.*

We can use *without a/an* in place of *with no* with singular countable nouns:

*How do you manage **with no watch**?*
→ *How do you manage **without a watch**?*

1 without (any) legal advice
2 without (any) friends
3 without a watch (Not **without watch**)
4 without a battery (Not **without battery**)
5 without (any) encouragement
6 without (a/any) government
7 without any comments (and note the expressions *without comment, with no comment*; *without comments* could be ambiguous here = the article didn't contain any comments)
8 without (any) regrets/regret

You can't teach managers

It's simple!

THE Harvard Business School is the ark of the tabernacle in management education. Many schools more or less ape the HBS, especially its 'case study' method of instruction - though
5 mulling over out-of-date business anecdotes is about as helpful in actual management as waging war by tramping over old battlefields. The specific management element in these mind-bending studies is hard to isolate.
10 Although managers should be numerate (and many are not), they don't require skills in higher algebra; and many great businesses have been created by men who all but count on their fingers.

15 A story tells of two schoolboy friends, one brilliant at maths, one innumerate to the point of idiocy, who meet much later when the first is a professor and the second a multi-millionaire. Unable to control his curiosity, the professor asks the figure-blind dunderhead how he managed
20 to amass his fortune. 'It's simple,' replies Midas. 'I buy things at £1 and sell them for £2, and from that 1% difference I make a living.' The business world is full of successful one-percenters who live, not by their slide rules, but by knowing the difference between a buying
25 price and a selling price. It is also full of clever fools who work out elaborate discounted cash flow sums to justify projects that a one-percenter would laugh out of sight.

The clever fool syndrome would explain why one controversial study of HBS students found that, after a
30 flying start, the alumni (presumably among the ablest young men of their day) gradually slipped back to the general level inside their chosen management hierarchies. An HBS graduate has no reason at all to suppose that he will manage more effectively than a less instructed
35 contemporary. The HBS man can only claim that he is more highly educated: and high education and high achievement in practical affairs don't necessarily go together. John F. Kennedy found that assembling America's brightest brains in Washington neither got bills through
40 Congress nor avoided the Bay of Pigs; and many companies have discovered that business school diplomas are a thin defence against incompetence.

The Naked Manager by Robert Heller *(BrE)*

Sentence structure

A Three of these sentences contain an extra word. Cross out the extra words, where necessary, and say why you have done so. Then check against the text.

1 The specific management element in these mind-bending studies is hard to isolate it. (ll. 8–9)

2 Even although managers should be numerate (and many are not), they don't require skills in higher algebra; and many great businesses have been created by men who all but count on their fingers. (ll. 10–14)

3 It is also full of clever fools who work out elaborate discounted cash flow sums for to justify projects that a one-percenter would laugh out of sight. (ll. 25–27)

4 'I buy things at £1 and sell them for £2, and from that 1% difference I make a living.' (ll. 20 22)

B Rewrite these sentences making any necessary changes. Use the help given.

1 It is hard to isolate the specific management element in these mind-bending studies. (ll. 8–9)
The specific ....

2 The professor isn't able to control his curiosity, so he asks the figure-blind dunderhead how he managed to amass his fortune. (ll. 18–20)
Unable ....

Grammar points

C Supply *a/an*, *the* or zero (–) in this paragraph, then refer to the text. (ll. 1–22) Give a reason or reasons beside each choice.

1........ Harvard Business School is
2........ ark of the tabernacle
in 3........ management education.
4........ many schools more or less ape the HBS,
especially its 'case study' method of 5........ instruction – though
mulling over 6........ out-of-date business anecdotes is about as helpful
in 7........ actual management as waging war
by tramping over 8........ old battlefields.
9........ specific management element in these mind-bending studies is
hard to isolate. Although 10........ managers should be numerate
(and many are not), they don't require 11........ skills in
12........ higher algebra;
and 13........ many great businesses have been created by
14........ men who all but count on their
15........ fingers.
16........ story tells of
17........ two schoolboy friends, one brilliant at
18........ maths, one innumerate to the point of idiocy,
who meet much later when 19........ first
is 20........ professor
and 21........ second
22........ multi-millionaire.
Unable to control his 23........ curiosity,
24........ professor asks
25........ figure-blind dunderhead how he managed to amass his fortune.
'It's simple,' replies 26........ Midas.
'I buy 27........ things at £1 and sell them for £2,
and from that 1% difference I make 28........ living.'

D How are *between* and *among* used in these two sentences?

a *The business world is full of successful one-percenters who live ... by knowing the difference **between** a buying price and a selling price.* (ll. 22–25)

b *One controversial study of HBS students found that, after a flying start, the alumni (presumably **among** the ablest young men of their day) gradually slipped back ...* (ll. 28–31)

Supply *between* or *among*. Sometimes both are possible.

1 I'm at my best ...*between*.... 7 and 11 in the morning.
2 .... the people I know there's no one who sings as well as you do.
3 Is there a doctor........................ the audience?
4 Don't interfere! Let them sort it out........................ themselves.
5 Where do you find all that spare time........................ raising a family, writing a book and holding down a full-time job?
6 I try very hard never to eat........................ meals.
7 .... the four of them, the boys managed to collect £500 for the new nursing home.
8 I found the ticket stuck........................ the pages of this book.
9 What do we find in common........................ the major oil companies?
10 As an anthropologist, she specialized in finding tiny communities and living........................ them.
11 I think your application must have got lost........................ our records.

SENTENCE STRUCTURE

A Answers and commentary

Numbers **1**, **2** and **3** have an extra word in them.

1 *The specific management element in these mind-bending studies is hard to isolate it.* [> LEG 16.30]
We can say:
　It is hard to isolate the specific management element in these mind-bending studies. [> LAG 1C]
Or:
　The specific management element in these mind-bending studies is hard to isolate.
(compare **B1** below)

2 ~~Even~~ *although managers should be numerate (and many are not), they don't require skills in higher algebra; and many great businesses have been created by men who all but count on their fingers.*
We can say:
　Although managers should be numerate . . .
Or:
　Even though managers should be numerate . . . (But not **even although**)
Although, *even though* and *even if* introduce adverbial clauses of concession. [> LEG 1.50. LAG 3A*ns*.2–3, 11B*n*.2]

3 *It is also full of clever fools who work out elaborate discounted cash flow sums ~~for~~ to justify projects that a one-percenter would laugh out of sight.*
The infinitive markers *to*, *in order to* and *so as to* express purpose. We never use *for* in front of them [> LEG 16.12.1, compare > LAG 6B*n*.5, 7B*n*.11, 10B*n*.2]:
　I went to live in France to/in order to/so as to learn French.
For is a preposition, so it would be possible to use an *-ing* form after it [> LEG 16.50–56, LAG 1D]:
　They work out elaborate discounted cash flow sums for justifying projects. (= to justify)

4 This sentence is correct.

B Answers and commentary

1 *The specific management element in these mind-bending studies is hard to isolate.*
The specific management element in these mind-bending studies is the subject of *is*.
We often prefer to begin sentences like this with *it*:
　It is hard to isolate the specific management element in these mind-bending studies.
We can call this a 'preparatory *it*' because it prepares us for the subject. [> LAG 1C] In this way we also avoid beginning a sentence awkwardly with a *to*-infinitive [> LEG 1.23.1, 4.13, 16.30, 16.47–48]:
　To isolate the specific management element in these mind-bending studies is hard.

2 *Unable to control his curiosity, the professor asks the figure-blind dunderhead how he managed to amass his fortune.*
We have two ideas here:
a) *The professor can't control his curiosity.*
b) *He asks the figure-blind dunderhead how he managed to amass his fortune.*
Can, to express ability, is 'defective' and requires *be able to* to make up its missing parts. There is no present participle form of *can*. (Not **canning**) [> LEG 11.4, 11.6.1, 11.12]
We can therefore join these two ideas in different ways:
　Not being able to control his curiosity, the professor asks . . .
　Being unable to control his curiosity, the professor asks . . .
Or we can drop the present participle and begin with *unable to* [compare > LEG 1.58.3]:
　Unable to control his curiosity, the professor asks . . .

GRAMMAR POINTS

C Articles [> LEG Chapter 3, LAG 8C, etc.]

1 *The*: *The Harvard Business School* is an institution. *The* is part of its title and is necessary here. [> LEG 3.22] However, we can also refer to it without *the* in e.g:

He attended Harvard Business School.

2 *the*: There is only one *ark*: the reference is highly specific, so *the* is required. [> LEG 3.22]

3 (–) *management education*: in general, therefore zero article with noun modifier (*management*) + uncountable noun (*education*). [> LEG 2.10, 6.13, 3.25–26]

4 (–) *Many schools*: The reference is general, so zero article with plural countable noun (*schools*). [> LEG 3.25–26] *Many* refers to number and doesn't need an article. [> LEG 5.13]

5 (–) *instruction*: in general, so zero article with uncountable noun (*instruction*). [> LEG 3.25–26]

6 (–) *out-of-date business anecdotes*: in general, so zero article with plural countable noun (*anecdotes*). [> LEG 3.25–26]

7 (–) *actual management*: in general, therefore zero article with uncountable noun (*management*). [> LEG 3.25–26]

8 (–) *old battlefields*: in general, therefore zero article with plural countable noun (*battlefields*). [> LEG 3.25–26]

9 *The specific management element*: The *element* has been specified: it is the one *in these mind-bending studies*, so *the* is required. [> LEG 3.20.3]

10 (–) *managers*: in general, so zero article with plural countable noun (*managers*). [> LEG 3.25–26]

11 (–) *skills*: in general, therefore zero article with plural countable noun (*skills*). [> LEG 3.25–26]

12 (–) *higher algebra*: in general, therefore zero article with uncountable noun (*algebra*). [> LEG 3.25–26] Note that *algebra* is an abstract uncountable noun. [> LEG 2.12, 2.15]

13 (–) *many great businesses*: The reference is general, therefore zero article with plural countable noun (*businesses*). [> LEG 3.25–26] *Many* refers to number and does not require an article. [> LEG 5.13, and **4** above]

14 (–) *men*: in general, therefore zero article with plural countable noun (*men*). [> LEG 2.26, 3.25–26]

15 (–) *fingers*: We already have a possessive adjective (*their*). We can use only one determiner in front of a noun (Not **men who count on their the fingers**). [> LEG 3.4]

16 *A story*: First mention and unspecified, therefore *a*. [> LEG 3.8, 3.10.2]

17 (–) *two schoolboy friends*: in general, therefore zero article with plural countable noun (*friends*). [> LEG 3.25–26] *Schoolboy* is a noun modifier here.

18 (–) *maths*: an uncountable noun (an academic subject), therefore no article (also **12** above, *algebra*). [> LEG 3.27.5 and compare > LEG 2.31]

19 *the first*: specific reference (to *the first* of the former *schoolboy friends*), so *the*. [> LEG 4.11]

20 *a professor*: We always use *a/an* before a singular countable noun when the reference isn't specific: *He's a professor*. (Not **He's professor.**) [> LEG 3.3, 3.9.3]

21 *the second*: follows *the first*. [> LEG 4.11]

22 *a multi-millionaire*: exactly as for **20** above. [> LEG 3.3, 3.9.3]

23 (–) *curiosity*: We already have a possessive adjective (*his*). We can use only one determiner in front of a noun (Not **his the curiosity**). [> LEG 3.4] Compare **15** above.

24 *the*: After the first mention (*the first is a professor*, see **20** above) the reference is specific. [> LEG 3.10.2, 3.20.1]

25 *the*: After the first mention (*a multi-millionaire*), the reference is specific. [> LEG 3.10.2, 3.20.1]

26 (–) *Midas*: proper noun, therefore no article. [> LEG 2.13, 3.25]

27 (–) *things*: in general, therefore zero article with plural countable noun (*things*). [> LEG 3.25–26]

28 *a living*: *make a living* is a fixed expression. [compare *do for a living* > LEG 13.34.4]

D 'Between' and 'among' [> LEG App 25.13]

a *Between* refers to two: *a buying price* and *a selling price*.

b *Among* refers to many: *the ablest young men of their day*.

Note that we sometimes use *between* to refer to more than two things when they are viewed separately and there are not many.

1 between (two times) **2** Among (an unspecified number) **3** among (unspecified number implied in the collective noun *audience*; *in* would also be possible) **4** between (more than two, but not many) or among (an unspecified number) **5** between (each item is listed) **6** between (one meal and another) **7** Between (a specified number) or among **8** between (the pages of a book) **9** between (one oil company and another) or among **10** among (an unspecified number of communities) **11** among (an unspecified number of records)

An English lesson

I SAT in on an English lesson at the Gamal Abdel Nasser Secondary School. The Scottish instructor - one of three Britons employed in the Yemeni school system - was drilling the class in the difference between the 'present simple' and the 'present continuous'. There were twenty very thin, very eager boys aged between about fourteen and twenty-two. They were part of that tiny educated leaven in a country which has an illiteracy rate of ninety per cent, and they had tense, ambitious faces. They had been trained to compete continually against each other, so that the lesson turned into a kind of noisy greyhound race. The moment that the instructor was half-way through a question, his voice was drowned by shouts of 'Teacher! Teacher! Teacher!' and I lost sight of him behind the thicket of urgently raised hands. If a student began to stumble over an answer, the others fought to grab the question for themselves, bellowing for Teacher's attention. I once taught for a term at a comprehensive school in England: had the children in my class ever shown a small fraction of the enthusiasm displayed by these Yemeni students, I might have stayed in the job a great deal longer. They were ravenous for the good marks and certificates which would take them out of their villages and tenements, and they behaved as if every minute spent in the classroom could make or break them.

Arabia Through the Looking Glass by Jonathan Raban *(BrE)*

Sentence structure

A Join these sentences using the suggestions in brackets and making any necessary changes. Then check against the text.

1 The Scottish instructor was drilling the class in the difference between the 'present simple' and the 'present continuous'. He was one of three Britons. He was employed in the Yemeni school system. (ll. 2–6) [dashes, past participle]

....

....

2 They were part of that tiny educated leaven in the country. It has an illiteracy rate of ninety per cent. They had tense, ambitious faces. (ll. 8–10) [*which, and*]

....

....

3 They had been trained to compete continually against each other. The lesson turned into a kind of noisy greyhound race. (ll. 10–12) [*so that*]

....

....

4 The instructor was half-way through a question. His voice was drowned by shouts of 'Teacher! Teacher! Teacher!' I lost sight of him behind the thicket of urgently raised hands. (ll. 12–16) [*The moment that, and*]

....

....

5 A student began to stumble over an answer. The others fought to grab the question for themselves. They were bellowing for Teacher's attention. (ll. 16–18) [*If, -ing* form]

....

....

6 I once taught for a term at a comprehensive school in England. The children in my class had never shown a small fraction of the enthusiasm displayed by these Yemeni students. I might have stayed in the job a great deal longer. (ll. 18–22) [colon (:), conditional with *ever*]

....

....

Grammar points

B *I **sat in on** an English lesson at the Gamal Abdel Nasser Secondary School.* (ll. 1–2)
Suggest a meaning for the verb in bold italics. What sort of verb is this?

....

Suggest meanings for the verbs in italics.

1 Don't accept their offer. You should *stick out for* more.   *insist on receiving*
2 Jimmy *has* already *grown out of* his new shoes!   ....
3 I must dash to the supermarket. We've nearly *run out of* coffee.   ....
4 What do I have to do to *brush up on* my English?   ....
5 We'll go ahead as soon as the bank *comes across with* the money.   ....
6 Take a short holiday, I'll be happy to *stand in for* you.   ....
7 Tony believes his teacher really *has it in for* him.   ....
8 We're going to Amsterdam soon and I want to *read up on* it.   ....
9 What have the children been *getting up to* in our absence?   ....
10 Don't worry! No matter what they say I'll *stick up for* you!   ....
11 She's been fiddling her expenses and *has been getting away with* it.   ....
12 *Cash in on* the high price of gold and sell your jewellery!   ....
13 He doesn't mean what he says. Don't *start in on* him!   ....
14 Monica's positively *bursting out of* her clothes!   ....
15 I've been away. Can you *fill me in on* the latest news?   ....
16 I'll never forgive her for *running out on* the children.   ....
17 It's going to be a difficult day, but we just have to *go through with* it.   ....
18 The homeless are just *crying out for* help.   ....
19 Franklin's new play has *come in for* a lot of criticism.   ....
20 Just tell me what happened. Don't *hold out on* me.   ....

C *Had the children in my class ever shown a small fraction of the enthusiasm displayed by these Yemeni students, I might have stayed in the job a great deal longer.* (ll. 19–22)
Show how this sentence could begin in a different way. What type of sentence is it?

....

Respond appropriately to these statements using the modals in brackets.

1 The management didn't act soon enough to prevent the strike. (would)
  Had they acted sooner, they would have prevented it
2 The weather forecast was inaccurate, so we didn't take the right precautions. (might)

3 We didn't know which horse would win, so we didn't bet any money. (would)

4 The temperature didn't fall below zero last night, so the crops weren't damaged. (might)

D *They **behaved** as if every minute spent in the classroom could make or break them.* (ll. 24–26)
Suggest at least three other verbs that might be used in place of *behave* here.

....

Respond appropriately to these statements using the verbs in brackets.

1 Janice doesn't own this company, you know! (behave)   *She behaves as if she does!*
2 I think it'll rain soon. (feel)   ....
3 This food's been burnt. (taste)   ....
4 I think Max is mad. (act)   ....
5 John knows something we don't. (behave)   ....
6 I thought he'd lose everyone's support. (look)   ....
7 Has she retired? (appear)   ....

SENTENCE STRUCTURE

A Answers and commentary

1 *The Scottish instructor – one of three Britons **employed** in the Yemeni school system – was drilling the class . . .*
We can mark off extra information by using a non-defining relative clause with commas:
    *The Scottish instructor, **who** was one of three Britons employed in the Yemeni school system, was drilling . . .*
Alternatively, we can just use commas or dashes (without a relative pronoun + *was*). The use of dashes emphasizes the addition of extra information. [> LEG 1.26, LAG 3B*n*.3] The past participle *employed* is used in place of a relative (*who were employed*). [> LEG 1.62.3]

2 *They were part of that tiny educated leaven **in a country which** has an illiteracy rate of ninety per cent, **and they** had . . .*
Which refers to *a country* and introduces a defining clause (that is, it adds essential information, therefore no commas are used):
    Yemen is a country. It has an illiteracy rate . . .
    → *Yemen is **a country which has** an illiteracy rate . . . .* [> LEG 1.26]
Because of the length of the clauses, the writer uses a comma before *and* and repeats the subject: *and they had . . . .* Note it is also possible to say *the Yemen.* [> LEG 3.31]

3 *They had been trained to compete continually against each other, **so that** the lesson turned into a kind of . . .*
So that introduces an adverbial clause of result. [> LEG 1.52] It would also be possible to use *so* on its own to express result:
    *They had been trained to compete continually against each other, **so** the lesson . . .* [> LEG 1.18, 1.20.4]
We should distinguish between *so that . . .* + modal to express purpose [> LAG 10B*n*.2]:
    *I arrived early **so that I might** get a good seat.*
and *so that* or *so (quickly) that* to express result [> LEG 1.51.1–2, LAG 10A*n*.2]:
    *We arrived **so early that** (as a result) we got good seats.*
    *We arrived early, **so (that)** (as a result) we got good seats.*

4 *The **moment that** the instructor was half-way through a question, his voice was drowned by shouts of 'Teacher! Teacher! Teacher!' **and** I lost sight of him . . .*
The moment (that) introduces an adverbial clause of time and is the equivalent of *as soon as* [> LEG 1.45.1, LAG 6B*n*.1, 34A*n*.4]:
    ***As soon as** the instructor was half-way through a question . . .*
and introduces a co-ordinate clause followed by a new subject (*I*). [> LEG 1.17–20, LAG 13B]

5 *If a student began to stumble over an answer, the others fought to grab the question for themselves, **bellowing** . . .*
If does not introduce a conditional here. It means 'on those occasions when' and introduces a time clause. [> LEG 14.23.1, LAG 6B*n*.2] The present participle *bellowing* is used in place of the simple past (*and they bellowed*) or past progressive (*and they were bellowing*). [> LEG 1.58.1, LAG 4B*n*.3]

6 *I once taught for a term at a comprehensive school in England: **had the children** in my class **ever shown** a small fraction of the enthusiasm displayed by these Yemeni students, **I might have stayed** in the job a great deal longer.*
The colon is used here to introduce the 'explanation' that follows. It would also have been possible to use a full stop. [> LAG 8B*n*.2] The author then uses a Type 3 conditional with *had* + inversion [> LAG 16C] rather than *if* + past perfect [> LEG 14.17, 14.18.3, LAG 50D]:
    ***If the children had ever shown** a small fraction of the enthusiasm displayed by these Yemeni students, **I might have stayed** . . .*
    → ***Had the children ever shown** a small fraction of the enthusiasm displayed by these Yemeni students, **I might have stayed** . . .*
We do not automatically use *will/would* in conditional sentences. We use other modals as well, to express possibility, ability, etc. Compare:
    ***Had the children ever shown** a small fraction of the enthusiasm displayed by these Yemeni students, **I would have stayed** . . .*
    ***Had the children ever shown** a small fraction of the enthusiasm displayed by these Yemeni students, **I might have stayed** . . .*
The second sentence is much less certain. [> LEG 14.7, 14.14, 14.19]

GRAMMAR POINTS

B Type 4 phrasal verbs (idiomatic meanings): 'sit in on' [> LEG 8.30, App 37, LAG 27C and compare > LAG 4D, 8D, 13C, 24C, 38D, 44D, 47E]

A possible meaning: *was present without taking part*. This is a three-part phrasal verb.

Some three part verbs have obvious meanings:
> We **drove on to** *Oxford.*

Others have little or no relation to their literal meanings:
> *I can't* **put up with** *this nonsense any longer.* (= tolerate)

Possible answers

1 *stick out for* (= insist on receiving)
2 *has grown out of* (= has got too big for)
3 *run out of* (= used up all we had)
4 *brush up on* (= improve)
5 *comes across with* (= provides)
6 *stand in for* (= act in your place)
7 *has it in for* (= dislikes him)
8 *read up on* (= improve my knowledge of)
9 *getting up to* (= doing, especially something mischievous)
10 *stick up for* (= defend)
11 *has been getting away with* (= has been managing to deceive)
12 *cash in on* (= take advantage of)
13 *start in on* (= begin to criticize)
14 *bursting out of* (= has got too fat for)
15 *fill me in on* (= inform me about)
16 *running out on* (= abandoning)
17 *go through with* (= finish a difficult thing)
18 *crying out for* (= are in great need of)
19 *come in for* (= received)
20 *hold out on* (= keep a secret from)

C Inversion with 'had' in Type 3 conditionals: 'Had the children in my class . . . ' [> LEG 14.18.3 and compare > LEG 14.19, LAG 50D and compare > LAG 9E, 22C, 37D]

The sentence could have begun: *If the children in my class had ever shown* . . . . It's a conditional sentence.

We can begin a Type 3 conditional sentence with *Had* instead of *If (he) had* . . . , especially in formal writing:
> *If* **he had told** *me earlier, I* **would have been able to** *do something about it.*
> → **Had he told** *me earlier, I* **would have been able to** *do something about it.*

1 Had they acted sooner, they would have prevented it.
2 Had it been accurate, we might have taken the right precautions.
3 Had we known which horse would win, we would have bet some money.
4 Had it fallen below zero, the crops might have been damaged.

D 'As if' after 'be', 'seem', etc. [> LEG 1.47.2, LAG 14E, 21An.2, 23Bn.6, 27An.4, 37D]

Three other verbs could be: *acted, looked, seemed.*

We can use *as if* (or *as though*) after *be, seem,* etc. to say that we think something might be true.

We use a variety of tenses after *as if*, not just the subjunctive (*were*). [> LEG 11.75.1, LAG 37D] We never use a *to*-infinitive:
> *He's ill. – Yes, he* **looks as if he's ill**. (Not *he looks to be ill**)
> *He was ill. – Yes, he* **looked as if he was/ were/had been ill**. (Not *he looked to have been ill**)

1 She behaves as if she does!
2 It feels as if it will!
3 It tastes as if it has (been)!
4 He acts as if he is/were!
5 He behaves as if he does/did!
6 It looked as if he would! (or *He looked* . . .)
7 It appears as if she has!

Minty

MINTY knew the moment that he got up in the morning that this was one of his days. He sang gently to himself as he shaved. 'This is the way that Minty
5 goes, Minty goes, Minty goes.' Although he had a new blade he did not cut himself once; he shaved cautiously rather than closely, while the pot of coffee, which his landlady had brought him, grew cold on the washstand.
10 Minty liked his coffee cold; his stomach would bear nothing hot. A spider watched him under his tooth glass; it had been there five days; he had expected his landlady to

clear it away, but it had remained a second day, a third day.
15 He cleaned his teeth under the tap. Now she must believe that he kept it there for study. He wondered how long it would live. He watched it and it watched him back with shaggy patience. It had lost a leg when he put the glass over it.
20 Above his bed was a house-group, rows of boys blinking against the sun above and below the seated figures of the prefects, the central figure of the housemaster and his wife. It was curious to observe how a moustache by being waxed at the tips could date a man as accurately as a woman's
25 dress, the white blouse, the whalebone collar, the puffed sleeves. Occasionally Minty was called on to identify himself; practice had made him perfect; there had been a time of hesitation when he could not decide whether Patterson seated on the housemaster's left or Tester standing
30 rather more obscurely behind, his jaw hidden by a puffed sleeve, best acted as his proxy. For Minty himself did not appear; he had seen the photograph taken from the sickroom window, a blaze of light, the blinking blackened faces, the photographer diving beneath his shade.
35 'This is the way that Minty goes.' He picked a stump of cigarette from the soap-tray and lit it. Then he studied his hair in the mirror of the wardrobe door; this was one of his days; he must be prepared for anything, even society.

England Made Me by Graham Greene (BrE)

Sentence structure

A Circle the item that fits the space, then refer to the text.

Minty knew the moment that he got up in
the morning [1]........ this was one of his days.
He sang gently to himself [2]........ he shaved.
[3]........ he had a new blade he did not cut himself
once; he shaved cautiously [4]........ closely,
[5]........ the pot of coffee,
[6]........ his landlady had brought him, grew cold.
Minty liked his coffee cold [7]........
[8]........ stomach would bear nothing hot. A
spider watched him under his tooth glass; [9]........
had been there five days; [10]........ had expected
his landlady to clear it away. (ll. 1–14)

	a	b	c
1	as	that	for
2	as	during	along
3	If so	Even	Although
4	instead	rather than	rather
5	while	during	just as
6	who	which	whom
7	so	;	then
8	his	whose	he's
9	who	it	which
10	it	he	which

B Supply the missing words only where necessary, then check against the text.

Above his bed [1].................... was a house-group, rows of boys [2](*blink*) .... against the sun above and [3].................... below the seated figures of the prefects, the central figure of the housemaster and his wife. [4].................... was curious to observe how a moustache by [5](*be*) .... waxed at the tips could date a man [6].................... accurately as a woman's dress, the white blouse, the whalebone collar, the puffed sleeves. Occasionally Minty was called on [7](*identify*) .... himself; practice had made him perfect; [8].................... had been a time of hesitation when he could not decide [9].................... Patterson [10](*seat*) .... on the housemaster's left or Tester [11](*stand*) .... rather more obscurely behind, his jaw [12].................... hidden by a puffed sleeve, best acted as his proxy. For Minty himself did not appear; he had seen the photograph [13](*take*) .... from the sickroom window. (ll. 20–33)

Grammar points

C *... the **pot of coffee**, which his landlady had brought him, grew cold.* (ll. 8–9)
What's the difference between *a pot of coffee* and *a coffee-pot*?

....

Suggest related pairs using the words below.
1 coffee *a cup of coffee / a coffee cup*   5 beer ....
2 tea ....   6 milk ....
3 sugar ....   7 toothpaste ....
4 matches ....   8 biscuits ....

D What does *must* mean in these sentences?
   a He **must be prepared** for anything, even society. (l. 38)
   b She **must believe** that he kept it there for study. (ll. 15–16)

Put the two above sentences into the past.
   c ....
   d ....

D1 Rewrite the following sentences in the past making only necessary changes.
1 Jo must believe fares are going up or he wouldn't be buying a season ticket.
   Jo must have believed fares were going up or he wouldn't have been buying a season ticket.
2 It's a standard rule in our office that we must be seen to be working when the boss comes in.
   ....
3 Our letter is unanswered, so John can't have seen it: he must be away.
   ....
4 The company secretary must know that the latest accounts will be found unacceptable.
   ....
5 I told him that I really must know what has been happening in my absence.
   ....
6 From what he says I can only conclude that he must be lying.
   ....
7 We don't have much time to get to the airport because we must be checking in before 8 a.m.
   ....
8 I don't follow what you're saying; I must be thinking of something else.
   ....

D2 Respond appropriately using either the simple present, or the correct form of *have to*.
1 Your mother must believe I'm rich or something.
   Yes, I'm sure she believes that.
2 Your mother must catch the next train.
   Yes, she has to catch it.
3 I can't understand why he's late for the meeting. He must be held up in a traffic jam.
   ....
4 Now that the boss is going to retire, I'm sure he must be arranging to appoint a successor.
   ....
5 He doesn't have much choice I'm afraid. He must sit for the exam again.
   ....
6 If they want any chance of buying this property, they must offer a lot more than that.
   ....
7 The way she's spending money, everyone must think she's inherited a fortune or something.
   ....
8 Unless we want to risk missing the next train, we must be leaving now.
   ....

SENTENCE STRUCTURE

A Answers and commentary

1 b *that*: subordinating conjunction, after the reporting verb *knew*, introducing a noun clause (*that this was one of his days*). *That* is often optional, but its use is preferable here because the verb and noun clause are separated by a clause. [> LEG 1.23.2, 15.12, LAG 14B]

2 a *as* (= while): time conjunction introducing an adverbial clause of time (*as he shaved*). [> LEG 1.45.1, LAG 21A*n*.3, 47A*ns*.9,12]

3 c *Although* (= Even though): conjunction introducing an adverbial clause of concession. [> LEG 1.50, LAG 3A*ns*.2–3]

4 b *rather than*: We can often use *instead of* in place of *rather than*, but not here, because *rather* intensifies *than* in the implied comparative construction: *He shaved **more cautiously** (rather) **than** closely* .... [> LEG 16.11, LAG 39D]

5 a *while* (= during the time that): time conjunction introducing an adverbial clause of time. [> LEG 1.45.1, 9.20.2] *While* and *during* are not interchangeable. [> LAG 10A*n*.1, 50A*n*.4]

6 b *which*: object relative pronoun referring to *the pot of coffee* [> LEG 1.34]:
*His landlady had brought him **the pot of coffee**. It grew cold.*
→ ***The pot of coffee**, **which** his landlady had brought him, grew cold.*

7 b *;* (semi-colon): We often use a semi-colon rather than a conjunction to separate closely related clauses. [> LEG 1.17]

8 a *his*: The possessive adjective + noun begins the new clause. [> LEG 4.21] Otherwise we would have to say:
*Minty, **whose** stomach would bear nothing hot, liked his coffee cold.*

9 b *it*: The subject pronoun, referring to *a spider*, begins a new clause. [> LEG 4.5.5] Otherwise we would have to say:
*A spider, **which had been there five days**, watched him under his tooth glass.*

10 b *he*: The subject pronoun, referring to *Minty*, begins the new clause. [> LEG 4.5.3]

B Answers and commentary

1 (–): Nothing is required here, though *there* would be acceptable. [compare > LEG 7.59.2, 10.19]

2 *blinking*: present participle construction replacing a relative clause [> LEG 1.58.6, LAG 9A*n*.1]:
*There were rows of **boys who were blinking** ... → There were rows of **boys blinking** ...*

3 (–): Nothing is required here.

4 *It*: The true subject of the sentence is the infinitive: *to observe how* .... *It* is 'preparatory' [> LEG 4.13, 16.30, 16.47]:
***To observe how**, etc. (subject) was curious.*
→ ***It** (preparatory it) was curious to observe how*, etc. [> LAG 1C]

5 *being*: We use the *-ing* form after prepositions. [> LEG 16.50–56, LAG 1D] We often use *by* + *-ing* to refer to method (answering the question *How?*) [> LEG 13.40.4, 16.51, App 25.17, LAG 20B*n*.1, 29A*n*.3]:
***How** does his moustache look like that? – **By being** waxed at the tips.*

6 *as*: ***as accurately as a woman's dress** (could date a woman)* is a shortened clause. [compare > LEG 1.53, 1.55, 4.7.3, LAG 19A*n*.2, 28B*n*.6]

7 *to identify*: infinitive of purpose. [> LEG 16.12.1, LAG 6B*n*.5, 7B*n*.11, 10B*n*.2, 15A*n*.3]

8 *there*: *There* combines with all forms of the verb *be*, not just *is/are* and *was/were* [> LEG 10.19]:
***There hadn't been** any rain for months. The earth was bare and dry.*

9 *whether* or *if*: *Decide* is a reporting verb which is followed by *if/whether* or a question-word [> LEG 15.17–20, App 45, LAG 10E, 14B, 29B, 50E]:
*I can't **decide whether/if** I should go on holiday.*
*I can't **decide when** I should go on holiday.*

10 *seated*: past participle construction in place of a relative clause [> LEG 1.62.3, LAG 6B*n*.4]:
*... decide whether Patterson, **who was seated** on the housemaster's left ...*
→ *... decide whether Patterson **seated** on the housemaster's left ...*

11 *standing*: present participle construction in place of a relative clause [> LEG 1.58.6, LAG 9A*n*.1]:
*... or Tester, **who was standing** rather ...*
→ *... or Tester **standing** rather ...*

12 (–): Nothing is required here.

13 *taken*: The past participle follows the verb of perception *see*. [> LEG 16.9.2, LAG 28D]:
*He had seen the photograph **taken** ...*
In the active, the bare infinitive (Not *to*) is used after *see*. There is also ambiguity, suggesting that the photographer was in the sickroom:
*He had seen the photographer **take** the photograph from the sickroom window.*

GRAMMAR POINTS

C Partitives and compound nouns: 'a pot of coffee/a coffee-pot' [> LEG 2.10.7, 2.18.2, App 5, compare > LAG 5B]

A pot of coffee describes a pot with coffee in it; *a coffee-pot* describes a container which may be full or empty.

We use *partitives* to describe:
- a single item (*a loaf of* bread)
- an amount of something (*a slice of* bread)
- a collection of things (*a packet of* biscuits).
Many partitives can be 'containers':
> *a pot of coffee*.
Some of these can be re-expressed as compound nouns:
> *a coffee-pot*.

Possible answers
1. a cup of coffee/a coffee-cup
2. a pot of tea/a teapot
3. a bowl of sugar/a sugar-bowl
4. a box of matches/a match-box
5. a can of beer/a beer-can
6. a jug of milk/a milk-jug
7. a tube of toothpaste/a toothpaste-tube
8. a tin of biscuits/a biscuit-tin

D Primary and secondary uses of 'must' [> LEG 11.4, 11.9, 11.27, 11.32–33, 11.46–48, 11.50–51]

a *he must be prepared* (necessity = it's necessary for him to be prepared)
b *she must believe* (deduction = it's possible she believes)
c *He **had to be prepared** for anything, even society.* (past necessity)
d *She **must have believed** that he kept it there for study.* (past deduction)

In its primary use, *must* refers to 'inescapable obligation' and is a 'defective verb'. This means we can use it to refer only to the present and the future:
> *They **must leave now**.* (present reference)
> *They **must leave tomorrow**.* (future reference)
If we want to refer to any other time, we have to 'make up the missing parts' of *must* by using a form of *have to*:
> *We **had to be** at the meeting at 11 yesterday*. (Not *We must be/We musted be*)
[> LAG 7D, 23F]

In its secondary use, *must* refers to degrees of certainty. [> LEG 11.3–4, 11.27, 11.32–33] In this use, it has only two forms:
> *They **must be** right*. (present form)
> *They **must have been** right*. (past or perfect form)

It follows that *had to (be)* and *must have (been)* have very different meanings.

D1

1. Jo must have believed fares were going up or he wouldn't have been buying a season ticket.
2. It was a standard rule in our office that we had to be seen (or *must be seen*, see note on **5** below) to be working when the boss came in.
3. Our letter was unanswered, so John couldn't have seen it: he must have been away.
4. The company secretary must have known that the latest accounts would be found unacceptable.
5. I told him that I really had to (or *must*) know what had been happening in my absence.
   Note that in indirect speech *must* (necessity) can remain unchanged when it refers to the past, or it can be replaced by *had to*. [> LEG 15.13n.6]
6. From what he said I could only conclude that he must have been lying.
   Note that *have to/have got to* can informally express deduction as well, so *he had to be lying* would be possible. [> LEG 11.33]
   Must be lying is also possible here (indirect speech). [> LEG 15.13n.6]
7. We didn't have much time to get to the airport because we had to be checking in before 8 a.m.
8. I didn't follow what you were saying; I must have been thinking of something else.

D2 Possible answers
1. Yes, I'm sure she believes that. (must = deduction)
2. Yes, she has to catch it. (must = necessity)
3. Yes, I'm sure he's held up in a traffic jam. (must = deduction)
4. Yes, I'm sure he's arranging to appoint a successor. (must = deduction)
5. Yes, he has to sit for it again. (must = necessity)
6. Yes, they have to offer a lot more than that. (must = necessity)
7. Yes, I'm sure everyone thinks so. (must = deduction)
8. Yes, we have to be leaving now. (must = necessity)

'The criminal look'

WITNESSES may pick out from an identification parade the person who most resembles their idea of what the criminal would look like, a
5 conference organized by the British Psychological Society was told on Saturday. Mr Ray Bull, a senior lecturer at the North East London Polytechnic, said research had shown
10 that the public tended to link abnormal appearance with abnormalities of behaviour. 'The public and police do agree about what face fits what crime,' he said.
15 'One apparently widely held belief is the "what is beautiful is good" stereotype. An individual's facial attractiveness has an effect on how threatening other people judge that
20 person to be. I have found that the addition of one or two small scars to a face leads to that face being judged more dishonest.'

Those beliefs also influence
25 length of sentence and verdict, he said. Research in mock-trial settings had shown that the more unattractive defendant was more heavily sentenced than one of attractive
30 character and appearance. Mr Bull, an expert on identification by witnesses, was addressing psychologists and lawyers at a conference in London held by Sir
35 Brian MacKenna, a retired high court judge, on the role of psychology in the legal system.

For decades it had been known that people often do not see or hear
40 things presented to their senses, but do 'see' and 'hear' things that have not occurred. But none of those factors meant that identification evidence was of little value.
45 Laboratory research based on photographs had shown recognition rates were high, about 80 per cent, even after delays of 35 days. But rates were lower when identification
50 was tested in mock criminal episodes in the streets because of stress and the inability of the witness to concentrate simultaneously on self-preservation and remembering
55 details of the culprit. Law enforcement authorities should be more aware of the factors that influence memory and identification, Mr Bull said. Apart from people's
60 prejudices about the 'look' of a criminal, the factors included the way questions were asked.

The Times (BrE)

Sentence structure

A Three of these sentences contain a word that is wrong. Provide the right words where necessary and give reasons for your choice. Then check against the text.

1 Witnesses may pick out from an identification parade the person who most resembles their idea of which the criminal would look like. (ll. 1–4)

....

2 The public and police do agree about that face fits what crime. (ll. 12–14)

....

3 I have found that the addition of one or two small scars to a face leads to that face being judged more dishonest. (ll. 20–23)

....

4 Mr Bull is an expert on identification by witnesses, was addressing psychologists and lawyers at a conference in London. (ll. 30–34)

....

B Join these notes to make sentences. Then check against the text.

1 Research – mock-trial settings – shown – more unattractive defendant – more heavily sentenced – one of attractive character and appearance (ll. 26–30)

....
....

2 For decades – known – people often – not see – hear things presented – senses – 'see' – 'hear' things – not occurred (ll. 38–42)

....

Grammar points

C What's the difference between *one* and *an* in these two sentences?

a *One* apparently widely held belief is the 'what is beautiful is good' stereotype. (ll. 15–17)

b *An* apparently widely held belief is the 'what is beautiful is good' stereotype.

In which of these sentences can we use: **a** both *a/an* and *one* **b** only *a/an* **c** only *one*? Why?

1 This is .... possible approach to the problem.   *a – a/one*
2 I agree that you're facing .... serious problem.
3 I've never met .... reader who doesn't like P.G. Wodehouse.
4 .... reader wrote to the publisher and ordered the complete works.
5 I wouldn't consider myself .... reader of novels.
6 What has happened is simply .... catastrophe.
7 The recent earthquake was just .... catastrophe among many.
8 You shouldn't expect too much from .... computer.
9 If you make .... mistake, they'll fire you.
10 We need .... additional assistant in this office.

D Join these sentences making any necessary changes, then compare your answer with ll. 18–20.
That person is threatening. That's how other people judge him.
Other people ....
What did you notice about the way the sentences are joined in the text?

Join or rewrite these sentences making any necessary changes.

1 Pat's really dependable. That's how I find her. *I find Pat (to be) really dependable.*
2 The case is closed. That's how I consider it.
3 Wise and clever – that's how I imagine her.
4 Suitable for the job – that's how they judge me.
5 John's incompetent. The company's always assumed it.
6 Ned's a bit of a fool. That's how I've always taken him.
7 A man of integrity – that's how I know him.
8 The only possible leader – that's how they see her.
9 Mozart's the greatest musician. Time has shown it.
10 His property is worth a million. Everyone estimates it.

E Analyze the structure in bold italics.
*The addition of one or two small scars to a face leads to **that face being judged** more dishonest.* (ll. 20–23)

Join these sentences making any necessary changes.

1 That social climber is invited to every single party. I dislike it.
   I dislike that social climber/social climber's being invited to every single party.
2 The boss's daughter is given a good job. Other employees resent it.

3 His private affairs are discussed by everyone. John can't stand it.

4 Her good looks are part of her success. Alison can't help it.

5 Pensioners are given extra money at Christmas. Everybody welcomes it.

6 The whole world is concerned about the ozone layer. Everyone's future depends on that.

SENTENCE STRUCTURE

A Answers and commentary

Numbers **1**, **2** and **4** contain a wrong word.

1 *Witnesses may pick out from an identification parade the person who most resembles their idea of* **what** (Not **which**) *the criminal would look like.*
what (= the thing which) *the criminal would look like* is an object noun clause after the preposition *of*. We often use *what* to introduce a noun clause. [> LEG 1.23.2, 1.24.2, LAG 42D, 50E] We often use *What + like?* to ask about appearance, etc. [> LEG 13.34.2]

2 *The public and police do agree about* **what** (Not **that**) *face fits what crime.*
what (= which) *face fits what crime* is an object noun clause after the preposition *about*. *What* and *which* (+ noun) are often interchangeable in noun clauses and questions [> LEG 13.34.1, 13.36.1, LAG 42D, 50E]:
> **What book/books** *did you buy?*
> **What boy/boys** *did you meet at the party?*
> → **Which book/books** *did you buy?*
> **Which boy/boys** *did you meet at the party?*

3 This sentence is correct. The first *that* introduces an object noun clause after the reporting verb *found*. [> LEG 1.23.2, App 45, LAG 4E, 14B] The second *that* (. . . *leads to* **that** *face being judged*) is a demonstrative adjective. [> LEG 4.32–36, App 7]

4 **Mr Bull, an expert on identification by witnesses**, *was addressing psychologists . . .*
We could say:
> **Mr Bull is** *an expert on identification by witnesses.* **He** *was addressing psychologists . . .*
Or:
> **Mr Bull, who** *is an expert on identification by witnesses, was addressing psychologists . . .*
Instead, the writer has used a noun phrase in apposition to *Mr Bull* to provide information about him. This style is common in journalism. [> LEG 1.39] The use of *an* (*Mr Bull, an expert . . .*) suggests that the reader may not have heard of Mr Bull. [> LEG 3.30, LAG 8B*n*.1]

B Answers and commentary

1 *Research in mock trial settings had shown that . . .*
The use of the past perfect (*had shown that*) is a case of reported speech backshift, or 'moving one tense back' from the present perfect (*has shown*), but the simple past, or in direct speech, the present perfect and present, would also have been possible. [> LEG 15.13*n*.3] *Show* is used as a reporting verb here with *that* introducing a noun clause. [> LEG 1.23.2, App 45]

. . . shown that the more unattractive defendant was more heavily sentenced than one of attractive character and appearance.
It would also be possible to leave out the first *more* here without changing the sense:
. . . the unattractive defendant was more heavily sentenced than one of attractive character and appearance. [> LEG 6.25–27] *More heavily* intensifies the verb *sentenced*. [> LEG 7.53, LAG 3C]

2 *For decades it had been known that people often do not see or hear things presented to their senses . . .*
The true subject of the sentence is the noun clause beginning with *that* (and ending with *their senses*):
> **That people often do not see or hear things presented to their senses** *had been known for decades . . .*
However, we generally avoid beginning a sentence with a subject noun clause and often prefer to use *It* instead. [> LEG 1.23.1–2] *It* is a 'preparatory subject'. [> LEG 4.13, LAG 1C] The past participle *presented* is used in place of a relative clause. [> LEG 1.62.3, LAG 6B*n*.4]

. . . but do 'see' and 'hear' things that have not occurred.
Do is used for emphasis here. [> LEG 10.4, compare > LAG 33B*n*.9] *. . . that* (or *which*) *have not occurred* is a defining relative clause which provides essential information, so there is no comma in front of *that*. [> LEG 1.26, LAG 5A*n*.3]

GRAMMAR POINTS

C 'A/an' and 'one' [> LEG 3.11]

a *One* (= one belief of many);
b *An* (= any, indefinite, unspecified)

We cannot normally use *a/an* and *one*
interchangeably, without changing the meaning.
[compare > LAG 29E, 40B*n*.4]
We use *a/an* to mean 'any one', not specified:
  *I'd like **a coffee** please.* ('any one')
We use *one* when we are counting (*one* and not
two or *three*):
  *I'd like **one coffee** please.* ('not more than
  one')
We rarely stress *a/an* in speech, but we often
stress *one* to show that we are counting.

1 **a** *a* (= any one possible approach); *one* (= one
of many possible approaches)
2 **a** *a* (= an unspecified problem); *one* (= and not
two or more)
3 **a** *a* (= any reader); *one* (= (not) a single)
4 **a** *a* (= an unspecified reader); *one* (shows that
this reader had been particularly noted)
5 **b** *a* (= deserving the label of 'reader', because I
don't read many novels [> LEG 3.9.3])
6 **b** *a* (= deserving the label of 'catastrophe' [> LEG
3.9.3])
7 **c** *one* (stressed in speech: = only one of the
catastrophes counted)
8 **a** *a* (= any computer); *one* (= you need more
than one computer)
9 **a** *a* (= any mistake); *one* (= just one/one is all it
takes)
10 **a** *a* (= any assistant); *one* (= one and not more
than one)

D Verb + object + 'to be': 'consider him to be' [> LEG 16.22, and compare > LEG 4.15, LAG 1E, 30F, 36C, 37B*n*.2]

*Other people judge **that person to be**
threatening.*
The infinitive *to be* is used after *judge that*
person, rather than the simple present *is* (also
possible).

We can use an object + *to be* after verbs like
acknowledge, assume, believe, calculate,
consider, declare, discover, find, imagine,
judge, know, prove, see, show, suppose, take (=
presume), *think* and *understand*.

We can often omit *to be*:
  *I find Pat **to be really dependable**.*
  → *I find Pat **really dependable**.*

1 I find Pat (to be) really dependable.
2 I consider the case (to be) closed.
3 I imagine her to be wise and clever.
4 They judge me (to be) suitable for the job.
5 The company's always assumed John to be
incompetent.
6 I've always taken Ned to be a bit of a fool.
7 I know him to be a man of integrity.
8 They see her to be the only possible leader.
9 Time has shown Mozart to be the greatest
musician.
10 Everyone estimates his property to be worth a
million.

E Verb (+ accusative or possessive) + '-ing': 'imagine my mother('s) approving' [> LEG 16.45, LAG 1F, 30D]

That face is the object (accusative) of *leads to*
and is followed by *-ing* (*being*).

Some verbs such as *dislike, excuse, fancy, hate,*
like, love, mind, etc. [> LEG 16.45.3] can be
followed by an object (accusative) or a
possessive + *-ing*. The most acceptable form after
these verbs is the possessive:
  *I can't **imagine my mother's approving**.*
  (*my mother's* = possessive)
In everyday speech, the accusative is often used
instead of the possessive, but not all native
speakers approve of its use:
  *I can't **imagine my mother approving**.*
  (*my mother* = object/accusative)

1 I dislike that social climber being invited to every
single party. (or *social climber's*)
2 Other employees resent the boss's daughter
being given a good job. (or *boss's daughter's*)
3 John can't stand his private affairs being
discussed by everyone. (The object is not a
person, therefore no possessive. [> LEG 2.44])
4 Alison can't help her good looks being part of
her success. (no possessive, as in **3** above)
5 Everybody welcomes pensioners being given
extra money at Christmas. (or *pensioners'*)
6 Everyone's future depends on the whole world
being concerned about the ozone layer. (or
whole world's, if we personalize 'world')

Alaska's dirty dollars

EXXON has spent more than $2bn cleaning up the oil which spilled from the tanker Exxon Valdez, making it one of the world's costliest industrial accidents. Much of this money has found its way into the pockets of a few thousand inhabitants who lived in the path of the oil slick. Yet Exxon's gold has not brought contentment to their small Alaskan fishing towns. It has set neighbour against neighbour and led to allegations that Exxon succeeded in buying off the anger of the local communities.

The largest US-based oil company invented a novel technique last summer to clean up the public relations mess left by the March 24 spill. It sprayed dollars around the shores of southern Alaska almost as liberally as its supertanker had

sprayed oil into the clear waters of Prince William Sound. Spending on this scale opened up unsuspected fissures in Alaska's inward-looking towns. Pragmatists were pitched against idealists; newcomers against oldtimers; and, at its crudest, those who welcomed against those who were appalled by the chance to take Exxon money. The idyllic self-image which these communities harboured - of the last great American frontier,

where hardy, self-reliant people came to escape the modern world - was shattered in the process.

The town of Homer is typical. It has just enjoyed one of the most prosperous years since its foundation in 1896 by a gold-digging adventurer from Michigan. Yet, like the gold rush itself, it is a feverish sort of prosperity which has divided Homer's 4,000 inhabitants.

John P. Calhoun, Homer's nervy, chain-smoking mayor, has only recently felt up to the task of talking to strangers about the impact on his town. 'The economics of the spill in the short term were very positive. It infused more money into our town than normal. The trouble was that not everyone gained to the same extent,' explains Mayor Calhoun in his pint-sized office in Homer's city hall.

The Financial Times (BrE)

Sentence structure

A A word is missing from three of these sentences. Put it in and give a reason.

1 Exxon has spent more than $2bn cleaning up the oil which spilled from the tanker Exxon Valdez, making it one of the world's costliest industrial accidents. (ll. 1–6)

....

2 It sprayed dollars around the shores of southern Alaska almost as liberally its supertanker had sprayed oil into the clear waters of Prince William Sound. (ll. 22–27)

....

3 The idyllic self-image which these communities harboured – of the last great American frontier, hardy, self-reliant people came to escape the modern world – was shattered in the process. (ll. 36–42)

....

4 Yet, like the gold rush itself, it is a feverish sort of prosperity has divided Homer's 4,000 inhabitants. (ll. 48–51)

....

B Replace or delete the word or words in italics. Then refer to the text.

1 Much of this money has found its way into the pockets of a few thousand inhabitants. *They* lived in the path of the oil slick. (ll. 6–10)

2 It has set neighbour against neighbour, *leading* to allegations that Exxon *managed to buy* off the anger of the local communities. (ll. 13–17)

3 Pragmatists were pitched against idealists; newcomers against oldtimers; and, at its crudest, those *welcoming* against those *appalled* by the chance to take Exxon money. (ll. 31–36)

4 John P. Calhoun, *who is* Homer's nervy, chain-smoking mayor, has only recently felt up to the task of talking to strangers. (ll. 52–55)

Grammar points

C Supply the right forms of the verbs in brackets then refer to the text. (ll. 1–36) Variations are possible. In each case give your reason for the tense you have chosen.

Exxon has spent more than $2bn cleaning up the oil
which [1](*spill*) .... from the tanker Exxon Valdez, ...
making it one of the world's costliest industrial accidents.
Much of this money [2](*find*) .... its way into the pockets ....
of a few thousand inhabitants who [3](*live*) ....
in the path of the oil slick. Yet Exxon's gold [4](*not bring*) ....
contentment to their small Alaskan fishing towns. It [5](*set*) ....
neighbour against neighbour and [6](*lead*) ....
to allegations that Exxon [7](*succeed*) ....
in buying off the anger of the local communities.
The largest US-based oil company [8](*invent*) .... a novel ....
technique last summer to clean up the public relations mess left by the
March 24 spill. It [9](*spray*) .... dollars around the shores of ....
southern Alaska almost as liberally as its supertanker
[10](*spray*) .... oil into the clear waters of Prince William Sound. ....
Spending on this scale [11](*open*) .... up unsuspected fissures ....
in Alaska's inward-looking towns. Pragmatists [12](*pitch*) ....
against idealists; newcomers against oldtimers; and, at its crudest,
those who [13](*welcome*) .... against those who ....
[14](*appal*) .... by the chance to take Exxon money. ....

D Choose the right word in this sentence, then check against the text. What's the difference?
*The idyllic self-image – of the **last/latest** American frontier – was shattered.* (ll. 36–42)

....

Supply words or phrases to replace the words or phrases in italics.

1 Is this your *most recent* publication?   *latest*
2 Is there any *additional* information?   ....
3 Do we have to go *a much greater distance*?   ....
4 I want the *final* edition of today's paper.   ....
5 Who *was born first* in your family?   ....
6 Which *house was put up first* in this town?   ....
7 *Was your sister born before* you?   ....
8 My house *didn't* cost *as much as* yours.   ....

E Why is the verb plural in **a**, but singular in **b**?

a *The economics of the spill in the short term **were** very positive.* (ll. 56–58)
b *Generally speaking, economics **isn't** taught at school.*

....

Write two sentences for each of these nouns, the first with a plural verb and the second with a singular one.

1 a economics ....
  b ....
2 a acoustics ....
  b ....
3 a statistics ....
  b ....
4 a ethics ....
  b ....

SENTENCE STRUCTURE

A Answers and commentary

Numbers 2, 3 and 4 have a word missing.

1 This sentence is correct.

2 *It sprayed dollars around the shores of southern Alaska almost **as liberally as** its supertanker had sprayed oil into the clear waters of Prince William Sound.*
An adverbial clause of comparison is introduced by *as liberally as* . . . . [> LEG 1.53, LAG 17Bn.6, 28Bn.6]

3 *The idyllic self-image which these communities harboured – of the last great American frontier, **where** hardy, self-reliant people came to escape the modern world – was shattered in the process.*
where introduces an adverbial clause of place [> LEG 1.46, LAG 31Bn.3, 44Bn.3]:
*It was **the last great American frontier**. Hardy, self-reliant people came **there** to escape.*
→ *It was **the last great American frontier**, **where** hardy, self-reliant people came to escape.*

4 *Yet, like the gold rush itself, it is a feverish sort of prosperity **which/that** has divided Homer's 4,000 inhabitants.*
*It refers back to the previous sentence (one of the most **prosperous** years since its foundation).* [> LEG 4.5.5, LAG 30An.1]
We can either say:
Yet, like the gold rush itself, a feverish sort of prosperity has divided Homer's 4,000 inhabitants.
Or:
. . . it is a feverish sort of prosperity which/ that . . .
Which/that is the subject of the relative clause. [> LEG 1.31, LAG 5An.3]

B Answers and commentary

1 *Much of this money has found its way into the pockets of a few thousand inhabitants **who** lived in the path of the oil slick.*
Who (or *that*) is the subject of the relative clause. It remains unchanged whether it refers to masculine, feminine, singular or plural. [> LEG 1.29] We do not use a comma in front of *who* because it introduces a defining clause which gives us essential information about the inhabitants it refers to. [> LEG 1.26, LAG 3Bn.2 and compare > LAG 9Bn.2, 22Ans.4–5]

2 *It has set neighbour against neighbour **and led** to allegations . . .*
A co-ordinate clause introduced by *and* is used in place of a present participle. [> LEG 1.17, 1.58.1, LAG 1Bn.2]
*. . . allegations that Exxon **succeeded in buying** off the anger of the local communities.*
We cannot use *could* to describe the successful completion of a specific action. In this context, we can use *was able to*, *managed to* or *succeeded in* (+ *-ing*). [> LEG 11.12.3, LAG 9C, 48C]
Could gives us a different meaning here:
*. . . it has led to allegations that Exxon **could buy off** the anger of the local communities.* (i.e. it is a possibility) [> LAG 22C]

3 *. . . and, at its crudest, those **who welcomed** against those . . .*
A relative clause introduced by *who* is used in place of a present participle. [> LEG 1.58.6, 1.29]
*. . . against those **who were appalled by** the chance to take Exxon money.*
A relative clause followed by a verb in the passive is used in place of a past participle. [> LEG 1.62.1, 1.29]

4 *John P. Calhoun, Homer's nervy, chain-smoking mayor, has only recently felt up to the task . . .*
A phrase in apposition with *John P. Calhoun* is used in place of a relative clause. The second phrase provides information about the first. [> LEG 1.39, LAG 2An.1, 5Ans 2,4]

GRAMMAR POINTS

C Verbs and verb tenses [> LEG Chapter 9, regular and irregular verbs, Apps 39–40, LAG 8E, 25C, 26C, 28C, 33B, 37C, etc.]

The simple past combines with other tenses, particularly in the kind of narrative we have here. [> LEG 9.21]

1 *spilled* (also spelt *spilt* [> LEG 9.14.1]): Simple past, implying the event is over: there is no more oil to spill. [> LEG 9.17.1] The present perfect *has spilt* would suggest up to now [> LEG 9.25.1, 9.26, LAG 25C]; the present perfect progressive *has been spilling* would suggest an action in progress throughout a period, up to the present. [> LEG 9.33.1, LAG 33B*n*.4]

2 *has found*: Present perfect without a time adverbial, pointing to consequences *now* of something which took place *then*. [> LEG 9.26.1]

3 *lived*: Simple past, though presumably they still live there. [> LEG 9.17.1] The simple present, *live*, would convey this more precisely. [> LEG 9.8.2]

4 *has not brought*: Present perfect without a time adverbial, as for 2 above.

5 *has set*: Present perfect without a time adverbial, as for 2 above.

6 *led*: Present perfect continuation of 5 above: *It has set ... and (has) led.*

7 *succeeded*: Simple past, suggesting the action is finished. [> LEG 9.17.1] The present perfect (*has succeeded*) would have different time implications, pointing to the consequences *now* of something which took place *then*. [> LEG 9.26.1, LAG 25C]

8 *invented*: Simple past + time adverbial *last summer*. [> LEG 9.18, LAG 38C]

9 *sprayed*: Simple past, suggesting the action is finished. [> LEG 9.17.1]

10 *had sprayed*: Past perfect, because this refers to an earlier occasion: 'an earlier past'. [> LEG 9.29.1, LAG 27B*n*.3, 33B, 37B*n*.3, 41B, 52B]

11 *opened*: Simple past, because the action is finished. [> LEG 9.17.1]

12 *were pitched*: Simple past (passive) referring to what happened. [> LEG 9.17.1, 12.2, 12.3*n*.1]

13 *welcomed*: Simple past, referring to what happened. [> LEG 9.17.1]

14 *were appalled*: Simple past (passive) referring to what happened. [> LEG 9.17.1, 12.2, 12.3*n*.1]

D Adjectives and adverbs often confused e.g. 'last/latest' [> LEG 6.24–26, 7.4–5, App 12]

last (= there are no others); *latest* would imply that new frontiers are still being created and this is 'the latest'.

Possible answers

1 latest (presumably you are going to publish some more)

2 further (= additional; Not *farther*)

3 (much) further/farther (both can refer to distance)

4 last (there will be no other editions)

5 *Who is the eldest/oldest in your family?*

6 *Which is the oldest house in this town?* (Not *the eldest house*)

7 *Is your sister older than you?* (Not *elder than you*; we can't use *than* after *elder*.)

8 *My house cost less than yours.* (Not *lesser*)

E Nouns with a plural form + singular or plural verb: 'economics' [> LEG 2.31]

a *Economics* is used here to make a specific reference to particular finances, therefore the verb is plural.

b *Economics* is used here to refer to the academic subject, therefore the verb is singular.

Some nouns ending in *-ics*, such as *acoustics, economics, ethics* and *statistics* take a singular or plural verb. When the reference is to an academic subject (e.g. *acoustics* = the scientific study of sound) then the verb must be singular:
Acoustics is a branch of physics.
When the reference is specific (e.g. *acoustics* = sound quality), then the verb must be plural:
The acoustics in the Festival Hall are extremely good.

Sample answers

1a The economics of this project are about right.

b Economics is a subject often studied by future politicians.

2a The acoustics in ancient Greek theatres are quite remarkable.

b Acoustics is something the ancient Greeks understood very well.

3a The statistics quoted in this article are quite inaccurate.

b Statistics is an inexact science.

4a The ethics of the situation are self-evident.

b Ethics is actively taught as part of our course in philosophy.

Fire message in plain English

FIRE INSTRUCTIONS (PART 1)

FIRE

COMMUNICATIONS experts are rewriting London Underground's fire instructions to staff 'in plain English', 15 months after the King's Cross fire in which 31 people lost their lives. This followed criticism that the size and wording of the fire emergency instructions had contributed to difficulties in staff - the Underground has 10,000 - getting the fire brigade quickly to the scene.

Under the changes, words like 'if' and 'but' are being jettisoned, along with clauses and sub-clauses added over decades. 'We are giving priority to rewriting in positive and easy-to-understand terms the Underground's instructions on what to do in case of fire,' said a spokesman yesterday.

He said that among examples of unacceptable 'chatty and verbose' wording was rule D2. This says: 'If fire or smouldering is small enough to be dealt with by members of staff, speed is of the utmost importance. If a member of staff observes or is informed of a small fire or smouldering in or around railway buildings, tracks, cables or other property (including tunnels and the sides of cuttings and embankments) he must take immediate action to extinguish it. Most fires can be extinguished or kept in check by buckets of water and/or hand pumps or beating with lengths of hose.'

The spokesman said that while the instructions included words like 'must' and 'speed', the approach was long-winded and softened its impact by using the words 'if' and 'smouldering'. These and similar regulations are being replaced by simply-worded instructions including:

'Fire or smoke in stations - Tell the line controller where the fire is and the best way for the fire brigade to reach it.'

And: 'Station evacuation: Close the station to incoming passengers.'

A Cambridge communications firm has been commissioned for the project.

The Daily Telegraph (BrE)

Sentence structure

A Three of the phrases below can be used in place of phrases in the text. Underline the phrases in the text that could be replaced.

what we should do
have been thrown out
which 31 people lost their lives in
isn't too large
Unless a member of staff observes

Now say why the two remaining phrases are wrong.

1 ....
2 ....

B Rewrite these sentences as one sentence beginning with the words provided. Then check against the text.

1 The spokesman said that the approach was long-winded. The instructions included words like 'must' and 'speed'. It softened its impact. It used the words 'If' and 'smouldering'. (ll. 39–44)
   The spokesman said that ....
   ....

2 Where is the fire? What's the best way for the fire brigade to reach it? Tell the line controller. (ll. 48–51)
   Tell the line controller ....
   ....

Grammar points

C Supply appropriate forms of *say* and *tell*, then check against the text.

 a He _____ that among examples of 'chatty and verbose' wording was rule D2. (ll. 22–24)
 b _____ the line controller where the fire is ... (ll. 48–49)
   What's the basic rule for the use of *say* and *tell*?
   ....

Respond to these statements using *say* or *tell*. Begin each answer with *Yes, that's what ....*

 1 So they're going to close the hotel. (say)   *Yes, that's what they said.*
 2 And they're going to decorate it. (tell)   *Yes, that's what they told me.*
 3 And replace the windows. (be tell)   ....
 4 And they'll refit the bar. (be say)   ....
 5 And change the fire-places. (tell)   ....
 6 And refit the bathrooms. (say)   ....

D Supply the missing preposition, then check against the text.
If a member of staff observes or is informed of a small fire or smouldering in or around railway buildings, tracks, cables or other property (_____ tunnels) he must take action. (ll. 27–34)

Write sentences using the following prepositions.

 1 barring ....
 2 concerning ....
 3 considering ....
 4 excluding ....
 5 including ....

E Give the right form of the verb in brackets, then check against the text.
These and similar regulations (replace) _____ by simply-worded instructions. (ll. 44–46)
Comment on the form of the verb *replace*.

Respond to these questions.

 1 Are they replacing the regulations?
    Yes, they're being replaced. As far as I know they've been replaced already.
 2 Are they paying the staff?
    ....
 3 Are they building the new hotel?
    ....
 4 Are they feeding the cows?
    ....
 5 Are they cleaning the carpet?
    ....

F Join these two sentences with *for*, then compare your answer with the text. (ll. 50–51)
The fire brigade want to reach it. What's the best way?
What's the best way ....

Join these sentences combining *for* with the adjectives in italics.

 1 She wants her daughter to succeed. She's very *anxious*.
    She's very anxious for her daughter to succeed.
 2 We want our team to win. We're very *keen*.
    ....
 3 I want those things to arrive. I feel very *impatient*.
    ....

SENTENCE STRUCTURE

A Answers and commentary

The following phrases in the text should be underlined:

1 in which 31 people lost their lives (ll. 5-6)
(→ *which 31 people lost their lives in*)
[> LEG 1.36, LAG 21An.1, 24An.7, 27An.3, 50An.2, 58C, etc.]
Which (not *that*) can be used directly after a preposition (*in which 31 people . . .*); this style is formal.
We can move the preposition to the end (*which 31 people lost their lives in*).
In informal style, we can omit the relative pronoun altogether:
  . . . the fire 31 people lost their lives in.

2 what to do (ll. 19-20)
(→ *what we should do*)
[> LEG 15.24.2]
We can report a direct request for information with a question-word + *should . . . ?* in two ways:
  What should I do? → He wanted to know what he should do.
  → He wanted to know what to do.
In the reported question, *what he should do* is a noun clause object of the verb *know* [> LEG 1.23.2, 1.24.2, LAG 50E,F]; *what to do* is an infinitive phrase replacing the noun clause.

3 is small enough (l. 25)
(→ *isn't too large*)
. . . is small enough to be dealt with/isn't too large to be dealt with [> LEG 16.32.1-2]
Enough comes after the adjective and means 'to the necessary degree'. [> LAG 34E]
Too comes before the adjective and has the sense of 'excessive', 'more than is desirable'. [compare > LAG 28Bn.5, 36Bn.2]

Remaining answers

1 *have been thrown out* does not replace *are being jettisoned* (l. 14); *have been thrown out* describes a completed action; *are being jettisoned* describes an action in progress. [> LEG 9.26.1, 9.34, 9.11.1, 12.2-3]

2 *Unless a member of staff observes* does not replace *If a member of staff observes* (ll. 27-28). *Unless* means 'except on the condition that', not 'on the condition that'. [> LEG 14.20.2, LAG 10F]

B Answers and commentary

1 *The spokesman said that **while** the instructions included words like 'must' and 'speed', the approach was . . .*
While means 'although' here and introduces an adverbial clause of concession. [> LEG 1.50]
Compare the use of *while* (= during the time that) to introduce adverbial clauses of time [> LEG 1.45.1, 9.20.2, LAG 10An.1]:
  ***While I fumbled/was fumbling** for some money, my friend paid the fares.*
*. . . the approach was long-winded **and** softened its impact . . .*
and introduces a co-ordinate clause. [> LAG 1Bn.2]
As the subject (*the approach*) is the same for *was* and *softened*, it isn't necessary to repeat it. [> LEG 1.17, 1.20, LAG 13B]
*. . . its impact **by using** the words 'if and 'smouldering'.*
By is a preposition. If we use a verb after it, the verb must be an *-ing* form. [> LEG 16.50-56, LAG 1D]
By + -ing can refer to 'method', answering the question *How?* [> LEG 13.40.4, 16.51, App 25.17, LAG 17Bn.5, 29An.3]:
  *How did they soften the impact of the instructions? – **By using** the words 'if and 'smouldering'.*

2 *Tell the line controller **where the fire is** and (tell him what) **the best way** (is) for the fire brigade to reach it.*
Tell must always be followed by an object (*tell me*) (Not **Say me**). [> LEG 15.9, LAG 20C]
In an indirect question the inversion after a question-word (*Where is the fire?*) changes back to statement word order (subject + verb) [> LEG 15.19-20, LAG 50E]:
  *Tell me where **the fire is** . . . .*

GRAMMAR POINTS

C 'Say' and 'tell' [> LEG 15.5–9, LAG 4E, 14B, 46A]

a *said*; **b** *Tell*

The basic rule is that *tell* must be followed by a personal indirect object (*tell somebody ...*). *Say* can be followed by an optional *to* + the person who is addressed:

'You haven't got much time,' **he told me/he said (to me)**. (Not **he told*/*he said me**)

1 Yes, that's what they said (to me).
2 Yes, that's what they told me.
3 Yes, that's what I was told.
4 Yes, that's what was said.
5 Yes, that's what they told me.
6 Yes, that's what they said.

D Prepositions ending in '-ing': 'including'
[> LEG App 20.2]

The missing preposition is *including*.

There are a small number of prepositions (words followed by an object) which end in -*ing*, some of the most common of which are given in the answers to the exercise below.

Other uses of the -*ing* form are:
- as part of a verb [> LAG 20E, 51E]:
  I've been **writing** *letters.*
- as a gerund (= a noun) [> LAG 34C, 37E]:
  Writing *letters is a chore.* (= the writing of)
- as an adjective [> LAG 13D, 23E]:
  We live in **interesting** *times.*

Sample answers
1 Barring delays, we hope to be with you before nightfall.
2 Concerning your application, I'm afraid we have no further news.
3 We have a right to expect better roads, considering the taxes we pay.
4 This amount covers the bill, excluding VAT. (= Value Added Tax)
5 I've paid the hotel bill, including service charge.

E The passive: present progressive and simple present perfect [> LEG 12.2, 12.3n.6]

are being replaced

Only present and past forms of the progressive are common in the passive:
It **is being replaced**.
It **was being replaced**.

It is important never to confuse *being* and *been* in the passive:
It is **being** *replaced.* (present progressive)
It has **been** *replaced.* (simple present perfect: no progressive; the form **has been being replaced** is too rare to account for.)

1 Yes, they're being replaced. As far as I know they've been replaced already.
2 Yes, they're being paid. As far as I know, they've been paid already.
3 Yes, it's being built. As far as I know, it's been built already.
4 Yes, they're being fed. As far as I know, they've been fed already.
5 Yes, it's being cleaned. As far as I know, it's been cleaned already.

F 'For' + noun/pronoun + 'to': 'the best way for the fire brigade to reach it' [> LEG 16.28]

What's the best way **for the fire brigade to reach it?**

We can use *for* + noun/pronoun after a few nouns and adjectives, followed by a *to*-infinitive:
1 She's very anxious for her daughter to succeed.
2 We're very keen for our team to win.
3 I feel very impatient for those things to arrive.

Another day begins

THE day on which Emily Stockwell Turner fell out of love with her husband began much like other days. As usual, Emmy lay in bed twenty minutes
5 later than she should have done, with her son Freddy playing cars over her legs, and when she finally got up it seemed as if things would never be sorted out. But somehow breakfast was made; Freddy was fed and
10 dressed and sent off to nursery school in the car pool, and at length Emmy stood outside the house watching her husband leave for work on time.

'Looks like snow,' said Turner, an instructor in the
15 Languages and Literature Division at Convers College, as he stood beside her on the frozen lawn in his overcoat. It was a chilly, dark morning early in November, and Emmy wore only an old cashmere sweater and slacks, but she was the kind that never feels the cold.
20 'Oh, good; do you think so? But it's only the first week in November. I'm afraid it's much too soon.'

'It probably snows early here,' Holman said, and climbed into his car and shut the door. Through the glass he could see Emmy look round at the clouds, smiling. What a
25 magnificent creature she is, he thought as he frequently did. She was a big girl, tall, tanned like a gypsy, and with a high colour. Her heavy, bright-brown hair had not yet been done up for the day; it hung down over one shoulder in a thick braid. She was twenty-seven, and still had, as on
30 the day he married her, the look of a carefully bred and beautifully groomed animal kept permanently at the peak of its condition for some high use which has not yet arrived and possibly never will arrive. Holman had seen it often on boys and girls of Emmy's class, though seldom to such a
35 degree or accompanied by so much beauty.

Emmy continued to stand beside the car, waiting for her husband to roll the window down, so he rolled it down.

'Goodbye, darling,' she said, stooping to kiss him.

'So long, baby,' Holman replied. He rolled the window
40 up again and drove away down the drive.

Love and Friendship by Alison Lurie *(AmE)*

Sentence structure

A Choose the words that fit, then refer to the text.

1 The day .... Emily Stockwell Turner fell out of love with her husband began much like other days. (ll. 1–3) [*which/on which*]

2 As usual, Emmy lay in bed twenty minutes later .... she should have done, with her son Freddy playing cars over her legs, and when she finally got up it seemed .... things would never be sorted out. (ll. 4–8) [*than/as, how/as if*]

3 'Looks like snow,' said Turner, an instructor in the Languages and Literature Division at Convers College, ... he stood beside her on the frozen lawn in his overcoat. (ll. 14–16) [*as/during*]

B Break these sentences down into short sentences, making any necessary changes. Write one short sentence beside each letter.

1 It was a chilly, dark morning early in November, and Emmy wore only an old cashmere sweater and slacks, but she was the kind that never feels the cold. (ll. 16–19)

a ....
b ....
c ....

2 Through the glass he could see Emmy look round at the clouds, smiling. (ll. 23–24)

a ....
b ....
c ....

Grammar points

C Which words can you use in place of *much* in these two sentences?

   a *The day ... began* **much** *like other days.* (ll. 1–3) ....

   b *I'm afraid it's* **much** *too soon.* (l. 21) ....

Suggest replacements for *much* in these sentences. Sometimes there is more than one possibility.

   1 Queen Victoria was seldom much amused.   *very*
   2 This is much the worst painting on display.
   3 Our government is much concerned about the hostages.
   4 I much prefer the picture on the right.
   5 We aren't much interested in your proposal.
   6 This essay isn't much better than the previous one.
   7 John's much more cautious since his operation.

D What are the principal parts of the verbs in bold italics?

   a *Emmy* **lay** *in bed twenty minutes later than she should have done.* (ll. 4–5) ....

   b *Do you think Emmy* **lied** *to her husband?* ....

   c *Emmy* **laid** *the mirror on her dressing table.* ....

Supply the right forms of the verbs *lie* and *lay* in these sentences.

   1 He took off his glasses and ...... *laid* ...... them on the table.
   2 I know it's Sunday morning, but how long do you intend to .... in bed?
   3 It's now clear that one of the witnesses .... to the jury.
   4 We'll have to .... the case before the jury and let them decide.
   5 I hope your goose has .... a golden egg.
   6 These eggs have .... under this bush for some time.
   7 When are you going to .... the table?

E *He stood* **beside** *her.* (l. 16) *Emmy continued to stand* **beside** *the car.* (l. 36)
Write a sentence using the word *besides* as a preposition or an adverb.

....

What's the difference between *beside* and *besides*?

....

Supply *beside* or *besides*.

   1 I think Tim should sit ...... *beside* ...... your mother at the dinner-table.
   2 Who else are we going to invite to the party .... your mother?
   3 .... the matter of cost, it will be very inconvenient to have the roof replaced.
   4 We won't have time to go to the Henry Moore exhibition. ...., it hasn't opened yet.
   5 What would you suggest to set .... Churchill's wartime achievements?
   6 I find it very inconvenient not to have a reading lamp .... my bed.
   7 You shouldn't need much else on your desk .... a reading lamp.

F Complete the following, then check against the text.
'Looks like snow.' – *'Oh, good; do you think* ....*?'* (l. 14, 1.20)

Respond in the negative (X) or affirmative (√). Give two negative forms where possible.

   1 Has your father got home from work yet? (√ think)   *I think so.*
   2 The train's going to be late. (X hope)
   3 Are there any letters for me? (X be afraid)
   4 Is John better now? (√ imagine)
   5 You won't be needing this book any more. (X suppose)
   6 It's going to rain. (√ seem)
   7 This new business isn't going to succeed. (X seem)

SENTENCE STRUCTURE

A Answers and commentary

1 *The day* **on which** *Emily Stockwell Turner fell out of love with her husband began much like other days.*
→ *The day began much like other days. Emily Stockwell Turner fell out of love with her husband* **on that day**.
Which, referring to *day*, is the relative pronoun object of the preposition *on*. [> LEG 1.36]
The day which is impossible unless *which* refers to *day* as the subject. Compare:

The day *began like any other.* **It was an ordinary day, but it turned out badly.**

→ **The day, which** *began like any other, turned out badly.*

2 *As usual, Emmy lay in bed twenty minutes later* **than** *she should have done, with her son Freddy . . .*
We use *than* (Not *as*) after the comparative (*later*). [> LEG 6.27.1, LAG 32D] *Than* introduces an adverbial clause of comparison here: *. . . than she should have done.* [> LEG 1.53]

. . . playing cars over her legs, and when she finally got up it seemed **as if** *things would never be sorted out.*
We can say: *Things would never be sorted out. That's* **how** *it seemed.* But not *it seemed how*. Though we often hear sentences like *It seemed like things would never be sorted out*, not all native speakers approve of the use of *like* to introduce a clause. [> LEG App 25.25] We need *as if/as though* to introduce an adverbial clause of manner after *be*, *seem*, etc. [> LEG 1.47.2, LAG 16D]

3 *'Looks like snow,' said Turner . . .* **as** *he stood beside her on the frozen lawn in his overcoat.*
During is not interchangeable with *as* or *while*. *As* and *while* can introduce an adverbial clause of time (as here). [> LEG 1.45.1] We can also use *during the time (that)*, but not *during* on its own. *During* is a preposition and must be followed by an object to produce an adverbial phrase (*during the summer*, etc.). [> LEG 8.4.2, 7.35]

B Answers and commentary

Most of the sentences you have written are simple sentences. A simple sentence has one finite verb. [> LEG 1.7] The basic word order in a sentence that is not a question or a command is:

(Time) Subject Verb Object Manner Place (Time)
[> LEG 1.3, 7.22, LAG 4A]

1a *It* (subject) *was* (be) *a chilly, dark morning* (complement) *early in November* (time).
Verbs like *be* and *seem* cannot be followed by an object. [> LAG 4A] We use a complement after them. This is usually an adjective, a noun or a pronoun which completes the sense by telling us something about the subject. In this case *a chilly, dark morning* tells us about *It*. [> LEG 1.9, 1.11] *It* is an empty subject because it carries no real information. It is present because every English sentence has to contain a subject and verb. [> LEG 4.12, LAG 58An.6, 60An.5]

b *Emmy* (subject) *wore* (verb) *only* (focus adverb) *an old cashmere sweater and slacks* (object).
We often put the adverb *only* in front of the word(s) we want to qualify, so as to focus attention on it.
Compare: **Only Emmy** *wore an old cashmere sweater.* (= She was the only one who did this)
[> LEG 7.54–55, compare > LAG 11An.1b]

c *She* (subject) *was* (be) *the kind that never feels the cold* (complement).
This sentence contains two ideas: *She was that kind of person. She never feels the cold.*
That (or *who*) is the relative pronoun subject of the relative clause (*that never feels the cold*).
[> LEG 1.29, LAG 3Bn.2]

2a *Through the glass* (place) *he* (subject) *could see* (verb) *Emmy* (object). Or: *He could see Emmy . . .*
We can emphasize location by mentioning it first. [> LEG 7.19.2 and compare > LAG 28An.2a]

b *Emmy* (subject) *looked round at* (verb) *the clouds* (object).
Look round at is a three-part verb. [> LEG 8.30] *He could see Emmy look round* means he observed the whole action, from start to finish. Verbs of perception like *see* can be followed by the bare infinitive or the *-ing* form. [> LEG 16.9.2]

c *She* (subject) *was smiling* (verb).
The verb *was smiling* is intransitive. [> LEG 1.10] In *. . . she looked round at the clouds, smiling*, *smiling* is a present participle construction used in place of a co-ordinate clause (*and she was smiling*). [> LEG 1.57]

GRAMMAR POINTS

C 'Much' as an intensifier and as an adverb of degree: 'much obliged', 'much worse' [> LEG 6.28.2, 7.45, 7.48, 7.50–51, compare > LAG 2F, 31D]

a *a lot* **b** *a lot/far*

We can use *much* as an intensifier, especially with past participles. In such instances, it can be replaced by *very* [compare > LAG 3C, 11C]:

*I'm **much/very obliged** to you.*

*I told them about it, but they weren't **much/very interested**.*

We can use *much* as an adverb of degree, especially with comparatives and superlatives. [> LAG 27E, 32D, 45F] In such instances it can often be replaced by *a lot* or *far*:

*His condition is **much/a lot/far worse**.*

Possible answers

1 very
2 (by) far
3 very
4 far
5 very
6 a lot
7 far/a lot

D The verbs 'lay' and 'lie' [regular and irregular verbs, > LEG Apps 39, 40, compare > LAG 49F]

a *Emmy **lay** in bed ...* lie, lay, have lain
(= be in a flat position); present participle: *lying*

b *Emmy **lied** to her husband ...* lie, lied, have lied
(= tell lies); present participle: *lying*

c *Emmy **laid** the mirror ...* lay, laid, have laid
(= put down); present participle: *laying*

The main problem arises from the fact that the past form *lay* (= was in a flat position) is the same as the present form *lay* (= put down).
Even native speakers regularly confuse these verbs and say e.g. **I laid in my bed.* **He's been laying there a long time.* The wholly regular verb *lie, lied, lied* (= to tell lies) adds to the confusion.

1 laid (= put)
2 lie (in bed)
3 lied (= told lies)
4 lay (= put)
5 laid (an egg)
6 lain/have been lying (= been resting)
7 lay (the table)

E 'Beside' and 'besides' [> LEG App 25.12]

Possible answer: *There were a lot of people at the meeting **besides** us.* (= in addition to)
Beside means 'next to'; *besides* means 'in addition to'.

We use *beside* as a preposition (always followed by a noun/pronoun object) [> LAG 12Bn.29]:
*Sit **beside Tim**. Sit **beside me**.*
We use *besides* as a preposition:
*There's a lot more in life **besides work**.*
or as an adverb [> LAG 55Bn.1]:
*It's a fast car. **Besides**, it's got four-wheel drive.*

1 beside (next to)
2 besides (in addition to)
3 Besides (in addition to)
4 Besides (in addition)
5 beside (next to)
6 beside (next to)
7 besides (in addition to)

F 'So', not 'it' after certain verbs [> LEG 4.17, compare > LAG 53E]

'Looks like snow.' – *'Oh, good; do you think **so**?'*

After verbs like *believe, expect, imagine*, etc. we use *so* when we're giving affirmative answers:
Are you free tomorrow?
*– I think **so**.* (Not **I think.* or **I think it.*)
With many of these verbs we can form negative answers in two ways:
Are you free tomorrow?
*– I think **not**.* Or:
*– I don't think **so**.*
With a few such verbs, we can only use *not*:
*I hope **not**.* (Not **I don't hope so.*)

1 I think so.
2 I hope not.
3 I'm afraid not.
4 I imagine so.
5 I suppose not./I don't suppose so.
6 It seems so.
7 It seems not./It doesn't seem so.

Patients get the message

PATIENTS recover more quickly from surgery when tapes with hypnotic suggestions are played to them on the operating table, doctors at St Thomas's Hospital, London have found. While under anaesthetic, they were told: 'You will not feel sick. You will not have any pain.' Those given such suggestions had fewer complications than others after surgery and left hospital sooner.

The experiment was set up at St Thomas's after doctors found patients could sometimes recall things said during operations. In a study at another hospital, many patients who were told during an operation that they should touch their ears at a later interview with a doctor did so. The experiment at St Thomas's was conducted on 19 women having a hysterectomy operation. The women, who had consented to

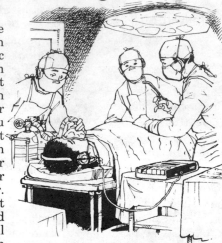

the experiment, were played a 12-minute recording repeated six times. Most of the tape gave details of the normal procedures following the operation and how to cope with them. It said, for example: 'How quickly you recover from your operation depends upon you - the more you relax, the more comfortable you will be.'

This was followed by two minutes of directly telling the patient she would feel well after the operation. Then came a minute of third-person suggestions - for example: 'the operation seems to be going very well and the patient is fine.'

A control group of patients was played blank tapes. Patients who received the suggestions were discharged from hospital 1.3 days earlier on average. If this could be achieved as a routine, the health service could save millions of pounds a year. Nurses rated the patients, and almost all those who had been given suggestions did better than expected. They suffered from less fever and had few stomach and bowel disturbances, which are common following an abdominal operation.

The Independent (BrE)

Sentence structure

A Supply punctuation marks, capital letters, etc. where necessary.
Explain why you have used them, then check against the text.

1 While under anaesthetic they were told you will not feel sick you will not have any pain (ll. 7–10)

....

....

2 Those given such suggestions had fewer complications than others after surgery and left hospital sooner (ll. 10–13)

....

3 The experiment was set up at St Thomas after doctors found patients could sometimes recall things said during operations (ll. 14–17)

....

....

4 In a study at another hospital many patients who were told during an operation that they should touch their ears at a later interview with a doctor did so (ll. 17–22)

....

5 The women who had consented to the experiment were played a 12-minute recording repeated six times (ll. 25–29)

....

....

6 It said for example how quickly you recover from your operation depends upon you the more you relax the more comfortable you will be (ll. 32–37)

....

....

Grammar points

B Supply *a/an*, *the* or zero (–) in this paragraph, then refer to the text. (ll. 1–37) Give a reason or reasons beside each choice.

1....... patients recover more quickly from
2....... surgery when tapes with
3....... hypnotic suggestions are played to them
on 4....... operating table,
5....... doctors
at 6....... St Thomas's Hospital, London have found. While
under 7....... anaesthetic, they were told: 'You will not feel sick.
You will not have any pain.' Those given such
suggestions had 8....... fewer complications than others after
9....... surgery and left
10....... hospital sooner.
11....... experiment was set up at St Thomas's after
12....... doctors found
13....... patients could sometimes recall
14....... things said during
15....... operations.
In 16....... study at another hospital,
17....... many patients who were told during
18....... operation that they should touch their ears
at 19....... later interview
with 20....... doctor did so.
21....... experiment at St Thomas's was conducted on 19 women
having 22....... hysterectomy operation.
23....... women, who had consented to
24....... experiment,
were played 25....... 12-minute recording repeated six times.
26....... most of the tape gave details of the normal procedures
following 27....... operation and how to cope with them.
It said, for example: 'How quickly you recover from your operation
depends upon you – 28....... more you relax,
29....... more comfortable you will be.'

C Supply the missing verb and give a reason for your choice, then refer to the text. (ll. 50–52)
If this .... be achieved as a routine, the health service could save millions ...

....

Write sentences beginning with *if* to respond to these statements.

1 We might be able to achieve this and save millions of pounds.
Yes, if we could achieve this, we could save millions of pounds.

2 We might be able to anticipate what's going to happen and make a lot of money.

....

3 We might have been able to stop and avoid the accident.

....

4 We might be able to meet tomorrow and discuss the matter.

....

5 We might have been able to take an earlier train and get to the meeting on time.

....

6 We might be able to spend the night in Brighton and not have to drive back to London tonight.

....

SENTENCE STRUCTURE

A Answers and commentary

1 *While under anaesthetic, they were told:*
We generally use a comma when the adverbial clause comes first. [> LEG 1.45.1] We can use a colon to introduce direct speech in a formal context of this kind and especially in American English. [> LEG 15.3*n*.2]

'You will not feel sick. You will not have any pain.'
We use quotation marks around what is actually spoken and enclosing other punctuation marks. The quotation marks may be single (' ... ') or double (" ... ") and are placed high above the base-line at the beginning and end of each quotation. [> LEG 15.3*n*.1, LAG 46A] A written sentence must begin with a capital letter and end with a full stop (.), a question mark (?) or an exclamation mark (!). [> LEG 1.2, LAG 46A*n*.1]

2 *Those given such suggestions had fewer complications than others after surgery and left hospital sooner.*
Only a full stop is needed to end the sentence. *Those (who were) given such suggestions* ... is a shortened defining relative clause, providing essential information, and therefore without commas. [> LEG 1.26, 1.62.3, LAG 7A*ns*.7c,8c]

3 *The experiment was set up at St **Thomas's** after doctors found patients could sometimes recall things said during operations.*
A full stop ends the sentence. Full stops are now optional after abbreviations like *St* (= Saint). [> LEG 3.27.2]

St Thomas's: we add *'s* to names ending in -*s*: *Charles's address*. However, we can sometimes use *'* or *'s* [> LEG 2.44.3]:
St Thomas' Hospital. Or:
St Thomas's Hospital.

4 *In a study at another hospital, many patients* ...
A longish adverbial at the beginning of a sentence is often marked off with a comma. [> LEG 7.19.2]

... who were told during an operation that they should touch their ears at a later interview with a doctor did so.
Who introduces a defining relative clause which provides essential information. Therefore the relative clause is not marked off by commas. They are *patients who were told* ... (not *patients, who were told* ...). The sentence ends with a full stop. [> LAG 3B*n*.2, 9B*n*.2] The original text is punctuated in the way shown above, but it would be improved with the addition of a comma after *ears* and a comma after *doctor*.

5 *The women, who had consented to the experiment, were played a 12-minute recording repeated six times.*
The sentence ends with a full stop. Commas mark off *who had consented to the experiment* because this is provided as extra information and is therefore non-defining [> LEG 1.26, LAG 3B*n*.2, 9B*n*.2]:

The women (= all 19 of them) were played a 12-minute recording. (Incidentally,) they had consented to the experiment.
→ *The women, who had consented to the experiment, were played* ...
Without commas, the above sentence would imply that some women didn't consent to the experiment and were not played the recording.

6 *It said, for example:*
Connecting words and phrases (adverbs) are marked off by commas, so we use a comma in front of *for example*. [> LEG 7.58, App 18.4, compare > LAG 56A*ns*.4–5] The colon after *it* formally introduces a quotation. [> LEG 15.3*n*.2]

'How quickly you recover from your operation depends upon you – the more you relax, the more comfortable you will be.'
How quickly you recover from your operation is the noun clause subject of *depends* and is not divided with a comma. [> LEG 1.24.2, compare > LAG 24A*n*.18, 29B, 50C] The single dash (–) serves in place of a colon (:) and introduces an explanation. [> LAG 8B*n*.2, 16A*n*.6] The construction with *the* ... *the* shows cause and effect: when one change is made, another follows. It is divided by a comma. [> LEG 6.27.3, LAG 41D]

GRAMMAR POINTS

B Articles [> LEG Chapter 3, LAG 8C, etc.]

1 (–) *Patients*: in general, so zero article with plural countable noun (*patients*). [> LEG 3.25–26]

2 (–) *surgery*: in general, so zero article with uncountable noun (*surgery*). [> LEG 3.25–26]

3 (–) *hypnotic suggestions*: in general, therefore zero article with (adjective +) plural countable noun (*hypnotic suggestions*). [> LEG 3.25–26]

4 *the operating table*: general statement with *the*; zero article with the plural, *operating tables*, or *an* (*an operating table*) would also be possible to make general statements. [> LEG 3.19.1 and compare > LEG 3.20.4]

5 (–) *doctors*: in general, therefore zero article with plural countable noun (*doctors*). [> LEG 3.25–26]

6 (–) *St Thomas's Hospital*: proper noun, therefore no article. [> LEG 2.13, 3.25, 3.31]

7 (–) *anaesthetic*: fixed prepositional phrase: *under anaesthetic*. [compare > LEG App 26.9]

8 (–) *fewer*: normal comparative (*fewer ... than*), so no article. [> LEG 6.24–27] We put only one determiner in front of a noun. [> LEG 3.4]

9 (–) *surgery*: in general, so zero article with uncountable noun (*surgery*). [> LEG 3.25–26]

10 (–) *hospital*: no article with nouns like *hospital* when we refer to their 'primary purpose'. [> LEG 3.28.3, App 22.5, LAG 45E]

11 *The experiment*: specific reference, therefore *the*. The experiment has already been described (in the preceding paragraph). [> LEG 3.18, 3.20.1]

12 (–) *doctors*: in general, therefore zero article with plural countable noun (*doctors*). [> LEG 3.25–26]

13 (–) *patients*: in general, so zero article with plural countable noun (*patients*). [> LEG 3.25–26]

14 (–) *things*: in general, therefore zero article with plural countable noun (*things*). [> LEG 3.25–26] *The things* would also have been possible if the writer had regarded *things* as specific (qualified by *said*: *the things said*). [> LEG 3.20.3]

15 (–) *operations*: in general, so zero article with plural countable noun (*operations*). [> LEG 3.25–26]

16 *a study*: first mention and unspecified, therefore *a*. [> LEG 3.3, 3.8, 3.10.2]

17 (–) *many patients*: in general, therefore zero article with plural countable noun (*patients*). [> LEG 3.25–26, LAG 31D] *Many* is simply added in front of the plural countable noun here. [> LEG 5.13] We normally use only one determiner in front of a noun. [> LEG 3.4, 2.52]

18 *an operation*: any operation, so *an* + countable noun . [> LEG 3.3, 3.8, 3.10.2]

19 *a later interview*: any interview, therefore *a* + countable noun . [> LEG 3.3, 3.8, 3.10.2]

20 *a doctor*: any doctor, not specified, therefore *a* + countable noun. [> LEG 3.3, 3.8, 3.10.2 and compare > LEG 3.9.3]

21 *The experiment*: specific reference (already mentioned at the beginning of the text and **11** above), therefore *the*. [> LEG 3.18, 3.20.1]

22 *a hysterectomy operation*: classifying what kind of operation, therefore *a* + countable noun. [> LEG 3.9.3] [For *a/an* with words beginning with *h* > LEG 3.7]

23 *The women*: already mentioned in the previous sentence, therefore *the*. [> LEG 3.18, 3.20.1]

24 *the experiment*: already mentioned, therefore *the*. [> LEG 3.18, 3.20.1]

25 *a 12-minute recording*: first mention, so *a* + countable noun . [> LEG 3.10.2] [For countable nouns like *a recording* > LEG 16.39.1]

26 (–) *Most of the tape*: *Most* means 'the largest number', or (as here) 'the greatest amount'. It is not a superlative. [> LEG 6.27.4] It is followed by *of* + *the* (specific reference). [> LEG 5.5.2]

27 *the operation*: already mentioned (**22** above), therefore *the*. [> LEG 3.18, 3.20.1]

28 - 29 *the more you relax, the more comfortable you will be*: We use this construction with adjectives or adverbs to show cause and effect. [> LEG 6.27.3, LAG 22A*n*.6, 41D]

C 'If' + 'could' and 'if' + 'could have' [> LEG 11.12, 14.10, 14.16–17, 14.19]

could, because we are referring to ability here.

We don't normally use *would* immediately after *if*, but we often use *could/could have* (ability).

Possible answers

1 Yes, if we could achieve this, we could save millions of pounds. (= we would be able to)

2 Yes, if we could anticipate what's going to happen, we could make a lot of money. (= we would be able to)

3 Yes, if we could have stopped, we could/might have avoided the accident. (= we would have been able to)

4 Yes, if we could meet tomorrow, we could discuss the matter. (= we would be able to)

5 Yes, if we could have taken an earlier train, we could/might have got to the meeting on time. (= we would have been able to)

6 Yes, if we could spend the night in Brighton, we wouldn't have to drive back to London tonight.

Spot of mutiny on the high Cs

IF you detect a look of refined pain on the faces of opera singers as their voices soar above the snow line, it is not because they are lesser vocal athletes than the great singers of the past. They are performing feats that Mozart and Verdi never demanded of their contemporaries. High Cs are getting higher and higher, and a boiling point of exasperation was reached last week when a starry cast of opera singers in Rome and Paris protested that the upward movement of orchestral concert pitches must stop or the voices of this generation would crack and the voices of the next be still-born.

'We are having to face the highest tuning in the history of music,' said Placido Domingo. 'And concert pitches continue to rise. We must fight back.'

Violin makers are also warning that Stradivariuses and other priceless old instruments, whose bass bars have already been reinforced to take the strain of the modern taste for a brighter, higher pitch, may not survive an even tenser tuning. When musicologists talk about the upward drift of concert pitch, it sounds as mysteriously inevitable as inflation. Pitch is based on the number of vibrations a second of a tuning fork to the A above middle C. Although pitch is imperceptible to most ears, there is a constant pressure in the expectancy of audiences towards the brighter sheen of faster vibrations.

An international agreement in 1939 set the number of vibrations at 440. In Germany and Vienna some pitches are now up in the higher forties and cases of 460 have been reported in the French Press. Marek Janowski, who is conducting Wagner's 'Ring' at Orange in Provence, says: 'My pitch is 442. Above that, it is true, there is a danger to both voices and instruments.' In Italy, two senators have introduced draft legislation to hold down concert pitch.

It sounds as if opera stars should instantly seek asylum in Britain where orchestras virtuously keep to 440. John Willan, the managing director of the London Philharmonic, says: 'Higher pitch is like shouting on the phone. It must put an additional strain on singers who have enough strain to contend with already.'

The Observer (BrE)

Sentence structure

A Which word(s) do the words in italics refer to? Check against the text and note them down.

1 *They* are performing feats that Mozart and Verdi ... (ll. 6–8) ....
2 *We* are having to face the highest tuning in the history of music ... (ll. 19–20) ....
3 ... *it* sounds as mysteriously inevitable as inflation. (ll. 32–33) ....
4 ... *who* is conducting Wagner's 'Ring' at Orange in Provence ... (ll. 47–49) ....
5 Above *that*, it is true, there is a danger to both voices ... (ll. 50–51) ....
6 *It* must put an additional strain on singers ... (ll. 61–62) ....

B Replace the words in italics, then refer to the text.

1 *When* you detect a look of refined pain on the faces of opera singers ..., it is ....
   not *that* they are lesser vocal athletes than the great singers of the past. (ll. 1–6) ....
2 Concert pitches continue *rising*. (ll. 21–22) ....
3 Violin makers are also warning that Stradivariuses, *the bass bars of which* ....
   have already been reinforced, may not survive a *still* tenser tuning. (ll. 24–30) ....
4 *While* pitch is imperceptible to most ears, ...
   a *constant pressure exists* in the expectancy of audiences. (ll. 36–39) ....
5 In Italy, two senators have introduced draft legislation ....
   because they want to hold down concert pitch. (ll. 51–54) ....
6 It sounds *as though* opera stars should instantly seek asylum in Britain ....
   in which orchestras virtuously keep to 440. (ll. 55–58) ....

Grammar points

C Supply *less* or *lesser*, then refer to the text. Give reasons for your choice.

    a *It is not because they are* .... *vocal athletes than the great singers of the past.* (ll. 4–6)

    b *It is not because they are* .... *athletic vocally than the great singers of the past.*

Supply *less* or *lesser*.

1 We just have to decide which is the ..*lesser*.. of two evils.

2 There's probably .... fossil fuel in the world than we think.

3 Fortunately, the situation has proved to be .... bad than we all thought.

4 Thomas Nashe is one of the .... known writers of the sixteenth century.

5 Your first suggestion is probably OK, but your second is .... acceptable.

6 There is still a lot of unemployment, though probably to a .... extent in the South.

7 For several years now we have had .... rain than we would wish.

8 She resigned when she had to. A .... person would have clung to power.

9 The .... able in this class are given extra tuition.

10 No one will think any the .... of you if you say what you believe.

D What does *are getting* mean in this sentence?
High Cs **are getting** *higher and higher.* (ll. 9–10) ....

Replace the verb *get* in these sentences. Do not use the same verb more than once.

1 Some species of butterfly *are getting* very rare.   *are becoming*

2 Your son *has* really *got* very tall in the last year. ....

3 The leaves *are getting* yellow early this year. ....

4 The soles of my shoes *are getting* very thin. ....

5 When did you realize you *were getting* ill? ....

6 These pears *are getting* a bit soft. ....

E What's the difference between the phrases in bold italics?

    a *A* **boiling point** *of exasperation was reached last week.* (ll. 10–12)

    b *You should sterilize those instruments in* **boiling water***.*

Suggest combinations with *-ing* in place of the words in italics.

1 What we need is a *pan we can use for frying.*   *a frying pan*

2 We sat by a *stream that was running.* ....

3 You ought to read a *book that is interesting.* ....

4 *Water* out of this tap isn't *fit for drinking.* ....

5 I need some *paper I can write on.* ....

6 I can hear the sound of *glass that is breaking.* ....

F Explain the meaning of the verb phrase in bold italics as accurately as you can.
We **are having to** *face the highest tuning in the history of music.* (ll. 19–20)

Suggest alternatives for the phrases in italics. Use the progressive forms of *have to*.

1 We owe so much money *we're obliged to* sell some of our furniture.   *we're having to*

2 Our car's getting old and *we'll be obliged to* replace it soon. ....

3 Business has been so bad, *we've been obliged to* close our shop early. ....

4 There were so many phone calls this morning, *I was obliged to* answer the phone every two minutes. ....

5 *Are you obliged to* wear warmer clothes than usual in this cold weather? ....

6 *Have you been obliged to* work longer hours ever since you changed jobs? ....

SENTENCE STRUCTURE

A Answers and commentary

The point of the exercise is to show how coherence is achieved in a piece of writing through constant back-reference especially by means of pronouns.

1 *They* refers to *opera singers*. [> LEG 4.5.7]

2 *We* refers to *opera singers* (including the speaker). [> LEG 4.5.6]

3 *... it* refers to *the upward drift of concert pitch*. [> LEG 4.5.5]

4 *... who* refers to *Marek Janowski*. We can't use *that* in place of *who* here because the *who*-clause is non-defining. [> LAG 5A*ns*.1–2] *That* is rarely possible in non-defining clauses. Compare:
   *He's the man **who's/that's** conducting Wagner's 'Ring'* (defining). [> LEG 1.26, 1.29, LAG 3B*n*.2]

5 *... that* refers to *442* (pitch). We often use *this/that* for back reference. [> LEG App 7.7, LAG 60A*n*.3]

6 *It* refers to *higher pitch*. [> LEG 4.5.5]

B Answers and commentary

1 ***If you detect a look of refined pain on the faces of opera singers, ...***
   If does not always mean 'provided that', introducing a condition (*If ... then*). [> LEG 14.1, LAG 9E] It can also mean 'on those occasions when' (as it does here). In such cases, the main clause (*it is not because they are lesser vocal athletes ...*) does not necessarily contain a modal (e.g. *will* or *would*). [> LEG 14.23.1]

   *... it is not **because** they are lesser vocal athletes than the great singers of the past.*
   It is not that provides a reason in the same way as *it is not because*. [For some uses of *because* > LEG 1.48, LAG 54A*n*.9].

2 ***Concert pitches continue to rise***.
   We use the *to*-infinitive or *-ing* form without a change of meaning after verbs like *begin, continue, start*. [> LEG 16.57, LAG 1E]

3 ***Violin makers are also warning that Stradivariuses, whose bass bars ...***
   Note how we can use *whose* to refer to things as well as to people. Native speakers often prefer to refer to things with *of which* rather than *whose* [> LEG 1.32, LAG 51A*n*.1 and compare > LAG 11B*n*.1]:
   *This is the house **the windows of which** were broken*.
   rather than:
   *This is the house **whose windows** were broken*.
   However, in this sentence, *whose* is probably less elaborate, and therefore preferable.

   *... **have already been reinforced, may not survive an even** tenser tuning.*
   Even is a focus adverb which goes before the word to be emphasized (*tenser*). [> LEG 7.54–55, compare > LAG 11A*n*.1b, 21B*n*.1b, 40A*n*.1, 50A*n*.1]

4 ***Although pitch is imperceptible to most ears, ...***
   Although and *while* introduce adverbial clauses of concession [> LEG 1.50, LAG 3A*n*.2, 20B*n*.1], though *while* also introduces adverbial clauses of time. [> LEG 1.45.1, 9.20.2–3, LAG 10A*n*.1]

   *... **there is a constant pressure** in the expectancy of audiences.*
   There is points to existence and can sometimes be replaced by the verb *exist*. [> LEG 10.19, 10.22, LAG 7B*n*.13, 14A*n*.2, 48B*n*.2b]

5 ***In Italy, two senators have introduced draft legislation to hold down concert pitch***.
   The infinitive of purpose generally conveys the idea of 'want to' [> LEG 16.12.1, LAG 7B*n*.11, 10B*n*.2, 15A*n*.3]:
   *I went to France. **I wanted to learn** French.*
   → *I went to France **to learn** French.*

6 ***It sounds as if opera stars should instantly seek asylum in Britain ...***
   As if and *as though* are interchangeable after *be, seem*, etc. to introduce adverbial clauses of manner. [> LEG 1.47.2, LAG 16D]

   *... **where** orchestras virtuously keep to 440.*
   Where introduces an adverbial clause of place. [> LEG 1.38.2, 1.46, LAG 19A*n*.3]

GRAMMAR POINTS

C 'Less' and 'lesser' [> LEG 6.24–26, 6.26n.4, 5.2n.2, 5.16, 5.6.2]

a *It is not because they are **lesser** vocal athletes than the great singers of the past.*

b *It is not because they are **less** athletic vocally than the great singers of the past.*
We use *less . . . than*, not *lesser*, in the comparative degree.

Less is an adverb meaning 'not so much'. We use *less*:
– with the positive form of one-syllable adjectives: *She's **less tall** than her brother.* (= shorter than)
– as the opposite of *more* to form the comparative with adjectives of two or more syllables: *less careful, less interesting.* [> LAG 32D]
– as a quantifier, usually with uncountable nouns: *less milk, less sugar, less time, less money* (. . . *than*). [> LAG 19D, 45F]

Lesser is not a true comparative and we cannot use *than* immediately after it. (Not *I have lesser than you.*)
We use *lesser* as an adjective to mean 'not so great' in fixed phrases like *to a lesser degree*. It goes in front of a noun:
   *Jonson and Shakespeare wrote plays, but Jonson is certainly **a lesser dramatist than** Shakespeare.*

1 lesser   2 less   3 less   4 lesser   5 less
6 lesser   7 less   8 lesser   9 less   10 less

D Process verbs related to 'be' and 'become': 'get', 'grow', etc. [> LEG 10.26]

*High Cs **are becoming** higher and higher.*

Process verbs (e.g. *become, come, fall, go, get, grow, run, turn, wear*) describe a change of state and we often use them in the progressive. [compare > LAG 51E]

1 are becoming
2 has grown
3 are turning
4 are wearing
5 were falling
6 are going

E Nouns formed with gerund + noun, compared with '-ing' form adjectives: 'boiling point' and 'boiling water' [> LEG 2.7, 2.11, 6.2–3, 6.14, 16.38, 16.39.3]

a A *boiling point* (which may be written with or without a hyphen) is a noun.

b In *boiling water*, *boiling* is an adjective (= water which is boiling) and no hyphen can be used.

Compound nouns formed with gerund + noun often mean 'something that is used for doing something':
a frying pan (= a pan that is used for frying)
Nouns like *frying pan*, *writing paper*, etc. are often fixed combinations.

When we use an *-ing* form as an adjective in front of a noun (*boiling water*), the resulting combination is not fixed (compare *boiling oil, boiling fat, boiling lava*, etc.). We never spell these combinations with a hyphen and we usually stress both parts in speech: 'boiling 'water.

1 a frying pan
2 a running stream
3 an interesting book
4 drinking water
5 writing paper
6 breaking glass

F 'Have to' as an ordinary verb used in the progressive: 'We're having to' [> LEG 11.4, 11. 47–48]

We are having to means: 'we are obliged to and we have no choice'.

We use *have to* to express 'inescapable obligation'. In this respect, *have to* is almost exactly the same as *must*. However, we can use *must* (= inescapable obligation) only to refer to the present or future:
   *I **must** see him **now**.* (present)
   *I **must** see him **tomorrow**.* (future)
We can use *have to* in place of *must* to refer to the present or future, or when it is impossible to use *must*: for example, in the progressive: e.g.
I am having to.
We can use *have to*, simple and progressive forms, in all tenses, just like any ordinary verb.

1 we're having to   4 I was having to
2 we'll be having to   5 Are you having to
3 we've been having to   6 Have you been having to

Homeopathy

ALTHOUGH during the past 200 years many people in Britain, Europe and America have felt better for consulting a homeopath, orthodox doctors are scornful. According to them, homeopathic remedies only work because the people who take them believe that they will work. Scientists are sceptical because they are convinced that the remedies do not contain enough of the substance to have any effect. But the idea of taking the smallest possible amount, or minimum dose, of the remedy is fundamental to homeopathy. The British Medical Association's 1986 report on alternative medicine rejected homeopathy out of hand - the theory of minimum dose was irrational.

Dr Samuel Hahnemann (1755-1843), the father of homeopathy, objected to the barbarous practices of allopathic medicine. 18th century doctors relied on blood letting and prescription of poisonous mixtures of drugs. Hahnemann noticed that substances which produced the same symptoms as a particular disease could be used to cure it. Hahnemann came across this phenomenon (first described by Hippocrates) when he experimented with cinchona or Peruvian bark, from which quinine is derived. Knowing that the drug was effective against malaria, he took it and found that he developed all the symptoms of malaria. Through extensive testing on himself, friends, and family, he drew the drug pictures of hundreds of substances and established the law of similars, or treatment of like by like.

Since the substances were often toxic, Hahnemann began to experiment with methods of diluting them to find the smallest possible dose - a cure without side effects. He diluted one part of the substance with 99 parts of a mixture of water and alcohol and gave the result 100 powerful shocks, or successions. He called this dilution the first centesimal potency.

In the London cholera epidemic of 1854, the death rate in orthodox London hospitals was 53.2 per cent, compared with a death rate in the London Homeopathic Hospital of 16.4 per cent. This striking difference may be accounted for by other aspects of homeopathy - its emphasis on diet, exercise, and fresh air and the patient's spiritual, emotional, and intellectual wellbeing. Whether the minimum dose is vindicated or not, patients will continue to seek relief from the ailments conventional medicine cannot cure. And they will continue to benefit from the time and attention they receive from homeopathic practitioners.

The Guardian (BrE)

Sentence structure

A Supply the connecting words, then check against the text.

Dr Samuel Hahnemann (1755–1843), the father of homeopathy, objected [1]............ the barbarous practices of allopathic medicine. 18th century doctors relied [2]............ blood letting and [3](*prescribe*) .... of poisonous mixtures of drugs. Hahnemann noticed [4]............ substances [5]............ produced the same symptoms as a particular disease could be used to cure it. Hahnemann came across this phenomenon (first described by Hippocrates) [6]............ he experimented with cinchona or Peruvian bark, from [7]............ quinine is derived. [8](*Know*) .... that the drug was effective against malaria, [9]............ took it and found that he developed all the symptoms of malaria. Through extensive testing on himself, friends, and family, [10]............ drew the drug pictures of hundreds of substances [11]............ established the law of similars, or treatment of like by like. [12]............ the substances were often toxic, Hahnemann began [13](*experiment*) .... with methods of diluting them [14](*find*) .... the smallest possible dose – a cure without side effects. He diluted one part of the substance with 99 parts of a mixture of water and alcohol [15]............ gave the result 100 powerful shocks, or successions. He called this dilution the first centesimal potency. In the London cholera epidemic of 1854, the death rate in orthodox London hospitals was 53.2 per cent, [16](*compare*) .... with a death rate in the London Homeopathic Hospital of 16.4 per cent. This striking difference may be accounted for by other aspects of homeopathy [17]............ its emphasis on diet, exercise, and fresh air and the patient's spiritual, emotional, and intellectual wellbeing. [18]............ the minimum dose is vindicated or not, patients will continue [19](*seek*) .... relief from the ailments conventional medicine cannot cure. (ll. 23–78)

Grammar points

B Comment on the verb phrase with *have* in **b** below.

  a *The remedies do not contain enough of the substance* **to effect** *a cure.*

  b *The remedies do not contain enough of the substance* **to have any effect.** (ll. 11–13)

....

Suggest combinations with *have* which you could use in place of the phrases in italics.

1 I think I've *been very lucky* really.   *had a lot of luck*
2 I *feel* that we're going to see a change in the political climate. ....
3 Joan *influences* her husband *a great deal*. ....
4 I think *it's* really *cheeky of him* to ask us for a loan. ....
5 We *discussed* the business *at length*, but came to no decisions. ....
6 *Can you suggest* what we should do? ....
7 I hope we're not going *to argue* about this. ....
8 I'd made up my mind, but at the last minute I *lost my confidence*. ....

C *Hahnemann* **came across** *this phenomenon when he experimented with cinchona.* (ll. 34–37)
Suggest a meaning for the verb in bold italics. What sort of verb is this?

....

Suggest meanings for the verbs in italics.

  1 The Robinsons have recently *come into* a lot of money.   *inherited*
  2 He wants to pay the bill himself, but I *won't hear of* it. ....
  3 Everything *turns on* clause 7b in the contract. ....
  4 I *gather from* our neighbours there's going to be a power cut. ....
  5 Frank's always *digging at* his wife in public. ....
  6 Two of my aunts are *descending on* us next weekend. ....
  7 I can't understand why you did that! What *came over* you? ....
  8 John keeps *falling for* every pretty girl he meets. ....
  9 I just hate the idea of *running into* debt. ....
10 Do you think we can *bank on* his support? ....
11 We're *toying with* the idea of retiring early. ....
12 I wish you'd stop *pecking at* your food! ....
13 I know the horse lost. How much did you *put on* it? ....
14 I can really *do without* sarcastic comments from you. ....
15 I wouldn't *touch on* that subject if I were you. ....
16 It's time we *saw about* that fence. ....
17 We're late and we really have to *step on it*. ....
18 I wish you'd stop *harping on* your past successes. ....
19 If you think I'm going to *fall for* that trick, you're mistaken. ....
20 We won't *go into* all that now. ....

D Why is *the* used once and omitted once in front of *London* here?
In the London *cholera epidemic of 1854, the death rate* **in orthodox London hospitals** *was*
53.2%. (ll. 62–65)

....

Supply *the* only where necessary.

1 ......*The*...... Chicago of the 1920s was a dangerous place.
2 .... Chicago rivals .... New York.
3 .... Chicago art galleries rival anything in Europe.
4 There's nothing in the world like .... Chicago meat industry.
5 Isn't .... Chicago on .... Lake Michigan?
6 Who conducts .... Chicago Symphony Orchestra?

SENTENCE STRUCTURE

A Answers and commentary

1 *to*: the verb *object* is followed by *to* (+ *-ing* where appropriate). *To* is a preposition, not an infinitive marker here. (Not **object to practise**) [> LEG 16.56, App 28]

2 *on*: *rely* is followed by *on*. [> LEG 8.27, App 28] Note the use of the *-ing* form (*blood letting*) after the preposition (*on*). [> LEG 16.50–56]

3 *prescription*: We could also use a gerund (*-ing* form) here [> LAG 60C]:
... *doctors relied on blood letting and the* **prescribing** *of poisonous mixtures* ...
Or we could use a verb:
... *doctors relied on blood letting and* **they prescribed** *poisonous mixtures* ...
The noun has been used instead:
...*they* **prescribed**
→ *(the)* **prescription** *of* [> LEG 16.33]

4 *that*: introduces a noun clause after the reporting verb *noticed*. The use of reporting verbs is not confined to indirect speech. [> LEG 1.23.2, App 45, LAG 4E, 14B]

5 *which*: relative pronoun subject of the relative clause. *Which* and *that* remain unchanged whether they refer to singular or plural:
These are the substances. They produced symptoms.
→ *These are the substances* **which/that** *produced symptoms.* [> LEG 1.31]

6 *when*: time conjunction introducing an adverbial clause of time (*when he experimented*). [> LEG 1.38.1, 1.45.1, LAG 6Bn.1]

7 *which*: relative pronoun object of the preposition *from*. We could say [> LEG 1.36]:
... *Peruvian bark,* **from which** *quinine is derived.* (formal word order)
... *Peruvian bark,* **which** *quinine is derived* **from**. (less formal)
In a defining clause we could say:
... *cinchona, the Peruvian bark quinine is derived* **from**. (colloquial word order with relative omitted)

8 *Knowing*: present participle construction in place of a clause of reason (*because/as he knew* ...). [> LEG 1.58.3, LAG 2Bn.2, 41An.1]
As he knew *that the drug was effective* ...
→ **Knowing** *that the drug was effective* ...

9 *he*: refers back to *Hahnemann* and serves as the subject of *knowing*. [> LEG 1.58.3, 4.5.3]

10 *he*: refers back to *Hahnemann*, the person who did the *testing*: *he tested ... and he drew* ... [> LEG 4.5.3]

11 *and*: introduces a co-ordinate clause. As the subject (*he*) is the same in all parts of the sentence, it isn't necessary to repeat it here [> LEG 1.17–20, LAG 4Bn.2, 13B]:
... **he drew** *the drug pictures of hundreds of substances* **and established** ...

12 *Since*: introduces an adverbial clause of reason and could be replaced by *as* or *because* [> LEG 1.48, LAG 30An.6, 34An.3]:
Since/As/Because *the substances were often toxic, Hahnemann began* ...
Compare the use of *since* as a time conjunction:
I haven't seen him **since he arrived**. [> LEG 1.45.1, 9.25.2, LAG 8Bn.1, 10Ans.2,4]

13 *to experiment* or *experimenting* can be used after *begin*, without affecting the meaning. [> LEG 16.57, LAG 1E, 23Bn.2]

14 *to find*: infinitive of purpose. We could also use *in order to find* or *so as to find*. [> LEG 16.12.1]

15 *and*: introduces a co-ordinate clause. As the subject (*he*) is the same in all parts of the sentence, it isn't necessary to repeat it here [> LEG 1.17–20, LAG 4Bn.2, 13B]:
... **he diluted** *one part of the substance ...* **and gave** *the result* ...

16 *compared*: past participle construction in place of a relative clause [> LEG 1.62.3, LAG 6Bn.4]:
... *the death rate was 53.2 per cent,* **(which can be) compared** *with ... 16.4 per cent.*
We could also use a prepositional phrase: *by comparison with, in comparison with, in comparison to*. [> LEG App 20.3]

17 a dash (–), a colon (:), or a phrase like *such as* would fit here because the author is introducing an explanatory list of examples. [> LAG 8Bn.2]

18 *Whether*: We can only use *whether* (Not **if**) to begin a sentence in this way. *Whether* introduces a noun clause in place of a direct question [> LAG 10E, 14B]:
Is the minimum dose vindicated?
→ **Whether** *the minimum dose is vindicated* ...
Or not is often used optionally with *whether* and in different positions [> LEG 1.24 1, 15.18n.7]:
Whether or not *the minimum dose is vindicated, patients will continue* ...
Whether *the minimum dose is vindicated* **or not**, *patients will continue* ... [> LAG 10An.4]

19 *to seek* or *seeking* can be used after *continue* without affecting the meaning. (See **13** above and [> LEG 16.57])

GRAMMAR POINTS

B Common combinations with 'have': 'have an effect' [> LEG 10.37–38, App 42, compare > LAG 41E]

In **b** a verb phrase with *have* (*to have an effect*) is used in place of the verb *to effect* in **a**.

Have combines with a great many nouns. These combinations may have straightforward meanings (*have a bath*) or idiomatic meanings (*have a brainwave*).

Possible answers
1 had a lot of luck
2 have a feeling
3 has a lot of influence on
4 he (really) has a cheek
5 had a long discussion about
6 Have you any suggestions about
7 have an argument
8 had cold feet

C Type 1 phrasal verbs (idiomatic meanings): 'come across (a phenomenon)' [> LEG 8.27, App 30, LAG 8D, 27C, 47E and compare > LAG 4D, 13C, 16B, 38D, 44D]

A possible meaning: *met. Come across* is a phrasal verb.

Some verbs followed by prepositions have obvious meanings [> LAG 8D]:

*He often **suffers from** colds.*

Others have little or no relation to their literal meanings:

*Has she **got over** her illness yet?* (= recovered from)

Possible answers
1 *come into* (= inherited)
2 *won't hear of* (= refuse to consider)
3 *turns on* (= depends on)
4 *gather from* (= understand from)
5 *digging at* (= finding fault with)
6 *descending on* (= visiting, perhaps inconveniently)
7 *came over* (= affected, happened to)
8 *falling for* (= falling in love with)
9 *running into* (= incurring)
10 *bank on* (= rely on)
11 *toying with* (= considering lightly)
12 *pecking at* (= eating without appetite)
13 *put on* (= bet on)
14 *do without* (= manage without)
15 *touch on* (= mention)
16 *saw about* (= arranged to do something about)
17 *step on it* (= hurry)
18 *harping on* (= always referring to)
19 *fall for* (= be deceived by)
20 *go into* (= consider or discuss)

D Use and omission of the article before proper nouns [> LEG 2.13.1, 3.20.3, 3.24–27, 3.31]

the London cholera epidemic:
London is a noun modifier and comes after *the*, specifying *which* cholera epidemic.

orthodox London hospitals:
London is a noun modifier after the adjective *orthodox*; *orthodox hospitals* in general, therefore no article.

We use no article (–) before proper nouns, which includes most place names [> LAG 8C, 30C, 44C, 54B]:

(–) ***London** is the capital of England.*
But if they are specified in some way as nouns, then it is possible to use definite and indefinite articles:

***The London** of the past was a foggy place.*
*We want **a London** which is bright and clean.*

1 The Chicago of the 1920s ... (specified, therefore *the*)
2 (–) Chicago ... (–) New York ... (proper nouns, no article)
3 (–) Chicago art galleries ... (art galleries in general; *Chicago* is a noun modifier; however *the* would also be possible if we were intending to specify)
4 ... the Chicago meat industry. (specified, therefore *the*)
5 (–) Chicago ... (–) Lake Michigan ... (proper nouns, no article)
6 ... The Chicago Symphony Orchestra? (*The* is part of the title: 'unique item' [> LEG 3.22])

Decision-thinking

DECISION-THINKING is not unlike poker -
it often matters not only what you
think, but also what others think you
think and what you think they think you
5 think. Interestingly poker, that most
subjective of games, has often been of
considerable interest to people who are, by
any standards, good thinkers.

The great mathematician John von
10 Neumann was, among his many other
accomplishments, one of the originators of
games theory. In particular, he showed that
all games fall into one of two classes: there are what he
called 'games of *perfect information*', games like chess
15 which are meant to involve no element of concealment,
bluff or luck - games where the players can, in principle,
discover the best move by the application of pure logic to
the available data. Then there are 'games of *imperfect
information*', like poker, in which it is impossible to know,
20 in advance, that one course of action is better than another.

One of the most dangerous illusions about business (or,
indeed, any activity involving human beings and human
institutions) is that it can be treated as a game of perfect
information. Quite the reverse. Business, politics, life itself
25 are games which we must normally play with very imperfect
information. Many a business decision involves odds that
would make a professional poker player shudder, for the
number and extent of the unknown and unknowable factors
are themselves often incalculable. But, as I have wished to
30 point out, few organizations find it comfortable or congenial
to admit that they are gambling, and many still prefer to
delude themselves that they are playing a sober, responsible
game of chess and are not engaged, as is often the case, in
a fling at the poker table.

The Professional Decision-Thinker
by Ben Heirs with Peter Farrell *(BrE)*

Sentence structure

A Sometimes an unnecessary word has been added. Sometimes a necessary word has been
omitted. Delete the unnecessary words or supply the necessary ones. Some lines need no
change at all. Then refer to the text.

Decision-thinking is not poker – it often matters not only what	1 ....
you think, but also what others think you think .... . Interestingly poker,	2 ....
that most subjective of games, has often been of considerable interest	3 ....
to people who they are, by any standards, good thinkers.	4 ....
The great mathematician John von Neumann, among his many other	5 ....
accomplishments, one of the originators of games theory. Particular,	6 ....
he showed that all games fall into one of two classes: there are	7 ....
what he was called 'games of *perfect information*', games like chess	8 ....
which are meant to involve no any element of concealment, bluff or	9 ....
luck – games where the players can, in principle, discover the best	10 ....
move by the application pure logic to the available data.	11 ....
Then there are 'games of *imperfect information*', like poker, which	12 ....
it is impossible to know, in advance, that one course of action is	13 ....
better than another.	14 ....
One of the most dangerous illusions about business (indeed,	15 ....
any activity involving in human beings and human institutions) is	16 ....
that it can be treated a game of perfect information.	17 ....
Quite the reverse. Business, politics, life itself are games	18 ....
which we must normally to play with very imperfect information.	19 ....
Many business decision involves odds that would make a	20 ....
professional poker player to shudder, for the number and extent	21 ....
of the unknown and unknowable factors are themselves often	22 ....
incalculable. (ll. 1–29)	23 ....

Grammar points

B Comment on the emphasis of the phrases in italics.

  a *Decision-thinking is **like poker**.*
  b *Decision-thinking is **not unlike poker**.* (l. 1)

Suggest phrases with *not* which will replace the words or phrases in italics.

1 *Very little* is happening in our office at the moment.   *Not much*
2 *Very few* people know about my interest in butterflies.
3 There's just *insufficient* evidence to proceed with charges.
4 This is *very similar* to your earlier proposal.
5 Money is *one of the greatest* of his worries.
6 We've had *no offers* for our house.

C Can we use *has been* in sentence **b**? Why/Why not?

  a *Poker **has** often **been** of considerable interest to people who are good thinkers.* (ll. 5–8)
  b *Poker **was** of considerable interest to von Neumann when he developed his games theory.*

Supply *was/were* or *have/has been*.

1 I   *was*   self-employed for over a year, but I'm glad to be employed again.
2 We   in the Sudan for a year before we moved to Egypt.
3 It   very cold for the past few days, but I expect the weather will improve.
4 What   the weather like when you were in Paris last week?
5 You   a teacher so you should have more understanding of children with problems.
6 When I   a teacher I enjoyed working with children who had learning difficulties.

D What could we use in place of *no* in these sentences?

  a *There are games like chess which are meant to involve **no** element of concealment.* (ll. 13–15)
  b *He's **no** expert on finance, but that never prevents him from expressing his opinion.*

Suggest alternative constructions to *no* in these sentences.

1 We can't act because we've received no information.   *haven't received any*
2 You can't expect him to believe that. He's no fool.
3 For years, we had no freedom to express our political opinions.
4 Don't bother to ask her. She has no ideas at all.
5 There's no idea that hasn't already been thought of.
6 You keep referring to her as a lady, but she's no lady.

E What's wrong with this sentence? Correct it, then rewrite it in the passive.
  These odds would make a professional poker player to shudder. (compare ll. 26–27)

Rewrite these sentences using suitable forms of *make*.

1 When we were children, mother obliged us to take a bath every day.
  When we were children, mother made us take a bath every day.
2 We were obliged to clean up the mess we had made.

3 The prisoners-of-war were obliged to build roads across the Burmese jungle.

4 The film was so moving, it caused the audience to weep.

5 Competition from rival firms caused us to try even harder.

SENTENCE STRUCTURE

A Answers and commentary

1 *not **unlike***: This means it is *like* poker: two negatives make a positive. We sometimes use *not* in this way to emphasize the opposite [> LEG 5.8, LAG 25B]:

> She's had **not a few** proposals of marriage in her time. (= a lot)

2–3 These lines are correct.

4 ... *who ~~they~~ are, by any standards, good thinkers*:

> They are people. **They** are good thinkers.
> → They are people **who** are good thinkers.

Who is the subject relative pronoun of the relative clause; we do not have two subjects. (Not *who they*) [> LEG 1.29, LAG 2Bn.2]

5 *The great mathematician John von Neumann **was**, among his many ...*: The phrase *among his many other accomplishments* is not in apposition with *John von Neumann* [> LEG 1.39]; the verb *was* is missing.

6 We have to say **In** particular, or *Particularly*, to introduce the sentence. This connecting adverb itemizes some details of von Neumann's theory. [> LEG 7.57–58, Apps 17, 18, LAG 56A]

7 This line is correct.

8 ... *what he ~~was~~ called 'games of perfect information'*. Compare:

> There are games. He called them 'games of perfect information'.
> → There are **what** he called ...

What (= that which) introduces a noun clause complement after *there are*. [> LEG 1.24.2, LAG 42D]

9 ... *which are meant to involve no ~~any~~ element of concealment*. We can say:

> ... *which **are not** meant to involve **any** element of concealment.*
> Or: ... *which **are** meant to involve **no** element of concealment.* [> LEG 5.11, 13.9–10, LAG 14G, 25D, 49G]

10 This line is correct.

11 ... *by the **application of** pure logic*. We can say:

> *They can **apply** pure logic.* (using a verb)
> or: *It's the **application of** pure logic.* (using a noun) [> LEG 16.33] We can also say:
> ... *by **applying** pure logic.* [> LEG 13.40.4, 16.51, App 25.17, LAG 60C]

12 ... *in which it is impossible to know, in advance, ...* Compare:

> **Poker** is a game. **It** is easy to learn.
> → Poker is a game **which** is easy to learn.

In the text, *which* is the object of the preposition *in*. [> LEG 1.36] It is not a relative pronoun subject. [> LEG 1.31, LAG 20An.1]

13–14 These lines are correct.

15 *(... **or**, indeed,) ...*: *Or* introduces an afterthought here. [> LEG 1.18, LAG 2Bn.1]

16 *(... any activity **involving** ~~in~~ human beings and human institutions)*: *Involved* can be followed by *in* (or *with*) [compare > LAG 43An.18]:

> *I don't want to get **involved in** this case.* [For other examples of adjective + preposition > LEG App 27, LAG 1D, 9D, 52D].

Involving is followed by an object: *There have been several crashes **involving coaches***. [> LAG 20D]

17 ... *that it can be treated **as** a game of ...*: *As* = 'in the capacity of' here. Compare:

> He works **as** a lawyer.
> Who's used this knife **as** a screwdriver?

[> LEG App 25.25, LAG 12Bn.18]

18 This line is correct. (It isn't always necessary to use *and* before the last item in a list, especially in conversational style.) [compare > LEG 6.21.2, LAG 4Bn.3, 5An.2]

19 ... *which we **must** normally ~~to~~ **play** with very imperfect information*: We do not use a *to*-infinitive after modal verbs. [> LEG 11.6.1n.2, 16.3]

20 *Many a business decision ...*: We can say:

> *Many business decisions **involve** ...* [> LEG 5.13, LAG 2F, 31D]

Or: *Many a business decision **involves** ...* *Many a* + singular noun is not generally interchangeable with *many* + plural noun. *Many a* is often used for stylistic effect in the sense of 'not a few'. [> LAG 25B]

21 ... *would **make** a professional poker player ~~to~~ shudder ...*

Make (= compel, cause to) is followed by a bare infinitive in the active voice. [> LEG 16.4.3, LAG 25E]

22–23 These lines are correct.

GRAMMAR POINTS

B 'Not' to emphasize the opposite: 'not unlike'
[> LEG 5.8, 5.13, 13.13]

a *Decision-thinking is **like poker**:* a straightforward comparison with the preposition *like* + object. [> LEG App 25.25, LAG 13An.1, 47An.4]

b *Decision-thinking is **not unlike poker**: not unlike* emphasizes the similarity. (= it is very much like)

This use of *not* makes a statement stronger, by drawing attention to whatever is asserted. We often use it with quantifiers like *enough*, *every*, *a few*, *a little*, *many*, *much*, etc. [> LAG 2F, 21C, 31D]

Possible answers

1 Not much
2 Not many
3 not enough
4 not unlike
5 not the least
6 not one offer

C 'Have/has been' and 'was/were' [> LEG 10.8–9, 10.12–13]

No, we can't use *has been* in **b**. In **b** the action is completed [> LEG 9.17–18] and the simple past is required.

Have/has been + noun or adjective is the present perfect of the verb *be* used as a full verb. It follows the normal rules for the present perfect, describing states, moods, etc. continuing up till now. [> LEG 9.25, compare > LAG 19C, 56C]

Was/were + noun or adjective is the simple past of the verb *be* used as a full verb. It describes states, moods, etc. which no longer apply and we use it when there is a past time reference, like *when*:

*I **was** lazy **when** I was a schoolboy.* (simple past: perhaps I'm not lazy now)

*I **have been** lazy all my life.* (present perfect: I still am)

1 was   2 were   3 has been   4 was
5 have been or were, depending on speaker's viewpoint   6 was

D 'Not any' and 'not a/an' in place of 'no': 'he's no expert' [compare > LAG 14G, > LEG 5.11, 13.10, LAG 49G, 53D]

a *... which aren't meant to involve **any** element of concealment ...*

b *He isn't an expert ...*

Not ... any replaces *no* when the reference is to:
- plural countable nouns:

*There **are no bananas** in the supermarket.*
→ *There **aren't any bananas** in the supermarket.*

- uncountable nouns:

*There **is no milk** in the fridge.*
→ *There **isn't any milk** in the fridge.*

This point is generally well-known. However, it is less well-known that *no* will replace *not a/an* when the reference is to a countable noun. The use of *no* with nouns describing people is not the exact equivalent of *not a/an* in meaning, because it often implies praise (*he's no liar*) or criticism:

*I could tell at a glance he **was no lawyer**.*
→ *I could tell at a glance he **wasn't a lawyer**.*

*There **was no garage** in sight.*
→ *There **wasn't a garage** in sight.*

1 haven't received any information
2 he isn't a fool
3 didn't have any freedom
4 She hasn't any ideas
5 There isn't an idea
6 she isn't a lady

E 'Make' (= compel) + bare infinitive: 'it makes him shudder' [> LEG 16.4.3]

*These odds **would make** a professional poker player ~~to~~ **shudder**.*

*A professional poker player **would be made to shudder** (by these odds).*

We use the bare infinitive after *make* (= compel) in the active:

*He **made** us **work** hard.* (Not **to work**)

We use the *to*-infinitive after *make* (= compel) in the passive:

*We **were made to work** hard.*

1 When we were children, mother made us take a bath every day.
2 We were made to clean up the mess we had made.
3 The prisoners-of-war were made to build roads across the Burmese jungle.
4 The film was so moving, it made the audience weep.
5 Competition from rival firms made us try even harder.

Pigeons 'not so bird-brained'

exhibiting four emotions - happiness, anger, surprise and disgust,' said Prof Edward Wasserman of the University of Iowa.

In each experiment, a bird was shown the picture, and was taught to reply by pecking at one of four keys. 'After being rewarded with pinches of grain for each correct answer, they all learned to identify the person and the emotion correctly,' he said. If they made a wrong identification, they were 'punished' by not being given the grain. 'To make it more difficult, the faces were photographed without any special distinguishing features such as clothing or jewellery.'

The people pictured were all about the same age; two men and two women, one of each fair-haired, the other dark-haired. Their slightly exaggerated expressions showed happiness, with broad grins; anger, with furious, threatening scowls; surprise, with wide open mouths and staring eyes, and disgust, with twisted lips and screwed-up eyes. After each bird had been shown an expression on one face, it was shown another photograph and 'asked' whether the new face had the same expression. Once the birds had recognized the expressions, they never mistook them.

'The experiments show that pigeons are more intelligent than any animals except for dogs and primates,' Prof Wasserman said. 'We suspected this since, in the countryside, they can tell the difference between a man with a shotgun and a man carrying a walking stick. They showed the same amount of intelligence as human babies, who are not born with the ability to recognize the expressions on people's faces, but have to be taught it. Charles Darwin speculated in the last century that some birds might have this ability, but it's amazing to have it proved.'

The Daily Telegraph (BrE)

PIGEONS can recognize individual human faces and the expressions on them, showing that they are far more intelligent than hitherto suspected, a psychologist said yesterday. 'We showed the birds black-and-white photographs of four people, each

Sentence structure

A Join these sentences making any necessary changes. Then refer to the text.

1 Pigeons can recognize individual human faces and the expressions on them. This shows that they are far more intelligent than hitherto suspected. A psychologist said this yesterday. (ll. 1–5)

....

....

2 They were rewarded with pinches of grain for each correct answer. They all learned to identify the person and the emotion correctly. (ll. 15–18)

....

....

3 Each bird was shown an expression on one face. It was shown another photograph. It was 'asked' whether the new face had the same expression. (ll. 35–39)

....

....

4 The birds recognized the expressions. They never mistook them. (ll. 40–42)

....

B One word or phrase is in the wrong position in each of these sentences. Show with an arrow where the wrongly-placed word(s) should be. Then check against the text.

1 If they made a wrong identification, they were 'punished' by being not given the grain. (ll. 19–21)

2 To make it more difficult, were the faces photographed without any special distinguishing features such as clothing or jewellery. (ll. 21–25)

Grammar points

C Supply the right forms of the verbs in brackets, then refer to the text. (ll. 12–25) Variations are possible. In each case, give your reason for the form you have chosen.

In each experiment, a bird ¹(*show*) .... the picture,
and ²(*teach*) .... to reply by pecking at one of four keys.
'After ³(*reward*) .... with pinches of grain for each
correct answer, they all ⁴(*learn*) .... to identify the person and
the emotion correctly,' he ⁵(*say*) ....
If they ⁶(*make*) .... a wrong identification, they
⁷('*punish*') ....
by ⁸(*not give*) .... the grain.
'To make it more difficult, the faces ⁹(*photograph*) ....
without any special distinguishing features such as clothing or jewellery.'

D Supply the plural forms of the nouns in brackets only where necessary. Give a reason for each of your decisions. Write /s/ or /z/ to show pronunciation of the plural where applicable.

The ¹(*people*) .... pictured were all about the same age;
two ²(*man*) ....
and two ³(*woman*) ...., one of each fair-haired, the other
dark-haired. Their slightly exaggerated ⁴(*expression*) ....
showed ⁵(*happiness*) ...., with broad
⁶(*grin*) ....; anger, with furious, threatening
⁷(*scowl*) ....; surprise, with wide open
⁸(*mouth*) .... and staring
⁹(*eye*) ...., and disgust, with twisted
¹⁰(*lip*) .... and screwed-up eyes. (ll. 26–35)

E Would you supply *say* or *tell* here? Why?
They can .... the difference between a man with a shotgun and ... . (ll. 48–50)

Supply correct forms of *say* or *tell*.

1 The children always like me to ....*tell*.... them a story before they go to sleep.
2 At the end of the meeting the chairman stood up to .... a few words.
3 Jimmy mentions everyone in the family whenever he .... his prayers.
4 George Washington told his father that he could never .... a lie.
5 I don't know how you distinguish between those two. I just can't .... them apart.
6 When in doubt, it's best to .... nothing.

F What's the difference in meaning between the phrases in bold italics? (ll. 56–59)

a *Darwin speculated that some birds might have this ability, but it's amazing **to have proved** it.*
b *Darwin speculated that some birds might have this ability, but it's amazing **to have it proved**.*

Supply the right forms of the verbs in brackets using suitable forms of *have* where necessary.

1 They claim that they (*test it*) *have had it tested* by experts.
2 I was curious about this new car and I was invited (*test it*).................... myself.
3 If you want to get a job done properly, it's best (*do it*).................... yourself.
4 We couldn't possibly tackle this job ourselves, so we (*do it*).................... by a local firm.
5 She shows such talent for swimming that her father (*train her*).................... by professionals.
6 Surely you (*explain the process*).................... to you before?
7 I don't think you've quite understood. I'll just (*explain the process*).................... to you again.

113

SENTENCE STRUCTURE

A Answers and commentary

Suggestions for joining these sentences were not provided in the exercise, so there are many possible answers. The commentary is based on the way the sentences have been joined in the text.

1 *Pigeons can recognize individual human faces and the expressions on them, **showing** that they* ...
The present participle construction is used in place of *which shows* or *and this shows*. [> LEG 1.42, 1.58, LAG 4Bn.3, 9An.1]

... *are far more intelligent than hitherto suspected, **a psychologist said yesterday***.
This is reported speech, so no quotation marks are used. [> LEG 15.18n.1, LAG 4E, and compare > 46A]
We can use noun + reporting verb (***a psychologist said** yesterday*) or reporting verb + noun (***said a psychologist** yesterday*, the latter use being particularly common in journalism). [> LEG 15.3n.4, App 45.1, LAG 46An.2]
The subject + reporting verb can come after what is reported as well as at the beginning.

2 ***After being** rewarded with pinches of grain for each correct answer, they all learned to identify the person and the emotion correctly.*
We can use the present participle construction in place of an adverbial clause of time [> LEG 1.58.2, 1.62.2, LAG 3Bn.1, 6C]:
***After they were rewarded** with pinches of grain, they* ...
→***After being rewarded*** ...
The construction is in the passive. [> LEG 12.3n.8 and compare > LEG 16.51]

3 ***After each bird had been shown** an expression on one face, it was shown another photograph* ...
After introduces an adverbial clause of time. [> LEG 1.45.1] The use of the past perfect here emphasizes that one action took place before another (first each bird was shown an expression, then it was shown another photograph). However, the use of the past perfect is not obligatory here. [> LEG 9.30, compare > LAG 33B, 41B, 52B]

... ***and** 'asked' whether the new face had the same expression.*
When the subject is the same in all parts of the sentence (*it*), it is usual not to repeat it after *and*. [> LEG 1.20, LAG 4Bn.2, 13B]

4 ***Once the birds had recognized the expressions**, they never mistook them.*
Once introduces an adverbial clause of time. Again (compare **3** above) the use of the past perfect is optional here. [> LEG 1.45.1, 9.30, compare > LAG 40An.2]

B Answers and commentary

1 *If they made a wrong identification, they were 'punished' by **not being** given the grain.* (Not **by being not given**)
Not goes before *-ing*. [> LEG 16.40, LAG 6C, 20Bn.1, and compare > LAG 53An.1]

2 *To make it more difficult, **the faces were photographed** without any special distinguishing features* ... (Not **were photographed the faces**)
The basic word order in a sentence that is not a question or a command is:
Subject | Verb | Object | Adverbials
[> LEG 1.3, LAG 4A]:
The faces (subject) *were photographed* (verb) ...
Inversion is only possible after a negative adverb, for example:
***The faces were** seldom photographed* ...
***Seldom were the faces** photographed* ....
[> LEG 7.59.3, LAG 30B, 33C, 49C]

GRAMMAR POINTS

C Verbs and verb tenses and the passive [> LEG Chapters 9 and 12, regular and irregular verbs > Apps 39–40, LAG 8E, 19C, 28C, etc.]

The passive dominates here as the language of scientific experiment.

1 *was shown*: Simple past, because the event is finished. [> LEG 9.17.1, 12.1–4]

2 *was taught*: Simple past, because the event is finished. [> LEG 9.17.1, 12.1–4]

3 *being rewarded*: -ing form construction in place of an adverbial clause of time. [> LEG 1.62.2, 12.3n.8] Alternatively, we could have:
　After they were rewarded ...,
　Or: *After they had been rewarded ...*, [> LEG 1.45.1, 9.17.1, 9.29–30, 12.1–4, LAG 36An.2]

4 *learned* (also spelt *learnt* [> LEG 9.14.1]): Simple past (active), because the event is finished. [> LEG 9.17.1, 12.1–4]

5 *said*: Simple past (active), because the event is finished. [> LEG 9.17.1, 12.1–4] *Said* reports direct speech here. [> LEG 15.1–3, LAG 46A]

6 *made*: Simple past (active), because the event is finished. [> LEG 9.17.1, 12.1–4]

7 *were 'punished'*: Simple past, because the event is finished. [> LEG 9.17.1, 12.1–4] *If* is not conditional in this sentence, but means 'on those occasions when'. [> LEG 14.23.1]

8 *not being given*: Participle construction after *by* (+ *-ing*). [> LEG 13.40.4, 16.51, App 25.17] Note the position of *not* before *being*. [> LEG 16.40, LAG 26Bn.1]

9 *were photographed*: Simple past, because the event is finished. [> LEG 9.17.1, 12.1–4]

D Number (singular and plural of nouns) [> LEG 2.20–38, LAG 34F, 39C]

1 *people*: collective noun with no plural form, but used with a plural verb (*the people were*). [> LEG 2.29, LAG 36E]

2 *men*: irregular plural. [> LEG 2.26]

3 *women*: irregular plural. [> LEG 2.26]

4 *expressions*: regular plural formation [> LEG 2.20]; pronunciation /z/. [> LEG 2.21]

5 *happiness*: uncountable (abstract) noun, no plural. [> LEG 2.14.2, 2.15, LAG 34F]

6 *grins*: regular plural formation [> LEG 2.20]; pronunciation /z/. [> LEG 2.21]

7 *scowls*: regular plural formation [> LEG 2.20]; pronunciation /z/. [> LEG 2.21].

8 *mouths*: regular plural formation [> LEG 2.20]; irregular pronunciation /z/. [> LEG 2.22]

9 *eyes*: regular plural formation [> LEG 2.20]; pronunciation /aɪz/. [> LEG 2.21]

10 *lips*: regular plural formation [> LEG 2.20]; pronunciation /s/. [> LEG 2.21]

E Expressions with 'say' and 'tell': 'tell the difference' [> LEG 15.7.2]
tell the difference; *tell the difference* is a fixed expression.

In addition to their primary uses as reporting verbs [> LEG 15.5–9], *say* and *tell* have secondary uses and can be used in fixed expressions like *say a few words* and *tell the difference*. [> LEG 15.7.2]

1 tell them a story
2 say a few words
3 says his prayers
4 tell a lie
5 tell them apart
6 say nothing

F The causative with 'have': 'have something done' [> LEG 12.10–12, compare > LAG 3E]

a *it's amazing to have proved it*: this can suggest that we proved it ourselves: adjective + *to*. [> LEG 16.30, LAG 1C]

b *it's amazing to have it proved*: this means that someone or something else proved it for us.

We use:
– the **active** to show we are doing, have done, etc. something ourselves:
　My theory is correct and I'll prove it to you.
(= I'll prove it myself)
– the **passive** to show that we may not know or may not need to name who is doing an action:
　It was proved centuries ago that you can sail round the earth.
– the **causative** (*have* + object + past participle) to stress the fact that we're 'causing' someone else to perform a service for us:
　We've had these photographs taken by a professional photographer.

1 they have had it tested
2 to test it
3 to do it
4 we had it done
5 her father is having her trained
6 you have had the process explained to you
7 explain the process to you

First impressions

WHEN I first met Nina, I disliked her
at once. She was wearing skintight
pedal pushers, a flashy, floppy top,
and sneakers with no socks - bizarrely
5 inappropriate even at our very informal
company. Soon, Nina was doggedly pumping
me for information about the new department
I was running, where she hoped to get a
permanent job. *Not a chance*, I thought. *Not if I*
10 *have anything to say about it.*

However, I didn't. Within a few days she was 'trying out' for
me. I gave her a moderately difficult, uninteresting, and
unimportant project that I didn't need for months. It took that
long for her successor to untangle the mess she had made out of it.
15 Although I couldn't have predicted *exactly* what Nina would do,
in three minutes flat I had assessed her as someone who could not
be relied upon to get a job done.

We all make snap judgments about strangers. Within seconds
after we meet someone, we take in a host of details and draw
20 rather large conclusions from them. We may decide in an instant
whether it is someone's nature to be warm or cold, friendly or
hostile, anxious or calm, happy or troubled. Unconsciously, we
often ask and quickly answer certain questions: *Will I enjoy talking
to him at this party? Will she make an interesting friend? Will he/she*
25 *make a good boss/sales manager/secretary/spouse/lover - for me?* If we
get to know the person better, we may change our minds. But we
may not have the chance.

From Nina's inappropriate dress and aggressive behavior
toward me, I'd decided she was pushy, insensitive, and had poor
30 judgment. I also had a lot of vague impressions I couldn't explain.
It was as if a warning bell went off in my head. Its message: this
person was not to be trusted; her behavior would be unpredictable;
she was motivated by an idiosyncratic agenda of her own that I
would never understand.

35 I was using a combination of observation, inference and
intuition.

New Woman (AmE)

Sentence structure

A Three of these sentences contain a wrong word. Replace the wrong word, where necessary, and say why you have done so. Then check against the text.

1 When I first met Nina, I disliked her at once. (ll. 1–2)

2 During a few days she was 'trying out' for me. (ll. 11–12)

3 Although I couldn't have predicted *exactly* what Nina would do, in three minutes flat I had assessed her as someone whom could not be relied upon to get a job done. (ll. 15–17)

4 It was like a warning bell went off in my head. (l. 31)

B Join these notes to make sentences. Then check against the text.

1 Soon, Nina – doggedly pumping me – information – new department – I – running – she hoped – get a permanent job (ll. 6–9)

2 It took that long – successor – untangle – mess – she – made – it (ll. 13–14)

3 From Nina's inappropriate dress – aggressive behavior – me, I – decided – she – pushy, insensitive – poor judgement (ll. 28–30)

Grammar points

C Rewrite this sentence putting the phrase in bold italics into the passive. What do you notice?

*I had assessed her as someone **I could not rely upon** to get a job done.* (ll. 16–17)

....

....

Respond to these statements beginning with *Yes* and using the passive.

1 Have you dealt with the problem? *Yes, the problem's been dealt with.*
2 Has anyone paid for these goods? ....
3 Have we kept to the rules? ....
4 Did anyone turn off all the lights? ....
5 Did someone give out the exercise books? ....
6 Did you write down what he said? ....
7 Is anyone seeing to my supper? ....
8 Have they approved of the plan? ....
9 Is anyone looking after the children? ....
10 Have you filed away the documents? ....

D What's the difference in emphasis between the phrases in bold italics?

a *When will you **have the job done**?* ....
b *When will you **get the job done**?* (compare ll. 16–17) ....

Respond to these statements by beginning with the words in brackets and following on with *get*.

1 My hair really needs cutting. (Why don't) *Why don't you get it cut?*
2 I thought no one would repair your car. (I finally) ....
3 Surely his book's unpublishable! (No, he) ....
4 This lock needs fixing. (Why don't) ....
5 My will needs changing. (Yes, you should) ....
6 This car needs servicing. (Yes, I must) ....

E Comment on the different uses of *better* in these two sentences:

a *If we get to know the person **better**, we may change our minds.* (ll. 25–26) ....
b *After all I've been through, I'm sure I'm now a **better** person.* ....

Complete these statements.

1 I'd like to get to know him better. I don't know him very *well.*
2 I think my golf is getting better, but I have to say it's never been very ....
3 Jane's beginning to feel better. She hasn't been .... for some time now.
4 I'm better-placed for promotion now, though I was quite .... before.
5 This reference is better than the last one, which wasn't very .... at all.
6 The situation is a great deal better now. It hasn't been very .... for a long time now.
7 What do you mean my cooking tastes better? Surely it's always tasted very ....
8 What do you mean he seems better? He seemed very .... when I last saw him.

F Use three words to complete this sentence, then describe the form you have used.

You can't trust this person. This person is not .... (ll. 31–32)

....

Respond to these sentences.

1 You mustn't take this medicine before meals. *It's not to be taken.*
2 We can't repeat this offer. ....
3 Please don't criticize him. ....
4 Don't open this before Christmas. ....
5 No one must read these letters. ....
6 Don't let the dogs out! ....

SENTENCE STRUCTURE

A Answers and commentary

Numbers **2**, **3** and **4** contain a wrong word.

1 This sentence is correct.

2 **Within** *a few days she was 'trying out' for me.* (Not **During**)
Within means 'before the end of a stated period of time' and is correct here. [> LEG 8.14, LAG 5C]
During, followed by a noun, can refer to a whole period of time [> LEG 7.35, LAG 10An.1, 21An.3, 35Bn.15]:
　During the week, *she was 'trying out' for me.* (Not **Within**)

3 *... I had assessed her as someone* **who** *could not be relied upon ...* (Not **whom**)
Who is the subject of the clause, not the object of the preposition *upon*. [> LEG 1.29, LAG 12An.12, 40An.3] Compare:
　I had assessed her. **She** *could not be relied upon.*
　→ *I had assessed her as someone* **who** *could not be relied upon.*
　I had assessed her. I couldn't rely upon **her***.*
　→ *I had assessed her as someone* (**whom**) *I couldn't rely upon.*
In the second sentence *whom* is the relative pronoun object of *upon* and could be omitted. [> LEG 1.36, LAG 20An.1, 24An.7]

4 *It was* **as if** *a warning bell went off in my head.* (Not **like**)
As if introduces an adverbial clause of manner and is the right conjunction here. [> LEG 1.47.2, LAG 16D, 21An.2, 23Bn.6]
Like is a preposition and is followed by a noun or pronoun [> LEG App 25.25, LAG 13An.1, 47An.4, 60An.13]:
　There's no business **like show business***.*
Like (= as/as if) is often used as a conjunction to introduce a clause, especially in informal American English. This use has not gained full acceptance in British English:
　She's spending money **like there was** *no tomorrow.* (= as if)

B Answers and commentary

1 *Soon, Nina was doggedly pumping me for information about the new department ...*
Here the past progressive describes a situation that was in progress at some time in the past. [> LEG 9.20.1, LAG 8En.1, 12An.16, 35C, 44An.4b]
About means 'concerning'. [> LEG App 25.1]
... about the new department I was running, ...
I was running is a relative clause in which *which/that* has been deleted [> LEG 1.34, LAG 6Bn.1, 22An.2]:
　This is the **department***. I was running* **it***.*
　→ *This is the department* (**which/that**) *I was running.*
... where she hoped to get a permanent job.
Where (= in which) introduces an adverbial clause of place. [> LEG 1.38.2, 1.46, LAG 19An.3, 31Bn.3; for *hope to* > LEG 16.12.3, 16.23, LAG 9An.4, 40C]

2 *It took that long for her successor to untangle the mess she had made out of it.*
The past perfect (*she* **had made** *out of it*) is obligatory here because it refers to an earlier period and suggests that Nina was dismissed (or left) and was replaced by someone else. [> LEG 9.29.1, 9.30; LAG 33B, 37Bn.3, 41B, 52B. For *It takes/took* > LEG 16.21, LAG 60An.5]

3 *From Nina's inappropriate dress and aggressive behavior toward me, I'd decided she was pushy, insensitive ...*
The past perfect (*I'd decided*) is necessary here because it refers to an earlier period. The author had already made up her mind about Nina. [> LEG 9.29.1, 9.30, LAG 26An.3, 33B, 37Bn.3, 41B, 52B]
Compare:
　From her aggressive behavior toward me, I **decided** *....* (i.e. I decided at that moment).
Towards would probably be more usual in British English. [> LEG App 25.34]
Note the contraction *I'd* for *I had* and compare it with *I'd* for *I would*. [> LEG 14.17n.3, LAG 35Bns.8–9]
The adjectives *pushy, insensitive* could be joined by *and* to make 'a pair' [> LEG 6.21.1]:
　... I'd decided she was **pushy and insensitive** *and had poor judgement.*
... and had poor judgement.
When the subject (*she*) is the same in all parts of the sentence, we don't need to repeat it. [> LAG 4Bn.2, 13B]

GRAMMAR POINTS

C **The passive with phrasal verbs: 'she couldn't be relied upon'** [> LEG 8.27.1*n*.d, 8.28.1*n*.d, 12.3*n*.7, Apps 28–30, 32, 33, LAG 4D, 8D, 13C, 44D, 47E]

*I had assessed her as someone **who could not be relied upon** to get a job done.*
The preposition or particle is an inseparable part of the passive verb.

We form the passive only with verbs which are transitive. [> LEG 12.3.*n*.2, compare > LAG 38D] In the case of phrasal verbs, the preposition or particle immediately follows the verb in passive constructions and can often end a sentence:
> *Our tent was **blown down**.*
> *The newsagent's has been **broken into**.*
Very few three-part phrasal verbs [> LEG 8.30, App 37, LAG 16B] can go into the passive, even though they are transitive:
> *The old rules **have been done away with**.*

1 Yes, the problem's been dealt with.
2 Yes, these goods have been paid for.
3 Yes, the rules have been kept to.
4 Yes, all the lights were turned off.
5 Yes, the exercise books were given out.
6 Yes, what he said was written down.
7 Yes, your supper is being seen to.
8 Yes, the plan has been approved of.
9 Yes, the children are being looked after.
10 Yes, the documents have been filed away.

D **The causative with 'get': 'get something done'** [> LEG 12.13.1, compare > LAG 23D]

a This is neutral in tone: a normal causative. [> LAG 26F]
b It has a stronger sense, suggesting that 'you' will take an active part in causing the job to be done.

The causative with *get* is more limited than the causative with *have*. It always suggests that the subject (*I, you, he*, etc.) will take positive action to 'have something done':
> *Why don't you **have your hair cut**?* (neutral suggestion)
> *Why don't you **get your hair cut**?* (almost an order = 'Take action. Do something about it.')

Possible answers
1 Why don't you get it cut?
2 I finally got it repaired.
3 No, he's got it published.

4 Why don't you get it fixed?
5 Yes, you should get it changed.
6 Yes, I must get it serviced.

E **'Better' as an adjective and as an adverb: 'a better person/know him better'** [> LEG 6.24, 7.4, 5.12.3, 6.17, LAG 32D and compare > LAG 39F]

a *Better* is an adverb here: *I'll get to **know** him **better**. I don't know him **well**.*
b *Better* is an adjective: *I'm now a **better person**. Before this, I wasn't very **good**.*

Better is the comparative of *good* (adjective) and the comparative of *well* (adverb).
We also use *better* as the comparative of *well* (= in good health):
> *I wasn't **well**, but now I'm **better**.*
We use adjectives after verbs relating to the senses like *look, taste, appear*, etc. [> LAG 2D, 14E, 16D, 46D]:
> *It tastes **good**.* (= it is good) (Not **well**)
But note:
> *He seems **well**.* (= appears to be in good health)
> *He seems **good**.* (= appears to be suitable, capable etc.)

1 well
2 good
3 well
4 well-placed
5 good
6 good
7 good
8 well

F **'Be' + passive infinitive as a future substitute: 'she is not to be trusted'** [> LEG 9.47–48, 16.2, 16.14]

*This person is **not to be trusted**.* The negative passive infinitive (*not to be trusted*) after *is*.

We can use *be to* to refer to the future [> LAG 29D]:
> *I **am to be met** on arrival.* (= Someone is going to meet me)

1 It's not to be taken.
2 It's not to be repeated.
3 He's not to be criticized.
4 It's not to be opened.
5 They're not to be read.
6 They're not to be let out.

Sherlock Holmes

The heath was covered with golden patches of flowering gorse, gleaming magnificently in the light of the bright spring sunshine. Behind one of these clumps I took up my
5 position, so as to command both the gateway of the Hall and a long stretch of the road upon either side. It had been deserted when I left it, but now I saw a cyclist riding down it from the opposite direction to that in which I had come.
10 He was clad in a dark suit, and I saw that he had a black beard. On reaching the end of the Charlington grounds he sprang from his machine and led it through a gap in the hedge, disappearing from my view.

A quarter of an hour passed and then a second cyclist
15 appeared. This time it was the young lady coming from the station. I saw her look about her as she came to the Charlington hedge. An instant later the man emerged from his hiding place, sprang upon his bicycle, and followed her. In all the broad landscape those were the only moving
20 figures, the graceful girl sitting very straight upon her machine and the man behind her bending low over his handle-bar, with a curiously furtive suggestion in every movement. She looked back at him and slowed her pace. He slowed also. She stopped. He at once stopped, too,
25 keeping two hundred yards behind her. Her next movement was as unexpected as it was spirited. She suddenly whisked her wheels round and dashed straight at him!

The Return of Sherlock Holmes by Sir A. Conan Doyle *(BrE)*

Sentence structure

A Break these sentences down into short sentences, making any necessary changes. Write one short sentence beside each letter.

1 The heath was covered with golden patches of flowering gorse, gleaming magnificently in the light of the bright spring sunshine. (ll. 1–3)
   a ....
   b ....

2 Behind one of these clumps I took up my position, so as to command both the gateway of the Hall and a long stretch of the road upon either side. (ll. 4–7)
   a ....
   b ....

3 On reaching the end of the Charlington grounds he sprang from his machine and led it through a gap in the hedge, disappearing from my view. (ll. 11–13)
   a ....
   b ....
   c ....
   d ....

B Replace the words in italics, then refer to the text.

1 It had been deserted *at the time* I left it, but now I saw a cyclist riding down it from the opposite direction to that *I had come in*. (ll. 7–9) ....

2 This time *the young lady was coming* from the station. (ll. 15–16) ....

3 In all the broad landscape those were the only *figures that were moving*, the graceful girl *who was sitting* very straight upon her machine and the man behind her *who was bending* low over his handle-bar, *and had* a curiously furtive suggestion in every movement. (ll. 19–23) ....

4 She looked back at him, *slowing* her pace. (l. 23) ....

5 He at once stopped, *as well*, *and kept* two hundred yards behind her. (ll. 24–25) ....

6 Her next movement was *unexpected and it was spirited, too*. (ll. 25–26) ....

Grammar points

C Supply the right forms of the verbs in brackets, then refer to the text. (ll. 1–13) Variations are possible. In each case give your reason for the form you have chosen.

The heath ¹(*cover*) .... with golden patches of flowering gorse, ...
gleaming magnificently in the light of the bright spring sunshine.
Behind one of these clumps I ²(*take*) .... up my position, ...
so as to command both the gateway of the Hall and a long
stretch of the road upon either side. It ³(*desert*) .... when ....
I ⁴(*leave*) .... it, but now ....
I ⁵(*see*) .... a cyclist riding down it from the opposite direction
to that in which I ⁶(*come*) ....
He was clad in a dark suit, and I ⁷(*see*) ....
that he ⁸(*have*) .... a black beard. On reaching the ....
end of the Charlington grounds he ⁹(*spring*) .... from his machine and
¹⁰(*lead*) .... it through a gap in the hedge, disappearing from my view. ....

D How does the bare infinitive in **a** differ in meaning from the *-ing* form in **b**?

a *I saw her **look** about her as she came to the Charlington hedge.* (ll. 16–17)
b *Now I saw a cyclist **riding** down it from the opposite direction.* (ll. 8–9)

Join these pairs of sentences.

1 John was cycling down the street. I saw him.
   I saw John cycling down the street.
2 He promised to take the children to school this morning. I heard him.
   ....
3 The children were coughing all night. I could hear them.
   ....
4 The factory was burning. I went out to watch it.
   ....

E What is the opposite of the adjective in bold italics?
*Her next movement was as **expected** as it was spirited.* ....(ll. 25–26)

Give the opposites of the adjectives in italics.

1 Her behaviour is very *agreeable*.   *disagreeable*
2 Isn't this court order *legal*?   ....
3 What you're asking me to do is just *possible*. ....
4 I can't imagine he's *honest*.   ....
5 Is a state of war really *thinkable*?   ....
6 I think his behaviour is quite *moral*.   ....

F What's the difference between *at* and *to* in these sentences?

a *She suddenly whisked her wheels round and dashed straight **at** him!* (ll. 26–28) ....
b *As soon as we arrived at the beach, we dashed **to** the sea.* ....

Supply *at* or *to*.

1 He raised the gun and aimed ...*at*... the target.
2 The shepherd threw a stone .... the wild dog.
3 Please throw the ball .... me not .... me.
4 Hasn't anyone ever told you it's rude to stare .... people?
5 When they tried to stop him, he drove straight .... them!
6 I'll drive .... the station and pick up your father.

SENTENCE STRUCTURE

A Answers and commentary

The sentences you have written are simple sentences. A simple sentence has one finite verb. [> LEG 1.7, LAG 1A] The basic word order in a sentence that is not a question or a command is: (Time) Subject Verb Object Manner Place (Time) [> LEG 1.3, 7.22, LAG 4A]

1a *The heath* (subject) *was covered with* (verb) *golden patches of flowering gorse* (object). [> LEG 1.3]

b *It/They* (*the gorse* or *the golden patches*: subject) *gleamed* (verb) *magnificently* (manner) *in the light of the bright spring sunshine* (place). We can use a co-ordinate main clause (*and gleamed . . .*) in place of a present participle construction (*gleaming*). [> LEG 1.58.1]

2a *I* (subject) *took up* (verb) *my position* (object) *behind one of these clumps* (place). An adverb of place usually comes after the object, but we can begin with place if we wish to emphasize location. [> LEG 7.19.2, LAG 4A]

b *I* (subject) *wanted* (verb) (*my position*) *to command both the gateway of the Hall and a long stretch of the road upon either side* (object). We can use the infinitive (*to, so as to, in order to*) to express purpose. [> LEG 16.12.1] After verbs like *want*, the *to*-infinitive is part of the object of the verb. [> LEG 16.13, 16.19]

3a *He* (subject) *reached* (verb) *the end of the Charlington grounds* (object). *On reaching* is a present participle construction in which *on* is used as a conjunction to mean 'when'. [> LEG 1.58.2, LAG 3Bn.1, 53An.2]

b *He* (subject) *sprang* (verb) *from his machine* (adverb of place). [> LEG 1.3]

c *He* (subject) *led* (verb) *it* (i.e. *the machine*: object) *through a gap in the hedge* (place). It wasn't necessary to repeat the subject: *and (he) led*. [> LEG 1.20, LAG 4Bn.2, 13B]

d *He* (subject) *disappeared* (verb) *from my view* (adverb of place). The present participle construction (*disappearing*) was used to connect this sentence. [> LEG 1.57]

B Answers and commentary

1 *It had been deserted **when** I left it . . .* *When* introduces an adverbial clause of time. [> LEG 1.45.1, LAG 6Bn.1]

*. . . but now I saw a cyclist riding down it from the opposite direction to that **in which I had come**.* The relative pronoun *which* is the object of the preposition (*in*). The use of the pronoun directly after the preposition (as in the text) is formal and rare in speech. [> LEG 1.36, LAG 20An.1]

2 *This time **it was the young lady (who was) coming** from the station.* → *This time it was **the young lady**. **She** was coming from the station.* The present participle construction is used in place of the relative clause. [> LEG 1.58.6, 4.14 and compare > LEG 10.20, LAG 34D, 9An.1]

3 *In all the broad landscape those were the only **moving figures**, . . .* *Moving* is an adjective here, not part of a compound noun like *frying pan* (= pan used for frying). [> LEG 2.7, 16.38, LAG 23E]

*. . . the graceful girl **sitting** very straight . . . and the man **bending** low . . .* Present participles (*sitting, bending*) are used in place of relative clauses. [> LEG 1.58.6]

*. . . **with** a curiously furtive suggestion . . .* Note this use of *with* to show possession. [> LEG 10.31, App 25.37, LAG 14D, 14G]

4 *She looked back at him **and slowed** her pace.* A co-ordinate clause (*and slowed*) is used in place of a participle (*slowing*). [> LEG 1.58.1]

5 *He at once stopped, **too**, **keeping** two hundred yards behind her.* *Too* replaces *as well*. [> LEG 7.56, LAG 36Bn.2] *keeping* (present participle) replaces a co-ordinate clause (*and kept*). (See **4** above)

6 *Her next movement was **as unexpected as it was spirited**.* *As .. as* introduces an adverbial clause of comparison here. [> LEG 1.53, LAG 17Bn.6]

GRAMMAR POINTS

C Verbs and verb tenses [> LEG Chapter 9, regular and irregular verbs > Apps 39–40]

The past and the past perfect are the dominant tenses here, reflecting the language of narration. [> LEG 9.21]

1 *was covered*: Simple past: description. [> LEG 9.17.1, 12.1–4]
2 *took*: Simple past: narration. [> LEG 9.17.1]
3 *had been deserted*: Past perfect, referring to an earlier past in the story. [> LEG 9.29.1, 9.30, 12.1–4, LAG 27Bn.3, 33B, 41B, 52B, 37Bn.3]
4 *left*: Simple past: narration. [> LEG 9.17.1]
5 *saw*: Simple past: narration. [> LEG 9.17.1] Alternatively, the use of *could* (*I could see*) would be possible with a verb of perception. [> LEG 11.13, LAG 28D]
6 *had come*: Past perfect, referring to an earlier past in the story. [> LEG 9.29.1, 9.30]
7 *saw*: Simple past: narration [> LEG 9.17.1]; *could see* would again be possible (See 5 above).
8 *had*: Simple past: statement of fact. [> LEG 9.17.1, and compare > LEG 10.31n.4]
9 *sprang* (*spring, sprang, sprung*): Simple past: narration. [> LEG 9.17.1]
10 *led* (*lead, led, led*): Simple past: narration. [> LEG 9.17.1]

D The bare infinitive or '-ing' after verbs of perception: 'saw him ride/saw him riding' [> LEG 16.9, compare > LAG 17Bn.13]

a *I saw her **look** about her* suggests that I saw the whole action from start to finish.
b *I saw a cyclist **riding*** suggests that the action was in progress before I noticed it.

The following verbs can be followed by a noun or pronoun object + bare infinitive or the *-ing* form: *feel, hear, listen to, look at, notice, observe, perceive, see, smell* and *watch*. The bare infinitive generally refers to the complete action [> LAG 21Bn.2b, 43An.23]:
    *I **watched** a pavement-artist **draw** a portrait in crayons.* (from start to finish)
The *-ing* form generally refers to an action in progress:
    *I **watched** a pavement-artist **drawing** a portrait in crayons.* (the action was in progress when I arrived)

We also use the bare infinitive for a single short action (*I **heard** him **cough***) and the *-ing* form for a repeated action (*I **heard** him **coughing***). [> LAG 35Bn.3]

1 I saw John cycling down the street.
2 I heard him promise to take the children to school this morning.
3 I could hear the children coughing all night.
4 I went out to watch the factory burning.

E Adjectives formed with prefixes: 'unexpected' [> LEG 6.2, App 8.2]
unexpected

Prefixes added to adjectives generally have a negative effect. For example, *dis-* added to *agreeable* gives us *disagreeable*; *un-* added to *interesting* gives us *uninteresting*. Not every 'positive' adjective can be turned into a negative one by the addition of a prefix. Sometimes we have to use *not* (*not taxable*). Similarly, not every 'negative' adjective (especially those formed with past participles) has a positive equivalent (*discontinued, mistaken*, but not **continued*, *unmistaken**).

1 disagreeable
2 illegal
3 impossible
4 dishonest
5 unthinkable
6 immoral (= not good or right). (Compare *amoral* = having no understanding of right and wrong.)

F 'To' (direction) and 'at' ('against') [> LEG 8.9, App 25.7]

a *dashed at him*: possibly to harm him.
b *dashed to the sea*: in that direction.

To after a verb often suggests direction (*we ran to the gate*); *at* after a verb or adjective often suggests aggression (*we ran at the gate*; *she's angry at me*):
    *She **shouted to** the children to warn them of the danger.* (direction/communication)
    *The children got very dirty and she **shouted at** them.* (to scold them)

1 aimed at
2 threw a stone at
3 throw to me not at me
4 stare at
5 drove straight at
6 drive to

Breaking the Portland Vase

M R NIGEL WILLIAMS, the British Museum's chief conservator of ceramics, is about to break a Roman glass vase, worth several million pounds, into more than 200 pieces and then put it together again. The Portland Vase, made of blue and white glass by the sculptor Dioscourides, was smashed into 200 pieces by a drop-out from Trinity College, Dublin, while it was on show in the British Museum in 1845. It was pieced together by the museum's restorer, John Doubleday, but a century later the glue began to weaken and, in 1949, the vase was re-assembled by the conservator James Axtell. Now the 1940s adhesive has become brittle and yellow and Mr Williams explained yesterday how he will take the vase apart and achieve a near perfect restoration that will last 200 years - including scores of tiny fragments left out by Doubleday.

'It is the most difficult restoration I have attempted in 28 years,' he said.

Mr Williams will begin by encasing the vase in a paper mould and placing it in an atmosphere of solvent which will release the joins. With the vase still in its mould, he will then remove tapes placed over each crack inside the vase and fish out the pieces, numbering and recording their positions. He will then replace the pieces after painting each edge with a glue that will not become fast until he is satisfied each is in exactly the right position, held by sticky tape. The tiny extra fragments will be positioned using tweezers which hold each piece with compressed air. When the vase is complete it will be 'shot' with ultraviolet light to activate the glue.

Although Mr Williams supervises a team of 12 conservators, the vase restoration will be his alone. He expects it to take 40 per cent of his time for the rest of the year.

The Times (BrE)

Sentence structure

A Combine the sentences below into single complete sentences. Make any necessary changes and use the help given. Then check against the text.

1 The Portland Vase was made of blue and white glass by the sculptor Dioscourides. It was smashed into 200 pieces by a drop-out from Trinity College, Dublin. At the time, it was on show in the British Museum in 1845. (ll. 8–15)
The Portland Vase, made of blue and white glass ....
....

....

2 The museum's restorer, John Doubleday, pieced it together. A century later the glue began to weaken. In 1949, the conservator James Axtell re-assembled the vase. (ll. 15–21)
It was pieced together by the museum's restorer, ...
....

....

3 Mr Williams will encase the vase in a paper mould. That's how he will begin. He will place it in an atmosphere of solvent. The solvent will release the joins. (ll. 33–37)
Mr Williams will begin by ....
....

....

B Choose the word that fits, then refer to the text.

Now the 1940s adhesive has become brittle and yellow and Mr Williams explained yesterday .... he will take the vase apart and achieve a near perfect restoration that will last 200 years – including scores of tiny fragments left out by Doubleday. (ll. 21–29) [*whether/how*]

Grammar points

C Supply the right forms of the verbs in brackets, then refer to the text. (ll. 33–53)

Mr Williams will begin by encasing the vase in a paper mould and placing it in an atmosphere of solvent which [1](*release*) .... the joins. With the vase still in its mould, he [2](*then remove*) .... tapes placed over each crack inside the vase and [3](*fish*) .... out the pieces, numbering and recording their positions. He [4](*then replace*) .... the pieces after painting each edge with a glue that [5](*not become*) .... fast until he [6](*satisfy*) .... each is in exactly the right position, held by sticky tape. The tiny extra fragments [7](*position*) .... using tweezers which hold each piece with compressed air. When the vase [8](*be*) .... complete it [9](*be*) .... 'shot' with ultraviolet light.

D What's the meaning of the phrase in bold italics?
*Mr Nigel Williams **is about to** break a Roman glass vase.* (ll. 1–5) ....

Supply the right forms of the phrases in brackets.

1 Quick! The race (*be about to*) *is about to* start.
2 You (*be to*) .... deliver this message and wait for an answer.
3 Sorry we can't chat with you – we (*be on the point of*) .... leaving.
4 This present (*be not to open*) .... before Christmas.
5 What time (*the plane be due*) .... to land?
6 If they ask you any questions you (*be not to*) .... tell them anything.
7 Sh! The play (*be about to*) .... begin.
8 It's too early to go to the airport. The plane (*be not due*) .... for ages.

E Supply suitable forms of the word *million* in these sentences.

a *The Roman glass vase is worth several* .... *pounds.* (ll. 4–6)
b *The Roman glass vase is worth* .... *of pounds.*
c *The Roman glass vase is worth more than a/one* .... *pounds.*

Supply the correct forms. Use words instead of numbers and symbols.

1 How much is the vase worth? It's worth more than (1 million) *a/one million* pounds.
2 (Thousand) .... of pounds have been spent on the new hospital.
3 There were (dozen) .... of complaints after the broadcast.
4 For a lot of people (£100) .... is a lot of money.
5 The whole collection of pictures at the National Gallery is worth (billion) ....
6 (Hundred) .... of people gathered at the stage door after the performance.
7 ($Billion) .... have been spent developing this new car.
8 Who's going to wade through a novel of more than (1000) .... pages?

F Supply *of*, *from* or *with* in these sentences and give reasons for your choice.

a *The Portland Vase, made* .... *blue and white glass, was smashed . . .* (ll. 8–12)
b *The sauce is delicious. It's been made* .... *fresh cream.*
c *Our cakes are made* .... *pure ingredients like eggs, butter and milk, with no additives.*

Supply *made of*, *made from* or *made with* in these sentences.

1 It's hard to believe that whisky is *made from* barley.
2 Most cheap toys are .... plastic these days.
3 What's plastic .... ?
4 You can't expect chocolates .... fresh cream to keep very long.
5 Chocolate is .... milk, cocoa and flavourings.
6 The entire building is .... steel and glass.
7 The metal used in these coins is a cheap alloy .... various metals.
8 I've just bought a nice flan .... fresh fruit which we can have for our tea.

SENTENCE STRUCTURE

A Answers and commentary

1 *The Portland Vase,* **made** *of blue and white glass by the sculptor Dioscourides . . .* , (subject)
, . . . made of blue and white glass, is short for *which was made of . . .* (a non-defining, passive relative clause). [> LEG 1.62.1 and compare > LEG App 25.26, LAG 6B*n*.4] The participle phrase is in apposition to *The Portland Vase*, that is, it adds information about the vase. [> LEG 1.39, LAG 2A*n*.1]
. . . by + agent (*Dioscourides*) is necessary here because it adds important information. [> LEG 12.5, LAG 49D]

. . . **was smashed** (verb) *into 200 pieces* (manner) *by a drop-out from Trinity College, Dublin, . . .* (agent)
Again, *by* + agent (*a drop-out . . .*) adds important information, following the passive verb *was smashed*. [> LEG 12.5, LAG 49D]

. . . **while** *it was on show in the British Museum in 1845.* (subordinate adverbial clause of time)
While (= during the time when) introduces this time clause [> LEG 1.45.1], which is subordinate to the main clause that has gone before. [> LEG 1.21]

2 *It was pieced together by the museum's restorer, John Doubleday, . . .* (main clause)
The focus is on the vase, so the description continues in the passive with *by* + agent (*John Doubleday*) adding important information. [> LEG 12.5, LAG 49D] *John Doubleday* is in apposition to *the museum's restorer*. [> LEG 1.39, LAG 2A*n*.1, 5A*ns*.2,4]

. . . **but** *a century later the glue began to weaken . . .* (co-ordinate main clause)
This clause, introduced by the conjunction *but*, stands beside the main clause. [> LEG 1.17–18]

. . . **and**, *in 1949,* **the vase was re-assembled by** *the conservator James Axtell.* (co-ordinate main clause)
A further co-ordinate main clause, introduced by *and*, is added. The passive follows the style of the rest of the sentence. [compare > LAG 26C, 33A–B]

3 *Mr Williams* **will begin by encasing** *the vase in a paper mould* **and placing** *it in an atmosphere of solvent . . .* (main clause)
By + (*-ing*) answers *How?* [> LEG 13.40.4, 16.51, App 25.17] and governs *encasing* and *placing*. [> LAG 1D, 17B*n*.5, 20B*n*.1]

. . . **which/that** *will release the joins.* (subordinate relative clause)
Which/that introduces a defining relative clause, so no comma is used: the clause provides essential information about the *solvent*. [> LEG 1.26, LAG 5A*n*.3, 22A*ns*.4–5] *Which/that* is the relative pronoun subject of the clause [> LEG 1.31]:
This is **the solvent**. *It will release the joins.*
→ *This is* **the solvent** *which/that will release the joins.*

B Answer and commentary

. . . Mr Williams explained yesterday **how** *he will take the vase apart . . .*
Explain is a reporting verb which can be followed by *whether* or any question-word (*how, when, why,* etc.). [> LEG 15.19–20, App 45]
Compare:
Does he have to take the vase apart? (yes/no question) *He didn't explain.*
→ *He didn't explain* **whether** *he had to take the vase apart.* (indirect question) [> LEG 15.17–18, LAG 10E, 14B]
How will he take the vase apart? (question-word question). *He explained.*
→ *He explained* **how** *he will* (or *would*) *take the vase apart . . .* (reported question) [> LEG 15.19–20, LAG 50E and compare > LAG 22A*n*.6, 41A*n*.3]
Note how the author of this text uses *will* rather than *would* in the reported statement. The sequence of tenses depends on the viewpoint of the person reporting, not on any abstract rule! [> LEG 15.10, 15.13*n*.1, 15.14–16, LAG 7F, 10C]

GRAMMAR POINTS

C The simple future tense and future reference

[> LEG 9.35–40, compare > LAG 5D, 9E]

We form the simple future tense with the modal verb *will* (though we can also use *shall* with *I* and *we*, especially in British English). We can use *will* and *shall* in this way for simple prediction:

> Tottenham **will win** on Saturday.
> I don't know if I **shall see** you next week.

However, *will* and *shall* have many other uses in English, e.g.

– requests: **Will you hold** the door open please?
– offers: **Shall I get** your coat for you?

Nearly all the verbs in this extract require *will* (= prediction). Reasons are given when *will* is not used.

1 will release   2 will then remove   3 (will) fish
4 will then replace   5 will not become
6 is satisfied (no future after temporal conjunctions like *until* [> LEG 1.45.2, passive 12.2])
7 will be positioned (passive [> LEG 12.2])
8 is (no future after temporal conjunctions like *when* [> LEG 1.45.2])   9 will be 'shot'

D Future substitutes: 'be about to', etc. [> LEG 9.47–48]

He's going to break it very soon.

We can also express the future with:
– *be to* for arrangements, duties, instructions:
> OPEC representatives **are to meet** in Geneva next Tuesday.
– *be about to* and *be on the point of* for the immediate future:
> We**'re about to** leave/**on the point of** leaving.
– *be due (to)*: for timetables:
> The next train **is due to leave** at 4.17.

1 is about to   2 are to   3 are on the point of
4 is not to be opened   5 is the plane due
6 are not to   7 is about to   8 is not due

E Numbers and their plurals [> LEG 2.37, 3.11, App 47]

a *The Roman glass vase is worth **several million pounds**.*
b *The Roman glass vase is worth **millions of pounds**.*
c *The Roman glass vase is worth more than **a/one million pounds**.* [compare > LAG 40B*n*.4]

With numbers and words like *dozen*, we use:
– the singular to refer to one. We can say *a* or *one dozen*, *a* or *one hundred*, etc.
– the singular when the reference is to more than one: *two hundred*, *three thousand*, etc. (Not *two hundreds*, *three thousands*)
– the singular with quantity words: *a few million*, *several hundred*. (Not *millions*, *hundreds*)
– the singular when we refer to the currency: *two million pounds*, *three thousand dollars*. (Not *millions*, *thousands*); but *3000 yen*. (Not *yens*)
– the plural when we use *of*: *thousands of pounds*, *millions of dollars*. (Not *thousands pounds*, *millions dollars*)
– the plural when the number is used as a plural:
> **Billions** have been spent on the new airport.

1 *a* or *one* million pounds   2 Thousands of pounds   3 dozens of complaints   4 *a* or *one* hundred pounds   5 billions   6 Hundreds of people   7 *a* or *one* billion dollars, or billions of dollars   8 *a* or *one* thousand pages

F 'Made of', 'made from' and 'made with' [> LEG App 25.26]

a **made of** blue and white glass (we can recognize the material)
b **made with** fresh cream (contains a material or materials we can identify)
c **made from** eggs, butter and milk (the ingredient or ingredients aren't immediately obvious)

1 whisky is made from barley (the ingredients aren't obvious)
2 toys are made of plastic (we can recognize the material)
3 What's plastic made from? (the 'ingredients' aren't obvious)
4 chocolates made with fresh cream (identifiable ingredient)
5 Chocolate is made from milk, etc. (the ingredients aren't obvious)
6 The entire building is made of steel and glass (we can recognize the materials)
7 a cheap alloy made from various metals (it isn't obvious which metals)
8 a nice flan made with fresh fruit (identifiable ingredient)

Fax-mad New Yorkers

to have gone as fax mad as New York. Radio stations, for example, are taking record requests by fax - the advantage is that office workers can do it without the boss hearing them telephone. To order lunch, you can zap off a completed 'le fax menu' to your favourite restaurant. If you are looking for a partner for the evening you fax your needs to a fax-dating service. Down in Greenwich Village, there are even artists busy developing the genre of fax art. Half the telephone calls from New York to Japan are between fax machines. This being New York, you can also, of course, use the machine to communicate with your 'shrink' for some fax therapy.

The craze, however, has its excesses and various spoilsports are already working on ways of reining in the more dubious joys of fax. First, there is the danger of faxing in the fast lane. The police have decreed that under no circumstances may you transmit from your car fax while

NOT SO LONG AGO, the typical New York sign-off used to be 'Have a nice day'. It is fast being replaced by a new one: 'What's your fax number?' From Tokyo to London to Los Angeles, the craze of the facsimile machine is sweeping the world, but no city seems

on the move, though of course you may receive.

People in the fax industry are also expecting restrictions on a growing menace in the new culture - junk faxes. The advertising companies which pack your letter box with 'personalized' brochures and telephone you to offer their goods just as you are sitting down to dinner, have latched on to the fax with a vengeance. Since they are presumed to be affluent, people with fax machines are a desirable target. Since machines cannot filter out unwanted callers, they are being increasingly clogged up with unsolicited advertising.

There is another hazard in faxing that can cause embarrassment - the wrong number. It can prove ticklish to fax a love letter to an office machine by mistake. More damaging, though, is the mis-faxed business letter. Things have gone so far that some experts are predicting an imminent 'fax-lash'.

The Times (BrE)

Sentence structure

A Replace the words in italics, then refer to the text.

1 Not so long ago, the typical New York sign-off used to be 'Have a nice day'. *This sign-off* is fast being replaced by a new one: 'What's your fax number?' (ll. 1–5) ....

2 Radio stations, for example, are taking record requests by fax – the advantage *being* that office workers can do it *when the boss can't hear* them telephone. (ll. 10–14) ....

3 *As this is* New York, you can also, of course, use the machine to communicate with your 'shrink' for some fax therapy. (ll. 24–27) ....

4 The police have decreed that under no circumstances may you transmit from your car fax *during the time you are* on the move, *but* of course you may receive. (ll. 33–37) ....

5 The advertising companies *who* pack your letter box with 'personalized' brochures ... have latched on to the fax with a vengeance. (ll. 41 47) ....

6 *As* they are presumed to be affluent, people with fax machines are a desirable target. (ll. 47–49) ....

B Which feature of word order is unusual in this sentence and why?

The police have decreed that under no circumstances may you transmit from your car fax while on the move, though of course you may receive. (ll. 33–37)

....

....

Grammar points

C Supply *a/an*, *the* or zero (–) in this paragraph, then refer to the text. (ll. 1–26)

Not so long ago, [1]...... typical New York sign-off used to be 'Have [2]...... nice day'. It is fast being replaced by [3]...... new one: 'What's your fax number?' From [4]...... Tokyo to [5]...... London to [6]...... Los Angeles, [7]...... craze of [8]...... facsimile machine is sweeping [9]...... world, but no city seems to have gone as fax mad as [10]...... New York. [11]...... Radio stations, for example, are taking record requests by fax - [12]...... advantage is that [13]...... office workers can do it without [14]...... boss hearing them telephone. To order [15]...... lunch, you can zap off [16]...... completed 'le fax menu' to your favourite restaurant. If you are looking for [17]...... partner for [18]...... evening you fax your needs to [19]...... fax-dating service. Down in [20]...... Greenwich Village, there are even [21]...... artists busy developing [22]...... genre of [23]...... fax art. [24]...... half the telephone calls from [25]...... New York to [26]...... Japan are between [27]...... fax machines. This being [28]...... New York, you can also, of course, use [29]...... machine to communicate with your 'shrink'.

D Correct this sentence, then refer to the text.
Office workers can do it without the boss to hear them telephone. (ll. 12–14)

Replace the phrases in italics using a suitable phrase with *without*.

1 To surprise her, he booked a table at a restaurant *and she didn't know*. *without her knowing*
2 He went into the house *and no one heard* him. ....
3 He went into the house *and the family didn't hear* him. ....
4 She left home *and the neighbours didn't see* her. ....
5 She left the meeting *and the chairman didn't ask* her any questions. ....
6 She sold her shares *and none of us found* out about it. ....
7 She sold her shares *and we didn't find* out about it. ....
8 He changed the figures in the books *and the manager didn't notice*. ....

E Would you use *-ing* or *to* here? Why?
In Greenwich Village, there are even artists busy (develop)..........*the genre ...* (ll. 19–21)

Supply the correct verb form. In which of these sentences can we use *-ing* only?

1 Can't you see I'm busy (get) *getting*...... the dinner ready?   *(-ing only)*
2 It is difficult (find) *to find / finding*...... work in some rural areas.   *(to or -ing)*
3 It isn't easy (speak) .... in public.
4 We're all fed-up (wait) .... for visas to visit our friends in the West.
5 Hazel was fully occupied (work at) .... her painting.
6 It's boring (be) .... at sea for days on end.
7 I got bored (be) .... at sea for days on end.
8 It's really strange him (behave) .... like that.

F Supply the right form of the verb in this sentence, then check against the text.
Since they (presume)..........*to be affluent, people with fax machines are a target.*
(ll.47–49)

Supply the right form of the verbs in brackets.

1 As he never returned from Vietnam, (presume) *he was presumed*...... to be dead.
2 She (consider) .... to be an expert on animal behaviour and often appears on television.
3 We hardly know him, but he (suppose) .... to have been a spy in World War II.
4 According to the radio, many of the passengers (believe) .... to be still alive.
5 After his death, his fortune (estimate) .... to be in excess of $5,000,000.
6 All the documents he produced (show) .... to have been forgeries.
7 No one (can find) .... to be guilty without a proper trial.
8 The expensive picture (declare) .... to be a fake.

129

SENTENCE STRUCTURE

A Answers and commentary

1 *Not so long ago, the typical New York sign-off used to be 'Have a nice day'. **It** is fast being replaced ...*

It refers to *sign-off*. *It* can refer to a thing, a quality, an event, a place, etc. [> LEG 4.5.5]

2 *Radio stations, for example, are taking record requests by fax – the advantage **is** that office workers can do it ...*

Being can replace *is* or *was* as a connecting present participle [> LEG 1.60, LAG 6C]:

*They **are/were** taking record requests by fax, the advantage **is/was** that ...*

→*They **are/were** taking record requests by fax, the advantage **being** that ...*

*... **without the boss hearing** them telephone.* Present participle constructions are common after *with* and *without* [> LEG 1.60, 16.51, compare > LAG 1D, 30D]:

The rail strike is continuing. People are driving to work.

→ *With the rail strike continuing, people are driving to work.*

*They debated for hours. **A decision wasn't taken**.*

→ *They debated for hours **without a decision being taken**.*

3 ***This being** New York, you can also, of course, use the machine to communicate with your 'shrink' ...*

Being can replace *is* or *was* as a connecting present participle. (See **2** above) [> LEG 1.60] Note the use of *being* after *this, it, there*, etc.:

*It **being** a bank holiday, all the shops were shut.*

*There **being** no further business, I declare the meeting closed.*

4 *... under no circumstances may you transmit from your car fax **while** on the move ...*

While (– during the time that, Not **during**) introduces an adverbial clause of time [> LEG 1.45.1, LAG 10An.1], which can be abbreviated [> LEG 1.55, LAG 4Bn.3]:

While you are on the move ...

→ *While on the move ...*

*... **though** of course you may receive.*

But can replace *though* in a contrast clause [> LEG 1.50, LAG 3Ans.2–3, 11Bn.2], except at the beginning of a sentence:

***Though** she can't spell very well, she's an excellent secretary.* (Not **But she can't spell ...**)

5 *The advertising agencies **which** pack your letter box with 'personalized' brochures ...*

The rule is that *which*, not *who*, applies to things [> LEG 1.31]:

*The building, **which** is very tall ...* (Not **who**)

However, with some nouns (especially collective nouns like *committee, government*) we use *which* when we think of them as a whole group, or *who* when we think of them in a more personal way. [> LEG 2.28.1, compare > LAG 36E]

6 ***Since** they are presumed to be affluent, ...*

Since (= because) can introduce adverbial clauses of reason. [> LEG 1.48, LAG 10An.4, 24An.12] Compare *since* (= from the time when), which can introduce adverbial clauses of time [> LEG 1.45.1, LAG 8Bn.1, 8En.5, 10An.2]:

*Traffic has greatly increased **since the motorway was completed**.*

B Answer and commentary

*... under no circumstances **may you transmit** ...*

There is inversion of verb and subject after a 'negative adverb' [> LEG 1.6, 7.59.3, App 19, LAG 33C, 49C]:

***You may not transmit** in/under any circumstances ...*

→ *In/Under no circumstances **may you transmit** ...*

GRAMMAR POINTS

C Articles [> LEG Chapter 3, LAG 8C, etc.]
Cross references are given to LEG for selected items only.

1 the typical New York sign-off **2** Have a nice day [compare > LEG 10.39] **3** a new one [compare > LEG 4.10] **4** from (–) Tokyo **5** to (–) London **6** to (–) Los Angeles **7** the craze **8** of the facsimile machine [> LEG 3.20.2] **9** the world [> LEG 3.20.4] **10** as (–) New York **11** (–) Radio stations **12** the advantage **13** (–) office workers **14** the boss **15** To order (–) lunch [> LEG 3.28.2] **16** a completed 'le fax menu' **17** a partner **18** the evening [> LEG 3.21.2] **19** a fax-dating service **20** (–) Greenwich Village **21** (–) artists **22** the genre **23** of (–) fax art **24** (–) Half the telephone calls [> LEG 5.18.2] **25** from (–) New York **26** to (–) Japan **27** between (–) fax machines **28** (–) New York **29** the machine

D Preposition + object + '-ing': 'without the boss hearing' [> LEG 16.51, LAG 1D and compare > LAG 1F, 18E]

*Office workers can do it **without the boss/ boss's hearing** them telephone.*

We can use a name or a noun (accusative or possessive) after a preposition and before *-ing*:
*They can do it **without the boss/boss's hearing** them telephone.*

We can sometimes use an object pronoun or a possessive adjective after a preposition and before *-ing*:
*They can do it **without him/his hearing** them telephone.*

1 without her knowing
2 without anyone hearing
3 without the family/family's hearing
4 without the neighbours/neighbours' seeing
5 without the chairman/chairman's asking
6 without any of us finding out
7 without us/our finding out
8 without the manager/manager's noticing

E 'It's difficult to find/finding' and 'I'm busy working' [> LEG 16.47 and compare > LAG 5E]

We use *-ing* here, because it's a participle.
*In Greenwich Village there are artists. They are **busy**. They are **developing** the genre of fax art.*

→ *In Greenwich Village there are artists **busy developing** the genre of fax art.*

We use the *-ing* form (participle) after adjectives such as *bored, busy, fed-up, frantic, happy, occupied* and *tired* with a personal subject (Not **It**). [compare > LAG 1C]

1 busy getting (*-ing* only)
2 difficult to find/finding (*to* or *-ing*)
3 easy to speak/speaking (*to* or *-ing*)
4 fed-up waiting (*-ing* only)
5 working at (*-ing* only)
6 boring to be/being (*to* or *-ing*)
7 bored being (*-ing* only)
8 strange him behaving (*-ing* only)

F Verb + object + 'to be' (passive): 'they are presumed to be' [> LEG 16.22 and compare > LAG 18D, > LAG 3D, 36C, 37Bn.2]

*Since **they are presumed** to be affluent, people with fax machines are a target.*

We can use an object + *to be* after verbs like *acknowledge, assume, believe, calculate, consider, declare, discover, find, imagine, judge, know, prove, see, show, suppose, take* (= presume), *think* and *understand*. These verbs are often used in the passive. We can often omit *to be*:
They have found Samantha (to be) really dependable.

→ ***Samantha has been found** (to be) really dependable.*

1 he was presumed to be dead
2 She is considered to be an expert
3 he is supposed to have been a spy
4 many of the passengers are believed to be still alive
5 his fortune was estimated to be in excess of $5,000,000
6 the documents were shown to have been forgeries
7 No one can be found to be guilty
8 The expensive picture was declared to be a fake

Japan's underground frontier

Proposed subterranean cities could help ease a space crunch

Underground. The word brings many unsavory adjectives to mind: dark, dank, clandestine, illegal.
5 But in Japan the 'underground' is becoming the new frontier and the best hope for solving one of the country's most intractable
10 problems. With a population nearly half the size of the U.S.'s squeezed into an area no bigger than Montana, Japan has virtually no room
15 left in its teeming cities. Developers have built towering skyscrapers and even artificial islands in the sea, but the space crunch
20 keeps getting worse. Now some of Japan's largest construction companies think they have the answer:

huge developments beneath
25 the earth's surface where millions of people could work, shop and, perhaps eventually, make their homes. 'An underground city
30 is no longer a dream. We expect it to actually materialize in the early part of the next century,' says Tetsuya Hanamura, the chief
35 of Taisei Corp.'s proposed development.

Taisei calls its project Alice City after Lewis Carroll's heroine who went
40 underground by way of a rabbit hole. The company, which has drawn up elaborate plans, envisions two huge concrete
45 'infrastructure' cylinders, each 197 ft. tall and with a diameter of 262 ft., that would be built as much as 500 ft. below ground. They
50 would house facilities for power generation, air conditioning and waste processing. Each cylinder would be connected by
55 passages to a series of spheres, which would accommodate stores, theaters, sports facilities, offices and hotels. Taisei's
60 initial $4.2 billion design could support 100,000 people.

Time (AmE)

Sentence structure

A Combine the sentences below into single complete sentences. Make any necessary changes and use the help given. Then check against the text.

1 Japan has a population nearly half the size of the U.S.'s. The population is squeezed into an area no bigger than Montana. Japan has virtually no room left in its teeming cities. (ll. 10–15)
With a population ....
....
....

2 The company has drawn up elaborate plans. It envisions two huge concrete 'infrastructure' cylinders, each 197 ft. tall and with a diameter of 262 ft. The cylinders would be built as much as 500 ft. below ground. (ll. 41–49)
The company, which ....
....
....

B Replace the words in italics, then refer to the text.

1 But in Japan the 'underground' is becoming the new frontier and the best hope *to solve* one of the country's most intractable problems. (ll. 5–10) ....

2 Developers have built towering skyscrapers and even artificial islands in the sea, but the space crunch *continues to get* worse. (ll. 16–20) ....

3 Now some of Japan's largest construction companies think they have the answer: huge developments beneath the earth's surface *in which* millions of people could work. (ll. 20–27) ....

4 'We expect *that it will actually materialize* in the early part of the next century,' says Tetsuya Hanamura, the chief of Taisei Corp.'s proposed development. (ll. 30–36) ....

5 They would house facilities *to generate power* ... and *to process waste*. (ll. 49–53) ....

Grammar points

C Supply the missing prepositions, then refer to the text. (ll. 1–25)

Underground. The word brings many unsavory adjectives to mind: dark, dank, clandestine, illegal. But [1]....... Japan the 'underground' is becoming the new frontier and the best hope [2]....... solving one [3]....... the country's most intractable problems. [4]....... a population nearly half the size [5]....... the U.S.'s squeezed [6]....... an area no bigger than Montana, Japan has virtually no room left [7]....... its teeming cities. Developers have built towering skyscrapers and even artificial islands [8]....... the sea, but the space crunch keeps getting worse. Now some [9]....... Japan's largest construction companies think they have the answer: huge developments [10]....... the earth's surface.

D Which of the two (**a** or **b**) doesn't sound quite right? Why?

a *Underground. The word brings many unsavory adjectives to mind.* (ll. 1–3)
b *My teacher says I use many adjectives when I write stories.*

Supply *much, many* or *a lot (of)*. Note where alternatives are possible.

1 *Many/A lot of*....... modern plays, like *Who's Afraid of Virginia Woolf?*, deal with relationships.
2 We all thought Frank was rich, but we later discovered he owed everyone .... money.
3 .... has been written about the high price of land in Japan.
4 With high interest rates, ... companies are cutting back on investment.
5 I'm impressed by your library. You really have .... books.
6 There aren't .... opportunities for people who haven't got good qualifications.
7 We thought there wasn't .... oil in this field before we used new drilling techniques.
8 Is there .... demand for second-hand cars in the present market?

E What do *left* and *over* mean in these sentences?

a *Japan has virtually no room **left** in its teeming cities.* (ll. 14–15)
b *We ordered some tiles for our roof and we have a lot **over**.*

Respond using combinations with *left* or *over*. Sometimes you can use either.

1 I'd love to have another one of those pies.   *I'm afraid there aren't any left.*
2 We prepared heaps of food for the party.
3 We're looking for land in the city centre.
4 There are twelve of us and I've got thirteen tickets.
5 We've sold nearly all our stock of winter coats.
6 All the books fit on to the shelf except this one.
7 We've completely run out of cooking oil.
8 We've got a lot of unsold lottery tickets.

F What is the effect of *keeps* in this sentence?
*Developers have built towering skyscrapers, but the space crunch **keeps** getting worse.* (ll. 16–20)

Respond appropriately using the verbs in brackets.

1 What do you think? Should I try to pass my driving test again? (keep)
Yes, you should keep trying.
2 What shall I do? Shall I wait any longer before writing to them again? (suggest)

3 What does John say? Did he take the ledger from my desk drawer? (deny)

4 What should we do? Should we travel in this bad weather? (postpone)

SENTENCE STRUCTURE

A Answers and commentary

1 **With a population** *nearly half the size of the U.S.'s* ...
With can sometimes be used in place of *have/have got* [> LEG 10.31, App 25.37, LAG 14D, 14G]:

It's a house **which has got** *a high fence round it.*
→ *It's a house* **with** *a high fence round it.*

... **squeezed** *into an area no bigger than Montana,* ...
The past participle construction has been used in place of a relative clause [> LEG 1.62.3, LAG 6B*n*.4]:

Japan has a population (**which is**) **squeezed** *into an area no bigger than Montana* ...

... *Japan has virtually no room left in its teeming cities.*
Note how mention of the subject (*Japan*) is delayed to this point [compare > LEG 1.21]:

When **she** *got on the train,* **Mrs Tomkins** *realized she had made a dreadful mistake.*

2 *The company,* **which has drawn up elaborate plans,** *envisions two huge concrete 'infrastructure' cylinders, each 197 ft. tall and with a diameter of 262 ft.,* ...
Which (referring to *the company*) introduces a non-defining relative clause here which supplies extra information, so commas are used round the clause. [> LEG 1.26, LAG 17A*n*.6]

... **that** *would be built as much as 500 ft. below ground.*
That, referring to *the cylinders*, introduces a further relative clause. Commas are used round the preceding phrase (*each 197 ft. tall and with a diameter of 262 ft.*) because it is in apposition to *the cylinders*. [> LEG 1.39, LAG 2A*n*.1, 5A*ns*.2,4]
This relative clause, though it has a comma in front of it, is a defining clause, providing essential information (*cylinders that would be built*). We can't introduce non-defining clauses with *that*. [> LEG 1.31.2, LAG 5A*n*.3, 17A*n*.6]

B Answers and commentary

1 ... *the 'underground' is becoming the new frontier and the best* **hope for solving** ...
We can use a *to*-infinitive as a complement after some nouns (*the best* **hope to solve**) or we can use a preposition + *-ing* (*the best* **hope for solving**). [> LEG 10.9.10, 16.33, 16.53, App 25.20, LAGP 1D, 7B*ns*.4,8]

2 ... *the space crunch* **keeps getting** *worse.*
We can use a *to*-infinitive or an *-ing* form after *continue* (*continues to get/continues getting worse*). [> LEG 16.57, LAG 42C, 57D] Or we can express the same idea of continuity with *keep* + *-ing* (not a *to*-infinitive). [> LEG 16.42, LAG 1F, 31F]

3 ... *huge developments beneath the earth's surface* **where** *millions of people could work.*
We often use *in which* in place of *where* to introduce a relative clause of place [> LEG 1.38.2]:

This is the place **in which** *I grew up.*
→ *This is (the place)* **where** *I grew up.*
Where introduces an adverbial clause of place [> LEG 1.46, LAG 19A*n*.3, 27B*n*.1, 44B*n*.3]:

You can't camp **where/wherever you like** *these days.*

4 '*We* **expect it to actually materialize** *in the early part of the next century.*'
Expect is a reporting verb which can be followed by *that* + future (*we expect that it will materialize*). [> LEG 9.37.3, 9.43.1, App 45, LAG 4E]
We can also use an object (here, *it*) + *to*-infinitive after *expect*. [> LEG 16.20, 16.23, LAG 10D] It is quite acceptable to split the infinitive (that is, to put an adverb after the infinitive marker *to*) here, though the writer could also have written:

We expect it **actually to materialize** ... .
[> LEG 16.15]

5 *They would house facilities* **for power generation** ...
We normally use a *to*-infinitive to express purpose (*facilities* **to generate power**). [> LEG 16.12, LAG 7B*n*.11, 15A*n*.3] An alternative correct answer is *for generating*. [> LEG 16.40.9, App 25.20]
We often express purpose with *for* + *-ing* (*facilities* **for generating power**), or a noun (as here): *facilities* **for power generation**.
Similarly, *to process waste* is an alternative to *for waste processing*. [> LEG 16.40.9, App 25.20, LAG 1D, 54A*n*.7, 60C]

GRAMMAR POINTS

C Prepositions [> LEG Chapter 8, Apps 20–30]

1 *in* Japan: *in* an area. [> LEG 8.9.2, 10.13.4, App 22.1]
2 hope *for*: *for* (= purpose) [> LEG App 25.20]; hope *of*: noun + preposition. [> LEG 16.33*n*.2] Both of them have to be followed by *-ing* if you want to continue with a verb. [> LAG 1D]
3 one *of*: specific reference. [> LEG 5.5.2 and compare > LEG 4.10, 5.30, LAG 58F]
4 *With* a population: (= having). [> LEG App 25.36, LAG 14D, 14G]
5 *of* the U.S.'s: (double) genitive. [> LEG 2.47, 2.50, 2.52, App 25.27, LAG 51D, 57E]
6 *into* an area no bigger than Montana: suggests movement, therefore *into*; *in* (an area) is also possible. [> LEG 8.9.5, LAG 12B*n*.25]
7 *in* its teeming cities: *in* an area; as for **1** above.
8 *in* the sea: *in* an area. [> LEG 8.9.5, compare > LAG 45E]
9 some *of*: specific reference. [> LEG 5.5.2]
10 *beneath*, *below* or *under*: *Beneath* is less common and more literary than *under*. [> LEG 25.18, 25.35]

D 'Much', 'many' and 'a lot of' [> LEG 5.13–14, LAG 2F, and compare > LAG 21C, 33D]

b doesn't sound quite right.
a is right because *brings many unsavory adjectives to mind* stands for an abstract idea. See below.

We normally use *much* (+ uncountable) and *many* (+ countable) in negative statements/ questions:
> *I haven't much time/many clothes.*
> *Is there much milk in the carton?*
> *Are there many eggs in the fridge?*

In everyday speech we usually avoid using *much* and *many* in affirmative statements and prefer *a lot of*:
> *We've got a lot of time to kill before the play starts.* (Not *much time*)

We avoid using *much* and *many* in the affirmative with concrete nouns in everyday speech: *He has much money* *We have many letters*.

Much and *many* occur in the affirmative in formal style:
> *Much money must be invested in developing countries.*
> *Many teachers dislike marking piles of exercise books.* [> LAG 15C*ns*.4,13, 22B*n*.17]

We can also use *not a lot of* in place of the neutral *not much*, *not many* for special emphasis:
> *I haven't got a lot of patience with hypochondriacs!* (= I haven't got much)

If in doubt, always stick to the basic rule of using *much* and *many* in the negative and in questions and using *a lot of* in the affirmative. Affirmative uses of *much* and *many* often sound wrong in ways which are hard to define.

1	Many/A lot of	**5**	a lot of
2	a lot of	**6**	many/a lot of
3	Much/A lot	**7**	much/a lot of
4	many/a lot of	**8**	much/a lot of

E The use of ' … left' and ' … over' after quantifiers: 'any left', 'some over' [> LEG 5.7, LAG 2F, 6D, 25B, 31D, 39E]

a *not used up*   **b** *more than we needed*

(None) left means 'not consumed or remaining'; *(a lot) over* means 'more than is/are wanted'. Depending on our viewpoint we can sometimes use *left* and *over* interchangeably, especially when talking about food.

Possible answers
1 I'm afraid there aren't any left.
2 There's a lot left/over.
3 There isn't much left.
4 You've got one over.
5 There are hardly any left.
6 You've got one book over.
7 We've got none left.
8 We've got a lot over/left.

F Verb + '-ing': 'keep trying' [> LEG 16.42 and compare > LAG 1E, 1F, 40C]

Keep + -ing suggests continuity. We sometimes use *on* after *keep* for greater emphasis. [> LEG App 32.9.1]

When we want to use another verb immediately after *keep*, the second verb can only be an *-ing* form, not a *to-*infinitive. A few other verbs like this are: *admit, avoid, consider, deny, dislike, enjoy, excuse, finish, imagine, keep, postpone, report, suggest, understand.*

Possible answers
1 Yes, you should keep trying.
2 Yes, I suggest waiting a bit longer. (Compare: *I suggest you wait.* [> LEG 11.75.2])
3 He denies taking it.
4 We should postpone travelling.

Schooldays

AT THE FIRST recess a large boy approached him, hit him hard in the face, and said, 'Come on, Chicken, let's see if you can fight.' They fought, and Francis
5 was beaten disastrously.

After that he had to fight twice a day for three weeks, and he was beaten every time. Small boys are not skilled fighters, and though he was hurt and shaken, he suffered no serious
10 damage. But after recess he sat at his desk, wretched and aching, and Miss McGladdery was angry with him because he was inattentive. Miss McGladdery was fifty-nine, and she was soldiering through her teaching career until, at
15 sixty-five, she would be able to retire and, with God's help, never see any of her former pupils again.

A strong Scots background, and thirty years at Carlyle Rural, had made her an expert disciplinarian. A short, fat, implacable woman, she ruled her three groups - for Carlyle
20 Rural had only two rooms and she took the most advanced classes - not with a rod of iron, but with the leather strap that was issued by the school board as the ultimate instrument of justice. She did not use it often; she had only to take it from a drawer and lay it across her desk to quell any ordinary
25 disobedience. When she did use it, she displayed a strength that even the biggest, most loutish boy dreaded, for not only did she flail his hands until they swelled to red, aching paws, but she tongue-lashed him with a virtuosity that threw her classes into an ecstasy of silent delight.
30 'Gordon McNab, you're a true chip off the McNab block. (*Slash!*) I've given the strap to your father (*Slash!*), and both your uncles (*Slash!*), and I once gave it to your mother (*Slash!*), and I'm here to tell the world that you are the stupidest, most ignorant, no-account ruffian of the whole caboodle. (*Slash!*)
35 And that's saying something. (*Slash!*) Now go to your seat, and if I hear a peep out of you except in answer to a question, you'll get it again and get it worse, because I've got it right here in my desk, all ready for you. Do you hear me?'

What's Bred in the Bone by Robertson Davies *(Canadian)*

Sentence structure

A Put the words in the right order in each sentence to prepare yourself for exercise **B** below.

1 a Fifty-nine Miss McGladdery was.

b Through her teaching career she was soldiering. At sixty-five she to retire would be able.

c Again with God's help any of her former pupils she would never see. (ll. 13–16)

2 a A short fat implacable woman she was.

b She her three groups didn't rule with a rod of iron.

c Only two rooms had Carlyle Rural and the most advanced classes she took.

d She with a leather strap ruled. By the school board it was issued.

e The ultimate instrument of justice it was. (ll. 18–23)

B Join the above into two separate sentences, then check against the text.

1 ....

2 ....

Grammar points

C Supply prepositions or particles *only where necessary*, then refer to the text.

1 At the first recess a large boy approached .... him. (ll. 1–2)
2 'Come ...., Chicken, let's see if you can fight.' (ll. 3–4)
3 He suffered .... no serious damage. (ll. 9–10)
4 After recess he sat .... his desk. (l. 10)
5 Miss McGladdery was angry .... him. (ll. 11–12)
6 She was soldiering .... her teaching career. (l. 14)
7 She ruled .... the leather strap that was issued .... the school board. (ll. 19–22)
8 She had only to take it .... a drawer and lay it .... her desk to quell any disobedience. (ll. 23–25)
9 She tongue-lashed him .... a virtuosity that threw her classes .... ecstasy. (ll. 28–29)

D Supply comparative or superlative forms, then check against the text.

1 Carlyle Rural had only two rooms and she took (advanced) .... classes. (ll. 19–21)
2 When she did use it, she displayed a strength that even (big) ...., (loutish) .... boy dreaded. (ll. 25–26)
3 'I'm here to tell the world that you are (stupid) ...., (ignorant) ...., no-account ruffian of the whole caboodle.' (ll. 33–34)
4 'If I hear a peep out of you except in answer to a question, you'll get it again and get it (bad) ...., because I've got it right here in my desk, all ready for you.' (ll. 36–38)

E Supply the missing words in these sentences.

a *You've got a smudge on* .... *face.*
b *A large boy hit him hard in* .... *face.* (ll. 1–3)

Supply possessive adjectives (*my*, etc.) or *the*.

1 A wasp appeared out of nowhere and settled on *my* nose.
2 A wasp stung me on .... nose.
3 She stopped suddenly, pulled me by .... sleeve, and cried, 'Look!'
4 Look out! You're putting .... sleeve into the dish.
5 How are you? How's .... family?
6 .... hair is really getting too long. I must have it cut.
7 You don't expect teachers to pull children by .... hair to attract their attention!
8 We dragged him out of the water by .... feet.
9 He stepped into a puddle and got .... feet wet.

F What's the difference between these -ed forms? Show whether they're pronounced /t/ or /ɪd/.

a *After recess he sat at his desk,* **wretched** *and aching.* (ll. 10–11) ....
b *The bomb explosion* **wrecked** *the entire building.* ....

Say what part of speech the -ed forms are and show whether they are pronounced /d/, /t/ or /ɪd/.

1 The attack without warning was a case of *naked* aggression. *adjective / ɪd/*
2 This sherry has been *aged* in oak casks. ....
3 It is now my responsibility to look after my *aged* parents. ....
4 They *ragged* him mercilessly when he was at school. ....
5 A horde of *ragged* urchins approached as we entered the town. ....
6 You have to be a *learned* professor to understand what he says. ....
7 What we *learned* at school didn't equip us for life. ....
8 She *crooked* her little finger and he came running. ....
9 Plastic surgery won't straighten a *crooked* nose. ....
10 This was the last letter I received from my *beloved* husband. ....

SENTENCE STRUCTURE

A Answers and commentary

1a *Miss McGladdery* (subject) *was* (be) *fifty-nine* (complement). [> LEG 1.11]

b *She* (subject) *was soldiering* (verb) *through her teaching career* ('place'). [> LEG 1.3, 1.10]

At sixty-five (time) *she* (subject) *would be* (be) *able* (adjective complement) *to retire* (+ *to*-infinitive). [> LEG 1.3, 1.11]
The time-phrase can come at the beginning or at the end of the clause. [> LEG 7.22, LAG 4A] We could also say:

> *She would be able to retire* **at sixty-five.**

c *With God's help* (manner) *she* (subject) *would never see* (verb) *any of her former pupils* (object) *again* (time). [> LEG 1.3, 1.12]
Adverbials of manner usually come after the object or after the verb. [> LAG 4A] In narrative writing, sentences often begin with adverbs of manner. [> LEG 7.16.3, LAG 48A*n*.1]
The meaning of *again* at the beginning of the sentence would be different from its meaning at the end:

> *Again with God's help* ... (= Once more with God's help – implying that God had helped her in the past)
> *She would never see any of her former pupils* **again**. (= another time)

2a *She* (subject) *was* (be) *a short, fat, implacable woman* (complement). [> LEG 1.11, LAG 4A]

b *She* (subject) *didn't rule* (verb) *her three groups* (object) *with a rod of iron* (manner).
[> LEG 1.3, 1.12, 7.16, LAG 4A]

c *Carlyle Rural* (subject) *had* (verb) *only two rooms* (object) *and* (conjunction) *she* (subject) *took* (verb) *the most advanced classes* (object).
Two simple sentences are joined by *and*. [> LEG 1.19] The two clauses have different subjects, which must both be used. [> LEG 1.20.1, LAG 13B]

d *She* (subject) *ruled* (verb) *with a leather strap* (manner). [> LAG 4A]
Note how the verb *rule* is used intransitively here, but transitively in **b** above. [> LEG 1.10, App 1.3]

It (subject) *was issued* (passive verb) *by the school board* (by + agent).
By + agent is necessary here because it introduces important information. [> LEG 12.5, LAG 49D]

e *It* (subject) *was* (be) *the ultimate instrument of justice* (complement). [> LEG 1.11, LAG 4A]

B Answers and commentary

1 *Miss McGladdery was fifty-nine,* **and** *she was soldiering through her teaching career* ...
and introduces a co-ordinate clause. [> LEG 1.17–20, LAG 1B*n*.2]

... **until**, *at sixty-five, she would be able to retire* ...
until introduces an adverbial clause of time.
[> LEG 1.45.1, LAG 1B*n*.2, 6B*n*.1, 53B*n*.1]

... **and**, *with God's help, never see any of her former pupils again.*
and introduces another co-ordinate main clause.
[> LEG 1.17–20]

2 *A short, fat, implacable woman, she ruled her three groups* ...
A short, fat, implacable woman is in apposition with *she*. [> LEG 1.39, LAG 2A*n*.1, 5A*ns*.2,4]

... *– for Carlyle Rural had only two rooms and she took the most advanced classes –* ...
For introduces a co-ordinate clause of reason. [> LEG 1.20.5, LAG 7A*n*.2a] It is separated here by dashes rather than by commas or brackets. [compare > LEG 1.26, LAG 3B*n*.3]

... **not with** *a rod of iron,* **but with** *the leather strap* **that** *was issued by the school board* ...
A contrasting negative is introduced by *not* here [compare > LEG 16.14]; *that was issued* ... is a defining clause, providing essential information, therefore no commas. [> LEG 1.26, LAG 5A*n*.3]

... **as** *the ultimate instrument of justice.*
as (= in the capacity of). [> LEG App 25.25, LAG 12B*n*.18]

GRAMMAR POINTS

C Prepositions and particles [> LEG 8.4, LAG 4C, 4D, 12B, 13C, 16B, 27C, etc.]

1 a large boy *approached him*: No preposition after *approach*. [> LEG 8.24n.5]

2 'Come *on*, Chicken': verb + particle (intransitive); Type 3 phrasal verb. [> LEG 8.29, App 32.9.2, LAG 13C, 38D]

3 He *suffered no serious damage*: *Suffer* (= experience something unpleasant) is followed directly by an object; compare *suffer from* (a condition like *nerves*, *rheumatism* [> LAG 8D]):
*Poor Margaret **suffers from** hay fever*. (Not *suffers hay fever*)

4 he sat *at his desk*: *at* a point. [> LEG 8.6]

5 angry *with* him: angry *with* someone; angry *at* something. [> LEG App 25.36, 27, LAG 1D, 9D, 52D]

6 soldiering *through*: (= from one end to the other, probably with difficulty). [> LEG App 25.4]

7 *with* the leather strap: (= by means of). [compare > LEG App 25.36–37, LAG 49D]
issued *by* the school board: passive + *by* + agent. [> LEG 12.5]

8 take it *from* (or *out of*): movement away from [> LEG 8.9.1]; movement out of. [> LEG 8.9.6]
lay it *across* her desk: position, lack of movement [> LEG 8.7, App 25.4]; lay it *on* (a surface). [> LEG 8.6]

9 *with* a virtuosity: referring to manner. [> LEG App 25.17, compare > LAG 14D, 14G]
threw her classes *into* ecstasy (an ecstasy of silent delight): 'movement' after verb of motion. [> LEG 8.9.5, LAG 12Bn.25, 31Cn.6]

D Adjectives: comparative and superlative forms [> LEG 6.22–29]

1 she took *the most advanced* classes: *the most* + adjective of two or more syllables. [> LEG 6.25–26, 6.26n.3, LAG 11C]

2 *the biggest*: regular comparison of shorter adjective; single consonant after single vowel-letter, so consonant doubles: *big – bigger – (the) biggest*; *(the) most loutish*: *the most* + adjective of two or more syllables. [> LEG 6.25–26]

3 *the stupidest* or *the most stupid*: two-syllable adjective which can form its comparative and superlative with *-er*, *-est* or with *more/the most* [> LEG 6.25n.1, 6.26n.1]; *(the) most ignorant*: as in **1** above.

4 get it *worse*: irregular comparison: *worse* is an adverb here. [> LEG 7.4 and compare > LEG 6.24, LAG 27E]

E The use of 'the' in place of 'my', 'your', etc.: 'punched me in the face' [> LEG 4.23]

a *your* **b** *the*

We sometimes use *the* where we might expect a possessive adjective, e.g. with parts of the body after prepositions, especially after verbs which suggest aggressive behaviour:
*He punched me **in the face***. (Not *in my face*)
We can extend this use to hair and clothes (i.e. things which are 'attached' to the body):
*Miss Pringle pulled Clarinda by **the hair**/by **the sleeve***. (attack, or rough movement)
In informal contexts, we often use *the* with words like *children* and *family*:
*How are **the** children? How's **the** family?*
We can't say *How's the husband?* and *How's the wife?* isn't universally acceptable.

1 settled on my nose   2 stung me on the nose   3 pulled me by the sleeve   4 putting your sleeve   5 How's the family?   6 My hair is getting too long   7 pull children by the hair   8 by the/his feet   9 got his feet wet

F Adjectives ending in '-ed' /ɪd/ compared with regular past participles /t/ or /d/: 'wretched', 'wrecked' [> LEG 6.14, 9.14.1, App 39]

a *wretched* /ɪd/ is an adjective.

b *wrecked* /t/ is the regular past form of the verb *wreck*.

In *a locked door*, *locked* (pronounced /lɒkt/) is a regular past participle used as an adjective. [> LAG 3C, 7C, 21C, 47D] Some adjectives ending in *-ed* are not past participles and are pronounced /ɪd/: an *aged* parent, a *crooked* path.

1 *naked* aggression /ɪd/ (adjective)
2 has been *aged* /d/ (verb)
3 my *aged* parents /ɪd/ (adjective)
4 they *ragged* him /d/ (verb = 'made fun of')
5 *ragged* urchins /ɪd/ (adjective = 'in rags')
6 *learned* professor /ɪd/ (adjective)
7 we *learned* /t/ or /d/ (verb)
8 she *crooked* /t/ (verb = 'bent')
9 a *crooked* nose /ɪd/ (adjective)
10 my *beloved* husband /ɪd/ (adjective)

Our tribal past

THE genetic 'footprints' of ancient tribal ancestors have been uncovered among the bustling populations of the world's cities. Some of the most intriguing evidence for this startling new finding has just come from Hiroshima and Nagasaki. Since atom bombs were dropped in 1945, their citizens, and their genes, have been studied in extensive detail. Scientists have been searching for signs that mutations, triggered by the A-bomb blasts, had passed on to survivors' children. A study of tens of thousands of parents and children, involving the investigation of several thousand genes which control the manufacture of proteins in the body, was carried out.

Against all expectations, researchers, led by Professor James Neel of Michigan University, found no sign that any new mutated genes, created by the blast, were passed on to offspring. But to their great surprise, the researchers did find

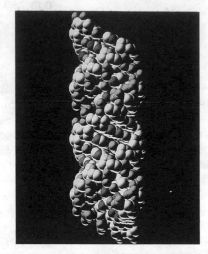

DNA structure

evidence of other mutations, ones laid down by the ancient tribes that had established the cities - 6,000 years ago when Nagasaki was founded by the Jomon culture and Hiroshima by the Yayoi people. The Jomon and the Yayoi evolved independently and carried genes that varied distinctively. Scientists found these genes still persist among modern Japanese.

Nor is Japan alone in displaying its ancient genetic heritage so openly. Italy provides another striking example. By testing blood groups and other genetically determined physical features, scientists have found significant differences between regions in the south, established by the ancient Greeks, and further north, round Orvieto, which was the centre of the Etruscan civilisation. In other words, the genes of ancient Greeks and Etruscans still flow - noticeably - through the veins of modern Italians. It is even possible to determine differences in spoken dialect between natives of these two regions, ones that exactly correlate to their separate genetic histories.

Scientists now believe that all countries display such characteristics. 'There are certainly noticeable differences in blood groups and other genetic features between modern Scots, English and Welsh - for all the intermingling that has gone on over the ages,' said Dr Jones.

The Observer (BrE)

Sentence structure

A Sometimes a wrong word has been used or added. Delete the wrong word, and suggest a replacement. Some lines need no change at all. Then refer to the text.

Scientists have been searching for signs that mutations, triggering by the A-bomb	**1** ....
blasts, had passed on to survivors' children. A study of tens of thousands	**2** ....
of parents and children, involved the investigation of several thousand genes	**3** ....
which control the manufacture of proteins in the body, was carried out.	**4** ....
Against all expectations, researchers, led by Professor James Neel	**5** ....
of Michigan University, was found no sign that any new mutated genes, created	**6** ....
by the blast, were passing on to offspring. But to their great surprise, the	**7** ....
researchers did find evidence of other mutations, ones laid down by	**8** ....
the ancient tribes that had established the cities – 6,000 years ago	**9** ....
where Nagasaki was founded by the Jomon culture and Hiroshima by the	**10** ....
Yayoi people. The Jomon and the Yayoi evolving independently and carried	**11** ....
genes that varied distinctively. Scientists found these genes still	**12** ....
are persisting among modern Japanese. Nor is Japan alone in displaying its	**13** ....
ancient genetic heritage so openly. Italy provides another striking example.	**14** ....
By test blood groups and other genetically determined physical features,	**15** ....
scientists have found significant differences between regions in the south,	**16** ....
establishing by the ancient Greeks, and further north, round Orvieto,	**17** ....
who was the centre of the Etruscan civilisation. In other words, the	**18** ....
genes of ancient Greeks and Etruscans still flowing – noticeably – through	**19** ....
the veins of modern Italians. (ll. 13–60)	

Grammar points

B Supply the right forms of the verbs in brackets, then refer to the text. (ll. 1–43)

The genetic 'footprints' of ancient tribal ancestors have been uncovered among the bustling populations of the world's cities. Some of the most intriguing evidence for this startling new finding [1](*just come*) .... from Hiroshima and Nagasaki. Since atom bombs [2](*drop*) .... in 1945, their citizens, and their genes, [3](*study*) .... in extensive detail. Scientists [4](*search*) .... for signs that mutations, triggered by the A-bomb blasts, [5](*pass*) .... on to survivors' children. A study of tens of thousands of parents and children, involving the investigation of several thousand genes which [6](*control*) .... the manufacture of proteins in the body, was carried out. Against all expectations, researchers, led by Professor James Neel of Michigan University, [7](*find*) .... no sign that any new mutated genes, created by the blast, [8](*pass*) .... on to offspring. But to their great surprise, the researchers [9](*find*) .... evidence of other mutations, ones laid down by the ancient tribes that [10](*establish*) .... the cities – 6,000 years ago when Nagasaki [11](*found*) .... by the Jomon culture and Hiroshima by the Yayoi people. The Jomon and the Yayoi [12](*evolve*) .... independently and [13](*carry*) .... genes that [14](*vary*) .... distinctively. Scientists [15](*find*) .... these genes still [16](*persist*) .... among modern Japanese.

C What's the basic difference in word order between these two sentences?

a *Japan isn't alone, either, in displaying its ancient genetic heritage so openly.*
b *Nor is Japan alone in displaying its ancient genetic heritage so openly.* (ll. 44–46)

....

Rewrite these sentences using the adverbs provided.

1 There has never been such a move to protect the environment of Antarctica.
Never *has there been such a move to protect the environment of Antarctica.*
2 The passengers don't realize how lucky they have been.
Little ....
3 We were able to enjoy the glory of the night sky only during a powercut.
Only during a powercut ....
4 The barrister questioned the witness so furiously that she broke down.
So furiously ....
5 We won't be allowed to enter the restricted area in any circumstances.
In no circumstances ....
6 We reported the fraud to the police only when we knew we had solid evidence.
Only when ....
7 The opposition to the new tax had been so great that it finally had to be abandoned.
So great ....

D Supply the missing adverbs, then check against the text.

a *Nor is Japan alone in displaying its ancient genetic heritage* .... *openly.* (ll. 44–46)
b *Scientists now believe that all countries display* .... *characteristics.* (ll. 66–68)

Supply *so, so many, so much,* or *such (a/an)*. Alternatives are sometimes possible.

1 It's been ....*so*.... quiet here since the children left home.
2 I feel .... better now that I think I can go back to work on Monday.
3 There are .... parking restrictions in our town, that I prefer to go everywhere on foot.
4 Weddings can be very formal and you must have the right clothes for .... occasions.
5 Dumping waste in the sea aroused .... hostility, the government had to think again.
6 Halley's Comet was last seen in 1989. .... occurrences are eagerly awaited.
7 Few projects have required .... colossal investment as the Channel tunnel.
8 I can't explain why I've been feeling .... run down.

SENTENCE STRUCTURE

A Answers and commentary

1 *triggered*: The past participle construction is used in place of a relative clause (passive) [> LEG 1.62.3, LAG 6B*n*.4]:

> ... *mutations*, *(which were)* **triggered** *by the A-bomb blasts*, ... Commas show that the clause is non-defining, that is it provides extra, not essential, information (from the point of view of the writer). [> LAG 17A*n*.6b]

2 This line is correct.

3 *A study of tens of thousands of parents and children*, **involving** ...
The present participle construction combines two ideas here [> LEG 1.57–58]:

> *A* **study** *was carried out.* **It involved** *the investigation* ...
> → *A* **study** ..., **involving** ..., *was carried out.*

4–5 These lines are correct.

6 ... *researchers, led by Professor James Neel of Michigan University*, **found** ...
Researchers is the subject of the active verb *found*. [> LEG 1.3, 1.21]
... **led** *by Professor James Neel of Michigan University*, ... is used in place of a passive relative clause, as in **1** above.

7 ... *any new mutated genes, created by the blast,* **were passed** *on to offspring.*
... *any new mutated genes* is the subject of the passive verb *were passed*. [> LEG 1.3, 1.21, 12.1, 12.3*n*.3]
... **created** *by the blast,* ... a past participle is used in place of a passive relative clause, as in **1** above.

8–9 These lines are correct.

10 ... *6,000 years ago* **when** *Nagasaki was founded by the Jomon culture and Hiroshima by the Yayoi people.*
We are concerned here with the time (*6,000 years ago*), not the place (*Nagasaki*), therefore we need the time conjunction *when* [> LEG 1.45.1], not the place conjunction *where*. [> LEG 1.46]

11 *The Jomon and the Yayoi* **evolved** *independently and carried genes* ...
A finite verb (*evolved*), not a present participle (*evolving*), is required here, to match with the finite verb in the co-ordinate clause (*and carried*). [> LEG 1.2, 1.17, 1.58]

12 This line is correct.

13 *Scientists found these genes still* **persist** *among modern Japanese.*
A finite verb may be required here. We have two ideas:

> 1 *These genes still* **persist** *among modern Japanese.*
> 2 *Scientists* **found** *this.*
> → *Scientists* **found** (reporting verb) *(that) these genes still* **persist**. (noun clause object of a verb [> LEG 1.23.2, LAG 4E, 14B])

Or we could say:

> *Scientists* **found** *these genes still* **persisting** *among modern Japanese.*
> where *persisting* is a present participle. [> LEG 2.7, 16.39.2, 16.45.1, LAG 1F]

14 This line is correct.

15 *By* **testing** *blood groups* ...
The *-ing* form is required after a preposition. [> LAG 1D] The *-ing* form answers *How?* here and refers to method. [> LEG 13.40.4, 16.51, App 25.17, LAG 17B*n*.5, 20B*n*.1, 29A*n*.3]

16 This line is correct.

17 ... *differences between regions in the south,* **established** *by the ancient Greeks,* ...
The past participle construction is used in place of a relative clause in the passive:

> *There were* **regions**. *They were* **established** *by the ancient Greeks.*
> → *There were* **regions**, *(which were)* **established** *by the ancient Greeks,* .... [> LEG 1.62.3, LAG 6B*n*.4]

18 ... *round Orvieto,* **which** *was the centre of the Etruscan civilisation.*
Orvieto is obviously a place, not a person. The relative pronoun *which*, referring to things, is required, not *who*, referring to persons. [> LEG 1.27–29, LAG 17A*n*.6b, 31A*n*.2]

19 *In other words, the genes of ancient Greeks and Etruscans still* **flow** *– noticeably – through the veins of modern Italians.*
A finite verb (*flow*) is required, not a present participle (*flowing*). [> LEG 1.2, LAG 1A]
Compare e.g:

> *The genes, still* **flowing** (participle) *noticeably,* **show** (finite verb) *the origin of these people.*

GRAMMAR POINTS

B Verbs and verb tenses [> LEG Chapter 9, regular and irregular verbs > Apps 39–40]

The present perfect and the simple past are the dominant tenses here. The opening paragraph clearly illustrates the use of the present perfect as a *present* tense. [> LEG 9.23] The contrast with the simple past as a narrative tense in the second paragraph is clearly marked. [> LEG 9.21]

1 *has just come*: We often use the present perfect when we don't specify the time: *just* is not an exact time reference. [> LEG 7.29, 9.26.2]

2 *were dropped*: Simple past: exact time reference (*in 1945*). [> LEG 9.17–18] Note the use of *since* + point of time. [> LEG 9.25.2]

3 *have been studied*: Present perfect to describe actions that began in the past and continue into the present. [> LEG 9.25, 12.1–4, LAG 8En.6]

4 *have been searching*: The present perfect progressive emphasizes that the activity has been in progress throughout a period with consequences *now*. [> LEG 9.33.1, LAG 19Cn.1]

5 *had passed*: The past perfect refers to an earlier past. [> LEG 9.29.1, 9.30, LAG 52B] The simple past or present perfect would also be possible here.

6 *control*: The simple present to describe a permanent truth. [> LEG 9.8.1, LAG 50C]

7 *found*: Simple past: narration. [> LEG 9.17.1]

8 *were passed*: Simple past: narration. [> LEG 9.17.1, 12.1–4] The simple past perfect (*had been passed*) would also be possible here.

9 *did find*: Simple past with emphatic *do*. The surprise referred to (*to their great surprise*) is emphasized by *did*. [> LEG 9.17.1, 10.4n.2]

10 *had established*: The simple past perfect referring to an earlier past [> LEG 9.31], but the simple past would also have been possible.

11 *was founded*: Simple past: narration. [> LEG 9.17.1] Compare: *find - found - found* (irregular verb, 15 below) and *found* (= establish) *- founded - founded* (regular verb).

12 *evolved*: Simple past: narration. [> LEG 9.17.1]

13 *carried*: Simple past: narration. [> LEG 9.17.1]

14 *varied*: Simple past: narration [> LEG 9.17.1]; or *vary* because it still applies.

15 *found*: Simple past: narration. [> LEG 9.17.1]

16 *persist*: The simple present to describe a permanent truth or 'the present period'. [> LEG 9.8.1–2, LAG 37C, 50C]

C Inversion after negative adverbs, etc.: 'nor is Japan alone' [> LEG 7.59.3, App 19]

The subject in **b** (*Japan*) comes after the verb (*is*).

If we begin a sentence with a negative adverb like *Never* we must follow with the word order we use in a Yes/No question. Beginning with a negative is very formal. Inversion occurs after:
- negative adverbs: e.g. *hardly* [> LAG 11E], *hardly ever, never*, etc.: **Never has there been** ... (= There has never been)
- phrases with *only*: e.g. *only after, only then, only when*, etc.: **Only then did I learn** ...
- *so* + adjective or adverb: **So difficult was this problem**, *Einstein couldn't solve it*. [> LAG 1Bn.2]

1 Never has there been such a move   2 Little do the passengers realize how lucky they have been.   3 Only during a powercut were we able to enjoy   4 So furiously did the barrister question the witness   5 In no circumstances will we be allowed to enter   6 Only when we knew we had solid evidence did we report the fraud   7 So great had been the opposition/had the opposition been to the new tax

D 'So', 'so many', 'so much', 'such (a/an)' [> LEG 7.51.1, LAG 1Bn.2, 16An.3]

a *so openly*
b *such characteristics*

We use *so, so many, so much* and *such (a/an)* as intensifiers/adverbs of degree. We can use:
- *so* + adjective: *It's **so quiet** here!*
- *so much* + comparative: *I feel **so much better**.* (Not **so better*) [compare > LEG 6.27.5]
- *so many* + plural countable noun: *We've had **so many letters**.* [compare > LAG 2F, 31D]
- *so much* + uncountable noun: *There's been **so much trouble**!* [compare > LAG 2F, 31D]
- *such a/an* + countable noun: *She's **such a nice person**. It's **such an opportunity**.*
- *such* + plural countable noun: *There have been **such changes** in this department.* (= so many)
- *such* + uncountable noun: *It's been a period of **such change**.* (= so much)

1 so quiet   2 so much better   3 such parking restrictions/so many parking restrictions   4 such occasions   5 so much/such hostility   6 Such occurrences 7 such (a) colossal investment   8 so run down

Village women

THE WOMEN play a great part in village politics. They do a lot of the organizing and if their men hold trade-union offices or party positions, they will do all the
5 writing for them. The women are political because it is they who spend the wages. A man will take his wage and think it fair enough but his wife will have a weekly experience of how inadequate it is. She soon comes to understand that
10 it is this constant just-too-little money which must always keep the family static. The Women's Institute has educated the village women. Women like organizations. They like committees for this and sub-committees for that. They don't care what they say to each other when
15 they are on a committee and when they come to a unanimous resolution about something - it has to be done! The women never lost their independence during the bad days as the men did. The men were beaten because the farms took every ounce of their physical
20 strength and, as they had no great mental strength because of lack of education, they were left with nothing. Their physical strength was their pride and as soon as it was gone they became timid. It was the farm versus their bodies, and the farm always won. The farms used to
25 swallow up men as they swallowed up muck and the men realized this quite early on in their lives. Things are different now, of course, but there is a legacy of beaten men in the Suffolk villages. Some of these men are surprisingly young. You don't find women in this
30 condition, no matter how hard their lives have been.

Akenfield by Ronald Blythe *(BrE)*

Sentence structure

A Six of the words or phrases below can be used in place of words or phrases in the text. Underline the words or phrases in the text that could be replaced.

organize a lot	*they hadn't nothing left*
on account of the fact that they are the ones	*the moment it had gone*
lost theirs	*in the same way*
since they possessed	*regardless of*

Now say why the two remaining phrases are wrong.

1 ....
....
....

2 ....
....
....

B Rewrite these sentences as one sentence beginning with the words provided. Then check against the text.

1 A man takes his wage. He thinks it is fair enough. His wife will have a weekly experience of how inadequate it is. (ll. 6–9)
A man will take ....
....

2 They were proud of their physical strength. As soon as it was gone they became timid. (ll. 21–23
Their physical strength ....
....

Grammar points

C Rewrite these phrases with *do*, making any necessary changes.

a *The women organize a lot.* (l. 2) ....

b *They will write everything.* (ll. 4–5) ....

Replace the phrases in italics using a phrase with *do* and making any necessary changes.

1 Who *irons the clothes* in this household? *does the ironing* ....

2 I *read a lot* when I'm on holiday. ....

3 We looked around and *shopped a bit*. ....

4 *I'm cooking* at the moment. ....

5 I like to *write* in my spare time. ....

6 Did you *see the sights* in Rome? ....

D Rewrite this sentence beginning with *It*, then compare your answer with the text. (ll. 5–6)
Women spend the wages, not men.

....

Rewrite these sentences beginning with *It*.

1 Freda phoned last night, not Rita. *It was Freda who phoned last night, not Rita.*

2 Angela signed the cheque, not her husband. ....

3 John arrived last Wednesday, not Thursday. ....

4 I wrote to Frank, not his brother. ....

5 I use a laptop computer, not a desktop. ....

E Why is *enough* in different positions in these two sentences?

a *A man will take his wage and think it fair* **enough**. (ll. 6–8)

b *I haven't got* **enough** *small change to get a bus ticket.*

....

Supply suitable phrases using *enough*.

1 Is the water *hot enough* for me to have a bath?

2 We can't have such an expensive holiday if we haven't got ....

3 I can't carve this meat. The carving knife isn't ....

4 Have we got .... and forks for our guests?

5 I don't think she runs .... to take part in this race.

6 Would you be .... to give her a message?

7 There just isn't .... in my room to fit in another piece of furniture.

F Explain the different uses of *experience* in these two sentences.

a *His wife will have a weekly* **experience** *of how inadequate it is.* (ll. 8–9)

b *The ability to handle money comes with* **experience**.

....

Write sentences using the following words.

1a power ....

  b a power ....

2a age ....

  b an age ....

3a youth ....

  b a youth ....

4a ice ....

  b an ice ....

5a education ....

  b an education ....

SENTENCE STRUCTURE

A Answers and commentary

The following words or phrases in the text should be underlined:

1 because it is they (l. 6)
(→ *on account of the fact that they are the ones*)
on account of is a preposition. [> LEG App 20.3] *The fact that* follows prepositions and prepositional phrases like *because of, in view of*, particularly in formal writing. [> LEG 1.23.3]
We often use *one* and *ones* as substitution words after *the, that/those* etc. to refer to people or things. We use them when we wish to avoid repeating the noun [> LEG 4.10, LAG 54E]:
> It is *the women* who . . .
> → They are *the ones* who . . .

2 did (l. 18)
(→ *lost theirs*)
*The women never lost their independence during the bad days as the men **did**/ . . . as the men **lost theirs**.*
We often use the appropriate form of *do* to avoid repeating the previous verb. [> LEG 4.18, 10.44.2, LAG 53E, 54Ans.10,18, 57A]

3 as they had (l. 20)
(→ *since they possessed*)
As and *since* interchangeably introduce adverbial clauses of reason. [> LEG 1.48]
We often use *have* and *have got* in the sense of 'possess'. [> LEG 10.31ns.3–4] *Have got* usually refers to the present. [> LEG 10.30n.4]

4 as soon as it was gone (ll. 22–23)
(→ *the moment it had gone*)
As soon as and *the moment (that)* are interchangeable in adverbial clauses of time. [> LEG 1.45.1, LAG 6Bn.1, 16An.4]
With a few verbs like *do, go* and *finish, be* can replace *have* [> LEG 10.9.8]:
> *I left my keys just there and the next moment they **were** (had) gone.*

5 as (l. 25)
(→ *in the same way*)
*The farms used to swallow up men **as** they swallowed up muck/ . . . **in the same way** they swallowed up muck . . .*
As and *in the (same) way (as)* are interchangeable in adverbial clauses of manner. [> LEG 1.47.1]

6 no matter (l. 30)
(→ *regardless of*)
*You don't find women in this condition, **no matter** how hard . . . /**regardless of** how hard . . .*
No matter and *regardless of* (= regardless of the degree to which) introduce adverbial clauses of concession. [> LEG 1.50]

Remaining answers

1 *organize a lot* does not exactly replace *do a lot of the organizing* (l. 2). *They organize a lot* can suggest that 'they organize a lot of things'. *They do a lot of the organizing* (= whatever organizing needs to be done). [compare > LEG 10.44.4, 16.40.4]

2 *they hadn't nothing left* does not replace *they were left with nothing* (l. 21). We usually have only one negative in any one clause [> LEG 7.39, 13.10]. [For the use of *left* (= not consumed, or remaining) > LEG 5.7, LAG 31E.]

B Answers and commentary

1 *A man **will take** his wage **and** think it fair enough **but** his wife will have a weekly experience of how inadequate it is.*
We can use *will* + verb in place of the simple present to describe characteristic habit or behaviour. [> LEG 11.63, LAG 5D]
and introduces a co-ordinate clause (*and think . . .*) and we don't repeat the subject + *will* here. [> LEG 1.17–20]
but introduces a contrast clause followed by a new subject (*but his wife*). [> LEG 1.20.2]

2 *Their physical strength was **their pride and** as soon as it was gone they became timid.*
We can use a noun (*Their strength was their pride*) in place of an adjective (*They were **proud** of their strength*). [> LEG 8.20, 16.34] Here is an analysis of the sentence [> LEG 1.17, 1.21]:
Their physical strength was their pride (main clause) ***and** they became timid* (co-ordinate main clause) ***as soon as** it was gone* (subordinate adverbial clause of time).

GRAMMAR POINTS

C 'Do' + '-ing': 'do the shopping' [> LEG 10.44.4, 16.39.1, 16.40.4]

a *The women **do a lot of the organizing***.
b *They **will do all the writing***.

We often use *do + -ing* (gerund) to refer to named tasks. We can use determiners like *the, this, a lot of, some, any* etc. in front of the gerund: *do the ironing, do some reading,* etc.

1 does the ironing
2 do a lot of reading
3 did a bit of shopping
4 I'm doing some cooking
5 do some writing
6 do some/any sightseeing

D The use of 'it' in 'cleft sentences': 'it's women who...' [> LEG 4.14, compare > LAG 1C, 28Bn.2]

It's women who spend the wages, not men.

We can begin sentences with *It is* or *It was* + subject + *that* or *who(m)/which*, if we wish to emphasize the word or phrase that follows. We call these *cleft* sentences because a simple sentence is split up (cleft) into two clauses using the *it*-construction:

Women spend the wages, not men.
→ *It's women who spend the wages, not men.*

1 It was Freda who/that phoned last night, not Rita.
2 It was Angela who signed the cheque, not her husband.
3 It was last Wednesday (when/that) John arrived, not Thursday.
4 It was Frank (who/that/whom) I wrote to, not his brother.
5 It's a laptop computer (that) I use, not a desktop.

E 'Enough' as an adverb of degree and as an adverb of quantity: 'fair enough', 'enough biscuits' [> LEG 5.17, 7.47–48, 16.32.2, 16.37]

In **a** *enough* is an adverb of degree, so it comes after the adjective (*fair enough*).
In **b** *enough* is an adverb of quantity, so it comes in front of the adjective + noun (*enough small change*).
Enough comes after adjectives and adverbs when we use it to express degree:

*It's **fair enough**.* (= to that degree)

Enough comes in front of plural countable nouns and uncountable nouns to describe quantity:

*Are there **enough biscuits** for everyone?*
*Is there **enough tea** for everyone?*

(= quantity) [> LAG 36Bn.1]

Possible answers
1 hot enough (degree)
2 enough money (quantity)
3 sharp enough (degree)
4 enough knives (quantity)
5 fast enough (degree)
6 good enough (degree) [> LEG 16.27.1]
7 enough space (quantity)

F Countable and uncountable uses of nouns: 'an experience', 'experience' [> LEG 2.14, 2.16]

a *An experience* is countable and refers to a single event: *a weekly experience*.
b *Experience* is uncountable and refers to the gaining of knowledge or skill.

Strict classifications of nouns into countable and uncountable are unreliable. It is better to think of countable and uncountable *uses* of nouns. [> LAG 37E, 42F, 44E]

Possible answers

1a Power tends to corrupt and absolute power corrupts absolutely. (= influence)
b What's the definition of a world power? (= a powerful nation)
2a Wisdom is supposed to come with age. (= the passing of years)
b You're at an age when you ought to know better. (= old enough)
3a Youth is the time for action. (= the period when you are young)
b He already knew what he was going to be when he was still a youth. (= young man) [> LEG 2.28.2]
4a Would you like some ice in your drink? (= frozen water)
b I'd like two milkshakes and an ice please. (= an ice cream) [> LEG 2.16.2]
5a The best investment any nation can make is in education.
b What can be said these days in favour of a classical education? [> LEG 2.16.4]

Dreams and nightmares

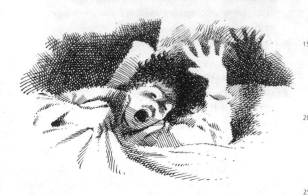

IRIS is like my former wife in that when she sleeps she sometimes has violent dreams. She thrashes around in bed during the night and wakes in the morning drenched with
5 sweat, the nightgown sticking to her body. And, like my former wife, she wants to tell me her dreams in great detail and speculate as to what this stands for or that portends. My former wife used to kick the covers off in the
10 night and cry out in her sleep, as if someone were laying hands on her. Once, in a particularly violent dream, she hit me on the ear with her fist. I was in a dreamless sleep, but I struck out in the dark and hit her on the forehead. Then we
15 began yelling. We both yelled and yelled. We'd hurt each other, but we were mainly scared. We had no idea what had happened until I turned the lamp on; then we sorted it out. Afterwards, we joked about it - fistfighting in our sleep. But when so much else began to happen that was far more serious
20 we tended to forget about that night. We never mentioned it again, even when we teased each other.

Once I woke up in the night to hear Iris grinding her teeth in her sleep. It was such a peculiar thing to have going on right next to my ear that it woke me up. I gave her a little shake, and
25 she stopped. The next morning she told me she'd had a very bad dream, but that's all she'd tell me about it. I didn't press her for details. I guess I really didn't want to know what could have been so bad that she didn't want to say. When I told her she'd been grinding her teeth in her sleep, she frowned and
30 said she was going to have to do something about that. The next night she brought home something called a Niteguard - something she was supposed to wear in her mouth while she slept. She had to do something she said. She couldn't afford to keep grinding her teeth; pretty soon she wouldn't have any. So
35 she wore this protective device in her mouth for a week or so, and then she stopped wearing it. She said it was uncomfortable and, anyway, it was not very cosmetic. Who'd want to kiss a woman wearing a thing like that in her mouth, she said. She had something there, of course.

Whoever was using this bed by Raymond Carver (*AmE*)

Sentence structure

A Circle the item that fits the space, then refer to the text.

Iris is like my former wife [1]........
[2]........ she sleeps she sometimes has violent dreams.
She thrashes around in bed during the night [3]........
wakes in the morning [4]........ with sweat,
the nightgown [5]........ to her body.
And, like my former wife, she wants [6]........ me
her dreams in great detail and speculate [7]........
[8]........ this stands for or that portends. (ll. 1–8)

1	a so	b that	c in that
2	a when	b during	c although
3	a but	b she	c and
4	a drench	b drenched	c to drench
5	a to stick	b stick	c sticking
6	a tell	b to tell	c telling
7	a as	b as to	c for
8	a who	b what	c which

B Supply the connecting words where necessary, then refer to the text.

[1]........ I woke up in the night [2](*hear*) .... Iris [3](*grind*) .... her teeth in her sleep. [4]........ was such a peculiar thing to have [5](*go*) .... on right next to my ear [6]........ it woke me up. I gave her a little shake, and [7]........ stopped. The next morning she told me she [8]........ had a very bad dream, but that's all she [9]........ tell me about it. I didn't press her for details. I guess I really didn't want to know [10]........ could have been [11]........ bad that she didn't want to say. [12]........ I told her she'd been grinding her teeth in her sleep, she frowned and said [13]..... she was going to have to do something about that. The next night she brought home something [14](*call*) .... a Niteguard – something she was supposed to wear in her mouth [15]........ she slept. She had to do something she said. She couldn't afford to keep [16](*grind*) .... her teeth; pretty soon she wouldn't have any. So she wore this protective device in her mouth for a week or so, and then she stopped [17](*wear*) .... it. She said it was uncomfortable and, anyway, it was not very cosmetic. Who'd want to kiss a woman [18](*wear*) .... a thing like that in her mouth, she said. (ll. 22–38)

Grammar points

C What's the difference in meaning between the verb phrases in bold italics?

   a *My former wife **used to kick** the covers off in the night and cry out in her sleep.* (ll. 8–10)
   b *I work in a bakery, so **I'm used to getting up** very early in the morning.*
   c *I had a wonderful view of the sun rising when **I was getting up** this morning.*

Supply suitable verb forms with *used to*, *be used to* or the past progressive.

   1 When we were children we (*spend*) .....*used to spend*..... our holidays on a farm.
   2 I seem to be more aware of traffic noise these days. I (*never mind*) .... it.
   3 As I live in the centre of the city, I (*hear*) .... traffic noise all the time.
   4 When I (*drive*) .... to work this morning, the streets were almost empty.
   5 I (*drive*) .... a 20-ton truck when I was in the army.
   6 I (*drive*) .... in heavy traffic: it doesn't bother me.
   7 You can't blame them for pushing. They (*not wait*) .... in queues.
   8 I (*wait*) .... all morning for a telephone call from you.
   9 I (*be*) .... patient, but as I get older I can't suffer fools gladly.
   10 You must give her clear instructions. She (*be told*) .... what to do.

D Would you use *after* or *afterwards* here? Why?
We had no idea what had happened. .... , *we joked about it.* (ll. 16–18)

Supply *after* or *afterwards*. Alternatives are sometimes possible.

   1 So you took the children to the zoo. Where did you go .....*after*..... that?
   2 .... a walk through the park, we visited the zoo.
   3 I watched the car-chase on TV, but I didn't see what came ....
   4 We had a very long wait for our flight .... we arrived at the airport.
   5 According to most fairy stories, everybody lives happily ever ....
   6 Let's have a meal first. .... we can watch this video.

E Which construction with *have* will fit in here?
It was such a peculiar thing (go on) .... *right next to my ear.* (ll. 23–24)

Use suitable constructions with *have*.

   1 We've told the police. We can't (*people play*) loud music.   *have people playing*
   2 We're ex-Directory now. We don't want to (*strangers ring*) us up. ....
   3 We often (*salesmen call*) at our door. ....
   4 We never (*the post arrive*) before eight o'clock. ....
   5 Shut the door. We don't want to (*anyone interrupt*) the meeting. ....

F Supply the missing construction with *be supposed to*. What does it mean?
Niteguard was something she (wear) .... *in her mouth while she slept.* (ll. 31–33)

Supply suitable constructions with *be supposed to*.

   1 I'm sorry. I'll have to phone you later. (*work*) .....*I'm supposed to be working*..... at the moment.
   2 You'd better ask Henry. (*know*) .... how this computer works.
   3 We'd better hurry. The train (*arrive*) .... at two minutes past four.
   4 Just look at the questionnaire! How (*we/answer*) .... questions like this?
   5 I don't think there are any buses today. There (*be*) .... a strike.
   6 We're already late. We (*submit*) .... this report five days ago.
   7 Don't breathe a word to anybody. (*You/not know*) .... anything about this.

SENTENCE STRUCTURE

A Answers and commentary

1 **c** *in that*: introduces a 'limiting clause', qualifying *Iris is like my former wife*. [> LEG 1.54]

2 **a** *when*: introduces a time-clause + present. [> LEG 1.45.2, LAG 6Bn.1] *While* could replace *when* here. [compare > LEG 9.20.2]

3 **c** *and*: introduces a co-ordinate main clause in which the subject (*she*) is not repeated. [> LEG 1.17–20]

4 **b** *drenched*: The past participle is used adjectivally in place of the passive [> LEG 1.62.1]:
She wakes up in the morning. She is drenched with sweat ...
→ *She wakes up in the morning **drenched** ...*

5 **c** *sticking*: The present participle is used in place of a co-ordinate clause [> LEG 1.58.1]:
*... drenched with sweat, **and the nightgown is sticking** to her body.*
→ *drenched with sweat, **the nightgown sticking** ...*

6 **b** *to tell*: When we use a verb after *want*, it must be a *to*-infinitive. [> LEG 16.19–20, App 46.1]

7 **b** *as to*: Preposition used in the sense of 'about'. [> LEG App 25.38]

8 **b** *what*: introduces a noun clause after *speculate as to*. [> LEG 1.24.2, LAG 14C, 42D, 50E]

B Answers and commentary

1 *Once* (= On one occasion): Adverb of indefinite time, common in narrative. [> LEG 7.23]

2 *to hear*: The *to*-infinitive is used here in place of *and heard* to describe a later event in a sequence. It is used to describe an event which is unexpected and perhaps unwelcome. It could be preceded by *only* [> LEG 16.12.2]:
*I woke up in the night **and heard** Iris ...*
→ *I woke up in the night **(only) to hear** Iris ...*

3 *grinding*: We can use a bare infinitive (*and heard Iris grind*) or the *-ing* form (*and heard Iris grinding*). The *-ing* form tells us that the writer heard part of the action only and emphasizes continuity [> LEG 16.9.2, LAG 28D]:
*Iris **was grinding** her teeth. I **heard** her.*
→ *I **heard** Iris **grinding** her teeth.*

4 *It*: The pronoun refers to the whole action of *Iris grinding her teeth*. [> LEG 4.5.5, LAG 23A]

5 *going*: The use of the *-ing* form after *have* here refers to happenings beyond the writer's control [> LEG 16.10.2, LAG 35E]:

*I **had** this peculiar thing **going** on right next to my ear ...*

6 *that*: (which could be omitted) introduces an adverbial clause of result after *such a* + adjective + noun. [> LEG 1.52.1, LAG 10An.2]

7 *she*: Compare *I gave her a shake and stopped* (= that's what I did) and *I gave her a shake and **she** stopped* (= that's what she did). *She* refers to *Iris*. [> LEG 4.5.4]

8 *had* or *'d*: *had had* is the past perfect form. [> LEG 10.28] *Have* can be both an auxiliary and a main verb. [> LEG 10.30n.3, 10.32, 10.36n.1] The short form *'d* should not be confused with *'d* (= would). (See **9** below.) [> LEG 14.17n.3]

9 *would* or *'d*: refers to willingness here. [> LEG 11.38.1, 14.24.1] See **8** above for *'d* (= had).

10 *what*: introduces a noun clause after the reporting verb *know*. [> LEG 15.19–20, 15.24.2]

11 *so*: goes in front of an adjective to introduce an adverbial clause of result (*so bad (that) she didn't want to say ...*). [> LEG 1.52.1]

12 *When*: introduces an adverbial clause of time (*When I told her ...*). [> LEG 1.45.1]

13 (–) or *that*: *that* is often omitted after a reporting verb like *say*. [> LEG 1.23.2, 15.9]

14 *called*: The past participle construction is used in place of a relative clause with the verb in the passive [> LEG 1.62.3, LAG 6Bn.4]:
*She brought home **something**. It **was called** a Niteguard.*
→ *She brought home **something** (which was) **called** a Niteguard.*

15 *while*: introduces an adverbial clause of time. [> LEG 1.45.1, 9.20.2] *During* cannot be used here because it is a preposition and must be followed by a noun (*during the night*). [> LEG 7.35] But we can say: *during the time she slept*.

16 *grinding*: *keep* has the sense of 'continue' here and is followed by an *-ing* form. (Not *keep to grind*) [> LEG 16.42, 16.45.1, LAG 31F]

17 *wearing*: We use the *-ing* form after *stop*. [> LEG 16.42] The *to*-infinitive after *stop* is not an acceptable alternative to *-ing*; it is the infinitive of purpose [> LEG 16.59]:
*On the way home I **stopped to buy** a paper.*

18 *wearing*: The present participle construction is used in place of a relative clause [> LEG 1.58.6]:
*Who'd want to kiss a **woman who is wearing** a thing like that ...*
→ *Who'd want to kiss a **woman wearing** a thing like that ...*

GRAMMAR POINTS

C 'Used to', 'be used to' and past progressive ('was/were getting up') [> LEG 11.58–62, 10.26.1, 16.56, 9.20]

a *used to kick*: past habit.
b *I'm used to getting up* (= I am accustomed to).
c *I was getting up* (= the action in progress).

– *She used to kick the covers off*: *used to* refers only to the past to talk about habits we no longer have.
– *I'm used to getting up*: *be used to + -ing* means 'be accustomed to'. [> LAG 1D] We can also use a noun after it, or use it with *get* [> LAG 23D]:
I'm used to noise. When you work in a factory, you soon get used to the noise.
– *I was getting up*: we use the past progressive to describe actions in progress at a particular time in the past [> LAG 10An.1, 41Bns.5,8]:
It was raining all night long. (Not *used to rain*)
Very occasionally, when meanings coincide, *used to* and the past progressive are interchangeable:
I was always arriving late for work/always used to arrive late for work, until I was told off.

1 used to spend
2 never used to mind
3 am used to hearing
4 was driving
5 used to drive
6 am used to driving
7 are not used to waiting
8 was waiting
9 used to be
10 is used to being told

D 'After' and 'afterwards' [> LEG 8.4.1, 8.4.4, App 25.5]

Afterwards

We use *after*:
– as a preposition (with a noun or pronoun after it): *I'll see you after lunch. I'll see you after that*.
– as a conjunction (followed by a clause): *I'll see you after I get back to the office*. [> LAG 6Bn.1]
– sometimes as an adverb, especially when modified, by e.g. *soon*: *We arrived first and they arrived soon after*.
We hardly ever use *after* as an adverb on its own at the beginning of a sentence.

We use *afterwards* only as an adverb (i.e. on its own), often to begin a sentence or clause:
We had a swim. Afterwards, we lay on the beach. (Not *After*)

1 after
2 After
3 after/afterwards
4 after
5 after/afterwards
6 Afterwards

E 'Have' + object + '-ing' form: 'have something going on' [> LEG 16.10.2, compare > LAG 12C, 26F]

It was such a peculiar thing to have going on right next to my ear.

We sometimes use *have* + object + *-ing* to refer to things that happen beyond our control:
I had this peculiar thing going on right next to my ear. (= I could do nothing about it)

1 have people playing
2 have strangers ringing
3 have salesmen calling
4 have the post arriving
5 have anyone interrupting

F 'Be supposed to' [> LEG 12.8n.3, compare > LAG 18D, 30F, 36C]

Niteguard was something she was supposed to wear in her mouth while she slept.

We often use *be supposed to* to suggest failure or inability to perform a duty:
She was supposed to wear it in her mouth. (= but she didn't)
We also use *be supposed to* to mean 'there is reason to believe that':
There's supposed to be a political broadcast before tonight's News.

1 I'm supposed to be working
2 He's supposed to know
3 is supposed to arrive
4 are we supposed to answer
5 is supposed to be
6 were supposed to submit/are supposed to have submitted
7 You're not supposed to know

Armageddon larder

BISCUITS thought to date from the Second World War and sweets from the 1960s have been discovered by Yorkshire children in a secret government store, stockpiled in case of a nuclear holocaust. This key element of British emergency planning came to light after pupils at Adwick comprehensive school, Doncaster, started complaining of stomach pains. The children admitted eating the sweets after some of them broke into the Second World War depot at Planet Road in Adwick village. Biscuits, said to date from 1943, were also discovered. The chairman of South Yorkshire emergency planning committee, Roger Barton, said he could only presume that the 20-year-old sweets and 40-year-old biscuits were part of the region's wartime food stocks, held in the secret depot. 'You would have thought kids would have enough problems in World War Three without being made ill by ancient sweets as their post-holocaust treat,' he said.

A spokeswoman for the Ministry of Agriculture, Fisheries and Food, confirmed that the depot was still

used to hold emergency food stocks. She denied reports that the biscuits had been attacked by vermin, but said it was possible they dated from the Second World War. The food was non-perishable and was regularly monitored by scientists, she said. The depot was one of many around the country, but their locations were classified. However, she said, the depot was being closed down. This had nothing to do with the break-in. After police identified the cause of the stomach-ache, workmen immediately removed hundreds of boxes of biscuits and sweets. This too had nothing, absolutely nothing, to do with the break-in.

As the people of South Yorkshire were digesting the revelation that London intends them to survive a nuclear strike on nothing more substantial than ancient barley sugar, a second horrible thought struck home. What would happen after the store closed? Perhaps the only alternative to barley sugar was ... no barley sugar? No, no said the Ministry. The Planet Road depot was being closed as part of a nationwide reorganization of emergency food storage, and the area would be covered by another secret depot. 'We haven't got anything against South Yorkshire,' she added, somewhat unconvincingly.

The Independent (BrE)

Sentence structure

A Join these sentences making any necessary changes. Then refer to the text.

1 Biscuits have been discovered by Yorkshire children in a secret government store. They are thought to date from the Second World War. Sweets from the 1960s have also been discovered. They were stockpiled in case of a nuclear holocaust. (ll. 1–7)

....

....

....

2 The children admitted eating the sweets. Some of them broke into the Second World War depot at Planet Road in Adwick village. (ll. 11–15)

....

....

B One word is in the wrong position in each of these sentences. Show with an arrow where the wrongly-placed word should be. Then check against the text.

1 'You would have thought kids enough would have problems in World War Three without being made ill by ancient sweets as their post-holocaust treat,' he said. (ll. 24–28)

2 This had nothing too, absolutely nothing, to do with the break-in. (ll. 47–49)

3 'We haven't got anything against South Yorkshire,' added she, somewhat unconvincingly. (ll. 64–67)

Grammar points

C What's the difference in meaning between these two sentences?

a *The biscuits date from the Second World War.*

b *The biscuits are thought to date/are said to date from the Second World War.* (ll. 1–2 and 15–16)

Rewrite these sentences using the present passive of the verbs in brackets.

1 The biscuits date from the Second World War. (think)
The biscuits are thought to date from the Second World War.

2 Prices will rise if interest rates remain high. (expect)

3 Most of the passengers survived the air crash. (believe)

4 Dr Griffiths knows all there is to know about Legionnaire's Disease. (suppose)

5 The two young men introduced a virus into the computer system. (allege)

D How has the noun in bold italics been formed?
*This had nothing to do with the **break-in**.* (ll. 42–43)

Write suitable responses with *Yes* using nouns in place of the verbs in italics.

1 Someone smashed the window and *broke in*. *Yes, there was a break-in.*
2 They began by *warming up* the audience.
3 I believe he *dropped out* of university.
4 The government has *covered up* the truth.
5 Don't ask me, I'm only *looking on*.
6 Are you going to *lie in* tomorrow morning?
7 I think they've really *ripped* us *off*.
8 I'll meet you where we *check* our bags *in*.

E Supply *has/have* in these sentences. What do you notice?

a *The police* _____ *identified the cause of the stomach-ache.* (compare ll. 44–45)

b *The crowd* _____ *been waiting for hours to see the princess.*

Supply *is/are* or *have/has*. Show where you can use either a singular or plural verb.

1 There's been an accident and the police __*are*__ already at the scene.
2 The committee _____ going to consider the proposal this morning.
3 I believe the jury _____ at last come to a decision.
4 The company _____ announced record profits for the first half-year.
5 How many people _____ waiting to see me?
6 Everybody knows the clergy _____ very poorly paid.

F What does *another* mean here?
*The area would be covered by **another** secret depot.* (ll. 63–64)

Say whether *another* means *an additional* or *a different* in these sentences.

1 Three shelves aren't enough. I think we need another one.   *an additional*
2 They took away the faulty cooker and installed another one.
3 What shall I do? One cookery book says this and another says that.
4 Throw your cookery book away and get another.
5 We need another secretary in this office. One isn't enough.
6 When our secretary left, it took us a long time to find another.

SENTENCE STRUCTURE

A Answers and commentary

Suggestions for joining these sentences were not provided in the exercise, so there are many possible answers. The commentary is based on the way the sentences have been joined in the text.

1 *Biscuits **thought** to date from the Second World War* ...

This is a shortened relative clause (*which/that are thought to date* ...). The past participle construction is used to join the simple sentence *They are thought to date from the Second World War.* [> LEG 1.62.3, LAG 6B*n*.4, 22A*n*.2]

... *and sweets from the 1960s have been discovered by Yorkshire children in a secret government store,* ...

Note how the subject of *have been discovered* has been extended here. [> LEG 1.5, LAG 11A*n*.2b] Alternatively, this could have read:

Biscuits and sweets, thought to date from the Second World War and the 1960s, have been discovered ...

However, this alternative is not as precise as the sentence in the text.

... ***stockpiled*** *in case of a nuclear holocaust.*
A second past participle construction is used to join the simple sentence *They were stockpiled* .... [> LEG 1.62.3]

2 *The children admitted eating the sweets **after** some of them broke into the Second World War depot at Planet Road in Adwick village.*

After introduces an adverbial clause of time. [> LEG 1.45.1, LAG 6B*n*.1] The author could have written:

... *after some of them **had broken** into the Second World War depot* ... [> LEG 9.30] but the past perfect (*had broken*) is optional here.

B Answers and commentary

1 *You would have thought kids would have **enough problems*** ... (Not **enough would have problems**)

When *enough* refers to quantity or number, we usually put it in front of the word it refers to [> LEG 5.17, LAG 34E]:

*Have we got **enough books** to read while we are on holiday?*

*Have we got **enough food** in the house to last for the next few days?*

However, there are instances when *enough* referring to quantity or number can go after the noun, though this is less usual. [> LEG 16.37, LAG 34E] The writer could have written:

*You would have thought kids would have **problems enough** in World War Three* ...

When *enough* refers to degree, we put it after the adjective or adverb it refers to [> LEG 5.17, 7.47–48, 16.27.1, 16.32.2, 16.37]:

*The water in the pool is **warm enough** (to swim in). (Not *enough warm*)*

2 ***This too*** *had nothing, absolutely nothing, to do with the break-in.*

Too and *as well*, used as focus adverbs, usually go in the end position in the affirmative; we use *either* in the negative:

*This had **something** to do with the break-in, **too/as well**. (affirmative)*

*This had **nothing** to do with the break-in, **either**. (negative)*

However, we can use *too* directly after the subject for special emphasis, or in formal writing, and it would be usual to separate it by commas. [> LEG 7.56] When used directly after the subject, *too* can occur in affirmative *or* negative sentences:

***This, too**, had something to do with the break-in.*

***This, too**, had nothing to do with the break-in.*

***This, too**, didn't have anything to do with the break-in.* (= This didn't have anything to do with the break-in, either.)

3 *'We haven't got anything against South Yorkshire,' **she added**, somewhat unconvincingly.*

In modern English we do not put a pronoun after a reporting verb when we are writing direct speech, though this was common in the past (*'Really,' said he*, etc.). However, we often put a noun subject after a reporting verb when we are writing direct speech [> LEG 15.3*n*.4, LAG 46A*n*.2, and LEG App 45.1 which marks verbs where this sort of inversion is usually possible]:

*'We haven't got anything against South Yorkshire,' **added the Ministry official**.*

GRAMMAR POINTS

C **The passive with verbs of 'saying' and 'believing': 'they are said to date from World War II'** [> LEG 12.8, LAG 30F and compare > LAG 18D, 37B*n*.2]

a The writer is sure that this is a fact.
b The writer is not sure that this is a fact.

When we are sure of our facts, we can make statements like:

*Muriel **pays** less income tax than she should.*
*Muriel **paid** less income tax than she should have.*

When we are not sure of our facts, it is safer to say:

*Muriel **is said to pay** less income tax than she should.*
*Muriel **was said to have paid** less income tax than she should have.*

We use verbs of 'saying' and 'believing' in this passive construction: e.g. *allege, believe, expect, know, say, suppose.* [> LAG 35F]

1 The biscuits are thought to date from the Second World War.
2 Prices are expected to rise if interest rates remain high.
3 Most of the passengers are believed to have survived the air crash.
4 Dr Griffiths is supposed to know all there is to know about Legionnaire's Disease.
5 The two young men are alleged to have introduced a virus into the computer system.

D **Nouns formed from phrasal verbs: 'a break-in'** [> LEG 8.28.1g, App 31, 8.29.1d, App 35, 2.11*n*.2]

It has been formed from the phrasal verb *break in*: *How did the thieves **break in**?*

We can form nouns from Types 2 (transitive) and 3 (intransitive) phrasal verbs [> LAG 4D, 38D, 44D]:

*He **knocked the champion out** in the fourth round.*
→ *It was a **knockout**.*
*At first they said they would go on strike, then they **climbed down**.*
→ *It was a **climb-down**.*

Possible answers
1 Yes, there was a break-in.
2 Yes, there was a warm-up.
3 Yes, he was a dropout.
4 Yes, there was a cover-up.
5 Yes, (s)he's only an onlooker.
6 Yes, I'm having a lie-in.
7 Yes, it was a rip-off.
8 Yes, I'll meet you at the check-in.

E **Collective nouns with singular or plural verbs: e.g. 'police', 'crowd'** [> LEG 2.28.1, 2.29, compare > LAG 7E, 30A*n*.5]

a *The police **have*** (plural verb only).
b *The crowd **has**/**have** been waiting* (singular or plural verb).

Some collective nouns like *audience, committee, company, crowd, family, jury* take a singular or plural verb.
Others like *cattle, the clergy, the military, people, the police, vermin* take a plural verb only.

1 the police are
2 the committee is/are
3 the jury has/have
4 the company has/have
5 people are
6 the clergy are

F **'Another' meaning 'an additional' or 'a different'** [> LEG 5.27, compare > LAG 49E, 58F]

In this context, *another* means 'a different'.

Another has two meanings ('additional' or 'different') depending on context.

1 an additional
2 a different
3 a different (one)
4 a different (one)
5 an additional
6 a different (one)

Alzheimer's telltale protein

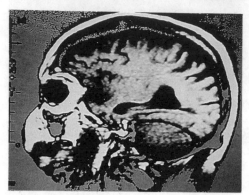

Brain scan showing Alzheimer's disease

A S IF THE CREEPING FORGETFULNESS it causes were not horrible enough, Alzheimer's disease carries an extra burden: a person must be dead before doctors can identify the disorder with absolute certainty. A discovery announced last week, however, could result in a simple and accurate skin test for living patients. The finding may also lead to new treatment for an incurable illness believed to afflict up to 4 million Americans.

Just how Alzheimer's ravages the brain isn't understood, but a protein molecule is thought to be involved. This protein, which pathologists look for in brain tissue after a suspected Alzheimer's sufferer has died, is also present in easily accessible skin cells, the new research indicates. Dr Dennis Selkoe and colleagues at the Brigham and Women's Hospital in Boston found the protein in the skin of 8 out of 11 people with Alzheimer's disease who had died. Selkoe's test must be confirmed by other laboratories and made easy to do on a large scale. But he is optimistic that a reliable skin test may be only two or three years away.

The finding suggests a fresh strategy for attacking the disease. Scientists have been trying to perfect drugs capable of repairing the damage Alzheimer's does to the brain. On the theory that the protein causes the disorder by traveling from other tissues to the brain, researchers may now seek to devise drugs that would block the protein before it gets there.

US News and World Report (AmE)

Sentence structure

A Three of these sentences are wrong. Correct what is wrong, where necessary, and say why you have done so. Then check against the text.

1 Like the creeping forgetfulness it causes were not horrible enough, Alzheimer's disease carries an extra burden: a person must be dead before doctors can identify the disorder with absolute certainty. (ll. 1–6)

....

2 The finding may also lead to new treatment for an incurable illness believed to afflict up to 4 million Americans. (ll. 8–9)

....

3 This protein, which pathologists look for it in brain tissue after a suspected Alzheimer's sufferer has died, is also present in easily accessible skin cells, the new research indicates. (ll. 11–14)

....

4 On the theory that the protein causes the disorder by traveling from other tissues to the brain, researchers may now seek to devise drugs that would block the protein before it will get there. (ll. 22–25)

....

B Choose the words that fit and say why you have made your choice. Then check against the text.

1 A discovery announced last week, ..., could result in a simple and accurate skin test for living patients. (ll. 6–8) [*however/moreover*]

....

2 Just how Alzheimer's ravages the brain isn't understood, but a protein molecule is thought ......involved. (ll. 10–11) [*that it is/to be*]

....

3 Dr Dennis Selkoe and colleagues at the Brigham and Women's Hospital in Boston found the protein in the skin of 8 out of 11 people with Alzheimer's disease who ...... (ll. 14–17) [*died/had died*]

....

Grammar points

C Supply the right forms of the verbs in brackets, then refer to the text. (ll. 1–18)

As if the creeping forgetfulness it causes were not horrible enough, Alzheimer's disease [1](*carry*) .... an extra burden: a person [2](*must dead*) .... before doctors [3](*can identify*) .... the disorder with absolute certainty. A discovery announced last week, however, [4](*can result*) .... in a simple and accurate skin test for living patients. The finding [5](*may also lead*) .... to new treatment for an incurable illness believed to afflict up to 4 million Americans. Just how Alzheimer's [6](*ravage*) .... the brain [7](*not understand*) ...., but a protein molecule [8](*think*) .... to be involved. This protein, which pathologists [9](*look for*) .... in brain tissue after a suspected Alzheimer's sufferer [10](*die*) ...., is also present in easily accessible skin cells, the new research [11](*indicate*) .... Dr Dennis Selkoe and colleagues at the Brigham and Women's Hospital in Boston [12](*find*) .... the protein in the skin of 8 out of 11 people with Alzheimer's disease who [13](*die*) .... Selkoe's test [14](*must confirm*) .... by other laboratories and [15](*make*) .... easy to do on a large scale.

D Why is *were* used here rather than *was*?
*As if the creeping forgetfulness it causes **were** not horrible enough ... (ll. 1–2)*

....

Complete these sentences using *were*.
1 He acted as if *he were mad.* ....
2 If I ....
3 I wish John ....
4 She shouldn't behave as if ....

E What part of speech is *finding* here and what does that imply in terms of usage?
*The **finding** suggests a fresh strategy for attacking the disease. (l. 20)*

....

Supply suitable *-ing* forms with or without *a/an* or *the*.
1 (*record*) *Recording* and (*sell*) .... CDs is a major growth industry.
2 I've just bought (*excellent record*) .... of Tchaikovsky's First Piano Concerto.
3 (*new record*) .... of this concerto on CD is far superior to my old LP.
4 There have been a great many (*record*) .... of this concerto.
5 There is still a lot of disagreement about the best way to teach (*read*) ....
6 There is nothing I like better on holiday than (*little light read*) ....
7 Dickens became exhausted by the large number of (*read*) .... he gave of his work.
8 (*slow read*) .... may lead to (*better understand*) .... of this text.

F Should it be *traveling* or *travelling*? Why?
*... the protein causes the disorder by **traveling** from other tissues to the brain. (ll. 22–24)*

....

Some of these verbs can be spelt in two ways, and some only in one. Which?
1 It took me some time to realize that I had been (*dial*) *dialing/dialling* the wrong number.
2 There is now general agreement that all goods for sale should be properly (*label*) ....
3 Sandra (*excel*) .... at school and at university, so I'm not surprised at her success.
4 I was (*signal*) .... a left hand turn, when the vehicle behind went into me.
5 The speaker was so smug, I was (*impel*) .... to ask a few awkward questions.
6 Some married couples are always (*quarrel*) ....
7 The flight to Helsinki has been (*cancel*) .... because of bad weather.
8 I'm really (*repel*) .... by racist remarks.

SENTENCE STRUCTURE

A Answers and commentary

Numbers **1**, **3** and **4** contain mistakes.

1 *As if the creeping forgetfulness it causes were not horrible enough, ...* (Not *Like*)
We can use *was* or *were* after *as if*. [> LEG 1.47.2 and compare uses of *were* in > LEG 11.42–43, 11.75.1, 14.13, 14.15, LAG 16D, 37D]
As if introduces an adverbial clause of comparison [> LEG 1.47.2, LAG 27An.4]:
*I feel **as if** I'm floating on air*.
However, in this text *as if* is used at the beginning of a statement to express incredulity [> LEG 14.23.3]:
***As if** it mattered!*
Like is a preposition and is followed by a noun [> LAG 13An.1, 47An.4, 60An.13]:
*Ageing brings with it things **like creeping forgetfulness***.
Like used as a conjunction (*like I told you*) has not gained universal acceptance. [> LEG App 25.25, LAG 27An.4]

2 This sentence is correct.

3 *This protein, which pathologists look for ~~it~~ in brain tissue ...* ,
Which is the relative pronoun object of the relative clause. We never use an object pronoun as well [> LEG 1.34, LAG 2An.2]:
*This is the protein. Pathologists look for **it***.
→ *This is the protein **which** pathologists look for ...*

4 *... researchers may now seek to devise drugs that would block the protein before **it gets** there.* (Not *will get*)
When the reference is to future time, the time conjunction *before* is followed by the simple present tense. [> LEG 1.45.2, LAG 6Bn.1]

B Answers and commentary

1 *A discovery announced last week, **however**, could result in a simple and accurate skin test ...*
However is used as a connecting adverb to draw a contrast here. It often occurs at the beginning of a sentence [> LAG 10Bn.1], but can also be used in mid-position (as here). When we use *however* (or any other connective adverb) in mid-position, we put commas before and after it. *Moreover* is also a connecting adverb, but is used for addition/reinforcing, not contrast. [> LEG App 18.2, 18.5, LAG 56A]

2 *Just how Alzheimer's ravages the brain isn't understood, but a protein molecule is **thought to be** involved.*
We use this construction in the passive with verbs of 'saying' and 'believing' when we are not entirely sure of our facts. [> LEG 12.8] Some verbs, like *believe, consider, find, suppose, think* and *understand* are often followed by an object + *to be* + noun or by a passive infinitive. [compare > LAG 27F] These verbs are often used in the passive (as here). [> LEG 16.22, LAG 18D, 30F, 36C]

3 *Dr Dennis Selkoe and colleagues at the Brigham and Women's Hospital in Boston found the protein in the skin of 8 out of 11 people with Alzheimer's disease who **had died**.* (Not *died*)
The use of the past perfect (*had died*) is critical here. It tells us the patients had died previously: they were already dead when the protein was found in their skin. If we say:
*They found the protein in the skin of 8 out of 11 people who **died**.*
it would mean that they found the protein, *and then* the people died. [> LEG 9.29.1, 9.30, LAG 18Bn.1, 26Ans.3–4, 28C, 33B, 41B, 52B]

GRAMMAR POINTS

C Verbs and verb tenses, modal verbs [> LEG Chapters 9 and 11, LAG 8E, 10C, etc.]

1 *carries*: Simple present for permanent truth. [> LEG 9.8.1, LAG 33B*n*.6, 50C]

2 *must be dead* (= it is necessary): Primary use of *must*. [> LEG 11.4, 11.9, 11.46–47, LAG 17D]

3 *can identify* (= are able to): Ability in the present with *can*. [> LEG 11.10–11] No future after temporal conjunctions like *before*. [> LEG 1.45.2, LAG 6B*n*.1]

4 *could result* (possibility): [> LEG 11.3, 11.28–30, compare > LAG 3B*n*.3, 10C*n*.2]

5 *may also lead* (possibility): *Might also lead* is also possible if we want to express greater uncertainty. [> LEG 11.3, 11.28–30]

6 *ravages*: Simple present for permanent truth. [> LEG 9.8.1] *(Just) how Alzheimer's ravages* ... is an indirect question, and is also the noun clause subject of *isn't understood*. [> LEG 1.24.2, 15.19–22, LAG 50E]

7 *isn't understood*: Simple present (passive) for permanent truth. [> LEG 9.8.1, 12.1–3]

8 *is thought*: Simple present passive with verbs of 'saying' and 'believing' to express uncertainty. [> LEG 12.8, LAG 18D, 30F, 36C, 37B*n*.2]

9 *look for*: Simple present, habitual action. [> LEG 9.8.3]

10 *has died*: The present perfect after a temporal conjunction. [> LEG 1.45.2] The simple present (*dies*) would also be possible. [> LAG 6B*n*.1]

11 *indicates*: Simple present to describe the present situation. [> LEG 9.8.2]

12 *found*: Simple past: completed action. [> LEG 9.17.1]

13 *had died*: Past perfect to refer to an earlier past. [> LEG 9.29.1, 9.30, LAG 37B*n*.3]

14 *must be confirmed* (= it is necessary): Primary use of *must* [> LEG 11.4, 11.9, 11.46–47, LAG 17D]; passive. [> LEG 12.2]

15 *made*: i.e. *must be made*, see **14** above.

D The subjunctive form 'were' [> LEG 1.47.2, 11.42.1, 11.75.1, 14.13, 14.15, Apps 44, 45.3]

Were is more formal and expresses more doubt than *was*.

We sometimes use the subjunctive form *were* (in all persons) as an alternative to *was*:
– after *(seem) as if*: *It seemed as if he* **were** *angry.*
– after *wish*: *I wish she* **were** *here.*
– in Type 2 conditionals: *If she* **were** *here now, she'd know what to do.*

Possible answers
1 He acted as if he were mad.
2 If I were you, I'd take the money.
3 I wish John were here now.
4 She shouldn't behave as if she were my mother.

E The gerund '-ing' form: 'dancing is fun' [> LEG 2.16.5, 3.26.2, 16.39.1, 16.39.3, LAG 20D, compare > LAG 34C, 60C]

Finding is a countable noun and may therefore be used with an article.

The most common use of -*ing* form gerunds is as uncountable nouns in general statements:
    Dancing *is fun.* (zero article)
Used as countable nouns -*ing* forms can have a singular and plural:
    This is **a new recording**.
    These are **new recordings**.

1 Recording . . . selling
2 an excellent recording
3 The new recording
4 recordings
5 reading
6 a little light reading
7 readings
8 Slow reading . . . (a) better understanding

F Doubling the consonant: British and American spellings: 'travelling/traveling' [> LEG 9.10, 9.14.2]

Traveling is correct here, since this is an American text. The British spelling is *travelling*.

If the stress is on the first syllable of a two-syllable verb, don't double the -*l* in American spelling, but double it in British spelling:
ˈtravel/ˈtraveling (American);
ˈtravel/ˈtravelling (British).
If the stress is on the second syllable, double the -*l*: exˈcel/exˈcelled (British and American).

1 dialing/dialling
2 labeled/labelled
3 excelled
4 signaling/signalling
5 impelled
6 quarreling/quarrelling
7 canceled/cancelled
8 repelled

Drug-war overkill

AS THE WAR on drugs and organized crime has expanded, pretrial property seizures have become
5 increasingly routine. Consider the experience of an Alaskan halibut fisherman named Kevin Hogan, whose only
10 significant business asset is his fishing boat, *Hold Tight*. Hogan, 37, paid $140,000 for the vessel and a year ago last May set out with a crew
15 of three on *Hold Tight's* maiden voyage, from Port Townsend, Washington, to halibut-fishing grounds in the Gulf of Alaska. En route,
20 *Hold Tight* was boarded and searched, with neither a warrant nor probable cause, by the U.S. Customs Service. In the pocket of one of the
25 crew members, an agent discovered a 35-mm.-film canister containing 1.7 grams of marijuana - enough

to make two cigarettes.
30 Hogan testified that he had no knowledge that any marijuana was aboard his boat, and crew members confirmed that he had
35 specifically warned them not to bring any drugs onboard. But it didn't matter. U.S. Customs Service seized Hogan's fishing boat - once
40 again, in advance of trial and with no finding of guilt on the part of anyone.
For Hogan, the results have been devastating. It
45 took him months to get his

boat back and operating after he found himself in a wildly lopsided struggle with the government. He has
50 alleged in court papers, for example, that when he told Customs officials that he intended to hire a lawyer to help recover his vessel, he
55 was warned not to. And when he contacted Alaska congressman Don Young to complain, Customs officials declared that he had simply
60 'made the matter worse.' Now Hogan is suing the federal government for $450,000 in compensatory and punitive damages, and
65 he can doubtless look forward to years of legal wrangling. (Ironically, the crew member who actually possessed the marijuana
70 wound up being sentenced to a $250 fine and a year's probation.)

New York (AmE)

Sentence structure

A Break these sentences down into short sentences, making any necessary changes. Write one short sentence beside each letter.

1 As the war on drugs and organized crime has expanded, pretrial property seizures have become increasingly routine. (ll. 1–5)

a ....

b ....

2 Consider the experience of an Alaskan halibut fisherman named Kevin Hogan, whose only significant business asset is his fishing boat, *Hold Tight*. (ll. 6–11)

a ....

b ....

c ....

3 En route, *Hold Tight* was boarded and searched, with neither a warrant nor probable cause, by the U.S. Customs Service. (ll. 19–23)

a ....

b ....

B Join these notes to make sentences. Then check against the text.

1 Hogan testified – had no knowledge – any marijuana – aboard his boat – crew members confirmed – specifically warned them – not bring any drugs onboard (ll. 30–36)

....

....

2 He has alleged in court papers, for example, – told Customs officials – he intended – hire a lawyer – help recover his vessel – warned not to (ll. 49–55)

....

Grammar points

C It is the month of June. Hogan bought his vessel in May last year. Write the phrase which tells us when he bought it, then check against the text. (ll. 13–14)

....

Today is **Wednesday, May 1**. Use 'point of time' phrases to say exactly when in each sentence.

1 You phoned on Tuesday at night.   *last night*
2 Your first wedding anniversary was on May 1 a year ago.
3 You're going to see me on Wednesday, May 8.
4 You phoned on Monday afternoon.
5 We met on Tuesday, April 16, two weeks ago.
6 We're going to meet on Thursday in a month's time.
7 You phoned on Monday at night.

D *A year ago last May Hogan* **set out** *with a crew of three on* Hold Tight's *maiden voyage.* (ll. 13–16) Suggest a meaning for the verb in bold italics. What sort of verb is this?

....

Suggest meanings for the verbs in italics.

1 Don't go so fast. I just can't *keep up*.   *stay equal with you*
2 I can't argue my case if you're always *cutting in*.
3 Jim and his wife have really *fallen out*.
4 Look who's just *blown in*!
5 I want to post this. *Pull in* by that letter-box.
6 In the middle of the conversation she suddenly *rang off*.
7 You really have to learn how to *wind down* after work.
8 Every time I raise the subject, he just *switches off*.
9 I don't think Jim and his wife really *get on*.
10 Are you going to *dress up* for this party?
11 Has Susie *settled down* in her new school?
12 We had to clear up the mess, so we all *set to*!
13 I'll say what I think and you won't get me to *shut up*.
14 If you get the opportunity, don't *hold back*!
15 Come on, *own up*. Who's responsible?
16 If you knew what I know, you'd really want to *speak out*.
17 What time did you *knock off* last night?
18 Grandad's always *dropping off* in front of the TV.
19 I tell you I just can't answer that. Why don't you *lay off*?
20 When she told us what had happened, we all *fell about*.

E Report this sentence with *warn*, then check against the text. (ll. 34–36 and ll. 54–55)
'Don't bring any drugs onboard,' he warned them.
He warned them ....

Rewrite these sentences using the verbs in brackets.

1 They didn't reply. (He told them)
   He told them not to reply. They wanted to reply, but he told them not to.
2 They didn't complain. (She advised them)

3 The soldiers didn't fire. (The officer ordered the soldiers)

4 We didn't talk about the project. (The boss reminded us)

5 I didn't take legal action. (My lawyer persuaded me)

SENTENCE STRUCTURE

A Answers and commentary

All the sentences you have written are simple sentences. A simple sentence has one finite verb. [> LEG 1.2, 1.7] The basic word order in a sentence that is not a question or a command is: (Time) Subject Verb Object Manner Place (Time) [> LEG 1.3, 7.22, LAG 4A]

1a *The war on drugs and organized crime* (subject) *has expanded* (verb).
The subject (*The war on drugs*) is lengthened by another noun phrase (*(and) organized crime*). [> LEG 1.5, 2.1, LAG 11A*n*.2b, 36A*n*.1]
The verb *has expanded* is used intransitively. [> LEG 1.9–10, App 1.3]

b *Pretrial property seizures* (subject) *have become* (verb) *increasingly routine* (complement).
Become is like *be* and cannot have an object. [> LEG 1.9, LAG 23D] A complement is often an adjective (as here) or a noun. [> LEG 1.11] The adverb *increasingly* intensifies the adjective *routine*. [> LEG 7.52–53, LAG 3C]

2a *Consider* (verb) *the experience of an Alaskan halibut fisherman* (object).
The subject of the imperative is hidden:
  You consider . . . .
There is only one form of the imperative whether we are addressing one person or several people. [> LEG 1.2, 9.54, LAG 46C]

b *He* (subject) *is named* (passive verb) *Kevin Hogan* (complement). [> LEG 1.14, LAG 3D]
This simple sentence is reduced to a past participle construction in the original sentence. [> LEG 1.62.3, LAG 6B*n*.4]

c *His only significant business asset* (subject) *is* (be) *his fishing boat*, Hold Tight (complement).
Whose is the subject of the relative clause and replaces *his* in the original sentence. [> LEG 1.32, LAG 6B*n*.3, 11B*n*.1]

3a *En route*, (Time/Place) Hold Tight (subject) *was boarded and searched* (verb) *by the U.S. Customs Service* (by + agent).
By + agent is used after the passive verbs here to supply important information: we need to know *who* boarded the vessel. [> LEG 12.5, LAG 29A, 49D]

b *They* (subject) *had* (verb) *neither a warrant nor probable cause* (object).
In the original sentence the idea of possession is conveyed by *with*. [> LEG App 25.37]
Neither . . . nor are used here to join two objects. [> LEG 1.16, compare > LAG 60A*n*.20]

B Answers and commentary

1 *Hogan testified that he had no knowledge* . . .
The reporting verb *testified* introduces a noun clause object *that he had no knowledge*. [> LEG 1.23.2, 15.12–13, App 45, LAG 4E, 14B]
. . . *that any marijuana was aboard his boat*, . . .
Instead of saying *Hogan testified* (reporting verb) *that he didn't know* (noun clause) *that any marijuana was aboard his boat* (noun clause), the writer uses the noun (*had no*) *knowledge* in place of the verb (*didn't*) *know*. [compare > LEG 16.33]
. . . *and crew members confirmed* . . .
and introduces a co-ordinate main clause. [> LEG 1.17–20]
. . . *that he had specifically warned them* . . .
This is a noun clause object after the reporting verb *confirmed*. [> LEG 1.23.2, 15.12–13, App 45, LAG 4E, 14B]
. . . *not to bring any drugs onboard.*
Warn must be followed by an object (*them*) when used with a *to*-infinitive. [> LEG 16.21]
The negative imperative *Don't bring any drugs onboard* is reported by *warned them*, which is stronger and more appropriate than *told them*. *Not* precedes the *to*-infinitive: . . . *warned them not to bring*. (Not *to not bring**) [> LEG 15.24.1]
Note that *onboard* is normally written as two words: *on board*.

2 *He has alleged in court papers, for example, that when he told Customs officials that he intended* . . .
The reporting verb *alleged* introduces a noun clause (*that* . . .) which contains an adverbial clause of time introduced by *when*, followed by another noun clause after *told Customs officials*. [> LEG 1.23.2, 1.45.1, LAG 4E, 20C]
. . . *that he intended to hire a lawyer* . . .
intended may be followed by a *to*-infinitive or *-ing* (*hiring*) without any change of meaning. [> LEG 16.57, LAG 42C, 57D]
. . . *to help recover his vessel*, . . .
to (or *so as to/in order to*) expresses purpose here. [> LEG 16.12.1] For *help* (*him*) (*to*) *recover* [> LEG 16.7, 16.20]
. . . *he was warned not to.*
Note how, to avoid repetition, we can leave out the verb after *to* [> LEG 16.17, LAG 38E]:
. . . *he was warned not to* (*hire a lawyer*).

GRAMMAR POINTS

C 'Points of time' (adverbs of definite time): 'last night' [> LEG App 48]

a year ago last May

Even elementary points of time can be tricky: e.g. *last night* (Not **yesterday night**); *this morning* (Not **today morning**), etc. More advanced points of time (*a year ago last May*) can be equally unpredictable. [> LAG 54An.1]

Possible answers
1 last night
2 a year ago today
3 a week (from) today/today week/
   in a week's time/this day week
4 the day before yesterday in the afternoon
5 a fortnight (from) yesterday (English requires
   fortnight (= fourteen nights), not **fifteen days**)
6 a month (from) tomorrow
7 the night before last

D Type 3 phrasal verbs (idiomatic meanings): 'set out' [> LEG 8.29, App 36, LAG 4D, 13C, 32C and compare > LAG 8D, 16B, 24C, 27C, 38D, 44D, 47E]

set out (= began a journey); *set out* is an intransitive phrasal verb.

Type 3 verbs followed by adverb particles are intransitive (i.e. they have no object). They may have obvious meanings:
Sit down. *Hurry up*. *We went in*. etc.
Or they may have little or no relation to the literal meanings of the verb and the particle:
We set out at 6. (= started our journey)

Possible answers
1 *keep up* (= stay equal with you)
2 *cutting in* (= interrupting)
3 *fallen out* (= quarrelled)
4 *blown in* (= arrived unexpectedly)
5 *pull in* (= stop the car at the roadside)
6 *rang off* (= ended the phone call)
7 *wind down* (= relax)
8 *switches off* (= stops paying attention)
9 *get on* (= have a good relationship)
10 *dress up* (= put on your best clothes)
11 *settled down* (= got used to)
12 *set to* (= began working energetically)
13 *shut up* (= be quiet: *very* informal)
14 *hold back* (= hesitate)
15 *own up* (= confess, admit it)
16 *speak out* (= make your views public)
17 *knock off* (= stop work)
18 *dropping off* (= falling asleep)
19 *lay off* (= stop being annoying)
20 *fell about* (= collapsed with laughter)

E Verb + compulsory noun/pronoun + *to*-infinitive: 'he warned me (not) to' [> LEG 15.24, 16.17, 16.21 and compare > LAG 1E, 10D, 18D]

*He warned them **not to bring** any drugs onboard.*
We can report an imperative accurately by using the appropriate reporting verb (*advise, ask, instruct, warn,* etc.). Other verbs which are not strictly 'reporting' are also followed by an object + *to* (*allow, encourage,* etc.). In the negative, *not* always goes in front of the *to*-infinitive:
*He **advised me to wait**.*
*He **advised me not to wait**.*
To avoid repetition, we can omit the verb after *to* [compare > LAG 40C]:
Why did you do that?
- I was advised to.
- I was advised not to.

1 He told them not to reply. They wanted to reply, but he told them not to.
2 She advised them not to complain. They wanted to complain, but she advised them not to.
3 The officer ordered the soldiers not to fire. The soldiers wanted to fire, but the officer ordered them not to.
4 The boss reminded us not to talk about the project. We wanted to talk about the project, but the boss reminded us not to.
5 My lawyer persuaded me not to take legal action. I wanted to take legal action, but my lawyer persuaded me not to.

Garbage

only partly in fun, that *Homo sapiens* may have been propelled
15 along the path toward civilization by his need for a class at the
bottom of the social hierarchy that could be assigned the task of
dealing with mounting piles of garbage.

This brings us to an important truth about garbage: There are
no ways of dealing with it that haven't been known for many
20 thousands of years. These ways are essentially four: dumping it,
burning it, converting it into something that can be used again,
and minimizing the volume of material goods - future garbage -
that is produced in the first place ('source reduction', as it is
called). Every civilization of any complexity has used all four
25 methods to varying degrees.

From prehistory through the present day dumping has been the
means of disposal favored everywhere, including in the cities. The
archaeologist C. W. Blegen, who dug into Bronze Age Troy in the
1950s, found that floors had become so littered that periodically a
30 fresh supply of dirt or clay had been brought in to cover up the
refuse. Of course, after several layers had been applied, the doors
and roofs had to be adjusted upward. Over time the ancient cities
of the Middle East rose high above the landscape on massive
mounds, called tells. In 1973 a civil engineer with the Department
35 of Commerce, Charles Gunnerson, calculated that the rate of
uplift owing to the accumulation of debris in Bronze Age Troy was
about 4.7 feet per century. If the idea of a city rising above its
garbage at this rate seems extraordinary, it may be worth
considering that 'street level' on the island of Manhattan is fully
40 six feet higher today than it was when Peter Minuit lived there.

The Atlantic (AmE)

FOR most of the past two and a half
million years human beings left their
garbage where it fell. Oh, they
sometimes tidied up their sleeping and
5 activity areas, but that was about all. This
disposal scheme functioned adequately,
because hunters and gatherers frequently
abandoned their campgrounds to follow game
or find new stands of plants. Man faced his
10 first garbage crisis when he became a
sedentary animal - when, rather than move
himself, he chose to move his garbage. The
archaeologist Gordon R. Willey has argued,

Sentence structure

A Supply the connecting words, then check against the text.

For the most of the past two and a half million years human beings left their garbage ¹............ it fell. Oh, they ²............ tidied up their sleeping and activity areas, ³............ that was about all. This disposal scheme functioned adequately, ⁴............ hunters and gatherers ⁵............ abandoned their campgrounds ⁶............ follow game ⁷............ find new stands of plants. Man faced his first garbage crisis ⁸............ he became a sedentary animal – ⁹............, rather than ¹⁰(*move*) .... himself, he chose to move his garbage. The archaeologist Gordon R. Willey has argued, only partly in fun, ¹¹............ *Homo sapiens* may have been propelled along the path toward civilization by his need for a class at the bottom of the social hierarchy ¹²............ could be assigned the task of ¹³(*deal*) .... with mounting piles of garbage.

¹⁴............ brings us to an important truth about garbage: There are no ways ¹⁵............ dealing with it that haven't been known for many thousands of years. ¹⁶............ ways are essentially four: dumping it, burning it, converting it into something ¹⁷............ can be used again, and minimizing the volume of material goods – future garbage – ¹⁸............ is produced in the first place ('source reduction', as it is called). Every civilization of any complexity has used all four methods to varying degrees.

From prehistory through the present day dumping has been the means of disposal favored everywhere, ¹⁹(*include*) .... in the cities. The archaeologist C. W. Blegen, ²⁰............ dug into Bronze Age Troy in the 1950s, found that floors had become ²¹............ littered ²²............ periodically a fresh supply of dirt or clay had been brought in to cover up the refuse. Of course, ²³............ several layers had been applied, the doors and roofs had to be adjusted upward. Over time the ancient cities of the Middle East rose high above the landscape on massive mounds, ²⁴(*call*) .... tells. (ll. 1–34)

Grammar points

B Supply *a/an*, *the* or zero (–), then refer to the text. (ll. 1–12)

For most of ¹........ past two and ²........ half million years ³........ human beings left their garbage where it fell. Oh, they sometimes tidied up their sleeping and activity areas, but that was about all. This disposal scheme functioned adequately, because ⁴........ hunters and ⁵........ gatherers frequently abandoned their campgrounds to follow ⁶........ game or find new stands of plants. ⁷........ man faced his first garbage crisis when he became ⁸........ sedentary animal - when, rather than move himself, he chose to move his garbage.

C Supply the plural forms of the nouns in brackets only where necessary. (ll. 26–32)

From prehistory through the present day dumping has been the ¹(*means*) .... of disposal favored everywhere, including in the ²(*city*) .... The archaeologist C. W. Blegen, who dug into Bronze Age Troy in the 1950s, found that ³(*floor*) .... had become so littered that periodically a fresh supply of ⁴(*dirt*) .... or ⁵(*clay*) .... had been brought in to cover up the ⁶(*refuse*) .... Of course, after several ⁷(*layer*) .... had been applied, the ⁸(*door*) .... and ⁹(*roof*) .... had to be adjusted upward.

D Correct this sentence and give a reason or reasons, then check against the text.

Man faced his first garbage crisis when he became a sedentary animal – when, rather than to move himself, he chose to move his garbage. (ll. 9–12)

....

Suggest alternative phrases using *rather than* in place of the phrases in italics.

1 Extend your house, *instead of moving* to another one.   *rather than move / moving*
2 Phone them *instead of waiting* for them to phone.   ....
3 I tried to repair it *instead of throwing* it away.   ....
4 I prefer to buy vegetables *instead of growing* them.   ....

E Explain the meaning of *any* in these two sentences.

a *I can't believe that we don't have **any** rubbish to be collected this week.*   ....
b *Every civilization of **any** complexity has used all four methods.* (ll. 24–25)   ....

Suggest meanings for *any* in these sentences.

1 You have to be really rich to go round without carrying *any* money.   *no (money) at all*
2 Margot Fonteyn wasn't just *any* ballerina you know.   ....
3 I want *any* advice you can give me.   ....
4 I'm afraid I still don't feel *any* better.   ....
5 I need a car. *Any* car will do.   ....

F What's the difference between *high* and *highly* in these two sentences?

a *Over time the ancient cities of the Middle East rose **high** above the landscape.* (ll. 32–33)
b *You know your boss thinks very **highly** of you, don't you?*

Read each sentence, then write another using the *-ly* form of the adjective or adverb in italics.

1 I can't imagine anyone sharing the view of the *hard* left or the *hard* right.
It's hardly right to tell others what to do when you don't follow your own advice.
2 Our candidate was just a few votes *short* of winning a place on the board.

....

3 I always feel very *full* indeed whenever I eat a curry.

....

4 The most *direct* route from here to Nottingham is also the most expensive.

....

SENTENCE STRUCTURE

A Answers and commentary

1 *where*: introduces an adverbial clause of place (*where it fell*). [> LEG 1.38.2, 1.46, LAG 19A*n*.3, 44B*n*.3]

2 *sometimes*: adverb of frequency used before the main verb (*tidied up*). [> LEG 7.40.1, LAG 45D]

3 *but*: co-ordinating conjunction introducing a co-ordinate main clause to express contrast. [> LEG 1.17–20, LAG 1B*n*.2]

4 *because*: introduces an adverbial clause of reason (*because hunters and gatherers abandoned...*). [> LEG 1.48, LAG 1B*n*.2, 54A*n*.9, 56A*n*.8]

5 *frequently*: adverb of frequency used before a main verb (*abandoned*) as in **2** above.

6 *to*: *to*-infinitive to express purpose. This could be replaced by *so as to* or *in order to*. [> LEG 16.12.1, LAG 10B*n*.2]
We can also express purpose with *so that* or *in order that + might*, though this is a more complex construction [> LEG 1.51.2]:
*... they abandoned their campgrounds **in order that they might follow** game...*

7 *or*: co-ordinating conjunction introducing a second (alternative) infinitive of purpose with *to* omitted. [> LEG 16.8, LAG 2B*n*.1]

8 *when*: time conjunction, introducing an adverbial clause of time (*when he became a sedentary animal*). [> LEG 1.45.1, LAG 3B*n*.1, 57A*n*.4]

9 *when*: as in **8** above.

10 *move*: the bare infinitive after *rather than* or *sooner than*. We could also use the *-ing* form [> LEG 16.11, LAG 39D]:
*Man became a sedentary animal **rather than moving** himself.*

11 *that*: introduces a noun clause as object of the reporting verb *has argued* (*that Homo sapiens may have been propelled...*). We don't usually omit *that* after *argue*. [> LEG 1.23.2, 15.12–13, App 45, LAG 4E, 14B]

12 *that*: is a relative pronoun here, subject of the relative clause, and could be replaced by *which*, referring back to *a class (at the bottom of the social hierarchy)*. [> LEG 1.31, LAG 5A*n*.3]

13 *dealing*: We need the *-ing* form after the preposition *of*. [> LEG 16.50–56, LAG 1D]

14 *This*: used as a connecting pronoun to refer to the previous paragraph. [> LEG 4.33, App 7.7, LAG 23A*n*.5]

15 *of*: a preposition which is followed by an *-ing* form (*dealing*), as in **13** above. We could also say [> LEG 16.33]:
*There is no **way to deal** with it.*
→ *There is no **way of dealing** with it.*

16 *These*: used as a demonstrative adjective referring to *ways*. *These* here emphasizes 'nearness'. [> LEG 4.33, LAG 45A]

17 *that*: relative pronoun subject of the relative clause; compare **12** above. [> LEG 1.31]:
*... converting it into **something**. It can be used again.*
→ *... converting it into **something that/which** can be used again...*

18 *that*: relative pronoun subject of the relative clause, referring back to *volume* [> LEG 1.31, LAG 5A*n*.3]:
*This is the **volume**. It is produced.*
→ *This is the **volume that/which** is produced...*

19 *including*: an *-ing* form preposition here [> LEG App 20.2], rather than a present participle construction. [> LEG 1.58, LAG 20D]

20 *who*: relative pronoun subject of the relative clause, referring to *C. W. Blegen*. Commas are used round the clause because it is non-defining, that is, it provides extra information [> LEG 1.26, 1.29, LAG 5A*ns*.1–2]:
*This is **C. W. Blegen**. He dug into Bronze Age Troy in the 1950s. He found that...*
→ *...**C. W. Blegen**, **who** dug into Bronze Age Troy in the 1950s, found that...*

21 *so*: adverb of degree combining with *that* (see **22** below).

22 *that*: introduces an adverbial clause of result [> LEG 1.52.1, LAG 2B*n*.1, 10A*n*.2]:
*Floors had become littered. **As a result**, periodically a fresh supply of dirt or clay had been brought in.*
→ *Floors had become **so** littered **that** periodically a fresh supply of dirt or clay had been brought in.*

23 *after*: time conjunction introducing an adverbial clause of time. [> LEG 1.45.1, LAG 36A*n*.2] The past perfect (*had been applied*) emphasizes the reference to an earlier past. [> LEG 9.29.1, 9.30]

24 *called*: past participle construction used in place of a relative clause [> LEG 1.62.3, 6B*n*.4]:
*... massive mounds, (which are) **called** tells.*

GRAMMAR POINTS

B Articles [> LEG Chapter 3, LAG 8C, 11C, 15C, 18C, 22B, 30C, 44C, 45E, 54B]

Cross references are given to LEG for selected items only.

1 most of the past [> LEG 5.5.2]
2 two and a half [> LEG 3.11]
3 (–) human beings [> LEG 3.26.1]
4 (–) hunters [> LEG 3.26.1]
5 (–) gatherers
6 (–) game (= wild animals, etc., uncountable [> LEG 2.27])
7 (–) man [> LEG 3.22]
8 a sedentary animal [> LEG 3.3, 3.9.3]

C Number (singular and plural of nouns) [> LEG 2.20–38, compare > LAG 26D, 34F]

1 *means* (= method): plural in form + singular or plural verb [> LEG 2.31]; compare *means* (= money). [> LEG 2.32]
2 *cities*: regular plural: consonant + *-y* (*city*) becomes *-ies* in the plural. [> LEG 2.20]
3 *floors*: regular plural. [> LEG 2.20]
4 *dirt*: uncountable noun, no plural. [> LEG 2.14.2]
5 *clay*: normally uncountable noun. [> LEG 2.14]
6 *refuse*: noun (stress on first syllable) not normally countable in English: no plural. [> LEG 2.17, App 4]
7 *layers*: regular plural. [> LEG 2.20]
8 *doors*: regular plural. [> LEG 2.20]
9 *roofs*: regular spelling, but sometimes irregular pronunciation (/fs/ or /vs/); compare *wife/ wives*. [> LEG 2.23]

D 'Rather than' + bare infinitive or '-ing' [> LEG 16.11, compare > LAG 17A*n*.4b]

... *rather than ~~to~~ move himself, he chose to move his garbage.* We don't use a *to*-infinitive after *rather than*.

We can use a bare infinitive or *-ing* after *rather than* and *sooner than* (= instead of):
Rather than waste/wasting time doing it yourself, why don't you call a builder?

1 rather than move/moving
2 rather than wait/waiting
3 rather than throw/throwing
4 rather than grow/growing

E Special uses of 'any' [> LEG 5.12.2–3, and compare > LEG 5.3, 5.10]

a *an amount of* (however small)
b *whatever, even the smallest amount of*

In its basic use, *any* refers to an indefinite number or amount:
*Are there **any apples** in the bag?*
*Is there **any milk** in the fridge?*

Apart from its basic use as a quantifier, *any* can be used to refer to an unspecified person or thing, etc. When used in this way, it is generally stressed in speech. See the answers to the exercises for possible meanings [and compare > LAG 6D].

Some possible meanings of 'any'

1 no (money) at all
2 like other (ballerinas)
3 as little or as much as
4 at all
5 it doesn't matter which

F Adjectives/adverbs with two forms, but different meanings: 'high/highly' [> LEG 7.14–15, Apps 14–16, compare > LAG 56B]

a *High* is an adverb referring to *height*: ***rose high above the landscape.***
b *Highly* is an adverb meaning 'in the highest degree': *he thinks very **highly** of you.* [> LEG 7.53.1]

Some words can be used as adjectives or adverbs without *-ly*:
*The plane **flew high**. (Not ***highly****)*
They have a completely different meaning when formed with *-ly*:
*He's **highly respected**. (= to a high degree)*

Possible answers

1 It's hardly right to tell others what to do when you don't follow your own advice. [compare > LAG 11E]
2 I think we'd better go to the departure gate. The plane will be leaving shortly. (= in a short time)
3 I am fully (= completely) aware that you're not allowed to stop on a motorway.
4 I'll be in touch with you directly (= immediately) she phones me. [> LEG 1.45.2]

The Japanese sense of beauty

THE JAPANESE have a strong aesthetic sense: they beautify, embellish, adorn and decorate everything they touch. A sandwich in Japan is not just a sandwich, it is a work of art. It is cut into an artistic shape - it can be circular, octagonal or star-shaped - and given a colour scheme with carefully placed bits of tomato, coleslaw and pickles. There is, as a rule, a flag or some other decoration hoisted on top. Every dish is aimed at the eye as well as the palate.

Every tiny parcel, from the humblest little shop, radiates some original charm or at least tries to, and reflects pride: look how well done it is! Every taxi-driver has a small vase in front of him, with a beautiful, fresh, dark-red or snow-white flower in it. Once I watched a man at the counter in a fish-restaurant. *Sushi* and *sashimi* - the famous raw fish of Japan - comes in many forms and cuts, and it takes about ten years for a man to reach the counters of a first-class establishment. The man I watched was not bored with his somewhat monotonous job: he enjoyed every minute of it to the full, took immense pride in it. Michelangelo could not have set a freshly carved Madonna before you with more pride and satisfaction than this cook felt when he put a freshly carved piece of raw fish on your plate.

The Japanese are unable to touch anything without beautifying it, shaping it into something pretty and pleasing to the eye. One evening I was walking in one of the slummy suburbs of Tokyo and saw a heap of rubbish outside the backyard of a factory. It was an immense mountainside of rubbish, but it was not just thrown out as it came: all the boxes were piled into a graceful if somewhat whimsical pyramid, while the loose rubbish was placed on top as artistic and picturesque decoration. Someone must have spent considerable time in converting that heap of rubbish into a thing of beauty.

The Land of the Rising Yen by George Mikes *(BrE)*

Sentence structure

A Replace the words in italics and give a reason. Then refer to the text.

1 A sandwich in Japan is not *only* a sandwich, it is a work of art. (ll. 3–4)

....

2 *On one occasion* I watched a man at the counter in a fish-restaurant. (ll. 16–17)

....

3 The man *whom* I watched was not bored with his somewhat monotonous job. (ll. 20–22)

....

4 He enjoyed every minute of it to the full, *was immensely proud of* it. (ll. 22–23)

....

5 All the boxes were piled into a graceful if somewhat whimsical pyramid, *and at the same time* the loose rubbish was placed on top as artistic and picturesque decoration. (ll. 32–35)

....

B Three of these sentences contain a wrong word. Replace the wrong word, where necessary, and say why you have done so. Then check against the text.

1 The Japanese have a strong aesthetic sense which they beautify, embellish, adorn and decorate everything they touch. (ll. 1–3)

....

2 There is, as a rule, a flag or some other decoration hoisted on top. (ll. 8–10)

....

3 It takes about ten years for a man to reach to the counters of a first-class establishment. (ll. 19–20)

....

4 An evening I was walking in one of the slummy suburbs of Tokyo and saw a heap of rubbish outside the backyard of a factory. (ll. 29–31)

....

Grammar points

C Use one word to complete these sentences.

 a *Every tiny parcel radiates some original charm or at least tries* ...... (ll. 12–14)
 b *Any customer who orders our food enjoys* ......

 Complete these sentences with *to* or *it*. Alternatives are sometimes possible.

 1 I didn't intend to take a holiday this year, but now I've decided *to*
 2 I don't eat raw fish because I don't enjoy *it*
 3 I go to the theatre as often as I can because I like ....
 4 Cindy isn't going to the party this evening because she doesn't want ....
 5 James isn't going to play tennis tomorrow because he doesn't feel like ....
 6 It wasn't my idea to take this path. I didn't suggest ....
 7 I know you don't want to make an effort, but you could at least try ....
 8 Are you going to pay in cash? – Yes, I'd prefer ....
 9 Do you always have tea without sugar? – Yes, I prefer ....
 10 Henry never does the washing-up. He always avoids ....
 11 Elizabeth isn't going to retire early. She won't even consider ....
 12 You needn't come shopping with us if you don't want ....
 13 You don't have to eat that sandwich if you don't want ....
 14 I'm going to study engineering at university – at least I hope ....
 15 Frank says he bites his nails because he can't help ....
 16 Did you have any lentil soup? – No, I don't like ....
 17 Why didn't you accept the money? – Because I didn't need ....
 18 Jane says she never travels abroad because she doesn't enjoy ....

D Which verb-form goes into the space?
 He enjoyed every minute of it to the full, ... *immense pride in it.* (ll. 22–23)

 Supply correct forms of *give* or *take*.

 1 I think I'll *take* a bath before we go out.
 2 When are you going to .... the exam?
 3 Just .... a look at this!
 4 You don't get a lucky break in life unless someone .... you an opportunity.
 5 I'm glad someone competent is going to .... charge of this company.
 6 Mrs Tomkins .... driving-lessons for a living.
 7 I .... six lessons from Mrs Tomkins and passed my driving-test first time.
 8 When driving in France, you have to .... way to traffic on the right.
 9 Would you like me to .... you a lift to the station?
 10 The new regulations .... effect from tomorrow.

E What goes into this space: *out of* or *outside*? Why?
 I saw a heap of rubbish .... *the backyard of a factory.* (ll. 30–31)

 Supply *out of* or *outside*.

 1 Someone has left a parcel for us *outside* the front door.
 2 He went straight .... the front door and never came back!
 3 I'm afraid you can't speak to Mr Jones. He's .... his office at the moment.
 4 As children, we often had to stand .... the headmaster's study.
 5 Don't play silly games in here. Why don't you play .... ?
 6 John doesn't have any interests .... his work.
 7 What are you going to get .... this?
 8 We'll go .... for five minutes or so, to let you discuss the matter privately.
 9 You should never throw anything .... the window.

SENTENCE STRUCTURE

A Answers and commentary

1 *A sandwich in Japan is not **just** a sandwich, it is a work of art.*
Just is a focus adverb here. We could also have used *simply*. Focus adverbs go in front of the word they qualify to focus attention on it. [> LEG 7.54–56, LAG 11A*n*.1b, 21B*n*.1b, 23B*n*.3, 50A*n*.1]
We can show addition or sequence with *not only . . . , (but) . . . (, too/as well)* [> LEG 1.20.1, LAG 36B*n*.2]:
> *A sandwich in Japan is **not only** a sandwich, **(but)** (it is) a work of art(, **too/as well**).*

2 ***Once** I watched a man at the counter in a fish-restaurant.*
Once is an adverb of indefinite time, often used in narrative. [> LEG 7.23, LAG 35B*n*.1]
Once (= when) can also introduce an adverbial clause of time [> LEG 1.45.1, LAG 26A*n*.4]:
> ***Once** you've seen one penguin, you've seen them all.*

3 ***The man I watched** was not bored with his somewhat monotonous job.*
Who(m) is the relative pronoun object of the relative clause, and is usually omitted [> LEG 1.33, LAG 12A*n*.12, 27A*n*.3]:
> *This is **the man**. I watched **him**.*
> → *He is the man **that/who(m)** I watched.*
> → *He is **the man I watched**.*

4 *He enjoyed every minute of it to the full, **took immense pride in** it.*
The verb *take* (like *have* [> LAG 24B, 41E] and *give*) combines with a large number of nouns: e.g. *take a decision* (= decide); *take pity on* (= feel sorry for); *take a seat* (= sit down), etc. [> LEG 8.20, App 42.3, LAG 40D]

5 *All the boxes were piled into a graceful if somewhat whimsical pyramid, **while** the loose rubbish was placed on top . . .*
While introduces adverbial clauses of time. [> LEG 1.45.1, LAG 10A*n*.1, 12A*n*.16, 20B*n*.1, 41A*n*.4] It is also used to emphasize parallel actions and situations, as here. [> LEG 9.20.3]

B Answers and commentary

Numbers **1**, **3** and **4** contain wrong words.

1 *The Japanese have a strong aesthetic sense: (~~which~~) they beautify, embellish, adorn and decorate everything they touch.*
The information following the colon (:) amplifies the preceding statement. [> LAG 8B*n*.2, 16A*n*.6, 22A*n*.6, 46A*n*.6]
The use of *which* misleadingly suggests that they *beautify, embellish* etc. *a strong aesthetic sense*.

2 *There is, as a rule, a flag or some other decoration hoisted on top.*
This sentence is correct.
[For this use of *some* > LEG 5.12.1, LAG 6D.]
[For the use of *other* > LEG 5.27, LAG 48E, 58A*n*.2.]
[For the use of the past participle *hoisted* > LEG 1.62.3.]

3 *It takes about ten years for a man to reach ~~to~~ the counters of a first-class establishment.*
Reach is a transitive verb, so it is followed directly by an object (*reach the counters*). [> LEG 1.9, App 1]
Compare *arrive* which must have *at/in* after it if it is followed by an object [> LEG 8.6, 8.9.3, 8.27.1, App 28]:
> *We **arrived in London** before midnight.*
> → *We **reached London** before midnight.*
> *We've **arrived at the other side** of the river bank.*
> → *We've **reached the other side** of the river bank.*

4 ***One evening** I was walking in one of the slummy suburbs of Tokyo . . .*
One + morning, evening, day etc. is often used as an adverb of time, especially in story-telling. [> LEG 3.11 and compare > LEG 7.23] We only use *one* in place of *a/an* to refer, for example, to:
Whole numbers:
a (or *one*) *hundred, thousand, million.* [> LEG App 47, LAG 18C, 29E]
Fractions:
a (or *one*) *quarter, third, half,* etc.
Money:
a (or *one*) *pound/dollar,* etc.
Weight/measure:
a (or *one*) *pound/kilo, foot/metre,* etc.

GRAMMAR POINTS

C Verb + 'to' or verb + noun/pronoun object: 'if you want to', 'if you want it' [> LEG 4.16.2, 16.17, 16.19–25, 16.42, 16.58]

a *tries **to***
b *enjoys **it***

We can avoid repeating whole phrases by using *to* to refer back to a verb (*radiates*), and *it* to refer back to a noun (*food*), a pronoun or a gerund [> LAG 1E, etc.]:

> *You don't **have to** eat it if you don't want **to**.*

Depending on context, we can also use a pronoun in such cases:

> *You don't have to eat **it** if you don't want **it**.*

We must use a noun/pronoun object after transitive verbs normally followed by *-ing*: *admit, appreciate, avoid, celebrate, consider, contemplate, defer, delay, deny, detest, discontinue, dislike, dispute, endure, enjoy, it entail(s), escape, excuse, explain, fancy, feel like, finish, forgive, can't help, hinder, imagine, it involve(s), keep, loathe, it mean(s), mention, mind (= object to), miss, it necessitate(s), pardon, postpone, practise, prevent, recall, report, resent, resist, risk, suggest, understand* [> LEG 16.42]:

> *I always go to Iceland for my holidays because I **enjoy it**.* (Not *to*)

1	decided to	**10**	avoids it (*doing*)
2	enjoy it (*raw fish*)	**11**	consider it (*retiring*)
3	like to/it (*theatre*)	**12**	want to
4	want to	**13**	want to/it (*sandwich*)
5	feel like it (*playing*)	**14**	hope to
6	suggest it (*taking*)	**15**	can't help it (*biting*)
7	try to	**16**	like it (*lentil soup*)
8	prefer to	**17**	need to/it (*the money*)
9	prefer to/it (*tea*)	**18**	enjoy it (*travelling*)

D 'Give' + noun and 'take' + noun [> LEG 10.37, App 42.2–3]

> *He enjoyed every minute of it to the full, **took** immense pride in it.*

There are many combinations with *give* and *take* (compare combinations with *have* > LAG 24B). *Give* is followed by an indirect object: *give (somebody) (something)*: *advice/information/news, an answer, one's attention, a bath, a call/a ring, a chance, a description, an explanation, a guess, help, a kiss, a lead, lessons, a lift, an opportunity*, etc.

Or it may occur in fixed phrases: *give birth to, give evidence, give one's life for, give a party, give place to, give thanks for*, etc.

Take combines with: *action, advice, aim, a bath, a break, care, charge of, a class, courage, a decision, effect, an exam, fright, a joke, a look*, etc.

1	take a bath	**6**	gives driving-lessons
2	take the exam	**7**	took six lessons
3	take a look	**8**	give way to
4	gives you an opportunity	**9**	give you a lift
5	take charge of	**10**	take effect

E 'Out of' and 'outside' [> LEG 8.9.6, App 25.31]

*I saw a heap of rubbish **outside** the backyard of a factory.*

We use *outside* here because there is no movement.

The basic rule is that we use *out of* as the opposite of *into* as prepositions which show movement:

> *We got **into** the car. We got **out of** the car.*

We use *outside* as a preposition when there is no movement:

> *I stood **outside** his office.*

We also use *outside* when we are not referring to physical space:

> *This is quite **outside my experience**.*

We can use *outside* as an adverb (that is, without an object), but we can never use *out of* in this way:

> *Where's John? – He's **outside**.* (= physically present)

We can use *out* as an adverb, e.g:

> *Where's John? – He's **out**.* (= out of this place/ elsewhere, I don't know where)

1 outside the front door
2 out of the front door
3 out of his office
4 outside the headmaster's study
5 play outside
6 outside his work
7 out of this
8 go outside
9 out of the window

Two topics of conversation

HAVING only two topics of conversation, the Second World War and the greengrocery trade, Sydney Faraday had talked exhaustively about battles and beetroot, the former slightly dominating. He had been a sergeant with a tank regiment, part of Montgomery's Second Army that swept across northern Germany in the spring of 1945. One of his favourite stories was how he and a corporal and a private had gone into a farmhouse kitchen near the Weser, found the occupants gone, nothing to eat but a sucking pig roasting, in fact ready to eat at that moment, in the oven. Another was the one about the gun. Outside Bremen Sydney had found a dead German officer lying in a ditch. He was still holding a gun in his hand which led Sydney to believe (on no other evidence) that he had shot himself out of despair at the way the war was going. On the altruistic grounds of not wanting the man branded a suicide, Sydney took the gun and kept it. It was a Luger.

'A German military small-bore automatic pistol,' Sydney would explain to the company, rather in the manner of an encyclopedia.

The first time Victor heard this story had been after Christmas dinner. He was only seventeen and still going about with his parents. He heard it again ten years later when his mother said she never saw him these days and then nagged him into going with them to Muriel's on Christmas Day. Things were just the same: the same under-cooked defrosted turkey, this time with canned potatoes, for there had been technological progress during the intervening decade, and greens that were perhaps sub-standard for the shop. While they ate the shop-bought, home-boiled pudding and drank the only pleasing constituent of the meal, Sydney's port, Sydney told the story of the German officer and the gun once more. Victor's mother murmured, though to no avail, that she had heard it before. Muriel, who had no doubt heard it many many times, interjected mechanically with 'My goodness!' and 'I say!', uttered expressionlessly as if she was learning these exclamations as part of a minor role in a play. She had grown fat, and the more fat she became the more withdrawn. It was as if whatever spirit she had ever had was being steadily suppressed, muffled and smothered under layers of flesh.

Live Flesh by Ruth Rendell *(BrE)*

Sentence structure

A Combine the sentences below into single complete sentences. Make any necessary changes and use the help given. Then check against the text.

1 Sydney Faraday had only two topics of conversation. These were the Second World War and the greengrocery trade. He had talked exhaustively about battles and beetroot. The former slightly dominated. (ll. 1–5)
Having only ....

2 He had been a sergeant with a tank regiment. This was part of Montgomery's Second Army. It swept across northern Germany in the spring of 1945. (ll. 5–8)
He had been a sergeant with a tank regiment ....

3 He and a corporal and a private had gone into a farmhouse kitchen near the Weser. They had found the occupants gone. There was nothing to eat but a sucking pig roasting. In fact it was ready to eat at that moment, in the oven. This was one of his favourite stories. (ll. 8–14)
One of his favourite stories was how ....

4 They ate the shop-bought, home-boiled pudding. They drank the only pleasing constituent of the meal. This was Sydney's port. Sydney told the story of the German officer and the gun once more. (ll. 34–37)
While ....

Grammar points

B Supply the right form of the verbs in brackets, then refer to the text. (ll. 1–19)

Having only two topics of conversation, the Second World War and the greengrocery trade, Sydney Faraday had talked exhaustively about battles and beetroot, the former slightly· dominating. He ¹(*be*) .... a sergeant with a tank regiment, part of Montgomery's Second Army that ²(*sweep*) .... across northern Germany in the spring of 1945. One of his favourite stories was how he and a corporal and a private ³(*go*) .... into a farmhouse kitchen near the Weser, found the occupants gone, nothing to eat but a sucking pig roasting, in fact ready to eat at that moment, in the oven. Another ⁴(*be*) .... the one about the gun. Outside Bremen Sydney had found a dead German officer lying in a ditch. He ⁵(*still hold*) .... a gun in his hand which ⁶(*lead*) .... Sydney to believe (on no other evidence) that he ⁷(*shoot*) .... himself out of despair at the way the war ⁸(*go*) ....

C Describe four different uses of *would* here.

  a '*A German military small-bore automatic pistol,*' Sydney **would explain** ... . (ll. 22–23)
  b *I promised I* **would write** *to you and I did.*
  c *Is Friday convenient for you? – Yes, Friday* **would be** *fine.*
  d **Would you like** *some more coffee?*

  ....
  ....

Describe four different uses of *would* in these sentences.

  1 I would often climb trees when I was a boy, but I don't now of course.   *past habit* ....
  2 Would you like to have dinner with us next week?   ....
  3 John explained how he would save money for the company.   ....
  4 I asked Joan if she would be in tomorrow.   ....
  5 Don't ask me questions like that! I wouldn't know.   ....
  6 Would you think that's too much to pay for a car?   ....
  7 He said he would see a specialist, but he hasn't done so yet.   ....
  8 As students, we would often stay up all night talking.   ....

D What meaning is conveyed by *the more ... the more* here? (ll. 42–43)
The more fat she became **the more** withdrawn. ....

Join these sentences using *the ... the*.

  1 You practise hard. You become better. *The harder you practise, the better you become.*
  2 You learn more. You know less. ....
  3 You shout louder. You get less attention. ....
  4 You get older. You remember less. ....

E In what way are the uses of *had had* different in these two sentences?

  a *It was as if whatever spirit she* **had** *ever* **had** *was being steadily suppressed.* (ll. 43–44)
  b *I asked him if he* **had** *ever* **had** *a swim in the Dead Sea.*

Supply *had had* and say whether the meaning is 'possessed' or something else.

  1 I fell asleep quickly after dinner because I ...*had had*... a large meal.   *had eaten* ....
  2 I .... a motorbike for several years before I bought a car.   ....
  3 The policeman wanted to know what they .... to drink.   ....
  4 She .... a quick temper as a child, but now things had changed.   ....
  5 He told me he (never) .... more than one pair of shoes.   ....
  6 I woke in a sweat because I .... a bad dream.   ....
  7 The doctor wanted to know if I (ever) .... German measles.   ....

SENTENCE STRUCTURE

A Answers and commentary

Detailed suggestions for joining these sentences were not provided in the exercise, so there are many possible answers. The commentary is based on the way the sentences have been joined in the text.

1 *Having only two topics of conversation, ...*
Having is the present participle of *have*, used as a full verb here. As a full verb, *have* means 'possess'. [> LEG 10.27–31, LAG 41E]
The present participle construction is used here in place of an adverbial clause of reason:
> *As he had* .... [> LEG 1.58.3]

Though *having* is a present participle form, there is no progressive tense when *have* means 'possess', so we have to say:
> *I have a car.* (Not *I'm having a car.*) [> LEG 10.30n.3, 10.33n.1, LAG 51E]

But we can say:
> *Having a car, I was able to drive to work during the railway strike.*

Compare the use of *having* as an auxiliary verb [> LEG 1.59, 10.3]:
> *Having invited him here to speak, we'd better go to his lecture.* (= As we have invited)

and the use of *having* when *have* is a full verb meaning something other than 'possess':
> *Having second thoughts, we decided to put off making a decision.* (= As we had ...) [> LEG 10.32–38, App 42]

... the Second World War and the greengrocery trade, ...
This phrase is used in apposition to *two topics of conversation*. It supplies additional information and replaces a relative clause [> LEG 1.39]:
> *He had only two topics of conversation, (which were) the Second World War and the greengrocery trade, ...*

... Sydney Faraday had talked exhaustively about battles and beetroot, ...
Participle phrases (*having* ...) must relate to the subject (*Sydney Faraday*) [> LEG 1.61]:
> Not *Having only two topics of conversation, the war was a boring subject.*

*... the former slightly **dominating**.*
The former refers to *battles*; *the latter* would refer to *beetroot*. [> LEG 4.11, LAG 4Bn.3]

The present participle *dominating* is used in place of a co-ordinate clause:
> *... and the former slightly dominated.* [> LEG 1.58.1]

2 *He had been a sergeant with a tank regiment, part of Montgomery's Second Army ...*
The phrase in apposition (see **1** above) replaces a relative clause [> LEG 1.39, LAG 5Ans.2,4]:
> *He had been a sergeant with a tank regiment, (which was) part of ...*

*... **that** swept across northern Germany in the spring of 1945.*
That (or *which*) is the relative pronoun subject of the defining relative clause [> LEG 1.31.1]:
> *This was part of Montgomery's Second Army. It swept across ...*
> → *... that/which swept across ...*

3 *One of his favourite stories was **how** he and a corporal and a private had gone into a farmhouse kitchen near the Weser, ...*
How introduces a noun-clause complement to *was* and the clause follows statement word order. [> LEG 1.24.2, LAG 29B, 50E]

... found the occupants gone, ... (= had found that the occupants had gone)
the occupants gone is the object of *(had) found*.

... nothing to eat but a sucking pig roasting, ...
(= nothing to eat except a sucking pig which was roasting) This is the second item in a list.

... in fact ready to eat at that moment, in the oven.
These phrases are in apposition to *a sucking pig* (above). The sense obliges the writer to put the phrase of place (*in the oven*) after the time phrase here. [compare > LEG 7.19, LAG 4A]

4 *While they ate the shop-bought, home-boiled pudding and drank the only pleasing constituent of the meal, Sydney's port, ...*
While introduces an adverbial clause of time and points to parallel actions. The progressive (*were eating/drinking*) could be used in place of the simple past (*ate/drank*). [> LEG 1.45.1, 9.20.2–3, LAG 10An.1, 12An.16, 20Bn.1] *And* introduces a co-ordinate clause. [> LEG 1.17–20]

... Sydney told the story of the German officer and the gun once more.
This is the main clause.

GRAMMAR POINTS

B Past tenses in narration [> LEG 9.31, Apps 39–40, LAG 8E, 19C, 26C, 28C, 33B, 53C, 58D]

This extract illustrates particularly well the use of past tenses in narration, with emphasis on the past perfect to refer to an earlier past.

1 *had been*: Past perfect referring to an earlier past. [> LEG 9.29.1, 9.30, 10.12–13, LAG 33B, 52B]
2 *swept* (*sweep - swept - swept*): Simple past for completed action [> LEG 9.17.1]; the past perfect would also be possible, as in **1** above.
3 *had gone*: Past perfect referring to an earlier past. [> LEG 9.29.1, 9.30, 10.13.4]
4 *was*: Simple past, narration. [> LEG 9.17.1, 10.8–9, LAG 33B, 53C]
5 *was still holding*: Past progressive: action in progress at the time. [> LEG 9.20.1, LAG 8En.1]
6 *led* (*lead - led - led*): Simple past, narration. [> LEG 9.17.1]
7 *had shot* (*shoot - shot - shot*): Past perfect referring to an earlier past. [> LEG 9.29.1, 9.30]
8 *was going*: Past progressive, because the war was still in progress at the time. [> LEG 9.20.1, LAG 8En.1] The past perfect (*had gone*) would suggest that the war had ended.

C Selected uses of 'would'

a *Sydney would explain*:
would to describe past habit. [> LEG 11.61, compare > LAG 5D]
b *I promised I would write*:
will becomes *would* when reported in the past. [> LEG 9.5, 15.12–13, 15.13n.6, LAG 7F, 10C]
c *Friday would be fine*:
less definite *would* in place of the simple present. [> LEG 11.3, 11.74.2, LAG 10Cn.7]
d *Would you like ... ?*:
would in suggestions/offers. [> LEG 11.37–38]

Would has a variety of uses in English, four of which are identified above.

1 past habit
2 invitation/suggestion
3 past sequence of tenses in indirect statement
4 past sequence in indirect question
5 less definite (possibly rude response), in place of simple present (*I don't know*)
6 less definite, in place of simple present (*Do you think ...?*); *would* is more tentative and more polite
7 past sequence in indirect statement
8 past habit

D 'The' + comparative + 'the': 'the more ... the more' [> LEG 6.27.3]

The first *the more* describes the cause; the second *the more* describes the effect. [> LAG 22An.6]

This construction with *the ... the* is used with comparative adjectives or adverbs to show cause and effect: when one change is made, another follows:

> **The more** money you make, **the more** you spend.

1 The harder you practise, the better you become.
2 The more you learn, the less you know.
3 The louder you shout, the less attention you get. (Not *the less you get attention*)
4 The older you get, the less you remember.

E The past perfect of 'had': 'had had' [> LEG 10.30n.3, 10.32, 10.35–36]

a possession **b** experience

Have as a full verb has two uses:
– possession:
> I **have** a Ford. I **had** a Ford last year.

Possession can include mental and emotional qualities, illnesses, etc. [> LEG 10.31, App 42.1]
– something other than possession (e.g. *take, experience, enjoy*):
> I'm **having** a drink. I **had** a ride in my brother's new car.

In both uses, *have* can be an auxiliary verb which 'helps itself'. That's why we have the form *had had*:

> I **had had** a Ford for several years, before I bought a different model. (possession)

> I **had** never **had** a ride on an elephant before I went to India. ('experienced')

1 had had (= had eaten)
2 had had (= possessed)
3 had had (= had drunk)
4 had had (= possessed)
5 had never had (= possessed)
6 had had (= experienced)
7 had ever had (= 'possessed'/experienced)

Invasion of the data snatchers!

FROMA JOSELOW was getting ready to bang out a newspaper story when the invisible intruder struck. Joselow, a financial reporter at the
5 Providence *Journal-Bulletin*, had carefully slipped a disk holding six months' worth of notes and interviews into one of the newsroom computers when the
10 machine's familiar whir was pierced by a sharp, high-pitched beep. Each time she tried to call a file to the screen, the warning DISK ERROR flashed instead. It was as if the
15 contents of her floppy disk had vanished. 'I got that sinking feeling,' recalls Joselow. 'Every writing project of mine was on that disk.'
20 In the *Journal-Bulletin's* computer centre, where Joselow took her troubled floppy, the detective work began immediately. Using a binary editor - the
25 computer equivalent of a high-powered magnifying glass - Systems Engineer Peter Scheidler examined the disk's contents line by line. 'What I saw wasn't pretty,' says
30 Scheidler. 'It was garbage, a real mess.' Looking for a way to salvage at least part of Joselow's work, he began peering into each of the disk's 360 concentric rings of data.
35 Suddenly he spotted something that gave him a chill. Buried near Sector 0, the disk's innermost circle, was evidence that the glitch that had swallowed six months of
40 Joselow's professional life was not a glitch at all but a deliberate act of sabotage. There, standing out amid a stream of random letters and numbers, was the name and phone
45 number of a Pakistani computer store and a message that read, in part: WELCOME TO THE DUNGEON ... CONTACT US FOR VACCINATION.
50 Joselow had been stricken by a pernicious virus. Not the kind that causes measles, mumps or the Shanghai flu, but a special strain of software virus, a small but deadly
55 program that lurks in the darkest recesses of a computer waiting for an opportunity to spring to life. The computer virus that struck Joselow had been hiding in the
60 memory of the newspaper's machine and had copied itself onto her data disk, scrambling its contents and turning the reporter's words and sentences into electronic
65 confetti.

Time (AmE)

Sentence structure

A Join these sentences making any necessary changes, then refer to the text.

1 Joselow is a financial reporter at the Providence *Journal-Bulletin*. She had carefully slipped a disk holding six months' worth of notes and interviews into one of the newsroom computers. The machine's familiar whir was pierced by a sharp, high-pitched beep. (ll. 4–11)

....

....

....

2 She tried to call a file to the screen. The warning DISK ERROR flashed instead. (ll. 11–14)

....

3 Systems Engineer Peter Scheidler examined the disk's contents line by line. He used a binary editor. This is the computer equivalent of a high-powered magnifying glass. (ll. 24–28)

....

B Explain why the first of these statements is not a true grammatical sentence. Then join the statements to make one complete sentence before checking your answer against the text.

Not the kind that causes measles, mumps or the Shanghai flu. It is a special strain of software virus, a small but deadly program. It lurks in the darkest recesses of a computer. It is waiting for an opportunity to spring to life. (ll. 51–57)

....

....

Grammar points

C What's the difference in meaning between these two sentences?

  a *Each time **she tried to call** a file to the screen, the warning DISK ERROR flashed.* (ll. 11–14)
  b *Each time **she tried calling** a file to the screen, the warning DISK ERROR flashed.*

....

Say whether the phrases in italics mean 'attempted' or 'experimented'.

  1 I *tried to dial* your number ten times this morning, but couldn't get through. *attempted*
  2 Why don't you *try dialling* again, using the new code number?
  3 *Try turning* the power *on* and see if the computer comes on.
  4 Even if you *try to turn* the power *on*, the computer is still dead.
  5 The salesman *tried to convince* me that I need a life insurance policy.
  6 You *try convincing* an unwilling customer to buy life insurance!

D What does *what* mean in this sentence?
  ***What** I saw wasn't pretty.* (l. 29)

Use phrases with *what* or *which* to replace the phrases in italics.

  1 Our teacher doesn't always correct *the things we write*. *what we write*
  2 *The thing that matters* most is to go on developing.
  3 You shouldn't pay any attention to *the things he says*.
  4 Honesty is the best policy, *a thing you know* only too well.
  5 I've taken all the things *that belong* to me.
  6 It's either a or b. *The one you choose* is your affair.
  7 *The thing I choose to do* is my affair, not yours.
  8 She keeps a record of *the things that happen*.

E What does *got* mean in this sentence?
  *'I **got** that sinking feeling,' recalls Joselow.* (ll. 16–17)

Suggest approximate meanings for *get* in these sentences.

  1 How did you *get* that idea? *'obtain'*
  2 Did you *get* your money back in the end?
  3 Where did you *get* that lovely jacket?
  4 Which train did you *get*?
  5 I'm *getting* very fed up with the weather.
  6 How did you *get* her to tell you what happened?
  7 Don't park there. You'll *get* your car vandalized.
  8 I had no key and *got in* through a window.

F Rewrite this sentence in the singular, then refer to the text. (l. 30) What did you notice?
  The things I saw on the screen were garbage. The thing ....

....

Choose the right word(s).

  1 Don't believe what he says. It's (a rubbish/rubbish). *rubbish*
  2 I'd like (an information/some information) please.
  3 Have you brought a lot of (luggage/luggages) with you?
  4 Please give me (some advices/an advice/some advice).
  5 Your (furnitures are/furniture is) so beautiful!
  6 Have (some fruits/a fruit/some fruit)!
  7 Don't talk (nonsense/nonsenses)!
  8 Could I have some more (macaronis/macaroni) please?
  9 Listen to (all those thunders/all that thunder)!
  10 She's bought lots of new (clothing/clothings).

SENTENCE STRUCTURE

A Answers and commentary

Suggestions for joining these sentences were not provided in the exercise, so there are many possible answers. The commentary is based on the way the sentences have been joined in the text.

1 *Joselow, a financial reporter at the Providence* Journal-Bulletin, ...
The two noun phrases are in apposition, the second adding information to the first. They are used in place of a relative clause [> LEG 1.39]:
   Joselow, (who is) a financial reporter at the Providence Journal-Bulletin, ...

... *had carefully slipped a disk holding six months' worth of notes and interviews into one of the newsroom computers* ...
Adverbs of manner like *carefully* usually come after the object or after the verb. [> LEG 7.16.1] However, we can also put them after the first auxiliary verb (here, *had*) if we want to emphasize the subject or if, as here, there is a very long object (*a disk holding six months' worth of notes and interviews*). [> LEG 7.16.2] This is also the usual position for adverbs of frequency like *often*, *never*, etc. [> LEG 7.40.1]

... *when the machine's familiar whir was pierced by a sharp, high-pitched beep.*
When introduces a subordinate adverbial clause of time. [> LEG 1.21, 1.45.1]

2 *Each time she tried to call a file to the screen, the warning DISK ERROR flashed instead.*
Each time is the equivalent of *whenever* and introduces an adverbial clause of time. [> LEG 1.45.1] The writer could have used *Every time* instead. *Each* is more individual and suggests 'one by one' or 'separately'. [> LEG 5.26.1]

3 *Using a binary editor* ...
The present participle construction is used in place of a co-ordinate clause [> LEG 1.57–58]:
   He used a binary editor and examined ...

... – *the computer equivalent of a high-powered magnifying glass –* ...
The flow of the sentence is interrupted by this extra information, which the writer considers necessary to explain to the reader what *binary editor* means. It is the equivalent of a relative, non-defining clause:

Using a binary editor – (which is) the computer equivalent of a high-powered magnifying glass – ...
The use of dashes, instead of commas, emphasizes the introduction of additional information. [> LEG 1.26, LAG 3B*n*.3]

... *Systems Engineer Peter Scheidler examined the disk's contents line by line.*
Note how the introduction of the subject (*Peter Scheidler*) has been delayed. Identifying people by profession before mentioning their names (*Systems Engineer Peter Scheidler*) is a common journalistic device. [> LEG 1.21 and compare > LEG 6.21.1]

B Answers and commentary

The first statement in the exercise (and the whole statement in the text) is not a true grammatical sentence because it doesn't have a subject and finite verb. [> LEG 1.2, 4.5, 4.12, LAG 1A] This doesn't mean the statement is wrong. We can write statements without verbs, especially when we want to keep the rhythms of speech, as is the case in this passage. The statement could have read:
It was not the kind that causes measles, mumps or the Shanghai flu ...
The subject *it*, referring back to *a pernicious virus*, is followed by the finite *was*.

... *but a special strain of software virus, a small but deadly program* ...
The subject and verb are not repeated after the first *but* (*but it was a special strain*). [> LEG 1.20.6] The second *but* means 'though': *Though it is a small program, it is a deadly one* .... [compare > LEG 1.50, LAG 12A*n*.1]

... *that lurks in the darkest recesses of a computer* ...
That (or *which*) is the relative pronoun subject of the relative clause [> LEG 1.31]:
   It is a special strain of software virus. It lurks ...
      → ... *a special strain that/which lurks* ...

   waiting for an opportunity to spring to life.
The present participle construction is used in place of a relative clause [> LEG 1.58.6]:
   It is a special strain of software virus (that/which is) waiting to spring to life.

GRAMMAR POINTS

C 'Try' + 'to' and 'try' + '-ing' [> LEG 16.59, compare >LAG 57D]

a *she tried to call* (= she made an effort to call)
b *she tried calling* (= she did this experimentally to see what might happen)

Try + *to*-infinitive means 'make an effort':
*You really must **try to overcome** your shyness.*
Try + *-ing* means 'experiment':
***Try holding** your breath to stop sneezing.*

1 'attempted'
2 'experiment'
3 'experiment'
4 'attempt'
5 'attempted'
6 'experiment'

D 'What' (= the thing(s) that): 'what I saw wasn't pretty' [> LEG 1.24.2, LAG 50E]

The thing that/that which

We use *what*, not 'that which', 'those which', in sentences like:
*Show me **what** you bought.*
We can use *what* in this way as a subject:
***What I bought** isn't expensive. (Not *That which*)*
or as an object of a verb or preposition:
*Show me **what you bought**.*
*Look **at what he does** instead of listening **to what he says**.*

We use *which* as a relative pronoun (subject or object), not *what* [> LEG 1.27–36]:
*I've got a watch **which works** without a battery. (Not *what*)*
*Your watch is better than **the one** (**which**) I bought. (Not *what*)*

Sometimes we may use *which* when the choice is limited:
*Show me **which you chose**. [compare > LEG 13.36.1]*
Or we may use *what* when the choice is not limited:
*Show me **what you chose**. [compare > LEG 13.34.1, LAG 18An.2]*

1 what we write
2 What matters
3 what he says
4 which you know
5 which belong
6 Which you choose
7 What I choose to do
8 what happens

E Some meanings of 'get' [> LEG 8.9.7, 10.26.1, 12.6, LAG 23D, 27D]

had

The basic meaning of *get* is 'receive' or 'obtain', but note the uses listed below.

1 How did you *get* that idea? (= 'obtain')
2 Did you *get* your money back in the end? (= 'receive')
3 Where did you *get* that lovely jacket? (= 'obtain', 'buy')
4 Which train did you *get*? (= 'catch')
5 I'm *getting* very fed up with the weather. (= 'becoming') [> LEG 10.26.1]
6 How did you *get* her to tell you what happened? (= 'persuade') [> LEG 12.13.2]
7 You'll *get* your car vandalized. (= 'it will happen beyond your control') [> LEG 12.13.3]
8 I had no key and *got in* through a window. (= 'entered with difficulty') [> LEG 8.9.7]

F Nouns not normally countable in English: 'information' [> LEG 2.17, App 4]

The thing I saw on the screen was garbage.
We do not use *garbage* in the plural (Not *garbages*) or with *a* (Not *a garbage*).

Some nouns, like *information*, are countable in other languages, but not countable in English. This means they can't be used with *a/an* and can't be used in the plural, so we have to say:
*I'd like **some information** please. (Not *an information*/*some informations*)*

1 rubbish
2 some information
3 luggage
4 some advice
5 furniture is
6 some fruit
7 nonsense
8 macaroni
9 all that thunder
10 clothing

The thoughts of Henry Wilt

WHENEVER Henry Wilt took the dog for a walk, or, to be more accurate, when the dog took him, or, to be exact, when Mrs Wilt told them both to go and take themselves out of
5 the house so that she could do her yoga exercises, he always took the same route. In fact the dog followed the route and Wilt followed the dog. They went down past the Post Office, across the playground, under
10 the railway bridge and out on to the footpath by the river. A mile along the river and then under the railway line again and back through streets where the houses were bigger than Wilt's semi and where there were large trees and gardens
15 and the cars were all Rovers and Mercedes. It was here that Clem, a pedigree Labrador, evidently feeling more at home, did his business while Wilt stood looking around rather uneasily, conscious that this was not his sort of neighbourhood and wishing it was. It was about the only
20 time during their walk that he was at all aware of his surroundings. For the rest of the way Wilt's walk was an interior one and followed an itinerary completely at variance with his own appearance and that of his route. It was in fact a journey of wishful thinking, a pilgrimage along trails of
25 remote possibility involving the irrevocable disappearance of Mrs Wilt, the sudden acquisition of wealth, power, what he would do if he was appointed Minister of Education or, better still, Prime Minister. It was partly concocted of a series of desperate expedients and partly in an unspoken
30 dialogue so that anyone noticing Wilt (and most people didn't) might have seen his lips move occasionally and his mouth curl into what he fondly imagined was a sardonic smile as he dealt with questions or parried arguments with devastating repartee. It was on one of these walks taken in
35 the rain after a particularly trying day at the Tech that Wilt first conceived the notion that he would only be able to fulfil his latent promise and call his life his own if some not entirely fortuitous disaster overtook his wife.

Wilt by Tom Sharpe *(BrE)*

Sentence structure

A Sometimes a wrong word has been used or added. Delete the wrong word and suggest a replacement where necessary. Some lines are correct. Then refer to the text.

However Henry Wilt took the dog for a walk, or, to be more accurate, when	**1**	....
the dog took him, or, to be exact, when Mrs Wilt told both them to go and take	**2**	....
themselves out of the house so that she did her yoga exercises, he always	**3**	....
took the same route. In fact the dog followed the route and Wilt followed	**4**	....
the dog. They went down passed the Post Office, across the playground, under	**5**	....
the railway bridge and out of on to the footpath by the river. A mile along	**6**	....
the river and then under the railway line again and backwards through	**7**	....
streets where the houses were bigger as Wilt's semi and where there	**8**	....
were large trees and gardens and the cars were all Rovers and Mercedes.	**9**	....
It was here that Clem, a pedigree Labrador, evidently feeling more at home,	**10**	....
did his business while Wilt stood and looking around rather uneasily,	**11**	....
conscious that this was not his sort of neighbourhood and wished it	**12**	....
was. It was about the only time during their walk that he was at all	**13**	....
aware of his surroundings. For the rest of the way Wilt's walk was an	**14**	....
interior one and following an itinerary completely at variance with his	**15**	....
own appearance and that from his route. It was in fact a journey of wishful	**16**	....
thinking, a pilgrimage along trails of remote possibility involving	**17**	....
with the irrevocable disappearance of Mrs Wilt, the sudden acquisition	**18**	....
of wealth, power, that he would do if he was appointed Minister of Education	**19**	....
or, better still, Prime Minister. It was partly concocted of a series	**20**	....
of desperate expedients and partly in an unspoken dialogue so that	**21**	....
anyone noticed Wilt (and most people didn't) might have seen his lips	**22**	....
moved occasionally and his mouth curl into ... a sardonic smile (ll. 1–33)	**23**	....

Grammar points

B Supply *do* or *make* in this sentence, then check against the text. (ll. 3–6)
Mrs Wilt told them to take themselves out so that she could .... her yoga exercises.

Supply the correct forms of *do* or *make* in these sentences.

1 You can't rely on him. He's always ..*making*.... excuses for never getting things done.
2 I hope you're not going to .... a habit of ringing me up in the middle of the night.
3 Just a minute, I have to .... a call home.
4 The recent storm has .... a lot of damage.
5 .... me a favour, will you, and post these letters when you're out.
6 Who .... the rules in this household?
7 You either know the answer or you don't. It's no good .... guesses.
8 Drink this. It will .... you a lot of good.
9 You can't come into the kitchen just now. We're .... the floor.
10 I've always liked the way you .... your hair.
11 Which modern languages are you ....? – I'm .... Russian and Polish.
12 We .... an agreement and you've broken it.
13 I've got a lot of jobs to .... this morning.
14 Please don't .... a noise or you'll disturb the people upstairs.
15 Peeling onions is the last thing I want to do after I've .... a day's work.
16 I shouldn't employ him. He's always .... trouble.
17 We've been learning Chinese for a year, but we haven't .... much progress.
18 Don't tell me you still .... the washing on Mondays!
19 A car that size only .... about 10 miles to the gallon.
20 I went all the way there for nothing. I .... an unnecessary journey.

C Suggest a few adverbs of direction you could use in front of *past* here, then refer to the text.
They went .... past the Post Office. (ll. 8–9)

Supply possible adverbs or prepositions in these sentences.

1 The accident happened because you cut in *in front of* me.
2 I don't like people who drive close .... behind you.
3 Will you boys please get down .... that tree!
4 The noise is coming from .... the floorboards.
5 I'd like to drive on .... the next service station before stopping for a break.
6 There's a stationer's just four shops along .... the left.
7 We're .... on our holidays next week.
8 We're entertaining our neighbours .... across the road next Sunday.
9 We were thrown .... against the wall by the blast.
10 I think we're going to have to walk back .... the jungle.

D What does *that of* replace in this sentence? (ll. 22–23)
*It was completely at variance with his own appearance and **that of** his route.* ....

Show where *that of* or *those of* can be used in these sentences.

1 The circumference of the earth is much larger than ~~the circumference of~~ the moon. *that of*
2 The area of Brazil is not as large as the area of the USA. ....
3 Beethoven's compositions are not as numerous as the compositions of Mozart. ....
4 The freezing point of nitrogen is lower than the freezing point of water. ....
5 The intelligence of a chimpanzee is higher than the intelligence of a donkey. ....
6 Our exam results are the same as the exam results of other schools. ....
7 The atmosphere here is less polluted than the atmosphere of other cities. ....
8 The hotels are less expensive here than the hotels of the south coast. ....
9 Your handwriting is different from the handwriting of your sister. ....

SENTENCE STRUCTURE

A Answers and commentary

1 *Whenever*: The meaning is *when* here and *whenever* is used emphatically to introduce an adverbial clause of time. [> LEG 1.45.1, 13.47] *However* means 'no matter which way' [> LEG 1.50], or introduces contrast. [> LEG 7.58]

2 *told them both*: We always use a personal indirect object after *tell*. We have to say *tell them both* or *tell both of them*. (Not **both them**) [> LEG 5.20.2, 15.7.1, LAG 20C]

3 *could do*: adverbial clause of purpose introduced by *so that*. We need *could* here because the narrative is all in the past [> LEG 1.51.1–2]; *so that she did* incorrectly suggests result [> LEG 1.52.2] which would be wrong here.

4 This line is correct.

5 *past*: preposition + object (*the Post Office*) [> LEG 8.1, App 20.1]; *passed* is the past tense of the verb *pass*. [> LEG 9.14.1, App 39.2]

6 *out of on to the footpath*: *Out* is an adverb and follows the verb *went* here:
They **went out** on to the footpath.
Out of is a preposition and is used in front of an object as the opposite of *into* to show movement:
into the building/out of the building. [> LEG 8.4.2, 8.9.5–6, App 25.31, LAG 40E]

7 *back*: is an adverb and follows the verb *went* from the preceding sentence. *Went back* means 'returned'; *went backwards* means 'with (your) back facing the direction (you) are going in'. [> LEG 7.18, 8.4.3, App 32.5 and compare *towards*, > LEG App 25.34, LAG 12Bn.21] The statement *A mile ... Mercedes* is not a true grammatical sentence because it does not contain a finite verb. [> LEG 1.2, LAG 1A]

8 *than*: We use *than* after a comparative (e.g. *bigger*), not as. *Than* is a preposition here because it is followed by a noun object (*Wilt's semi*). *Than* also functions as a conjunction when it is followed by a clause. [> LEG 1.53, 4.7.3, 6.27.1]

9–10 These lines are correct.

11 *stood looking*: *stood and looked* would be all right, but **stood and looking** would be wrong here. The *-ing* form is a participle. [> LEG 1.57, and compare > LEG 16.45.1, LAG 4Bn.3, 8An.3]:
Wilt **stood** there. He **was looking** around ...
→ *Wilt* **stood looking** around ...

12 *wishing*: relates to *conscious* here, not to *(stood) looking*: *Wilt, conscious that it was not his sort of neighbourhood and wishing (that) it was ...* (Not **Wilt stood looking ... and wishing ...**)

13–14 These lines are correct.

15 *followed*: a finite verb is required here, not a present participle. *And* introduces a co-ordinate main clause [> LEG 1.17, LAG 1Bn.2]:
Wilt's walk was an interior one. **It followed** ...
→ *Wilt's walk was an interior one* **and followed** ...
However, if *and* were replaced with a comma, *following* would be all right:
Wilt's walk was an interior one, **following** *an itinerary ...*

16 *of*: *that of* is used here (Not **that from**) to avoid repeating *the appearance* [> LEG App 7.10, LAG 43D]:
Wilt's walk was an interior one and followed an itinerary completely at variance with his own appearance and **the appearance of** *his route.*
→ *... completely at variance with his own appearance and* **that of** *his route.*

17 This line is correct.

18 *involving with*: We don't use *with* after *involving*. [> LAG 20D] Compare the transitive verb *involve*:
Protection of the environment is an issue that **involves everybody**.
and *to be involved with/in* [> LAG 25An.16]:
The police interviewed everyone **involved with/in** *the case.*

19 *what* (= the thing(s) that): introduces a noun clause after *involving*. The word order is that of an indirect question. [> LEG 1.24.2, 15.19–20, LAG 42D, 50E–F]

20–21 These lines are correct.

22 *noticing*: The present participle is used here in place of a relative clause [> LAG 9An.1]:
... so that **anyone** *(who might have been)* **noticing** *Wilt ... might have seen his lips ....*
so that introduces an adverbial clause of result. [> LEG 1.52.2]

23 *move*: The sequence is: *...* **might have seen** *his lips* **move** *occasionally and his mouth* **curl** *...* We can use a bare infinitive or the *-ing* form after the verb of perception *see*. The bare infinitive refers to the complete action. [> LEG 16.9.2, LAG 17Bn.13, 21Bn.2b, 35Bn.3] Compare:
... might have seen **that his lips moved** *...* where *that* introduces a noun clause as object of the verb *might have seen*.

GRAMMAR POINTS

B Combinations with 'do' and 'make': 'do yoga', 'make an appointment' [> LEG 10.45, App 43, compare expressions with *have* > LAG   24B]

*. . . so that she could **do** her yoga exercises.*

Make conveys the sense of 'create'; *do*, often suggesting 'be engaged in an activity', is a more general term.

Do and *make* occur in a variety of fixed combinations:

- *do your best, do business with someone, do damage to something, do your duty, do someone a favour,* etc.
- *make an accusation against someone, make an appointment with someone, make an arrangement,* etc.
- in some instances *do* can replace *make,* when *making something* is seen as *doing a job*:

*I haven't **made the beds** yet. I'll **do them** after I've finished this.*

There is no general rule to guide you when to use *do* rather than *make.* Learn the combinations as you encounter them.

1 making excuses
2 make a habit of
3 make a call
4 has done a lot of damage
5 Do me a favour
6 Who makes the rules
7 making guesses
8 do you a lot of good
9 doing the floor
10 do your hair
11 languages are you doing ?. . . doing Russian and Polish
12 made an agreement
13 jobs to do
14 make a noise
15 done a day's work
16 making trouble
17 made much progress
18 do the washing
19 does about 10 miles to the gallon
20 made an unnecessary journey

C Combinations of particles and prepositions: 'down past the Post Office' [> LEG 8.18, 8.30.2, compare > LAG   13C]

Possible combinations:

*They went **down/up/along past** the Post Office.*

Sometimes we can use an adverb particle in front of prepositions:

*I'm going **down to** the beach.* [compare > LAG 16B]

Sometimes we can use two (or even more) prepositions together:

*Come out **from under** there, will you?*

Possible answers

1 cut in in front of me
2 drive close up behind you
3 please get down from that tree
4 coming from under the floorboards
5 drive on to the next service station
6 four shops along on the left
7 we're off on our holidays
8 entertaining our neighbours from across the road
9 thrown back against the wall
10 walk back through the jungle

D Comparisons using 'that of' and 'those of' [> LEG App 7.10]

that of replaces *the appearance of* so it isn't necessary to write: *his own appearance and the appearance of his route.*

In formal use, we may use *that of* and *those of* to replace a noun with *of* or a possessive when we are making comparisons. This saves us from having to repeat the noun:

*The area of the USA is larger than **that of** Brazil.* (= than the area of)

*Tom's essays are better than **those of** the other boys.* (= than the other boys' essays)

1 ~~the circumference of~~ that of
2 ~~the area of~~ that of
3 ~~the compositions of~~ those of
4 ~~the freezing point of~~ that of
5 ~~the intelligence of~~ that of
6 ~~the exam results of~~ those of
7 ~~the atmosphere of~~ that of
8 ~~the hotels of~~ those of
9 ~~the handwriting of~~ that of

Dinosaurs on a tidal wave?

IN A RIVER VALLEY not far from Houston, Texas, a team of American scientists have found geological evidence that a vast tidal wave swept the whole Caribbean region 65 million years ago, just as the Cretaceous period - the age of the dinosaurs - was ending. Writing in the latest issue of the US journal *Science*, the geologists claim that a tidal wave on this scale could only have been caused by the impact of an asteroid, probably five to ten kilometres in diameter, plunging through the Earth's atmosphere and into the sea. That spectacular picture fits well with the view of the 'catastrophists', geologists who think that the sudden disappearance of the dinosaurs, along with a diverse range of other living things, was caused by a series of asteroid impacts.

Each impact would have thrown up a world-embracing dust cloud, blotting out the Sun and lowering temperatures to the point where many plants and animals could not survive. Evidence for that view already comes in clays from the end of the Cretaceous period. They are enriched in iridium, an element which is very rare in the Earth's crust but much more abundant in asteroids.

Of course, the clinching evidence for the catastrophic view would be the discovery of the remains of the craters where the asteroids struck. Unfortunately, no crater of the right age has been definitely identified, although if they are all at the bottom of the sea that is not so surprising. But the new work published in *Science* does provide the next best thing - if not the crater itself, evidence of the wave the asteroid created when it struck the sea. The evidence comes in a puzzling layer of rippled sandstone found in the Brazos River valley, Texas. The sandstone is curious because, at first, there seems no good reason why it should be there. It is a sudden, thin interruption in a thick deposit of mudstone. That, as its name suggests, is compacted mud that quietly accumulated over the millions of years that the region lay at the bottom of a shallow, undisturbed sea.

The Times (BrE)

Sentence structure

A Circle the item that fits the space, then refer to the text.

In a river valley not ¹...... Houston, Texas, a team of American scientists have found geological evidence ²..... a vast tidal wave ³...... the whole Caribbean region 65 million years ago, ⁴...... the Cretaceous period – the age of the dinosaurs – was ending. ⁵...... in the latest issue of the US journal *Science*, the geologists claim ⁶...... a tidal wave on this scale could only have been caused ⁷...... the impact of an asteroid, probably five to ten kilometres in diameter, ⁸..... through the Earth's atmosphere. (ll. 1–16)

1 a far from	**b** far away	**c** away from
2 a which	**b** who	**c** that
3 a had swept	**b** swept	**c** sweeping
4 a until	**b** just as	**c** along with
5 a Wrote	**b** Written	**c** Writing
6 a that	**b** so that	**c** what
7 a by	**b** from	**c** with
8 a to plunge	**b** plunging	**c** by plunging

B Supply the connecting words, then check against the text. (ll. 25–52)

Each impact would have thrown up a world-embracing dust cloud, ¹(*blot*) .... out the Sun and ²(*lower*) .... temperatures to the point ³............. many plants and animals could not survive. Evidence for that view ⁴............. comes in clays from the end of the Cretaceous period. ⁵............. are enriched in iridium, an element ⁶............. is very rare in the Earth's crust ⁷............. much more abundant in asteroids.

Of course, the ⁸(*clinch*) .... evidence for the catastrophic view would be the discovery of the remains of the craters ⁹............. the asteroids struck. ¹⁰(*Unfortunate*) .... , no crater of the right age has been definitely identified, ¹¹............ if they are all at the bottom of the sea that is not so surprising. But the new work ¹²(*publish*) .... in *Science* does provide the next best thing – if not the crater itself, evidence of the wave the asteroid created ¹³............. it struck the sea.

Grammar points

C Supply *a/an, the* or zero (–) in this paragraph, then refer to the text. (ll. 1–17)

In ^{1}..... river valley not far from ^{2}..... Houston, ^{3}..... Texas, ^{4}..... team of American scientists have found geological evidence that ^{5}..... vast tidal wave swept ^{6}..... whole Caribbean region 65 million years ago, just as ^{7}..... Cretaceous period – ^{8}..... age of ^{9}..... dinosaurs – was ending. Writing in ^{10}..... latest issue of ^{11}..... US journal *Science*, ^{12}..... geologists claim that ^{13}..... tidal wave on this scale could only have been caused by ^{14}..... impact of ^{15}..... asteroid, probably five to ten kilometres in diameter, plunging through ^{16}..... Earth's atmosphere and into ^{17}..... sea.

D *Each impact would have thrown up a world embracing dust cloud,* **blotting out** *the Sun ...* (ll. 25–27)
What sort of verb is *blotting out*? Comment on the position of *out*.

....

Suggest meanings for the verbs in italics.

1 Mrs Hanson *put* her hip *out* in an accident.   *dislocated*
2 Miss Jones *told* the girls *off* for making so much noise.
3 You don't seem to understand. Let me *spell* it *out* for you.
4 I don't believe that story. You're *making* it *up*.
5 There's a programme on TV that's always *sending up* politicians.
6 Is there any way we can *put off* tomorrow's meeting?
7 Don't do that! You're *putting* me *off* my food.
8 The caterers at our wedding reception really *let* us *down*.
9 Jane's always *dashing* letters *off* to the newspapers.
10 I just don't believe you're *packing in* smoking again.
11 This'll do. Just *drop* me *off* here.
12 I know the medicine's awful. Shut your eyes and *knock* it *back*!
13 How many workers will the factory be *keeping on*?
14 Sally didn't make the team. They just *passed* her *over*!
15 It's a big deal and I don't know if I can really *bring* it *off*.
16 Look where you're going, unless you want to get *run over*.
17 I'll be OK. Don't bother to *see* me *off*.
18 As she isn't present, it isn't fair to *run* her *down*.
19 There's so much I have to *look up* in this difficult text.
20 I'm glad the dentist can *fit* me *in* this morning.

E *Evidence for that view already comes in* **clays** *from the end of the Cretaceous period.* (ll. 31–33)
What does *clays* mean? Comment on the plural here.

....

Use plural forms where appropriate.

1 Yesterday we had the opportunity to sample a variety of different (*wine*) *wines*
2 It's never advisable to drink a lot of (*wine*) ....
3 One thing we'll never be able to control is the (*weather*) ....
4 Even at the age of eighty-five, she goes out in all (*weather*) ....
5 The (*soil*) .... in this region is rich and fertile.
6 Scientists have just completed a major analysis of different (*soil*) ....
7 (*Fabric*) .... vary in price according to their weight.
8 We're going to need an awful lot of (*cloth*) .... for these curtains.
9 (*Religion*) .... is central to most human societies.
10 I'm just completing my study of world (*religion*) ....
11 Do you know you've had seven cups of (*tea*) ....?
12 Is this tea from one region, or is it a blend of different (*tea*) ....?

SENTENCE STRUCTURE

A Answers and commentary

1 a *far from*: *not far from* is the equivalent of *near*. We rarely use *far from* in the affirmative: *London is a long way from here*. (Not **far from**) [> LEG App 25.15, and compare > LEG App 25.8 for *far away*.]

2 c *that*: introduces a noun clause, dependent on *geological evidence*. [> LEG 1.23.2, App 45, compare > LAG 5An.5, 38Bn.1]

3 b *swept*: the simple past is required here, not the past perfect (*had swept*) even if the events described occurred 'a long time ago'. [> LEG 9.29]

4 b *just as*: introduces an adverbial clause of time [> LEG 1.45.1]; *just as* often introduces a past progressive (*was ending*). [> LEG 9.20.2] The past progressive describes a situation or action in progress in the past, and the simple past (*swept*) describes a shorter action or event. See **3** above.

5 c *Writing*: The present participle construction comes before the main clause (*the geologists claim*). [> LEG 1.57, compare > LAG 4Bn.3] The participle relates to the subject of both verbs (*the geologists*) [> LEG 1.61]:
> **The geologists** are writing ... **They** claim ...
> → **Writing** in the latest issue of Science, **the geologists claim** ...

6 a *that*: introduces a noun clause object of the reporting verb *claim*. [> LEG 1.23.2, App 45, compare > LAG 4E, 5An.5]

7 a *could only have been caused by*: *by* + agent (*the impact of an asteroid*) follows the passive verb *have been caused*. It is necessary here because it supplies essential information. [> LEG 12.5, LAG 49D]

8 b *plunging*: The present participle construction replaces a relative clause [> LEG 1.58.6, LAG 9An.1]:
> ... an asteroid ... **(which was) plunging** through the Earth's atmosphere ...

B Answers and commentary

1 *blotting*. The present participle construction replaces a relative clause [> LEG 1.58.6, LAG 9An.1]:
> *Each impact would have thrown up a world-embracing dust cloud, **which blotted** ...*
> → *a world-embracing dust cloud, **blotting** ...*

2 *lowering*: exactly as in **1** above:
> ... **which lowered** → **lowering** ...

3 *where*: introduces an adverbial clause of place. [> LEG 1.46, LAG 19An.3] It could be replaced by *at which*. [> LEG 1.38.2] ... *where many plants and animals could not survive* is a defining clause because it provides essential information here.

4 *already*: The position of *already* is the same as for adverbs of frequency: it can come before the main verb, as here. [> LEG 7.26, 7.40, LAG 45D]

5 *They*: The pronoun refers back to *clays* in the previous sentence. [> LEG 4.5.7]

6 *which* (or *that*): The relative pronoun subject of the relative clause [> LEG 1.31, LAG 5An.3]:
> **Iridium** is an element. **It** is very rare.
> → **Iridium** is an element **which/that** is very rare.

7 *but* (or *though*): It isn't necessary to repeat *which* + verb [> LEG 1.20.6]:
> ... an element which is very rare in the Earth's crust **but** *(is)* **much more abundant** in asteroids.

8 *clinching*: The *-ing* form is a present participle used as an adjective here. It is not a present participle construction used in place of a clause, nor is it a gerund used as part of a compound noun [> LEG 2.7, 6.14, 16.38, 16.39.3, LAG 13D, 20D, 23E, 28Bn.3, 47An.10]:
> ... the **clinching** evidence
> → the evidence that is **clinching** ...

9 *where*: introduces an adverbial clause of place (also a relative clause). [> LEG 1.38.2, 1.46, LAG 19An.3]

10 *Unfortunately*: a viewpoint adverb which tells us about the writer's attitude. He or she considers that the information that follows is 'unfortunate'. We always use a comma after a viewpoint adverb when it begins a sentence. [> LEG 7.57, App 17.9, LAG 11Ans.1–2, 52An.1C, 54An.5]

11 *although* (or *though*): introduces an adverbial clause of concession (*although ... that is not so surprising*), expressing a contrast. [> LEG 1.50, LAG 3An.2]

12 *published*: The past participle construction is used in place of a relative clause [> LEG 1.62.3, LAG 6Bn.4]:
> ... the new work **(which has been) published** in Science ...

13 *when*: introduces an adverbial clause of time. [> LEG 1.45.1, 9.18, compare > LAG 3Bn.1, 6Bn.1]

GRAMMAR POINTS

C Articles [> LEG Chapter 3, LAG 8C, etc.]

Cross references are given to LEG for selected items only.

1 a river valley
2 (–) Houston
3 (–) Texas [> LEG 2.13.1, 3.24–25, 3.31]
4 a team of American scientists [> LEG 2.19, App 6]
5 a vast tidal wave
6 the whole Caribbean region [> LEG 3.31, 5.2n.4, 5.22]
7 the Cretaceous period [> LEG 3.22]
8 the age of [> LEG 3.20.2]
9 the dinosaurs [> LEG 3.22]
10 the latest issue [> LEG 7.5n.4]
11 the US journal *Science*
12 the geologists [> LEG 3.20.1]
13 a tidal wave
14 the impact of
15 an asteroid
16 the Earth's [> LEG 2.49]
17 the sea [> LEG 3.20.4]

D Type 2 phrasal verbs (idiomatic meanings): 'blotting out the sun' [> LEG 8.28, App 33, LAG 4D, 13C, 27C, and compare > LAG 8D, 16B, 24C, 38D, 47E]

blot out is a transitive phrasal verb [compare > LAG 4D]; we could also say ***blotting* the sun *out***.

Type 2 phrasal verbs followed by adverb particles are transitive (i.e. they have an object). They may have obvious meanings:

Write *their names* **down**.
Write down *their names*.

Or they may have idiomatic meanings:

*A cloud **blotted out** the sun.* (= hid)

The adverb particle is mobile with noun objects [> LEG 8.28.2, LAG 4D, 13C]:

*The cloud **blotted out** the sun./ ... **blotted** the sun **out***.

A pronoun object always comes before the particle:

*The cloud **blotted it out**.* (Not *blotted out it*)

Possible answers

1 *put her hip out* (= dislocated)
2 *told the girls off* (= reprimanded them)
3 *spell it out* (= make it absolutely clear)
4 *making it up* (= inventing it)
5 *sending up politicians* (= ridiculing them e.g. by imitating them)
6 *put off tomorrow's meeting* (= postpone it)
7 *putting me off my food* (= making me feel it's repulsive)
8 *let us down* (= didn't fulfil our expectations)
9 *dashing letters off* (= quickly writing)
10 *packing in smoking* (= stopping it)
11 *drop me off* (= let me get out of the vehicle)
12 *knock it back* (= swallow it quickly)
13 *keeping on* (= continuing to employ)
14 *passed her over* (= didn't choose her)
15 *bring it off* (= complete it successfully)
16 *run over* (= knocked down by a vehicle)
17 *see me off* (= accompany me to my departure point)
18 *run her down* (= criticize her)
19 *look up* (= check e.g. in a dictionary)
20 *fit me in* (= give me an appointment)

E Countable and uncountable uses of nouns: 'clay' and 'clays' [> LEG 2.14, 2.16.3]

Clays means 'different varieties of clay'; *clay* (= a substance) is normally uncountable with no plural.

It is a basic rule in English that we can't use uncountable nouns like *bread* or *wine* in the singular or plural. (Not *I want a bread*, **I want some breads**) However, we sometimes use nouns like this, which are normally uncountable, as countable nouns when we refer to particular varieties. When we do this, we often put an adjective in front of the noun: *a nice wine*, or we specify the noun in some way: *a wine of high quality*. We can use nouns like this in the plural as well, as if they were countable [compare > LAG 34F, 42F]:

*This region produces **some awful wines** as well as good ones.*

1 a variety of different wines
2 a lot of wine
3 the weather
4 all weathers
5 The soil
6 different soils
7 Fabrics
8 an awful lot of cloth
9 Religion
10 world religions
11 tea
12 different teas

When mothers work

SCHOOL-AGED daughters of employed mothers tend to have consistently high academic performance. They also tend to develop close relationships with
5 their fathers if they are warm, supportive, and participate actively in parenting. School-aged sons tend to have better social and personality adjustments as well as higher
10 academic achievement if their mothers work outside the home. However, sons of lower socioeconomic families with a working mother may be less admiring of their fathers, perhaps because of the perceived notion of economic failure on their part.

15 Adolescents benefit when their mothers work. Employed women (or those with significant interests or activities outside the home) usually are happier, more satisfied, and more likely to encourage their children to be independent. Sons tend to demonstrate better social
20 and personal adjustments at school, and daughters tend to be more outgoing, independent, motivated, and better adjusted to their environment. Children of working mothers also are less likely to have stereotyped perceptions of life roles on the basis of being male or
25 female.

The newly evolved role of fathers and the concept of shared parenting have led some corporations to develop paternity-leave policies, but fewer than one percent of eligible men make use of them. Barriers include the
30 financial burden on the family from loss of income and the subtle psychological pressure that defines work as the highest priority for men. Federal legislation has been introduced to guarantee paternity leave with provisions for reinstatement and with protection from harassment.

USA Today (AmE)

Sentence structure

A Six of the words or phrases below can be used in place of words or phrases in the text. Underline the words or phrases in the text that could be replaced.

These are also likely	*women who have*
assuming	*similarly are not so*
Nevertheless	*are, for example,*
if	*like*

Now say why the two remaining phrases are wrong.

1 ....
....
2 ....
....

B Rewrite these sentences as one sentence beginning with the words provided. Then check against the text.

1 Women who are employed (or those with significant interests or activities outside the home) usually are happier. They are more satisfied. They are more likely to encourage their children to be independent. (ll. 16–19)
Employed ....
....

2 Some corporations have been led to develop paternity-leave policies because of the newly evolved role of fathers and the concept of shared parenting. Fewer than one percent of eligible men make use of them. (ll. 26–29)
The newly evolved ....
....

Grammar points

C Supply the missing adjective, then check against the text. (ll. 5–6)
Fathers who warmly support their children can be described as warm and ....

Complete these statements with appropriate adjectives.

1 The author describes the scene well. His writing is very   *descriptive* ....
2 That class is impossible to manage. It is really   ....
3 Those kittens really like to play. Aren't they   ....
4 He has the sort of manner you expect in business. He's really   ....
5 I would say he's around forty – yes, definitely   ....
6 Such behaviour cannot be permitted. It's truly   ....
7 She treats me like a friend. Her behaviour towards me is so   ....
8 We've driven in a huge circle. Our route has been truly   ....

D *Employed women **usually** are happier.* (ll. 16–17)
What would be the more usual position for *usually*? ....

Respond to these statements, changing the position of the adverb of frequency for emphasis.

1 Philip is never on time.   *I agree. He never is on time.*
2 Bob has always been a rebel.   ....
3 Jane can never keep appointments.   ....
4 You could usually rely on Jim.   ....
5 Ann would frequently leave work early.   ....
6 Alan isn't normally depressed.   ....

E Why is a definite article used before *school* in **a**, but not in **b**?

a *My wife and I have to attend a meeting at **the school** this evening.*
b *Sons tend to demonstrate better social and personal adjustments **at school**.* (ll. 19–20)

....

Supply *a/an*, *the* or (–).

1 Our children attend .... *a* .... very good school.
2 Some people think they know about education just because they were once at ....
school.
3 When we were children we were always in .... bed before 8.30.
4 .... bed is not something you buy very often.
5 Make sure you sweep in all the corners and under .... bed.
6 People who spend time in .... prison rapidly become institutionalized.
7 As soon as the riot broke out, police surrounded .... prison.
8 A lot of people think .... prison should be just like any other building.
9 The trial attracted a lot of attention and .... court was crowded.
10 A lot of people have been taken to .... court for failing to pay local taxes.
11 Though it's a small town, it has .... school, ... church and ....
court.

F Supply *fewer* or *less* here, then refer to the text. Give a reason for your choice.
.... *than one percent of eligible men make use of [paternity-leave policies].* (ll. 28–29)

....

Supply *fewer* or *less*.

1 .... *Fewer* .... unemployed can expect to find work during a recession.
2 .... people these days expect to stay in the same job all their lives.
3 You'll have .... chance of success if you don't change jobs reasonably often.
4 It just isn't true that there are .... opportunities for young people.
5 Newspapers in the past had .... pictures and .... pages.
6 Previously, ... paper was used in newspapers, so .... trees were destroyed.

189

SENTENCE STRUCTURE

A Answers and commentary

The following words or phrases in the text should be underlined:

1 if (they are warm, supportive) (l. 5)
(→ *assuming*)
... *if they are warm, supportive* ... /*assuming they are warm, supportive* ...
Conjunctions like *as long as, assuming (that), on (the) condition (that), provided/providing (that)* can sometimes replace *if* to introduce a condition, as here. [> LEG 14.21]

2 However (l. 11)
(→ *Nevertheless*)
However, *sons of lower socioeconomic families* ... /**Nevertheless**, *sons of lower socioeconomic families* ...
We can use adverbs like *however* or *nevertheless* to express a contrast. Such adverbs often come at the beginning of a sentence and are followed by a comma. They help us to present information in a coherent fashion. [> LEG 7.58, App 18.6–7]

3 when (their mothers work) (l. 15)
(→ *if*)
Adolescents benefit **when** *their mothers work.*/
Adolescents benefit **if** *their mothers work.*
If does not always mean 'on the condition'. It can also be used to mean 'when' if the reference is to a permanent truth (as is suggested here). [> LEG 14.23.1, LAG 6Bn.2, 26Cn.7]

4 those with (l. 16)
(→ *women who have*)
Employed women (or **those with** *significant interests* ...)/*Employed women (or* **women who have** *significant interests* ...)*
Those is used as a pronoun here and replaces *those women*. Although we use a plural noun after *these* and *those* to refer to people (see **1** below), we can use *those* on its own to refer to people if it is followed by *who* or *with* [> LEG 4.34]:
Those *(of you)* **who** *wish to go now may do so quietly.*
Those with *tickets in rows 19 to 44 may now board the aircraft.*
We often use *with* to show possession. [> LEG 10.31, App 25.37, LAG 14D, 14G]

5 also are less (l. 23)
(→ *similarly are not so*)
Children of working mothers **also are less** *likely to have* ... /*Children of working mothers* **similarly are not so** *likely to have* ...

Note the position of *also* before *be* for special emphasis here. [> LEG 7.40.6, 7.56]

6 include (l. 29)
(→ *are, for example,*)
Barriers **include** *the financial burden* ...
/*Barriers* **are**, **for example**, *the financial burden* ...
We can use the verb *include* to cite examples, as well as using the phrase *for example*. [> LEG App 18.4, LAG 22An.6]

Remaining answers

1 *These are also likely* does not replace *They also tend* (ll. 3–4) because we use a plural noun after *these* and *those* to refer to people, though we don't have to use a noun after *these/those* to refer to things [> LEG 4.34 and see **4** above]:
These girls also tend to develop close relationships ... Compare:
These are for you. (e.g. books)

2 *like* does not replace *as* in: ... *that defines work* **as** *the highest priority for men.* (ll. 31–32) We cannot use *like* in place of *as* to mean 'in the capacity of'. [> LEG App 25.25, LAG 12Bn.18]

B Answers and commentary

1 *Employed women (or those with significant interests or activities outside the home)* (subject) *usually* (adverb of frequency) *are (be) happier, more satisfied,* **and** *more likely to encourage their children to be independent* (complement).
Employed is a past participle used as an adjective here. [> LEG 6.14] Note how the clauses are listed and separated by commas and with *and* after the final comma. [compare > LEG 9.30]

2 *The newly evolved role of fathers and the concept of shared parenting* (compound subject) **have led** (verb) *some corporations* (object) *to develop paternity-leave policies* (infinitive construction), *but fewer than one percent of eligible men make use of them* (co-ordinate main clause).
The sentence is re-expressed in the active voice. [> LEG 12.1] The verb *have led* is followed by an object + *to*-infinitive. [> LEG 16.20, App 46.1, LAG 38E] *But* introduces a contrasting co-ordinate main clause. [> LEG 1.17, 1.21]

GRAMMAR POINTS

C Adjectives formed with suffixes:'supportive'
[> LEG 6.2, App 8.1]

supportive (*supporting* is also possible).

Some words function only as adjectives (*tall*). Others function as adjectives or nouns (*cold*). Many adjectives which are related to verbs or nouns have a characteristic ending (or *suffix*). For example, *-able* added to a verb like *enjoy* gives us the adjective *enjoyable*; *-ful* added to a noun like *truth* gives us the adjective *truthful*.

Note that some of these answers have prefixes (which have a negative effect [> LAG 28E]) as well as suffixes.

1 descriptive
2 unmanageable
3 playful
4 businesslike
5 fortyish
6 impermissible
7 friendly [> LEG 7.12]
8 circular/circuitous

D Position of adverbs of indefinite frequency: 'they are usually happier' [> LEG 7.40]

*Employed women are **usually** happier.*

The usual position of adverbs of frequency (*always*, *never*, etc. [> LEG 7.39, LAG 48D]) is after auxiliaries like *be*, *have*, *can*, *must*, but before an ordinary verb. They also come after *be* and *have* when these are used as full verbs:

> *I **was never** very good at maths.*
> *John **is always** complaining.*
> *Gerald **often made** unwise decisions.*

However, we sometimes use adverbs of frequency before auxiliaries for special emphasis:

> *You **can never rely** on Philip.*
> → *You **never can rely** on Philip.*

Possible answers

1 I agree. He never is on time.
2 I agree. He always has been a rebel.
3 I agree. She never can keep appointments.
4 I agree. You usually could rely on him.
5 I agree. She frequently would leave work early.
6 I agree. Alan normally isn't depressed.

E The use of the article with nouns like 'school', 'hospital', etc. [> LEG 3.28.3, 10.9.7, 10.13.4, Apps 21–23]

a ... *the school* because we are referring to it as a building and saying which one we mean.

b ... *at (–) school* because we are referring to its 'primary purpose'.

We use no article (zero) in front of nouns like *bed, church, class, college, court, hospital, prison, school, sea, town, university* when we refer to their 'primary purpose', that is the activity associated with them:

> *He's **in** (–) **bed**.* (for the purpose of sleeping)
> *The children went **to** (–) **school** this morning.* (for the purpose of learning)

Otherwise, articles with these nouns follow the usual rules:

> *There's a meeting at **the** school at 6.* ('not for the purpose of learning')

1 a very good school	7 the prison
2 at (–) school	8 a prison
3 in (–) bed	9 the court
4 A bed	10 to (–) court
5 under the bed	11 a school, a
6 in (–) prison	church and a
	court

F 'Fewer' and 'less' [> LEG 5.16]

Fewer than one percent of eligible men ...
We use *fewer* with plural countables. However, *less* would also be possible here if we wanted to put the emphasis on *one percent* (= an uncountable amount) rather than *men*.

The basic rule is that we use *fewer* with plural countable nouns and *less* with uncountable nouns:

> *fewer boys, fewer girls, fewer books, fewer times*
> *less time, less money, less sugar, less water*

[> LAG 19D, 23C]
In practice, many native speakers informally use *less* with plural countables (*less people, less newspapers*), but a lot of people still do not approve of this usage. The problem only arises with plural countables (*fewer people* or *less people*), never with uncountables (*less money*; not *fewer money*).

1 Fewer unemployed   2 Fewer people
3 less chance of success   4 fewer opportunities   5 fewer pictures ... fewer pages   6 Less paper ... fewer trees

Peter

PRESENTLY an old man in a grubby cream apron appeared, trundling a wheelchair from the back of the house. Anna moved smartly to the side of the car and opened the door. 'Right, Tom,' she said, 'if you take him at the top and I grab his legs, OK?' Their hands reached into the car, tangling with each other, fumbling with the seat-belt, feeling for their quarry. 'Come on, Peter,' said the old man, his nose moist and capillaried. 'Into this chair,' he said. 'But don't get too used to it, mind.' He grinned, his lips thick and pink, as he took my weight, hoisting me into the wheelchair before bending back into the car for the black polythene bag containing my 'belongings'. He put the bag in my lap and curled my hand over it. Then he reached back into the car for my history which he handed to Anna. The bag slid from under my moist palm, creased shirts and odd socks spilling on to the slushy gravel. A shadow of irritation passed over his face before he bent down to pick up my things. 'Never mind, Peter,' he said. 'Never you mind.'

As they wheeled me round to the back of the house I felt a curious sensation: the building had jerked, slipped somehow, bounced a little in its foundations. But the other two seemed to have noticed nothing and I readily attributed it to my considerable fatigue. Tom negotiated a troublesome step with the chair, pushing me into a big, warm kitchen dominated by two yellow-topped tables pushed together in the centre. The place was alive with the smell of freshly baked food and my stomach stirred unpleasantly. 'Has he eaten?' asked Tom. Anna silently and tartly indicated that he should direct his question to me. 'I'm sorry,' he said to her, compounding his error. 'Have you had anything to eat, Peter?' he bawled, unnecessarily. The two looked down at me in silence. Anna pursed her lips. 'They've been using a syringe to feed him,' she said.

The Comforts of Madness by Paul Sayer (*BrE*)

Sentence structure

A Supply punctuation marks where necessary.
Say why you have used them, then check against the text.

1 Right Tom she said if you take him at the top and I grab his legs OK (ll. 5–6)

2 Come on Peter said the old man his nose moist and capillaried (ll. 9–10)

3 Into this chair he said but don't get too used to it mind (ll. 10–11)

4 He grinned his lips thick and pink as he took my weight hoisting me into the wheelchair before bending back into the car for the black polythene bag containing my belongings (ll. 11–15)

5 Never mind Peter he said never you mind (ll. 20–21)

6 As they wheeled me round to the back of the house I felt a curious sensation the building had jerked slipped somehow bounced a little in its foundations (ll. 22–24)

7 Have you had anything to eat Peter he bawled unnecessarily (ll. 33–34)

Grammar points

B Supply the missing prepositions, then refer to the text. (ll. 1–19)

Presently an old man [1]..... a grubby cream apron appeared, trundling a wheelchair [2]..... the back [3]..... the house. Anna moved smartly [4]..... the side [5]..... the car and opened the door. 'Right, Tom,' she said, 'if you take him [6]..... the top and I grab his legs, OK?' Their hands reached [7]..... the car, tangling [8]..... each other, fumbling [9]..... the seat-belt, feeling [10]..... their quarry. 'Come on, Peter,' said the old man, his nose moist and capillaried. '[11]..... this chair,' he said. 'But don't get too used [12]..... it, mind.' He grinned, his lips thick and pink, as he took my weight, hoisting me [13]..... the wheelchair before bending back [14]..... the car [15]..... the black polythene bag containing my 'belongings'. He put the bag [16]..... my lap and curled my hand [17]..... it. Then he reached back [18]..... the car [19]..... my history which he handed [20]..... Anna. The bag slid [21]..... [22]..... my moist palm, creased shirts and odd socks spilling [23]..... the slushy gravel. A shadow [24]..... irritation passed [25]..... his face.

C What's the difference between *Don't get too used to it!* (l. 11) and *Don't you get too used to it!*?

....

Rewrite these imperatives using the words in brackets.

1 Never mind! (you)   *Never you mind!* ....
2 Get dinner this evening. (you) ....
3 Wait here please. (Sally) ....
4 Don't say anything! (you) ....
5 Stand up! (everybody) ....
6 You meet them at the station. (Tim and Liz) ....
7 Try preparing food for a hundred people! (you) ....
8 Don't breathe a word about this! (nobody) ....

D Rewrite this sentence using *didn't seem* or *seemed*. Different versions are possible.
They didn't notice anything. (ll. 24–25)

....

Rewrite these sentences with suitable forms of *seem*.

1 He knows the answer.   *He seems to know the answer.*
2 He isn't well. ....
3 Everything was quiet. ....
4 Everybody was leaving. ....
5 Liz has lost the game. ....
6 The letter has been stolen. ....
7 They knew what had happened. ....
8 John had forgotten my birthday. ....

E Rewrite this question with *Have you had*, then check against the text.
Have you eaten anything, Peter? (l. 33) ....

Respond appropriately to these sentences.

1 What are you wearing this evening? *I haven't got anything to wear. / I've got nothing to wear.*
2 Why don't you read something? – ....
3 Why don't the children play with something? – ....
4 For heaven's sake, cut the string with something. – ....
5 How is it you're so hungry? – ....
6 You look really bored! Do something! – ....
7 Open the letter properly! Don't tear it! – ....
8 So you're going to the party alone! – ....

SENTENCE STRUCTURE

A Answers and commentary

Note: A written sentence must begin with a capital letter and end with a full stop (.), a question mark (?), or an exclamation mark (!). [> LEG 1.2]

1 *'Right, Tom,' she said, 'if you take him at the top and I grab his legs, OK?'*

Quotation marks, single (' . . . ') or double (" . . . ") go round what is actually spoken and enclose other punctuation marks such as commas, full stops, question marks and exclamation marks. [> LEG 15.3*n*.1]

When the subject + reporting verb (*she said*) comes in the middle of the quotation, as here, the second part of the quotation doesn't begin with a capital letter if it isn't a separate sentence. [> LEG 15.3*n*.2]

What Anna says is a rhetorical question (that is, it doesn't require an answer). The *if*-construction is used in place of the imperative. [> LEG 14.9] It is the equivalent of [> LAG 46C]:

'. . . (you) take him at the top and I'll grab his legs, OK?'

2 *'Come on, Peter,' said the old man, his nose moist and capillaried.*

We use a comma before a name when we address somebody. [> LEG 15.3*n*.1]

We may invert a noun subject + reporting verb: *said the old man* instead of *the old man said* (which would be the normal word order). But we don't do this with pronouns (Not **said he**) in modern English. [> LEG 15.3*n*.4, App 45.1, LAG 36B*n*.3]

The phrase *his nose moist and capillaried* is in apposition to *the old man* and is separated by a comma. [> LEG 1.39, LAG 2A*n*.1, 5A*ns*.2,4]

3 *'Into this chair,' he said. 'But don't get too used to it, mind.'*

The writer has chosen to treat *Into this chair* as a complete sentence. (It is an abbreviated imperative: *(Get) into this chair.*) The comma goes before the second quotation mark. He then begins a new sentence with *But*. There is a comma before *mind* because it is a kind of imperative form (which doesn't mean very much). Alternatively, the writer could have written:

'Into this chair,' he said, 'but don't get too used to it, mind.'

treating the whole statement as a single sentence.

4 *He grinned, his lips thick and pink, as he took my weight, hoisting me into the wheelchair before bending back into the car for the black polythene bag containing my 'belongings'.*

He grinned and *his lips thick and pink* are in apposition and are separated by commas. [> LEG 1.39, LAG 2A*n*.1, 5A*ns*.2,4]

We generally use a comma to separate an adverbial clause (*as he took my weight*). [> LEG 1.45.1]

The quotation marks round the word *belongings* are ironic: Peter has hardly any 'belongings'.

5 *'Never mind, Peter,' he said. 'Never you mind.'*

There are two separate sentences here. The first one ends with a full stop after *he said*. The second one begins with a capital letter and ends with a full stop. See notes **1** and **3** above and [> LEG 15.3*n*.2]. *Never mind* is a fixed expression, though *Never* is sometimes used in the imperative as a stronger form of *Don't*. [> LEG 9.52*n*.6] *You* is used for special emphasis here. [> LEG 9.54, LAG 46C]

6 *As they wheeled me round to the back of the house I felt a curious sensation: the building had jerked, slipped somehow, bounced a little in its foundations.*

It would have been possible to use a comma after the introductory time clause (*As they wheeled me round to the back of the house, I felt . . .*). The information after the colon (:) amplifies and explains what has gone before (*a curious sensation*). [> LAG 8B*n*.2, 16A*n*.6, 22A*n*.6, 40B*n*.1]

The clauses are a list and are separated by commas. [compare > LEG 6.21, 9.30]

7 *'Have you had anything to eat, Peter?' he bawled, unnecessarily.*

The quotation ends with a question mark; a comma is not used as well. [> LEG 15.3*n*.2] Note that only one question mark is used at the end of the question (not before and after the question). The noun or pronoun in front of the reporting verb (*bawled*) is lower case: *he*, not **He**.

The adverb (*unnecessarily*) is separated by a comma after the reporting verb *bawled*, though the use of a comma here would be optional.

GRAMMAR POINTS

B Prepositions [> LEG Chapter 8, Apps 20, 25–30, LAG 12B, 31C, 32C, 55C]

Cross references to LEG are provided without explanations.

1 *in* a grubby cream apron [> LEG App 25.37]
2 *from* the back [> LEG 8.9]
3 the back *of* the house [> LEG App 25.11, 2.47, 2.50]
4 *to* the side [> LEG 8.9]
5 the side *of* the car [> LEG 2.50]
6 *at* the top [> LEG 8.6]
7 reached *into* [> LEG 8.9.5]
8 tangling *with* [compare > LEG Apps 28, 30]
9 fumbling *with* [compare > LEG Apps 28, 30]
10 feeling *for* [compare > LEG Apps 28, 30]
11 *Into* this chair [> LEG 8.9.5]
12 get too used *to* it [> LEG 10.26.1, 16.56]
13 hoisting me *into* the wheelchair [> LEG 8.9.5]
14 bending back *into* the car [> LEG 8.9.5]
15 *for* the black polythene bag [> LEG App 25.20]
16 put the bag *in/into* my lap [> LEG 8.9.5]
17 and curled my hand *over* it [> LEG App 25.32]
18 reached back *into* the car [> LEG 8.9.5]
19 *for* my history [> LEG App 25.20]
20 he handed *to* Anna [> LEG 1.13.2]
21 *from*
22 *under* my moist palm [> LEG 8.18, LAG 43C]
23 *on to/onto* the slushy gravel [> LEG 8.9.4]
24 a shadow *of* irritation [> LEG 2.50]
25 passed *over/across* his face [> LEG App 25.3]

C The imperative to address particular people: 'Don't you get too used to it' [> LEG 9.54]

Don't get too used to it. (negative imperative [> LEG 9.51–52])

Don't you get too used to it. (personally addresses Peter)

We use the imperative (*Wait here!*) to address one person or several people: *you* is implied. However, we can use words like *you*, *everyone* etc. combined with the imperative, to get the attention of particular people.

Possible answers

1 Never you mind!
2 You get dinner this evening.
3 Sally, wait here please.
4 Don't you say anything!
5 Everybody stand up!
6 Tim and Liz, you meet them at the station.
7 You try preparing food for a hundred people!
8 Nobody breathe a word about this!

D 'Seem' [> LEG 10.23–25 and compare > LAG 14E]

They didn't seem to notice anything.
→ *They seemed not to notice anything.*
→ *They seemed not to have noticed anything.*
→ *They seemed to have noticed nothing.*

We use *seem* in place of *be* or a full verb to express uncertainty:

> *He **is** tired.*
> → *He **seems (to be)** tired.*
> *He **knows** the answer.*
> → *He **seems to know** the answer.*

We don't have to use *to be* in front of an adjective or noun after the simple present or past of *seem*:

> *He **seems/seemed (to be)** tired.*

But we must use *to*, *to be* or *to have* if what follows *seem* is a verb:

> *He seems/seemed **to know**.*
> *He seems/seemed **to be thinking**.*
> *He seems/seemed **to have left**.*

Possible answers

1 He seems to know the answer.
2 He doesn't seem (to be) well./He seems not to be well.
3 Everything seemed (to be) quiet.
4 Everybody seemed to be leaving.
5 Liz seems to have lost the game.
6 The letter seems to have been stolen.
7 They seemed to know what had happened.
8 John seemed to have forgotten my birthday.

E 'Have you had anything to eat?' [> LEG 4.41, 13.8–10, 16.36, LAG 11E]

> *Have you eaten anything, Peter?*
> → *Have you had **anything to eat**, Peter?*

We can use a *to*-infinitive after indefinite pronouns like *anything*, *nothing*, etc. We can have only one negative in a sentence [> LAG 34A]:

> *I **haven't** got anything to eat.* → *I've got **nothing** to eat.* (Not *I haven't got nothing*)

Sentences like this often end in prepositions:

> *She's got nothing to play **with**.*

Possible answers

1 I've got nothing to wear.
2 I haven't got anything to read.
3 They've got nothing to play with.
4 I haven't got anything to cut it with.
5 I haven't had anything to eat all day.
6 I've got nothing to do.
7 I've got nothing to open it with.
8 I haven't got anyone to go with.

Life on a desert island

THE weeks that followed were unremittingly hot and dry. We seemed to have entered a new phase of weather. There were no longer grey clouds gliding by to taunt us with 5 unreliable promises of rain. The magnesium flare dazzle of the sun hovered in the pricking blue of the sky like the vapour of a burning breath. The hours of cool, after dawn and before sunset, seemed shorter and shorter. The dry heat brought 10 sounds of its own to the quiet interior. Brittle branches crumbled off trees with the softest brush of a shoulder and fell in powdery lumps among paper-dry grasses. Petrified streamers of heat-faded pandanus leaves detached themselves from the moistureless sockets and crackled like 15 Christmas wrapping paper as they broke on the baked ground. Footsteps through the rustling tissues of the dying undergrowth were loud. Daily it became easier to see through to the blue distance on the other side of the island as the trees sloughed off their bleached foliage. The colours, 20 russets, ochres, bronze, reminded me of autumn, but here death came from the sun and there was no rich, dark winter to come.

G wrestled with the lifeless soil. Deeper and deeper he went, pocking the surface of the island with waterless 25 wells. The spindly vegetable shoots that had come through so eagerly fell like pieces of straw, there was nothing to hold their roots in the earth. Older plants, like the tomatoes and sweetcorn, stayed upright, electing to die on their feet. A recently planted bed of kohlrabi, tiny purple leaves just 30 formed, stayed two inches high for weeks on end and then died as a body. It was a struggle without hope and yet we hoped all the time.

Castaway by Lucy Irvine *(BrE)*

Sentence structure

A Supply the missing words, then check against the text.

The weeks [1]............. followed were unremittingly hot and dry. We seemed [2](*have*) .... entered a new phase of weather. There were no longer grey clouds [3](*glide*) .... by to taunt us with unreliable promises of rain. The magnesium flare dazzle of the sun hovered in the pricking blue of the sky [4]............. the vapour of a burning breath. The hours of cool, after dawn and before sunset, [5](*seem*) .... shorter and shorter. The dry heat [6](*bring*) .... sounds of its own to the quiet interior. Brittle branches crumbled off trees with the softest brush of a shoulder [7]............. fell in powdery lumps among paper-dry grasses. Petrified streamers of heat-faded pandanus leaves detached themselves from the moistureless sockets and [8](*crackle*) .... like Christmas wrapping paper [9]............. they broke on the baked ground. Footsteps through the [10](*rustle*) .... tissues of the dying undergrowth were loud. [11]............. it became easier to see through to the blue distance on the other side of the island [12]............. the trees sloughed off their bleached foliage. The colours, russets, ochres, bronze, reminded me of autumn, [13]............. here death came from the sun [14]............. there was no rich, dark winter to come. (ll. 1–22)

B One word or phrase is in the wrong position in each of these sentences. Show with an arrow where the wrongly-placed word or phrase should be. Then check against the text.

1 With the lifeless soil G wrestled. (l. 23)

2 Deeper and deeper went he, pocking the surface of the island with waterless wells. (ll. 23–25)

3 The spindly vegetable shoots that had come through so eagerly fell like pieces of straw, was there nothing to hold their roots in the earth. (ll. 25–27)

4 Older plants, like the tomatoes and sweetcorn, stayed upright, to die on their feet electing. (ll. 27–28)

Grammar points

C What is the effect of *no longer* in this sentence?
*There were **no longer** grey clouds gliding by to taunt us with unreliable promises ...* (ll. 3–5)

....

Write these sentences again using *any longer* or *no longer*. The position of *no longer* can vary.
1 It isn't raining.   *It isn't raining any longer.*
2 My children collect stamps.   ....
3 Mr Watkins is in charge of this department. ....
4 We don't have to pay this tax.   ....

D What part of speech is *baked* here and what does it derive from?
*They crackled like Christmas wrapping paper as they broke on the **baked** ground.* (ll. 14–16)

....

Match a word in column A with the most likely word in column B.

A	B	
1 spoilt	goods	*spoilt child*
2 paid	food	
3 stolen	offerings	
4 sworn	angel	
5 frozen	head	
6 forbidden	child	
7 burnt	ship	
8 fallen	fruit	
9 shrunken	enemy	
10 sunken	assistant	
11 hidden	promise	
12 broken	catch	

E Complete this sentence with the words in brackets, then check against the text. (ll. 19–20)
The colours, russets, ochres, bronze, (reminded/autumn) ....

Supply the missing prepositions.
1 Celia often reminds me __of__ her mother.
2 Share your good fortune .... others.
3 Can I interest you .... insurance?
4 You should divide the number .... seven.
5 I congratulate you .... your success.
6 Who'll compensate me .... my loss?
7 I admire her .... so many qualities.
8 Don't lend anything .... him.
9 It isn't easy to steal money .... a bank.
10 They appointed her .... a senior post.
11 Please reserve this seat .... me.
12 Who informed you .... this?
13 I always identify myself .... the hero.
14 Has everything been included .... this bill?
15 You can't combine oil .... water.
16 Please charge the clothes .... my account.
17 Her parents were charged .... neglect.
18 Please describe him .... me.
19 The fairy turned the frog .... a prince.
20 I'll have to refer you .... the manager.
21 Just add what I've had .... the bill.
22 How do you convert miles .... kms?
23 I'll discuss the matter .... your father.
24 Please return the book .... the library.
25 They were all searched .... drugs.
26 She'll adapt herself .... our way of life.
27 They charged Dr Crippen .... murder.
28 I can't excuse you .... your behaviour.
29 Who'll defend us .... our friends?
30 I can't compare my flat .... yours.
31 I'm not investing money .... oil.
32 You can't accuse me .... laziness.
33 I don't blame you .... what happened.
34 We assessed the damage .... £400.
35 I use the cellar .... storing wine.
36 Don't repeat what I said .... anybody.
37 You should claim damages .... them.
38 Attach this label .... the handle.
39 We've insured ourselves .... fire.
40 She was robbed .... her life savings.

SENTENCE STRUCTURE

A Answers and commentary

1 *that* (or *which*): relative pronoun subject of the clause (defining) [> LEG 1.26, 1.31, LAG 5A*n*.3]:
> **The weeks** *followed.* **They** *were unremittingly hot and dry.*
> → **The weeks that/which** *followed were unremittingly hot and dry.*

2 *to have*: We need the perfect infinitive (*to have entered*) after *seemed* here because the event described had already happened [> LEG 9.29.1, 10.23, 16.2]:
> *We* **had entered** *a new phase of weather.*
> → *We* **seemed to have entered** *a new phase of weather.* [> LAG 46D]

3 *gliding*: present participle construction in place of a relative clause [> LEG 1.58.6, LAG 9A*n*.1]:
> *There were no longer grey clouds* (**which were**) **gliding** *by to taunt us* ...

4 *like*: preposition *like* + noun phrase object (*the vapour of a burning breath*). [> LEG App 25.25]

5 *seemed*: A finite verb, following the subject *The hours of cool, after dawn and before sunset* [> LEG 1.2, LAG 46D]; *to get* after *seemed* would be optional here. [> LEG 10.23–26]

6 *brought*: A finite verb, following the subject *The dry heat.* [> LEG 1.2]

7 *and*: This co-ordinating conjunction introduces a co-ordinate main clause. [> LEG 1.17] When the subject is the same in all parts of the sentence, it is usual not to repeat it. [> LAG 13B] We do not usually put a comma in front of *and*:
> **Brittle branches** *crumbled off trees.* **They fell** *in powdery lumps.*
> → **Brittle branches** *crumbled off trees* **and fell** ...

8 *crackled*: finite main verb of the second co-ordinate clause (see 7 above):
> *Petrified streamers of leaves* **detached themselves.** **They crackled** *like Christmas wrapping paper.*
> → *Petrified streamers of leaves* **detached themselves and crackled** ....

9 *as*: time conjunction introducing an adverbial clause of time (*as they broke on the baked ground*). [> LEG 1.45.1, LAG 17A*n*.2a]

10 *rustling*: a present participle used as an adjective (*tissues that are rustling*). [> LEG 2.7, 6.14, 16.38, 16.39.3] This use of *-ing* should not be confused with a present participle construction in place of a clause. [> LEG 1.57–58]

11 *Daily*: Normally, a time adverbial like this would come at the end. It is necessary in this position to avoid ambiguity. Otherwise, we might think that *the trees sloughed off their bleached foliage daily*. [> LEG 7.38, LAG 4A]

12 *as*: conjunction introducing an adverbial clause of time (*as the trees sloughed off their bleached foliage*). [> LEG 1.45.1, LAG 17A*n*.2a]

13 *but*: co-ordinating conjunction introducing a contrast. [> LEG 1.17–20, LAG 1B*n*.2]

14 *and*: co-ordinating conjunction introducing an addition. [> LEG 1.17–20, LAG 1B*n*.2]

B Answers and commentary

1 *G* (subject) **wrestled with** (verb) *the lifeless soil.*
The sentence follows the basic word order of an English sentence. [> LEG 1.3, LAG 4A]

2 *Deeper and deeper* **he went**, *pocking the surface* ...
Two comparatives joined by *and* convey the idea of general increase. [> LEG 6.27.2, LAG 32D] They are followed by normal word order (subject + verb). Inversion can occur after negative adverbs (*never, rarely, seldom*, etc.), when they are used at the beginning of a sentence. They must then be followed by auxiliary verbs (*be, do, have, can, must*, etc.). The order would then be [> LEG 7.59.3, LAG 30B, 33C, 49C, 51B–C]:
> *Never* **did he** *go* ... (Not **Never he went/ Never went he**)

3 *The spindly vegetable shoots that had come through so eagerly fell like pieces of straw,* **there was** *nothing to hold their roots in the earth.* ...
was there would introduce a yes/no question. [> LEG 13.1, 13.3] The writer has chosen to separate these statements with a comma. As they are complete sentences, it would have been possible to use a full stop after *straw* and then begin a new sentence. [> LEG 1.7–16]

4 *Older plants, like the tomatoes and sweetcorn, stayed upright,* **electing** *to die on their feet.*
The present participle construction is used in place of a co-ordinate clause [> LEG 1.58.1, LAG 4B*n*.3, 43A*n*s.11–12]:
> *Older plants, like the tomatoes and sweetcorn, stayed upright* **and elected** *to die on their feet.*
> → *... stayed upright,* **electing** *to die* ...

GRAMMAR POINTS

C 'No longer' [> LEG 7.36, compare > LAG 48D]

No longer suggests that something had been going on for a period of time and then stopped.

The adverb *long* emphasizes duration:
> *It rained all night **long**.*

We use *not ... any longer, not ... any more* and *no longer* to show that an action that has been going on has now stopped, or must stop:
> *Hurry up! I can't wait **any longer**.*
> → *I **can** wait **no longer**.*

No longer comes before a full verb or (more formally) at the end of a sentence
> *I was told that he **no longer worked** there.*
> *I was told that he worked there **no longer**.*

Possible answers
1 It isn't raining any longer.
2 My children no longer collect stamps./ ... collect stamps no longer.
3 Mr Watkins is no longer in charge of this department./ ... is in charge of this department no longer.
4 We don't have to pay this tax any longer.

D Past participles as adjectives: 'the baked ground'

[> LEG 6.14, App 40, and compare > LAG 3C, 7C, 32F]
Baked is an adjective deriving from the verb *to bake*.

Many past participles, regular and irregular, can be used as adjectives: *baked apples, broken glass.* However, it is not possible to use all past participles as adjectives. We wouldn't normally say **the taught children**, for example. Some past participles naturally combine (or 'collocate') with particular nouns. Note the adjectives *shrunken* (from *shrink – shrank – shrunk*) and *sunken* (from *sink – sank – sunk*).

The most likely combinations are probably:
1 spoilt child
2 paid assistant
3 stolen goods
4 sworn enemy
5 frozen food
6 forbidden fruit
7 burnt offerings
8 fallen angel
9 shrunken head
10 sunken ship
11 hidden catch
12 broken promise

E Verb + object + preposition: 'remind me of' [> LEG 8.27.3, 16.21, App 29, LAG 8D, 24C, 27C and compare > LAG 4D, 13C, 16B, 38D, 44D]

*The colours, russets, ochres, bronze, **reminded me of** autumn.*

Some verbs are followed directly by prepositions: *agree with, suffer from, insist on,* etc. [> LEG 8.27.2, App 28, LAG 8D]
Other verbs take an object before the preposition:
> *She **reminds me of** her mother.*

1	reminds ... of	21	add ... to
2	share ... with	22	convert ... to/into
3	interest ... in	23	discuss ... with
4	divide ... by	24	return ... to
5	congratulate ... on	25	searched for
6	compensate ... for	26	adapt ... to
7	admire ... for	27	charged ... with
8	lend ... to	28	excuse ... for
9	steal ... from	29	defend ... from
10	appointed ... to	30	compare ... with
11	reserve ... for	31	investing ... in
12	informed ... of	32	accuse ... of
13	identify ... with	33	blame ... for
14	included in	34	assessed ... at
15	combine ... with	35	use ... for
16	charge ... to	36	repeat ... to
17	charged with (see 27)	37	claim ... from
18	describe ... to	38	attach ... to
19	turned ... into	39	insured ... against
20	refer ... to	40	robbed of

The crowd

MR SPALLNER put his hands over his face.

There was the feeling of movement in space, the beautifully tortured scream, the impact and tumbling of the car with wall, through
5 wall, over and down like a toy, and him hurled out of it. Then - silence.

The crowd came running. Faintly, where he lay, he heard them running. He could tell their ages and their sizes by the sound of their
10 numerous feet over the summer grass and on the lined pavement, and over the asphalt street; and picking through the cluttered bricks to where his car hung half into the night sky, still spinning its wheels with a senseless centrifuge.
15 Where the crowd came from he didn't know. He struggled to remain aware and then the crowd faces hemmed in upon him, hung over like the large glowing leaves of down-bent trees. They were a ring of shifting, compressing, changing faces over him, looking down, looking down, reading the time
20 of his life or death by his face, making his face into a moon-dial, where the moon cast a shadow from his nose out upon his cheek to tell the time of breathing or not breathing any more ever.

How swiftly a crowd comes, he thought, like the iris of an
25 eye compressing in out of nowhere.

A siren. A police voice. Movement. Blood trickled from his lips and he was being moved into an ambulance. Someone said, 'Is he dead?' And someone else said, 'No, he's not dead.' And a third person said, 'He won't die, he's not going to die.'
30 And he saw the faces of the crowd beyond him in the night, and he knew by their expressions that he wouldn't die. And that was strange. He saw a man's face, thin, bright, pale; the man swallowed and bit his lips, very sick. There was a small woman, too, with red hair and too much red on her cheeks
35 and lips. And a little boy with a freckled face. Others' faces. An old man with a wrinkled upper lip, an old woman, with a mole upon her chin. They had all come from - where? Houses, cars, alleys from the immediate and the accident-shocked world. Out of alleys and out of hotels and out of streetcars and
40 seemingly out of nothing they came.

The Crowd by Ray Bradbury (*AmE*)

Sentence structure

A Order each sentence in two different ways. Then check against the text.

1 where faintly he running them lay he heard (ll. 7–8)
  a ....
  b ....

2 where he crowd the from know came didn't (l. 15)
  a ....
  b ....

B Comment on these statements.

1 Explain the use of *picking* and *spinning* in this sentence.
   He could tell their ages and their sizes by the sound of their numerous feet over the summer grass and on the lined pavement, and over the asphalt street; and picking through the cluttered bricks to where his car hung half into the night sky, still spinning its wheels with a senseless centrifuge. (ll. 8–14)

   ....
   ....

2 What's the difference between these two statements?
   a And that was strange. (ll. 31–32)
   b And a little boy with a freckled face. (l. 35)

   ....
   ....

Grammar points

C In which of these sentences can you use *could*?
What would you use instead of *could* in one of these sentences and why?

a *He* .... *tell their ages and their sizes by the sound of their numerous feet.* (ll. 8–10)
b *He regained consciousness before he died and* .... *tell the police what had happened.*
c *He* .... *read without glasses till he was sixty.*

Supply *could* or a suitable alternative in these sentences.

1 The atmosphere was so clear we ..... *could* ...... see as far as the blue mountains in the distance.
2 She .... sing beautifully till her mid-twenties and then she lost her voice.
3 There was a lot of demand for bread before the holiday, but I .... get the last loaf.
4 I .... get some petrol yesterday, just before the price went up again.
5 We rushed to the kitchen because we .... smell something burning.
6 When I was young, I .... walk for hours without getting tired.
7 In the old days, you .... buy a loaf of bread for a penny.
8 I .... understand why she retired at 50, but I wouldn't do it myself.
9 There was a terrible traffic jam this morning, but I .... get to work on time.
10 I .... avoid the traffic jam this morning by travelling to work on my bike.

D What's the difference in emphasis between these two sentences?

a *He won't breathe any more ever.* (compare ll. 22–23)
b *He will never breathe any more.*

Change the emphasis in these sentences by rewriting them with *not ... ever again*.

1 When we emigrated to Australia I knew I would never see my relations again.
When we emigrated to Australia, I knew I wouldn't see my relations ever again.
2 I know he has misbehaved, but I promise you he will never do that again.

3 John promised the doctor he wouldn't smoke and he has never smoked again.

4 I swear I'll never gamble again.

5 Following his accident he will never be able to play football again.

6 Never repeat what I told you to anyone again.

E Supply *else* or *other*, then check against the text.

a *Some* .... *person should chair this meeting.*
b *And someone* .... *said, 'No, he's not dead.'* (l. 28)

Supply *else* or *other* in these sentences.

1 I can't answer your question, you'll have to ask someone ..... *else* ......
2 Is there anyone .... than you who objects to these proposals?
3 Who .... are you going to invite to your party?
4 There's no .... person I can think of who would be more suitable for this job.
5 Who's going on this excursion .... than you and me?
6 A screwdriver won't do. Is there anything .... you can use?
7 A screwdriver won't do. Is there any .... tool you can use?
8 Nothing .... but the best will do as far as you're concerned.
9 She left me nothing .... than a few bits and pieces in her will.
10 This certainly isn't my umbrella. It belongs to someone ....

SENTENCE STRUCTURE

A Answers and commentary

The author employs an impressionistic style in this text to convey as vividly as possible the experience of a car accident from the point of view of the protagonist, Mr Spallner. The word order and sentence structure often depart from the norms of English to achieve this. [> LAG 4A]

1a *Faintly,* (adverb of manner) *where he lay,* (clause of place) *he heard them running* (main clause).

It is not unusual to begin a sentence with an adverb of manner in narrative writing, though this would be unusual in speech. [> LEG 7.16.3, LAG 32An.1c] Reference to place can come at the beginning of a sentence, especially in descriptive writing. [> LEG 7.19.2, LAG 28An.2a]

b *He faintly heard them running, where he lay.*

This would be the more normal word order, but less effective stylistically in terms of what the author is trying to achieve. *Faintly* comes between the subject and the verb and emphasizes the verb. [> LEG 7.16.2, LAG 42An.1] This position also avoids the possible ambiguity of:

He heard them running faintly.

which could suggest that the act of running was 'faint'. [compare > LEG 6.8.1, 7.19.2, LAG 52An.2d]

... where he lay is an adverbial clause of place. [> LEG 1.46]

2a *Where the crowd came from* (noun clause) *he didn't know* (main clause).

We don't say **Where did the crowd come from he didn't know**, though we could express this idea in two sentences:

Where did the crowd come from? He didn't know.

We use statement word order (i.e. subject + verb) in a reported question. [> LEG 15.19–20, LAG 50E] *Where the crowd came from* is a noun clause object of the verb *know*. [> LEG 1.23.2]

b *He didn't know where the crowd came from.*

This would be the more normal word order, where the noun clause object follows the verb. [> LEG 1.23.2, LAG 29B, 50E]

B Answers and commentary

1 The subject of *picking* is *their numerous feet*: *He could tell their ages and their sizes by the sound of **their numerous feet** over the summer grass ... and (by the sound of their numerous feet) **picking** (their way) through the cluttered bricks to where his car hung ....* [compare > LEG 1.56–58]

The subject of *spinning* is *his car. Spinning* is used here as a transitive verb in the active. [> LEG 1.9, 1.10.2] The object of *spinning* is *its wheels*:

*... (their numerous feet picked their way) through the cluttered bricks to where **his car** hung half into the night sky, (and was) still **spinning its wheels** with a senseless centrifuge.*

2a *And* (conjunction) *that* (subject) *was* (verb) *strange* (complement).

This is a normal simple sentence with a subject, followed by the verb *be*, followed by a complement. [> LEG 1.11] The author's use of the conjunction *and* to begin a sentence is a matter of style. The normal use of *and* would be as a co-ordinating conjunction to join simple sentences. [> LEG 1.17–20, LAG 1Ans.2–3]

b *And* (co-ordinating conjunction) *a little boy with a freckled face* (complement).

This is not a grammatical sentence because it doesn't contain a finite verb (that is, a verb which has a subject and a tense), e.g. [> LAG 1An.3]:

There was a little boy with a freckled face. [> LEG 1.2, compare > LAG 14An.2]

The statement follows the previous sentences: *There was a small woman, too, with red hair and too much red on her cheeks and lips.* The statements that follow are all without verbs, depending on the first *There was ...* , perhaps to convey shock and immediacy:

And a little boy with a freckled face. Others' faces. An old man with a wrinkled upper lip, an old woman, with a mole upon her chin. [compare > LAG 14An.2]

GRAMMAR POINTS

C 'Could' and 'managed to' [> LEG 11.8.3, 11.12–13, LAG 9C]

a *He **could** tell their ages ...*

b *... and **was able to/managed to** tell the police what had happened.*

c *He **could** read without glasses till he was sixty.*

We have to use *was able to* or *managed to* in **b** because the reference is to a specific action.

We use *could* for general ability in the past [> LAG 9C]:

*I **could run** very fast when I was a boy.*

For the successful completion of specific actions we use *managed to (do)*, *was/were able to (do)* or *succeeded in (doing)*:

*For a change, I **managed to** get to work on time this morning.* (Not **could**)

But note that we can use *could* for specific actions with verbs of perception: *see, hear, taste, smell*, and also with verbs like *tell* (*He **could tell** their ages*), *understand* and *imagine*.

1 *could see* (*could* + verb of perception; *were able to* would also be possible, but not **managed to/ succeeded in**)

2 *could sing* (general ability in the past; *was able to* is possible, but not **managed to**)

3 *managed to get/succeeded in getting/was able to get*: specific action (Not **could**)

4 *managed to get/succeeded in getting/was able to get*: specific action (Not **could**)

5 *could smell* (*could* + verb of perception; but not **were able to**, **managed to** or **succeeded in**)

6 *could walk* (general ability in the past; *was able to* is possible, but not **managed to**)

7 *could buy* (general ability in the past; *were able to* is possible, but not **managed to**)

8 *could understand* (*could* + verb of perception; *was able to* is also possible); *managed to* if we think of it as a specific action

9 *managed to get/succeeded in getting/was able to get*: specific action (Not **could**)

10 *managed to avoid/succeeded in avoiding/was able to avoid*: specific action (Not **could**)

D 'Never' and 'not ever' [> LEG 7.39, 7.40.5, LAG 45D]

a (*not any more ever*) is more emphatic than **b** (*never*).

The basic rule for *ever* and *never* is that we use *ever* (= at any time) in questions:

***Do you ever see** him these days?*

We use *not ever* and *never* interchangeably to express a negative:

*I **don't ever go** to London these days.*

*→ I **never go** to London these days.*

However, we sometimes prefer *not ever* to *never* for extra emphasis in promises, warnings, etc. especially in combination with *again*:

*I promise you, he **won't ever** trouble you again.* (more emphatic than *he'll never*)

Ever can also go to the end for even greater emphasis (especially when stressed):

*... he **won't** trouble you **ever** again.*

Combined with *any more/any longer* it is even stronger [compare > LAG 47C]:

*... he **won't** trouble you **any more ever** again.*

1 *... I knew I wouldn't ever see my relations again./ ... wouldn't see my relations ever again.*

2 *... he won't ever do that again./ ... he won't do that ever again.*

3 *... he hasn't ever smoked again./ ... he hasn't smoked ever again.*

4 *... I won't ever again gamble./ ... won't gamble ever again.*

5 *... he won't ever be able to play football again./ ... he won't be able ever to play football again./ ... he won't be able to play football ever again.*

6 *Don't ever repeat what I told you to anyone again./ ... what I told you to anyone, ever again.*

E 'Else' and 'other' [> LEG 4.42, 5.27]

a *some other person*

b *someone else said*

Else is an adverb which we often use after indefinite pronouns like *someone, something* and question words like *Who*, etc. In *Some other (person), other* is an adjective, so we must put a noun after it (*the other person*). *Other than* is almost always preferable to *else than*.

1 someone else
2 anyone other than you
3 Who else
4 no other person
5 other than you and me
6 anything else
7 any other tool
8 Nothing else
9 nothing other, *else* is also possible
10 someone else

All politics is local

WHEN Tip O'Neill said, 'All politics is local,' he was talking about the way political issues are shaped by local interests. Defense policy, for example, logically calls for
5 an overview of national-security needs, yet it is often dictated by employment levels in factories that happen to depend on defense contracts and are in the district of an influential congressman. In such cases, local
10 interest debases the issue with a shortsighted and self-serving perspective. But there's another kind of local politics, and it works in a way that's almost completely opposite. For instance, the City Council of Irvine, California, recently passed legislation restricting the use of chlorofluorocarbons within
15 the city limits. This legislation will cause hardships for local businesses and raise the cost of some consumer goods for local people, and these sacrifices will not be rewarded by any special environmental benefits to the citizens of Irvine. Everyone in the world, and for generations to come, will benefit, but only by an
20 infinitesimal amount, and the citizens of Irvine no more than anyone else. From a realist's point of view, Irvine's action seems almost unnatural; it's idealistic, even quixotic, for little Irvine to take responsibility for the sky. And yet on an emotional level the action seems exactly right.
25 As global problems become overwhelming, the idea of locality assumes a new political importance. The issue of nuclear armaments, for example, presents two conflicting perspectives. From the international, panoramic perspective of the government in Washington, a nuclear defense seems reasonable, but from the
30 perspective of, say, someone sitting under a tree in his back yard the idea of a nuclear defense appears insane. People sitting in their back yards have no power - none, anyway, that might have a meaningful impact on the nuclear situation. Nor, usually, do they have much knowledge about defense strategy. And yet home is
35 the place where the deepest response to the nuclear situation takes place.

Suzannah Lessard, *The New Yorker (AmE)*

Sentence structure

A Join these sentences making any necessary changes, then refer to the text.

  1 Defense policy, for example, logically calls for an overview of national-security needs. It is often dictated by employment levels in factories. These happen to depend on defense contracts. They are in the district of an influential congressman. (ll. 4–9)

  ....

  ....

  2 This legislation will cause hardships for local businesses. It will raise the cost of some consumer goods for local people. These sacrifices will not be rewarded by any special environmental benefits to the citizens of Irvine. (ll. 15–18)

  ....

  ....

  ....

B What do the following refer to in the text? What's their general effect?
  for example (l. 4); *In such cases* (l. 9); *For instance* (l. 13); *say* (l. 30)

  ....

  ....

  ....

C Comment on the word order in this sentence.

  Nor, usually, do they have much knowledge about defense strategy. (ll. 33–34)

  ....

  ....

Grammar points

D Explain when we use *by* + agent in the passive.

Rewrite these sentences in the passive, then check your answers against the text.

1 Local interests shape political issues. (compare l. 3)

2 Employment levels in factories often dictate defense policy. (compare ll. 4–7)

E Rewrite this sentence in the singular, then check against the text.
There are other kinds of local politics. (ll. 11–12)

What three things did you notice when you rewrote the sentence?

Make the singular sentences plural and the plural sentences singular.

1 There is another kind of Arctic bird which is rarely seen in this country.
There are other kinds of Arctic birds which are rarely seen in this country.
2 There are other sorts of problems which no one has mentioned so far.

3 Do you know of any other kinds of computer which can be easily carried?

4 I always avoid these sorts of places.

5 We should do everything we can to prevent this kind of thing from happening again.

F Supply *rise* or *raise* in this sentence, then refer to the text. Give a reason for your choice.
This legislation will .... the cost of some consumer goods. (ll. 15–16)

Supply suitable forms of *raise* or *rise*.

1 We can't get better-qualified employees without ....*raising*.... standards in education.
2 Standards in education simply have to .... before we get better-qualified employees.
3 It isn't often I get the opportunity to see the sun ....
4 Your loaf looks as if it has .... nicely.
5 Those in favour of this motion should .... their right arms.

G Explain the difference between *no* and *none* in this sentence (ll. 31–33):
*People sitting in their back yards have **no** power – **none**, anyway, that might have an impact.*

Supply *no* or *none*.

1 There's ......*no*...... reason to suppose that there will be serious traffic delays today.
2 Is there any reason to suppose that there will be serious traffic delays today? – No,
   ....
3 .... of this meat is suitable for human consumption.
4 There are .... goods for sale which don't carry Value Added Tax.
5 I can't lend you any money because I've got ....
6 There's .... sense in asking me the same question again and again.
7 Einstein is among the greatest scientists. Perhaps there were .... greater.
8 There's .... advice you could give me which will help in this situation.

SENTENCE STRUCTURE

A Answers and commentary

1 *Defense policy, for example, logically calls for an overview of national-security needs, **yet** it is often dictated by employment levels in factories ...*

Yet is used to introduce a co-ordinate main clause expressing contrast. [> LEG 1.17–20, LAG 3A*ns*.1–2] It would also have been possible to use *but* or *(al)though*.

*... **that** happen to depend on defense contracts ...*

That (or *which*) is the relative pronoun subject of a relative clause [> LEG 1.31]:

> *It is often dictated by employment levels in* **factories**. ***These** happen to depend on defense contracts ...*
> → *It is often dictated by employment levels in* **factories that/which** *happen to depend on defense contracts ...*

No comma is used after *factories*, because the clause is defining, providing essential information. [> LEG 1.26, LAG 5A*n*.3]

*... **and** are in the district of an influential congressman.*

And introduces a co-ordinate relative clause [> LEG 1.21, LAG 1B*n*.2]:

> *... **and that/which** (i.e. *factories*) are in the district of an influential congressman.*

2 *This legislation will cause hardships for local businesses **and raise** the cost of some consumer goods for local people ...*

And introduces a co-ordinate main clause. [> LEG 1.17–20] It would have been possible to use a present participle construction here [> LEG 1.58.1, LAG 4B*n*.3, 43A*ns*.11–12, 47B*n*.4]:

> *... for local businesses, **raising** the cost of some consumer goods ...*

*... **and** these sacrifices will not be rewarded by any special environmental benefits to the citizens of Irvine.*

And introduces a co-ordinate main clause with a new subject (*these sacrifices*). [> LEG 1.17–20, LAG 1B*n*.2] It would have been possible to use a relative clause here, following the noun *sacrifices* used in apposition to the preceding clause [> LEG 1.39, LAG 5A*ns*.2,4]:

> *... and raise the cost of some consumer goods for local people, **sacrifices which** will not be rewarded ...*

B Answer and commentary

– *for example* refers to *Defense policy*, but also illustrates the idea that 'all politics is local';

– *In such cases* refers to employment levels in factories where (we presume) local interests conflict with 'national-security needs';

– *For instance* refers to the story about 'the City Council of Irvine', but also refers to *another kind of local politics* in the previous sentence;

– *say* refers to 'the perspective of someone sitting under a tree', but also refers to *two conflicting perspectives* in the previous sentence. [compare > LEG Apps 17–18]

As a result, the coherence of this text is fairly loose.

C Answer and commentary

*Nor, usually, **do they have** much knowledge about defense strategy.*

Nor (like *neither*) is a 'negative adverb'. When we use a negative adverb at the beginning of a sentence, we must use an auxiliary verb (*be, do, have, can, must*, etc.) + subject after it. (Not **Nor, usually, they have ...**) This kind of inversion, which may be used for particular emphasis, is typical of rhetoric and formal writing. [> LEG 7.59.3, App 19, LAG 30B, 33C]

Usually has been used, with commas, before the auxiliary for special emphasis. Its normal position and punctuation in a negative sentence would be [> LEG 7.40.2, 7.40.6, LAG 45D]:

> *Nor do they **usually** have much knowledge about defense strategy.*

Note that *nor* and *neither* can replace each other here without any change of meaning [> LEG 13.28–29]:

> ***Nor/Neither**, usually, **do they have** much knowledge about defense strategy.* Or:
> ***Nor/Neither do they** usually **have** much knowledge about defense strategy.*

GRAMMAR POINTS

D 'By' + agent after a passive: 'It was composed by Mozart' [> LEG 12.5]

We use *by* + agent in the passive only when it is important to say who or what did something.

In most passive constructions, we don't need *by* + agent:

I've been asked to deal with this matter.

In most situations, a statement like the above conveys as much information as is necessary. We add *by* + agent to supply important information:

I've been asked by the boss himself to deal with this matter. [> LAG 29Ans.1–2]

1 Political issues are shaped by local interests.
2 Defense policy is often dictated by employment levels in factories.

E 'Kind of' and 'sort of' [> LEG App 7.17, compare > LAG 55F]

There is another kind of local politics.

1 We use *another* in the singular.
2 *kinds of* becomes *kind of*.
3 *politics* (here) is a singular noun. It is always spelt with an *s* (Never *politic*). [> LEG 2.31, compare > LAG 19E]

Kind of and *sort of* follow *this/that* and *kinds of/sorts of* follow *these/those*:

I like that kind of/sort of film.
→ *I like those kinds of/sorts of films.*

However, in informal usage, native speakers often say:

**I like those kind of/sort of films.*

We can also say:

I like films of that kind. (Not *of those kinds*)

Note, incidentally, how *another* is followed by a singular noun and *other* by a plural noun [> LEG 5.27]:

There is another kind of Arctic bird …
→ *There are other kinds of Arctic birds …*

1 There are other kinds of Arctic birds which are rarely seen in this country.
2 There is another sort of problem which no one has mentioned so far.
3 Do you know of another kind of/any other kind of computer which can be easily carried?
4 I always avoid this sort of place.
5 We should do everything we can to prevent these kinds of things from happening again.

F 'Raise' and 'rise' [> LEG Apps 1.1, 39–40: regular and irregular verbs, compare > LAG 21D]

This legislation will raise the cost …

We need *raise* here because it is followed by an object (*the cost*).

Raise (= 'lift something') is transitive, that is, it is always followed by an object:

Raise *your hand.*

Rise (= 'lift myself/itself') is intransitive:

'Rise!' said the queen. (= 'get off your knees')

1 raising standards
2 standards have to rise
3 see the sun rise
4 your loaf has risen
5 raise their right arms

G 'No' and 'none' [> LEG 5.5.2, 5.11, 13.9]

No is followed by a noun (*power*); *none* stands on its own. [compare > LAG 14G, 25D, 53D]

No means 'not a/an' (*I'm no expert*) or 'not any' (*We've got no apples/milk*). We use *no* as an alternative form to *not … any* to talk about quantity.

None is a pronoun, which means it stands on its own and we can't use it in front of a noun:

We've got no apples/milk.
→ *We've got none.*

We can use *of* after *none*, but we can't use *of* after *no*:

None of this milk can be used.
I've used none of it.

1 There's no reason
2 No, none
3 None of this meat
4 no goods
5 I've got none
6 There's no sense
7 none (We could also say *no greater*, but then we would be using *no* as an adverb of degree, not a quantifier. [> LEG 5.12.3])
8 no advice

What is the soul?

BUT what is the soul? From Plato onwards many answers have been given to this question, and most of them are but modifications of his conjectures. We use the word constantly, and it must be presumed that we mean something by it. Christianity has accepted it as an article of faith that the soul is a simple spiritual substance created by God and immortal. One may not believe that and yet attach some signification to the word. When I ask myself what I mean by it I can only answer that I mean by it my consciousness of myself, the I in me, the personality which is me; and that personality is compounded of my thoughts, my feelings, my experiences and the accidents of my body. I think many people shrink from the notion that the accidents of the body can have an effect on the constitution of the soul. There is nothing of which for my own part I am more assured. My soul would have been quite different if I had not stammered or if I had been four or five inches taller; I am slightly prognathous; in my childhood they did not know that this could be remedied by a gold band worn while the jaw is still malleable; if they had, my countenance would have borne a different cast, the reaction towards me of my fellows would have been different and therefore my disposition, my attitude to them, would have been different too. But what sort of thing is this soul that can be modified by a dental apparatus? We all know how greatly changed our lives would have been if we had not by what seems mere chance met such and such a person or if we had not been at a particular moment at a particular place; and so our character, and so our soul, would have been other than they are.

A Writer's Notebook by W. Somerset Maugham *(BrE)*

Sentence structure

A Replace the words in italics and give reasons. Then refer to the text.

1 From Plato onwards many answers have been given to this question, and most of them are *only* modifications of his conjectures. (ll. 1–4)

2 There is nothing for my own part I am more assured *of*. (ll. 17–18)

3 My soul would have been quite different *had I not* stammered. (ll. 18–19)

4 In my childhood they did not know that this could be remedied by a gold band worn *during the time that* the jaw is still malleable. (ll. 20–22)

5 We all know how greatly changed our lives would have been if we had not by *something which* seems mere chance met such and such a person. (ll. 27–29)

B Which form of the verb would be preferable to the form in italics and why?

When I ask myself what *do I mean* by it I can only answer that I mean by it my consciousness of myself. (ll. 11–12)

C Which words could you add to this sentence without changing its meaning and why?

Christianity has accepted it as an article of faith that the soul is a simple spiritual substance created by God and immortal. (ll. 6–9)

Grammar points

D Supply the right forms of the verbs in brackets, then refer to the text. (ll. 18–32)

My soul would have been quite different if I [1](*not stammer*) .... or if I [2](*be*) .... four or five inches taller; I [3](*be*) .... slightly prognathous; in my childhood they [4](*not know*) .... that this [5](*can remedy*) .... by a gold band worn while the jaw [6](*be*) .... still malleable; if they [7](*have*) .... , my countenance [8](*bear*) .... a different cast, the reaction towards me of my fellows [9](*be*) .... different and therefore my disposition, my attitude to them, [10](*be*) .... different too. But what sort of thing is this soul that [11](*can modify*) .... by a dental apparatus? We all [12](*know*) .... how greatly changed our lives [13](*will be*) .... if we had not by what seems mere chance [14](*meet*) .... such and such a person or if we [15](*not be*) .... at a particular moment at a particular place; and so our character, and so our soul, [16](*be*) .... other than they are.

E Rewrite this question beginning with the words provided, then check against the text. (l. 11)
What do I mean by it? I ask myself ....
What major change did you make and why?
....

E1 Rewrite these questions with the words provided.
1 What does he mean by the word 'soul'? I asked him *what he meant by the word 'soul'.*
2 What does she know about their plans? Ask her ....
3 When will they leave? He wanted to know ....
4 What's the time? Please tell me ....
5 How does she manage? I'd like to know ....
6 How did she manage? I'd like to know ....
7 What will she do? I asked her ....
8 What shall I do? Please tell me ....

E2 Rewrite this question beginning with the words provided. How is this different from E1 above?
Who makes the rules round here? I want to know ....

Rewrite these questions with the words provided.
1 Which firm has the greatest exports? I want to know *which firm has the greatest exports.*
2 What made that noise? I wanted to know ....
3 Which film will be shown? I asked ....
4 What's happening? Please tell me ....
5 Who replaced him when he left the company? I asked ....

F Suggest which words could be used in place of the words in bold italics.
*So our character, and so our soul, would have been **other than** they are.* (ll. 31–32) ....

Combine these clauses with *different from what*.
1 They told you something different. It is not the same as they told me.
What they told you *is different from what they told me.*
2 She says something different. It is not the same as she does.
What she says ....
3 You bought something different. It is not the same as I bought.
What you bought ....
4 Jack has done something different. It is not the same as he said he would do.
What Jack has done ....

SENTENCE STRUCTURE

A Answers and commentary

1 ... *many answers have been given to this question, and most of them are but modifications* ...

But (= only) is used as a focus adverb here [compare > LEG 7.54–55], not as a conjunction. [> LEG 1.17–20] As a focus adverb, *but* has limited uses compared with *only* and is rather formal. [> LAG 21Bn.1b, 23Bn.3, 40An.1]

2 *There is nothing of which for my own part I am more assured.*

This use of the relative (*which*) after a preposition (*of*) is very formal. In spoken English, we usually drop the relative and move the preposition to the end of the sentence [> LEG 1.36, LAG 20An.1]:

There is nothing which for my own part I am more assured of.

There is nothing (-) for my own part I am more assured of.

3 *My soul would have been quite different if I had not stammered.*

This is a normal Type 3 Conditional (*If* + past perfect + *would have*). [> LEG 14.16–19, LAG 50D] Inversion with *had* (*had I not stammered*) is a formal variation of *If I had not stammered*. [> LEG 14.18.3, LAG 16C]

4 ... *remedied by a gold band worn while the jaw is still malleable.*

While introduces an adverbial clause of time and can be replaced by *during the time (that)*. [> LEG 1.45.1] *While* cannot be replaced by *during* on its own. (Not *during the jaw is still malleable*) [> LEG 7.35, LAG 4Bn.3, 10An.1, 21An.3, 41An.4]

5 ... *if we had not by what seems mere chance met such and such a person.*

What seems mere chance is a noun clause following the preposition *by*. *What* (= the thing(s) which) can introduce a noun clause. [> LEG 1.24.2, 15.19–20, LAG 8An.2, 35An.8b, 42D]

B Answer and commentary

In indirect questions, the inversion in the direct question usually changes back to statement word order, so *When I ask myself what I mean* ... would be the normal word order here. [> LEG 15.18n.2, 15.20ns.1–2, LAG 50E]

However, a direct question (with question word-order) can sometimes be embedded in indirect speech, especially in colloquial usage [> LEG 15.18n.3]:

She said she was going to the shops and asked me did I want anything while she was out.

→ *She said she was going to the shops and asked me if I wanted anything while she was out.*

C Answer and commentary

Christianity has accepted it as an article of faith that the soul is a simple spiritual substance which/that is created by God and (which/that is) immortal.

The writer has combined the idea of two relative clauses:

1 (*that is*) *created by God*
2 (*that is*) *immortal*

Both the past participle construction, *created by God*, and the adjective, *immortal*, depend on *that is* which could be added to this sentence. [> LEG 1.62.3] The use of the simple present (*is*) suggests a permanent truth. [> LEG 9.8.1, LAG 33Bn.6, 37C]

GRAMMAR POINTS

D Past tenses and Type 3 conditionals: 'if I had ... I would have' [> LEG 9.13–31, 14.16–19, modal passive 12.2, compare > LAG 16C, 9E (Type 1), 22C, 37D (Type 2)]

The topic here is hypothetical (what Somerset Maugham might have been like if things had been different) and this is well-illustrated in the use of tenses.

1 if I had not stammered
2 If I had been
3 am
4 did not know
5 can/could be remedied
6 is
7 if they had (known)
8 would have borne (*bear* has two past participles: *born*, as in *I was born in 1960* and *borne*, as in *She has borne three children*. [> LEG App 40])
9 would have been different
10 would have been different
11 can be modified
12 we all know
13 would have been
14 met
15 if we had not been
16 our soul would have been

E Indirect question-word questions: 'I ask myself what I mean by it.' [> LEG 15.19–20, LAG 29B and compare > LAG 42D]

I ask myself what I mean by it.
The major change here was in word order:
  What do I mean ... ?
  → *... what I mean ....*

There are three important facts to remember about indirect question-word questions:
– The word order of the direct question changes back to statement word order (subject/verb/object).
– The tenses may change when reported: 'present may become past, past may become past perfect'. [> LEG 15.13, LAG 29B]
– Quotation marks and question marks are not used in indirect questions.

E1

1 I asked him what he meant by the word 'soul'.
2 Ask her what she knows about their plans.
3 He wanted to know when they would leave.
4 Please tell me what the time is.
5 I'd like to know how she manages.
6 I'd like to know how she managed. [> LEG 15.13n.3]
7 I asked her what she would do.
8 Please tell me what I should do/what to do. [> LEG 15.24.2]

E2 *I want to know who makes the rules round here.*

The word order does not change because this is a subject-question [> LEG 15.21–22]:
  He makes the rules round here.
  → *Who makes the rules round here?*
  → *I'd like to know who makes the rules round here.*

1 I want to know which firm has the greatest exports.
2 I wanted to know what made/had made that noise.
3 I asked which film would be shown.
4 Please tell me what's happening.
5 I asked who replaced/had replaced him .... [> LEG 15.13n.3]

F 'Different from' + 'what'-clause [> LEG 6.30.4]

So our character, and so our soul, would have been different from what they are.

Other than + clause (*other than they are*) is relatively rare and highly formal. [compare > LAG 48E]

Native speakers have difficulty with this construction. Careful speakers want to avoid *different than*, but the correct alternative, *different from what* (= that which [> LAG 42D]) + clause can sometimes be awkward.

1 What they told you is different from what they told me.
2 What she says is different from what she does.
3 What you bought is different from what I bought.
4 What Jack has done is different from what he said he would do.

The ultimate quest

THE elevator doors opened into a cavernous room in an underground tunnel outside Geneva. Out came the eminent British astrophysicist Stephen Hawking, in a wheelchair as always. He was there to behold a wondrous sight. Before him loomed a giant device called a particle detector, a component of an incredible machine whose job is to accelerate tiny fragments of matter to nearly the speed of light, then smash them together with a fury far greater than any natural collision on earth.

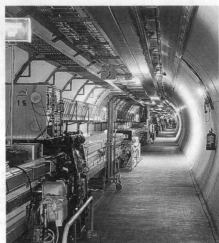

Paralyzed by a degenerative nerve disease, Hawking is one of the world's most accomplished physicists, renowned for his breakthroughs in the study of gravitation and cosmology. Yet the man who holds the prestigious Cambridge University professorship once occupied by Sir Isaac Newton was overwhelmed by the sheer size and complexity of the machine before him. Joked Hawking: 'This reminds me of one of those James Bond movies, where some mad scientist is plotting to take over the world.'

It is easy to understand why even Hawking was awed: he was looking at just a portion of the largest scientific instrument ever built. Known as the large electron-positron collider, this new particle accelerator is the centerpiece of CERN, the European Organization for Nuclear Research and one of Europe's proudest achievements. LEP is a mammoth particle racetrack residing in a ring-shaped tunnel 27kms (16.8 miles) in circumference and an average of 110 meters (360 ft.) underground. The machine contains 330,000 cubic meters (431,640 cu. yds.) of concrete and holds some 60,000 tons of hardware, including nearly 5,000 electromagnets, four particle detectors weighing more than 3,000 tons each, 160 computers and 6,600 km (4,000 miles) of electrical cables. Tangles of brightly colored wires sprout everywhere, linking equipment together in a pattern so complicated, it seems that no one could possibly understand or operate the device. In fact, it takes the combined efforts of literally hundreds of Ph.Ds to run a single experiment.

Time (AmE)

Sentence structure

A Combine the sentences below into single complete sentences. Make any necessary changes and use the help given. Then check against the text.

1 A giant device loomed before him. It is called a particle detector. It is a component of an incredible machine. Its job is to accelerate tiny fragments of matter to nearly the speed of light. Then it smashes them together with a fury far greater than any natural collision on earth. (ll. 8–15)
Before him ....
....
....

2 Hawking is one of the world's most accomplished physicists. He is paralyzed by a degenerative nerve disease. He is renowned for his breakthroughs in the study of gravitation and cosmology. (ll. 16–21)
Paralyzed ....

3 This new particle accelerator is the centerpiece of CERN, the European Organization for Nuclear Research. It is known as the large electron-positron collider. It is one of Europe's proudest achievements. (ll. 36–41)
Known as ....
....

B Comment on the word order of this sentence.

Out came the eminent British astrophysicist Stephen Hawking, in a wheelchair as always. (ll. 4–6)
....

Grammar points

C Rewrite this sentence so that it begins with *Out*, then refer to the text.
The eminent British astrophysicist Stephen Hawking came out. (ll. 4–6)

Rewrite these sentences making a change in word order in each case.

1 The crowd had been waiting for hours, when the President came out and waved to them.
The crowd had been waiting for hours, when out came the President and waved to them.

2 The hot-air balloons went up – the very moment the crowd had been waiting for.

3 You go in now and I'll follow you.

4 The walkers stopped at the inn for a glass of beer and then they went off.

5 I can't possibly look after you so you must go back to your mother.

D Replace a phrase in this sentence with a construction with *'s*, then refer to the text. (ll. 36–41)
This new particle accelerator is one of the proudest achievements of Europe.

Replace phrases in these sentences with *'s/s'* constructions.

1 Which is the tallest skyscraper in New York?   *New York's tallest skyscraper*
2 What's the policy of the European Community about this?
3 We'll never solve the mysteries of Easter Island.
4 We were married in the church of St Andrew.
5 The recovery of post-war Germany was a miracle.
6 The theatres of London are justly famous.
7 It's the resolution of the United Nations.
8 What's the policy of the Labour Party?
9 Did you read the leader in *The Times* on that?
10 I agree with the point of view in *The Economist*.

E Delete the wrong form here. Write your reason, then check against the text.
The machine (is containing/contains) 330,000 cubic meters of concrete. (ll. 47–49)

Supply simple or progressive forms of the verbs in brackets, using appropriate tenses.

1 I don't need a fill-up just yet. My petrol tank (contain) *contains* at least 50 litres.
2 This property (belong) .... to our family for over a hundred years.
3 Any photograph from outer space immediately (prove) .... that the earth is round.
4 John died of a heart-attack while he (prove) .... that he could run the Marathon.
5 You ate sea cucumber when you were in China. What (taste) .... like?
6 I scalded my mouth while I (taste) .... the soup.
7 Pollution (concern) .... our children more than it (concern) .... us.
8 You look great! That hair style really (suit) .... you!
9 Politics is a rough trade and politicians (not normally deserve) .... much sympathy.
10 What've you been up to? For a month now, I (hear) .... strange reports about you.
11 He expresses surprise if you tell him you (never hear) .... of something he knows.
12 I tell you inflation will come down. – I (completely disagree) .... with you.
13 They (weigh) .... the parcel and told me it would cost a fortune to send.
14 Some people (weigh) .... themselves every time they pass a weighing machine.
15 She looks down on everybody just because she (have) .... a house in the country.
16 We (have) .... a house built on this site and it will take years to finish.
17 John (believe) .... anything I tell him.

SENTENCE STRUCTURE

A Answers and commentary

Detailed suggestions for joining these sentences were not provided in the exercise, so there are many possible answers. The commentary is based on the way the sentences have been joined in the text.

1 *Before him loomed a giant device **called** a particle detector, ...*
The past participle construction with *called* is used in place of a relative clause [> LEG 1.62.3, LAG 6B*n*.4]:

> *Before him loomed a giant device **which is called** ...*
> → *... a giant device **called** ...*

Subject and verb are reversed after the adverb phrase *Before him* ... [> LEG 7.59.2, LAG 51B–C]:

> *A **giant device** (subject) **loomed** (verb) before him (adverb phrase).*
> → *Before him **loomed a giant device** ....*

... a component of an incredible machine ...
This phrase, which supplies more information, is in apposition to *a giant device called a particle detector*. [> LEG 1.39, LAG 2A*n*.1, 5A*ns*.2,4]

*... **whose** job is to accelerate tiny fragments of matter to nearly the speed of light, ...*
Whose replaces *its* and is used here in connexion with a thing. *Of which* would also have been possible [> LEG 1.32, LAG 11B*n*.1, 23B*n*.3]:

> *... an incredible machine **the job of which** is to accelerate ...*

*... then **smash** them together with a fury far greater than any natural collision on earth.*
The infinitive marker, *to*, is understood here:

> *Its job is **to accelerate** tiny fragments of matter ... and then **(to) smash** them together.*

[For noun + *to*-infinitive > LEG 10.9.10, 16.16, 16.33–36, LAG 7B*ns*.4,8]

2 ***Paralyzed** by a degenerative nerve disease, Hawking is one of the world's most accomplished physicists, ...*
The past participle is used in place of the passive [> LEG 1.62.1, LAG 6B*n*.4]:

> *He **is paralyzed** by a degenerative nerve disease ...*
> → ***Paralyzed** by a degenerative nerve disease, ...*

*... **renowned** for his breakthroughs in the study of gravitation and cosmology.*
This phrase replaces a relative clause (*who is renowned* ... [> LAG 6B*n*.4]) and is used in apposition to *Hawking is one of the world's most accomplished physicists* to supply additional information. [> LEG 1.39, LAG 2A*n*.1, 5A*ns*.2,4]

3 ***Known as** the large electron-positron collider, this new particle accelerator is the centerpiece of CERN, ...*
The past participle is used in place of the passive [> LEG 1.62.1, LAG 6B*n*.4]:

> *It **is known** as the large electron-positron collider ...*
> → ***Known** as the large electron-positron collider, **this new particle accelerator** ...*

... the European Organization for Nuclear Research ...
This phrase is in apposition to *CERN* and provides the English explanation for it. [> LEG 1.39 LAG 2A*n*.1, 5A*ns*.2,4] *CERN* is actually a French acronym standing for ***Conseil Européen pour la Recherche Nucléaire***. [For English abbreviations and acronyms > LEG 3.7, 3.17, 3.24.]

*... **and** one of Europe's proudest achievements.*
A further phrase in apposition, joined by *and*.

B Answer and commentary

'Normal' word order would require [> LEG 1.3, LAG 4A]:

> *The eminent British astrophysicist, Stephen Hawking, (subject) came out (verb) in a wheelchair as always (adverb).*

However, it is possible to begin with adverbs like *back, down, off, out, up* for dramatic effect, especially with verbs of motion like *come* and *go*. The noun subject comes after the verb [> LEG 7.59.1, LAG 51C]:

> ***Out** (adverb) **came** (verb) the eminent British astrophysicist Stephen Hawking, ...* (subject)

GRAMMAR POINTS

C Inversion after adverbs like 'back', 'down', 'off', 'out' etc.: 'out came Stephen Hawking' [> LEG 7.59.1 and compare > LAG 33C]

***Out came** the eminent British astrophysicist Stephen Hawking.*

If we begin a sentence with an adverb particle like *Back*, we continue with verb + noun subject. We use this inverted word order for special dramatic effect. Compare:

> ***The answer came back** - No!*
> → ***Back came the answer** - No!*

If the subject is a pronoun, it stays in front of the verb:

> ***It came back**.*
> → ***Back it came**. (Not *Back came it.*)*

1 The crowd had been waiting for hours, when out came the President and waved to them.
2 Up went the hot-air balloons – the very moment the crowd had been waiting for.
3 In you go now and I'll follow you.
4 The walkers stopped at the inn for a glass of beer and then off they went.
5 I can't possibly look after you so back to your mother you must go. (Or: . . . back you must go to your mother.)

D The genitive with place names and institutions: 'one of Europe's proudest achievements' [> LEG 2.49, 3.22, 3.31 and compare > LAG 5B]

*. . . one of **Europe's proudest achievements***

We use *'s* and *s'* mainly to show possession for people and some living things [> LEG 2.42–48]:

> ***Gus's** car, the **horses'** stables.*

However, we often use the genitive for place names and buildings:

> ***New York's** tallest skyscraper, **St Paul's Church**;*

and institutions:

> *The **European Community's** experts.*

'Institutions' as a concept is broad enough to include the press:

> ***Time's** Person of the Year.*

1 New York's tallest skyscraper
2 the European Community's policy
3 Easter Island's mysteries
4 St Andrew's Church
5 post-war Germany's recovery

6 London's theatres
7 the United Nations' resolution
8 the Labour Party's policy
9 *The Times'* leader
10 *The Economist's* point of view

E Stative and dynamic verbs [> LEG 9.3, App 38]

The machine contains . . .

The verb *contain* cannot be used in progressive tenses (Not *is containing*).

Verbs describing states (*stative* verbs, like *contain*) can't be used in the progressive:

> *This box **contains** matches.*

Verbs describing deliberate acts are *dynamic* and can be used in the progressive [compare > LAG 23D]:

> ***I'm unlocking** the door.*

Some verbs have stative or dynamic uses, with changes of meaning:

> *The radiator **feels** hot. (= that's its condition; stative, therefore simple present)*
> ***I'm feeling** the radiator. (= that's what I'm doing; dynamic, therefore present progressive)*

Stative verbs fall into five classes:

1 Feelings: *like, love,* etc.
2 Thinking/believing: *believe, think,* etc.
3 Wants and preferences: *prefer, want,* etc.
4 Perception and the senses: *hear, see,* etc.
5 Being/seeming/having, etc.: *seem, belong,* etc.

Suggested answers

1 contains
2 has belonged
3 proves/will prove
4 was proving
5 does it/did it taste like
6 was tasting the soup
7 will concern . . . concerns
8 suits
9 don't normally deserve
10 have been hearing [compare > LEG 9.11.4]
11 have never heard
12 completely disagree [> LEG 9.8.5]
13 weighed
14 weigh
15 has [> LEG 10.33n.1]
16 are having [> LEG 12.10]
17 believes

Henry Ford

WHEN he turned seventy-one Henry showed up to meet the press wearing two different shoes. Asked about it by reporters, he looked down and, obviously making up an answer
5 on the spot, said that he always wore one old shoe on his birthday to remind himself that he had once been poor and might be again. He still had his loose-limbed walk and springy gait; the netted wrinkles around his eyes
10 collaborated with his mouth when he smiled. He was still automatic news, charming even the reporters who came to 'get' him. Even his rare refusals to do journalists' bidding were endearing. A photographer once asked him to pose between two boys with
15 a hand on the head of each, and he refused. When asked why, he reminded the photographer about the picture of John Dillinger with an arm around the sheriff whose jail he later broke out of. 'You can see for yourself the spot I'd be in if these two boys turned out badly,' he said.
20 But if he was the same old Ford to the outer world, the employees close to him saw him as a different man. The practical jokes of a prior era had fermented into episodes of intentional cruelty; the belief in individuality and independence had become a sclerotic insistence on having his
25 own way. It was Edsel who absorbed most of the punishment. It was clear to everyone that Ford loved his son deeply, but it was the same sort of love as when Edsel was the little boy to whom he had been unusually close. Henry could not relinquish the role of father, and as Edsel tried to find ground he could
30 occupy Henry tried to push him back into dependence, capriciously overturning the decisions Edsel made as president and humiliating him in front of others. When Edsel learned that yet another of his orders had been countermanded, his jaw would tighten and his features cloud. 'Well, I thought
35 Father understood about this,' he would say. 'Apparently somebody talked to him about it ...' Finally he would shrug and repeat the only explanation he had for such behavior: 'Well, after all, my father built this business. It is his business.'

The Fords, An American Epic
by Peter Collier and David Horowitz *(AmE)*

Sentence structure

A Break these sentences down into short sentences, making any necessary changes. Write one short sentence beside each letter.

1 Asked about it by reporters, he looked down and, obviously making up an answer on the spot, said that ... he had once been poor and might be again. (ll. 3–7)

a ....

b ....

c ....

d ....

e ....

2 Henry could not relinquish the role of father, and as Edsel tried to find ground he could occupy Henry tried to push him back into dependence, capriciously overturning the decisions Edsel made as president and humiliating him in front of others. (ll. 28–32)

a ....

h ....

c ....

d ....

e ....

B Join these notes to make one sentence. Then check against the text.

The practical jokes – prior era – fermented into episodes – intentional cruelty – the belief – individuality – independence – become a sclerotic insistence – have his own way (ll. 21–25)

....

....

Grammar points

C Which verb does *belief* derive from here? (l. 23)
*The **belief** in individuality ... became a sclerotic insistence on having his own way.* ....

Rewrite these sentences with nouns in place of the verbs in italics and make any other changes.

1 He wanted to have his own way. He *insisted*, and this led to difficulties.
His *insistence on having his own way led to difficulties.* ....

2 This is an important scheme and we want him to *approve*.
We want his ....

3 You must congratulate her. She's passed the exams. She's *succeeded*.
You must congratulate her on her ....

4 He's staying with us. Why do you *object*? I can't understand it.
I can't understand your ....

5 It's either this or that. You must *choose*.
It's a ....

6 Tell me about the two schemes. How do they *differ*?
What's the ....

7 She doesn't pass exams. She *fails* and this depresses her.
Her ....

8 We need to get at the facts in this case. What do you *know*?
What's your ....

9 There was a whole series of crimes. He *confessed* and this amazed everybody.
His ....

10 He must leave this job. He must *resign*. We require it.
We require his ....

11 We didn't take legal action. You *advised* and we followed.
We followed your ....

12 He was in obscurity. Then he *emerged*. It was sudden.
His ....

D Supply the missing preposition, then refer to the text.
It was clear .... *everyone that Ford loved his son deeply.* (l. 26)

Supply the missing prepositions after the adjectives.

1 I think Celia is very angry *with* me.
2 He's really ashamed .... what he did.
3 We're all very obliged .... you.
4 I think he's capable .... anything.
5 This service is free .... charge.
6 Some people are very bad .... spelling.
7 London's full .... tourists at the moment.
8 He's quite careless .... danger.
9 They went ahead contrary .... my advice.
10 We're quite safe .... danger here.
11 You were wrong .... the election results.
12 She's very nervous .... the new boss.
13 Are you aware .... the cost of this?
14 We're grateful .... you for all your help.
15 I'm not afraid .... taking risks.
16 How long has she been absent .... class?
17 We're angry .... the way she's behaved.
18 He was married .... Sue for a day.
19 I hope you're satisfied .... my work.
20 Jane's busy .... the baby at the moment.
21 I'm faithful .... my principles.
22 I know you'll be annoyed .... me.
23 I've been so anxious .... you.
24 I've always been fond .... oysters.
25 She's so clever .... solving problems.
26 I'm really amazed .... your behaviour.
27 I'm sorry .... the trouble I caused.
28 I'm going to be late .... work again.
29 I hear you're very keen .... football.
30 Why is he so jealous .... his sister?
31 The twins are different .... each other.
32 Jane is very careful .... her money.
33 Alice is kind .... everybody.
34 We lost and we're very sad .... it.
35 Be careful .... talking to strangers.
36 The issues are separate .... each other.
37 John's very good .... his hands.
38 John's very good .... carpentry.
39 You need to be certain .... your facts.
40 We're ready .... action.

SENTENCE STRUCTURE

A Answers and commentary

Most of the sentences you have written are simple sentences. A simple sentence has one finite verb. [> LEG 1.2, 1.7] The basic word order in a sentence that is not a question or command is: (Time) Subject Verb Object Manner Place (Time) [> LEG 1.3, 7.22, LAG 4A]

1a *He* (subject) *was asked about* (verb) *it* (object) *by reporters* (by + agent).
The verb is passive in form. (Compare the active: *Reporters **asked him** about it.*) *By* + agent supplies essential information. [> LEG 12.5]

b *He* (subject) *looked down* (verb).
Looked down is a phrasal verb used intransitively here (without an object). [> LEG 1.10, 8.29]

c *He* (subject) *obviously* (viewpoint adverb) *made up* (verb) *an answer* (object) *on the spot* ('place'). Depending on the emphasis we wish to make, we can begin the sentence with *obviously*, or put it between the subject and the verb, as here. [> LEG 7.16.2, 7.57, App 17.1, LAG 54An.5]
Made up (= invented) is a transitive phrasal verb with an idiomatic meaning. [> LEG 8.28.5, App 33, LAG 44D] It would be possible to transpose the particle [> LEG 8.28.2, LAG 4D, 13C]: *He obviously **made** an answer **up** on the spot.*

d *He said* (reporting verb) *that he had once been poor* (noun clause object).
The reporting verb *said* introduces an indirect statement, which is the noun clause object of the verb. *That* is optional after *said*. [> LEG 1.23.2, 15.12–13, App 45] The direct speech equivalent of this would be: *'I was once poor.'* The tense change to the past perfect (*had (once) been*) is essential here because it emphasizes that the reference is to 'an earlier past'. [> LEG 9.29.1]

e *He might be again.*
The direct speech equivalent would be: *'I might be again'*. (*Poor* is understood after *might be*.) The sequence of tenses in the past is maintained for consistency. [> LEG 9.5, LAG 7F] 'Modal present' (*may*) becomes 'modal past' (*might*) after *said that*. [> LEG 15.13n.6, LAG 10C]

2a *Henry* (subject) *could not relinquish* (verb) *the role of father* (object).
Could not refers to general ability in the past here. [> LEG 11.8.3, 11.12.1, LAG 9C, 48C]

b *Edsel* (subject) *tried* (verb) *to find ground (that) he could occupy* (object, which includes a relative clause).

The *to*-infinitive can be the object of a verb. [> LEG 1.12, 16.13] *Try* is followed by *to* when it means 'make an effort' (as here) and by *-ing* when it means 'experiment'. (***Try holding** your breath to stop sneezing.*) [> LEG 16.59, LAG 42C]
(That) is the relative pronoun object of the relative clause, often omitted in defining clauses [> LEG 1.34, LAG 6Bn.1]:
*He tried to find ground. **He could occupy it**.*
→ *He tried to find ground **(that) he could occupy**.*

c *Henry* (subject) *tried* (verb) *to push him back into dependence* (object).
Try is used as in **2b** above. *Push back* is a Type 2 phrasal verb. As the object is a pronoun (*him*), it must come before the particle (*back*). [> LEG 8.28.2, App 32, LAG 4D, 13C, 44D] The object can be a *to*-infinitive. [> LEG 1.12, 16.13]

d *He* (subject) *capriciously* (adverb of manner) *overturned* (verb) *the decisions (that) Edsel made as president* (object, which includes a relative clause).
Note that the meaning would change if the adverb of manner, *capriciously*, were moved to the end of the sentence (= Edsel's capricious decisions). [compare > LEG 7.16.2, LAG 4A, 48Ans.1a–b] If the authors had used *had made*, they would have been pointing to decisions made in an earlier past. [> LEG 9.29.1] The use of *made* here suggests that Henry overturned decisions as Edsel made them (i.e. at the same time).

e *He* (subject) *humiliated* (verb) *him* (object) *in front of others* ('place').

B Answer and commentary

*The practical jokes **of** a prior era **had fermented** into episodes **of** intentional cruelty;*
The past perfect (*had fermented*) pervades the whole piece. There is constant comparison between a point 'now' (or in the past) and things as they were 'then' (further back in the past). Here the comparison is between 'Henry at 71' and 'Henry as he once was'. [> LEG 9.29.1, 9.31]

*… the belief **in** individuality **and** independence **had become** a sclerotic insistence **on** having his own way.*
We nearly always use the same preposition after nouns like *belief* and *insistence* as we do after the verbs they are related to: *believe/a belief **in**, insist/insistence **on***. [> LEG App 28] The past perfect emphasizes the idea of 'by that time'. [> LEG 9.29.2] We must use the *-ing* form (*having*) after the preposition *on*. [> LEG 16.53–54]

GRAMMAR POINTS

C Noun + preposition: 'belief in' [> LEG 8.20, 16.53, App 28–29, compare > LAG 60C]

believe

Many verbs, like *believe* and *insist*, are commonly followed by prepositions [> LAG 8D, 24C, 47E]:

   believe in, insist on.

Nouns formed from these verbs are nearly always followed by the same prepositions:

   belief in, insistence on.

1 His insistence on having his own way led to difficulties.
2 We want his approval of/for this important scheme.
3 You must congratulate her on her success in passing the exams.
4 I can't understand your objection to his/him staying with us.
5 It's a choice between this and that.
6 What's the difference between the two schemes?
7 Her failure in passing/to pass exams depresses her.
8 What's your knowledge of the facts in this case?
9 His confession to a whole series of crimes amazed everybody.
10 We require his resignation from this job.
11 We followed your advice against taking legal action.
12 His emergence from obscurity was sudden.

D Adjective + preposition: 'angry with' [> LEG 6.8.4, 8.19–20, 16.53, 16.60, App 27, LAG 1D, 9D]

clear to

Many adjectives are followed by prepositions. Sometimes different prepositions can follow the same adjective, though not always with the same meanings:

angry with someone, angry at/about something.

1 angry with me
2 ashamed of/at what he did
3 obliged to you
4 capable of anything
5 free of charge
6 bad at spelling
7 full of tourists
8 careless of danger
9 contrary to my advice
10 safe from danger
11 wrong about the election results
12 nervous of/about the new boss

13 aware of the cost of this
14 grateful to you
15 afraid of taking risks
16 absent from class
17 angry at/about the way she's behaved
18 married to Sue
19 satisfied with my work
20 busy with the baby
21 faithful to my principles
22 annoyed with me
23 anxious about/for you
24 fond of oysters
25 clever at solving problems
26 amazed at/by your behaviour
27 sorry about/for the trouble
28 late for work
29 keen on football
30 jealous of his sister
31 different from each other
32 careful of/with her money
33 kind to/about everybody
34 sad about it
35 careful of/about talking to strangers
36 separate from each other
37 good with his hands
38 good at carpentry
39 certain of your facts
40 ready for action

The healer

Hᴇᴀʟᴇʀs were initially suspicious of my 'clinic' until they had satisfied themselves that I limited myself to the treatment of infectious diseases with white
5 men's roots and was not in competition with them. One particular case raised certain moral and strategic difficulties. The Chief's brother, who lived several huts away, used to come and visit me quite often. He was a
10 gangling, awkward and affable man who had a reputation for being not too bright. I realized one day that he had not been to see me for several weeks and, on inquiring whether he was away, I was informed that he was dying. He had suffered a
15 severe bout of amoebic dysentery and the healer from up the cliff had been called. The examination of the entrails of a chicken had revealed that he was being afflicted by the spirit of his dead mother who wanted beer. This had been flung upon the skull but there was no improvement. Another
20 healer was called. He revealed that, in fact, the illness derived from another spirit masquerading as the spirit of the man's mother. Offerings were made but the young man still weakened. The Chief's third wife, who had looked after him as a boy, was very distressed and came and wailed
25 outside my hut asking if I had no roots that might save him. It was impossible to refuse, since I indeed had some powerful amoebicides and antibiotics. I explained to everyone that I was not a healer and that I did not know whether my roots might help but that if they wished me to
30 try to heal him I would do so. I had been afraid of alienating the healers by this but they were quite prepared to find that a wrong diagnosis had been made. The man's recovery was swift. He passed from a skeletal condition to good health in a matter of days and there was general rejoicing. The healers
35 were in no way put out. They merely explained that this was a complex case of a man ill with an infectious disease but that various spirits had taken advantage of it to increase his sufferings. They had dealt with the spirits; I had dealt with the disease.

The Innocent Anthropologist by Nigel Barley *(BrE)*

Sentence structure

A Three of these sentences are wrong. Correct what is wrong, where necessary, and say why you have done so. Then check against the text.

1 He was a gangling, awkward and affable man who had a reputation for be not too bright. (ll. 9–11)

2 I realized one day that he had not being to see me for several weeks and, on inquiring whether he was away, I was informed that he was dying. (ll. 11–14)

3 I explained everyone that I was not a healer and that I did not know whether my roots might help but that if they wished me to try to heal him I would do so. (ll. 27–30)

4 He passed from a skeletal condition to good health in a matter of days and there was general rejoicing. (ll. 33–34)

B Choose the words that fit and say why you have made your choice. Then check against the text.

1 Healers were initially suspicious of my 'clinic' ...... they had satisfied themselves that I limited myself to the treatment of infectious diseases with white men's roots. [*providing that/until*] (ll. 1–5)

2 I explained to everyone that I was not a healer and that I did not know ...... my roots might help but that if they wished me to try to heal him I would do so. [*that/whether*] (ll. 27–30)

Grammar points

C Supply the right form of the verbs in brackets, then refer to the text. (ll. 1–34)

Healers were initially suspicious of my 'clinic' until they had satisfied themselves that I
¹(*limit*) .... myself to the treatment of infectious diseases with white men's roots and
²(*not be*) .... in competition with them. One particular case ³(*raise*) ....
certain moral and strategic difficulties. The Chief's brother, who ⁴(*live*) .... several
huts away, used to come and visit me quite often. He ⁵(*be*) .... a gangling, awkward
and affable man who ⁶(*have*) .... a reputation for being not too bright. I ⁷(*realize*)
.... one day that he ⁸(*not be*) .... to see me for several weeks and, on
inquiring whether he was away, I ⁹(*inform*) .... that he ¹⁰(*die*) .... He
¹¹(*suffer*) .... a severe bout of amoebic dysentery and the healer from up the cliff
¹²(*call*) .... The examination of the entrails of a chicken ¹³(*reveal*) .... that
he ¹⁴(*afflict*) .... by the spirit of his dead mother who ¹⁵(*want*) .... beer. This
¹⁶(*fling*) .... upon the skull but there was no improvement. Another healer ¹⁷(*call*)
.... He ¹⁸(*reveal*) .... that, in fact, the illness ¹⁹(*derive*) .... from
another spirit masquerading as the spirit of the man's mother. Offerings ²⁰(*make*) ....
but the young man still weakened. The Chief's third wife, who ²¹(*look*) .... after him
as a boy, was very distressed and ²²(*come*) .... and ²³(*wail*) .... outside my hut
asking if I ²⁴(*have*) .... no roots that might save him. It was impossible to refuse, since I
indeed ²⁵(*have*) .... some powerful amoebicides and antibiotics. I ²⁶(*explain*)
.... to everyone that I ²⁷(*not be*) .... a healer and that I ²⁸(*not know*)
.... whether my roots might help but that if they ²⁹(*wish*) .... me to try to
heal him I would do so. I ³⁰(*be*) .... afraid of alienating the healers by this but they
were quite prepared to find that a wrong diagnosis ³¹(*make*) .... The man's recovery
³²(*be*) .... swift. He ³³(*pass*) .... from a skeletal condition to good health in a
matter of days and there was general rejoicing.

D What is the effect of *any* and *no* in these two sentences?

a *The Chief's third wife came ... asking if I had* **any** *roots that might save him.*
b *The Chief's third wife came ... asking if I had* **no** *roots that might save him.* (ll. 23–25)

Write questions using *no* and *no* compounds (*no one, nowhere*).

1 You want to know if there is a medicine that will cure a bad cough.
   Is there no medicine that will cure a bad cough?
2 You want to know if there is a place you can hide.

3 You want to know if there is a person who can advise you about tax.

4 You want to know if there is something that can be done to repair your radio.

E Complete this sentence using a suitable combination with *do*, then check against the text.
I explained that if they wished me to try to heal him I .... (ll. 27–30)

Complete these sentences using combinations with *do*.

1 If you want me to post these letters for you when I am out, *I'll do so.*
2 She asked me to write a letter on her behalf and later that day ....
3 Don't post all those invitations yet, will you? – I'm sorry, ...
4 I haven't had time to call them yet, but now it's quiet ....
5 Are you going to the party tomorrow? – I don't know. (*might*) ....
6 Did mother ring in my absence? – I don't know. (*might*) ....
7 I thought he was going to pay this bill on our behalf, but (*can't*) ....
8 If you wanted me to work late this evening, then ....

221

SENTENCE STRUCTURE

A Answers and commentary

Numbers **1**, **2** and **3** contain mistakes.

1 *He was a gangling, awkward and affable man who had a reputation **for being not too bright**.* (Not **for be**)
This is made up of three ideas joined by *who* and *for*:
1 *He was a gangling, awkward and affable man.*
2 *He was not too bright.*
3 *He had a reputation for it.*
We use the *-ing* form after a preposition:
    ... **for being not** *too bright*. [> LEG 16.51, LAG 1D, 6C]
Not could also come before *being* here [> LEG 16.40, LAG 26Bn.1]:
    *He had a reputation **for not being** too bright.*

2 *I realized one day that he had not **been** to see me for several weeks and, on inquiring whether he was away, I was informed that he was dying.* (Not **he had not being**)
... *he had not been* is the past perfect of the verb *be*. [> LEG 10.12–13]
We can use the participle form *being*:
– in present participle constructions [> LEG 1.58.3, 1.60, LAG 20D]:
    ***Being** anxious to please him, I bought him a nice present.*
– as a gerund [> LEG 16.40.2]:
    ***Being** lost can be a terrifying experience.*
– in the present and past progressive [> LEG 10.10–11, 12.3n.6, compare > LAG 10An.1]:
    *He's **being** silly/He **was being** interviewed.*
– after conjunctions like *on* and *after* [> LEG 1.62.2, 12.3n.8, compare LAG 1D, 3Bn.1, 4Bn.3, 57An.4]:
    *On **being** informed ....*

3 *I **explained to everyone** that I was not a healer and that I did not know whether my roots might help but that if they wished me to try to heal him I would do so.* (Not **I explained everyone**)
We use a direct object followed by *to* + noun/pronoun after *explain, introduce, say, suggest,* etc. [> LEG 1.12.1, LAG 11F and compare > LAG 13F]:
    *Gerald **explained the situation to me**.* (Not **explained me the situation**/*explained to me the situation**)

However, when the object is very long, we use *to* + noun/pronoun before e.g. a *that*-clause (as in the text):
    *I explained **to everyone** that I was not a healer ...*
rather than:
    I explained that I was not a healer to everyone.

4 This sentence is correct.

B Answers and commentary

1 *Healers were initially suspicious of my 'clinic' **until** they had satisfied themselves that I limited myself to the treatment of infectious diseases with white men's roots.*
Until (= at any time before and not later than) introduces an adverbial clause of time. [> LEG 1.45.1, LAG 1Bn.2, 6Bn.1]
Until is commonly used with the past perfect, as here (***until** they **had satisfied** themselves*) [> LEG 9.29.2] and with the future perfect (*I **won't have retired until** the year 2020*). [> LEG 9.43.1]
Until should not be confused with *by*. [> LEG 7.34]
Providing (that) means 'on the condition that' [> LEG 14.21]:
    *You can borrow my car **providing (that)** you return it by this evening.*

2 *I explained to everyone that I was not a healer and that I did not know **whether** my roots might help but that if they wished me to try to heal him I would do so.*
We use *whether* (or *if*) to report a Yes/No question, as in the text [> LEG 15.17–18, LAG 10E, 14B]:
    Are you good at maths?
    → *I don't know **whether** (or **if**)/I asked **whether** (or **if**) you are good at maths.*
We use *that* to report a statement [> LEG 15.12–13, LAG 4E, 14B]:
    I'm not very good at maths.
    → *I know **that**/I said **that** I'm not very good at maths*

GRAMMAR POINTS

C Past tenses in narration (including the passive)
[> LEG 9.31, 10.8–9, 10.12–13, 10.28, 10.30–33, 12.2–4, Apps 39–40, LAG 8E, 19C, 28C, 33B, 37C, 41B, 58D]

Note the combination of past tenses used here to tell a story, particularly the references to an earlier past by means of the past perfect tense.

1 limited
2 was not
3 raised
4 lived
5 was
6 had (Not *was having* [> LEG 10.30n.3])
7 realized
8 had not been [> LEG 10.13.5]
9 was informed
10 was dying
11 had suffered
12 had been called
13 had revealed
14 was being afflicted [> LEG 12.3n.6]
15 wanted
16 had been flung (*fling - flung - flung*)
17 was called
18 revealed
19 derived
20 were made
21 had looked
22 came
23 wailed
24 had
25 had
26 explained
27 was not
28 did not know
29 wished
30 had been
31 had been made
32 was
33 passed

D 'No' and 'no' compounds in questions: '. . . asking me if I had no roots' [> LEG 4.37–39, 5.10, 5.11, 13.9–10, LAG 14G, 25D, 49G]

a The question with *any* (*if I had any roots*) is an open question.
b The question with *no* (*if I had no roots*) is more emphatic. (= no roots of any description)

The elementary rule about *some* and *any* is that we use *some* in the affirmative, *any* in questions and negatives. We generally use *no* as an alternative to *not any* in statements. However, we can use *no* in questions for extra emphasis to replace *any*. This use makes a question more searching.

Possible answers
1 Is there no medicine that will cure a bad cough? (= of any description)
2 Is there nowhere/no place I can hide? (= a place of any description)
3 Is there no one who can advise me about tax? (= a person of any description)
4 Is there nothing that can be done to repair my radio? (= action of any description)

E The use of 'do so' to avoid repeating the previous verb: 'I did so' [> LEG 4.18, 10.44.2]
I would do so

We can use appropriate forms of *do* followed by *so* (and often by *it* or *that* when referring to a specific action) to avoid repeating the previous verb [compare > LAG 21F]:
Take the dog for a walk.
*- I've already **taken** him.*
*→ I've already **done so/done it**.*
Note how *do (so)* can combine with modals [> LEG 11.31]:
Will she go to the shops this morning?
*- She **might (do/do so)**.*
Has she gone to the shops this morning?
*- She **might have (done/done so)**.*
With modals, we can often omit *do* or *done*, as well as the original verb.

Possible answers
1 . . . I'll do so./I'll do that.
2 . . . I did so./I did it./I did.
3 . . . I've done so./I've done it.
4 . . . I'll do so.
5 I might do so./I might do./I might.
6 She might have done so./She might have done./She might have.
7 . . . he can't have done (so).
8 . . . I'd do so./I would do./I would./I'd do it.

Tax

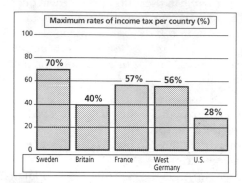

Maximum rates of income tax per country (%)

Sweden 70% · Britain 40% · France 57% · West Germany 56% · U.S. 28%

BRITAIN long ago surrendered its dubious pride of place as the heaviest taxer to Sweden. In 1976, Britons enjoyed the spectacle of Swedish
5 filmmaker Ingmar Bergman fleeing to their country in search of a tax haven! In comparisons among nations, Sweden holds the world record, claiming half of its gross domestic product in taxes.
10 Surprisingly, corporate tax burdens are light in socialist Sweden - even by U.S. standards. And many of the wealthy also escape heavy taxation. The reason: Sweden uses its tax code aggressively to
15 encourage government-approved investments (e.g., in steelmaking or shipbuilding) that promote economic stability. Perhaps because it never

experienced the sharp break with feudalism that most of
20 Western Europe did, Sweden is the ultimate 'nanny' state. Capital invested 'properly' is taxed lightly; investments not deemed to be socially useful (e.g., yachts, private estates, jewelry) are taxed at confiscatory rates. Likewise, while Sweden claims much of its citizens'
25 personal income, it gives much back. In the United States, many government benefits are means-tested; but 75 percent of all Swedes receive some sort of benefit - family allowances, tuition assistance, job training.

West Germany funds a large share of its social welfare
30 outlays, as it did in Bismarck's time, through regressive payroll taxes. Like Sweden, it uses tax incentives to lower certain burdens on the wealthy. Capital gains on stocks and bonds, subject to a tax of up to 33 percent in the United States, are exempt in West Germany - as well as
35 the Netherlands, Belgium, and Japan. (But the United States, virtually alone among Western nations, leaves gains from the sale of one's home, in most cases, untouched.)

In France, one of the most heavily taxed nations in
40 Europe, successive governments after World War II clung to the tradition of indirect taxation. France adopted a value added tax (VAT), a consumption tax on goods and services, in 1954, more than a decade before the rest of Europe. The French, like other people, have shaped the
45 tax system to reflect their culture. Wine is taxed at a lower rate than mineral water or Coca Cola; a tax on yachts, horses, limousines, and other 'signs of wealth' remains as a legacy of the Revolution.

The Wilson Quarterly (AmE)

Sentence structure **A** Sometimes a wrong word has been used or added. Delete the wrong word and suggest a replacement where necessary. Some lines need no change at all. Then refer to the text.

Britain long before surrendered its dubious pride of place as the heaviest	**1**
taxer to Sweden. In 1976, Britons enjoyed the spectacle of Swedish filmmaker	**2**
Ingmar Bergman to flee to their country in search of a tax haven! In comparisons	**3**
among nations, Sweden holds the world record, to claiming half of its gross	**4**
domestic product in taxes. Surprising, corporate tax burdens are light in socialist	**5**
Sweden – even by U.S. standards. And many of the wealthy also escape heavy	**6**
taxation. The reason: Sweden uses its tax code aggressively for encourage	**7**
government-approved investments (e.g., in steelmaking or shipbuilding)	**8**
that promote economic stability. Perhaps why it never experienced the sharp	**9**
break with feudalism that most of Western Europe has, Sweden is the ultimate	**10**
'nanny' state. Capital invested 'properly' is taxed lightly; investments	**11**
which not deemed to be socially useful (e.g., yachts, private estates,	**12**
jewelry) are taxed at confiscatory rates. Similar, while Sweden claims	**13**
much of its citizens' personal income, it gives much back. In the United	**14**
States, many government benefits are means-tested; but 75 percent of all	**15**
Swedes receiving some sort of benefit – family allowances, tuition assistance,	**16**
job training. West Germany funds a large share of its social welfare outlays,	**17**
as it does in Bismarck's time, through regressive payroll taxes. (ll. 1–31)	**18**

Grammar points

B Supply *a/an*, *the* or zero (–), then refer to the text.

[1]........ West Germany funds [2]........ large share of its social welfare outlays, as it did in Bismarck's time, through [3]........ regressive payroll taxes. Like [4]........ Sweden, it uses [5]........ tax incentives to lower certain burdens on [6]........ wealthy. [7]........ capital gains on [8]........ stocks and bonds, subject to [9]........ tax of up to 33 percent in [10]........ United States, are exempt in [11]........ West Germany – as well as [12]........ Netherlands, [13]........ Belgium, and [14]........ Japan. (But [15]........ United States, virtually alone among [16]........ Western nations, leaves gains from [17]........ sale of one's home, in most cases, untouched.) In [18]........ France, one of [19]........ most heavily taxed nations in [20]........ Europe, [21]........ successive governments after [22]........ World War II clung to [23]........ tradition of [24]........ indirect taxation. [25]........ France adopted [26]........ value added tax (VAT), [27]........ consumption tax on [28]........ goods and services, in 1954. (ll. 29–43)

C Put an X beside the sentences that are wrong here and say why they are wrong.

   a *He is a wealthy man.* ....
   b *He is wealthy.* ....
   c *He is a wealthy.* ....
   d *Tax the wealthies.* ....
   e *Tax the wealthy.* (l. 12, l. 32) ....

Write sentences using *the* + adjective (the group as a whole) in place of the phrases in brackets.

   1 (wealthy people)   *People often say the wealthy escape taxation.*
   2 (blind people) ....
   3 (unemployed people) ....
   4 (young people) ....
   5 (dead people) ....
   6 (handicapped people) ....
   7 (poor people) ....
   8 (elderly people) ....

D Identify the three forms in bold italics.

   a *Sweden uses **its** tax code aggressively.* (l. 14) ....
   b ***It's** subject to 33 per cent tax.* ....
   c ***It's** got a high value added tax.* ....

Cross out the wrong *its* or *it's*.

   1 You're welcome to my advice for what (its/it's) worth.
   2 (Its/It's) been known for years that sunspots affect the weather.
   3 The paintwork on my car is beginning to lose (its/it's) shine.
   4 (Its/It's) a wonder people put up with appalling governments.
   5 Inflation will come down, they say, once the government has got (its/it's) policies working.

E Identify the three forms in bold italics.

   a *I'll take only the **ones** I've paid for.* ....
   b *The US leaves gains from the sale of **one's** home.* (ll. 35–37) ....
   c *The large **one's** paid for.* ....

Cross out the wrong *ones* or *one's*.

   1 In such a situation one must rely on (ones/one's) common sense.
   2 (Ones/One's) first duty is to (ones/one's) family.
   3 One always wants the (ones/one's) who have worked hardest to succeed.
   4 This seat is free, but the next (ones/one's) reserved.
   5 Surely there's nothing more precious than (ones/one's) life.

SENTENCE STRUCTURE

A Answers and commentary

1 *ago*: The sense is: *Britain surrendered its dubious pride of place long ago*. We generally use time-phrase + *ago* (e.g. *three weeks ago*, meaning 'back from now') with past tenses. [> LEG 9.18] *Ago* normally comes at the end of a clause [> LEG 7.31] and often combines with *long*. [> LEG 13.40.5] *Ago* should not be confused with *before*, which commonly occurs with the present perfect [> LEG 9.25.1] or the past perfect. [> LEG 9.29.1]

2 This line is correct.

3 *fleeing*: The present participle construction is required here [> LEG 1.57, LAG 4Bn.3]:
　　*Ingmar Bergman **was fleeing** to their country. Britons enjoyed **the spectacle**.*
　　→ *Britons enjoyed **the spectacle of Ingmar Bergman fleeing** to their country.*

4 ~~to~~ *claiming*: *To* is not required here, though *in* would be possible. The present participle construction replaces an adverbial clause of reason (*as it claims*) to combine these ideas. [> LEG 1.58.3, LAG 2Bn.2]

5 *Surprisingly,*: *Surprising* is an adjective:
　　*What you say is **surprising**.* [> LEG 6.15, App 10] *Surprisingly* is a viewpoint adverb and expresses the writer's attitude to what she is about to tell us. Note how we can turn adjectives ending in *-ing* into viewpoint adverbs (*surprisingly, interestingly, amazingly,* etc.). We always use a comma after an *-ly* viewpoint adverb when it begins a sentence. [> LEG 7.57, App 17, LAG 11Ans.1–2, 44Bn.10, 52An.1c]

6 This line is correct.

7 *to encourage*: We can't use *for* + bare infinitive or **for to** to express purpose. We use the *to-*infinitive (*to, so as to, in order to*). [> LEG 16.12, LAG 7Bn.11, 10Bn.2, 31Bn.5] However, we can express purpose with *for* + *-ing* [> LEG 16.40.9, App 25.20], so here we could say:
　　*Sweden uses its tax code aggressively **for encouraging** government-approved investments.*

8 This line is correct.

9 *because*: *Because* and *why* are not interchangeable. *Why* questions may ask for a reason or reasons which can be supplied with *Because* [> LEG 13.37.1, LAG 56An.8]:
　　***Why** didn't you ~~tell~~ me about it?*
　　*– **Because** (Not *Why*) you didn't ask me.*

The use of *why* in place of the correct *because* is particularly misleading here because it might suggest 'the reason why' [> LEG 1.38.3, LAG 50E]:
　　*Perhaps (the reason) **why** it never experienced the sharp break with feudalism (**was because**) ...*

10 *did*: *Perhaps because it never **experienced** the sharp break with feudalism that most of Western Europe **did***.
We often use the verb *do* to avoid repeating a verb, but *do* is usually in the same tense as the original verb. In this example the past of *do* (*did*) is required to match *experienced*, not the present perfect, *has (done)*. [> LEG 4.18, 10.44.2, 11.31, 13.41–42, LAG **18** below, 34An.2, 53E, 57A]

11 This line is correct.

12 *investments ~~which~~ not deemed*: We either use the past participle construction, as in the text [> LEG 1.62.3], or a full relative [> LEG 1.26, 1.31]:
　　*...investments **which are** not deemed to be socially useful ...*.

13 *Likewise*: As in **5** above, a suitable adverb is required here. It would have been possible to use *Similarly*, but not the adjective *Similar* (*Those two cars are **similar***). [> LEG 7.57–58, Apps 17,18] The writer has used the connecting adverb *likewise* [> LEG App 18.5]; *-wise* (= in this way) is a suffix which is often used to form adverbs of manner. [> LEG 7.9]

14–15 These lines are correct.

16 *receive*: *Receiving* could be mistaken for a participle construction. In fact, what is required here is the simple present, *receive*, as it is essential to have a finite verb in this clause (beginning with *75 percent ...*). [> LEG 1.2, LAG 1A] The present progressive (*are receiving*) is also possible here. There is very little difference in meaning between the idea of 'the present period' (simple present) [> LEG 9.8.2] and 'current trends' (the present progressive). [> LEG 9.11.2] However, it is essential to have a finite verb in the sentence. [> LEG 1.2]

17 This line is correct.

18 *did*: *Does* might seem correct (to replace the simple present verb *funds*), but we need *did*, as the reference is to the past (*in Bismarck's time*), not to the present [> LAG note **10** above]:
　　*Germany **funds** a large share of its social welfare outlays. It **funded** a large share in Bismarck's time ...*
　　→ *Germany **funds** a large share of its social welfare outlays, as it **did in Bismarck's time** ...*

GRAMMAR POINTS

B Articles [> LEG Chapter 3, App 49, LAG 8C, 11C, 15C, 18C, 22B, 24D, 30C, 39B, 44C]

Cross references are given to LEG for selected items only.

1 (–) West Germany [> LEG 3.31 for all place names] **2** a large share **3** through (–) regressive payroll taxes [> LEG 3.26.1 for all plural countable nouns] **4** Like (–) Sweden **5** it uses (–) tax incentives **6** burdens on the wealthy [> LEG 6.12.2, App 9] **7** (–) Capital gains on **8** (–) stocks **9** subject to a tax **10** in the United States **11** in (–) West Germany **12** the Netherlands **13** (–) Belgium **14** (–) Japan **15** the United States **16** among (–) Western nations (*Western* is an adjective; *nations* a plural countable noun; *the Western nations* would also be possible) **17** the sale of [> LEG 3.20.2] **18** (–) France **19** the most heavily taxed nations [> LEG 6.28] **20** in (–) Europe **21** (–) successive governments **22** (–) World War II (proper noun [> LEG 2.13.1, 3.25]) (compare: *the Second World War* [> LEG 3.22]) **23** clung to the tradition **24** (–) indirect taxation **25** (–) France **26** a value added tax; (–) is also possible if we treat *value added tax* as a proper noun **27** a consumption tax. **28** on (–) goods [compare > LEG 2.32]

C 'The' + adjective: 'the wealthy' [> LEG 6.12.2, App 9]

c X *He is a wealthy*:
We use the indefinite article *a/an* with a countable noun or an adjective + countable noun (*a wealthy man*), not with an adjective on its own.

d X *Tax the wealthies*:
Wealthy is an adjective and has no plural. We can say *the wealthy* (+ plural verb) to refer to the group as a whole.

We can refer to a group as a whole with certain adjectives: *the rich, the poor, the unemployed*, etc. We cannot say *a rich*, *the riches*.

Sample answers
1 People often say the wealthy escape taxation.
2 People always give generously to good causes connected with the blind.
3 The unemployed depend on state support.
4 It is always the young that die in battle.
5 On November 11, I attended a memorial service for the dead of two World Wars.

6 Facilities for the handicapped should be available in all public buildings.
7 A caring society is one in which the poor are housed.
8 It is only proper that the elderly should enjoy low-cost rail travel.

D 'Its' (pronoun) and 'it's' (= it is, it has) [> LEG 4.1, 4.19–21, 10.6, 10.29, 10.30n.7]

a *its* (= possessive adjective (*its tax code*))
b *it's* (= *it is subject to* ...)
c *it's* (= *it has got a high* ...)
Even at advanced EFL levels (and constantly among native speakers) these forms are confused.

1 (its) ... for what it's worth (= it is)
2 (Its) It's been known for years ... (= It has)
3 (it's) ... beginning to lose its shine. (= possessive)
4 (Its) It's a wonder ... (= It is)
5 (it's) ... has got its policies working. (= possessive)

E 'Ones' (prop word), 'one's' (possessive adjective) and 'one's' (= one is/has) [> LEG 4.9–10, 4.19–20]

a *the ones I've paid for*: pronoun (prop word) used in place of a noun. [> LAG 55D, 58F]
b *the sale of one's home*: (= anyone's/everyone's); possessive adjective (like *my*, *your*, *his*, etc.).
c *the large one's paid for*: (= the large *one is* paid for). [> LEG 10.6]

We use *one/ones* as pronouns/prop words to replace nouns because we don't normally use an adjective on its own in place of a noun:
I want the big one. (Not *I want the big.*)

We use *one/one's* (= everyone('s)/anyone('s)) as indefinite pronouns only in very formal contexts, often in general statements.
One's (= one is/one has) is like *it's* (= it is, it has). Note the possessive forms *one's* (apostrophe) and *its* (no apostrophe).

1 (ones) ... rely on one's common sense
2 (Ones) ... (ones) One's first duty is to one's family.
3 (one's) ... the ones who have worked hardest ...
4 (ones) ... the next one's reserved (= one is)
5 (ones) ... than one's life.

The Marquess of Queensberry

ALFRED DOUGLAS is perhaps best understood in relation to his
5 father, John Sholto Douglas, ninth Marquess of Queensberry. The impression that
10 has been given of Queensberry is that he was a simple brute. In fact he was a complex one. Insofar as he was brutal, he practiced a rule-bound brutality. That was why at the age of twenty-four he had
15 changed the nature of boxing by persuading England and America to agree to the Queensberry rules, and also by securing adoption of weight differences, so that boxers might be evenly matched. He had channeled
20 together his belligerence and his litigiousness. He made himself known as a fulminator against Christianity, and was always raging publicly and indecorously against someone else's creed. He fancied himself as an aristocratic rebel, socially ostracized
25 because of his iconoclasm.

Besides being a good boxer and an excellent hunter, Queensberry was a poet of sorts. In the *Spirit Lamp* Douglas printed one of his father's poems, 'Lines Suggested by Fred Leslie's Death 3 Feb. 1893,' lines perhaps suggested also by a
30 poem of Christina Rossetti. 'When I am dead, cremate me,' was its resonant opening. In 1880 Queensberry published in pamphlet form his most ambitious poem, *The Spirit of the Matterhorn.* (His brother, Lord Francis Douglas, had died climbing that mountain.) In it he expressed certain views
35 which he thought might placate the Scottish nobility. The Scottish lords had just then voted not to re-elect him as one of their representatives to the British House of Lords (something he and his ancestors considered their due because of their ancient title), on the grounds that he had publicly denied the
40 existence of God. This rebuff wounded Queensberry deeply. He explained in a preface to his poem that he did not deny the existence of God, but preferred to call him the Inscrutable. His poem was mostly a versification of a theory that the soul is not distinct from the body, but is a result of the body itself.
45 Consequently, one must choose one's mate carefully so that the descent will be as eugenic as possible, since we reproduce not only our children's bodies but their souls. 'Go, tell mankind, see that thy blood be pure.' The Godfearing Scottish lords were not mollified.

Oscar Wilde by Richard Ellmann *(AmE)*

Sentence structure

A Circle the item that fits the space, then refer to the text.

Alfred Douglas is perhaps best understood in [1]........ to his father. The impression [2]........ has been given of Queensberry is [3]........ he was a simple brute. [4]........ he was a complex one. [5]........ as he was brutal, he practiced a rule-bound brutality. That was [6]........ at the age of twenty-four he had changed the nature of boxing by [7]........ England and America [8]........ to the Queensberry rules and [9]........ by securing adoption of weight differences [10]........ boxers might be evenly matched. (ll. 1–19)

1	a related	b relative	c relation
2	a –	b who	c that
3	a that	b because	c as
4	a The fact	b In fact	c In effect
5	a Insofar	b So far	c In that
6	a because	b why	c reason
7	a persuade	b persuading	c persuaded
8	a to agree	b agreeing	c agree
9	a too	b either	c also
10	a in order to	b for that	c so that

B Supply the connecting words, then check against the text.

[1]................ being a good boxer and an excellent hunter, Queensberry was a poet of sorts. [2]................ the *Spirit Lamp* Douglas printed one of his father's poems, 'Lines [3](*Suggest*)................ by Fred Leslie's Death 3 Feb. 1893,' lines perhaps [4](*suggest*)................ also by a poem of Christina Rossetti. 'When I [5](*be*)................ dead, cremate me,' was its resonant opening. [6]................ 1880 Queensberry published in pamphlet form his most ambitious poem, *The Spirit of the Matterhorn.* (His brother, Lord Francis Douglas, [7](*die*)................ [8](*climb*)................ that mountain.) In it he expressed certain views [9]................ he thought might placate the Scottish nobility. The Scottish lords had just then voted [10](*not re-elect*)................ him as one of their representatives. (ll. 26–37)

Grammar points

C Supply the missing prepositions, then refer to the text. (ll. 1–25)

Alfred Douglas is perhaps best understood [1]........ relation [2]........ his father, John Sholto Douglas, ninth Marquess of Queensberry. The impression that has been given [3]........ Queensberry is that he was a simple brute. In fact he was a complex one. Insofar as he was brutal, he practiced a rule-bound brutality. That was why [4]........ the age [5]........ twenty-four he had changed the nature [6]........ boxing [7]........ persuading England and America to agree [8]........ the Queensberry rules, and also [9]........ securing adoption [10]........ weight differences, so that boxers might be evenly matched. He had channeled together his belligerence and his litigiousness. He made himself known [11]........ a fulminator [12]........ Christianity, and was always raging publicly and indecorously [13]........ someone else's creed. He fancied himself [14]........ an aristocratic rebel, socially ostracized [15]........ .... his iconoclasm.

D What is the function of *one* in this sentence?
*Many people think that Queensberry was a simple brute. In fact he was a complex **one**.*
(ll. 8–12)

....

Respond appropriately with sentences using *one* or *ones*.

1 What happened after the company secretary resigned? – *A new one was appointed.*
2 I'd like to have a word with your daughter. ....
3 Do you know our neighbours? ....
4 I love teaching children. ....
5 I've met that man somewhere. ....
6 Who's that woman over there? ....
7 Two postmen deliver letters here, don't they? ....
8 Which secretary typed this letter? ....

E Supply *-ly* adverbs here. What do you notice?

a *The problem is (basic)* .... *simple.*
b *He was always raging (public)* .... *and indecorously ...* (ll. 22–23)

....

Supply *-ly* adverbs.

1 She listened to my story (*sympathetic*) *sympathetically*
2 This strike is (*political*) .... motivated.
3 What you're suggesting should be (*logical*) .... possible.
4 I don't think such a sentence is possible (*grammatical*) ....
5 They all set to work (*energetic*) ....
6 Sometimes we tend to think of the past (*nostalgic*) ....
7 He was (*public*) .... humiliated.
8 I'm afraid I was never (*musical*) .... educated.

F What is the effect of *of sorts* here? Suggest another way we could express this with *sort*.
*Queensberry was a poet **of sorts**.* (l. 27)

....

Rewrite these statements using either *a sort of* or *of sorts*.

1 He an artist.   *He's a sort of artist/an artist of sorts.*
2 It's a sculpture. ....
3 She's a healer. ....
4 It's a fricassee. ....
5 It's employment. ....
6 It's a melodrama. ....

SENTENCE STRUCTURE

A Answers and commentary

1 c *relation*: Prepositions may be single words (e.g. *across*); two words (*according to* [> LAG 2E]) or three words (*in relation to*). [For other examples > LEG App 20.3.]

2 c *that*: relative pronoun subject of a relative clause [> LEG 1.31, LAG 2An.2]:
> *This is the impression. **It** has been given ...*
> → *This is the impression **that/which** has been given ...*

3 a *that*: conjunction introducing a noun clause complement to *is* (*that he was a simple brute*). [compare > LEG 1.23, LAG 4E, 5An.5, 14B]

4 b *In fact*: This is a connecting adverb which makes a point of fact. [> LEG 7.58, App 18] Alternatively, *The fact is (that)* would have been possible. We use *in effect* when commenting on the outcome of a situation or event. [> LEG App 18.10]

5 a *Insofar as* or *In so far as*: introduces a 'limiting clause' (*Insofar as he was brutal*), which qualifies the main clause (*he practiced a rule-bound brutality*). This conjunction is used in formal style. [> LEG 1.54, LAG 35An.1c]

6 b *why*: *(the reason) why* introduces a relative clause of reason: *why ... he had changed the nature of boxing*. [> LEG 1.38.3]

7 b *persuading*: The *-ing* form of a verb follows a preposition (*by*). *By + -ing* answers the question *How?* and refers to method. [> LEG 13.40.4, 16.51, App 25.17, LAG 1D, 17Bn.5, 20Bn.1, 29An.3]

8 a *to agree*: The verb *persuade* is followed by an object + a *to*-infinitive (*persuade **someone to do** something*). [> LEG 16.21, LAG 38E]

9 c *also*: *Too* is usually interchangeable with *also*, but it is inappropriate here. *Either* (= also) is used only in negative sentences. [> LEG 7.56, LAG 49C]

10 c *so that*: introduces an adverbial clause of purpose. It can be replaced by *in order that*. *Might* often follows *so that/in order that* as it does here. [> LEG 1.51, LAG 10Bn.2] *In order to* is a variation of the *to*-infinitive, also used to express purpose: *(in order) to match boxers evenly*. [> LEG 16.12]

B Answers and commentary

1 *Besides* (= in addition to): It should not be confused with *beside*, which means 'next to' (*Come and sit **beside** me.*). [> LEG App 25.12, LAG 21E]

2 *In*: *In* refers to space, and has the sense of 'enclosed within' something, here, a publication. [> LEG 8.6, LAG 12B] The phrase *In the Spirit Lamp* introduces an illustration for the statement that Queensberry was 'a poet of sorts'.

3 *Suggested*: The past participle construction is used in place of a relative clause [> LEG 1.62.3, LAG 6Bn.4]:
> *'Lines (which have been) suggested by Fred Leslie's death'.*

4 *suggested*: Exactly as in **3** above.

5 *am*: We use the simple present tense to refer to the future after temporal conjunctions like *when, after, as soon as*, etc. (Not **When I will be dead**) [> LEG 1.45.2, LAG 6Bn.1]

6 *In*: + year (*1880*) refers to time [> LEG 8.13, LAG 4C] and naturally connects to the preceding remarks on Queensberry's activities as a poet.

7 *had died*: Though the simple past (*died*) would be possible here, the past perfect strongly reinforces the reference to 'an earlier past', that is to the idea that Lord Francis Douglas was already dead when *The Spirit of the Matterhorn* was published. [> LEG 9.28–31, LAG 18Bn.1, 26Ans.3–4, 27Bn.3, 37Bn.3, 52B]

8 *climbing*: The present participle construction is used here in place of an adverbial clause of time [> LEG 1.58.2, LAG 4Bn.3]:
> *His brother, Lord Francis Douglas, had died **(while he was) climbing** that mountain.*

9 *which* (or *that*): relative pronoun subject of a defining relative clause [> LEG 1.31, LAG 5An.3]:
> *In it he expressed **certain views**. He thought **they** might placate the Scottish nobility.*
> → *In it he expressed **certain views which/ that** he thought might placate the Scottish nobility.*

10 *not to re-elect*: We put *not* before *to* to form the negative of the *to*-infinitive [> LEG 15.24.1, 16.14, LAG 38E]:
> *They voted **to re-elect** him.*
> → *They voted **not to re-elect** him.*

GRAMMAR POINTS

C Prepositions [> LEG Chapter 8, Apps 20, 25–30, LAG 12B, 31C, 32C, 46B]

1/2 *in relation to* his father: *in relation to* is a three-word preposition. [compare > LEG App 20.3]

3 *of* Queensberry: noun (*impression*) + preposition (*of*). [compare > LEG Apps 28–29]

4/5 *at the age of* (twenty-four): time phrase with *at*. [> LEG 8.11, LAG 4C]

6 *of* boxing: genitive. [compare > LEG 2.50]

7 *by* persuading: *by* + *-ing* to express method. [> LEG 13.40.4, 16.51, App 25.17, LAG 17Bn.5]

8 *agree to* (something): verb + preposition. [> LEG App 28, LAG 8D]

9 *by* securing: as for **7** above.

10 adoption *of*: genitive. [compare > LEG 2.50]

11 *as* a fulminator: (= in the capacity of [> LEG App 25.25, LAG 12Bn.18])

12 *against* Chrisitianity: compare *to fulminate against/at something*. [compare > LEG App 25.7]

13 *against* someone else's creed: as for **12** above.

14 fancied himself *as* an aristocractic rebel: as for **11** above.

15 *because of* his iconoclasm: (= as a result of [> LEG App 25.9, 25.19])

D 'One/ones' as prop words referring to people: 'He wasn't a simple brute. He was a complex one.'
[> LEG 4.10, and compare > LAG 18C, 54E, 58F]

We use *one* to avoid repeating the noun:
People think Queensberry was a simple brute. In fact he was a complex brute/one.

We can avoid repeating a noun by using *one/ones*. In fact they are often grammatically necessary because we cannot normally use an article + adjective without a following noun:
He was a complex one. (Not *He was a complex.*)
We often use *one/ones* in connexion with things:
Which one/ones do you want? – The red one/ones.
But we can use them just as easily to refer to people.

Possible answers
1 A new one was appointed.
2 Which one? My younger one or my older one?
3 The ones next door, or the ones opposite?

4 You mean you love teaching clever ones.
5 Is he the one we met at a cocktail party recently?
6 Which one? The tall one in the blue dress?
7 Yes, a young one and an old one.
8 I don't know which one.

E Adverbs ending in '-ally': 'basically' [> LEG 7.8n.4]

a *The problem is **basically** simple.*
b *He was always raging **publicly** and indecorously…*
Basically is spelt *-ally*; *publicly* is spelt *-ly*.

With the exception of *public/publicly*, all adjectives ending in *-ic* or *-ical* form adverbs ending in *-ically*:
comic/comically, tragic/tragically, fanatical/fanatically, geographical/geographically.

1 sympathetically
2 politically
3 logically
4 grammatically
5 energetically
6 nostalgically
7 publicly
8 musically

F 'A sort of'/'of sorts': 'a sort of poet/a poet of sorts' [> LEG 2.18.2, 3.9.3, 13.34.7, App 7.17, compare > LAG 49E]

Of sorts is uncomplimentary, suggesting he wasn't a very good poet.
Queensberry was a sort of poet.

We often use *a sort of* and *a kind of* to classify something precisely:
It's a sort of/a kind of beetle.
We can also use them with reference to people and things which we find hard to describe:
He's a sort of engineer./It's a sort of cake.
(= That's the nearest I can get to a description.)
This second use can also be uncomplimentary:
He's a sort of poet/a poet of sorts. (= He is no poet at all.)

1 He's a sort of artist/an artist of sorts.
2 It's a sort of sculpture/a sculpture of sorts.
3 She's a sort of healer/a healer of sorts.
4 It's a sort of fricassee/a fricassee of sorts.
5 It's a sort of employment/employment of sorts.
6 It's a sort of melodrama/a melodrama of sorts.

The center of our galaxy

On a clear, moonless night the shimmering light of the Milky Way glows especially bright toward the constellation Sagittarius. For years astronomers have been aware, from the distribution of groups of stars and from measurements of stellar motions, that objects in our galaxy must travel in orbits around a center located in that direction. Astronomers also have found that in most cases other galaxies are especially bright toward the center because the density of stars increases markedly there. In many instances the central regions also seem to be the sites of intriguing behavior, including the generation of enormous quantities of energy, peculiar radiations and other unusual effects. More and more, it seems that massive, unimaginably dense objects - black holes - lie at the heart of some of these galaxies. Could our own galaxy also harbor such an exotic object at its center?

The central region of the Milky Way has fascinated astronomers for many decades. After all, our galactic center is only about 25,000 light-years away as opposed to millions of light-years for centers of the nearest other galaxies, and so it is the one astronomers might reasonably hope to see and to understand best. Yet for a long time there was no direct way to see the center of our galaxy or to learn much about it, because it is cloaked in large and dense clouds of gas and dust.

Recent discoveries and new technologies have made it possible at last to study the center of our own galaxy in some detail. These developments include improved techniques for collecting and analyzing astronomical radio waves and infrared radiation as well as space flights above the earth's atmosphere, which have made possible the detecting of energetic X-ray and gamma-ray radiation emanating from the center of the galaxy.

All these types of waves - radio, infrared, X-ray and gamma-ray - are similar to visible light in that they are all forms of electromagnetic radiation and differ only in their wavelengths and energy levels. Unlike light, however, they can penetrate interstellar clouds of dust with some ease and hence provide a window into the structure and dynamics of the galactic center.

from 'What is Happening at the Center of Our Galaxy?' by Charles H Townes & Reinhard Genzel, © 1990 by Scientific American, Inc. All rights reserved. (AmE)

Sentence structure

A Eight of these connecting words and phrases will fit into the spaces below. Make your choices, then refer to the text.

after all	for years	hence	which
as a result	meanwhile	more and more	however
and so	also	yet	in many instances
similar to	at last	because	unlike

On a clear, moonless night the shimmering light of the Milky Way glows especially bright toward the constellation Sagittarius. [1]................. astronomers have been aware, from the distribution of groups of stars and from measurements of stellar motions, that objects in our galaxy must travel in orbits around a center located in that direction. Astronomers [2]................. have found that in most cases other galaxies are especially bright toward the center because the density of stars increases markedly there. [3]................. the central regions also seem to be the sites of intriguing behavior, including the generation of enormous quantities of energy, peculiar radiations and other unusual effects. [4]................., it seems that massive, unimaginably dense objects – black holes – lie at the heart of some of these galaxies. Could our own galaxy also harbor such an exotic object at its center?

The central region of the Milky Way has fascinated astronomers for many decades. [5]................., our galactic center is only about 25,000 light-years away as opposed to millions of light years for centers of the nearest other galaxies, [6]................. it is the one astronomers might reasonably hope to see and to understand best. [7]................. for a long time there was no direct way to see the center of our galaxy or to learn much about it, [8]................. it is cloaked in large and dense clouds of gas and dust. (ll. 1–41)

Grammar points

B Which two forms of *bright* can we use here? Why?
The light of the Milky Way glows especially .... *toward Sagittarius.* (ll. 1–4)

Where possible, supply two forms in these sentences.

1 On a clear moonless evening, the stars shine very (bright) *bright/brightly*
2 Teachers like students who answer questions (bright) ....
3 We bought our last car (dear) .... and sold it (cheap) ....
4 We had our car repaired quite (cheap) ....
5 The train always goes very (slow) .... along this part of the track.
6 I took a mouthful and chewed it (slow) ....
7 Please cut the next slice (thin) ....
8 I wish you wouldn't play that awful music so (loud) ....
9 I suddenly heard someone shouting (loud) .... for help.
10 For weeks, two detectives watched the house (close) ....
11 We came very (close) .... to an accident that time!
12 It was cut (clean) .... in two.
13 The sale of the house was completed very (clean) .... in about four days.
14 Thank you for explaining the situation so (clear) ....
15 The outline of the castle could be seen (clear) .... against the sky.

C Comment on the use of *have been* here.
For years astronomers **have been** *aware that objects in our galaxy must travel in orbits.* (ll. 4–9)

Supply suitable forms of *have been*.

1 You don't have to rub it in. I know I (a real fool) *have been a real fool.*
2 What's the matter with Moira? She (gloomy) .... for days.
3 We (terribly extravagant) .... and booked a holiday to the Seychelles.
4 I don't know what's the matter with me. I (so tired) .... lately.
5 The children (very quiet) .... We'd better go and see what they're getting up to.
6 That brother of yours (so annoying) ....
7 The little boy (missing) .... for a fortnight now.
8 I'm not surprised you're feeling sick. You (very greedy) ....
9 'You (a brave boy) .... , Jimmy,' the dentist said.

D Rewrite this sentence in the active, then check against the text. (ll. 42–43)
It has been made possible by recent discoveries and new technologies.
Recent discoveries and new technologies ....

Rewrite these sentences in the active.

1 It was made plain to us that we had little choice.
   They *made it plain to us that we had little choice.*
2 I'm driven crazy by loud music.
   Loud music ....
3 The door was held open.
   He ....
4 The room was kept cool by an electric fan.
   An electric fan ....
5 It was found difficult to explain how the accident had happened.
   They ....
6 Your plate has been wiped clean.
   You ....

SENTENCE STRUCTURE

A Answers and commentary

The general reference for viewpoint adverbs and connecting words and phrases is: [> LEG 7.57–58, Apps 17–18].

The following words or phrases fit into the spaces:

1 For years (ll. 4–5)
For years astronomers have been aware . . . .
This phrase immediately contrasts the eternity (in human terms) of the Milky Way and the short time-scale of astronomers. We often use *for* to express duration: *for days, for months*, etc. [> LEG App 25.20]
The phrase *more and more* could fit in here as well.

2 also (l. 11)
*Astronomers **also** have found that in most cases other galaxies are especially bright* . . .
The repetition of *astronomers* and the use of *also* continue the thread of the argument begun in the previous sentence. The normal position of *also* would be after the auxiliary (*have*). Compare the normal position of *also* in the next sentence in the text, immediately before the main verb [> LEG 7.56, LAG 45A*n*.5]:
*In many instances the central regions **also** seem to be* . . . .
Changing the position to before the auxiliary gives *also* a special emphasis. [> LEG 7.40.6]

3 In many instances (ll. 15–16)
In many instances the central regions also seem to be . . .
This phrase expands the point made in the previous sentence, namely that *galaxies are especially bright toward the center*. Other possible phrases that could fit here are: *In a number of cases, Very often, More and More*. *Also* would not be appropriate here, as it doesn't sound right at the beginning of a sentence in formal style. [> LEG 7.56]

4 More and more (l. 21)
More and more, it seems that massive, unimaginably dense objects . . .
The phrase emphasizes the conclusion to be drawn from the evidence in the preceding paragraph and prepares the reader for the final sentence, which asks the question whether our own galaxy might be like others. Another word that could fit in here is: *increasingly. Hence* and *As a result* wouldn't be right here because they say what the result is of the previous statement, instead of exemplifying it, like *more and more*.

5 After all (l. 29)
After all, our galactic center is only about 25,000 light-years away . . .
We often use *after all* at the beginning of a sentence to introduce an explanation or justification relating to what has just been said (in this case e.g. 'It's not surprising (they're fascinated by it) because it's much easier to study than more distant galaxies').
When we use *after all* at the end of a sentence, we are saying that one thing has or hasn't happened in spite of something else:
*We thought the flat was going to be expensive, but we didn't have to pay too much for it **after all***.

6 and so (l. 33)
*. . . **and so** it is the one astronomers might reasonably hope to see and to understand best. And* connects; *so* points to a result or conclusion. [> LEG 1.17–20] The adverb *hence* (after a semicolon, colon or a dash) would also fit here.

7 Yet (l. 36)
Yet for a long time there was no direct way to see the center of our galaxy or to learn much about it, . . .
Yet immediately draws a contrast and prepares us for the argument that there now might be a way of seeing *the center of our galaxy*. We need *Yet* here, not *Because*, to follow the fact that *our galactic centre* makes us part of the *Milky Way*. [> LEG 1.17–20, LAG 3A*n*.1] *However* would also fit here. [> LEG 7.58]

8 because (l. 39)
*. . . **because** it is cloaked in large and dense clouds of gas and dust.*
Because introduces the reason for the statement made in the first half of the sentence and introduces an adverbial clause of reason. We often use *because* in the second half of a statement to emphasize a reason which is probably not known to the reader or listener. [> LEG 1.48.2, LAG 1B*n*.2, 54A*n*.9]

GRAMMAR POINTS

B Adverbs with two forms often used in the same way: 'it glows bright/brightly' [> LEG 7.14, App 15.1, compare > LAG 39F]

*... glows especially **bright/brightly** toward Sagittarius.*
Some adverbs have two forms which can be used in the same way.

A word like *bright* is an adjective in:
*There was a **bright light** overhead.* [compare > LEG App 14]
Bright and *brightly* can be used interchangeably as adverbs:
*The light glowed **bright/brightly**.*
However, it is not usually made clear that the two forms are not always interchangeable.
We have to use the *-ly* form when it is an adverb of manner with a dynamic verb saying how something is/was done:
*He answered my question **brightly**.* (Not **bright**)
We often use the same form as the adjective:
– when we can replace the verb with *be* or *become* without really changing the meaning:
*The moon **shone**/(was) **bright**.*
– after verb + object combinations where the adjective form could be regarded as describing the state of the object:
*We **bought** it. It **was cheap**.*
*→ We **bought** it **cheap**.*
However, many native speakers say:
*We **bought** it **cheaply**.*
*The moon **shone brightly**.*
because they think the *-ly* form sounds 'more correct', even though it can sometimes be quite wrong.

1 shine bright/brightly
2 answer brightly
3 bought the car dear/dearly ... sold it cheap/cheaply
4 had our car repaired cheaply
5 goes slow/slowly
6 chewed it slowly
7 cut the next slice thin/thinly
8 play music so loud/loudly
9 shouting loudly
10 watched the house closely
11 came very close (came = *were*)
12 cut clean/cleanly
13 completed very cleanly
14 explaining the situation so clearly
15 could be seen clear/clearly

C 'Have been' + noun or adjective: 'have been aware' [> LEG 10.13.1, 10.13.3, App 41, compare > LAG 25C and 8E, 19C, 33B]

Have been is the present perfect of *be*. It combines with an adjective here (*aware*).

Many European languages use *is* (present) or *was* (past) where English uses *have been*. *Have been* is a normal present perfect form [> LEG 9.22–27] which combines with a limited range of adjectives (*have been aware*) and nouns (*have been a fool*).

1 I have been a real fool.
2 She has been gloomy for days.
3 We have been terribly extravagant ...
4 I have been so tired lately.
5 The children have been very quiet.
6 That brother of yours has been so annoying.
7 The little boy has been missing ...
8 You have been very greedy.
9 You have been a brave boy ...

D Verb + object + adjective/noun: 'made it possible' [> LEG 1.14]

*Recent discoveries and new technologies **have made it possible**.*

There are many combinations like *make it possible*: e.g. *drive me crazy, get it clean, find it difficult, hold it still, keep it cool, leave it open, like it hot, make it plain, open it wide*, etc.

1 They made it plain to us that we had little choice.
2 Loud music drives me crazy.
3 He held the door open.
4 An electric fan kept the room cool.
5 They found it difficult to explain how the accident had happened.
6 You have wiped your plate clean.

Mrs Radcliffe

MRS RADCLIFFE walked to the station with a springy tread. It was a radiant morning. The air was balmy, the sun was shining and a procession of large white
5 clouds was advancing across the sky. They looked beautiful, she thought, so majestic, so removed from the pettiness, the insignificant sorrows and joys of human existence. Mrs Radcliffe often derived great
10 pleasure from the changing sky. Times out of number she had sat at her window just gazing up into that vast infinity and allowing her thoughts to wander whither they would, occasionally chiding herself humorously
15 for the extravagant fancies that took shape in her mind. How fortunate to be blessed with imagination, to possess that inestimable gift of being able to distinguish beauty in the ordinary. Many of her acquaintances, she knew for a fact, hardly glanced at the sky from one year's end to the other
20 unless to see if it was going to rain. She remembered once saying to Cecil, Marjorie's husband, who after all was supposed to be a painter, when they were standing in the garden one summer evening before dinner, that sunset and sunrise were God's loveliest gifts to mortals if only they
25 were not too blind to be able to appreciate them. Cecil had laughed, that irritating, cynical laugh of his, and replied that many thousands of people would appreciate them more if they were edible. She recalled how annoyed she had been, she could have bitten her tongue out for betraying a
30 fragment of her own private self to someone who was obviously incapable of understanding it. On looking back, she realized that that was the first moment that she really knew that she disliked Cecil. Of course, she had never let Marjorie suspect it for an instant, and never would. What
35 was done, was done, but still it was no use pretending. 'Know thyself,' was one of the cornerstones of her philosophy. Poor Marjorie. Poor wilful, disillusioned Marjorie. That Marjorie was thoroughly disillusioned by now, Mrs Radcliffe hadn't the faintest doubt. Nobody could
40 be married for seven years to a man like Cecil with his so-called artistic temperament, his casualness about money, her money, and his complete inability to earn any for himself, without being disillusioned. Mrs Radcliffe sighed as she turned into Station Road. What a tragedy!

Mrs Radcliffe by Noël Coward *(BrE)*

Sentence structure

A Five of the words or phrases below can be used in place of words or phrases in the text. Underline the words or phrases in the text that could be replaced.

She couldn't remember how many times
that she was
barely

When she looked
and never did
and not be

Now say why the remaining phrase is wrong.

....
....
....
....

B Rewrite these sentences as one sentence, then check against the text.

Cecil was Marjorie's husband. He after all was supposed to be a painter. They were standing in the garden one summer evening before dinner. Sunset and sunrise were God's loveliest gifts to mortals. If only they were not too blind to be able to appreciate them. She remembered once saying this to Cecil. (ll. 20–25)
She remembered once saying to Cecil, ...
....
....

Grammar points

C Identify the two forms in bold italics.

   a *How fortunate **to be blessed** with imagination.* (ll. 15–16) ....

   b *How fortunate **to have been blessed** with imagination.* ....

Rewrite these sentences.

   1 I am fortunate. You give me so much help.   *I am fortunate to be given so much help.*

   2 I am fortunate. You gave me so much help.   *I am fortunate to have been given so much help.*

   3 I am lucky. You taught me a foreign language. ....

   4 She was annoyed. You interrupted her. ....

   5 He was proud. You trust him. ....

   6 John is ashamed. They found out about him. ....

   7 We are pleased. They employ us. ....

D What's the difference in meaning between these two sentences?

   a *She **remembered saying** to Cecil that sunset and sunrise were God's loveliest gifts.* (ll. 20–24)

   b *She **remembered to say** to Cecil that he shouldn't take everything for granted.*

Rewrite these sentences with *remember*.

   1 I didn't forget to post your letters.   *I remembered to post your letters.*

   2 I met him years ago.   *I remember meeting him years ago.*

   3 You mustn't forget to give him my message. ....

   4 They had one of the first television sets. ....

   5 I took that photograph on your birthday. ....

   6 I won't forget to lock the door next time. ....

   7 I was given a prize for sewing at school. ....

E Complete this sentence with *him* or *his*, then check against the text.
Cecil had laughed, that irritating, cynical laugh of .... (ll. 25–26)

Rewrite these sentences using an *of*-construction to express the possessive. Make any necessary changes.

   1 John is my friend.   *John is a friend of mine.*

   2 I'm really getting fed up with your brother. ....

   3 We're putting on one of Ayckbourn's plays. ....

   4 I can't stand his motorbike. ....

   5 It's her relations that are really the problem. ....

   6 He recited one of Keats' poems. ....

   7 It's their house that is so expensive to run. ....

F Describe two different uses of *let* in these two sentences.

   a ***Let's** ask Marjorie.*

   b *Of course, she had never **let** Marjorie suspect it for an instant, and never would.* (ll. 33–34)

Rewrite these sentences with suitable forms of *allow* to replace *let*, only where possible.

   1 They'll never let him forget his debt.   *They'll never allow him to forget his debt.*

   2 Letting you use my car was a real mistake. ....

   3 Don't let's argue about it. ....

   4 Let's take a taxi, shall we? ....

   5 You can't let people camp wherever they like. ....

   6 She was cross because I'd let the dog out. ....

   7 They didn't let us pay. ....

SENTENCE STRUCTURE

A Answers and commentary

The following words or phrases should be underlined:

1 Times out of number (ll. 10–11)
(→ *She couldn't remember how many times*)
Times out of number *she had sat at her window*/**She couldn't remember how many times** *she had sat at her window* ...
Times out of number and *time out of mind* are idiomatic 'frequency' expressions which suggest that we have lost count of the number of times something has happened.

2 (How fortunate) to be (blessed) (l. 16)
(→ *that she was*)
How fortunate **to be** *blessed with imagination*/*How fortunate* **that she was** *blessed with imagination* ...
We can use an adjective + *to*-infinitive in exclamations. These often begin with a negative or *How* [> LEG 16.27.3]:
  Wasn't she fortunate *to be blessed* ... !
  → **How fortunate** *(she was) to be blessed* ...!
The adjective *fortunate* can be followed by a *to*-infinitive:
  She was fortunate **to be** *blessed* ...
or a *that*-clause:
  She was fortunate **that she was blessed** ... .
[> LEG 1.23–24, 11.75.3, 15.6, 16.27–28, App 44, LAG 57C]

3 hardly (l. 19)
(→ *barely*)
Many of her acquaintances, she knew for a fact, **hardly** *glanced*/**barely** *glanced at the sky* ...
Hardly and *barely* are interchangeable as adverbs of frequency, as here [> LEG 7.39] and adverbs of degree. [> LEG 7.41] They are sometimes called 'negative adverbs' because they can be replaced by *almost never* [> LEG 13.8]:
  We **hardly**/**barely** *ever see them these days.*
  → *We* **almost never see** *them these days.*

4 On looking (l. 31)
(→ *When she looked*)
On looking *back, she realized* ... /**When she looked** *back, she realized* ...
When introduces an adverbial clause of time.
[> LEG 1.45.1] We can sometimes use *on* (= when) as a conjunction followed by the *-ing* form, as in the text. [> LEG 1.58.2, 12.3n.8, LAG 1D]

5 without being (l. 43)
(→ *and not be*)
Nobody could be married to ... Cecil ... **without being**/**and not be** *disillusioned* ...
The preposition *without* may be followed by the *-ing* form of the verb (Not *to*). [> LEG 1.60, 16.51]; ... *not be* follows *could*, not *without*.

Remaining answer
and never did does not replace *and never would* (l. 34). The sense is: *She had never let Marjorie suspect it for an instant* (i.e. in the past) *and never would* (i.e. in the future). *And never did* would fit into a sentence like this:
  She said she'd never speak to him again **and never did**.
We can use auxiliary verbs to avoid repeating the main verb. [> LEG 4.18, 10.4n.3, 11.31, 11.45, 13.28–29, 13.41, LAG 34An.2, 53E]

B Answer and commentary

She remembered once saying to Cecil, **Marjorie's husband**, ...
Marjorie's husband is in apposition to *Cecil*. The phrase provides us with more information about *Cecil*, while avoiding the use of a relative clause (*who was Marjorie's husband*). [> LEG 1.39]

... **who** *after all was supposed to be a painter,* ...
Who is the subject relative pronoun introducing a relative clause (non-defining) [> LEG 1.26, 1.29, LAG 5Ans.1–2, 16An.1]:
  This is **Cecil**. **He** *is supposed to be a painter.*
  This is **Cecil, who** *is supposed to be a painter.*

... **when** *they were standing in the garden one summer evening before dinner,* ...
When introduces an adverbial clause of time.
[> LEG 1.45.1, LAG 6Bn.1]

... **that** *sunset and sunrise were God's loveliest gifts to mortals* ...
That introduces a noun clause object of the reporting verb *saying*. [> LEG 1.23.2, App 45]

... *if only they were not too blind to be able to appreciate them.*
If only both suggests a wish here [> LEG 11.41–42] and introduces a condition. [> LEG 14.15, 14.21]

GRAMMAR POINTS

C Passive infinitive forms: 'to be given/to have been given' [> LEG 12.2n.3, 16.2]

a *to be blessed*: present passive infinitive form.

b *to have been blessed*: perfect or past passive infinitive form.

We can use a *to*-infinitive after some verbs [> LEG 16.19–25, LAG 1E] and after some adjectives. [> LEG 16.26–32, LAG 7Bn.4, 30E] Whether we use the present or past/perfect form (active or passive) depends on the context:

*How fortunate **to be blessed** with imagination.* (now)
*How fortunate **to have been blessed** with imagination.* (then)

1 I am fortunate to be given so much help.
2 I am fortunate to have been given so much help.
3 I am lucky to have been taught a foreign language.
4 She was annoyed to have been interrupted.
5 He was proud to be trusted.
6 John is ashamed to have been found out.
7 We are pleased to be employed.

D 'Remember' + 'to' and 'remember' + '-ing' [> LEG 16.59, compare > LAG 14B–C, 42C]

a She said this and she remembered it.

b She didn't forget to do this.

Remember + to means 'don't forget to':
Remember to post *my letter.*
Remember + -ing refers to the past:
I remember posting *your letter.*
We can use *remember + that* in place of *remember + -ing*:
I remember that I posted *your letter.*

1 I remembered to post your letters.
2 I remember meeting him years ago.
3 You must remember to give him my message.
4 They remember having one of the first television sets.
5 I remember taking that photograph on your birthday.
6 I'll remember to lock the door next time.
7 I remember being given a prize for sewing at school.

E The double genitive: 'a friend of mine/John's' [> LEG 2.52, compare > LAG 5B]

*Cecil had laughed, that irritating, cynical laugh **of his**.*

We can use *of* + possessive pronoun (e.g. *mine*) instead of possessive adjective (e.g. *my*) + noun:
*He is **my/your friend**.*
→ *He is **a friend of mine/yours**.* (Not *a friend of me/of your's*)
If we want to use a noun instead of a possessive pronoun, we must use the genitive (*'s/s'*) form:
He is my father's friend.
→ *He is **a friend of my father's**.* (Not *of my father*)
We often use this construction with *that* to criticize:
*…**that irritating, cynical laugh of his**.*

1 John is a friend of mine.
2 I'm really getting fed up with that brother of yours.
3 We're putting on a play of Ayckbourn's.
4 I can't stand that motorbike of his.
5 Those relations of hers are really the problem./It's those relations of hers that are really the problem.
6 He recited a poem of Keats'. [> LEG 2.44.3]
7 That house of theirs is so expensive to run./It's that house of theirs that is so expensive to run.

F Uses of 'let' [> LEG 16.4.1–2]

a *Let's*: suggestion (imperative form)

b *she **had** never **allowed** Marjorie **to suspect** …*

We can use the imperative form *let's* + bare infinitive for suggestions:
***Let's agree. Let's not argue** about it.*
We can use *let* as a full verb in the sense of *allow*:
*Please **let us** have more time, will you.*
(= allow us to) (Not *let us to have*)

1 They'll never allow him to forget his debt.
2 Allowing you to use my car was a real mistake.
3 Not replaceable by *allow*.
4 Not replaceable by *allow*.
5 You can't allow people to camp wherever they like.
6 … because I had allowed the dog (to go) out.
7 They didn't allow us to pay.

Spiders

Two of the worst Australian spiders are the funnel-web and the trap-door. One is even more lethal than the other but I can't remember which. It doesn't matter, because
5 either can put a child in peril of its life. The funnel-web is a ping-pong ball in a fox-fur. It inhabits a miniature missile silo in the ground, from which it emerges in a savage arc, ready to sink its mandibles into anything
10 that breathes. The trap-door spider is really a funnel-web plus cunning, since it conceals the mouth of its silo with a tiny coal-hole door. Both kinds of spider can leap an incredible distance. A wood-pile might contain hundreds of each kind. If you even suspected the presence of either species
15 in your garden you were supposed to report immediately to the responsible authorities. After the war an English immigrant lady became famous when she was discovered gaily swatting funnel-webs with a broom as they came flying at her in squadrons. Any one of them, if it had got close enough
20 even to spit at her, would have put her in bed for a year.

I somehow managed to avoid meeting trap-door spiders or funnel-webs. Quite often I came face to face with a harmless relative, which Aunt Dot called a tarantula and I called a triantelope. Actually it was just a common garden
25 spider called the huntsman, whose idea of a big thrill was to suck a wasp. The huntsman wove big vertical webs which I used regularly to walk into when heading tentatively down the back path to the lavatory after dark. Getting mixed up in the web, to which I knew the triantelope must be at some point
30 attached, was a frightening sensation which I attempted to forestall by inching forward very slowly, with one hand held out. It didn't help.

But the real horror among spiders was more likely to be encountered in the lavatory itself. This was the red-back. The
35 red-back is mainly black, with a scarlet stripe down where its spine would be if it were a vertebrate. Looking like a neatly rigged and painted single-seater that might once have been flown by von Richthofen, the red-back had enough poison in it to immobilise a horse.

Unreliable Memoirs by Clive James (*Australian*)

Sentence structure

A Supply the connecting words, then check against the text.

Two of the worst Australian spiders are the funnel-web and the trap-door. ¹........ is even more lethal than ²........ but I can't remember ³........ . It doesn't matter, because ⁴........ can put a child in peril of its life. The ⁵........ is a ping-pong ball in a fox-fur. ⁶..... inhabits a miniature missile silo in the ground, from which it emerges in a savage arc, ready to sink its mandibles into anything that breathes. The ⁷........ spider is really a funnel-web plus cunning, since ⁸........ conceals the mouth of its silo with a tiny coal-hole door. ⁹........ kinds of spider can leap an incredible distance. A wood-pile might contain hundreds of ¹⁰........ kind. If you even suspected the presence of ¹¹........ species in your garden you were supposed to report immediately to the responsible authorities. (ll. 1–16)

B Comment briefly on the way the author creates balance in **A** above.

....

....

....

C Join the following into one sentence. Make any necessary changes, then refer to the text.

Getting mixed up in the web was a frightening sensation. I knew the triantelope must be at some point attached to it. I attempted to forestall the sensation. I inched forward very slowly. I had one hand held out. (ll. 28–32) ....

....

Grammar points

D Supply the right forms of the verbs in brackets, then refer to the text.

1 Both kinds of spider can leap an incredible distance. A wood-pile might contain hundreds of each kind. If you even suspected the presence of either species in your garden you ¹(*suppose*) .... to report immediately to the responsible authorities. After the war an English immigrant lady ²(*become*) .... famous when she ³(*discover*) .... gaily swatting funnel-webs with a broom as they ⁴(*come*) .... flying at her in squadrons. Any one of them, if it ⁵(*get*) .... close enough even to spit at her, would have put her in bed for a year. (ll. 12–20)

2 But the real horror among spiders was more likely to be encountered in the lavatory itself. This was the red-back. The red-back is mainly black, with a scarlet stripe down where its spine would be if it ¹(*be*) .... a vertebrate. Looking like a neatly rigged and painted single- seater that ²(*may once fly*) .... by von Richthofen, the red-back ³(*have*) .... enough poison in it to immobilise a horse. (ll. 33–39)

E Explain what the words in bold italics refer to.

  a ***Either*** *can put a child in peril of its life.* (l. 5) ....

  b ***Neither*** *spider would make a nice pet.* ....

  c ***Both*** *kinds of spider can leap an incredible distance.* (ll. 12–13) ....

Rewrite these sentences using *either*, *neither* or *both*. Alternatives are sometimes possible.

1 You can have one of these books or you can have the other, but not both.
You can have either of these books, but not both.

2 This keyboard doesn't work very well. That keyboard doesn't work very well.
....

3 This keyboard works very well and that keyboard works very well.
....

4 This candidate isn't suitable and that candidate isn't suitable.
....

5 This jacket is expensive and that jacket is expensive. Don't buy either of them.
....

F What's the difference between the words in bold italics?

  a ***Any one*** *of them would have put her in bed for a year.* (ll. 19–20)

  b ***Anyone*** *would have been terrified by these spiders.*

Rewrite these sentences, with necessary changes, using *one of* after the words in italics.

1 I don't like *any* painting on show.
I don't like any one of the paintings on show.

2 *Either* vehicle will do more than 120 miles an hour. They're both fast.
....

3 I thought you'd fancy *another* truffle.
....

4 *Each* page has been carefully checked for spelling and punctuation.
....

5 The wretched train stopped at *every* station on the line.
....

6 Both these pictures are fakes. *Neither* of them is genuine.
....

7 Not a *single* prisoner escaped.
....

SENTENCE STRUCTURE

A Answers and commentary

1 *One*: A pronoun (or 'prop word') used here to refer to both types of spider. (The author can't remember which.) [> LEG 4.10–11, 5.27]

2 *the other*: used as a pronoun in contrast to *one*: *(the) one ... the other*. It is used here to refer to either *the funnel-web (spider)* or *the trap-door (spider)*. (See note **1** above.) [> LEG 4.11, 5.27]

3 *which* (= which one): *Which* (question-word or relative pronoun) often combines with *one*. [> LEG 4.10] As a question-word, *which* often refers to a choice between 'two'. [> LEG 13.36.2]

4 *either* (= the one or the other): *Either* is used as a pronoun here to refer both to *the funnel-web (spider)* and *the trap-door (spider)*. [> LEG 5.29]

5 *The funnel-web*: The author names the spider here to tell the reader which of the two spiders he is referring to. [compare > LEG 6.12.1]

6 *It*: The third person neuter pronoun refers directly to *the funnel-web*, which has just been mentioned. [> LEG 4.5.5] Compare this use of *it* with **It** *doesn't matter*, where *it* is an 'empty subject'. [> LEG 4.12, LAG 21Bn.1a, 60An.5]

7 *trap-door*: The author names the second spider to contrast it with *the funnel-web* in the previous sentence.

8 *it*: The third person neuter pronoun refers directly to *the trap door spider*, which has just been mentioned. [> LEG 4.5.5]

9 *Both*: refers to two and is followed by a plural verb. [> LEG 5.18–21, LAG 58E] We can say *both kinds of spider* (as here) or *both kinds of spiders*, but not *both kind of spiders* or *both kind of spider*. [> LEG App 7.17]

10 *each* (Not *both*): We use *each* to refer to more than two when we want to show how separate they are [> LEG 5.26.1, LAG 11D]: **Each child in the school was questioned**. (= Many children were questioned one by one.) Or we use *each* to refer to both members of a pair (as here) [> LEG 5.26.2]: *... hundreds (of spiders) of* **each kind**.

11 *either* (= one or the other): We use *either* to refer to two people, things, etc. (singular nouns). [> LEG 5.29, LAG 58E] *Species* is plural in form and can refer to a single unit, or to more than one [> LEG 2.31, compare > LAG 19E]:
  This **species** *of spider* **is** *dangerous.* (one)
  There **are** *thousands of* **species** *of spider(s).* (more than one)

B Answer and commentary

The contrast between two species of spider, *funnel-web* and *trap-door*, is carefully maintained in these lines. The author begins by introducing the two species of spider in the first sentence. He then goes on to compare them using the connecting words *one ... the other*. This is followed by a description of the funnel-web spider (*The funnel-web is a ping-pong ball ...*), after which there is a description of the trap-door spider. In the last three sentences, both kinds of spider are considered together. Balance is achieved through the careful sequencing of sentences and the use of words like *two, both, either, each, one ... the other*.

C Answer and commentary

Getting mixed up in the web, ... (subject)
Getting mixed up is a gerund, that is, a noun form, ending in *-ing*, used here as a subject. [> LEG 16.39, LAG 20D]

... **to which** *I knew the triantelope must be at some point attached, ...* (relative clause)
Which is the relative pronoun object of the preposition *to*. The use of the relative pronoun directly after the preposition is formal and rare in speech. The possibilities are [> LEG 1.36, LAG 20An.1, 24An.7]:
  the web **to which** *I knew it must be attached*
  the web **which** *I knew it must be attached* **to**
  the web (–) *I knew it must be attached* **to**

... *was* (verb) *a frightening sensation ...* (complement) [> LEG 1.11, LAG 4A]

... **which** *I attempted to forestall ...* (relative clause)
Which is the relative pronoun object of the relative clause [> LAG 6Bn.1]:
  It was **a sensation***. I attempted to forestall* **it**.
  → *It was* **a sensation** (**which**) *I attempted to forestall.*

... **by inching forward** *very slowly, ...*
By + -ing answers the question *How?* [> LEG 13.40.4, App 25.17, LAG 17Bn.5, 20Bn.1]

... **with** *one hand held out.*
We can convey the sense of 'having' with *with*. [> LEG 25.37, LAG 14D]

GRAMMAR POINTS

D Past tenses in narration and conditional sentences [> LEG 9.31, Chapter 14, LAG 8E, 19C, 26C, 33B, 41B, 50D, 53C]

1 1 were supposed to [> LEG 12.8n.3, 14.23.1]
   2 became
   3 was discovered
   4 came [compare > LEG 16.43]
   5 if it had got [> LEG 14.16–18]

2 1 if it were [> LEG 14.13]
   2 might once have been flown [> LEG 11.28–29, 12.2]
   3 had

E Distributives: 'both', 'either' and 'neither' [> LEG 5.18–21, 5.29]

a *either*: one or the other (considered separately)
b *neither*: not one and not the other
c *both*: one and the other (considered together)

We can use *either*, *neither* and *both* to refer to people and things:
– *Either* refers to two people or things separately:

> **Either (candidate)** *is suitable.*
> **Either (dictionary)** *will give you the answer.*

– *Neither* refers to two people or things separately:

> **Neither (candidate)** *is suitable.*
> **Neither (dictionary)** *will give you the answer.*

Any noun after *either* and *neither* is singular and takes a singular verb.
– *Both* refers to two people or things, considered together:

> **Both candidates** *are suitable.*
> **Both dictionaries** *will give you the answer.*

Any noun after *both* is plural and takes a plural verb.

We can use *of* (+ determiners like *the*, *these*, *my*) after all three distributives:

> **Either of/Neither of** *the candidates is suitable.* (singular verb, but [> LEG 5.31])
> **Both of the candidates are** *suitable.* (plural verb [> LEG 5.18.1])

Any noun after *either of* and *neither of* is plural; the verb that follows is singular.
Any noun after *both of* is plural + plural verb.

Possible answers.
(Some of these sentences can be re-expressed with *of* after *either*, *neither*, *both*.)

1 You can have either of these books, but not both.
2 Neither keyboard works well.
3 Both (these) keyboards work very well./Either keyboard works well.
4 Neither candidate is suitable.
5 Both (these) jackets are expensive./Either jacket is expensive.

F The use of 'one of' after distributives: 'any one of the spiders' [> LEG 5.30, compare > LAG 18C, 54E, 55D]

a *any one* of the spiders considered separately.
b *Anyone* (= any person)

Some/any/no compounds (*someone*, *anyone*) are written as one word, with the exception of *no one*. [> LEG 4.37–38]
Quantifiers like *any*, *some*, *many*, *much* can be followed by *of* when we are making specific references [> LEG 5.5.2]:

> *I don't want* **any/many of these things**.
> *I don't want* **much of this stuff**.

Distributives like *another*, [> LAG 36F] *any*, *each*, *either*, and *neither* refer to single items. We can use *of* after them:

> *I want to look at* **each of** *them.*
> *I don't want to look at* **any of** *them.*

If we want to emphasize the items singly, we can use *one* in front of *of*:

> *I want to look at* **each one of** *them.*
> *I don't want to look at* **any one of** *them.* (Not *anyone of them*)

Sample answers

1 I don't like any one of the paintings on show.
2 Either one of the vehicles will do more than 120 miles an hour.
3 I thought you'd fancy another one of those truffles.
4 Each one of these pages has been carefully checked for spelling and punctuation.
5 The wretched train stopped at every one of the stations on the line.
6 Both these pictures are fakes. Neither one of them is genuine.
7 Not a single one of the prisoners escaped.

My mother

MY MOTHER arrived at the port of Harwich some time in February, and was immediately apprehended by the British authorities for having filled up her landing
5 form with undue accuracy. To the question: Where born? she had answered St Petersburg. To the question: Where educated? she had answered Leningrad. The immigration authorities were convinced that she was
10 making light of the questionnaire, and I feel bound to add with a certain pride that it was only my presence that saved her from further unpleasantness. This tendency to answer official questions too literally seems
15 to run in the family, perhaps owing to the many frontiers we all have crossed since such encumbrances were invented.

Once she had been released by the pernickety British authorities, my mother travelled to London by train
20 through a thick industrial murk, which culminated in a swirling yellow fog, impenetrable, choking, and claustrophobic. She records that she had never seen or smelt such unadulterated filth in her life. Before the names of the stations were entirely obliterated towards the end of
25 the journey, the impression of Kafkaesque horror was increased by the fact that every station seemed to be called Bovril. It is necessary to explain to the uninitiated that Bovril was, and is, a most excellent beef-tea. Being the fruit of private enterprise in a highly competitive capitalist
30 society, it had bright and brilliant advertisements, unlike the names of stations which, although privately owned, were without direct competition, and so tended to conceal their identities behind layers of grit and grime.

The train finally pulled in to the greatest Bovril of them
35 all, and my mother was taken by her old governess to a boarding home run by an elderly Puritan couple where nothing was allowed except total silence. She knew, as she conversed in surreptitious whispers with Miss Rose, who had taught her all she knew in St Petersburg, that she had
40 made the mistake of her life in coming to this nightmare of a country with her unborn child. And yet, such is the power of acquired tastes in those of sensibility that this is the selfsame country she was to die in fifty-four years later, refusing for the last ten years of her life to leave even for a
45 brief vacation, wrapping up against the pervasive damp, making casual excuses for every discomfort, deeply involved in village life, warmed by soulless electric stoves and the great hearts of her neighbours.

Dear Me by Peter Ustinov *(BrE)*

Sentence structure

A Rewrite these sentences using the words provided and making any necessary changes. Then check against the text.

1 My mother was immediately apprehended by the British authorities when she arrived at the port of Harwich some time in February because she had filled up her landing form with undue accuracy. [*My mother arrived ... and ... for ...*] (ll. 1–5)

....

....

2 We tend to answer official questions too literally and this seems to run in the family, perhaps because of the many frontiers we have all crossed from the time such encumbrances were invented. [*This tendency ... owing to ... since ...*] (ll. 13–17)

....

....

....

3 After the train finally pulled in to the greatest Bovril of them all, my mother was taken by her old governess to a boarding home which was run by an elderly Puritan couple in which only total silence was allowed. [*The train ... and ... run ...where nothing ...*] (ll. 34–37)

....

....

....

Grammar points

B Supply the right active and passive forms and tenses of the verbs in brackets, then refer to the text. (ll. 1–30)

My mother arrived at the port of Harwich some time in February and [1](*immediately apprehend*) .... by the British authorities for having filled up her landing form with undue accuracy. To the question: Where born? she [2](*answer*) .... St Petersburg. To the question: Where educated? she [3](*answer*) .... Leningrad. The immigration authorities [4](*convince*) .... that she [5](*make*) .... light of the questionnaire, and I feel bound to add with a certain pride that it was only my presence that [6](*save*) .... her from further unpleasantness. This tendency to answer official questions too literally [7](*seem*) .... to run in the family, perhaps owing to the many frontiers we [8](*all cross*) .... since such encumbrances were invented.

Once she [9](*release*) .... by the pernickety British authorities, my mother travelled to London by train through a thick industrial murk, which [10](*culminate*) .... in a swirling yellow fog, impenetrable, choking, and claustrophobic. She records that she [11](*never see or smell*) .... such unadulterated filth in her life. Before the names of the stations [12](*entirely obliterate*) .... towards the end of the journey, the impression of Kafkaesque horror [13](*increase*) .... by the fact that every station [14](*seem*) .... to be called Bovril. It is necessary to explain to the uninitiated that Bovril was, and [15](*be*) .... , a most excellent beef-tea. Being the fruit of private enterprise in a highly competitive capitalist society, it [16](*have*) .... bright and brilliant advertisements.

C What phrase using the word *fact* fits into this space? (ll. 25–27)
The impression of Kafkaesque horror was increased .... *every station seemed to be called Bovril.*

Join these sentences using *the fact that* In suitable phrases. Use the words in brackets where these are given and make any necessary changes.

1 His proposal makes sense. This should be recognized.
   The fact that his proposal makes sense should be recognized.
2 So many people have seen the show. It proves how popular it is.
   ....
3 The new motorway went ahead. So many people were opposed to it. (despite)
   ....
4 Sally did very well at university. This was because she worked hard. (due to)
   ....
5 You still haven't paid the bill. You have received several reminders. (in spite of)
   ....

D Which words could you delete from this sentence? (compare ll. 31–33)
Some stations, although they were privately owned, tended to conceal their identities behind layers of grit and grime.

Delete words from these sentences.

1 While ~~she was~~ at college, Delia wrote a novel.
2 Improvements will be made where they are necessary.
3 I want to know if he owes us any money and if this is so, when he's going to pay us.
4 Squid is nice and crispy when it has been fried.
5 The train which is arriving at Platform 8 is the 17.50 from Crewe.
6 I'd like to change the date of my appointment if this is at all possible.
7 Though it had been clearly addressed, the letter failed to reach me.
8 I'd like the eggs to be hard boiled please.

SENTENCE STRUCTURE

A Answers and commentary

1 *My mother arrived at the port of Harwich some time in February, ...*

The clause follows standard word order [> LEG 1.3, 7.19.1, LAG 4A]: *My mother* (subject) *arrived at* (verb) *the port of Harwich* (object) *some time in February* (time). Adverbs of time can come at the beginning or end of a clause, so it would have been equally possible to write:

Some time in February my mother arrived at the port of Harwich ...

The author chooses *at* rather than *in* after *arrive* because he regards *Harwich* as a point on a route, not as a destination. [> LEG 8.6, 8.9.3, LAG 8D]

... and was immediately apprehended by the British authorities ...

It would have been possible to write *and she was immediately apprehended ...* , but it is usual not to repeat the subject after *and*. [> LEG 1.20.1, LAG 1An.2, 4Bn.2, 13B, *passim*]

The adverb *immediately* could have come after *apprehended* or after *the British authorities*. It is placed after the auxiliary verb *was* here to emphasize the unstated subject *she*. [> LEG 7.16, LAG 42An.1]

... for having filled up her landing form with undue accuracy.

The *-ing* form must be used after the preposition *for*. [> LEG 16.51, App 25.20, LAG 1D, 53Ans.1–2] The phrase *for having filled up* could be replaced by the adverbial clause of reason *because she had filled up*. [> LEG 1.48, LAG 1Bn.2, 2Bn.2, 56An.8]

2 *This tendency to answer official questions too literally seems to run in the family, ...*

This tendency to answer official questions too literally is the subject of *seems*. The author has chosen to use the noun *tendency* instead of the verb *tend*. This use of a noun or noun phrase instead of a verb is common in English and is called 'nominalization' in grammar [> LEG 2.50, 8.20, 16.33, LAG 3Bn.1]:

You shouldn't remove any books.
→ *The removal of books is forbidden.*

... perhaps owing to the many frontiers we have all crossed ...

Owing to (= because of) refers back to the verb phrase *seems to run* and can be contrasted with *due to* (= caused by), which usually follows a noun + *be* [> LEG Apps 25.9, 25.19]:

Our delay (noun) *was* (be) *due to/caused by heavy traffic.*

In practice, *owing to* and *due to* are often interchangeable.

... since such encumbrances were invented.

Since (= from the time when). Here *since* is used as a conjunction introducing an adverbial clause of time. [> LEG 1.45.1] Compare *since* as a preposition followed by an object:

I've been waiting since 4 o'clock. (Not **from 4 o'clock**). [> LAG 10An.2]

3 *The train finally pulled in to the greatest Bovril of them all, ...*

The clause follows standard word order [> LEG 1.3, 7.19.1]: *The train* (subject) *pulled in to* (verb) *the greatest Bovril of them all* (object or place depending on whether *to* is considered to be a preposition after the intransitive verb *pull in*, or whether *to* is considered to be part of a three-part transitive verb *pull in to* [> LEG 8.18, 8.29–30]).

... and my mother was taken by her old governess to a boarding home ...

We have a change of subject after *and*, so we have to say *my mother* to contrast with the earlier subject *the train*. [> LEG 1.20.1, LAG 13B]

... run by an elderly Puritan couple ...

The past participle is used in place of a relative clause [> LEG 1.62.3, LAG 6Bn.4, 8An.2]:

... to a boarding home ~~which was~~ run by ...
→ *... to a boarding home run by ...*

... where nothing was allowed except total silence.

In which is replaced by *where* to introduce a relative clause. [> LEG 1.38.2, LAG 31Bn.3, 44Bn.3] *Nothing ... except* replaces *only*. [> LEG 7.54–55] We could use *nothing but* here, preferably without separating them [> LEG 4.42, LAG 48E]:

... nothing but total silence was allowed.

GRAMMAR POINTS

B Verbs and verb tenses [> LEG Chapter 9, regular and irregular verbs Apps 39–40, LAG 8E, 25C, 26C, 33B, 37C]

The ruling tenses in this passage are past, active and passive.

1 *was immediately apprehended*: past passive to follow the governing tense established by the verb *arrived*. [> LEG 9.5, 9.13–18, 12.1–3]

2–3 *had answered*: past perfect because the reference is to an earlier past. [> LEG 9.29–30]

4 *were convinced*: past passive, as in **1** above.

5 *was making*: the use of the past progressive suggests her attitude as she was going through immigration. [> LEG 9.20]; *had made* would have suggested her attitude before this.

6 *saved*: simple past, the subject of which is *my presence*; the passive would be: *she was saved by my presence*. [> LEG 9.5, 9.13–18, 12.1–3]

7 *seems*: the author switches to the simple present to refer to a general truth as far as his family is concerned. [> LEG 9.8.1]

8 *have all crossed*: the use of the present perfect suggests 'up to the present time' (= and we are still doing it) [> LEG 9.22–26], compared to the past perfect *had all crossed*, which would have referred to an earlier past. [> LEG 9.29–30]

9 *had been released*: past perfect passive, referring to an earlier past, as in **2–3** above. *Once* (= when) introduces an adverbial clause of time [> LEG 1.45] and often occurs with the present perfect or past perfect.

10 *culminated*: the simple past tense picks up the narrative established by *arrived* in the opening sentence.

11 *had never seen or smelt*: the past perfect refers to an earlier past and follows on directly from the present tense *records* (i.e. 'which can still be read'). It clearly illustrates how the sequence of tenses reflects the viewpoint of the speaker and doesn't follow inflexible rules. [> LEG 9.5.2]

12 *were entirely obliterated*: past passive, resuming the narrative.

13 *was increased*: as in **12** above.

14 *seemed*: past active.

15 *is*: the reference switches to the present.

16 *had*: the simple past resumes the narrative. [> LEG 10.28, 10.30n.4]

C 'the fact that' [> LEG 1.23.3, 14.13.3, App 25.23]

by the fact that
the fact that is a formal phrase which we often use as follows:

1 to avoid the awkwardness of beginning a sentence with *that*:
The fact that his proposal makes sense should be recognized.

2 in combination with phrases like *because of, in view of, on account of, owing to, due to, in spite of, despite* and *notwithstanding*:
Our late arrival is due to the fact that so many trains have been cancelled.

Possible answers

1 The fact that his proposal makes sense should be recognized.

2 The fact that so many people have seen the show proves how popular it is.

3 The new motorway went ahead despite the fact that so many people were opposed to it.

4 Sally did very well at university due to the fact that she worked hard.

5 You still haven't paid the bill in spite of the fact that you have received several reminders.

D Abbreviated clauses [> LEG 1.55, 1.58–63, 12.3n.13, 14.5n.4]

Some stations, although ~~they were~~ privately owned, tended to conceal their identities behind layers of grit and grime.
We can often abbreviate clauses by:
- deleting the subject and *be*:
Although ~~she was~~ exhausted, she went to bed very late.
- deleting a relative pronoun and *be*:
The train ~~which is~~ arriving at Platform 8 has been delayed.
- making deletions after requests with *'d like*:
I'd like it ~~to be~~ repaired please.

1 While ~~she was~~ at college, Delia wrote a novel.

2 Improvements will be made where ~~they are~~ necessary.

3 I want to know if he owes us any money, and if ~~this is~~ so, when he's going to pay us.

4 Squid is nice and crispy when ~~it has been~~ fried.

5 The train ~~which is~~ arriving at Platform 8 is the 17.50 from Crewe.

6 I'd like to change the date of my appointment if ~~this is~~ at all possible.

7 Though ~~it had been~~ clearly addressed, the letter failed to reach me.

8 I'd like the eggs ~~to be~~ hard boiled please.

Forbidding fruit

INDUSTRIAL robots are the bolshiest workforce you can imagine. The slightest variation in their working conditions or duties, and the whistle will blow: they are off the job.
5 That applies even to a task as simple (for humans) as fruit-picking. Last month researchers from the University of Florida put an experimental robot picker into the orange groves of Catania in Sicily. It will be a long
10 while yet before the poor thing can cope.

Two problems confront a fruit picker (be it hydraulic or human): recognizing the fruit, and harvesting it quickly and thoroughly without damaging the fruit or the tree. So far, the

15 Florida team, led by Dr Roy Harrell, has solved only the first - and even that took some of the newest tricks in robotics. Their one-armed picker, which is mounted on a trailer, is fitted with a colour-television camera, sonar equipment, and a computer to make sense of what it sees and hears.

20 Like the human eye, television cameras split the world into the three primary colours: red, green and blue. It is not easy to define exactly which mixture of these colours should count as 'orange'. The definition must be wide enough to include most of the oranges on most of the trees, but not so wide as to encompass
25 unripe fruit or other objects in the vicinity. At sunset, for example, when the light becomes redder, everything starts to appear more orange. At that stage, either harvesting has to stop or the definition must be recalculated.

Television only tells the robot in which direction to pursue its
30 orange. To discover how far away it is, the machine has to rely on bat-like sonar. The robot makes high-pitched squeaks and measures the time taken for its squeaks to bounce back to build up an orange-map. The map is overlaid on to the television image. Faced with more than one orange, the robot chooses the one
35 nearest the centre of its field of view and makes a bee-line for it.

At best, the Sicilian prototype picks an orange every three to four seconds. An employable machine would need to be able to sustain such a rate all day. It would probably have up to 12 arms, each with its own camera, sonar and computer. If such machines
40 are to pay their way and harvest a profit, Dr Harrell thinks they will have to learn to pick at least 85% of the oranges on any given tree. At the moment, the prototype can only manage 75% of the fruit within its limited grasp.

The Economist (BrE)

Sentence structure

A Supply the connecting word or words where necessary, then refer to the text.

Industrial robots are the bolshiest workforce ¹........ you can imagine. The slightest variation in their working conditions or duties, ²........ the whistle will blow: they are off the job. ³........ applies even to a task as simple (for humans) as fruit-picking. ⁴........ month researchers from the University of Florida put an experimental robot picker into the orange groves of Catania in Sicily. ⁵........ will be a long while yet before the poor thing can cope. Two problems confront a fruit picker (⁶........ it hydraulic or human): recognizing the fruit, and harvesting it quickly and thoroughly ⁷........ damaging the fruit or the tree. ⁸......., the Florida team, ⁹(*lead*) .... by Dr Roy Harrell, has solved only the first – and even that took some of the newest tricks in robotics. Their one-armed picker, ¹⁰........ is mounted on a trailer, is fitted with a colour-television camera, sonar equipment, and a computer ¹¹(*make*) .... sense of ¹²........ it sees and hears. ¹³........ the human eye, television cameras split the world into the three primary colours: red, green and blue. It is not easy ¹⁴(*define*) .... exactly which mixture of these colours should count as 'orange'. The definition must be wide ¹⁵........ to include most of the oranges on most of the trees, but ¹⁶........ wide ¹⁷........ to encompass unripe fruit or other objects in the vicinity. At sunset, for example, ¹⁸........ the light becomes redder, everything starts to appear more orange. At that stage, ¹⁹........ harvesting has to stop ²⁰........ the definition must be recalculated. Television only tells the robot ²¹........ direction to pursue its orange. ²²(*discover*) .... how far away it is, the machine has to rely on bat-like sonar. The robot makes high-pitched squeaks and measures the time taken ²³........ its squeaks to bounce back to build up an orange-map. The map is overlaid on to the television image. (ll. 1–33)

B What does *they are off the job* mean here?
... *the whistle will blow:* **they are off the job.** (l. 4) ....

Suggest meanings for the phrases with *off*.

1 Well, see you later then. *We're off.*   *We're leaving.* ....
2 You've heard about tomorrow's match? *It's off.*   ....
3 I've checked the cooker. *It's off.*   ....
4 Just smell this meat! *It's off.*   ....
5 I'd like fish please. – I'm afraid *it's off* today.   ....
6 His behaviour *is a bit off*, isn't it?   ....
7 Where's Millie? - *She's off* today.   ....
8 *John's off* sick.   ....
9 She's *off her head.*   ....
10 Another button's *come off* my shirt.   ....
11 We live *well off* the main road.   ....
12 Are you *off your food* or something?   ....
13 Our new neighbours seem to be quite *well off*.   ....
14 *Be off* with you!   ....
15 Which direction is *off*? Up or down?   ....
16 How are you *off* for money?   ....
17 Why don't you *finish off* those potatoes?   ....
18 Can you help me *get* my boots *off*?   ....
19 She put it in her bag and just *walked off*.   ....
20 We manage to get to the theatre *off and on*.   ....

C *Two problems confront a fruit picker:* **recognizing** *the fruit and* **harvesting** *it.* (ll. 11–13)
Recognizing and *harvesting* are *ing*-form nouns (gerunds). What other nouns can you form from the verbs *recognize* and *harvest*? ....

Supply two noun forms for each of the verbs in brackets, providing any necessary additions.

1 *Discussing/A discussion of* the details of this contract is essential. (discuss)
2 .... a new clause in the contract is essential before I can sign it. (include)
3 .... adult responsibilities is never easy. (assume)
4 .... to negotiate is the only way to deal with dictators. (refuse)
5 .... guilt is never easy in a court of law. (prove)
6 .... what happened will be difficult. (describe)
7 .... property is a serious crime. (damage)
8 .... your own affairs comes with practice. (manage)
9 .... the factory caused many problems for the employees. (close)
10 .... the rich to help the poor won't help either. (rob)
11 .... a cocoon must be quite an experience for a moth. (emerge)
12 .... develops naturally in most young children. (speak)
13 .... your natural faculties is essential for success. (develop)
14 .... the survivors has proved difficult. (rescue)
15 .... involvement may be the best course of action for us. (deny)
16 .... injustice should be a basic requirement for politicians. (hate)
17 .... fatty foods is no bad thing. (avoid)
18 .... your rights should have its limits. (insist)
19 .... stamps is a hobby pursued not only by children. (collect)
20 .... guilt is not proof of guilt. (admit)
21 .... the muscles is important for pianists. (relax)
22 .... these census forms is required by law. (complete)
23 .... is supposed to be good for the system. (laugh)

SENTENCE STRUCTURE

A Answers and commentary

1 (–) or *which/that*: the object of the relative clause [> LEG 1.34, 6.28.1, LAG 7A*ns*.7c–8c]:

They are the bolshiest **workforce***. You can imagine* **them***.*

→ *They are the bolshiest workforce (**which/ that***) you can imagine.*

2 *and*: This construction is a variation on a Type 1 conditional sentence [> LEG 14.9, LAG 9E]:

If there is *the slightest variation, the whistle* **will blow***.*

→ *The slightest variation* **and** *the whistle* **will blow***.*

3 *That*: refers back to the previous statement. We can use *that* or *this* for backward reference, but not for forward reference, when we have to use *this*. [> LEG App 7.7, LAG 23A*n*.5]

4 *Last*: The adverbial phrase referring to past time (*last week, last month, last year*, etc.) is formed with *last* (Not **the last*). [> LEG 3.21.2, 8.12, App 48, LAG 19D, 38C]

5 *It*: an 'empty subject' referring to *a long while*. Note that *while* (= time) is a noun here. *It* carries no information. It is present because every English sentence has to contain a subject and verb. [> LEG 4.12, LAG 21B*n*.1a, 58A*n*.6]

6 *be*: This is a relatively rare use of the subjunctive with *be* in a Type 1 conditional sentence [> LEG 14.5n.4, LAG 9E]:

… *whether* **it is***/whether* **it be** *hydraulic or human.*

→ **be it** *hydraulic or human.* [For this kind of inversion, compare also > LEG 14.15, 14.18.3.]

7 *without* + *-ing* [> LEG 1.60, 16.51, LAG 1D]: an alternative way of saying *so as not to (damage)*. (Not **without to*) [> LEG 16.12.1]

8 *So far* (= up till now): The adverbial phrase relates to the present and must be followed by the perfect (*has solved*), not the simple past. [> LEG 9.18, 9.25.1, LAG 8E*n*.4, 25C]

9 *led*: The past participle construction is used in place of a relative clause, in apposition to *the Florida team* [> LEG 1.62.3, 1.39]:

… **the Florida team***, (which is)* **led** *by Dr Roy Harrell, has solved only the first [problem].*

10 *which*: relative pronoun (subject) introducing a relative clause. [> LEG 1.31]:

This is **their one-armed picker***. It is mounted on a trailer,* …

→ …**their one armed picker***,* **which is** …

Commas are used because this is a non-defining clause, providing extra information. [> LEG 1.26, LAG 5A, 22A*ns*.4, 5]

11 *to make*: infinitive of purpose after a noun (*computer*). [> LEG 10.9.10, 16.12, 16.33]

12 *what* (= that which): introduces a noun clause object of the preposition *of*. [> LEG 1.24.2, 15.19–24, LAG 8A*n*.2, 42D]

13 *Like*: a preposition here, followed by an object (*the human eye*). (Not **as*) [> LEG App 25.25]

14 *to define*: *It* is a preparatory subject here. The *to*-infinitive or *-ing* form could be the subject [> LEG 4.13, 16.29, 16.47, LAG 1C]:

To define/Defining *exactly which mixture isn't easy.*

→ **It isn't easy to define/defining** …

15 *enough*: comes after the adjective (*wide*) and means 'to the necessary degree'. [> LEG 5.17, 16.27.1, 16.32.2, LAG 34E]

16 *not so* (= not to the necessary degree): We can use *so* with an adjective as an adverb of degree [> LEG 7.51.1, LAG 33D]:

This new cheese is **so good***.*

17 *as*: part of the infinitive marker begun in **16** above [> LEG 16.12.1, 16.27.1]:

*It is wide enough (**so as***) to include most oranges* …

→ *It isn't* **so** *wide* **as** *to encompass unripe fruit.*

18 *when*: introduces an adverbial clause of time. [> LEG 1.45.1] The simple present *becomes* refers to a permanent state [> LEG 9.8.1] and is not used here in place of a future. [> LEG 1.45.2]

19 *either*: introduces alternatives. See **20** below.

20 *or*: follows *either* (above) just as *nor* follows *neither*. [> LEG 1.15, 1.17–20, 5.29.1]

21 *in which*: introduces a reported question [> LEG 15.24.2, also see 13.31*n*.4 for the position of prepositions in *Wh*- questions, LAG 20A*n*.1]:

Television only tells the robot **in which direction** *to pursue its orange.*

Television only tells the robot **which direction** *to pursue its orange* **in***.*

22 *To discover*: infinitive of purpose. [> LEG 16.12.1, LAG 6B*n*.5, 10B*n*.2, 15A*n*.3]

23 *for*: *It takes* may be followed by an indirect object [> LEG 1.13.3, 16.21, LAG 27B*n*.2]:

It takes **(me)** *ten minutes to walk to the station.*

→ *It takes ten minutes* **for me** *to walk to the station.* (= I take ten minutes to walk to the station.)

GRAMMAR POINTS

B Phrases with 'off' [> LEG 8.4.1, 8,28, 16.55, Apps 20.1, 25.27, 25.29, 26.5, 32.8]

they are refusing to work

Off is a preposition (*fall **off** the shelf*) or an adverb particle (*drive **off*** [> LAG 13C]). It has a basic sense of 'removal', 'detachment' and 'separation' and this meaning is apparent in the many phrases it occurs in. Expressions with *off* range from the literal (*fall off the shelf*) to the idiomatic/figurative (*the meat's off*). Combinations with *be* have a variety of different meanings, as the exercise demonstrates.

1 We're leaving.
2 It isn't going to happen.
3 The power isn't on.
4 It's gone bad. (= gone off)
5 It's not on the menu.
6 not correct or appropriate
7 She's not working
8 John's not at work (because he's sick).
9 mad
10 'removed itself from'
11 a good distance from
12 (Have you) lost your appetite?
13 rich
14 Go away!
15 (referring e.g. to a power switch)
16 supplied (compare *well off* in **13**)
17 eat them all completely
18 remove (them)
19 walked away from here
20 occasionally

C Nouns derived from verbs: 'recognizing', 'recognition' [> LEG 2.3, 2.16.5, 3.26.2, 16.33, 16.39.1, Apps 28–29, compare > LAG 37E, 52C]

recognition, harvest

We can turn almost any verb in English into a noun by adding *-ing* to it to make it a gerund:
> *I often **ride** my bike to work.*
> → ***Riding** my bike to work is good exercise.*

In addition to the *-ing* form, many verbs have their own noun forms:
> *Why don't we go for **a ride** on our bikes?*

Some verbs and nouns have the same form, e.g. *to harvest/a harvest, to ride/a ride*.

Many verbs, particularly those of Latin origin, have their own noun forms with characteristic endings: e.g. *-(t)ion*. The *-ing* form noun is an alternative of Saxon origin:
> *describe* (verb) → *description* → *describing*

There is a difference between an *-ing* form noun and an ordinary noun. The *-ing* form noun points to 'the act of'; an ordinary noun tells us what someone or something is called. [> LEG 2.1, LAG 52B, 52C] The ordinary noun is often followed by a preposition, usually *of* (*a **description of** someone* or *something*).

Some *-ing* form nouns may also be followed by prepositions, e.g. *emerging **from**, insisting **on***.

Possible answers

1 Discussing/A discussion of
2 Including/The inclusion of
3 Assuming/The assumption of
4 Refusing/Refusal
5 Proving/Proof of
6 Describing/A description of
7 Damaging/Damage to
8 Managing/Management of
9 Closing/The closure of
10 Robbing/Robbery of
11 Emerging from/Emergence from
12 Speaking/Speech
13 Developing/The development of
14 Rescuing/Rescue of
15 Denying/Denial of
16 Hating/Hatred of
17 Avoiding/Avoidance of
18 Insisting on/Insistence on
19 Collecting/The collection of
20 Admitting/Admission of
21 Relaxing/Relaxation of
22 Completing/Completion of
23 Laughing/Laughter [> LEG 2.1, 2.16.6]

Text references

These notes provide brief explanations for references in some of the texts. The criterion for listing items here is that explanations are not to be found in the *Longman Dictionary of Contemporary English* (LDOCE). There are also brief notes on newspaper and magazine sources and on some of the authors and their work.

1 Watching children (BrE)

Joyce Grenfell
Joyce Grenfell, British actress and writer (1910–1979). She achieved outstanding success as an entertainer in revues, first appearing in 1939. Later, her one-woman shows included songs and sketches written by herself. She was famous for her humorous sketches of female 'types', from the charlady to the Oxford don's wife. Perhaps her best-known creation was the harassed nursery school teacher, whose constant cry was 'George, don't do that!' Her first volume of autobiography, *Joyce Grenfell Requests the Pleasure* (1976), reached a wide and admiring audience.

2 Pop Art absurdists (BrE)

The Sunday Telegraph
The Sunday Telegraph is a British Sunday newspaper, founded in 1961 as sister-paper to *The Daily Telegraph*. It has a similar readership: middle-to-upper class, mainly right-wing. It is famous for the forthright and challenging views of its columnists, both on political and social issues. Published in London, in two sections (news/sport and a review of literature and the arts), its circulation is around 600,000.

Jasper Johns (lines 2–3)
(born 1930, Allendale, South Carolina) U.S. painter. Best known for presenting images of common objects such as numbers, letters, flags, beer cans and light bulbs.

absurdist (title and l. 4)
Noun or adjective from *absurd*, more commonly applied to literature than to painting, especially in the phrase 'the Theatre of the Absurd'. 'Absurdist' writers such as Camus, Ionesco and Beckett were interested in the idea of the 'absurdity' of the human condition and the view that all existence is pointless.

Christie's (l. 5)
International auctioneers specializing in works of art.

Geraldine Norman (l. 9)
British newspaper correspondent specializing in the art market.

keeps this . . . pantomime on the road (ll. 12–13)
A sarcastic adaptation of the phrase *keep the show on the road* (= allow it to continue). A *pantomime*, besides being a Christmas show for children, is sometimes used to refer to an activity which the speaker regards with contempt.

'modern art' (l. 18)
The term is used with contempt here, emphasized by the use of inverted commas.

Rolling Bones (ll. 36–37)
A joke. Mick Jagger (born 1944) is founder of the rock group the *Rolling Stones*, who first performed in 1962.

Marx's theory of Surplus Value (l. 40)
'The part of the value of the product produced by labour that exceeds the wages paid, regarded, in Marxian economics, as the profit of the capitalist.' (Random House Dictionary)

3 The man who discovered Britain (AmE)

The Reader's Digest
The *Reader's Digest* publishing company produces high-quality, beautifully illustrated books on a variety of mainly non-fiction topics, from do-it-yourself and gardening to natural history and guidebooks. It arose from the phenomenally successful magazine *Reader's Digest*, founded in the USA in 1922 by De Witt Wallace and his wife Lila Acheson. This monthly, pocket-sized magazine is published in 16 languages, and has a world-wide readership of 30 million. At first it was a 'digest' of condensed articles from other publications, and in the 1930s it began to include whole condensed books. Today, it mainly publishes original commissioned material: general-interest articles and regular features designed to instruct and entertain.

Pytheas (l. 13)
(flourished 300 B.C.; born Massalia – modern Marseilles – Gaul) Greek explorer who first visited and described the British Isles and the Atlantic coast of Europe. His main work, *On the Ocean*, has not survived.

Strabo (l. 31)
(born 64/63 B.C., died after AD 21) Greek geographer and historian who wrote the 17 volume *Historical Sketches*, most of which has been lost. Much of his 17-volume *Geographica* has survived.

Thule (l. 32)
No one knows exactly which bit of land is meant by Thule, except that it was thought to be the northernmost limit of the world. The Roman scholar Pliny said it was six days' sail from northern Britain. It may have been Iceland or some part of the Norwegian coast.

4 Heroic failures (BrE)

The Sunday Times
The British newspaper *The Sunday Times* was founded in London in 1822. The sister paper of *The Times*, it is particularly strong on investigative journalism (especially by its *Insight* team) and has a high reputation for its reviews of literature and the arts. In 1961 it was the first British newspaper to publish a colour magazine. The fattest of all British Sundays, it consists of seven sections (News, News Review and Sport, Style, Business Review, Books, and the *The Funday Times* for children), plus the colour magazine. *The Sunday Times* is published in London and has over a million readers. This extract, by the newspaper's columnist, Stephen Pile, has also appeared in book form, *The Return of Heroic Failures* (1988).

our man (l. 10)
Jocular phrase like *our hero*: the person who represents us all.

5 Little queens sweep the board (BrE)

The Observer
The Observer is Britain's oldest Sunday newspaper, founded in 1791. After 1814 it was the first newspaper in the world to use illustrations (woodcuts). It is published in three sections (The Observer, Observer Business, Observer Review), plus a colour magazine. With its high reputation for responsible reporting, penetrating editorial comment, and its coverage of literature and the arts, *The Observer* appeals mainly to the educated middle-classes. It is published in London, with a circulation of around 550,000.

Title
The title contains a pun. *Little queens* refers to chess pieces, as well as to the Polgar sisters.
Sweep the board means 'win easily' (LDOCE), but also refers to the chess board.

6 The cup that cheers (BrE)

The Daily Express
The British *Daily Express* was founded by Sir Arthur Pearson in 1900. Intended for a mass popular readership, it soon became noted for its wide coverage of international affairs, as well as for lively reporting and enthusiastic patriotism. In 1916 it was bought by the press magnate Lord Beaverbrook, who turned it into the most widely-read daily in the world. The *Express* now appeals to broadly middle-class, right-wing, but independently-minded readers. At first a broadsheet, it became a tabloid in 1977, in line with the newer popular newspapers such as *The Sun*. Published in London, it has a circulation of around 1,600,000.

Title
A saying commonly used to refer to tea (i.e. a drink that makes you feel cheerful). It's a quotation from the poem *The Task* by the English poet William Cowper (1731–1800):
Now stir the fire, and close the shutters fast,
Let fall the curtains, wheel the sofa round,
And, while the bubbling and loud-hissing urn
Throws up a steamy column, and the cups
That cheer but not inebriate, wait on each,
So let us welcome peaceful ev'ning in.

bergamot (l. 16)
Here *bergamot* is used to refer to the oil obtained from a citrus fruit, the bergamot orange, which is sometimes used to flavour tea.

7 Junket for robbers was police trap (BrE)

The Times
For a large part of its history, *The Times* has been the most influential British daily newspaper, essential reading for the traditional ruling classes. It was founded by John Walter in 1785 as *The Daily Universal Register*, renamed *The Times* in 1788. By the mid-19th century it had earned the nickname 'The Thunderer' for its formidable editorials, and was renowned for its coverage of world affairs (it was the first paper to employ foreign correspondents). After a period of decline, its prestige revived under the editorship of William Haley in the 1960s and 70s, marked by a famous – and controversial – advertising slogan, *Top People Read the Times*. *The Times*, like its sister paper *The Sunday Times*, is now owned by the international press magnate Rupert Murdoch. It is published in London, with a circulation of between 400,000 and 450,000.

Good Buy/Goodbye (l. 3)
An obvious pun which has been used as a slogan in airport shops: *Goodbye to the Good Buys*.

Atlantic City (l. 8)
Seaside resort in New Jersey, about 130 km south of New York.

Manhattan (l. 16)
A borough of New York City with a land area of 57 km^2, obtained from the Manhattan Indians in 1626 in exchange for trinkets worth $26 and first known as New Amsterdam. It is the commercial, cultural and financial heart of New York City.

Brooklyn (l. 36)
A borough of New York City with a land area of 184 km^2. It is separated from downtown Manhattan by the East River (hence the famous Brooklyn Bridge).

8 Roman regimental brewery (BrE)

The Independent
The Independent is Britain's newest 'quality' daily paper, founded in 1986, at a time when several other

newly-established papers were failing. Its survival was attributed to a long and careful period of planning, and to the excellence of its design, photography and graphics. It appeals particularly to educated, middle-class readers who don't care for the earnestness of *The Guardian*, or who find *The Daily Telegraph* stuffy, or who are worried by changes in *The Times* since its acquisition by the international businessman, Rupert Murdoch. It is published in London, with a circulation of over 400,000.

Roman Britain (general note)
The Roman invasion of Britain which resulted in lasting occupation began in AD 43. Britain was governed as a Roman province till about AD 410. The Romans maintained a large army in Britain and had military bases throughout most of the country. The northernmost point of occupation was the Antonine Wall (AD 142) which ran between the Forth Estuary and the Clyde.

Hadrian's Wall (l. 7)
The most important northern frontier of Roman Britain, in Northumberland. Hadrian's wall was built across the north of England by the emperor Hadrian between AD 122 and 128 to keep back the Picts (ancient inhabitants of Scotland).

Vindolanda (l. 9)
Roman camp near Chesterholm, 4 km south of Hadrian's Wall.

Northumberland (l. 10)
Northern county in England.

Virgil's Aeneid (ll. 54–55)
A 12-book Latin epic by the Roman poet Virgil (Publius Vergilius Maro, 70–19 B.C.). The hero of the poem is *Aeneas*, a Trojan prince who escaped from Troy and went to Carthage, where he met Dido, the Carthaginian queen. He finally went to Italy where his descendants founded Rome.

9 Plane-load of 400 lobsters (BrE)

The Guardian
The British daily newspaper *The Guardian* was founded in Manchester in 1821 as *The Manchester Guardian*. In 1959 its name was changed to *The Guardian*, and since 1961 it has been printed simultaneously in London and Manchester. A 'quality' daily, *The Guardian* is owned by a trust, not a proprietor, and therefore has a reputation for independence. Noted for its political comment, arts reviews, and women's page, its stance is leftwards, and it appeals mainly to middle-class readers who regard themselves as liberal-minded. Though it has been called 'Britain's nonconformist conscience', it has its lighter side, and is famous for its punning headlines. (The original headline for this extract was PLANE-LOAD OF 400 LOBSTERS ESCAPES PREMATURE PICKLE AS PILOT PLUMPS FOR PRISON IN NICK OF TIME). Its circulation is over 400,000.

lobster pot, bisque and quadrille (ll. 5–6)
The only real name for a dish is *lobster bisque*, a kind of soup. The other two references are jokes. *A lobster pot* is a kind of basket used to trap lobsters. *Lobster quadrille* is a reference to a lobster dance in *Alice in Wonderland* by Lewis Carroll (Charles Lutwidge Dodgson, 1832–1898). A *quadrille* was a ballroom dance for four couples in square formation, popular in the late 18th and early 19th centuries.

11 Memories of a great actress (BrE)

Sir John Gielgud
The British actor and director Sir John Gielgud /giːlgəd/ was born in 1904. He made his debut at the Old Vic Theatre, London, in 1921. His first great success was as Hamlet in 1929, and he went on to become one of Britain's most important interpreters of Shakespearian roles. He has also directed many productions, notably at the Shakespeare Festival, Stratford-on-Avon. Later he appeared in films, including *The Prime Minister* (as Disraeli, in 1940) and *Murder on the Orient Express*, winning an Oscar for his performance in *Arthur* in 1982. He was knighted in 1953. His published work includes an edition of Chekhov's *The Cherry Orchard*, theatrical memoirs, and his autobiography *An Actor and His Time* (1975).

Eleonora Duse (l. 5)
Eleonora Duse (1859–1924) was an Italian actress, particularly famed for her interpretations of Ibsen. She retired in 1909, but made a comeback in 1921.

Ghosts (l. 5)
A play (1881) by the great Norwegian dramatist, Henrik Ibsen (1828–1906).

Tottenham Court Road (ll. 6–7)
A street in the West End of London.

Charlie Chaplin (l. 26)
Sir Charles Chaplin (1889–1977); world-famous actor and director-writer, best remembered for the tramp character in his early films, such as *The Gold Rush* (1924).

Tree (l. 28)
Sir Herbert Beerbohm Tree (1853–1917); English actor and theatre manager.

12 La belle Monique (BrE)

The Daily Telegraph
The British *Daily Telegraph* was founded in 1855. As the first cheap daily newspaper in London, it was at the start rather radical in outlook (and enormously popular). Today its readers are mainly middle-to-upper class, with conservative views (and probably Conservative politics). *The Telegraph* has a reputation for wide and accurate reporting, and is considered to be one of Britain's 'quality' dailies (along with *The Times*, *The Guardian*, *The Financial*

Times and *The Independent*). It is published in London with a circulation of over 1,000,000.

Title
La belle Monique (= the beautiful Monique.) *La belle* + woman's name is sometimes used in English to suggest a 'femme fatale' (a woman of fatal attractions), especially a French one.

Jealousy of the Long Distance Lorry Driver (ll. 3–5)
This contains an intentional echo of *The Loneliness of the Long-Distance Runner*, a short story (1959) by Alan Sillitoe (born 1928), made into a successful film in 1962.

Autoroute (l. 6)
(= Motorway)

the Auvergne (l. 11)
A mountainous region of France, once a province, which includes the *départements* of Puy-de-Dôme, whose capital is Clermont-Ferrand, and the Upper Loire.

Route Nationale (l. 42)
Main trunk road in France, below the status of an *autoroute*.

knight of the road (l. 51)
A term once applied to highwaymen, and later used to mean 'a good and considerate driver' (used ironically here). The use of the word *knight* also implics a reference to duelling.

Honour still unsatisfied (l. 59)
An 'affair of honour' was a dispute which had to be settled, or 'satisfied', by a duel.

13 Patagonia (BrE)

Bruce Chatwin
Bruce Chatwin, British author and anthropologist (1940–1989). In 1965–66 he was a director of Sotheby's (the London auctioneers dealing in art and antiques), but left to study anthropology. His continuing interest in nomadic peoples took him to some of the remotest places in the world. He became a full-time writer in 1975 and his first book, *In Patagonia*, won the 1978 Hawthornden Prize. Other books include *The Viceroy of Ouidah* and *The Black Hill*, winner of the Whitbread Award for best first novel. As a travel writer, Chatwin was much more than a mere describer: what makes his books unique is his love for strange facts and his curiosity about human beings.

Title
Patagonia is a sparsely-populated region of South America, including the southern part of Argentina, and stretching from the Andes to the Atlantic.

thornscrub (l. 22)
An invented word made up of *thorn* and *scrub* (= low-growing plants and bushes, thickly covering the ground).

Río Negro (l. 26)

A river in southern Argentina.

dustclouds (l. 41)
An invented word (= clouds of dust).

14 You're Marlowe? (AmE)

Raymond Chandler
World-famous as the creator of the tough, deadpan Los Angeles private eye, Philip Marlowe, Raymond Chandler was born in Chicago in 1888. He was educated in London, France and Germany, moving to southern California in 1912. After serving with the Canadian Army in the First World War, he began writing stories for US detective magazines, but it was not until 1939 that the first novel featuring Marlowe, *The Big Sleep*, was published. Films based on Chandler's work include *Farewell my Lovely*, *The Long Goodbye* and *The Big Sleep*, with Humphrey Bogart as Marlowe. Raymond Chandler died in La Jolla, California, in 1959.

Title
Marlowe (= Philip Marlowe), fictional character and tough hero of several detective thrillers by Raymond Chandler, US author (1888–1959).

going on fifty (l. 20)
(= about or approaching the age of fifty)

pictures (l. 25)
(= movies, or films, here)

15 You can't teach managers (BrE)

Robert Heller
The best-selling British business writer, Robert Heller, trained as a journalist, joining *The Financial Times* in 1955. He left in 1966 to head the City pages of *The Observer*. In 1966 he was founding editor of Britain's leading monthly business magazine, *Business Today*, and also helped launch other magazines, including *Campaign* and *Computing*. His books include *The Naked Manager* (an international best-seller, 1974) and *Culture Shock: The Office Revolution* (1990). As well as writing, Robert Heller speaks to company and management audiences all over the world.

The Harvard Business School (l. 1)
Prestigious business school which is part of Harvard University, Cambridge, Massachusetts, U.S.A.

the ark of the tabernacle (ll. 1–2)
In the Old Testament of the Bible, the ark of the tabernacle, or ark of the covenant, was a box made of wood and gold containing the religious laws and representing God, carried by the Israelites during their wanderings in the desert and later kept in Solomon's Temple. It is now lost. The part of the tabernacle (= portable shrine) where the ark was kept was called the Holy of Holies. Hence the *ark of the tabernacle* is used to refer to something which is superlative and not to be questioned, often, as here, when the writer is about to challenge it.

Midas (l. 20)
A king in Greek mythology who turned everything he touched into gold.

John F. Kennedy (l. 38)
John F. Kennedy, born May 29, 1917, elected President of the USA in 1960 and assassinated on November 22, 1963.

the Bay of Pigs (l. 40)
The unsuccessful invasion of Cuba by 1,200 US trained and supplied, anti-Castro Cuban exiles on April 17, 1961 at the Bay of Pigs (Bahia de los Cochinos). The event led to the Cuban missile crisis in October, 1962, a major Cold War confrontation between the USA and the Soviet Union, which nearly precipitated World War III.

16 An English lesson (BrE)

Jonathan Raban
The British writer and journalist Jonathan Raban /reɪbən/ was born in London in 1942, and educated at the University of Hull. In the 1960s he lectured in English and American literature at the University College of Wales, Aberystwyth, and at the University of East Anglia. He became a full-time writer in 1969. As well as perceptive and highly-praised travel books such as *Arabia Through the Looking Glass* and *Old Glory* (1981, winner of the Heinemann Award and the Thomas Cook Award), he has written plays for the stage, TV and radio, and articles, short stories and reviews for newspapers and literary magazines.

Gamal Abdel Nasser Secondary School (ll. 1–2)
Named after *Gamal Abdel Nasser* (1918–1970), President of Egypt, 1956–1970, and founder of the United Arab Republic, principally an alliance of Egypt and Syria.

17 Minty (BrE)

Graham Greene
Graham Greene, one of Britain's most distinguished authors, was born in 1904, and educated at Berkhamsted School (where his father was Headmaster) and at Balliol College, Oxford. In 1926 he became a convert to the Roman Catholic Church. He worked in London as a journalist and film critic, and later as a publisher and freelance writer. His first novel, *England Made Me*, was published in 1935. In many of his books Greene, often using the format of the detective story or thriller, explores the nature of good and evil and the question of salvation, in settings ranging from the south coast of England (*Brighton Rock*) to Mexico (*The Power and the Glory*), or Vietnam (*The Quiet American*). He once said that if he could choose an epigraph for his novels, it would be a quotation from a poem by Robert Browning: 'Our interest's on the dangerous edge of things,/The honest thief, the tender murderer,/The superstitious

atheist ...'. Graham Greene also wrote travel books, plays, filmscripts (notably *The Third Man*), short stories, essays and autobiography. He was the most famous writer never to win the Nobel Prize for Literature. For the last part of his life he lived in Antibes on the French Riviera. He died in 1991.

this was one of his days (ll. 2–3)
This means it was sure to be a good day for him. The phrase often occurs in the expression 'It's not one of my days' (= everything is going wrong for me today).

This is the way that Minty goes (ll. 4–5)
This is an adaptation of a line from the well-known children's nursery song, 'Here we go round the mulberry bush' or 'Here we go gathering nuts in May': *This is the way we clap our hands*.

tooth glass (l. 12)
This refers here to a glass used for holding toothbrushes, etc.

shaggy patience (l. 18)
The spider gave the impression of shagginess (= covered with hair) and patience.

a house-group (l. 20)
A photograph of all the boys and staff living in a boarding-house at a British public (= private, fee-paying) school.

19 Alaska's dirty dollars (BrE)

The Financial Times
The Financial Times, a British daily, was founded in 1888. It provides full daily reports on the Stock Exchange and on world markets, and a comprehensive coverage of business affairs. But it is also greatly respected for its general news reporting and analysis, and for its reviews of literature and the arts. More expensive than other daily papers, and printed on distinctive pink paper, *The Financial Times* is published in London, with an international edition published in Frankfurt, New York, and Paris. Its circulation is around 290,000.

General
The background to this piece is the large spill of oil on March 24, 1989, when the oil tanker *Exxon Valdez* ran aground on Bligh Reef, Prince William Sound, Alaska, and seriously polluted the bay with crude oil.

Exxon (l. 1)
The largest US-based oil company, formerly known as Esso (= Standard Oil).

20 Fire message in plain English (BrE)

General
On November 18, 1987, 31 people were killed and 80 injured (12 of them seriously) in a fire in the Underground Railway Station at King's Cross Station, London.

21 Another day begins (AmE)

Alison Lurie
The American author Alison Lurie /liːuːrɪ/ was born in Chicago in 1926, and educated at Radcliffe College. In 1976 she was appointed Professor of English at Cornell University, where she teaches several subjects, including folklore and children's literature. Her highly acclaimed novels include *Love and Friendship* (1967), *Nowhere City* (1975) and *The Truth About Lorin Jones* (1988). Alison Lurie specializes in witty, sharply observed, and strongly characterized pictures of middle-class families in crisis. Her non-fiction books include *The Language of Clothes* (a study of the way people dress) and *Not in Front of the Grown-ups: Subversive Children's Literature*. She has also written books for children, including *Clever Gretchen* and *The Heavenly Zoo*.

23 Spot of mutiny on the high Cs (BrE)

Title
This is a joke, based on a pun: *a spot of mutiny on the high seas*. *High C* (two octaves above middle C) is at the very top of a singer's range.

snow line (l. 4)
An imaginary line, for example on a mountainside, above which snow never melts.

Placido Domingo (l. 21)
World-famous tenor, born Madrid, 1941.

bass bar (l. 26)
'A strip of wood glued lengthways inside the belly of instruments of the violin family, used to spread the vibrations over the surface'. (Random House Dictionary)

the A above middle C (l. 36)
This is the note used to tune up the instruments of the orchestra before a performance.

Provence (l. 49)
A region in the south of France.

24 Homeopathy (BrE)

allopathic medicine (l. 26)
The meaning intended here is 'conventional medicine exclusive of homeopathy'. *Homeopathy* implies treating like with like. *Allopathy* implies treating an ailment with its opposite.

Hippocrates (l. 36)
c.460–c.370 B.C., Greek physician, known as 'the father of medicine'.

successions (l. 59)
The meaning given in the text (= shocks) is peculiar to homeopathy and departs from the normal meanings of this word.

centesimal (l. 60)
Division into *hundredths* (noun); *centesimal* is an adjective (= hundredth).

25 Decision-thinking (BrE)

Ben Heirs
Ben Heirs heads a company that provides strategic advice to the senior management – in most cases the chief executive – of a wide range of international businesses.

John von Neumann (ll. 9–10)
U.S. mathematician, born in Budapest (1903–1957). His work in other fields includes quantum mechanics, logic and meteorology. His theory of games was influential in economics.

26 Pigeons 'not so bird-brained' (BrE)

Charles Darwin (l. 56)
British naturalist (1809–1882). His researches led to the formulation of his theory of evolution, set out in his work *The Origin of Species* (1859).

27 First impressions (AmE)

New Woman
New Woman is an American glossy magazine, founded in 1971 and published monthly in New York. It is designed to appeal not so much to the traditional housewife, as to professional working women between 25 and 45, and it publishes articles on such topics as work and financial problems, legal rights, relationships, health, diet, clothes and cosmetics, besides interviews and high-quality fiction. Its current circulation is around 1,350,000, and it also publishes a London edition.

pedal pushers (l. 3)
Calf-length trousers, originally worn for cycling.

trying out (l. 11)
(= being tested) American English usage, used intransitively here: 'Over a hundred boys came to try out for the football team'. (Random House Dictionary) The normal meaning of *try out* is to 'test something to see if you like it': *I'd like to try out this CD player before I buy it*.

28 Sherlock Holmes (BrE)

Sir Arthur Conan Doyle
Sir Arthur Conan Doyle, creator of Sherlock Holmes, the world's most famous detective, was born in Edinburgh, Scotland, in 1859. He studied medicine in Edinburgh and practised as a doctor for a while before becoming a writer. Sherlock Holmes, whose character was based on an Edinburgh surgeon, first appeared in Doyle's first book, *A Study in Scarlet* (1887) and was instantly popular. Holmes' brilliant deductions won the constant admiration of his assistant, Dr Watson. Later, Doyle grew tired of Holmes, and tried to kill him off, but was persuaded by popular pressure to revive him. He also wrote historical novels, such as *The White Company* (1891)

and science fiction, such as *The Lost World* (1912). In 1926 he wrote *A History of Spiritualism*, to which, in later life, he became converted. He died in 1930.

the Hall (l. 6)
Common name in England for the most important house, often belonging to a landowner, in or near a village. This one is presumably *Charlington Hall*.

29 Breaking the Portland Vase (BrE)

the Portland Vase (title)
A funerary urn discovered near Rome in the 17th century, first owned by the Barberini family, and then bought by the Duke of Portland. It was sold to the British Museum in 1845. Made of dark blue glass with white figures, it is the finest example of Roman cameo glass.

conservator (l. 3)
A museum official whose job is the upkeep and restoration of stock.

30 Fax-mad New Yorkers (BrE)

fax (title)
Fax is an abbreviation for *facsimile (machine)*. It can be part of a compound *(fax-mad)*; or a noun with a plural *(junk faxes)*; or a verb *(faxing in the fast lane)*.

sign-off (l. 2)
Sign off, as a verb, usually means 'cease broadcasting'. Here it is used as a noun to mean for example 'the end of a telephone conversation'.

record requests (l. 11)
A request for records here (not 'a record number of requests').

le fax menu (l. 15)
The use of *le* here (French for *the*) follows a fashion for labelling merchandise to suggest 'the one and only', e.g. *Le car*.

dating service (l. 19)
An agency which provides partners for single people who are interested in forming short-term or long-term relationships.

Greenwich Village (ll. 19–20)
A district of lower Manhattan in New York City, popular with artists and writers.

you transmit from your car fax (l. 35)
Transmit is used intransitively here (= send messages). *Car fax* (= a fax machine in a car).

junk faxes (ll. 40–41)
Junk faxes are unwanted fax messages, just as *junk mail* is unwanted material sent through the post.

fax-lash (l. 62)
This is a play on *backlash* (= a reaction against something) and therefore suggests 'a reaction against fax'.

31 Japan's underground frontier (AmE)

Time
In 1922 Henry R. Luce and Briton Haddon formed the communications company *Time Inc.* in New York. *Time*, the world's first weekly news magazine, and still the most popular, appeared in the following year. It is now published in several languages, selling all over the world, with a circulation of over 5 million. Besides world and US news, *Time* covers business, sport, science and technology, social issues and the arts, with a gossip column under the heading *People*. *Time* is famous for its informal, racy style of reporting, and for its pictures and picture-captions.

Montana (l. 13)
A state in the northwest U.S. with an area of 378,497 km².

Alice ... Lewis Carroll (ll. 38–39)
Alice City is a reference to *Alice in Wonderland* (1865), a famous story by Lewis Carroll (Charles Lutwidge Dodgson, 1832–1898).

32 Schooldays (Canadian)

Robertson Davies
The Canadian writer, dramatist and journalist, Robertson Davies, was born in Thamesville, Ontario, in 1913. He was educated at Queen's University, Kingston, Ontario, and at Balliol College, Oxford (1936–38), where he was awarded a B.Litt. He worked as a teacher and actor in London until 1940, when he returned to Canada, where he worked as an editor and publisher before being appointed Professor of English at the University of Toronto. His novels, including *A Mixture of Frailties* and *What's Bred in the Bone*, often portray, in a satirical but affectionate way, life in small-town Canadian society.

Carlyle Rural (ll. 17–18)
This is presumably short for *Carlyle Rural Elementary* (or *Junior*) *School*, that is, a small village school for young children. The school is probably named after Thomas Carlyle, British man of letters (1795–1881).

33 Our tribal past (BrE)

A-bomb (l. 15)
Short for *Atom Bomb*, or *Atomic Bomb*.

Etruscan (l. 56)
An early (pre-Roman) civilization in Italy which flourished between the 8th and the 3rd centuries BC in the region now known as Tuscany.

34 Village women (BrE)

Ronald Blythe
Born in 1922 in Suffolk, England, where he has lived since becoming a full-time writer in 1955, Ronald Blythe is highly praised by critics for his evocative

descriptions, based on tape-recorded interviews, of rural life in eastern England. *Akenfield: Portrait of a Village* (1969) summons up the life of the village largely through the words of its inhabitants, while in *The View in Winter* old people look back at their lives. Ronald Blythe is the editor of several volumes of Penguin Classics, including Jane Austen's *Emma*.

General

This piece refers to conditions in the 1920s and 1930s.

the Women's Institute (l. 11)

This is an organization for the education, entertainment, etc. of women, especially in rural areas, founded in Canada in 1897 and in Britain in 1915.

the bad days (l. 18)

This is a reference to the agricultural depression in Britain, which was originally caused by the importing to the UK of cheap grain from America and frozen meat from Australia and New Zealand. It caused massive unemployment and low wages, etc. in the countryside.

Suffolk (l. 28)

A county in eastern England, mainly agricultural.

35 Dreams and nightmares (AmE)

Raymond Carver

Raymond Carver, one of America's best short-story writers, was born in Clatskanie, Oregon, in 1938. He married for the first time at 19, and to support his family, worked at various jobs for many years, including as a janitor, a sawmill worker, a delivery man and a textbook editor. During this time he wrote several volumes of poetry, but his first real success came with his first book of stories, *Will You Please Be Quiet, Please?* in 1976, followed in the 1980s by works like *What We Talk About When We Talk About Love*, and *Elephant and Other Stories*. His work received many awards, and he is valued especially for the understated but poignant way in which he portrays the unfulfilled, often desperate lives of ordinary, rather inarticulate men and women. He married the poet Tess Gallagher in 1988, shortly before his death.

Niteguard (l. 31)

This kind of phonetic spelling (for 'Nightguard') is commonly used when naming consumer products: e.g. *Kleenex*, from 'clean', etc.

36 Armageddon larder (BrE)

Armageddon (title)

This is the name given in the Bible (Revelations 16: 14) to the site of the last great 'battle of that great day of God almighty' between the forces of good and evil. It is now used to describe any great battle or scene of slaughter.

The Second World War (l. 2)

Also referred to as *World War II* (1939–45) to distinguish it from the *First World War* or *World War I* (1914–18).

Doncaster (l. 10) *Yorkshire* (l. 4)

Doncaster is a town in *Yorkshire*, a county of north-eastern England.

37 Alzheimer's telltale protein (AmE)

US News and World Report

The American weekly news magazine *US News and World Report* was founded in 1933 as *US News*. It followed the same formula as the highly successful *Time* founded ten years earlier, but tended to take a more serious approach (for example, it gave whole texts of important speeches and documents). In 1945, its founder, David Lawrence, introduced *World Report* to cover world events and the two were amalgamated in 1948. It once had a reputation for dullness ('U.S. Snooze'), but was revamped in the late 1980s in a more attractive format, including colour photos. Its approach is moderate to conservative. *US News and World Report* is published in Washington, DC, with a circulation of well over 2 million.

Alzheimer's (title)

This is a reference to *Alzheimer's disease*, named after the German neurologist, Alois Alzheimer (1864–1915). He was the first to describe a condition, which can affect people from middle-age onwards, in which degeneration of brain and nerve tissue eventually destroys the personality.

38 Drug-war overkill (AmE)

New York

The weekly magazine *New York* was founded in 1968. Besides material of special interest to New Yorkers, such as a comprehensive entertainment guide and listings for restaurants, radio and TV, etc., it publishes book reviews and articles on politics, business, psychology, literature and the fine arts. It is noted for the grace and wit of its style, and for the excellence of its illustrations. It has a circulation of over 400,000.

39 Garbage (AmE)

The Atlantic

The Atlantic, founded in 1857 as *Atlantic Monthly*, is one of the most respected monthly reviews in the United States, and in the English-speaking world. At first, it was exclusively a literary magazine, publishing the work of American writers such as James Russell Lowell (its first editor), Oliver Wendell Holmes, Longfellow, Emerson, Mark Twain and Bret Harte. In the 1920s it began to extend its scope to include articles on economics, sociology, current events and politics. Today it contains extended analyses of

American society or foreign affairs, as well as poetry, fiction, humour and articles on leisure and fashion. *The Atlantic* is published in Boston, with a circulation of over 450,000.

stands of plants (l. 9)
(= groups or clumps of plants growing together in a continuous area)

Bronze Age (l. 28)
The Bronze Age is the name given to a pre-historic period (c. 3000–2000 B.C.) during which bronze was used for making tools. It followed the Neolithic Age (or Stone Age) and came immediately before the Iron Age.

Troy (l. 28)
Ruined city in what is now Turkey. There were at least nine successive settlements on this site in ancient times, the most famous being at the time of the Trojan war between the Greeks and the Trojans, described in Homer's *Iliad*.

island of Manhattan/Manhattan island (l. 39)
Part of *Manhattan*, the commercial, cultural and financial heart of New York City. It is 19.31 km long and 3.22 km wide at its widest point.

Peter Minuit (l. 40)
Peter Minuit (1580–1638) was the first director general (1626–31) of New Netherland, a Dutch colony (1613–64). Its capital was New Amsterdam, on Manhattan Island, which Peter Minuit bought from the Manhattan Indians. It was renamed New York when the colony was captured by the British in 1664.

40 The Japanese sense of beauty (BrE)

George Mikes
George Mikes /miːkeʃ/, a Hungarian author writing in English, achieved fame as a humorist in the years after the Second World War. His first book, *How to be an Alien* (1946), was a funny, bewildered look at the British way of life ('Continental people have sex-lives. The English have hot water bottles.') and was a best-seller. He wrote numerous other works, including *How to be God* and *The Land of the Rising Yen*. Born in Siklós, Hungary in 1912, he received his doctorate in literature at Budapest University, then worked as a theatre critic. In 1938 he was sent to England as a newspaper correspondent. He later worked for the Hungarian Service of the BBC, before becoming a full-time writer and broadcaster. He died in 1987.

sushi, sashimi (ll. 17–18)
Raw fish dishes served in Japanese restaurants and *Sushi* bars. *Sushi* is thinly-sliced raw fish coated in rice and wrapped in seaweed; *sashimi* is thinly-sliced raw fish served with vinegar.

Michelangelo (l. 23)
Michelangelo Buonarroti (1475–1564) was one of the greatest artists of the Italian Renaissance. The statues of the *Pietà* (St Peter's, Rome) and *David* (Academy, Florence) are among his many famous sculptures.

Madonna (l. 24)
A representation of the mother of Jesus Christ, a universal image in Christian art.

41 Two topics of conversation (BrE)

Ruth Rendell
The best-selling British crime and mystery writer, Ruth Rendell, was born in London. She worked as a journalist and as managing director of a local newspaper before writing her first novel *From Doon to Death* (1964), which introduced her famous detective, Chief Inspector Wexford. As well as the stories featuring Wexford, Ruth Rendell has written many hugely successful mystery novels, often about ordinary people trapped by obsession, for example, *A Judgement in Stone* and *Live Flesh*. She also writes under the pseudonym Barbara Vine. She has won many awards in Britain and America and her work has been translated into 15 languages.

The Second World War (l. 2)
Also referred to as *World War II* (1939–45) to distinguish it from the *First World War* or *World War I* (1914–18).

Montgomery (l. 7)
Bernard Law Montgomery, 1st Viscount Montgomery of Alamein (1887–1976), British field marshal, famous for his victory over Rommel at Alamein in the north African desert in 1942. Montgomery was commander of all ground forces in the invasion of Normandy, which led to the end of the Second World War in Europe in May 1945.

Weser (l. 11)
A river in north-west Germany.

Bremen (l. 15)
Germany's second largest port, after Hamburg, which extends 47 km along the river Weser.

42 Invasion of the data snatchers! (AmE)

Title
The title contains a reference to *Invasion of the Body-snatchers*, the title of a novel by Jack Finney, filmed twice, in which aliens take over a small American town. Originally, *body snatchers* were people who stole or dug up recently dead bodies to sell to medical schools for dissection, a practice which was stopped by the Anatomy Act of 1832.

Providence (l. 5)
The capital of Rhode Island, a state in the north-east of the United States.

Sector 0 (l. 37)
Disks in computers (floppy disks and hard disks) are divided into numbered segments, known as *sectors*.

glitch (l. 38)
A technical problem or malfunction, particularly in electrical or electronic equipment.

the Shanghai flu (l. 53)
An American English term given to any of the flu
epidemics that periodically spread across the
northern hemisphere, from East to West, often
referred to in British English as *Asian flu*.

43 The thoughts of Henry Wilt (BrE)

Tom Sharpe
Tom Sharpe, the best-selling British novelist of 'black
humour', was born in 1928. He attended Pembroke
College, Cambridge before working in South Africa.
On being deported for political reasons, he returned
to England and taught at Cambridge College of Arts
and Technology. His first (and very successful) novel,
Riotous Assembly, was published in 1971, since
when he has been a full-time writer. Many of his
books have been filmed or televised, including *Wilt*
and *Porterhouse Blue*. In 1986 he won the Grand
Prix de l'Humour Noir Xavier Forneret.
did his business (l. 17)
Informal expression for *defecated*, often used in
connexion with dogs and other animals.

44 Dinosaurs on a tidal wave? (BrE)

the Caribbean region (l. 6)
An area which includes the Caribbean Sea, the West
Indies, the Gulf of Mexico, the south-west United
States, Central America and the northern countries of
South America.
the Cretaceous period (l. 7)
A period in geological time, the third phase of the
Mesozoic Era, that began about 136,000,000 years
ago and lasted about 71,000,000 years. This period
was marked by great changes to the earth's surface.
Dinosaurs were the main life-form on land, with
mammals just beginning to appear.
'catastrophists' (l. 19)
There are several theories why the dinosaurs
disappeared; this refers to the proposition that their
disappearance was caused by a 'catastrophe', a
sudden violent event such as the one described here,
of an asteroid colliding with the Earth.
Brazos River (l. 55)
The Brazos River is formed in north-west Texas and
flows more than 1287 km south-east to Freeport on
the Gulf of Mexico.

45 When mothers work (AmE)

USA Today
USA Today was founded in 1915, as *Intellect*. It is
published monthly in Valley Stream, New York, by
the Society for the Advancement of Education. It
publishes articles on economics, national and
international affairs, medicine, mass media, culture
and other topics. Most of its writers are university

professors. In some respects similar to other news
magazines such as *Time* and *Newsweek*, its approach
is deeper, and its design is of a higher quality. Its
circulation is around 90,000.

46 Peter (BrE)

Paul Sayer
The young British novelist Paul Sayer was born and
brought up near Leeds, Yorkshire, England. When his
first book, *The Comforts of Madness*, was published,
he was working as a staff nurse in a large psychiatric
hospital in York. The book was a runaway success,
winning the Whitbread Book of the Year Award and
the Constable Trophy for Fiction in 1988. As one
critic said, 'it forces the reader to confront the fact
that behind the rigid stiffness of the ill or
handicapped there may be keen minds and
flourishing imaginations'. Paul Sayer now writes full
time, and has published a successful second novel,
Howling at the Moon.
capillaried (l. 10)
An adjective formed from *capillary* (= a bloodvessel
as fine as hair).

47 Life on a desert island (BrE)

Lucy Irvine
Lucy Irvine was born in England in 1956. At 12, she
ran away from school and had no regular education
after the age of 13. By 16 she was travelling round
Europe on her own. Adventurous by nature, she
answered a newspaper advertisement which resulted
in her spending a year on an uninhabited tropical
island with a complete stranger ('G'), an experience
which led to her highly successful first book,
Castaway. Her second autobiographical book,
Runaway, tells the story of her life before her year on
the island. In 1989 she published her first novel, *One
is one*. Lucy Irvine lives with her three sons in a
remote part of Scotland.
pandanus (l. 13)
A tropical palm-like plant, also known as *screw pine*.
pocking (l. 24)
Pock (= make holes) occurs unusually as a verb here.
Compare *pocked* or *pockmarked* (= covered with
hollow marks), especially to describe the condition of
the skin after a disease such as smallpox.

48 The crowd (AmE)

Ray Bradbury
Ray Bradbury was born in Waukegan, Illinois, USA, in
1920, and educated in Los Angeles, where he now
lives. As a child, he was a skilled conjuror and enjoyed
fantasy and horror magazines, and it is as a science
fiction and fantasy writer that he is best known. He
sold his first story to *Weird Tales* in 1942. Since then,

he has written more than 500 short stories, novels, plays and poems, including such classics as *The Martian Chronicles* (1950) and *Fahrenheit 451* (1953). Numerous films, including *The Illustrated Man*, have been based on or inspired by Bradbury's work. Since the 1960s Bradbury has become less interested in fantasy and more in writing about the predicaments of ordinary people.

49 All politics is local (AmE)

The New Yorker
The New Yorker, founded in 1925 by Harold Ross, is one of America's leading weekly magazines, also enjoyed throughout the English-speaking world. In its traditional 3-column layout, it presents a sophisticated and entertaining mix of stories, poems, humorous writing, essays, biographies and foreign reports, and has published work by America's best writers. It has always been famous for its cartoons, in particular those of Charles Addams and James Thurber, and is also noted for the glossiness of its advertisements. It appeals mainly to a smart, well-educated audience. Its present circulation is over 600,000.

Tip O'Neill (l. 1)
Thomas Phillip ('Tip') O'Neill, born 1912, Speaker, House of Representatives, USA.

chlorofluorocarbons (l. 14)
Commonly known as *CFCs* (= compounds containing chlorine and fluorine), chlorofluorocarbons are widely used as refrigerants and as propellants in aerosol sprays and in the production of foam packaging. They are believed to deplete the ozone layer, the shield that protects the earth from ultraviolet radiation, over the poles.

50 What is the soul? (BrE)

W. Somerset Maugham
The British author W. Somerset Maugham /mɔːm/ was born in 1874 in Paris, where his father was a lawyer with the British Embassy. Orphaned before he was 11, and suffering from a severe stammer, he was sent to live with relations in England, where he was educated at The King's School, Canterbury. Later, he went to Heidelberg University, Germany, and then trained as a surgeon at St Thomas's Hospital, London. His first novel, *Lisa of Lambeth,* appeared in 1897, but his first real success came as a playwright in the 1900s. His huge popular reputation rests on his later novels and in particular on his short stories, many of which, such as *Rain*, were filmed. He settled at Cap Ferrat in the south of France in 1926, and died in Nice in 1965.

Plato (l. 1)
The Greek philosopher, Plato, (c.427–c.347 B.C.) is one of the most influential thinkers of all time. He

recorded the ideas of his teacher, Socrates, as well as developing a philosophical system of his own. In his dialogue *Phaedo*, Plato distinguished between the soul (*psyche*) and the body (*soma*), observing that death liberated the soul from its 'tomb', the body.

51 The ultimate quest (AmE)

Stephen Hawking (ll. 5–6)
Stephen Hawking (born 1942) suffers from a devastating physical handicap, but has been Lucasian Professor of Mathematics at the University of Cambridge since 1979 (a post once held by Sir Isaac Newton). He is considered to be one of the world's most eminent physicists. His bestselling book, *A Brief History of Time: From the Big Bang to Black Holes* (1988), has reached a wide audience.

Sir Isaac Newton (l. 24)
Sir Isaac Newton (1642–1727) was an English physicist, mathematician and philosopher, Lucasian Professor of Mathematics at Cambridge (1669–1701) and President of the Royal Society (1703–27). His most famous discoveries were concerned with gravity, motion, calculus and the spectrum.

52 Henry Ford (AmE)

Peter Collier/David Horowitz
The American writer Peter Collier was born in Hollywood in 1939 and educated at the University of California, Berkeley, where he taught English until 1969. Since then he has been an editor and freelance writer, contributing to magazines such as *Esquire* and *Mademoiselle*. David Horowitz, born in New York in 1939, was educated at Columbia University and at the University of California, Berkeley. Besides *The Fords*, Collier and Horowitz have co-authored *The Rockefellers: An American Dynasty* (a Book-of-the-Month Club main selection in 1976), and *The Kennedys: An American Drama* (1984).

Henry Ford (title)
Henry Ford (1863–1947), U.S. motor engineer, car manufacturer and industrialist. He founded Ford Motors in 1903 and developed the world's first mass-produced car, the Model T (1908) which sold to a mass market. In 1936 Henry Ford and his son Edsel (1893–1943) set up the Ford Foundation with the general purpose of advancing human welfare.

John Dillinger (ll. 16–17)
John Dillinger (1902–34), U.S. bank robber who terrorized the Mid-West with a gang of criminals. He murdered sixteen people and was known as Public Enemy Number 1. He was finally shot by FBI agents.

sclerotic (l. 24)
Adjective from *sclerosis*, a condition in which body tissues become hardened. Here, it is used metaphorically to mean 'obstinate' or 'pig-headed'.

53 The healer (BrE)

Nigel Barley

After a degree in foreign languages at Cambridge University, England, Nigel Barley trained as an anthropologist at Oxford, where he was awarded a doctorate for his work on the Anglo-Saxons (early inhabitants of Britain). In the 1970s and 80s Nigel Barley made two fieldwork trips to the Cameroons, West Africa, on which he based two very successful books about the Dowayo society, *The Innocent Anthropologist* and *A Plague of Caterpillars*. In 1981 Dr Barley joined the British Museum.

white men's roots (ll. 4-5)
This is how the Dowayos referred to Western medicines, such as the 'amoebicides and antibiotics' mentioned in the text.

54 Tax (AmE)

The Wilson Quarterly
The Wilson Quarterly, published since 1976, is an American quarterly magazine written by academic specialists to appeal to the academically-educated non-specialist. It is published by the Woodrow Wilson International Center for Scholars, Washington DC, which was founded in 1968 as a 'living memorial' to the 28th President of the United States. Every issue features two important themes of current interest, with three or four articles on each. It also explains and summarizes developments in academic research on such topics as politics, the environment, social sciences and foreign affairs. Its circulation is around 75,000.

Ingmar Bergman (l. 5)
Ingmar Bergman (born 1918) is an internationally renowned film director and writer whose films include *The Seventh Seal*, *Wild Strawberries* and *Fanny and Alexander*.

gross domestic product (l. 9)
This is also referred to as the GDP and represents the total monetary value of the goods and services in a country within a specified period (usually a year) not including investments, etc. abroad.

corporate tax burdens (l. 10)
These are the taxes levied on the profits of a company or corporation.

the 'nanny' state (ll. 20-21)
This term, often derogatory, is used to describe a country in which the government plays a dominant part in taking care of the welfare of its citizens. *Nanny* here refers to a children's nurse.

Bismarck (l. 30)
Otto von Bismarck (1815-98), Prusso-German statesman, known as the Iron Chancellor. Resenting the power of Austria, he was responsible for bringing the southern states of Germany into a confederation led by Prussia, and in 1871 he became the first Chancellor of the German Empire under Kaiser Wilhelm I. Bismarck pursued a vigorous industrial and colonial policy and initiated numerous reforms in social welfare and education.

regressive payroll taxes (ll. 30-31)
Regressive payroll tax is a tax levied on the number of people employed (the *payroll*) which decreases ('regresses') as its base increases when more and more people are employed.

tax incentives (l. 31)
These may be, for example, incentives to encourage investments by relieving them of tax: such as not levying tax on capital gains made on stocks and bonds.

stocks and bonds (ll. 32-33)
Stocks refers to shares of ownership in a company, held in the form of certificates; *bonds* refers to money raised by local authorities or governments on which interest is paid and the capital 'redeemed' after a fixed term.

the Revolution (l. 48)
That is, the French Revolution, 1789-99, which resulted in the reorganization of the law and of national and local government to the advantage of the middle classes, instead of the aristocracy.

55 The Marquess of Queensberry (AmE)

Richard Ellman
The American academic and biographer Richard Ellman was born in Detroit, Michigan, in 1918, and graduated from Yale University in 1941. After wartime service in the US Navy, he went to Trinity College, Dublin, Ireland, where he wrote a biography of the poet William Butler Yeats. He was Assistant Professor of English at Harvard (1948-52), Professor of English at North Western University, Illinois (1951-68), and Goldsmiths' Professor of English Literature at Oxford University, England (1970-84). His biography of the Irish writer James Joyce (1952, revised 1982) won several important prizes, including the National Book Award. His widely-acclaimed *Oscar Wilde* was published after his death at Oxford in 1987.

The Marquess of Queensberry (title)
The Marquess of Queensberry (1844-1900) is known for his connexion with the Queensberry Rules, and especially for his connexion with the trials of Oscar Wilde (1854-1900), the Irish poet, dramatist and aesthete. In 1895, enraged by Wilde's association with his son, Lord Alfred Douglas, Queensberry publicly insulted Wilde, who retaliated by suing him – unsuccessfully – for libel. Wilde was subsequently tried, convicted and imprisoned for homosexuality. *Marquess* (or *Marquis*) is a hereditary title in the British nobility.

Alfred Douglas (l. 1)
Lord Alfred Douglas (1870-1945), known principally as Queensberry's son and Wilde's friend, but also as a

(not very good) poet. *Lord* is a title customarily given to younger sons and brothers of marquesses.

the Queensberry Rules (ll. 16–17)
These are the regulations governing boxing matches, which are the basis of modern boxing rules. Drafted in 1866–7 by Queensberry and John G. Chambers of the British Amateur Athletic Club, they were first used at a tournament in London in 1872, and in a world championship in 1892. The best-known of these rules is the one forbidding 'hitting below the belt'.

an excellent hunter (l. 26)
This is a reference to fox hunting, a traditional country activity in England.

the Spirit Lamp (l. 27)
An Oxford literary magazine, edited in 1893 by Douglas, then an undergraduate.

Christina Rossetti (l. 30)
British poet (1830–94). One of her most famous poems begins *When I am dead, my dearest,/Sing no sad songs for me.* Cremation was, until surprisingly recently, an unacceptable idea for many Christian believers. The ban against it by the Roman Catholic church was lifted only in 1963.

the Scottish nobility (l. 35)
Unlike English peers, Scottish lords do not have the automatic right to sit in the House of Lords in Westminster, but they elect their own representatives.

56 The center of our galaxy (AmE)

Scientific American
Scientific American, the respected American monthly, has the aim of explaining new developments in the sciences to non-scientific readers, without 'talking down' to them. It was founded in New York in 1845 by an inventor, Rufus Porter, as a weekly magazine describing new inventions. By the 1850s it was associated with a patent agency, advising inventors on patent law, and its circulation had risen to 30,000. It soon began reporting in general on such topics as medicine, science and technology. It has always been noted for its quality artwork and was one of the first journals to make use of photography. Its popularity and standing have increased with the pace of new scientific developments from the 1950s onwards. Still published in New York, its circulation is currently well over 600,000.

the Milky Way (ll. 2–3)
This refers to our galaxy, including our solar system, as well as to what can be seen in the sky. The term derives from *galaxy*, from the Greek *gala* (= milk), hence *Milky Way*.

57 Mrs Radcliffe (BrE)

Noël Coward
Noël Coward, the British playwright, actor, writer, composer and entertainer was born near London in 1899. He was the author of many elegant and sophisticated comedies, such as *Hay Fever*, *Private Lives* and *Blithe Spirit*, which were enormously popular from the 1920s to the 1940s, as well as hit musicals such as *Bitter Sweet* and *Cavalcade*. He briefly went out of fashion after the war and became a successful cabaret entertainer, performing the work of composers like Cole Porter and his own songs, the most famous of which is probably *Mad Dogs and Englishmen*. He also wrote screenplays (notably *Brief Encounter*), a novel (*Pomp and Circumstance*), short stories and an autobiography. In the English-speaking world his very name conjures up a picture of wit, sophistication, elegance and style. He died in Jamaica in 1973.

Know thyself (l. 36)
This saying was inscribed on the temple of Apollo at Delphi.

58 Spiders (Australian)

Clive James
The writer, journalist and TV broadcaster Clive James was born in Sydney, Australia in 1939, and educated at Sydney University and Cambridge, England where he was President of Footlights, the University dramatic society. He has published three best-selling volumes of autobiography (*Unreliable Memoirs*, *Falling Towards England* and *May Week was in June*), two novels, four satirical epic poems, a book of travel writing (*Flying Visits*) and poetry. Between 1972 and 1982 he made his reputation as the witty TV critic for *The Observer* newspaper in London. He appears regularly as a TV presenter and interviewer, with his own shows such as *Clive James on Television* and *Saturday Night Clive*. He is renowned for his wit, fluency and brilliant turn of phrase.

fox-fur (l. 6)
That is, a coat made of fox fur (not a fox's skin).

triantelope (l. 24)
A word, approximating to *tarantula*, invented by the writer when he was a child.

a single-seater (l. 37)
That is, a (small) plane.

von Richthofen (l. 38)
Manfred von Richthofen (1892–1918), German pilot who shot down 80 enemy planes in World War I. He was nicknamed the Red Baron and died in action in 1918.

59 My mother (BrE)

Peter Ustinov
The British actor, director, producer and writer Peter

Ustinov was born in London in 1921 after his parents left Russia, following the October Revolution of 1917. He was educated at Westminster School. After service in World War II, he worked mainly in films, acting in many roles, including the Emperor Nero and Hercule Poirot.

Harwich (l. 1)
Harwich is a seaport in Essex, about 44 km north east of London.

St Petersburg ... Leningrad (ll. 6–8)
The Russian Baltic seaport St Petersburg, founded in 1703 by tsar Peter the Great, was renamed Leningrad in honour of Lenin, the Russian revolutionary leader, in 1917. It reverted to its original name St Petersburg in 1991.

Kafkaesque (l. 25)
That is a feeling of helplessness and anxiety at being controlled by an organization or bureaucracy you don't understand. Writing in German, the Czech author Franz *Kafka* (1883–1924) explored this aspect of the human condition in novels like *The Trial* (1925) and *The Castle* (1926).

the greatest Bovril of them all (ll. 34–35)
That is, Liverpool Street Station, the London terminus for trains from the east of England.

60 Forbidding fruit (BrE)

The Economist
The Economist, a British weekly founded in 1843, covers not just economic and business affairs of Britain and the world, but also current affairs, politics, science and technology, literature and the arts. It is read by influential businessmen and politicians all over the world, besides having a wide general readership. *The Economist* is noted for the clarity of its style and for the fact that all its contributors are anonymous. Published in London, with editorial offices in America, Europe and the Far East, it has a circulation of over 400,000.

Forbidding fruit (title)
That is, fruit which is *forbidding*, meaning here 'not easy to pick'. It is a play on the phrase *forbidden fruit* (= fruit which it is forbidden to eat), a Biblical reference to the apples on the apple tree in the Garden of Eden, which Adam and Eve were forbidden to eat.

the whistle will blow (l. 4)
The phrase is used here to refer to industrial stoppage, when the shop steward blows his whistle for everyone to down tools and begin a strike.

A few statistics

1 *British English compared with others*

British English:	40 texts
American English:	18 texts
Canadian English:	1 text
Australian English:	1 text

2 *Book material compared with the press*

Book material:	27 texts
The press:	33 texts

'The press' breaks down to nine newspapers and ten magazines/journals.

3 *Non-fiction compared with fiction*

Non-fiction:	49 texts
Fiction:	11 texts

4 *Literary style compared with journalism*

Literary style:	23 texts
Journalism:	37 texts

5 *Number of texts published in the 1980s and beyond:* 48

6 *Analysis by difficulty*

Medium difficulty:	12 (Texts 1–12)
Difficult:	29 (Texts 13–41)
Very difficult:	19 (Texts 42–60)

Summary of sources

	Sources		Number of texts
BrE	*Newspapers*	The Daily Express	1
		The Daily Telegraph	3
		The Financial Times	1
		The Guardian	2
		The Independent	3
		The Observer	3
		The Sunday Telegraph	1
		The Sunday Times	2
		The Times	5
	Journals	The Economist	1
AmE	*Journals*	The Atlantic	1
		New Woman	1
		New York	1
		The New Yorker	1
		Scientific American	1
		Time Magazine	3
		US News and World Report	1
		USA Today	1
		The Wilson Quarterly	1
BrE	*Books*	Non-fiction	12
		Fiction	6
AmE	*Books*	Non-fiction	3
		Fiction	4
Australian	*Books*	Non-fiction	1
Canadian	*Books*	Fiction	1
Total:			60

Grammar terms and concepts

Words appearing in SMALL CAPITALS have their own entries.

abbreviated clause [> LEG 1.55]

Most kinds of CLAUSES can be *abbreviated* by deleting the SUBJECT and the VERB *be* after a CONJUNCTION. For example:
- time:
    While (she was) at college, Delia wrote a novel.
- place:
    Where (it is) necessary, improvements will be made.
- manner:
    He acted *as if (he was) certain of success*.

abbreviations [> LEG 2.24, 3.7, 3.17, 3.24, 3.27.2]

Here is a selection of items that are commonly abbreviated:

LEXICAL ITEMS: e.g. *kilos* (for *kilograms*); *photos* (for *photographs*).

Degrees, institutions etc. used with:
- *a/an*:
    a B.A. (a Bachelor of Arts); *an I.Q.* (an Intelligence Quotient).
- *the*:
    the B.B.C. (the British Broadcasting Corporation), *the EC* (the European Community).
- zero:
    ACRONYMS like *NATO* (North Atlantic Treaty Organization); H_2O (chemical symbol for *water*).
    Titles: *Mr, Mrs, Miss, Ms, Dr*.

The use of FULL STOPS is generally optional in abbreviations, except in small-letter abbreviations like *e.g.* and *a.m.*, and with abbreviations formed by cutting a word off in the middle: *Min. of Ag. and Fish.* (= Ministry of Agriculture and Fisheries).

ability [> LEG 11.10–18]

This is a NOTION generally expressed by the MODAL VERBS *can/could*:
I can/can't run 1500 metres in 5 minutes.
I could/couldn't run very fast when I was a boy.

abstract noun [> LEG 2.15]

An *abstract* NOUN refers to a quality or a concept which is not CONCRETE: e.g. *friendship, hope*. Abstract nouns can have COUNTABLE and UNCOUNTABLE uses:
- countable uses:
    an education, a friendship, a hope, a noise, etc.
- uncountable uses:
    education, friendship, hope, noise, etc.

accusative [> LEG 16.45]

This is another term for OBJECT and is used to describe the form of NOUNS and PRONOUNS, especially in languages like Latin and Greek. The *accusative* shows that the noun or pronoun is the DIRECT OBJECT of a VERB. After some verbs in English, we have a choice between the accusative and POSSESSIVE after certain verbs and in front of *-ING*:

- verb (+ accusative: *me*, etc.) + *-ing*:
    When are you going to start John/him working?
- verb (+ possessive: *my*, etc.) + *-ing*:
    The children don't enjoy John's/his teasing.
- verb (+ accusative or possessive) + *-ing*:
    I can't imagine my mother/my mother's approving.
    Please excuse him/his not writing to you.

acronym [> LEG 3.24]

Acronyms are words made up of the first letters of other words, for example *NATO* for North Atlantic Treaty Organization. Some acronyms are now used as real words, in that we may not be aware that they are 'made up': for example the computer programming language, *BASIC* (= Beginners' All-purpose Symbolic Instruction Code), or the method for finding the position for solid objects, *radar* (= Radio Detection and Ranging).

active voice [> LEG 12.1]

The terms *active voice* and PASSIVE VOICE refer to the form of a VERB. In the active, the SUBJECT of the verb is the person or thing doing the action:
John cooked the food last night.

adjectival clause [> LEG 1.25]

An *adjectival* or *adjective clause* is another name for a RELATIVE CLAUSE. In:
Holiday resorts which are crowded are not very pleasant.
the CLAUSE ... *which are crowded* ... is doing the same work as an ADJECTIVE: it is describing (or QUALIFYING) the COMPOUND NOUN *holiday resorts*. Compare:
Crowded (adjective) *holiday resorts* (noun) *are not very pleasant.*

adjectival participle [> LEG 6.14–15, 7.51, 12.7, App 10]

An *adjectival* PARTICIPLE is the same form as the PRESENT PARTICIPLE of a VERB (e.g. *frightening*) or the PAST PARTICIPLE of a verb (e.g. *frightened*) and is used exactly like an ADJECTIVE:
She told us a frightening story.
The frightened children hid in the attic.
We can distinguish between a past participle adjective and verb as follows:
I was worried about you all night.
(adjective: a state)
I was worried by mosquitoes all night.
(PASSIVE: a DYNAMIC verb)
If the word is an adjective, it cannot be used with *by* + AGENT and cannot be turned into a sentence in the ACTIVE.

adjective [> LEG 6.1]

An *adjective* describes (or QUALIFIES) the person, thing, etc. which a NOUN refers to. We use adjectives to say what a person, etc. is like or seems like. For example, adjectives can give us information about:
- quality: *a beautiful dress; a nice day.*

– size: *a **big** car; a **small** coin; a **tall** man.*
– age: *a **new** handbag; a **young** man.*

adjective + preposition [> LEG 8.19, 16.53, 16.60, App 27]
Many ADJECTIVES are followed by PREPOSITIONS, for example: *afraid **of**, good **at**, obliged **to***.

adverb [> LEG 7.1]
Adverb ('ad-verb') suggests the idea of adding to the meaning of a VERB. This is what adverbs do. They tell us something about the action in a SENTENCE by MODIFYING a verb, that is, by telling us *how, when, where*, etc. something happens or is done:
   *Paganini must have played the violin **beautifully**.*
   (How did he play?)
Adverbs can also modify other words, besides verbs, like GRADABLE ADJECTIVES, for example:
   *I'm **awfully** hungry.*

adverb of degree [> LEG 7.41–49]
Adverbs of degree are words like *enough, fairly, hardly, quite* and *rather* which broadly answer the question *To what extent?* They MODIFY:
– ADJECTIVES: ***quite good***.
– ADVERBS: ***quite quickly***.
– VERBS: *I **quite like** it.*
– NOUNS: ***quite an experience***.
Adverbs of degree change the meaning of a SENTENCE, often by weakening the effect of the word they modify. In speech, the information they provide can vary according to STRESS:
   *The film was **quite/good**.*
   (RISING TONE: = I enjoyed it on the whole)
   *The film was **quite\good**.*
   (FALLING TONE: = I didn't particularly enjoy it)

adverb of frequency [> LEG 7.37–40]
Adverbs of frequency answer the question *How often?* They may refer to:
– definite frequency:
   once, twice, hourly, every day, on Mondays, etc.
– indefinite frequency:
   always, almost always, usually, often, sometimes, almost never, hardly ever, never, etc.

adverb of manner [> LEG 7.7–16]
Adverbs of manner answer the question *How?* Most of them end in *-LY* and are formed from ADJECTIVES: *bad-badly, careful-carefully, happy-happily, day-daily, noble-nobly, fantastic-fantastically*, etc.

adverb of place [> LEG 7.17–19]
Adverbs of place are words and PHRASES that answer the question *Where?* or *Where to? Where from?* They may be:
– single words:
   abroad, anywhere, away, here, upstairs, etc.
– phrases:
   at my mother's, from New York, in hospital, on the left, etc.

adverb of time [> LEG 7.20–36, App 48]
Adverbs of time are words and PHRASES that answer the question *When (exactly)?* They refer to:
– duration:
   since Monday, for six weeks, etc.

– definite time:
   tomorrow, on Monday, etc.
– indefinite time:
   now, another time, any more, etc.

adverb particle [> LEG 8.4, 8.23–30]
An *adverb particle* is an ADVERB which is closely related to a VERB and does not 'govern' an OBJECT. This is what makes it different from a PREPOSITION:
   *We drove **round**.* (no object = adverb particle)
   *We drove **round the city**.* (*round* + object = preposition)
Some words can function as prepositions or adverb particles: *about, across, before, down, past*, etc. Others function only as adverb particles (not prepositions): *away, back, downwards, out*, etc. We use adverb particles to make up PHRASAL VERBS.

adverbial [> LEG 7.1]
We use the term ADVERB to describe single words like *slowly*. We use the term *adverbial* to describe single words (*slowly*) or PHRASES (*in the garden*).

adverbial clause [> LEG 1.44]
Adverbial clauses are introduced by CONJUNCTIONS (*as soon as, when*, etc.) and they are SUBORDINATE to a MAIN CLAUSE in a SENTENCE. Like ADVERBS, they answer the questions *When? Where? How? Why?* etc. They refer to e.g.:
– time: *Tell him **as soon as he arrives**.*   (**When?**)
– place: *You can sit **where you like**.*   (**Where?**)
– manner: *He spoke **as if he meant business**.*   (**How?**)
– reason: *He went to bed **because he felt ill**.*   (**Why?**)

adverbial clause of comparison [> LEG 1.53]
ADVERBIAL CLAUSES of *comparison* are introduced by *as ... as, -er than*, etc.:
   *He's as quick at answering questions **as his sister (is)**.*

adverbial clause of concession [> LEG 1.50]
ADVERBIAL CLAUSES of *concession* introduce an element of CONTRAST into a SENTENCE and are sometimes called contrast clauses. They are introduced by CONJUNCTIONS like *although, even if, while, however (much)* and *no matter how*:
   *We intend to go to India, **even if air fares go up again between now and the summer**.*

adverbial clause of manner [> LEG 1.47]
ADVERBIAL CLAUSES of *manner* answer the question *How?* and are introduced by CONJUNCTIONS like *as, in the way*, and *as if*:
   *Type this again **as I showed you a moment ago**.*
   (= in the way I showed you a moment ago)

adverbial clause of place [> LEG 1.46]
ADVERBIAL CLAUSES of *place* answer the question *Where?* and are introduced by CONJUNCTIONS like *where, wherever*, and *anywhere*:
   *You can't camp **where/wherever/anywhere you like** these days.*

adverbial clause of purpose [> ŁEG 1.51, 1.52.2]
ADVERBIAL CLAUSES of *purpose* answer the questions *What for?* and *For what purpose?* and are introduced by CONJUNCTIONS like *so that, in order that, in case,*

lest and *for fear (that)*:
> *I've arrived early **so that I can get a good view of the procession***.

adverbial clause of reason [> LEG 1.48]
ADVERBIAL CLAUSES *of reason* answer the question *Why?* and are introduced by CONJUNCTIONS like *as, because, seeing (that)* and *since*:
> ***As there was very little support***, *the strike was not successful.*

adverbial clause of result [> LEG 1.52]
ADVERBIAL CLAUSES *of result* describe consequences and are introduced by *that* after, for example, *so* + ADJECTIVE to answer e.g. *How (quick)?*:
> *His reactions are **so quick (that) no one can match him**.*

adverbial clause of time [> LEG 1.45]
ADVERBIAL CLAUSES *of time* broadly answer the question *When?* and are introduced by CONJUNCTIONS like *when, after, as soon as* and *since*:
> *You didn't look very well **when you got up this morning***.

adverbial of duration [> LEG 7.30–36]
Duration (periods of time) can be expressed by ADVERBIAL PHRASES like *all (day) long, during the week, for six months, since January*:
> *I haven't seen Tim **since January***.

adverbial phrase [> LEG 7.3.3]
Adverbial phrases of manner, place and time are often formed with a PREPOSITION + NOUN: *in a hurry, in the garden, at the station*. Phrases like this tell us *how, where, when*, etc. Because they are introduced by prepositions (*in, at*, etc.) they are also called PREPOSITIONAL PHRASES.

advisability [> LEG 11.46–47, 11.52, 11.54]
This is a NOTION generally expressed by the MODAL VERBS *should, ought to*, and *must*:
> *You **should smoke** less. You **shouldn't smoke** so much.*

affirmative [> LEG 13.4]
Affirmative refers to a STATEMENT the opposite of which is a NEGATIVE:
> – affirmative: *He's leaving.*
> – negative: *He is**n't** leaving.*

agent [> LEG 12.5]
An *agent* is a 'doer', that is, a person or thing that performs the action indicated by the VERB. *By* + agent in PASSIVE constructions tells us who or what did something:
> *The window was broken **by the boy who lives opposite***.

agreement [> LEG 1.4, 1.61, 1.63, *passim*]
Also called CONCORD, this usually refers to the way SUBJECT and VERB must match:
> ***John likes*** *ice-cream.* (Not **John like**)
Compare DANGLING PARTICIPLE.

AmE [> LEG 9.10, 9.14, 10.30, *passim*]
(= American English).The abbreviation *AmE* may be used to describe distinctively American forms relating, for example, to:
> – SPELLING: *traveling* (for British English *travelling*)

> – USAGE: *Do you have …?* (for British English *Have you got …?*)
The differences in STRUCTURE (as opposed to LEXIS) between American English and British English (BrE) are slight.

apostrophe [> LEG 2.42–52, 10.34, *passim*]
An *apostrophe* (') is a PUNCTUATION MARK which is used:
> – to show where a letter or letters have been omitted in a CONTRACTION:
> *I **haven't** (= have not) seen John lately.*
> – to show POSSESSION (the GENITIVE):
> *This is **John's** idea of a joke.*

apostrophe s/s apostrophe [> LEG 1.1, 2.42–52]
The *-es* GENITIVE ending of some classes of NOUNS in old English has survived in the modern language as *'s* (*apostrophe s*) for some nouns in the SINGULAR and *s'* (*s apostrophe*) for some nouns in the PLURAL to show POSSESSION. Such nouns usually refer to people, not things:
> *a **boy's** jacket* (one boy: *'s*)
> *a **girls'** school* (more than one girl: *s'*)

apposition [> LEG 1.39, 3.30, 6.21.1]
NOUN PHRASES, placed side by side, and separated by COMMAS are *in apposition*. The second phrase adds information to the first:
> ***Mr Watkins**, **a neighbour of mine**, never misses the opportunity to tell me the latest news.*
Phrases used in apposition are commonly used in journalism:
> ***Ageing**, **recently-widowed popular dramatist**, **Milton Fairbanks**, announced recently that 'Athletes' was to be his last play.*

article [> LEG 3.1–3]
Articles are used with NOUNS. We can describe three forms of the article in English:
> – the INDEFINITE ARTICLE, *a/an*:
> *I've ordered **a** new car.*
> – the DEFINITE ARTICLE, *the*:
> ***The** new car I ordered has arrived.*
> – the ZERO ARTICLE (or active non-use of the article):
> *(–) Cars pollute our atmosphere.*
The use and non-use of articles depends, among other things, on whether a noun is used as a SINGULAR COUNTABLE, a PLURAL countable, or an UNCOUNTABLE.

aspect [> LEG 9.2]
Aspect refers to the form of a VERB which tells us, for example, whether an action is in progress or completed.
> – progressive aspect:
> *It **is snowing**. It **has been snowing**. It **was snowing**.* (in progress)
> – perfective aspect:
> *It **has snowed**. It **had snowed**.* (completed)

attributive adjective [> LEG 6.7]
The term *attributive* is the opposite of PREDICATIVE and refers to the position of an ADJECTIVE in a PHRASE or a SENTENCE. We say that an adjective is attributive or is used *attributively* when it comes before a NOUN (and

is therefore part of a NOUN PHRASE):

> an **old** ticket, a **young** shop-assistant, he is an **old** man.

auxiliary verb [> LEG 10.1–4, 11.1]

An *auxiliary verb* (or HELPING VERB) contrasts with a FULL VERB. There are two kinds of auxiliary verbs in English:

- *be*, *have* and *do*, when they are used with other verbs to 'help' them complete their grammatical functions:

> I **am** working.

(*am* helps *work* complete its grammatical function: *be* helps create PROGRESSIVE TENSES)

> I **have** eaten.

(*have* helps *eat* complete its grammatical function: *have* helps create PERFECT TENSES)

> **Do** you know Tom?

(*do* combines with *know* to make a QUESTION: *do* helps express questions and NEGATIVES in the SIMPLE PRESENT and SIMPLE PAST)

- *Modal auxiliaries*, sometimes called MODAL VERBS, like *can*, *may*, *will* and *shall*, which we combine with other verbs to ask for PERMISSION, grant permission, make REQUESTS, make OFFERS, etc.:

> **Can/May I borrow** your car please?
> **You may borrow** my car if you want to.
> **Will you hold** the door open for me please?
> **Shall I hold** the door open for you?

backshift [> LEG 15.13*n*.3]

We use this term to refer to the 'moving back' of TENSES in INDIRECT SPEECH. Reporting usually takes place in the past, so the REPORTING VERB is often in the past. As a result, the tenses of the reported CLAUSES are usually 'moved back', so there is a uniform SEQUENCE OF TENSES. A general rule is that 'present becomes past and past or present perfect becomes past perfect':

> 'I **have lived** in the south for years,' Mrs Duncan **said**.
> Mrs Duncan **told me** (that) she **had lived** in the south for years.

bare infinitive [> LEG 16.1–6]

The *bare* INFINITIVE is the BASE FORM of the VERB: e.g. *go*, used without *to* (*to go*). In GRAMMAR, we distinguish the bare infinitive from the *TO*-INFINITIVE. We use the bare infinitive (without *to*) mainly after:

- MODAL VERBS:

> You **may go**. I **can see** you. She **might agree**.

- verbs like *let* and *make*:

> **Let's take** a taxi. Please **let me pay**.

base form [> LEG 9.51, 16.1]

This term is applied to VERBS to describe their basic form, which is a BARE INFINITIVE: e.g. *go*, which we use after MODAL VERBS and as an IMPERATIVE form:

> I must **tell** her immediately. (bare infinitive after modal verb *must*)
> **Tell** her immediately. (bare infinitive used as an imperative)

brackets [> LEG 1.26]

We can use *brackets* round NON-DEFINING CLAUSES

when we are adding extra information. We would use them in place of COMMAS or DASHES to emphasize that the information is additional and could be omitted without affecting the meaning of the MAIN CLAUSE:

> *The Portland Vase (which originally belonged to the Barberini family) is in the British Museum.*

BrE [> LEG 9.10, 9.14, 10.30, *passim*]

(= British English). The abbreviation *BrE* may be used to describe distinctively British forms relating, for example, to:

- SPELLING: *travelling* (for American English *traveling*).
- USAGE: *Have you got . . .?* (for American English *Do you have . . .?*)

The differences in STRUCTURE (as opposed to LEXIS) between British English and American English (AmE) are slight.

capital letter [> LEG 1.2, 2.13.1, 4.5.1, 15.3*n*.2]

Capital letters are *A, B, C, D*, etc. as opposed to small letters (*a, b, c, d*, etc.). We use them in a number of ways. For example:

- to begin a SENTENCE:

> *The purpose of war is peace.* (Not **the**)

- for PROPER NOUNS:

> *Everybody needs to learn English these days.* (Not **english**)

- for the PERSONAL PRONOUN *I*:

> *I agree with you.* (Not **i**)

- in DIRECT SPEECH:

> *John said, 'It's good to see you.'* (Not **it's**)

case [> LEG 1.1, 2.43, 4.1, 4.3, 4.19]

Case (not very common in English) refers to the form of a NOUN or PRONOUN to show whether it is SUBJECT, OBJECT or POSSESSIVE. Only six subject and object case forms survive in modern English: *I/me, he/him, she/her, we/us, they/them* and *who/whom*. There are a few POSSESSIVE CASE forms such as *mine, yours, his, hers, ours* and *theirs*. The GENITIVE form (*'s/s'*) also has limited uses.

causative [> LEG 12.10–13]

We form the *causative* with *have* (*have something done*) and sometimes *get* (*get something done*). We use it to stress the fact that we are 'causing' someone else to perform a service for us:

> *I'm having* my car *serviced*. (= I'm responsible for causing someone to do the job.)

The causative always has a different emphasis from the PASSIVE:

> *My car's being serviced*. (= Someone is doing the job for me.)

certainty/uncertainty [> LEG 11.3, 11.27–33]

Certainty and *uncertainty* are NOTIONS generally expressed by all MODAL VERBS (except *shall*) in their SECONDARY USE. Modal verbs can be arranged on a scale to express degrees of certainty, with *might* expressing the greatest uncertainty and *can't/must* expressing the greatest certainty. The order of modals between *might* and *must* is not fixed absolutely, but varies according to situation. One arrangement might be:

	might	***very uncertain***
	may	
	could	
	can hardly	
You	*should*	*be right.*
	ought to	*have been right.*
	would	
	will	
	can't	
	must	***almost certain***

clause [> LEG 1.2]

A *clause* is a group of words consisting of a SUBJECT +
FINITE VERB (+ COMPLEMENT or OBJECT if necessary). A
clause may be:
a complete, SIMPLE SENTENCE:
  I got in late for work this morning.
CO-ORDINATE:
  I unlocked the door *and* ***went into the house***.
  (two co-ordinate clauses here)
MAIN:
  I got in late for work this morning *because
  there was a traffic jam.*
SUBORDINATE (DEPENDENT):
  I got in late for work this morning ***because there
  was a traffic jam***.
ABBREVIATED (VERBLESS):
  While *(she was)* ***at college***, *Delia wrote a novel.*

clause analysis [> LEG 1.21]

The term describes the analysis of a SENTENCE into its
constituent parts or CLAUSES:
  (a) *Free trade agreements are always threatened*
       (MAIN CLAUSE)
  (b) *when individual countries protect their own
       markets*
       (SUBORDINATE CLAUSE dependent on (a))
  (c) *by imposing duties on imported goods*
       (PARTICIPLE CONSTRUCTION dependent on (b))
  (d) *to encourage their own industries.*
       (INFINITIVE CONSTRUCTION dependent on (c))

cleft sentence [> LEG 4.14]

This is a SIMPLE SENTENCE which is split up (*cleft*) when
it is re-expressed with *It is/was* + SUBJECT + *that/
who(m)*. By splitting a simple sentence in this way we
can express particular emphasis:
  Freda phoned Jack last night.
  (simple sentence, no emphasis)
  It was Freda who *phoned Jack last night.*
  (Freda phoned and not, for example, Rita)
  It was Jack who(m) *Freda phoned last night.*
  (She phoned Jack and not, for example, Richard)
  It was last night that *Freda phoned.*
  (and not this morning)

collective noun [> LEG 2.19, 2.28, App 6]

Collective nouns describe:
- groups or 'collections' of people or things: *an* ***army***
  of soldiers, a ***flock*** *of sheep, a* ***bunch*** *of flowers,*
  etc.
- groups of people or things considered as a unit:
  audience, committee, crowd, family, team, union,
  etc.

collocation

This term refers to the way words are drawn to each
other so that the resulting combinations sound
natural. When this happens we say the words
collocate. For example, we would *load a camera*, but
not **fill a camera**; we may *have a chat*, but not
make/do a chat; we might *eat heartily*, but not **eat
fully**. *Load* collocates with *camera*, *have* with *a chat*
and *eat* with *heartily*.

colloquial

The very INFORMAL language of everyday speech is
often referred to as *colloquial* (compare SLANG):
  I'm ***wiped out***. (colloquial style)
  I'm ***dead tired***. (informal style)
  I'm ***exhausted***. (neutral/FORMAL STYLE)

colon [> LEG 15.3n.2]

A *colon* (:) is a PUNCTUATION MARK which we use in
writing to introduce an explanation, an example, a
QUOTATION or a list:
  *I'm going to take the following subjects: History,
  Geography and Business Studies.*

comma [> LEG 1.17, 1.26, 1.39, 1.45.1, 6.21, 7.57, *passim*]

A *comma* (,) is a PUNCTUATION MARK which we use in
writing to express a short pause:
  *After she got married, Madeleine changed
  completely.*

command

We sometimes use the term *command* in place of
IMPERATIVE, when it is used for giving orders. A
command is one of the four types of SENTENCE:
  Open *the package carefully!*

common noun [> LEG 2.12–19]

A NOUN that is not the name of a particular person,
place, thing or idea is a *common noun* (not a PROPER
NOUN). We use *a/an*, *the* or the ZERO ARTICLE in front of
common nouns. Common nouns have COUNTABLE and
UNCOUNTABLE uses and may be CONCRETE (*a book,
clothing*) or ABSTRACT (*an idea, courage*).

comparative [> LEG 6.22–29, 7.4–6]

Comparatives of adjectives and adverbs are formed
with *-er . . .(than)* or *more/less . . . (than)*:
– ADJECTIVES:
  This tie is ***nicer***/*This tie is* ***more/less expensive***
  than that one.
– ADVERBS:
  Dave drives ***faster***/*Dave drives* ***more/less
  carefully*** *than anyone I know.*
We use the comparative form when we are comparing
one person or thing, etc. with another. COMPARISON
may be between:
– single items:
  Jane is ***taller than*** *Alice.*
– a single item and a group:
  Jane is ***taller than*** *other girls.*
– two groups:
  The girls in class 3 are ***taller than*** *the girls in
  class 1.*

comparison [> LEG 6.22–30]

The term *comparison* may refer to:
– the way we form the COMPARATIVE and SUPERLATIVE of

ADJECTIVES, sometimes called 'the comparison of adjectives':

tall, taller, tallest.

- the way we make comparisons in general, for example, with *the same as, different from*:

    My mountain bike is the same as/different from yours.

- the way we make comparisons with ADVERBIAL CLAUSES OF COMPARISON:

    He's as quick at answering questions as his sister (is).

complement [> LEG 1.8–9, 1.11]

A *complement* follows the VERB *be* and verbs related to *be*, such as *seem*, which cannot be followed by an OBJECT. A complement (generally an ADJECTIVE, a NOUN or a PRONOUN) completes the sense of an utterance by telling us something about the SUBJECT. For example, the words following *is* tell us something about the subject of the sentence, *Frank*:

Frank (subject) is (be) clever (adjectival complement).

Frank (subject) is (be) an architect (noun complement).

complementation [> LEG Chapter 16, Apps 44–46]

Complementation refers to constructions that might follow, for example, VERBS or ADJECTIVES to 'complete' their meaning. For example:

Some verbs, like MODAL VERBS, are followed by a BARE INFINITIVE: *You may go*.

Some verbs, like *fail*, may be followed by a TO-INFINITIVE: *He failed to turn up at the meeting.*

Some verbs, like *enjoy*, may be followed by the *-ING* FORM: *I enjoy walking in the mountains.*

Some verbs, like *begin*, may be followed by a TO-INFINITIVE or the *-ING* FORM: *We began to work/began working*.

Some adjectives may be followed by *to*, THAT or *-ing*:, for example, *it's certain to, it's certain that, it's funny seeing*.

complex sentence [> LEG 1.21–63]

Complex sentences are formed by linking SIMPLE SENTENCES together, but the elements in a complex sentence (unlike those of a COMPOUND SENTENCE) are not of equal importance. There is always one independent (or MAIN) CLAUSE and one or more DEPENDENT (or SUBORDINATE) CLAUSES. If removed from a sentence, a main clause can often stand on its own. We form complex sentences in two ways:

- by joining subordinate clauses to the main clause with SUBORDINATING CONJUNCTIONS:

    The alarm was raised (main clause) as soon as the fire was discovered (subordinate clause).

- by using INFINITIVE or PARTICIPLE CONSTRUCTIONS. These are non-FINITE and are PHRASES rather than clauses, but they form part of complex (not simple) sentences because they can be re-expressed as clauses which are subordinate to the main clause:

    To get to university you have to pass a number of examinations.

    (= If you want to get to university . . .)

Seeing the door open, the stranger entered the house.

(= When he saw the door open . . .)

compound adjective [> LEG 6.3]

Compound adjectives usually consist of two or three words and are often written with HYPHENS. Some of the commonest types are:

- compound adjectives formed with PARTICIPLES: *a candle-lit table, a horse-drawn cart, a self-employed author*.

- compound adjectives of measurement: *a twenty-year-old man, a four-hour meeting, a three-hour journey*.

- compound adjectives formed with other PARTS OF SPEECH: *tax-free, well-behaved, vacuum-sealed*.

compound noun [> LEG 2.4–11]

Compound nouns are NOUNS formed from two parts (*classroom*) or, less commonly, three or more (*son-in-law*). Sometimes they are spelt with a HYPHEN, sometimes not. A few common forms are:

- single word compound nouns:

    a cupboard, a raincoat, a saucepan.

- ADJECTIVE + noun:

    a greenhouse, a heavyweight, longhand.

- GERUND + noun:

    drinking water, a frying pan, a walking stick.

- noun + gerund:

    window-cleaning, sight-seeing, sunbathing.

- noun + noun:

    a car key, a kitchen sink, a bookcase, a cotton blouse, a horror film, a teapot, morning tea, self denial, a chairperson, a Ford car.

We generally prefer a compound noun (e.g. *a car key*) to an OF-CONSTRUCTION (*the key of the car*) because it is neater.

compound/complex sentence [> LEG 1.21]

CO-ORDINATE and SUBORDINATE CLAUSES can combine in a single SENTENCE to form a *compound/complex sentence*:

The racing car went out of control and hit the barrier several times before it came to a stop on a grassy bank.

compound sentence [> LEG 1.17–20]

We form *compound sentences* by linking SIMPLE SENTENCES with CONJUNCTIONS like *and*, *but*, and *so*. In a compound sentence, there is no single MAIN CLAUSE with SUBORDINATE CLAUSES depending on it: all the clauses are of equal importance and can stand on their own, though of course, they follow a logical order as required by the context. We often refer to clauses in a compound sentence as CO-ORDINATE (MAIN) CLAUSES:

I parked my car in the car park and walked to the station.

concession [> LEG 1.50]

This term refers to ADVERBIAL CLAUSES OF CONCESSION which are introduced by CONJUNCTIONS like *although*, *even if*, *while*, *however (much)* and *no matter how*:

We intend to go to India, even if air fares go up again between now and the summer.

concord [> LEG 1.4, 1.61, 1.63, *passim*]

Also called AGREEMENT, this usually refers to the way SUBJECT and VERB must match:

John likes ice-cream. (Not *John like*)

Compare: DANGLING PARTICIPLE

concrete noun [> LEG 2.15]

A NOUN which refers to people and things that have physical existence is *concrete*. Concrete nouns can have COUNTABLE and UNCOUNTABLE uses:

- countable uses (physical and individual existence): *a girl, a desk, an army, a litre, a packet*, etc.
- uncountable uses (physical but not individual existence): *cotton, barley, rice, camping*, etc.

conditional clause [> LEG 1.49, Chapter 14]

ADVERBIAL CLAUSES of *condition* are introduced by CONJUNCTIONS such as *assuming (that), if, on (the) condition (that), provided (that), providing (that), so/as long as* and *unless*. *Conditional clauses* are about events that can or might occur or that might have occurred. Sometimes these events are highly probable:

*If the price of oil comes down, **more people will buy it***.

Sometimes they are impossible (they did not or cannot happen):

*If my horse had won, **I would have made a lot of money***.

For convenience, conditional SENTENCES are often divided into three basic types:

- Type 1: *if* + SIMPLE PRESENT + *will*:

*If **I lose** my job, **I will go** abroad.*

- Type 2: *if* + SIMPLE PAST + *would*:

*If **I lost** my job, **I would go** abroad.*

- Type 3: *if* + SIMPLE PAST PERFECT + *would have*:

*If **I had lost** my job, **I would have gone** abroad.*

However, these sequences are not invariable and we can say, for example:

*If **I am** as clever as you think* (Type 1), *I **should have been** famous by now* (Type 3).

conjunction [> LEG 1.15–24, 1.44–55, 8.4.4]

Conjunctions are 'joining words' like *and, but, as soon as, since, when* and *until*. They fall into two classes:

- CO-ORDINATING CONJUNCTIONS which we use to form COMPOUND SENTENCES consisting of two or more CO-ORDINATE CLAUSES:

*I **parked my car in the car park** and **walked to the station***.

- SUBORDINATING CONJUNCTIONS which we use to introduce SUBORDINATE or DEPENDENT CLAUSES in COMPLEX SENTENCES:

The alarm was raised (MAIN CLAUSE) *as soon as the fire was discovered* (subordinate clause).

Words like *after, as, before, since, till* and *until* can function as PREPOSITIONS (when followed by an OBJECT) and conjunctions when followed by a CLAUSE:

*I haven't seen him **since this morning***. (preposition)

*I haven't seen him **since he left** this morning*. (conjunction)

connecting adverb [> LEG 7.58, App 18]

Connecting adverbs may show us that a speaker or writer wants to expand, modify, or summarize what has already been said. They are essential when we wish to present information in a coherent fashion in speech or writing. For example, a speaker or writer may use adverbs such as *however* or *on the contrary* to draw a CONTRAST; *at the same time* or *meanwhile* to tell us about something else that was happening at the same time; *as a result* or *consequently* to draw our attention to results; *furthermore* or *moreover* to add information:

*The room was in a real mess. **However**, nothing had been stolen.*

consonant [> LEG 3.7, *passim*]

Any letter (*b, c, d, f, g,* etc.) in the English alphabet except the VOWELS *a, e, i o, u.*

consonant sounds [> LEG 3.7]

There is a difference between CONSONANTS and *consonant sounds*. We use the INDEFINITE ARTICLE *a* before consonant sounds, not just consonant letters; we use *an* before VOWEL SOUNDS, not just vowel letters:

an umbrella but *a uniform*

an unusual case but *a union*

a year, a university, a European, but *an eye, an ear.*

continuity verb [> LEG 9.33.1]

Some VERBS like *learn, lie, live, rain, sit, sleep, stand, study, wait* and *work* naturally express *continuity* and convey nearly the same meaning when used in SIMPLE or PROGRESSIVE tenses. Progressive tenses reinforce the idea of continuity:

*I **live** in London.* (SIMPLE PRESENT TENSE)

→ *I'm **living** in London.* (PRESENT PROGRESSIVE TENSE)

continuous tenses [> LEG 9.2]

Terms like *present continuous tense, past continuous tense*, etc. are commonly used to describe actions in progress. Some grammarians consider the term *continuous* to be misleading because it suggests 'all the time'. On this basis, a statement like *I lived in London for three years* (SIMPLE PAST TENSE) might be described as 'continuous'. That's why PROGRESSIVE is often preferred to emphasize the idea of an action in progress.

contraction [> LEG 13.31, *passim*]

Contractions are shortened forms of words like *I've* for *I have* and *isn't* for *is not*. The letters that are 'missing' are represented by an APOSTROPHE ('). We often use contractions:

for VERBS like *be* and *have. I'm* (= I am), *you're* (= you are), *he's* (= he is *or* he has), *we've* (= we have).

- after QUESTION-WORDS: *When's* (= When is), *How's* (= How is *or* How has).
- in NEGATIVES in which the short form of *not* is spelt *n't: isn't, haven't, didn't, won't, needn't.*

contrast [> LEG 1.18–20, 1.50]

Contrast can be expressed by:

- CONJUNCTIONS like *but* and *yet*:

*The tower is leaning dangerously **but** is still standing.*

– conjunctions like *although* which introduce ADVERBIAL CLAUSES OF CONCESSION:

> **Although** *the tower is leaning dangerously, it's still standing.*

contrast clause [> LEG 1.50]

This is another term for ADVERBIAL CLAUSE OF CONCESSION.

co-ordinate clause [> LEG 1.17–20]

Co-ordinate CLAUSES, sometimes called *co-ordinate* MAIN CLAUSES, often occur in COMPOUND SENTENCES. They are of equal importance and can stand on their own, unlike SUBORDINATE CLAUSES. Co-ordinate clauses are joined by CONJUNCTIONS like *and*, *but* and *so*:

> *I parked my car in the car park and walked to the station.*

co-ordinating conjunction [> LEG 1.17–20]

We use *co-ordinating* CONJUNCTIONS to form COMPOUND SENTENCES. Co-ordinating conjunctions are: *and, and then, but, for, nor, or, so, yet; either ... or; neither ... nor; not only ... but ... (also/as well/too):*

> *I parked my car in the car park(,) and walked to the station.*

countable and uncountable nouns [> LEG 2.14–18]

All COMMON NOUNS fall into two sub-classes: they may be either *countable* (sometimes known as *unit* or *count*) nouns, or *uncountable* (sometimes known as *mass* or *non-count*). We say a noun is countable when we can use it with *a/an* (*a book*) and it has a PLURAL (*books*). We say a noun is uncountable when we don't normally use *a/an* in front of it and it has no plural (*sugar*). However, it is important to realize that most nouns cannot be strictly classified as countable or uncountable. Most nouns have countable and uncountable uses. For example, a noun we might think of as typically countable like *an egg* may have an uncountable use:

> *I had an egg for breakfast.* (countable)
> *You've got egg on your tie.* (uncountable)

A noun we might think of as typically uncountable like *wine* may have countable uses:

> *This region produces a lot of wine.* (uncountable)
> *This region produces a fine light wine.* (countable)
> *This region produces many fine wines.* (countable)

dangling participle [> LEG 1.61, 1.63]

Also called an UNRELATED PARTICIPLE, a *dangling participle* is one that does not relate to its SUBJECT and therefore lacks CONCORD:

> **Watching TV, time passes quickly.** (*Watching* is a dangling participle.) (= *Time watches TV*)

Compare:

> *Watching TV, I completely forgot what the time was.* (= I was watching TV and I forgot what the time was.)

In the above PARTICIPLE CONSTRUCTION, the UNDERSTOOD subject of the participle is the same as the expressed subject of the MAIN VERB: *I.*

dash [> LEG 1.26]

A *dash* (–) is a PUNCTUATION MARK which can be used like a COLON to introduce an explanation:

> *The phone rang and rang – there was no answer.*

Dashes may be used if we want to add extra

information in a NON-DEFINING CLAUSE. We would use them in place of COMMAS or BRACKETS to emphasize that the information is additional and could be omitted without affecting the meaning of the MAIN CLAUSE:

> *The Portland Vase – which originally belonged to the Barberini family – is in the British Museum.*

deduction [> LEG 11.32–33]

This is a NOTION generally expressed by the MODAL VERBS *can't* and *must* in their SECONDARY USE. *Can't* and *must* express the highest degree of CERTAINTY:

> *He can't be thirsty. He must be hungry.*
> *He can't have been thirsty. He must have been hungry.*

defective verb [> LEG 11.4, 11.6.1]

Defective verb is the term applied to MODAL VERBS like *can* and *must*, which, in their PRIMARY USE require another FULL VERB to make up their missing parts. So, for example, *can* requires *be able to* and *must* requires *have to*:

INFINITIVE:	*I'm sorry to have to leave so early.*
-ING FORM:	*It's a pity having to leave so early.*
PRESENT:	*We must leave now.*
FUTURE:	*We must leave tomorrow.*
PERFECT:	*They have had to leave early.*
PAST:	*They had to leave early.*
PAST PERFECT:	*They didn't take much with them because they had had to leave in a hurry.*
FUTURE PERFECT:	*As they're both unemployed, I imagine they will have had to leave their flat.*
CONDITIONAL:	*If we hadn't paid the rent, we would have had to leave this flat immediately.*

defining clause [> LEG 1.26]

A *defining clause* (sometimes called *restrictive* or *identifying*) is a RELATIVE CLAUSE (beginning with *who, which* or *that*) which provides essential information which we cannot omit. Because of this, we don't use COMMAS to separate the relative clause when it is defining:

> *I've never met anyone who can type as fast as you can.*
> *The magazine which arrived this morning is five days late.*

We never use commas with *that* in relative clauses:

> *The wallet (that) you lost has been found.*

definite article [> LEG 3.1–4, 3.16–23]

The word *the* is the *definite* ARTICLE in English and is used for definite reference: that is, the person or thing referred to is assumed to be known to the listener or reader. *The* never varies in form whether it refers to people or things, SINGULAR or PLURAL:

> *He's the man/She's the woman/That's the book I was telling you about.*
> *They're the men/They're the women/They're the books I was telling you about.*

degree [> LEG 7.41–49]

The term refers to ADVERBS OF DEGREE: that is, adverbs

like *enough*, *fairly*, *hardly*, *quite* and *rather* which broadly answer the question *To what extent?*

deletion [> LEG 1.55]

We use the term *deletion* with reference to e.g. ABBREVIATED CLAUSES in which SUBJECT and VERB have been omitted (or *deleted*):

While (she was) at college, Delia wrote a novel.

demonstrative adjective [> LEG 4.32–34, 4.42, App 7]

The *demonstrative adjectives* are *this*, *that*, *these* and *those*. They function as ADJECTIVES (not as DEMONSTRATIVE PRONOUNS) when they are followed by a NOUN. *This* and *these* refer to what is 'near'. *That* and *those* refer to what is 'distant':

I bought this shirt and these ties when I was out.
That office block and those houses next to it are going to be pulled down.

demonstrative pronoun [> LEG 4.32–34, 4.42, App 7]

The *demonstrative pronouns* are *this*, *that*, *these* and *those*. They function as PRONOUNS (not as DEMONSTRATIVE ADJECTIVES) when they stand on their own. *This* and *these* refer to what is 'near'. *That* and *those* refer to what is 'distant':

Look at this!/I'll have these please.
Look at that!/I'll have those please.

dependent clause [> LEG 1.21–63]

A *dependent clause* is another name for a SUBORDINATE CLAUSE. It is called 'dependent' because it cannot stand on its own and depends on a MAIN CLAUSE for the completion of its meaning. Dependent clauses are introduced by CONJUNCTIONS (words like *as soon as*, *when*, etc.):

The alarm was raised (main clause) *as soon as the fire was discovered* (dependent clause).

descriptive grammar [> LEG Introduction, and, for example, App 25.25]

This is GRAMMAR which describes grammatical FORM and USAGE as it is, rather than as it ought to be (= PRESCRIPTIVE GRAMMAR). A *descriptive grammar* will, for example, point out that the use of *like* as a CONJUNCTION has not gained full acceptance, but it will not forbid its use. For example:

Like I told you, it's an offer I can't refuse. (= As I told you . . .)

determiner [> LEG 3.1, 4.2]

Determiners are words we use in front of COMMON NOUNS (or ADJECTIVE + common noun). We call them 'determiners' because they affect or 'determine' the meaning of the noun. Determiners make it clear, for example, which particular thing(s) we are referring to or how much of a substance we are talking about. It's a basic rule in English that a SINGULAR COUNTABLE NOUN must have a determiner in front of it. There are two classes of determiners:

- words that classify or identify, like *a/an*, *the*, *this/ that/these/those* and *my*, *your* etc.:

I bought a new shirt yesterday. (but it's not necessary to say which)
The shirt I'm wearing is new. (i.e. I'm telling you which)
I bought this/that shirt yesterday. (i.e. the one I'm showing you)

Do you like my new shirt? (i.e. the one that belongs to me)

- words that indicate quantity, like numbers and QUANTIFIERS (*some*, *many*, etc.):

I bought two shirts yesterday. (i.e. that's how many I bought)
There wasn't much material in the shop. (i.e. not a great quantity)

direct object [> LEG 1.9]

A *direct object* refers to the person or thing affected by the action of the VERB. It comes immediately after a TRANSITIVE VERB:

Please don't annoy me.
Veronica threw the ball over the wall.

direct speech [> LEG 15.1–4]

We use 'direct speech' when we speak. We use the term *direct speech* to describe the way we represent the spoken word in writing. For example, QUOTATION MARKS go round what is actually spoken and enclose other PUNCTUATION MARKS such as COMMAS, FULL STOPS, QUESTION MARKS and EXCLAMATION MARKS:

'Is that you, Jane?' Bob asked.

distributives [> LEG 5.4, 5.18–31]

Distributives are words like *all*, *both*, *each*, *every*, *either* and *neither*. They contain the idea of 'distributing' because they refer to whole amounts/ collections or separate items:

- whole amounts/collections:

all/both the children, *all/both the books*, *all the cheese*.

- separate items:

each child, *either of the books*, *neither book*.

double genitive [> LEG 2.52, 3.4]

The GENITIVE shows POSSESSION, which can be expressed by APOSTROPHE S/S APOSTROPHE (*a boy's jacket*, *a girls' school*) or by an OF-CONSTRUCTION (*the book of the film*). The *double genitive* makes use of both these constructions in the same PHRASE, so that we say:

a friend of my father's (Not *of my father*)
(= one of my father's friends)
a play of Shakespeare's (Not *of Shakespeare*)
(= one of Shakespeare's plays)

The double genitive arises because in English we can't use two DETERMINERS together, so we can't say, for example, *This my son*. Instead we have to say: *This son of mine*.

double negative [> LEG 13.8–10]

If we want to express a NEGATIVE in English, we can have only one negative word in a SENTENCE, for example, *not* or *never*:

We don't go to the cinema. We never go to the cinema.

The problem of the *double negative* arises with NEGATIVE ADVERBS like *hardly*, *seldom*, *rarely*, etc. As these adverbs already express a negative, we do not use them in the same clause as *not*:

We hardly ever go to the cinema. (Not *We don't hardly ever go to the cinema.*)

It also arises with negative INDEFINITE PRONOUNS like *no one*, *nobody*, *none*, *nothing*, *nowhere*. As these pronouns already express a negative, we do not use them in the same clause as *not*:

> *I saw **no one***. (Not **I didn't see no one*.*)

Two negatives in a sentence make an AFFIRMATIVE:

> ***Nobody** did **nothing***. (= Everybody did something.)

duty [> LEG 11.46–48, 11.50–52]

This is a NOTION generally expressed by the MODAL VERBS *should, ought to*, and *must*:

> *You **should smoke** less. You **shouldn't smoke** so much. You **must look after** yourself.*

dynamic verb [> LEG 9.3, App 38]

VERBS used in PROGRESSIVE TENSES (e.g. *I am writing*) are called *dynamic*. We draw a distinction in English between dynamic verbs and verbs which describe states (STATIVE VERBS), which are used in SIMPLE TENSES (e.g. *I love you*). Stative verbs refer to states over which we have no control (e.g. *I see very well*). Dynamic verbs refer to actions which are deliberate (e.g. *I'm making a cake*). We can describe three classes of verbs:

- dynamic verbs which have SIMPLE AND PROGRESSIVE forms (most verbs in English):
  > *I often **listen** to records.* (SIMPLE PRESENT TENSE)
  > *I'm **listening** to a record.* (PRESENT PROGRESSIVE TENSE)
- verbs which are always stative:
  > *This coat **belongs** to you.* (Not **is belonging**)
- verbs that have stative or dynamic uses:
  > *I **weigh** 65 kilos.* (a state) (Not **I'm weighing 65 kilos*.*)
  > *I'm **weighing** myself.* (a deliberate action: present progressive tense)

echo tag [> LEG 13.24–27]

An *echo tag* is a response, in TAG form, to an AFFIRMATIVE or NEGATIVE STATEMENT by which we may or may not request further information depending on the INTONATION we use:

> *He's resigned. -**He has?***
> *He hasn't resigned. -**Hasn't he?***

empty subject [> LEG 4.12]

We often use *it* in sentences referring to time, the weather, temperature or distance. When used in this way, *it* is sometimes called an *empty subject* because it carries no real information. It is present because every English SENTENCE has to contain a SUBJECT and a VERB. Here are a few examples:

> *It's 8 o'clock. It's Tuesday. It's May 25th.*
> *It's hot. It's raining. It rains a lot here.*
> *It's 37° Celsius.*

exclamation [> LEG 3.13, 11.30, 13.3.3n.7, 13.16]

An *exclamation* is an expression of surprise, disbelief, etc. Exclamations can be expressed in many ways, for example:

- with *What*:   ***What** a lot of flowers!*
- with MODALS: *It **can't** be true!*
- through QUESTIONS: *Is he mad! Isn't it hot!*

exclamation mark [> LEG 1.2]

An *exclamation mark* (!) is a PUNCTUATION MARK which is used to end a SENTENCE and convey surprise, etc: *What a slow train this is!*

exponent [compare > LEG 11.34–40]

This term is generally used to refer to an example of a FUNCTION. Thus *I'm sorry* is one of the possible *exponents* of the language function 'apologizing'.

falling tone [> LEG 7.41, 13.22, 13.26]

This term refers to the pitch or INTONATION of the voice when it 'goes down'. We use a *falling tone* to confirm what is known, or to express a lack of enthusiasm:

- requesting confirmation:
  > *You locked the door, $\overline{didn't}$ you? - Yes, I did.*
- expressing lack of enthusiasm:
  > *The film was **quite** good.* (= I didn't particularly enjoy it.)

feminine [LEG 2.39–41]

There is no grammatical GENDER in English. We use *he* and *she* to refer to people and *it* to refer to everything else. Only a few MASCULINE and *feminine* word forms (like *man* and *woman*) survive. Otherwise, it is the PRONOUNS, not the NOUNS, that tell us whether the reference is male or female:

> *He is the **person** you spoke to. She is the **person** you spoke to.*

finite verb [> LEG 1.2]

A *finite verb* is a VERB that has a SUBJECT and TENSE. *He writes, she wrote* and *he has written* are finite, but *written* by itself is not. The INFINITIVE (e.g. *to go*) and PRESENT/PAST PARTICIPLES (e.g. *going, gone*) are non-finite forms. MODAL VERBS are also finite even though they do not have tense forms like other verbs (e.g. *he may arrive*). IMPERATIVES (e.g. *Stand up!*) are also finite. A complete SENTENCE must contain a finite verb.

focus adverb [> LEG 7.54–56]

Focus adverbs are ADVERBS like *even, just, merely* and *only* which can precede the word they MODIFY to focus attention on it:

> ***Only** Tom knows the answer.* (i.e. nobody else does)
> *Tom knows **only** half of it.* (i.e. nothing else)

foreign plurals [> LEG 2.34]

This term refers to some PLURALS of NOUNS not formed with *s*. There is a natural tendency to make all nouns conform to the REGULAR rules for pronunciation and SPELLING of English plurals. The more commonly a noun is used, the more likely this is to happen. Some native speakers avoid *foreign plurals* in everyday speech and use them only in scientific and technical contexts. There are:

- nouns of foreign origin with anglicized plurals like *genius/geniuses* (Not **genii**).
- nouns with both foreign and anglicized plurals like *cactus/cacti/cactuses*.
- nouns with foreign plurals only like *stratum/strata, basis/bases, phenomenon/phenomena*.

form [> LEG 10.6, *passim*]

Form is often contrasted with USAGE. It refers to the way in which language is put together rather than the way it is used. For example, *he is* (third PERSON) is different in form from *I am* (first person).

formal style [> LEG 7.59.3]

This refers to speech or writing which is very careful, correct and polite. For example, reports, business letters and public speeches might be in *formal style*. A construction like the following would be typical of formal style, as it makes use of INVERSION (e.g. *never has there been*) as well as LEXICAL ITEMS which derive from Latin and Greek, such as *environmental* and *catastrophe*:

> **Never has there been** so much protest against **environmental catastrophe**.

frequency [> LEG 7.37–40]

This term refers to ADVERBS OF FREQUENCY: that is, adverbs like *always*, *often* and *usually* which answer the question *How often?*

fronting [> LEG 1.6]

Placing an item at the beginning of a SENTENCE for special emphasis is called *fronting*:

> *A **fine mess** you've made of this.*
> (= You've made a fine mess of this.)

full form [> LEG 9.52, *passim*]

This is the opposite of a CONTRACTION or short form. For example, *don't* is the contraction of the *full form do not*.

full stop [> LEG 1.2, 3.17]

A *full stop* (.) is a PUNCTUATION MARK which is used:
– to end a SENTENCE:

> *The shops close at 7 tonight.*

– with some ABBREVIATIONS:

> *He got his M.A. (= Master of Arts) at Princeton.*

full verb [> LEG 9.1, 10.1, *passim*]

This is a term used to distinguish between an ordinary VERB (e.g. *work*) and an AUXILIARY VERB (e.g. some uses of *be, have, do,* or MODAL auxiliary verbs like *can, may* and *must*).

function [> LEG 11.34–40]

The term refers to 'language acts': things we do with language: for example, 'apologizing' is a *function* which may be expressed by the EXPONENT *I'm sorry*. Words describing functions often end with *-ing*: agreeing, complaining, refusing, etc.

future [> LEG 9.35–50]

There are many ways of expressing the *future* in English, for example, with:
– *be going to*:

> *My aunt's **going to** arrive tomorrow afternoon.*

– *be to/be about to*, etc.

> *The committee **is to meet** next week.*

– present TENSES:

> *The train **leaves** at 5.*
> *The train's **leaving** in ten minutes.*

future-in-the-past [> LEG 9.49–50]

The *future-in-the-past* can be expressed by *was going to, was about to, was to, was to have*, etc. It describes events which were planned to take place and which did or did not take place:

> *I couldn't go to Tom's party as **I was about to go** into hospital.*
> ***I was to have seen** Mr Kay tomorrow, but the appointment has been cancelled.*

future perfect progressive tense [> LEG 9.42–43]

This is the PROGRESSIVE form of the FUTURE PERFECT SIMPLE TENSE (*will have been* + *-ING* FORM). What is in progress now can be considered from a point in the future:

> *By this time next week, I **will have been working** for this company for 24 years.*

future perfect simple tense [> LEG 9.42–43]

Formed with *will have* + PAST PARTICIPLE, the *future perfect simple tense* describes an action that will be already completed by a certain time in the future:

> *I **will have retired** by the year 2020.*

future progressive tense [> LEG 9.40–41]

This is the PROGRESSIVE form of the SIMPLE FUTURE TENSE (*will/shall* + *be* + *-ING* FORM), which describes actions which will be in progress in the immediate or distant future:

> *Hurry up! Our guests **will be arriving** at any minute!*

gender [> LEG 2.39–41]

In many languages, the names of things such as *book, chair, radio, table* may be grammatically MASCULINE, FEMININE or NEUTER. Often *gender* doesn't relate to sex, so that the word for 'girl' might be neuter and the word for 'chair' might be feminine. There is no grammatical gender in English. We use *he* and *she* to refer to people and *it* to refer to everything else. Only a few masculine and feminine word forms (like *man* and *woman*) survive. Otherwise, it is the PRONOUNS, not the NOUNS, that tell us whether the reference is male or female:

> *He is the **person** you spoke to. She is the **person** you spoke to.*

genitive [> LEG 1.1, 2.42–52]

The *genitive*, sometimes called 'the possessive case', refers to POSSESSION. The genitive can be expressed in two ways in English:
– with APOSTROPHE *S/S* APOSTROPHE: *a **boy's** jacket, a **girls'** school*.
– with the *OF*-CONSTRUCTION: *the book **of the film***.
Apostrophe *s/s* apostrophe are used mainly for people, not things. If we want to show the genitive of a thing, we may use *of* (e.g. *the key of the car*), but, where possible, we prefer to use a COMPOUND NOUN (*the car key*).

gerund [> LEG 16.38–40]

Gerunds are NOUNS formed from VERBS, and they always end in *-ing*. Many verbs, particularly those of Latin origin, have their own noun forms with characteristic endings:, for example, *-(t)ion*. The *-ING* FORM noun is an alternative of Saxon origin: *describe* (verb) → *description* → *describing*.
The gerund points to 'the act of'; the ordinary noun tells us what something is called. Gerunds can be:
– UNCOUNTABLE:

> ***Dancing** is fun. I love it.*
> *I've done **a bit of shopping**.*

– COUNTABLE:

> *I've just bought **a new recording** of 'Figaro'.*
> *I've got three **recordings** of 'Figaro'.*

gradable/ungradable [> LEG 6.5]

Gradable is a term that is mainly applied to ADJECTIVES, though it can also apply to some ADVERBS and VERBS. Most adjectives are gradable. This means we can imagine degrees in the quality referred to, so we can:
- use an adjective with *very*, *too* and *enough*: *very good*, *too good*, *not good enough*.
- form a COMPARATIVE and SUPERLATIVE: *(big), bigger, biggest; (good), better, best.*

An adjective is *ungradable* when we can't modify it with *very*, *too*, etc. and can't make comparative and superlative forms:, for example, *daily, dead, medical, unique*, etc.

grammar [> LEG 1.1, 2.20, 9.6, *passim*]

Grammar deals with with three areas of language:
- SYNTAX (= the way words are combined to make acceptable SENTENCES): *I've met John.*
- MORPHOLOGY (= the rules governing the forms of words used in sentences): *book - books, write - writes*, etc.
- PHONOLOGY (= the rules governing the sounds of language):, for example, /s/ after /f/, /k/, /p/, /t/, /θ/: *cup/cups.*

habit [> LEG 9.8.3, 11.58–64]

This is a NOTION generally expressed by the SIMPLE PRESENT TENSE and MODAL VERBS like *will/would* or by *used to*:
> *I get up at 7.*
> *In fine weather, he will/would often sit in the sun for hours.*
> *I used to collect stamps when I was a child.*

helping verb [> LEG 10.1–4, 11.1]

This is another term for AUXILIARY VERB: that is, verbs like *be* which help other verbs complete their grammatical function (e.g. *I was writing*), and MODAL VERBS like *can* which combine with other verbs (e.g *I can swim*).

hyphen [> LEG 2.7, 2.11, 6.3]

A *hyphen* (-) is a PUNCTUATION MARK which is shorter than a DASH and which is used to join syllables (e.g. *co-operate*) or in COMPOUND ADJECTIVES and COMPOUND NOUNS. There are no precise rules for the use of hyphens in compound nouns. Two short nouns joined together are written without a hyphen (*teacup*). The use of the hyphen in longer compounds is at the discretion of the writer (*writing paper* or *writing-paper*), but the tendency is to avoid hyphens where possible.

idiom [e.g. > LEG 8.23–8.30]

A fixed PHRASE the meaning of which bears no relation to the meanings of the individual words that make up the phrase. PHRASAL VERBS can often have literal or idiomatic meanings:
> *The teacher told me to sit up.* (= sit upright: non-idiomatic)
> *We're going to sit up all night during the general election.* (= not go to bed: idiomatic)

Apart from phrasal verbs, there are numerous expressions which are idiomatic. For example:
- fixed phrases:
> *John imagines he'll be a millionaire before he's 25, but that's just pie in the sky.*
> (= wishful thinking, something which is impossible to achieve)
- proverbs:
> *Deal with the problem now. Remember, a stitch in time saves nine.*
> (= When something goes wrong, deal with it immediately before it gets worse.)

***if*-clause** [> LEG Chapter 14]

This is another term for CONDITIONAL CLAUSE.

imperative [> LEG 9.51–56]

The *imperative* is the same form as the BARE INFINITIVE (*go, run, stand*, etc.). The NEGATIVE is formed with *Don't*. We use the imperative not only for direct orders or COMMANDS (*Stand up!*), but also for warnings (*Look out!*), directions (*Take the 2nd turning on the right*), instructions (*Use a moderate oven*), etc.

indefinite article [> LEG 3.1–15]

The word *a/an* is the *indefinite* ARTICLE in English and is used for indefinite reference: that is, the person or thing referred to may not be known to the listener or reader, so *a/an* has the sense of 'any' or 'I can't/won't tell you which'. *A* and *an* have exactly the same meaning. We use *a* in front of CONSONANT SOUNDS (*a man, a year*) and *an* in front of VOWEL SOUNDS (*an umbrella, an eye, an hour*). When the reference is indefinite, we always use *a/an* in front of COUNTABLE NOUNS: *He's a doctor. It's a good book.*

indefinite pronoun [> LEG 4.9, 4.37–42]

Indefinite pronouns include:
- *one* (used in FORMAL STYLE):
> *World trade is improving, but one can't expect miracles.*
- compounds of *some-, any-, no- and every-*:
> *someone, anyone, no one, everyone*, etc.

These pronouns are called *indefinite* because they don't refer to anyone in particular:
> *There's someone on the phone who wants to speak to you.*

indirect object [> LEG 1.9, 1.13]

An *indirect object* usually refers to the person who 'benefits' from the action expressed in the VERB: someone you give something *to* or buy something *for*:
> *Throw me the ball.* (= Throw the ball to me.)
> *Buy your father a present.* (= Buy a present for your father.)

indirect question [> LEG 15.9, 15.17–24]

An *indirect question* is one that follows a REPORTING VERB like *ask if/whether*. We may report:
- YES/NO QUESTIONS:
> *'Are you ready?'*
> possible indirect question:
> *He asked me if/whether I was ready.*
- QUESTION-WORD QUESTIONS:
> *'Where are you going?' 'What caused the accident?'*
> possible indirect questions:
> *He asked me where I was going.*
> *He asked me what (had) caused the accident.*

indirect speech [> LEG 15.5–27]

We use *indirect speech* (sometimes called *reported speech*) when we are telling someone what another person says or said. The REPORTING VERB (e.g. *say, tell*) may be in the present or past (most often in the past) and the tenses of the INDIRECT STATEMENT are often (but not always) affected by this:
- actual spoken statement:
    'I'm busy.'
- recorded as DIRECT SPEECH:
    'I'm busy,' the boss says/said.
- indirect statement (present):
    *The boss **says** (that) he's busy.*
- indirect statement (past):
    *The boss **said** (that) he was busy.*
- indirect statements (mixed tenses):
    *The boss **says** (that) he was busy.*
    *The boss **said** (that) he's busy.*

A number of reporting verbs like *think* and *wonder* do not strictly report 'speech' (actual spoken words), but thoughts, feelings, etc. That's why *indirect speech*, as a term, is preferable to 'reported speech'.

indirect statement [> LEG 15.9–14]

An *indirect statement* is a STATEMENT that follows a REPORTING VERB like *say, tell, think*:
- actual spoken statement:
    'I made a good impression.'
- possible indirect statements:
    *He **said** (that) he (**had**) **made** a good impression.*
    *I **think** (that) I **made** a good impression.*

infinitive [> LEG 16.1–2, *passim*]

There are two forms of the *infinitive* in English:
- the BARE INFINITIVE, which is the BASE FORM of the VERB: e.g. *go*.
- the TO-INFINITIVE, which is the base form preceded by *to*: e.g. *to go*; also *so as to, in order to go*.

Some verbs, like MODAL VERBS, are followed by a bare infinitive: *You **may go**.*
Some verbs, like *fail*, may be followed only by a *to*-infinitive: *He **failed to turn** up at the meeting.*
Some verbs, like *enjoy*, may be followed only by the *-ING* FORM: *I **enjoy walking** in the mountains.*
Some verbs, like *begin*, may be followed by a *to*-infinitive or the *-ing* form: *We **began to work/began working**.*
Some ADJECTIVES, like *easy*, are followed by a *to*-infinitive or *-ing*: *It's easy **to add/adding up** with a calculator.*
Some NOUNS, like *opportunity*, are followed by a *to*-infinitive or a preposition: *Don't miss the **opportunity to buy/of buying** shares while prices are low.*
The forms of the infinitive are:

	ACTIVE	PASSIVE
present	*(to) ask*	*(to) be asked*
progressive	*(to) be asking*	–
perfect	*(to) have asked*	*(to) have been asked*
progressive	*(to) have been asking*	–

infinitive construction [> LEG 1.21, 1.51.2, 1.57, 16.12]

An *infinitive construction* involves the use of the INFINITIVE and may be part of a COMPLEX SENTENCE. We may use an infinitive construction, for example:
- in the sense of *want to*:
    ***To order** a vehicle, you have to pay a deposit.* (= If you want to . . .)
- to express purpose:
    *I went to live in France **to/so as to/in order to learn** French.*

infinitive marker [> LEG 16.1, *passim*]

The *infinitive marker* is the word *to* which we may use in front of the BASE FORM of a VERB, thereby changing the BARE INFINITIVE into a TO-INFINITIVE. *To* may often be expanded to *so as to* or *in order to*:
    *I arrived at the cinema early **to/so as to/in order to get** a good seat.*

inflexion [> LEG 1.1]

Many European languages are *inflected*, that is they make use of *inflexions* (also spelt *inflections*). For example:
- NOUNS have endings which change depending on whether they are, for example, the SUBJECT or OBJECT of a VERB.
- There are complex AGREEMENTS between ARTICLES, ADJECTIVES and nouns to emphasize the fact that a noun is, for example, subject or object, MASCULINE or FEMININE, SINGULAR or PLURAL.
- Verbs 'conjugate', so that it is immediately obvious from the endings which 'PERSON' (first, second, third) is referred to and whether the 'person' is singular or plural.

English was an inflected language up to the Middle Ages, but the modern language retains very few inflexions:, for example, the third person in the SIMPLE PRESENT TENSE: *I work – he **works**.*

informal style [> LEG 10.7*n*.4, 10.30*n*.8]

This refers to speech or writing which is used among friends (e.g. in private conversations or letters). 'Sub-standard' forms may occur in *informal style* (*you **ain't seen nothing** yet*), but usually informal style is correct and STANDARD, while avoiding COMPLEX SENTENCES and a 'high-sounding' tone:
- informal: *More than ever, we know we've got to look after nature.*
- FORMAL: *Our environmental awareness and protectiveness towards nature have increased.*

-ing form [> LEG 1.56–61, 2.7, 16.38]

Some people avoid the terms GERUND and PARTICIPLE because it is often difficult (and unnecessary) to distinguish between the two. Instead, the term *-ing form* is used to describe any word ending in *-ing*. The *-ing* form derives from a VERB (e.g. *write - writing*) and has three uses in English:
- as PRESENT PARTICIPLE used in the PROGRESSIVE TENSES or in PARTICIPLE CONSTRUCTIONS:
    *I'm **writing** a letter.* (PRESENT PROGRESSIVE)
    *He walked out of the room, **slamming** the door behind him.* (participle construction)

– as a gerund (NOUN) (= the act of):
> *Writing anything is never easy.* (= the act of writing)

– as an ADJECTIVE:
> *She told the children a frightening story which kept them awake for a long time.*

The gerund is often used in COMPOUND NOUNS and should not be confused with the adjectival form:
> *Here are your running-shoes.* (= shoes which you use for running: gerund; HYPHEN optional)
> *I love the sight of running water.* (= water which is running: adjective; no hyphen)

instrument [> LEG 12.5 and compare App 25.17]
This refers to the use of *with* in PASSIVE constructions and may be contrasted with the use of *by* + AGENT:
> *He was killed by a falling stone.* (accidental)
> *He was killed with a knife.* (deliberate)

intensifier [> LEG 7.50–53]
Intensifiers are ADVERBS which are used with GRADABLE ADJECTIVES and adverbs (e.g. *very slow/very slowly*) and, in some case, VERBS (e.g. *I entirely agree*). While an ADVERB OF DEGREE normally weakens or limits the meaning of the word it modifies, an intensifier normally strengthens (or 'intensifies') the meaning:
> *Your work is good.*
> *Your work is very good.* (intensifier: strengthens the meaning)
> *Your work is quite good.* (adverb of degree: weakens the meaning)

Typical intensifiers are *very*, *such (a/an)*, *so*, and *-LY* ADVERBS used in place of *very* (e.g. *extremely*).

interrogative [> LEG Chapter 13, *passim*]
We use this term to mean 'having the form of a QUESTION':
> *Has she returned? When did she arrive?*

intonation [> LEG 13.22]
Intonation refers to the rise and fall (or *pitch*) of the voice during speech. For example, we use:
– a RISING TONE not only to ask for information, but to express surprise, anger, interest, etc.:
> *You left the gas on, / didn't you?* (= Did you leave the gas on?)
> *You didn't leave the gas on, / did you?* (= I hope you didn't)
> *You couldn't do me a favour, / could you?* (= I hope you can)

– a FALLING TONE to confirm what we already know to be true:
> *You locked the door, didn't \ you?* – (Expecting: *Yes, I did* or no reply at all.)
> *You didn't lock the door, did \ you?* – (Expecting: *No, I didn't* or no reply at all.)

intransitive verb [> LEG 1.9–10, 8.29, App 1]
An *intransitive verb* is not followed by an OBJECT and can never be used in the PASSIVE.
There are verbs which:
– are always intransitive (e.g. *ache, appear, arrive, come, cough, disappear, fall, go*):
> *The train arrived late.* (No object is possible after *arrived*: Not *arrived the station*)

– have TRANSITIVE and intransitive uses (e.g. *break, burn, close, drop, fly, hurt, move, open*):
> *Someone opened the door.*
> (verb + object: transitive)
> *The door opened.*
> (verb without object: intransitive)

Some intransitive verbs may be PHRASAL: *come in, sit down, die away*, etc.

inversion [> LEG 1.6, 7.59, 13.1–3, 14.8, 14.15, 14.18.3]
The basic WORD ORDER in English is: SUBJECT, VERB, OBJECT, manner, place, time (SVOMPT). In a few instances, this has to be varied, so that the SUBJECT comes after the VERB. For example, this can happen:
– in QUESTIONS with *be* and *have* as FULL VERBS:
> *Am I late?* (STATEMENT: *I am late.*)
– after NEGATIVE ADVERBS:
> *Seldom have I heard such rubbish.*
– with *should*, *were* and *had* in CONDITIONAL CLAUSES:
> *Should you be interested in our offer, please contact us.* (If you should be . . .)
> *Were the government to cut Value Added Tax, prices would fall.* (If the government were to . . .)
> *Had the management acted sooner, the strike wouldn't have happened.* (If the management had . . .)

inverted commas [> LEG 15.3]
Inverted commas is another term for QUOTATION MARKS.

invitation [> LEG 11.37]
This is a NOTION generally expressed by the MODAL VERBS *will* and *would*:
> *Will you come for a walk with me?*
> *Would you like to come for a walk with me?*

irregular [> LEG 6.24, 7.4, 9.15–16, 9.22, Apps 39–40]
The term *irregular* is used in GRAMMAR to refer to anything that does not follow the same pattern as most others of its kind. It is often used in connexion with:
– ADJECTIVES like *bad - worse - worst* (which isn't REGULAR like *tall - taller - tallest*).
– VERBS like *begin - began - begun* (which isn't regular like *play - played - played*).

lexical item
Lexical item simply means 'word'. However, it is used in GRAMMAR specifically to refer to sets or classes of words with meanings that are not limited to their grammatical functions. Typical lexical items are words like *book, chair, umbrella* and *soap*, which may be contrasted with STRUCTURAL WORDS (like *this, I, me, is*), the use of which is grammatically defined. The use of lexical items is sometimes described as 'open'. For example, we can use a great variety of lexical items to complete this sentence:
> *I sat on the . . .* (*chair, stool, floor, tree-trunk*, etc.)

The use of structural words is sometimes described as 'closed', that is, limited by grammatical function. For example, if you want to talk about yourself, you can only use the structural word *I*:
> *I sat on the stool.*

lexis

Lexis simply means 'vocabulary'. All the words and phrases in a particular language are sometimes referred to as the *lexicon*.

limiting clause [> LEG 1.54]

A MAIN CLAUSE can be QUALIFIED or 'limited' by clauses introduced by *in that*, *in so far as* and *inasmuch as*:
> *The demonstration was fairly peaceful **in that there were only one or two clashes with the police**.*

link verb [> LEG 1.9, 10.23–26]

The term *link verb* (or *linking verb*) describes VERBS like *be* and *seem* which are followed by COMPLEMENTS (not OBJECTS):
> *Frank **is/seems/looks/sounds** clever.*

-ly adverb [> LEG 7.7–16, 7.52–53, 7.57]

There are three classes of adverbs ending in -*ly*:
- ADVERBS OF MANNER like *badly, carefully, happily*, etc.: *We played **badly** and lost.*
- INTENSIFIERS, that is adverbs like *extremely*, which we can used in place of *very*: ***very** tired/**extremely** tired.*
- VIEWPOINT ADVERBS like *frankly, generally*, etc.:
> ***Frankly**, I'm not satisfied with your work.*

main clause [> LEG 1.21]

In any COMPLEX SENTENCE there is always one independent (or *main*) CLAUSE and one or more DEPENDENT (or SUBORDINATE) elements. The *main clause* is the one that could stand as a SENTENCE on its own:
> ***The alarm was raised** (main clause) as soon as the fire was discovered (subordinate clause).*

main verb [> LEG 1.2, 1.21]

The *main verb*, sometimes called the main FINITE VERB, is the verb in a MAIN CLAUSE:
> *The alarm **was raised** (main verb) as soon as the fire was discovered (SUBORDINATE CLAUSE).*

masculine [> LEG 2.39–41]

There is no grammatical GENDER in English. We use *he* and *she* to refer to people and *it* to refer to everything else. Only a few *masculine* and FEMININE word forms (like *man* and *woman*) survive. Otherwise, it is the PRONOUNS, not the NOUNS, that tell us if the reference is male or female:
> ***He** is the **person** you spoke to. **She** is the **person** you spoke to.*

mass noun

Mass noun is another term for UNCOUNTABLE NOUN.

mid-position [> LEG 7.10]

This term is often used in connexion with ADVERBS OF FREQUENCY, which normally come after *be* when it is the only VERB in a SENTENCE (*He's **often** late*), after the first AUXILIARY (*He's **often** travelling abroad*) or before the MAIN VERB (*He **often** travels abroad*).

modal verb [> LEG 11.1, 16.3]

VERBS like *can* and *may* are called *modal* AUXILIARIES, *modal verbs* or simply *modals*. We frequently use modals when we are concerned with our relationship with someone else. We may, for example, ask for PERMISSION to do something; grant permission to someone; give or receive advice; make or respond to REQUESTS and OFFERS, etc. Modals sharing the same grammatical characteristics are: *can/could, may/might, will/would, shall/should, must* and *ought to*. Verbs which share some of the grammatical characteristics of modals (SEMI-MODALS) are: *need, dare* and *used to*. Some of the important characteristics of modals are:
- we do not use a TO-INFINITIVE after them:
> *I can **see** you.*
- they have no -*ING* FORM.
- they have no -*(e)s* in the third PERSON:
> *He can **see** you.*
- they make QUESTIONS and NEGATIVES without using *do/did*:
> ***Can** I come in? I **mustn't** be late.*
- they have PRIMARY AND SECONDARY USES:
> *You **must stop** at the lights.* (OBLIGATION/DUTY)
> *You **must be** right.* (near-CERTAINTY)

modify [> LEG 2.10, 7.1]

We say that an ADVERB *modifies* a VERB and in doing so tells us something about the action in a SENTENCE. For example, in the sentence *Paganini must have played the violin **beautifully**, beautifully* modifies *played*. Note, too, that a NOUN can modify another and act as a NOUN MODIFIER:, for example, *a **cotton** dress* (telling us what kind of dress).

morphology

Morphology refers to the rules governing the forms of words which we use in SENTENCES: for example, the rule for forming a PLURAL by adding *s* to a SINGULAR: *book/books*; or the rule for forming the third PERSON in the SIMPLE PRESENT by adding -*s* to some VERBS: *I play - he plays*.

necessity [> LEG 11.46–57]

This is a NOTION generally expressed by the MODAL VERBS *must* (necessity), *needn't* (lack of necessity) and *mustn't* (PROHIBITION):
> *You **must take care** of yourself.* (= it's necessary)
> *You **needn't come into work** tomorrow.* (= lack of necessity)
> *You **mustn't smoke** in the lift.* (= prohibition)

negative [> LEG 13.4]

A *negative* STATEMENT is the opposite of an AFFIRMATIVE statement. It says or means 'no' and contains a negative word such as *not* or *never*:
- affirmative: *He's leaving.*
- negative: *He isn't leaving.*

negative adverb [> LEG 7.59.3, 13.8, App 19]

Negative adverbs are ADVERBS like *never, seldom, rarely, hardly ever*, etc. Two important facts about them are:
- We use only one negative word in a SENTENCE: *I **hardly know** him.* (Not *I don't hardly know him.*)
- There is INVERSION if we begin a sentence with a negative adverb: ***Seldom have I** heard such rubbish.*

negative question [> LEG 13.14–16]

A *negative question* usually begins with a

CONTRACTION like *Can't*, or *Don't*. We ask negative questions, for example, when:
- we hope for the answer *Yes*:
    Don't you remember *that holiday we had in Spain?*
- we want to express surprise:
    Can't you ride *a bicycle?*

neuter [> LEG 2.39–41]

There is no grammatical GENDER in English. We use *he* and *she* to refer to people and *it* to refer to everything else. Only a few MASCULINE and FEMININE word forms (like *man* and *woman*) survive. Otherwise, it is the PRONOUNS, not the NOUNS, that tell us if the reference is male or female:
    He *is the* **person** *you spoke to.* **She** *is the* **person** *you spoke to.*

nominalization [> LEG 2.50]

This refers to the use of a NOUN PHRASE in place of a VERB PHRASE or in place of an INFINITIVE:
    It's forbidden **to remove books** *from this reference library.*
    → **The removal of books** *from this reference library is forbidden.*

non-defining clause [> LEG 1.26]

A *non-defining clause* (sometimes called *non-restrictive* or *non-identifying*) is a RELATIVE CLAUSE (beginning with, for example, *who*, or *which*) which provides 'extra information' that could be omitted without seriously changing the meaning of the SENTENCE. We always use COMMAS round a non-defining clause:
    Our new secretary, **who can type faster than anyone I have ever met**, *has completely reorganized our office.*
    Time Magazine, **which is available in every country in the world**, *is published every week.*
Non-defining clauses with *that* are not normally possible.

notion [> LEG 11.34]

A *notion* is an idea or concept like *ability, duty, existence, permission* which combines with a FUNCTION to suggest the true meaning behind what we say or write. If, for example, we say:
    Is there a hotel near here?
we are *inquiring about* (function) the *existence* (notion) of a hotel.
If we say:
    Can I use your phone please?
asking is the function and *permission* is the notion. The words used are the EXPONENT of the function.

noun [> LEG 2.1, 2.12]

A *noun* tells us what someone or something is called. For example, a noun can be the name of a person (*John*); a job title (*doctor*); the name of a thing (*radio*); the name of a place (*London*); the name of a quality (*courage*); or the name of an action (*laughter/laughing*). Nouns are the names we give to people, things, places, etc. in order to identify them. We can classify nouns as follows:

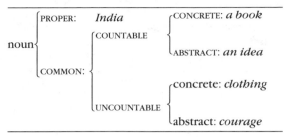

noun clause [> LEG 1.22–24, 15.5–27, Apps 44–45]

Noun clauses may follow REPORTING VERBS like *ask, say, think* and *wonder*, and ADJECTIVES like *certain*. They are a feature of INDIRECT SPEECH and are introduced by:
- *THAT* (introducing INDIRECT STATEMENTS):
    He said **that he would be late**.
- *if/whether* (introducing indirect YES/NO QUESTIONS):
    He asked me **if/whether I would be late**.
- a QUESTION-WORD such as *when* (introducing indirect WH-QUESTIONS):
    He wanted to know **when I would be arriving**.
Noun clauses are usually the OBJECT of a VERB (or a COMPLEMENT after *be*). However, a noun clause can be a SUBJECT as well (just like any NOUN):
    That crime is on the increase *is something no one can deny. = No one can deny* **that crime is on the increase**.
    What I like best *is a day at the races. = A day at the races is* **what I like best**.

noun modifier [> LEG 2.10, 6.13]

A *noun modifier* MODIFIES another NOUN to form a COMPOUND NOUN. It may, for example, refer to:
- use: *a* **kitchen** *chair* (= a chair for use in the kitchen)
- what something is made of: *a* **cotton** *blouse* (= a blouse made of cotton)
- what type of thing something is: *a* **horror** *film* (i.e. what kind of film)
Noun modifiers are sometimes confused with ADJECTIVES because they appear to behave like adjectives. However, they are nouns because they don't have COMPARATIVE and SUPERLATIVE forms and can't be used with *very*.

noun phrase [> LEG 1.2, 2.1]

We use a NOUN after a DETERMINER, for example, *a, the, this*, to form a *noun phrase*:, for example, *the man*. We can combine other words into the noun phrase:, for example, *the man next door, that tall building, the old broom in the cupboard*.

noun + preposition [> LEG 8.20, 16.53, 16.60, App 27–29]

Many NOUNS are followed by particular PREPOSITIONS. These nouns are often related to ADJECTIVES or VERBS, for example:
    absent *from* (adjective) → **absence** *from* (noun);
    advise *against* (verb) → **advice** *against* (noun).

number [> LEG 2.20]

The *number* of a NOUN is whether it is SINGULAR or PLURAL. Nouns may have plurals which are:
- REGULAR (ending in *-s, -es* or *-ies*):
    cats, potatoes, countries.

281

– IRREGULAR:
men, sheep, phenomena.

object [> LEG 1.4, 1.9, 1.12–14, 12.3n.2]
An *object* is normally a NOUN, PRONOUN or NOUN PHRASE.
It usually goes after the VERB in the ACTIVE and can
become the SUBJECT of a verb in the PASSIVE. Only a
TRANSITIVE VERB can have an object or be used in the
passive:
– active:
*They drove **him** (object) away in a police car.*
– passive:
***He** (subject) was driven away in a police car.*

obligation [> LEG 11.2, 11.46–48, 11.52–57]
This is a NOTION generally expressed by the MODAL
VERBS *should, ought to, must* and *needn't*:
*You **should phone** home now. You **shouldn't
keep** them waiting.*
*You **must wait** here.*
*You **needn't come into work tomorrow**.*
Should and *ought* to express escapable *obligation*,
must/mustn't express inescapable obligation and
needn't expresses absence of obligation.

of-construction [> LEG 2.10.1, 2.47–50]
The *of-construction* is a GENITIVE that shows
POSSESSION. We use it:
– to show possession by people if APOSTROPHE *S/S*
APOSTROPHE is not possible:
*Can't you look at the book **of the boy behind
you**?* (Not *... the boy behind you's book*)
– to show possession by things, rather than people:
*the key **of the car*** (Not *the car's key*). (If a
COMPOUND NOUN is possible, it is usually preferable to
of: *a car key* (Not *a key of a car*).

offer [> LEG 11.34–40, 16.4]
This is a NOTION generally expressed by the MODAL VERB
shall and the VERB *let*:
***Shall I carry** your bag for you? **Let me carry**
your bag for you.*

paradigm [> LEG 10.6, *passim*]
A *paradigm* is a complete example of, for instance, all
the forms of a VERB. For example, here is a paradigm of
the SIMPLE PRESENT TENSE of *be* (affirmative):

AFFIRMATIVE		SHORT FORM	
I	am	I'm	
You	are	You're	
He	is	He's	
She	is	She's	
It	is	It's	(old).
We	are	We're	
You	are	You're	
They	are	They're	

participle [> LEG 1.56–63, 16.1, 16.38, 16.41]
A *participle* is a non-FINITE form of a VERB. It may be a
PRESENT *-ING* FORM (*playing/writing*) or a PAST *-ed/-en*
form (*played/written*) or a PERFECT form (*having
played/having written*):

	present	**perfect**	**past**
ACTIVE:	*finding*	*having found*	–
PASSIVE:	*being found*	*having been found*	*found*

participle construction [> LEG 1.21, 1.57–63]
We use *participle constructions* in place of CLAUSES to
form COMPLEX SENTENCES. We may use:
– PRESENT PARTICIPLE constructions:
***Since phoning** you this morning, I have
changed my plans.*
(in place of the ADVERBIAL CLAUSE ***Since I phoned**
you this morning, I have changed my plans.*)
– PAST PARTICIPLE constructions in place of a PASSIVE:
***Viewed from a distance**, the island of Nepenthe
looked like a cloud.*
(in place of the adverbial clause ***When it was
viewed** from a distance ...*)

particle
This is another way of referring to an ADVERB PARTICLE.

partitive [> LEG 2.18, App 5]
A *partitive* is a NOUN which contains the idea of 'a part
of something'. We use partitives to refer to:
– one item: *a **loaf** of bread*
– a part of a whole: *a **slice** of bread*
– a collection of items: *a **packet** of biscuits*
The most common partitives are *a piece of* and (in
everyday speech) *a bit of*:
*Can I have **a piece of** bread/**a bit of** bread/**two
pieces of** bread please?*
There are partitives which go with some words but
not with others. So we can say *a slice of bread, a slice
of cake, a slice of meat*, but not *a slice of soap*.

part of speech
This term, now considered by many grammarians to
be old-fashioned, refers to word classes like 'NOUN',
'PREPOSITION', 'VERB'.

passive voice [> LEG 12.1–2]
The terms *passive voice* and ACTIVE VOICE refer to the
form of a VERB. In the passive, the action is done to the
SUBJECT:
*This food **was cooked** last night.*
We can form the passive only with TRANSITIVE VERBS:
that is, verbs which can be followed by an OBJECT.

past participle [> LEG 1.62, 6.14–15, 7.51, 9.22, 10.3, 12.7,
Apps 39–40]
The *past participle* is the third part of a VERB, which
may be REGULAR (e.g. *arrive - arrived - **arrived***) or
IRREGULAR (e.g. *begin - began - **begun***). We use the
past participle:
– with *have/had* to form PERFECT TENSES:
*I have **eaten**.*
– with *be* to form the PASSIVE:
*The train is **delayed**.*
– as an ADJECTIVE:
*a **locked** door, a **frozen** lake.*
– in PARTICIPLE CONSTRUCTIONS:
***Viewed** from a distance, the island of Nepenthe
looked like a cloud.*

past perfect progressive tense [> LEG 9.32–34]
This is the PROGRESSIVE form of the SIMPLE PAST PERFECT
TENSE. It is formed with *had been* + the *-ING* FORM
PARTICIPLE which emphasizes that an activity had been
in progress throughout a period with consequences
then. It is often used with CONTINUITY VERBS:

I had been working for Exxon for 15 years before I got a job with Shell.

past progressive tense [> LEG 9.19–21]
This is the PROGRESSIVE form of the SIMPLE PAST TENSE. It is formed with *was/were* + the *-ING* FORM PARTICIPLE which describes past situations or actions that were in progress at some time in the past:
> *I was living abroad in 1987, so I missed the general election.*

pattern [> LEG 1.8, 16.27–32, Apps 44–45]
A *pattern* is an accepted and often-used arrangement of words which conveys meaning. In GRAMMAR we can refer, for example, to:
- a VERB PATTERN:
> *My head aches.* (SUBJECT + INTRANSITIVE VERB)
- an ADJECTIVE PATTERN:
> *John is eager to please.*

perception
See VERBS OF PERCEPTION.

perfect [> LEG 9.22–27, 9.28–32, 9.42, 11.4, 11.7, 11.8.4, 11.28–33]
The *perfect* is the form of a VERB (*have* + the PAST PARTICIPLE) which we use to describe actions taking place up to a point in the present or a point in the past. Common examples are:
- SIMPLE PRESENT PERFECT:
> *I have just cleaned my teeth.*
- SIMPLE PAST PERFECT:
> *I didn't want to eat anything after I had cleaned my teeth.*
- MODAL combinations:
> *John must have arrived last night.*

perfect infinitive [> LEG 11.8.4, 16.1–2]
This is a form of the INFINITIVE which may be PERFECT or past in meaning:
> *It's important to have slept well the night before you take an exam.*

perfect participle [> LEG 1.56–63, 16.41]
This is composed of *having* + PAST PARTICIPLE and may be PERFECT or past in meaning:
> *Having found no one in when we called, we were obliged to leave a message.*

permission [> LEG 11.19–26]
This is a NOTION generally expressed by the MODAL VERBS *can/could* and *may/might*. We can ask for *permission* or grant and refuse it:
> *Can/Could/May/Might I borrow your umbrella please?*
> *You can(not)/may (not) watch TV for as long as you like.* (Not *could/might*)

person [> LEG 4.4]
PERSONAL PRONOUNS refer to grammatical *persons* (1st, 2nd, 3rd) and can be grouped like this:
- 1st person: *I, we*
- 2nd person: *you*
- 3rd person: *he, she, it, one, they*

personal pronoun [> LEG 4.3–8]
Personal pronouns may be:
- SUBJECT: *I, you, he, she, it, one, we, they*
- OBJECT: *me, you, him, her, it, one, us, them*

Though they are called 'personal' PRONOUNS, they do not refer only to people. We call them 'personal' because they refer to grammatical PERSONS.

phonology [> e.g. LEG 2.21]
This term refers to the rules that apply to the sounds we make when we speak. For example, we pronounce *s* as /s/ (Not */z/*) after /f/, /k/, /p/ and /θ/: *proofs, cakes, drops, pets, months. Phonology* is an important aspect of GRAMMAR.

phrasal verb [> LEG 8.23–30, Apps 28–37]
We often combine VERBS with PREPOSITIONS and ADVERB PARTICLES to form *phrasal verbs*. These verbs can have non-idiomatic meanings (*Come in!*) or IDIOMATIC meanings (*She's run down* = exhausted). We can identify four types of phrasal verbs with different characteristics:
- Type 1: verb + preposition (TRANSITIVE):
> *get over (an illness)*
- Type 2: verb + particle (transitive):
> *bring up (the children)*
- Type 3: verb + particle (INTRANSITIVE):
> *come about (= happen)*
- Type 4: verb + particle + preposition (transitive):
> *run out of (matches)*

phrase [> LEG 1.2]
A *phrase* is a group of words which can be part of a SENTENCE. A phrase may take the form of:
- a NOUN PHRASE:
> e.g. *a tube of toothpaste*
- a PREPOSITIONAL (or ADVERBIAL) PHRASE:
> e.g. *over the bridge*
- a VERB PHRASE:
> e.g. *will tell, will have done*
- a QUESTION-WORD + INFINITIVE:
> e.g. *what to do, when to go*

plural [> LEG 2.20, 4.5.6–7, 10.27, *passim*]
Plural is the grammatical form that describes more than one. For example, plural may refer to:
- the plural form of NOUNS (plural NUMBER):
> *cats, potatoes, wives, men, phenomena*
- the plural form of PRONOUNS: *we, they*
- the plural form of a VERB TENSE: *they have*

points of time [> LEG 9.4, 9.18, App 48, *passim*]
This term is often contrasted with periods of time to describe exact time references in the past, present or future with ADVERBS OF TIME: *yesterday, today, tomorrow,* etc.

possession [> LEG 2.10, 2.42–50, 4.1, 4.21, 13.39]
We can express *possession* in a variety of ways in English, for example:
- with COMPOUND NOUNS:
> *the table leg*
- with APOSTROPHE *S/S* APOSTROPHE:
> *a boy's jacket, a girls' school*
- with the *OF*-CONSTRUCTION:
> *the poetry of Keats*
- with POSSESSIVE ADJECTIVES AND PRONOUNS:
> *This is my book. This book is mine.*
- with *Whose?*:
> *Whose is this book?*

possessive adjectives and pronouns [> LEG 4.1, 4.21]
Possessive adjectives are:
   my, your, his, her, its, one's, our, your, their.
Possessive pronouns are:
   mine, yours, his, hers, ours, yours, theirs.
We use possessive adjectives in front of a NOUN:
   *This is **my book**.*
We use possessive pronouns on their own:
   *This book is **mine**.*

possessive case [> LEG 2.43]
This is another term for GENITIVE.

possibility [> LEG 11.3, 11.27–33]
Like CERTAINTY, the NOTION of *possibility* is generally expressed by all MODAL VERBS (except *shall*) in their SECONDARY USE. Modal verbs can be arranged on a scale to express degrees of certainty/possibility, with *might* expressing the greatest uncertainty and *can't/must* expressing the greatest certainty:
   *She **might be** right. → She **must be** right.*

pre-determiner [> LEG 3.4]
Pre-determiners are words like *both* and *all*, which we can use in front of DETERMINERS like *the, this* and *these*: **both the** girls, **all this** money, **all these** complaints.

predicate [> LEG 1.1, 1.4]
This term describes the VERB group, that is, what is said about the SUBJECT: all the words in a SENTENCE except the subject:

subject group	verb group (predicate)
The dog	*bit the man.*
The man	*bit the dog.*

predicative adjective [> LEG 6.7]
The term *predicative* is the opposite of ATTRIBUTIVE and refers to the position of an ADJECTIVE in a PHRASE or a SENTENCE. We say that an adjective is predicative or is used *predicatively* when it comes directly after *be, seem*, etc. It can be used on its own as a COMPLEMENT:
   *This ticket **is old**. Your mother **seems angry**.*

prediction [> LEG 9.37]
This is a NOTION generally expressed by the MODAL VERBS *will*, and *shall* after *I/We* in BrE. It is sometimes referred to as the pure FUTURE to distinguish it from other uses of *will* and *shall*:
   *It **will rain** soon.*
   *Can we find our way home? - I'm sure **we shall**.*

prefix [> LEG 6.2, App 8.2]
A *prefix*, sometimes called an *affix*, is added to the beginning of an ADJECTIVE, generally with a NEGATIVE effect: e.g. **dis**agreeable, **un**interested. Other typical prefixes are: **il**legal, **im**possible, **ir**responsible, **anti**septic.

preparatory object [> LEG 4.15, 16.22]
It + ADJECTIVE, used after VERBS like *find* and *think*, is a *preparatory object*, preparing us for the INFINITIVE or the *THAT*-CLAUSE that follows:
   – + infinitive:
      *Tim finds **it** difficult to concentrate.*
   – + *that*-clause:
      *Jan thinks **it** funny that I've taken up yoga.*

preparatory subject [> LEG 4.13, 16.27.2, 16.47]
Sometimes SENTENCES beginning with *It* continue with an INFINITIVE, a GERUND or a NOUN CLAUSE. It would be possible to begin the sentence with the infinitive, the gerund or the noun clause, but we generally prefer *it*:
   – infinitive: ***It**'s pleasant to lie in the sun.*
                     *(**To lie in the sun** is pleasant.)*
   – gerund: ***It**'s pleasant lying in the sun*
                     *(**Lying in the sun** is pleasant.)*
   – noun clause: ***It**'s a shame that Tom isn't here.*
                     *(**That Tom isn't here** is a shame.)*
                     ***It** doesn't matter when we arrive.*
                     *(**When we arrive** doesn't matter.)*
The true subject in these sentences with *it* is the infinitive, gerund or noun clause and *it* is preparatory to the subject. *It* as a *preparatory subject* combines with ADJECTIVES (*it's **easy to***), NOUNS (*it's **a pleasure to***) and VERBS (*it **appears** that*).

preposition [> LEG 8.1, App 20]
Prepositions are words we use in front of NOUNS or NOUN PHRASES, PRONOUNS or GERUNDS to express a relationship between one person, event, etc. and another. Some relationships expressed by prepositions are:
   – space: *We ran **across** the field.*
   – time: *The plane landed **at** 4.25 precisely.*
   – cause: *Travel is cheap for us **because of** the strength of the dollar.*
   – means: *You unlock the door **by** turning the key to the right.*

prepositional phrase [> LEG 1.2, 7.3.3]
PHRASES introduced by PREPOSITIONS like **in** a hurry, **in** the garden, **at** the station tell us *how, where, when*, etc. and are called *prepositional* or ADVERBIAL PHRASES.

prepositional verb [> LEG 8.26–27, Apps 28–30, 37]
A *prepositional verb* is a kind of PHRASAL VERB (verb + PREPOSITION) which may be:
   – non-idiomatic in meaning:
      ***Look at** this picture.*
   – IDIOMATIC in meaning:
      *I can't explain what **came over me**. (= affected)*
Some grammarians maintain that we can't call prepositional verbs 'phrasal'. But if we say that a VERB is phrasal when it has two or more parts, then it is difficult to argue that a verb like *look at* isn't phrasal. Similarly, it is difficult to argue that, for example, *come over*, used idiomatically (as in the above example), is not a phrasal verb.

prescriptive grammar [> LEG Introduction, App 25.25]
This is GRAMMAR which recommends particular grammatical FORMS and USAGES in preference to others and is not merely DESCRIPTIVE. A *prescriptive grammar* will, for example, actively discourage the use of *like* as a CONJUNCTION in:
   ***Like** I told you, it's an offer I can't refuse. (= As I told you . . .)*

present participle [> LEG 1.56–61, 16.38–39]
The *present* PARTICIPLE is the *-ING* FORM of a VERB. We use it:
   – as PRESENT PARTICIPLE in the PROGRESSIVE TENSES or in PARTICIPLE CONSTRUCTIONS:

*I'm **writing** a letter.* (PRESENT PROGRESSIVE)
*He walked out of the room, **slamming** the door behind him.* (participle construction)
– as an ADJECTIVE:
*She told the children a **frightening** story which kept them awake for a long time.*

present perfect progressive tense [> LEG 9.32–34]
This is the PROGRESSIVE form of the SIMPLE PRESENT PERFECT TENSE (formed with *have/has been* + the *-ING FORM PARTICIPLE*) which emphasizes that an activity has been in progress throughout a period with consequences 'now'. It is often used with CONTINUITY VERBS:
*I've **been working** for Exxon for 15 years.*

present progressive tense [> LEG 9.9–12]
This is the PROGRESSIVE form of the SIMPLE PRESENT TENSE (formed with *am/is/are* + the *-ING* FORM PARTICIPLE) which describes actions or events which are in progress at the moment of speaking:
*Someone's **knocking** at the door. Can you answer it?*

primary and secondary uses of modals [> LEG 11.2–4]
MODAL VERBS have two main uses: *primary* and *secondary*. In their primary use, they closely reflect the meanings often given first in most dictionaries and are DEFECTIVE, that is, they need other FULL VERBS to make up their 'missing parts'. For example, *must* has no 'past' form, so we refer to OBLIGATION in the past with *had to*: *I **must** go* (now). *I **had to** go* (then). The primary meanings of modal verbs are as follows:
– *can/could* relate mainly to ABILITY:
*I **can lift** 25 kg.*
– *may/might* relate mainly to PERMISSION:
*You **may leave** early*.
– *will/would* relate mainly to PREDICTION:
*It **will rain** soon.*
– *shall* after *I/We* relates mainly to prediction:
*Can we find our way home? – I'm sure **we shall**.*
– *should/ought to* relate mainly to escapable obligation:
*You **should do** as you're told.*
– *must* relates mainly to inescapable obligation:
*You **must be** quiet.*
– *needn't* relates to absence of obligation:
*You **needn't** wait.*
In their secondary use, all modal verbs (except *shall*) express degrees of CERTAINTY, with *might* expressing the highest degree of uncertainty and *can't/must* expressing the highest degree of certainty. In their secondary use, modal verbs have only two forms:
– present: *You **must be** right.*
– PERFECT and past: *You **must have been** right.*

process verb [> LEG 10.26]
Process verbs are verbs like *become, come, fall, go, get, grow, run, turn* and *wear*, which refer to a change of state:
*It **was** gradually **growing dark**.*
*Old Mr Parsons **gets tired** very easily since his operation.*

progressive tenses
SEE SIMPLE AND PROGRESSIVE TENSES

prohibition [> LEG 11.52, 11.54–57]
This is a NOTION generally expressed by the MODAL VERB *mustn't*:
*You **mustn't turn** left.*

pronoun [> LEG Chapter 4]
A *pronoun* is a word like *he* or *she* that can be used in place of a NOUN or NOUN PHRASE, as the word itself tells us: 'pro-noun'. We use pronouns like *he, she, it* and *they* when we already know who or what is referred to. This saves us from having to repeat the name or the noun whenever we need to refer to it:
*John arrived late last night. **He** had had a tiring journey.*
We use *I/me, you* and *we/us* for direct reference to ourselves or the person(s) addressed and not in place of nouns. Categories of pronouns include PERSONAL, POSSESSIVE, REFLEXIVE and INDEFINITE.

proper noun [> LEG 2.13, 3.9.4, 3.27, 3.31]
A *proper noun* (sometimes called a 'proper name') is used for a particular person, place, thing or idea which is, or is imagined to be, unique. It is generally spelt with a CAPITAL LETTER. ARTICLES are not normally used in front of proper nouns, which may include personal names (e.g. *Andrew Smith*), place names (e.g. *Asia, Madison Avenue*) and months of the year (e.g. *January*).

prop word [> LEG 4.10]
The INDEFINITE PRONOUN *one(s)* is sometimes called a *prop word* because it 'supports' the meaning of the NOUN it replaces:
*Have you seen **this dictionary**? – Is it **the one** that was published recently?*
*Have you met **our neighbours**? – Are they **the ones** who moved here recently?*

punctuation [> LEG 1.2, 15.3, *passim*]
Punctuation is the system we use in the written language to mark SENTENCES, PHRASES, etc. with PUNCTUATION MARKS, so that they are easy to read.

punctuation mark [> LEG 1.2, 15.3, *passim*]
Punctuation marks include FULL STOPS, COMMAS, etc. We can show the end of a SENTENCE with a full stop (.), a QUESTION MARK (?) or an EXCLAMATION MARK (!). We can show a pause in a sentence with a comma (,) and indicate spoken words with QUOTATION MARKS (' . . . ').

qualify [> LEG 6.1]
An ADJECTIVE describes (or *qualifies*) the person, thing, etc. which a NOUN refers to. We use adjectives to say what a person, etc. is like or seems like. For example: *a **tall** man; a **beautiful** dress; a **nice** day.*

quantifier [> LEG 5.1]
Quantifiers are words or PHRASES like *(a) few, (a) little, plenty (of)*, which often MODIFY NOUNS and show how many things or how much of something we are talking about. Some quantifiers combine with COUNTABLE nouns (*a few books*), some with UNCOUNTABLE nouns (*a little butter*) and some with both kinds (*a lot of books/butter*).

question [> LEG Chapter 13]
A *question* asks for information. It may elicit a SHORT ANSWER like *Yes, I have*, an ADVERBIAL of time, etc.

(*Yesterday*) or a complete STATEMENT:

Did Elaine go to her mother's yesterday?
– *Yes, she did.*
When did Elaine go to her mother's?
– *Yesterday.*
What did Elaine do yesterday?
– *She went to her mother's.*

question mark [> LEG Chapter 13, *passim*, 1.2, 15.3]
A *question mark* (?) is the symbol which we use in writing to indicate a DIRECT QUESTION:
'Is that you, Jane?' Bob asked.

question tag [> LEG 13.17–22]
A *question tag* (or *tag* QUESTION) is a short QUESTION (e.g. *have you?/haven't you?*) that follows a STATEMENT. AUXILIARY VERBS (*be, have, can, may*, etc.) used in the statement are repeated at the end, followed by a SUBJECT (always a PRONOUN):
John was annoyed, **wasn't he?**
He wasn't annoyed, **was he?**

question-word [> LEG 13.30]
A *question-word*, sometimes called a '*wh*-word', is a word we use to ask QUESTION-WORD QUESTIONS. Words like *When, Where*, etc. are question-words. *How* is the only question-word that doesn't begin with the letters '*wh*'.

question-word question [> LEG 13.30–47]
Question-word questions (sometimes referred to as WH-QUESTIONS) are questions asked with the following question-words:
Who(m) *did you invite to your party?*
What *will you buy at the sales?*
When *can you visit us?*
Which *do you like best?*
Why *don't you join us for dinner?*
Where *do you live?*
Whose *running shoes did you borrow?*
How *can I answer you?*
SUBJECT-QUESTIONS (identifying the SUBJECT of a SENTENCE) are also possible:
Who invited *us to the party?* – **Jane** did.
What/Which stores *begin their sales tomorrow?*
– **Department stores** (*do*).

quotation marks [> LEG 15.3]
We use *quotation marks*, also called *inverted commas*, to indicate spoken words. They may be single ('...') or double ("...") and are placed high above the base-line at the beginning and end of each quotation:
'Is that you, Jane?' Bob asked.
"Is that you, Jane?" Bob asked.

reflexive pronoun [> LEG 4.24–31]
Reflexive pronouns, sometimes called *emphatic pronouns*, are words like *myself, yourself, himself, herself* which we use after VERBS like *amuse, blame, cut, dry, enjoy, hurt* and *introduce* to point the action back to the SUBJECT:
I cut myself *shaving this morning.*
We really enjoyed ourselves *at the party.*

regular [> LEG 6.22, 7.4, 9.13–14, 9.22, Apps 39–40]
The term *regular* is used in GRAMMAR to refer to

anything that follows the same pattern as other words in the same class. It is often used in connexion with:
– ADJECTIVES like *tall - taller - tallest* (which isn't IRREGULAR like *bad - worse - worst*).
– VERBS like *play - played - played* (which isn't irregular like *begin - began - begun*).

reinforcement tag [> LEG 13.24–27]
A *reinforcement tag* is similar to an ECHO TAG and is used to emphasize the speaker's point of view:
You're *in in trouble,* **you are**.

relative clause [> LEG 1.25–42]
A *relative clause* is a CLAUSE introduced by a RELATIVE PRONOUN like *who* or *which*. Relative clauses can be:
– SUBJECT of the VERB:
He is **the man**. **He lives** *next door.*
→ *He is the man* **who lives** *next door.*
– OBJECT of the verb:
He is **the man**. *I met* **him** *on holiday.*
→ *He is* **the man** (**who(m)**) *I met on holiday.*
– object of a PREPOSITION:
He is **the man**. *I gave the money* **to him**.
→ *He is the man* (**who(m)**) *I gave the money* **to**.
– POSSESSIVE (subject/object):
He is **the man**. **His car** *was stolen.*
→ *He is* **the man whose car** *was stolen.*
He is **the man**. *The pictures were stolen* **from his house**.
→ *He is* **the man from whose house** *the pictures were stolen.*
Relative clauses may be DEFINING or NON-DEFINING.

relative pronoun [> LEG 1.27–42]
Relative pronouns introduce RELATIVE CLAUSES and relate to people or things:
– *who* or *that* (relating to people):
He is the man **who/that** *lives next door.*
– *which* or *that* (relating to things):
This is the photo **which** *shows my house.*
Relative pronouns remain unchanged whether they refer to MASCULINE, FEMININE, SINGULAR or PLURAL:
He is the **man**/*She is the* **woman who** *lives next door.*
They are the **men**/*They are the* **women who** *live next door.*

reported speech
Reported speech is another term for INDIRECT SPEECH.

reporting verbs [> LEG 15.5–9, *passim*, App 45]
Reporting verbs introduce INDIRECT SPEECH. The most common reporting verbs are *say, tell* and *ask*. However, there are a great many other verbs, such as *admit, agree, claim, know* and *wonder*, which introduce indirect speech, even if this is not always 'reported':
I often **wonder what happened** *to the people I knew at college.*

request [> LEG 11.34–40]
This is a NOTION generally expressed by MODAL VERBS like *will* and *could*:
Will you open *the window for me please?*
Could you help me *with this problem?*

rising tone [> LEG 7.41, 13.22, 13.26]

This term refers to the pitch or INTONATION of the voice when it 'goes up'. We use a *rising tone* not only to ask for information, but to express surprise, anger, interest, etc.:

You left the gas on,↗didn't you? (= Did you leave the gas on?)

You didn't leave the gas on,↗did you? (= I hope you didn't)

You couldn't do me a favour,↗could you? (= I hope you can)

RP

This is an abbreviation for *received pronunciation*: that is, the pronunciation of English which is considered to be the least regionally marked and thought to be used by educated speakers in southern England. Compare STANDARD ENGLISH.

secondary uses of modal verbs

see PRIMARY AND SECONDARY USES OF MODALS, CERTAINTY, DEFECTIVE VERB

semi-colon [> LEG 1.17]

A *semi-colon* (;) is a PUNCTUATION MARK which we use in writing to separate parts of a SENTENCE, for example, by introducing an element of CONTRAST:

The war was over; the shattered countryside was bleak and desolate.

semi-modal [> LEG 11.1]

The verbs *need*, *dare* and *used to* are sometimes called *semi-modals* because they can behave like MODAL VERBS verbs or like FULL VERBS, for example:

*You **needn't leave** yet.* (*need* behaving like a modal verb)

*You **don't need to leave** yet.* (*need* behaving like an ordinary verb)

sense verb [> LEG 6.17, 9.3, 16.9, App 38.4]

Sense verbs, sometimes called *verbs of perception*, are STATIVE VERBS that refer to the senses (e.g. *hear*, *see*, *smell*, *taste*). Verbs like *look* and *taste* behave like *be* in that they may be followed by a COMPLEMENT:

*That pie **looks good**, but it **tastes awful**.* (= it is good; it is awful)

sentence [> LEG 1.2]

A *sentence* is a complete unit of meaning. When we speak, our sentences may be involved or even unfinished, yet we can still convey our meaning through INTONATION, gesture, etc. When we write, these devices are not available, so sentences have to be carefully structured and punctuated. A written sentence must begin with a CAPITAL LETTER and end with a FULL STOP (.), a QUESTION MARK (?) or an EXCLAMATION MARK (!). A sentence may take any one of four forms:

– a STATEMENT: *The shops close/don't close at 7.*
– a QUESTION: *Do the shops close at 7?*
– a COMMAND: *Shut the door!*
– an EXCLAMATION: *What a slow train this is!*

One-word ABBREVIATED utterances (*All right! Good!*) can also be complete units of meaning, particularly in speech or written dialogue, but they are not real sentences because they don't contain a FINITE VERB. Sentences may be SIMPLE, COMPOUND, COMPLEX or COMPOUND-COMPLEX.

sentence adverb [> LEG 7.57]

see VIEWPOINT ADVERB

sentence pattern [> LEG 1.9–14]

see VERB PATTERN

sequence of tenses [> LEG 9.5, 15.13n.1, 15.14, *passim*]

In extended speech or writing we usually select a governing TENSE which affects all other tense forms. A present tense in the MAIN CLAUSE (for example, in a REPORTING VERB) normally attracts a present tense in the SUBORDINATE CLAUSE:

*He **tells** me he's a good tennis-player.*

A past tense normally attracts another past:

*He **told** me he **was** a good tennis-player.*

In the second example, only a more complete context would tell us whether *he was a good tennis-player* refers to the past (i.e. 'when he was a young man') or to present time. The speaker's or writer's VIEWPOINT determines the tenses, which may be mixed:

*He **told** me he **is** a good tennis-player.* (i.e. he still is)

*He **tells** me he **used to be** a good tennis-player.*

short answers [> LEG 13.5–7, *passim*]

Short answers are short responses to QUESTIONS and may take many forms, one of the commonest being *yes/no* short answers in response to YES/NO QUESTIONS:

Has the postman delivered the letters?
- Yes, he has.

short form

A *short form* is another term for CONTRACTION.

simple and progressive tenses [> LEG 9.2]

TENSES have two forms, SIMPLE and PROGRESSIVE. Both forms give a general idea of when an action takes place, but the progressive forms also tell us that an activity is (or was or will be etc.) in progress, or thought of as being in progress at a particular time.

	simple	
present:	*I work.*	
past:	*I worked.*	
present perfect:	*I have worked.*	
past perfect:	*I had worked.*	
future:	*I will work.*	
future perfect:	*I will have worked.*	

	progressive	
present:	*I am*	*working.*
past:	*I was*	*working.*
present perfect:	*I have been*	*working.*
past perfect:	*I had been*	*working.*
future:	*I will be*	*working.*
future perfect:	*I will have been*	*working.*

simple future tense [> LEG 9.35–38]

The *simple future tense* is formed with *will/won't*, though *shall/shan't* may be used as an alternative after *I/We* in BrE. We use it for PREDICTION, for example to say what we think will happen, or to invite prediction:

*It **will rain** tomorrow.*

***Will** house prices **rise** again next year?*

This is sometimes called the 'pure' future and should be distinguished from other uses of *will* and *shall* (for example in REQUESTS like **Will you open** *the window please?* or OFFERS like **Shall I carry** *that bag for you?*). *Will* and *shall* have so many uses as MODAL VERBS that some grammarians maintain that English does not have a future TENSE.

simple past perfect tense [> LEG 9.28–31]
The *simple past perfect tense* (formed with *had* + the PAST PARTICIPLE) describes actions that occurred during 'an earlier past':
> *The doctor arrived quickly, but the patient **had already died**.*

simple past tense [> LEG 9.13–18, Apps 39–40]
The *simple past tense*, which is formed with the past of REGULAR VERBS (e.g. *arrived*) and the past of IRREGULAR VERBS (e.g. *began*) describes events, actions or situations which occurred in the past and are now finished. A time reference is usually given or strongly implied:
> *Sam **phoned a moment ago**.*

simple present perfect tense [> LEG 9.22–27]
The *simple present perfect tense* (formed with *have/ has* + the PAST PARTICIPLE) describes:
– actions continuing up to the present moment and possibly the FUTURE:
> *I've **planted** fourteen rose-bushes **so far this morning**.*
– actions occurring or not occurring at an unspecified time in the past:
> *John's **passed** his driving test.* (no time reference)

simple present tense [> LEG 9.6–8]
The *simple present tense* (the BASE FORM of the verb with *-s* or *-es* endings in the third PERSON singular) is used to refer to actions which may be habitual, or generally true:
> *I **get up** at 7 every morning. John **gets up** at 7.30.*

simple sentence [> LEG 1.2, 1.7]
A *simple sentence* is the smallest sentence-unit possible and normally has one FINITE VERB. It has a SUBJECT and a PREDICATE:
> *One of our aircraft* (subject) *is missing* (predicate).

simple tenses
See SIMPLE AND PROGRESSIVE TENSES.

singular [> LEG 2.20, 4.5, 10.27, *passim*]
Singular is the grammatical form that describes one person, thing, etc. For example, singular may refer to:
– the singular form of NOUNS (singular NUMBER).
> *cat, potato, wife, man, phenomenon.*
– the singular form of PRONOUNS:
> *I, he, she, it.*
– the singular form of a VERB TENSE:
> *I have, he has, she has, it has*

slang
Slang is COLLOQUIAL language which is so INFORMAL and often impolite that it is not normally used in serious speech or writing:
> *I'm knackered.* (= extremely tired, exhausted)

spelling [> LEG 2.20, 6.22–23, 9.6–7, *passim*]
Correct *spelling* is a matter of observing spelling rules. Common rules cover, for example, forming the PLURAL of NOUNS (*potato - potato**es***), the COMPARISON of ADJECTIVES (*big - bigg**er***) and the addition of *-s* or *-es* to the third PERSON in the SIMPLE PRESENT (*I carry - he carries*).

split infinitive [> LEG 16.15]
This refers to putting an ADVERB or *please* between the INFINITIVE MARKER *to* and the VERB (*to boldly go*). Infinitives are sometimes *split* with adverbs like *completely, fully* and *really*. This is only possible with GRADABLE verbs:
> *I want **to completely/fully/really** etc. **understand** what your argument is.*
Many native speakers object to splitting the infinitive on the grounds of style and insist on:
> *I want **completely to understand** what your argument is*, etc.
even if this often sounds distorted.

standard English [e.g. > LEG 10.7*n*.4, 10.30*n*.8]
This is considered to be the kind of English which is generally acceptable, especially to educated users. USAGE that departs from *standard English* is often referred to as SUB-STANDARD:
> *You haven't seen anything yet.* (standard)
> *You ain't seen nothing yet.* (sub-standard)

statement [> LEG 1.2–3, 13.32]
A *statement* is an AFFIRMATIVE or NEGATIVE utterance that is not a QUESTION or a COMMAND. It is one of the four types of SENTENCE:
> *Elaine went/didn't go to her mother's yesterday.*

statement-question [> LEG 13.23]
A *statement-question* has the same word order as a STATEMENT (often with, for example, *surely*) but is expressed with a RISING TONE to ask for information in the same way a QUESTION asks for information:
> *(Surely) **you're coming** with us? **You aren't** hungry? **It isn't** 4 o'clock?*

stative verb [> LEG 9.3, App 38]
Stative verbs contrast with DYNAMIC VERBS because they describe states over which we have no control. They are not normally used in the PROGRESSIVE unless with a different meaning:
> *I **see** very well.* (a natural *stative* ability)
> *I'm **seeing** Barbara tomorrow.* (= I'm going to meet: deliberate, progressive)
Stative verbs may be classified in five groups:
– feelings, emotions:
> e.g. *hate, like, love.*
– thinking, believing:
> e.g. *agree, believe, know, think.*
– wants and preferences:
> e.g. *fancy, need, prefer, want, wish.*
– perception and the senses:
> e.g. *hear, see, smell, taste.*
– states of being, seeming, having, owning:
> e.g. *belong, have, seem, own.*

stress [> LEG 2.3–10, *passim*]

Stress is a matter of how prominent we make some sounds in relation to others when we speak. We use heavy stress for words and syllables that carry important information. Stress is part of the system of INTONATION:

I tell you, I've 'lost my keys.

strong form [> LEG App 40]

This term describes the form of IRREGULAR VERBS. For example *spoke* and *spoken* (from *speak*) are *strong forms*, compared with *arrived* (from *arrive*) which is a WEAK FORM. Unlike weak forms, strong forms are STRESSED in speech.

structural word

A *structural word* can be defined grammatically and has limited or 'closed' (grammatical) uses:, for example, *I, this, the*. It may be contrasted with a LEXICAL ITEM, for example, *book, desk, umbrella*, the use of which is 'open' and not grammatically defined.

structure

Structure refers to *grammatical structure*, that is the way words are arranged to form PATTERNS.

subject [> LEG 1.4]

A *subject* is normally a NOUN, PRONOUN or NOUN PHRASE; it usually goes before the VERB. The verb must 'agree' with the subject, so the subject dictates the form of the verb (e.g. *I wait, John waits, I am, you are, I have, the new edition has*). This AGREEMENT between subject and verb is often called CONCORD.

subject-question [> LEG 13.41–43]

Subject-questions ask for the identity of the SUBJECT. There is no INVERSION after the QUESTION-WORD and the question has the same WORD ORDER as a STATEMENT:

John (subject) *paid* (VERB) *the waiter* (OBJECT).
Who (subject question-word) *paid* (verb) *the waiter* (object)? – *John* (subject) *did*.

Compare these with a QUESTION-WORD QUESTION that has the subject and verb inverted:

Who(m) *did John pay?* – ***The waiter*** (object).

subjunctive [> LEG 11.75.1–3, 14.13]

The *subjunctive* is rare in English. It has two forms: present and past. In the case of the verb *be*, the present form is *be* and the past form *were*. These forms remain the same in all PERSONS. We use the subjunctive:

– after VERBS like *suggest*:

*I suggest he **be** told immediately.*

– after ADJECTIVES like *essential*:

*It's essential he **be** informed.*

– after *if*:

*If Jane **were** here now, she'd know what to do.*

With verbs other than *be*, only the present 3rd person SINGULAR is identifiable:

*I suggest she **phone** home at once.* (subjunctive)
*I suggest she **phones** home at once.* (normal 3rd person SIMPLE PRESENT)
*It's important she **make** up her mind as soon as possible.* (subjunctive)
*It's important she **makes** up her mind as soon as possible.* (normal 3rd person simple present)

subordinate clause [> LEG 1.21–63]

A *subordinate clause* is another name for a DEPENDENT CLAUSE. It is called 'subordinate' because it cannot stand on its own and is subordinate to a MAIN CLAUSE on which it depends for its meaning. Subordinate clauses are introduced by SUBORDINATING CONJUNCTIONS (words like *as soon as, when*, etc.):

The alarm was raised (main clause) ***as soon as the fire was discovered*** (subordinate clause).

subordinating conjunction [> LEG 1.21–63]

We use *subordinating* CONJUNCTIONS to form COMPLEX SENTENCES. Subordinating conjunctions are words like *after, as, as long as, as soon as, before, directly, since, so that, that, till, when* and *where*, which introduce ADVERBIAL CLAUSES or NOUN CLAUSES:

After he got married (adverbial clause of time), *Robin changed completely* (MAIN CLAUSE).

sub-standard English [e.g. > LEG 10.7*n*.4, 10.30*n*.8]

This is considered to be the kind of English which is generally unacceptable, especially to educated users. USAGE that departs from STANDARD ENGLISH is often referred to as *sub-standard*:

You ain't seen nothing yet. (sub-standard)
You haven't seen anything yet. (standard)

suffix [> LEG 2.2, 6.2, Apps 2, 8.1]

A *suffix* or *word ending* may be used to form, for example:

– NOUNS:

*play/play**er**, assist/assist**ant**, discover/discov**ery**, active/activ**ity**, mouth/mouth**ful**.*

– ADJECTIVES:

*change/change**able**, beauty/beauti**ful**, red/redd**ish**, attract/attrac**tive**, care/care**less**.*

suggestion [> LEG 11.34–40, 16.4]

This is a NOTION generally expressed by the MODAL VERB *shall* and the VERB *let*:

Shall *we go swimming?* ***Let's*** *go swimming.*

superlative [> LEG 6.22–29, 7.4–6]

Superlatives of ADJECTIVES and ADVERBS are formed with *-est* or *the most/the least*. We use the superlative when we are comparing one person or thing with more than one other in the same group. The DEFINITE ARTICLE *the* is used before a superlative in a PHRASE or SENTENCE:

– ADJECTIVES:

*This tie is **the nicest**/This tie is **the most/least expensive** on display.*

– ADVERBS:

*Of anyone I have ever met, Dave drives **the fastest**/Dave drives **the most/least carefully**.*

syntax [> LEG Chapter 1, *passim*]

Syntax (= putting together) is the term we use to describe the way words are combined to make meaningful PHRASES or SENTENCES.

tag [> LEG 13.19, *passim*]

A *tag* takes two forms:

– a QUESTION TAG (AUXILIARY VERB + SUBJECT):

*John was annoyed, **wasn't he**?*

– a TAG ANSWER (subject + auxiliary verb):

*Was John annoyed? – Yes, **he was**.*

tag answer [> LEG 13.5–7]

A *tag answer* is a SHORT ANSWER, usually to a YES/NO QUESTION, in which the first VERB in the question (i.e. the AUXILIARY OR MODAL) is usually repeated in the answer:

*Was James late? – Yes, he **was**./No, he **wasn't**.*

tag question

A *tag question* is another term for QUESTION TAG.

tense [> LEG 1.2, 9.1–2]

We express distinctions in time (past, present, FUTURE) through *tense*. Some grammarians believe that tense must always be shown by the actual FORM of the VERB, and in many languages, present, past and future are indicated by changes in verb forms. On this reckoning, English really has just two tenses, the present and the past, since these are the only two cases where the form of the basic verb varies: *love, write* (present); *loved, wrote* (past). However, it is usual (and convenient) to refer to all combinations of *be* + PRESENT PARTICIPLE and *have* + PAST PARTICIPLE as *tenses*. The same goes for *will* + BARE INFINITIVE to refer to the SIMPLE FUTURE TENSE. But we must remember that tense in English is often only loosely related to time. The key factor in choice of tense in English is the VIEWPOINT of the speaker in relating to what he/she is saying. Tenses have two forms in English: SIMPLE and PROGRESSIVE.

that-clause [> LEG 1.22–24, 11.75, 15.5–16, Apps 44–45]

A *that-clause* is another way of describing a NOUN CLAUSE, which we use after a REPORTING VERB. We use *(that) ... should*, particularly after verbs like *ask, propose, recommend, suggest*:

*I suggest **(that) he should apply for the job**.*

to-infinitive [> LEG 16.1–2, 16.7, 16.12–37]

We use the term *to*-INFINITIVE (e.g. *to go*) to distinguish it from BARE INFINITIVE (*go*).

tone

Tone is a feature of INTONATION. The rise and fall of the voice is referred to as RISING TONE and FALLING TONE.

transferred negative [> LEG 1.23.5]

After VERBS like *believe, imagine, suppose* and *think*, we can transfer the NEGATIVE from the verb to the *THAT-CLAUSE* without really changing the meaning:

*I **don't believe she**'ll arrive before 7.*
→ *I **believe she won't** arrive before 7.*

transitive verb [> LEG 1.9, 1.12–14, 8.27–28, 8.30, App 1]

A *transitive verb* is always followed by an OBJECT and can never be used on its own:

*I like **it**. I enjoyed **it**. (Not *I like, I enjoyed*")*

There are verbs which:
– are always transitive (e.g. *afford, blame, contain, enjoy, fix, have, let, like, make*):

*I **can't afford a car**.*

– have transitive and INTRANSITIVE uses (e.g. *break, burn, close, drop, fly, hurt, move, open*):

*Someone **opened the door**.*
(verb + object: transitive)
*The door **opened**.*
(verb without object: intransitive)

Some transitive verbs may be PHRASAL: *look at, get over, give away, make up, put up with*.

true subject

See PREPARATORY SUBJECT.

uncertainty

See CERTAINTY/UNCERTAINTY.

uncountable noun

See COUNTABLE AND UNCOUNTABLE NOUNS.

understood [> e.g. LEG 1.2]

We often use the term *understood* to mean 'assumed to be present'. For example, in *Open the door*, the SUBJECT *you* (***You** open the door*) is 'understood'.

unreal past [> LEG 14.12]

The term refers to a VERB which is past in FORM, but which does not refer to past time. The reference is 'hypothetical':

*If you **went** by train, you would get there earlier.*

unrelated participle

This is another term for DANGLING PARTICIPLE or *hanging participle*.

usage [> LEG 9.8, *passim*]

Usage (or the noun *use*) is often contrasted with FORM. It refers to the way language is actually used. For example, we can say that one generally accepted way of using the SIMPLE PRESENT TENSE is to describe permanent truths:

*Summer **follows** spring.*
*Gases **expand** when heated.*

verb [> LEG 9.1]

A *verb* is a word (e.g. *run*) or a PHRASE (e.g. *run out of*) which expresses the existence of a state (e.g. *like, seem*) or the doing of an action (e.g. *take, play*). Two facts are basic:

1 Verbs are used to express distinctions in time (past, present, FUTURE) through TENSE (often with ADVERBIALS OF TIME or FREQUENCY).

2 AUXILIARY VERBS are used with FULL VERBS to give other information about actions and states. For example, *be* may be used with the PRESENT PARTICIPLE of a full verb to say that an action was going on ('in progress') at a particular time (e.g. *I **was swimming**); have* may be used with the PAST PARTICIPLE of a full verb to say that an action is completed (e.g. *I **have finished**). We use the term ASPECT to indicate whether the form of a verb is progressive or completed.

verbless clause

This is another term for ABBREVIATED CLAUSE.

verb of perception [> LEG 6.17, App 38]

Verbs of perception are one of the classes of STATIVE VERBS. They refer to perception and the senses, for example: *hear, see, smell, taste*.

verb pattern [> LEG 1.8–14]

SENTENCES may be classified according to their *verb patterns*. A verb pattern refers to what, if anything, happens after the VERB. There are five basic verb patterns:

– *My head aches.* (SUBJECT + INTRANSITIVE VERB)
– *Frank is clever.* (subject + *be* + COMPLEMENT)
– *My sister answered the phone.* (subject + verb + DIRECT OBJECT)
– *They gave him a watch.* (subject + verb + INDIRECT OBJECT + direct object)

– *They appointed him chairman.* (subject + verb + OBJECT + complement)

verb phrase [> LEG 1.2]

A *verb phrase* may contain a single VERB:, for example, **built** *in stone*, or a combination of verbs: for example, *will tell, have done, may have been misunderstood.*

verb tense

This is another way of referring to the TENSE of a VERB.

viewpoint [> LEG 8.6, 15.13n.1]

A speaker's or writer's *viewpoint* is an important concept in English GRAMMAR and accounts for the reason why some 'rules' can be applied in different ways. For example, viewpoint may affect the choice of PREPOSITION. If a speaker says: *I live in London*, he or she feels 'enclosed' by London. But if a speaker says: *We stopped at London on the way to New York*, he or she sees London as a point on a route. In the same way, it is impossible to make rigid rules about the SEQUENCE OF TENSES in English, since this depends on the speaker's viewpoint: where he/she perceives him/herself to be in relation to what is said.

viewpoint adverb [> LEG 7.57, App 17]

Viewpoint adverbs (sometimes called *sentence adverbs*) tell us about a speaker's or writer's attitude to what he or she is saying. Viewpoint adverbs MODIFY a whole SENTENCE. That is why they often come at the beginning or end of a sentence, marked off by COMMAS. They do not affect the WORD ORDER of the rest of the sentence. For example, a speaker or writer may use adverbs such as *clearly* or *evidently* to tell us he/she is drawing conclusions; *frankly* or *honestly* to impress us with his/her sincerity; *generally* or *normally* to make generalizations, etc. The most common position for viewpoint adverbs is at the very beginning of a sentence. They are followed by a brief pause in speech or a comma in writing:

> **Frankly**, *I'm not satisfied with your work.*

voice

See ACTIVE, PASSIVE.

vowel [> LEG 3.7, *passim*]

The letters *a, e, i, o, u* are *vowels*. Compare CONSONANTS.

vowel sounds [> LEG 3.7]

There is a difference between VOWELS and *vowel sounds*. We use the INDEFINITE ARTICLE *an* before vowel sounds, not just vowel letters; we use *a* before CONSONANT SOUNDS, not just consonant letters:

> *an umbrella* but *a uniform*
> *an unusual case* but *a union*
> *a year, a university, a European*, but *an eye, an ear*

weak form [> LEG App 39]

This term describes the form of REGULAR VERBS. For example, *arrived* (from *arrive*) is a *weak form* and (unlike a STRONG FORM, e.g. *spoke, spoken*) is not STRESSED in speech.

wh-question [> LEG 13.30–43]

This is another term for QUESTION-WORD QUESTION. We often use it to include QUESTIONS with *How*, not just questions beginning with *Wh-*, like *When*.

word order [> LEG 1.1, 1.3, 1.6, 1.10–14, *passim*]

We use this term principally to refer to SENTENCE *word order*. The absence of INFLEXIONS makes English a word order language, not an inflected language: that is, the order of words is essential to the meaning of a sentence. A change in order means a complete change in meaning:

> *The dog bit the man.*
> *The man bit the dog.*

Word order also affects QUESTION forms and ADVERBS OF TIME/FREQUENCY. Departure from the standard word order pattern often involves INVERSION.

yes/no question [> LEG 13.1, 13.3]

A *yes/no question* is one that asks for *Yes* or *No* in the answer. We normally ask yes/no questions with AUXILIARY VERBS like *be, have* and *do* and MODAL auxiliary verbs like *can* and *may*:

> *Have you ever been to Egypt?*
> – **Yes**, *I have./***No**, *I haven't.*

zero article [> LEG 3.2, 3.24–31]

ARTICLES are frequently not used in general statements in English where they would be required in other European languages. We refer to this deliberate non-use of the article as *the zero article*, which is more accurate than saying that an article has been omitted. (It was never there in the first place to omit.) We use zero articles:

– with PLURAL COUNTABLE NOUNS:
> (–) **Beans** *contain a lot of fibre.*

– with UNCOUNTABLE nouns:
> (–) **Water** *must conform to EC standards of purity.*

– with PROPER NOUNS:
> (–) **Elizabeth** *was my mother's name.*

zero plural [> LEG 2.27]

Zero plural refers to NOUNS which do not change in FORM to show they are PLURAL:

> *This sheep is from Australia.*
> *These sheep are from Australia.*

Structural Index

This index is based mainly on grammar points presented on the right-hand study pages. All references are to the Notes that follow each set of study pages. Items that appear on the left-hand study pages are referred to briefly, with a *passim* reference (where this applies) because they occur in many places throughout the work. See pages 266–291 for index to terms.

A

a/an: 8C, 15C, 18C, 22B, 30C, 39B, 44C, 54B; in phrases in apposition 8B*n*.1; not specifying 8C*n*.5, 15C*n*.16 *passim*; *a/an* (= per) (*six gallons a day*) 8C*n*.14 *passim*; *he's a professor* 15C*n*.20; and *one* 18C, 40B*n*.4; with proper nouns 24D; *not a/an* and *no* 25D; *a/one million* 29E; with countable nouns 34F, 44E; *at (a) school* 45E

abbreviated clauses: 1B*n*.3, 59D *passim*

abbreviations: e.g. *St* for *Saint* 22A*n*.3

ability: with *could, was able to* 9B*n*.1, 9C, 15B*n*.2, 19B*n*.2, 48C

-able: 45C

able to: and *could, manage to, succeed in* 9B*n*.1, 9C, 15B*n*.2, 19B*n*.2, 48C; *could* and *would be able to* 22C

about: + noun clause 18A*n*.2; (= concerning) 27B*n*.1; *be about to* 29D; (*dream*) *about* 8D, 24C, 38D; (*curious*) *about* 9D, 52D

absent: *absent from* 52D

absolutely: 3C

abstract nouns: 15C*n*.12 *passim*

according to: and *by* 2E, 8A*n*.1

account: *on account of the fact that* 34A*n*.1

accusative: verb + accusative + *-ing* (*stop him knowing*) 1F, 18E; *want you to* 10D, 38E; preposition + accusative + *-ing* (*without the boss hearing*) 30D

accuse: *accuse of* 47E

accustomed: *be accustomed to* and *be used to* 35C

acknowledge: + *him to be* 18D; *he was acknowledged to be* 30F

acoustics: 19E

across: 32C*n*.8; and *over* 12B*n*.6; (*come) across (with)* 16B, 24C

act: *act as if* 16D

active voice: verbs active in form, passive in meaning (*It sold for £2.2m*) 2C; and passive/causative 26F, 45B*n*.2

adapt: *adapt to* 47E

add: *add to* 47E; reporting verb 36B*n*.3

adjectival clauses: see **relative pronouns and clauses**

adjectives: adjective + preposition (*afraid of*) 1D, 9D, 52D; predicative adjectives beginning with *a-* (*alive*) 2D; adjective as complement 2D, 3D; adjectival past participles (*extremely bored*) 3C, (*Tired of this ...*) 4B*n*.1 *passim*; separated by commas 5A*n*.4; adjective + *to* (*willing to*) 7B*n*.4 *passim*; compound adjectives (*hand-drawn*) 7C, (*nice-looking*) 13D; attributive and predicative 13E; and adverbs often confused 19D; with *too* and *enough* 20A*n*.3; *anxious for her daughter to succeed* 20F; comparative/superlative 21A*n*.2, 32D; *boiling water* 23E, 28B*n*.3, 44B*n*.8, 47A*n*.10; after sense verbs (*taste good*) 27E; pairs joined by *and* 27B*n*.3, separated by *but* 12A*n*.1; formed with prefixes 28E, suffixes 45C; *it's difficult to find/finding* 30E; ending in *-ed* (*wicked*) 32F; after *so* 33D; compared with nouns (*proud/pride*) 34B*n*.2; with two forms (*high/highly*) 39F; adjectival present participles 44B*n*.8, 47A*n*.10; *stolen goods* 47D; *the* + adjective (*the wealthy*) 54C

admire: *admire for* 47E

admit: + *-ing* 1E, 31F, 40C; *admitting/admission* 60C

adverbial clauses: of time with *till* 1B*n*.2 *passim*; of reason with *because* and *so* 1B*n*.2; of result with *so much (that)* 2B*n*.1, with *so/such ... (that)* 10A*n*.2; of purpose with *so that* 10B*n*.2, 39A*n*.6; of concession 3A*n*.2, 34A*n*.6 *passim*; of manner with *as if* 16D, 21A*n*.2, 23B*n*.6, with *in the same way* 34A*n*.5; of comparison with *as ... as* 17B*n*.6, 19A*n*.2, 28B*n*.6; of place 19A*n*.3 *passim*

adverb particles: in Type 2 phrasal verbs (*knocked the heater over*) 4D, 13C, 44D; in Type 4 (*sit in on*) 16B; in passive with phrasal verbs 27C; in Type 3 (*sit down*) 32C, 38D; *down past the post office* 43C

adverbs/adverbials: intensifying: *so* 1B*n*.2, 33D, *-ly* 3C, *much* 21C, *such* 33D; of manner, place, time: basic word order 4A; of indefinite time (*soon*) 7B*n*.10 *passim*; connecting (*however*) 10B*n*.1 *passim*; viewpoint (*perhaps*), focus (*alone*) 11A*n*s.1–2, 54A*n*.5 *passim*; *here* + inversion 11A*n*.2; *last summer* 19C, 38C *passim*; and adjectives often confused 19D; degree (*much, a lot, far*) 21C; beginning a sentence 28A*n*.2a, 47A*n*.11, 48A*n*.1, 51B–C *passim*; inversion after *seldom*, etc. 26B*n*.2, 30B, 33C, 49C; manner (position) 32A*n*.1c, 42A*n*.1, 48A*n*.1, 52A*n*.2d; quantity and degree compared 34E, 36B*n*.1; *however*, etc. 37B*n*.1; points of time 33B*n*.2, 38C; of frequency 39A*n*.2, 42A*n*.1, 45D, 49C; with two forms (*high/highly*) 39F, 56B; and see *-ly* **adverbs**

advice: 40D, 42F, 52C

advise: *advise against* 8D; *advised them not to* 38E; and *advice* 52C

afford: *can('t) afford to* 1E

afloat: and *floating* 2D

afraid: *afraid of* + *-ing* 1D, 52D; and *frightened* 2D; *I'm afraid so* 21F

after: + simple present 6B*n*.1 *passim*; + simple past 7B*n*.1; + present perfect 37C*n*.10; + past perfect 36A*n*.2 *passim*; *after being* 6C, 26A*n*.2, 53A*n*.2; and *afterwards* 35D; *look after* 27C

after all: 56A*n*.5